B. IOANNIS DUNS SCOTI

OPERA PHILOSOPHICA
V

Editor Generalis: Timothy B. Noone

THE CATHOLIC UNIVERSITY OF AMERICA PRESS
WASHINGTON, D. C.

FRANCISCAN INSTITUTE PUBLICATIONS
ST. BONAVENTURE UNIVERSITY
ST. BONAVENTURE, N. Y.

B. IOANNIS DUNS SCOTI

QUAESTIONES SUPER SECUNDUM ET TERTIUM DE ANIMA

Ediderunt
C. BAZÁN, K. EMERY, R. GREEN, T. NOONE,
R. PLEVANO, A. TRAVER

THE CATHOLIC UNIVERSITY OF AMERICA PRESS
WASHINGTON, D. C.

THE FRANCISCAN INSTITUTE: ST. BONAVENTURE UNIVERSITY
ST. BONAVENTURE, N. Y.

2006

The preparation of this volume was supported in part by grants from the Collaborative Research Program of the *National Endowment for the Humanities*, an independent federal agency.

Copyright © 2006

The Catholic University of America Press
The Franciscan Institute: St. Bonaventure University

ISBN 13: 978-0-8132-1422-1
10:     0-8132-1422-X

FOREWORD

Volume V is the fifth and last of five volumes published containing the critical edition of the philosophical writings of Blessed John Duns Scotus.

We gratefully acknowledge the authorization by the Minister General of the Order of Friars Minor for the Franciscan Institute to prepare the critical edition of Scotus' philosophical works.

The present volume has been made possible, in large part, by grants from the National Endowment for the Humanities. It has also been made possible by the financial and institutional support of St. Bonaventure University, The Catholic University of America, the Delmas Foundation, the Preston Foundation, and the Homeland Foundation ; in addition, we gratefully acknowledge the generosity of Fr. Richard D. Brigham, Mr. David Wroe, Mr. and Mrs. James D. Johnston, Dr. Michael Novak, Professor Stephen Brown of Boston College, Brother Owen Sadlier of the Brooklyn Franciscan Brothers, the Dominican Sisters of the Perpetual Rosary of Milwaukee, the Franciscan Friars of the Australian Provinces, and the Franciscan Friars of the North American Franciscan Provinces.

We wish to thank the past Directors of the Franciscan Institute, Maurice Sheehan, O.F.M.Cap., and Edward Coughlin, O.F.M., and Sr. Margaret Carney, O.S.F., under whose directorships much of the research was conducted, as well as the current Director, Fr. Michael Cusato, O.F.M. We express our deepest thanks, as well, to Rev. Kurt Pritzl, O.P., Dean of the School of Philosophy, The Catholic University of America, whose kind and unswerving support has helped to bring this volume to completion.

We would like to thank the following librarians for their invaluable assistance in securing for us materials: Mr. Paul Spaeth and Brother Anthony LoGalbo, O.F.M., of the Franciscan Institute; Dr. Christine Ferdinand and Ms. Sally Speirs of Magadalen College, Oxford; and Mr. Kevin Gunn and Dr. Bruce Miller of The Catholic University of America. We would also like to thank Dr. Stephen Dumont of the University of Notre Dame for providing us with an electronic text of the Wadding edition for the purposes of collation.

We also wish to thank the editorial assistants who helped us enormously in the final stages of preparation: Ms. H. Francie Roberts, Ms. Sarah Insley, Mrs. Kristina Hanning, and Ms. Daniela Petchik. We thank also Cheryl M. Jones, John A. Hall, Patrick M. Gardner and Stephen M. Metzger of the *Bulletin de philosophie médiévale*-Notre Dame for their help in the computer production of this volume.

Finally, we acknowledge our tremendous debt to those who made it possible for us to prepare in-house camera-ready copy of the complicated pages of this volume. The computer program that made this possible was first written in a simple form in 1984 by Ms. Rosalie Dieteman, a St. Bonaventure University student. It was then taken in hand by Mr. Terrence Dobbelsteyn of Toronto and New Brunswick, and, with a great amount of labor over a number of years, was developed for us into a very comprehensive program named **Imprimatur**. To appreciate the complications Terry overcame, one has only to look at the arrangement of an *additio interpolata*, with its accompanying variants and citations. Our debt to Terry is incalculable.

QUAESTIONES SUPER SECUNDUM ET TERTIUM DE ANIMA

§ 1: DESCRIPTIONS OF THE MANUSCRIPTS

A. The Manuscripts Collated in the Edition

1. *Modena, Biblioteca Estense, Cod. α M.5.29 (Lat. 302)* [= **F**].

   Italian (Franciscans, Milan), early 15th c. (1404); paper, 285 x 210 mm, i + 196 + i ff. The manuscripts in this book were copied by three scribes: the writer of an alphabetical table of questions in Nicolaus Bonetus' *Metaphysica* (ff. 1v-6r); the copyist of Bonetus' philosophical treatises (items 1-3, ff. 7ra-83va); and the copyist of Scotus' *Quaestiones De anima* and the *Quaestiones de cognitione Dei* (ff. 167ra-189va). The latter copyist and the user of the book sign their names and give the date 1404 on f. 184vb. The texts are written in Italian scripts, in 2 cols., ca. 43 lines per col. Nicolaus Bonetus (Nicolas Bonet, †1343) was an early disciple of Scotus known alternately as *Doctor Pacificus*, *Doctor Proficuus* and/or *Doctor Imaginativus*. The book contains texts suitable for a 'Scotistic' pedagogy in the Arts. Folio 6v is blank.

   1) NICOLAUS BONETUS, *Metaphysica*, ff. 7ra-83va:
      Omnes homines ymmo omnes naturae intellectuales naturaliter scire desiderant. Ideo a primis scibilibus secundum naturam est incipiendum....
      The text contains questions on the first nine Books of the *Metaphysics*.

   2) NICOLAUS BONETUS, *Praedicamenta*, ff. 83va-108va:
      Incipiunt praedicamenta Boneti ordinis Minorum cuius anima feliciter quiescat (*rubr.*). Quoniam autem secundum ordinem subiectorum est ordo passionum sic mediorum....

   3) NICOLAUS BONETUS, *Physica*, ff. 108va-162va:
      Incipit liber primus Physicorum.... Et hic terminantur capitula octo librorum Physicae naturalis. Praecedentibus tractatu de Praedicamentis philosophia naturali et methaphisica editis a fratre Nicholo Boneti Sacrae theologiae doctore etc.
      Folios 163r-166v are blank.

   4) IOANNES DUNS SCOTUS, *Quaestiones super secundum et tertium De anima*, ff. 167ra-184vb:
      Quaeritur utrum sensus tactus sit unus vel plures.... ergo ab obiecto et species obiecti est ratio sibi intelligendi per quam est in actu etc. Expliciunt quaestiones venerabilis D. subtilis magistri Ioannis Scoti de ordine minorum super 2 et 3 De anima etc. scriptae per me Maffenanthonem de Perabiago Mediolanense. (*Al. man.*): Expliciunt quaestiones venerabilis doctoris subtilis magistri Ioannis Scoti de ordine minorum super primo (*del.* F¹) et secundo et tertio De anima etc. Et sunt ad usum fratris Guidonis de Alba ordinis minorum MCCCC4.
      The text contains qq. 1-23 in the order established by the edition. Immediately following the colophon, the same scribe in the same format copies, *sine nomine et sine titulo*, five of the questions

that Wadding (V:318-37) attributed to Scotus and published under the title *De cognitione Dei*:

5) ANONYMUS, [*Quaestiones de cognitione Dei*], ff. 184*vb*-189*va*:
(ff. 184*vb*-186*ra*): Quaestio est utrum de Deo posset haberi cognitio media inter cognitionem fidei et patriae....
(ff. 186*ra*-187*rb*): Quaeritur utrum cognitio abstractiva possit dici cognitio scientialis....
(ff. 187*rb*-187*vb*): Quaeritur utrum cognitio abstractiva proprietatum personalium possit habere rationem scientiae....
(f. 188*ra*-188*vb*): Quaeritur utrum talis cognitio abstractiva quae ponitur media possit haberi de Deo per aliquod repraesentativum limitatum....
(ff. 188*vb*-189*va*): Quaeritur utrum cognitio intuitiva (*corr*. F^2 intellectiva F^1) et abstractiva possibilis haberi (*add. in marg.* F^1) de Deo sint eiusdem speciei....

These five questions plus one more are appended to Scotus' *Quaestiones De anima* in MS **W**, ff. 41*r*-42*v*, and are incorporated, with six other questions concerning the same topic, within the *Quaestiones De anima* in MS **C**, ff. 139*ra*-148*va*; all eleven of the questions are listed in the register of questions pertaining to Scotus in MS **Z**^{2} (items 77-87; see Description nr. 27). Scotus almost certainly was not the author of these questions; concerning their authorship and their relationship to Scotus' *Quaestiones De anima*, see the comments on MS **C**, item 2 (Description nr. 15, below), and also the comments on MS **V**, item 4 (Description nr. 24, below).

2. *Oxford, Balliol College Library, Ms. 117* [= **H**].

English, mid-15th c.; parchment, 339 x 222 mm, i + 246 + i ff.^{1} This Folio-size book comprises three separate manuscripts (ff. 1-108, 109-169, 170-246); the scripts of the three manuscripts are similar and the decoration and rubrication is uniform throughout the book, which suggests that the manuscripts were probably produced at the same place and rubricated just before binding. There are no indications of ownership in the present book, but in his catalogue of Balliol manuscripts, Gerard Langbaine (1609-1658) records a label on the old cover of the book: "Donum Georgii Nevyl Exoniensis episcopi cuius insignia coloribus suis depicta a tergo visuntur" (Mynors, 96). George Nevil was Bishop of Exeter, 1458-1465; if one presumes that it was he who had the book compiled, it would suggest that MS **H** was written in the early 1450s; this would make MS **H** the oldest surviving integral copy of Beta (see Introduction § 2). The manuscript contains texts suitable for a 'Scotistic' pedagogy in the Arts.

MS 1, ff. 1-108: (f. 1*r* is blank). *Gatherings*: i^3 (1-3, originally 8), ii-ix^{12} (4-99), x^9 (100-108, originally 12). The gatherings are signed a-h; catchwords are written at the bottom right corner of the last verso in each gathering; pricked and frame-ruled for 2 cols., 242 x 160 mm (centerspace: 12 mm), 51-62 lines per col.; written in a small English *currens* script. The ornamented initial beginning the text on f. 2*va* has been cut out; the border of the text on this folio is filled with foliage and vines in rose, blue, green and gold ink; 3- and 4-line blue initials ("Lombards"), infilled and flourished in red, begin each question. The opening words of questions are written in *litterae notabiliores*; alternating red and blue paraphs mark further text-divisions. The text-marking in this manuscript is similar to that in MSS **N** and **O** (Description nrs. 6-7, below). Folio 1*r* is blank; a table of contents is written by a later hand

---

^{1}H.O. Coxe, *Catalogus codicum mss. qui in collegiis aulisque oxoniensibus hodie adservantur* I.2 (Oxford, 1852), 33; R.A.B. Mynors, *Catalogue of the Manuscripts of Balliol College Oxford* (Oxford, 1963), 95-96.

on f. 1v:

> Contenta huius libri et In primis questiones:
> Questiones Ioannis Canonici super libros Phisicorum
> 23 questiones doctoris subtilis super libros De anima
> a. questiones doctoris subtilis super libros Metheororum
> Dedecus super libros Ethicorum

Folio 2r is blank; the end of the commentary on the *Metaphysics* by ANTONIUS ANDREAE is written on f. 2ra:

> (2ra) ....ideo sequitur maior quod omne ens per participationem etc.... qui est benedictus vivens et regnans super vniversam creaturam a saeculo et usque in saeculum. Amen. Explicit totaliter Metaphysica fratris Antonii.
>
> Mynors (95) comments that the rest of Antonius' commentary had already been removed in the fifteenth century, "perhaps in the process of dividing the bulky volume in half."

1) IOANNES CANONICUS, *Quaestiones super libro Physicorum*, ff. 2va-108vb:

   [Venite] ad me omnes qui laboratis.... Ecclesiastici xxiiij capitulo. Quot [et quan]tos fructus scientiarum notitia.... cum dicitur de ratione praeteriti est quod sit totum pertransitum. Deo gratias. Amen.

   Ioannes Canonicus refers often to Scotus' *Quaestiones De anima* in his questions on the *Physics*, and the two works likewise travel together in MS **G**, ff. 1r-225r.

* * *

MS 2, ff. 109-169: *Gatherings*: xi-xv^{12} (109-168), xvi^1 (169). Catchwords are written at the bottom right corner of the last verso in each gathering; pricked and frame-ruled for 2 cols., 254 x 154 mm (centerspace: 12 mm), 42-51 lines per col.; written in an English *currens* script, similar to the script of MS 1. Again, the opening ornamented initial on f. 109ra has been cut out; an elaborate border surrounds the text and runs down the center-space, decorated with flowers, leaves and vines in rose, green and blue ink sprinkled with gold; bar-border with rose, blue and gold bands; 5-line raised gold initials on a blue and deep rose block on ff. 146ra, 158rb; other text-divisions are marked by 3-line blue initials infilled and flourished in red ink; alternating red and blue paraphs.

2) [PS.-] IOANNES DUNS SCOTUS, *Quaestiones super libros Metheororum*, ff. 109ra-169rb:

   Circa primum Meteororum quaeritur utrum de impressionibus meteoricis sit scientia tanquam de subiectis.... Ad quartum dictum est in corpore convenienter. Consequenter....

   The text breaks off in q. 7 of Book III (Wadding ed., p. 169); f. 169v is blank. This work has frequently been ascribed to Scotus as it is in the table of contents in this manuscript; the work is printed in Vivès-Wadding IV:3-263. For these questions, likewise attributed to Scotus (or *Scotulus*), cf. MS **L**, ff. 121r-215r; MS **N**, ff. 185ra-233vb; MS **O**, ff. 86ra-134rb.

* * *

MS 3, ff. 170-246: *Gatherings*: xvii-xxii^{12} (170-241), xxiii^5 (242-246, originally 10). Quire-marks on the first 6 rectos and catchwords on the last verso of each gathering; ff. 170-190 are pricked and frame-ruled for 2 cols., 253 x 156 mm (centerspace: 12 mm), 53-57 lines per col., ff. 191-246 are written in 2 cols., 250 x 152 mm, 53-60 lines per col.; the manuscript is written in an English *textualis currens* script. The decoration and rubrication are the same as MSS 1-2. The initial beginning the *Quaestiones De anima* on f. 170*ra* has been cut out; this opening folio has the same border design as in MS 2, above; the initial beginning the next work (f. 190*vb*) has been preserved: 4-line two-tone blue U, infilled with rose and green floral leaf design on a gold block.

3) IOANNES DUNS SCOTUS, *Quaestiones super secundum et tertium De anima*, ff. 170*ra*-190*vb*:
Quaeritur utrum sensus tactus [sit] unus vel plures. Videtur quod unus quia si esset plures tunc [es]sent sex sensus.... igitur ab obiecto et species obiecti est ratio sibi intelligendi per quam est in actu; ergo etc. Expliciunt quaestiones D. super secundum et tertium de anima. Amen etc.
   The text contains the 23 questions of the collection but in the following order: qq. 1-5, 10-12, 7-9, 6, 13-23. The questions are attributed to Scotus in the book's table of contents. The colophon is written, presumably by the scribe, in the same *litterae notabiliores* as the opening words of the beginning of each question in the text. The 'D.' in the colophon is ambiguous, for it could refer to "Doctor subtilis" or to "Dedecus," to whom the next work is attributed in the table of contents.

4) IOANNES DEDECUS? *Super libros Ethicorum*, ff. 191*vb*-246*rb*:
Utrum ad felicitationem sub ratione finis ultimi appetitus rationalis debeat habitualiter dirigi.... ex virtute operantibus quod praemium nobis concedat qui sine fine vivit et regnat. Amen (f. 246*vb* is blank).
   Ioannes Dedecus purportedly taught at Oxford. This commentary on Aristotle's *Ethics* is preserved also in Balliol College Library, Ms. 93; All Souls College, Ms. 88; Worcester Cathedral, Ms. F.86; Cambridge, Gonville and Caius College, Ms. 369, and was formerly preserved in the libraries of Lincoln College in Oxford, Peterhouse in Cambridge, and Syon Abbey; it was printed in Oxford in 1518.[2]

3. *Oxford, Bodleian Library, Ms. Digby 44 [=* **K***].*

English (Oxford), later 15th c. (1470s); parchment, 190 x 125 mm, ii + 198 ff. (includes 8 unnumbered leaves).[3] The codex comprises a number of booklets all copied by one scribe, John Saunder (see below), in a *bastarda formata* script, in 1 col., 24-31 lines per col. Gatherings: I-II + 1, i-v^{10} (2-51), vi^9 (52-60, wants one), vii^{10} (61-70), viii^{10} (71-77, + 3 unnumbered blank folios), ix^{10} (77-79, unnumbered 79*), x-xi^{10} (87-106), xii^{10} (107-114, + 2 unnumbered blank folios), xiii^9 (115-121, + 2 unnumbered blank folios), xiv^{10} (122-131), xv-xx^{10} (132-190, + pasted down final leaf). Saunder writes catchwords at the foot of nearly every verso; catchwords at the end of gatherings are boxed. Items 1-4, 7, below, which are all listed in the book's table of contents, are decorated and rubricated in the same way. These texts have a deluxe appearance: each work begins with a 4- or 5-line gold initial, infilled in blue or deep rose and set on a deep rose or blue block, with marginal vine flourishes flecked in

---

[2] A.B. Emden, *A Biographical Register of the University of Oxford to A.D. 1500* I (Oxford, 1957; henceforward *BRUO*), 555; see also J.P.H. Clark, "John Dedecus: Was He a Cambridge Franciscan?" *Archivum Fratrum Historicum* 80 (1987): 1-38.

[3] Falconer Madan and H.H.E. Craster, *A Summary Catalogue of Western Mss. in the Bodleian Library at Oxford* II.1 (Oxford, 1922), 71; A.G. Watson, *A Descriptive Catalogue of the Medieval Manuscripts of All Souls College* (Oxford, 1997), 270 (Appendix II nr. 11); *Bodleian Library Quarto Catalogues IX: Digby Manuscripts 1: A Reproduction of the 1883 Catalogue by W.D. Macray*, cols. 40-41, and 2: *Notes on Macray's Descriptions of the Manuscripts* by R.W. Hunt and A.G. Watson (published together at Oxford, 1999), 24.

gold, sometimes with a bar-border with gold, blue and rose bands (see ff. 2r, 34v, 87r, 104r and 134v); 2-line blue initials, infilled and flourished in red, begin each question; red paraphs mark other text-divisions; title-incipits, the opening lines of each question, and Explicits are written in *litterae notabiliores* underlined in red. Items 5-6, below, are not listed in the book's table of contents and their opening initials are not so decorated, but their system of internal text-marking is the same as the other works in the book, suggesting that Saunder later added these texts which he copied to the five others he evidently copied as a set.

John Saunder, who copied the texts in this book (see the colophons, ff. 34v, 86v, 134r, 185r), was a fellow of All Souls College (1471-82), and of Eton College from 1483 until his death in 1495. A note written by Saunder himself at the bottom of f. 3r states: "Liber collegij animarum fidelium defunctorum in Oxon. Ex dono magistri Johannis Saundyr nuper socij eiusdem collegij cuius anime propicietur deus Amen." This book is recorded in the Vellum Inventory of All Souls College: "91. quaestiones de sompno et vigilia cum aliis contentis 2° folio elevantur quidem." In his will given at Eton, Saunder states that he wishes this book to be chained, as in fact it was, and notes that the book had been on deposit in the Selton Chest at All Souls, from which it was to be redeemed by the sale of five hoods and "volumina doctoris subtilis et volumina doctoris de lira." [4] The book later was obtained by Thomas Allen (1540-1632), who acquired many other books from Oxford colleges. Allen subsequently bequeathed the book to the polymath and bibliophile Kenelm Digby, who in turn bequeathed it to the Bodleian library in 1634.[5] (An inscription on f. 1v reads: "Vindica te tibi Kenelm Digby.") Saunder seemingly bequeathed another manuscript containing the *Quaestiones De anima* to All Souls College;[6] see MS **G** (Description nr. 18, below).

The manuscript contains texts suitable for a pedagogy in the Arts. Folio Ir bears the title "Quaestiones in Physica Aristotelis" (17th c. hand); ff. IIr-v and 1r are blank. Saunder writes a table of contents on f. 1v:

Contenta huius libri:
Quaestiones super libros de sompno et vigilio
Quaestiones super libros de sensu et sensato
Quaestiones super librum de memoria et reminiscentia
Quaestiones super librum de longetudine et brevitate vitae
Quaestiones medicinales
Expositio quaedam super librum de motu animalium
Doctor Subtilis super libros De anima
Tituli quaestionum cuiuslibet libri suprascripti
Tabula super omnes libros praedictos

1) ANONYMUS, *Quaestiones super libros de somno et vigilia*, ff. 2r-34v:
Circa librum de somno et vigilia quaeritur primo utrum somnus sit privatio vigiliae.... Auctoritas post oppositum est pro prima conclusione primi articuli. Expliciunt quaestiones super libros de somno et vigilia per manus domini Iohannis Saundyr.

---

[4] See N.R. Ker, *Records of All Souls College Library* (Oxford Bibliographical Society Publications 16; Oxford, 1971), 35 nr. 1016 (List XIII), and 109 (List XXVIA).
[5] This information concerning the book is recorded by Watson, *A Descriptive Catalogue*, 270 (Appendix II nr. 11).
[6] Emden, *BRUO* III (1959), 1643. Emden does not identify the All Souls manuscript but lists its contents from an archival document. See also M.B. Parkes, "The Provision of Books," in *The History of the University of Oxford II: Late Medieval Oxford*, ed. J.I. Catto and R. Evans (Oxford, 1992), 427.

2) IOANNES DE PISA? *Quaestiones super librum de sensu et sensato*, ff. 34v-86v:
Incipiunt quaestiones super librum de sensu et sensato. Quaeritur primo utrum de operationibus et passionibus animatorum sit. Scientia distincta a scientia libri de anima et aliorum librorum naturalium.... (74r) ....est falsa. Respondetur quod causa est haec quia aqua colata.

The rest of f. 74r and ff. 74v-75r is blank; the text of *De sensu et sensato* resumes on f. 75v with a new q. 9 (the text already includes qq. 1-10):

Quaestio nona (*in marg.*) Quaeritur nono utrum humidum sit substantium odoris vel siccum.... (76r) ....de ista quaestione sufficiant.

Hereafter in ff. 76v-77v follow three questions that do not belong to the text:

(76v) Quaestiones sequentes non sunt de substantia huius libri (*in marg. sup.*). Quaeritur utrum siccum igneum vel terrenum sit substantia odoris.... (77r) ...quod est calidum si hoc recipit odorem Quaeritur de agente odorem Utrum humidum aliquid faciat ad generationem odoris.... confert ad naturam odoris Quaeritur utrum frigidum aliquid agat ad generationem odoris (77v) ....quod sunt penitus caliditate. Nota quod iste quatuor quaestiones ultimae non sunt eiusdem doctoris cuius sunt octo aliae ut patet modus procedendi sed tamen suplent vicem. Nam deest finis quaestionis decimae et est deest quaestio undecima totaliter et primum quaestionis duodecimae et ideo illae quatuor praedictae non numerantur inter quaestiones huius libri ut patet in tabula eiusdem.

The next three unnumbered leaves are blank; then follows q. 12 (*in medias res*) of *De sensu* (q. 11 is missing):

(78r) Quaestio 12ª (*in marg. sup.*). Ex quo sequuntur corellariae quod species odoris realis dicitur odor spiritualis.... (86v) ....Dicta post oppositum sunt pro secunda conclusione primi articuli. Expliciunt quaestiones super libros de sensu et sensato secundum magistrum Iohannem Pisiensis dictum Spengen scriptae a Domino Iohanne Saundre.

3) ANONYMUS, *Quaestiones super librum de memoria et reminiscentia*, ff. 87r-104r:
Quaeritur circa librum de memoria et reminiscentia utrum memoria sit solum praeteritorum. Et arguitur quod non.... Auctoritas post oppositum est pro conclusione responsali primi articuli haec de ista quaestione. Expliciunt quaestiones super librum de memoria et reminiscentia.

4) [GUALTERUS BURLAEUS?] *Quaestiones super librum de longitudine et brevitate vitae*, ff. 104v-114r:
De longitudine et brevitate vitae (*in marg. sup.*) Circa librum de longitudine et brevitate vitae quaeritur primo utrum callidum et humidum sunt causae longae vitae.... et unius membri alicuius corporis ad aliud membrorum....

The text breaks off abruptly in q. 4. This work, which here is anonymous, also appears in MS **N**, ff. 180va-184vb, where it is attributed to Walter Burley. Folio 114v is blank, and is followed by 2 unnumbered blank folios.

5) ANONYMUS, *Quaestiones medicinales*, ff. 115r-121r:
Quaestiones medicinales intermixtae. Quaeritur primo utrum prius debeant exhiberi grossa cibaria vel subtilia.... (120v) ....Utrum fetus in utero maturo nutriatur lacto....

The set includes 8 questions; f. 121v is blank, followed by 2 unnumbered blank folios.

6) [GUALTERUS BURLAEUS?] *Liber de motu animalium*, ff. 122r-134r:
   De motu autem eo. Dividitur iste liber in duas partes. In prima dat intentionem suam.... In libro de generatione et hic sit modus huius libri. Explicit Liber de motu animalium. Quod D[ominum] I[ohannem] Saunder.

   This work also appears in MS **N,** ff. 177va-180va, described below, where it is explicitly attributed to Walter Burley.

7) IOANNES DUNS SCOTUS, *Quaestiones super secundum et tertium libros De anima*, ff. 134v-185r:
   Quaeritur circa secundum librum De anima utrum sensus tactus sit unus vel plures. Videtur quod sit unus primo sic quia si esset plures tunc essent sex sensus.... per quam est in actu etc. Expliciunt quaestiones doctoris subtilis super secundum et tertium libros de anima scriptae a domino Iohanne Saundr etc.

   The *notabilior* script of the *Expliciunt* is the same as the script of the question titles in the text. The *Quaestiones* are copied in six gatherings of this Quarto manuscript: xv-xx^{10} (132-190). The text contains the 23 questions of the collection but in the following order: qq. 1-5, 10-12, 7-9, 6, 13-23. Saunder numbers the questions sequentially 1-23, indicating that he did not know that there was anything wrong with the order. A *tabula quaestionum in voluminae tractatarum* is written by Saunder on ff. 186v-188r (ff. 185r-186r are blank, as are ff. 188v-190v following the table). The table for Scotus' *Quaestiones De anima* appears first (186v):

Quaestiones De anima:
Prima Utrum Sensus tactus sit unus vel plures
2^a Utrum Caro sit organum sensus tactus
3^a Utrum Ad tactum requiritur medium extrinsecum in quo sit
4^a Utrum Sensibile positum supra organum sensus sentiatur
5^a Utrum Sensus sit receptivus specierum sine materia
6^a Utrum Sensus communis sit unus vel plures
7^a Utrum Corpora caelestia possunt agere in intellectum nostrum
8va Utrum Potentia intellectiva et sensitiva sint tantum passivae
9^a Utrum Actio et passio sint idem motus
10^a Utrum Sensus particularis possit contraria sentire
11^a Utrum Sit necesse ponere sensum communem praeter haec
12^a Utrum Sint tantum quinque sensus
13^a Utrum de intentione Philosophi fuerit ponere intellectum agentem
14^a Utrum Species maneant in intellectu cessante actu intelligendi
15^a Utrum Intellectus noster sit immaterialis
16^a Utrum Magis universale prius intelligitur quam minus universale
17^a Utrum In intellectu nostro sint species intelligibiles priores actu intelligendi
18^a Utrum Intellectus noster possit intelligere sine phantasmate
19^a Utrum Quiditas sensibilis sit obiectum intellectus nostri
20^a Utrum ens sub ratione veri sit obiectum primum intellectus nostri
21^a Utrum Ens sit obiectum primum intellectus nostri
22^a Utrum Singulare sit ab intellectu modo per se intelligibile
23^a Utrum In electione actus intelligendi intellectus sit movens motum ab obiecto

4. *Oxford, Corpus Christi College Library, Ms. 227* [= **L**].

English (Oxford, Greyfriars), late 15th c. (1470s, 1491); paper, 207 x 144 mm, vi + 218 ff.[7] This Quarto-size volume binds together three manuscript booklets (ff. 1-48, 49-120, 121-218). The gatherings of the book, however, are numbered sequentially, *primus quaternus* through *18⁹ quaternus*, indicating that they were imposed when the separate manuscripts were bound together. The gatherings of MS 3 also bear a different sequence of quire marks, 14-20, indicating that this booklet had been bound in another volume. *Gatherings*: i-xviii^{12} (1-206), xix^2 (217-218). The manuscripts in this volume, bearing texts suitable for a 'Scotistic' pedagogy in the Arts, were copied in the convent of the Franciscans at Oxford. The first (ff. 1r-45v), which contains Scotus' *Quaestiones De anima*, was copied by the friar Petrus Pauli from Nyköping in Sweden, who studied in Oxford in the 1470s. The second and third manuscripts (ff. 49r-215r) were copied by the friar William Vavasor in 1491.[8] This book once belonged to the encyclopedic scholar John Dee, as an inscription in the top margin of f. 1r indicates: "Joannes Dee, 1559., Novembris 24 Ebonici."[9] On f. ir is a fifteenth-century inscription: "cetus in excelsis te laudas"; ff. iv-vir are blank; an old shelf-mark, F.1.12 [CCCO] N° 1694 227, is found on f. viv. A table of contents is written on the same page:

Quaestiones Scoti in secundum et tertium librum De anima
Quaestiones Antonii Andreae de 3 principiis naturalibus
Quaestiones Scoti in 3 libros Meteor.

MS 1, ff. 1-48: Frame-ruled for 1 col. of long-lines, 130 x 80 mm, 33-35 lines per col. The beginnings of questions are signaled by 2-line red initials and the first words of the questions are written by the scribe in *litterae notabiliores*; red paraphs mark internal text-divisions.

1) IOANNES DUNS SCOTUS, *Quaestiones super secundum et tertium De anima*, ff. 1r-45v:
Quaeritur utrum sensus tactus sit unus vel plures. Videtur quod unus quia si plures tunc essent sex sensus.... ergo ab obiecto et species obiecti est ratio sibi intelligendi per quam est in actu igitur etc. Expliciunt quaestiones Doctoris subtilis super secundo et tertio De anima Oxoniae scriptae per fratrem Petrum Pauli de Nycopia. (*Rubricator*): Lord Ihesu Mercy.

The text contains the 23 questions of the collection but in the following order: qq. 1-5, 10-12, 7-9, 6, 13-23. The scribe notes arguments, objections, responses, etc., in the margins, but he does not number the questions. Folios 46-48 are blank.

* * *

---

[7]Coxe, *Catalogus* II.4, 92.
[8]For Petrus Pauli, see Parkes, "The Provision of Books," 441-42, and R.B. Dobson, "The Religious Orders 1370-1540," in *The History of the University of Oxford* II, ed. Catto and Evans, 559. For William Vavasor, see Emden, *BRUO* III, 1943. Vavasor also copied a work titled *Quaestiones de anima* now preserved in Oxford, Corpus Christi College Library, Ms. 228, ff. 52-61: "Hic suppono quod in uno corpore est una anima.... Amen. quod frater Wyllelmus Vavysur. Expliciunt questiones de anima valde perutiles anno Domini 1490"; see Coxe, *Catalogus* II.4, 92-93, and A.G. Watson, *Catalogue of Dated and Datable Manuscripts c. 435-1600 in Oxford Libraries* I (Oxford, 1984), 129 nr. 780 (this manuscript also was once owned by John Dee). The incipit of the first question does not belong to the collection by Scotus, but because the latter's *Quaestiones* sometimes traveled with others, one ought to examine this text carefully, which we have not had the opportunity to do.
[9]See *Renaissance Man: The Reconstructed Libraries of European Scholars, 1450-1700. Series One: The Books and Manuscripts of John Dee, 1527-1608. Part 2: John Dee's Manuscripts from Corpus Christi College, Oxford. A Listing and Guide to the Microfilm Collection* (Marlborough: Adam Matthew Publications, 1992), 46-47.

MS 2, ff. 49-120: Frame-ruled for 1 col., 142 x 90 mm, 34-36 lines per col. An 8-line red initial begins the treatise on f. 49r, 3-line red initials mark the opening of chapters, the beginning words of which are written in *litterae notabiliores*; red paraphs mark other text-divisions.

2) ANTONIUS ANDREAE, *Tractatus de tribus principiis naturalibus*, ff. 49r-120r:
Cum secundum doctrinam Aristotelis in pluribus locis ex notitia principiorum videatur notitia cuiuscumque rei essentialiter.... (119v) ....non sunt sine generatione et corruptione. Sic igitur terminatus est tractatus iste. Amen. Explicit tractatus de tribus principiis veri et egregii doctoris fratris Anthonii Andreae ordinis minorum de provincia Aragoniae exceptus de dictis doctoris subtilis eiusdem ordinis scriptus per me Fratrem Wyllelmum studentem Oxoniae anno incarnationis Dominicae 1419. Quaestiones secundum primum principium naturae scilicet de materia.... (120r) ....Explicit Tabula.

The date in the colophon is an error, and should read 1491; see the Explicit for the next work. A table of questions in the *Tractatus* appears on ff. 119v-120r.

* * *

MS 3, ff. 121-218: Frame-ruled for 1 col., 137 x 86 mm, 41-43 lines per col. The rubrication is essentially the same as in MS 2.

3) [PS.-]IOANNES DUNS SCOTUS, *Quaestiones super Meteororum*, ff. 121r-215r:
Circa primum Meteorum quaeritur utrum de impressionibus meteoricis sit scientia tanquam de subiecto. Arguitur quod non.... Ad rationes dicitur quod salutae sunt ex praecidentibus etc. Expliciunt quaestiones tertii libri Meteororum secundum Doctorem Subtilem ordinis Minorum ac scriptae per manum fratris Wyllelmi Vavysur eiusdem ordinis anno Dominicae incarnationis 1491. Amen then. [Tabula quaestionum].... Explicit Tabula tertii libri meteororum etc. Finito libro sit laus et gloria Christo.

Folios 215v-218r are blank; f. 218v bears the inscription of a seventeenth-century owner: "The booke does belonge to me Christopher Thurske...." In the manuscript the questions on meteors are wrongly attributed to Duns Scotus; for these questions, often attributed to Scotus, cf. MS **H**, ff. 109ra-169rb; MS **N**, ff. 185ra-223va; MS **O**, ff. 86ra-134rb.

5. *Oxford, Magdalen College Library, Ms. lat. 16* [= **M**].

English (Oxford), mid-15th c. (1450s); parchment and paper, 218 x 135 mm, iii + 156 (numbered 1-145 + 11 unnumbered) + i (numbered 146) + 54 (numbered 147-200) + iii (numbered 201-203) ff.[10] The book comprises seven manuscript booklets (ff. 1-12, 13-58*, 59-96, 97-113*****, 114-119*****, 120-145, 146-200). This Quarto-size book was owned by Thomas Wyche, a fellow of Oriel College (M.A. by 1445, B.Th. by 1452), who purchased it from a certain Robert Law in the 1450s, as an inscription on f. 203v states: "[Iste?] liber Constat Magistro T Wyche sumptus per eundem a Magistro Roberto law anno domini M°CCCC^{mo}x [...] cum alio quaterno veteri de questionibus metephisicis pro xx s." Wyche was an active acquirer of books. He purchased two other manuscripts from Law; between the

---

[10]Coxe, *Catalogus* II.10, 14-15. Kent Emery profoundly thanks Ralph Hanna, Keble College, Oxford, for giving him a copy of his description of this codicologically complicated manuscript. Hanna's description will appear in his forthcoming catalogue of Latin manuscripts in Magdalen College Library.

years 1440 and 1458 he bought at least five books from the University Stationer, John More, including copies of works by Henry of Ghent and Giles of Rome. Significantly, two other books he owned today rest, like this manuscript, in Magdalen College Library, Ms. 4 (1454-55), and Ms. 134 (1552). In 1458, Thomas Gascoigne, likewise a fellow of Oriel College, lent Wyche a copy of Duns Scotus' commentary on the *Sentences*. In the present manuscript, Wyche himself copied Scotus' *Quaestiones De anima* (MS 3, ff. 59r-96r), as a scribal tag ("Quod Wyche") at the end of the text (f. 96r) indicates; Wyche seems also to have copied the following questions by Robert Cowton (MS 4, ff. 97r-109r), as well as the texts in MS 1 (ff. 1r-12r).[11] The original owner of the book, Robert Law, was the copyist of MSS 5-7; a third hand copied MS 2. As Hanna observes, the quire signatures in the book suggest that Wyche bought from Law a volume containing MSS 5-7, to which he added material of his own (MSS 1, 3-4) as well as another booklet in his possession (MS 2).

Our critical examination of the text of Scotus' *Quaestiones De anima* reveals that Wyche's copy (MS **M**) bears a special relationship with another copy of the *Quaestiones* in Magdalen College since the Middle Ages, Ms. 80 (MS **N**; see the next Description). Altogether, the manuscript contains texts suitable for a 'Scotistic' pedagogy in the Arts at the highest level (physics, on the soul, metaphysics). A table of contents, written by a fifteenth-century hand, appears on f. IIr (ff. Ir-v, IIv-IIIv are blank); the first two titles and titles 5-6 are no longer bound in the book:

> Contenta huius libri per ordinem:
> Tractatus magistri Walteri Burley de divisione scientiarum
> Tractatus Kylwardi de eadem (*17th c. note*: Eruuntque e libro)
> Bona quaestio et conclusiones primum librum Physicorum
> Expositio prohemij Physicorum cum quibusdam quaestionibus
> Quidam tractatus alicuius certi doctoris
> Burlaeus de potentiis animae
> Quaestiones Scoti super secundum et tertium libros de Anima
> Quaestiones Cowton super primum librum Sententiarum dist. 16
> Quaestio bona metaphysicalis de ente
> [deleted rubric]
> Alia quaestio metaphysicalis optima
> Quaestiones de distinctione formalitatum determinatae a Petro Thoma de ordine
>   fratrum minorum de provincia Sancti Iacobi
> Alias quaestiones formalitatum

MS 1, ff. 1-12: Parchment and paper (ff. 1, 4, 6-7, 9, 12 are parchment; ff. 2-3, 5, 8, 10-11 are paper). *Gatherings*: iii + i^{12} (1-12). The texts were copied by Thomas Wyche in 1 col., 148 x 95 mm, 32-37 lines per col., in a "mixed *Anglicana*-Secretary" script (Hanna). Blue initials, 2 to 4 lines, flourished in red, begin the texts and distinctions; alternating red and blue paraphs mark internal text-divisions. As Hanna points out, one hand has written text-headings, marginal rubrics and Explicits in black ink, underlined in red, in a *textualis formata* (Hanna: *quadrata*) display-script throughout the book (including the texts copied by Law and the third hand). This writer was Thomas Wyche, which is proved by the fact that he wrote his signature in this script in the Explicit to the *Quaestiones De anima* (see below).

---

[11] See Emden *BRUO* III, 2102, and Parkes, "The Provision of Books," 412, 419-20 and n. 62, 422 and n. 76.

1) [IOANNES CANONICUS], *Bona quaestio concernens primum librum Physicorum*, ff. 1r-5v:
   Bona quaestio concernens primum librum Physicorum (*in marg. sup.*). Utrum magis universalia sint nobis prius nota. Videtur quod non.... esse presentes quia earum similitudo est expressiva in anima etc.
   See C. Lohr, *Traditio* 26 (1970): 183-84.

2) [GUALTERUS BURLAEUS], *Expositio super Prohemium primi Physicorum*, ff. 6r-9v:
   Expositio super Prohemium primi Physicorum (*in marg.*). Quoniam autem intelligere et scire contingit etc. Iste liber dividitur in duas partes principales videlicet in prohemium et tractatum.... quod est magis consequens et ideo non oportet quod species etc.

3) IOANNES CANONICUS, *Super primum Physicorum q. 2 etc.*, ff. 10r-12r:
   Utrum magis universalia sunt nobis magis nota et videtur quod non quia secundum Philosophum 2° Post. difficilius est cognoscere universale quam singulare.... Avicenna primo Metaphysicae suae quod species specialissimae sunt magis intente a natura etc. (*litt. notab.*): Hanc quaestionem principalem nota bene declarata a Iohanne Canonico super primum Physicorum quaestione 2ᵃ etc.
   Folio 12v is blank.

* * *

MS 2, ff. 13r-58*v: Parchment and paper sheets. *Gatherings*: ii^{12} (13-24), iii^{10} (25-36, wants 2 leaves), iv^{12} (37-48), v^{11} (49-58*, wants 1 leaf), stubs of 4 missing leaves. Written in "*Anglicana* with Secretary" script (Hanna), 1 col., 145 x 90 mm, 26-27 lines per col.

4) [ANTONIUS ANDREAE], *Quaestio de tribus principiis naturalibus*, ff. 13r-58v:
   Bona quaestio de tribus principiis naturalibus (*in marg. sup.*). Utrum per se principia naturalia habeant in anima coniuncta actu esse intelligibile.... quae magis complet illud cui advenit quam forma alia perfectior complet suam et sic non procedit argumentum.
   Folio 58* is blank. The *quidem tractatus alicuius certi doctoris* and *Burlaeus de pontentiis animae* listed at this position in the table of contents (above) are now missing in the manuscript.

* * *

MS 3, ff. 59-96: Parchment. *Gatherings*: vi^{12} (59-70), vii^{12} (71-82, + 2 stubs), viii^{14} (83-96); the quires are signed (e-f-g) and numbered (1-6) on the first six rectos of each gathering. The *Quaestiones* were copied by Thomas Wyche, who signs his name on f. 96r, in an *Anglicana*-Secretary script (Hanna), 1 col. of long lines, 157 x 90 mm, 36 lines per col.

5) IOANNES DUNS SCOTUS sive 'SCOTULUS', *Quaestiones super secundum et tertium libros De anima*, ff. 59r-96r:
   Quaestiones Scotuli super secundum et tertium libros de Anima (*litt. notab., in marg. sup.*). Quaestio prima (*in marg.*). Quaeritur utrum sensus tactus sit unus vel plures. Videtur quod unus.... et species obiecti est ratio sibi intellegendi per quam est in actu igitur etc. (*Litt. notab.*): Quod Wyche. Expliciunt quaestiones super secundum et tertium libros de anima secundum Scotum alias doctorem subtilem.
   The text contains the 23 questions of the collection but in the following order: qq. 1-5, 10-12, 7-9, 6, 13-23. Wyche numbers the questions sequentially, 1-23; the question-numbers are marked by blue paraphs in the margin at the beginning of each question (e.g., Quaestio prima, Quaestio tertia); the questions are not numbered in the other manuscripts as this one copied from Beta, **H** and **L**, indicating that the questions were not numbered in the model but are here an editorial

introduction by Wyche. Wyche also wrote the title-heading and the *Expliciunt* in his *textualis formata* display script. The name *Scotulus*, to whom Wyche attributes the *Quaestiones* in the title-heading, sometimes refers to Antonius Andreae, but in his *Expliciunt* Wyche assigns the work unambiguously to Scotus. The reference to *Scotulus* in the title-heading led Balić and others to think that the questions might have been compiled, if not authored, by Antonius, but Wyche's use of the diminutive in the title and Scotus' proper name in the *Expliciunt* suggests that the term *Scotulus* here may signify "the young Scotus." Folio 96v is blank.

MS 4, ff. 97-113***:** Parchment. *Gatherings*: ix^{12} (97-108), x^{10} (109-113*****). The texts were copied by Thomas Wyche in 1 col., 158 x 90 mm, 32 lines per col.

6) ROBERTUS COWTON, *Quaestio inceptoris* d.3 qq.16-21 et 23, ff. 97r-109r:
    Quaestio inceptoris Cowton super primum librum Sententiarum distinctione 3^a quaestione 16 (*in marg. sup.*). Utrum intellectus noster pro statu viae posset per creaturas cognoscere de Deo quid est etc. Quod non arguitur per illud secundi Metaphysicae.... cui nomen potentiae imponitur et sic aliud est a quo imponitur nomen et aliud cui imponitur nomen etc.

7) RICHARDUS ARMACHANUS, *In 1 Sent.* q. 4, ff. 109r-113r:
    Armachanus s[uper] primum Sententiarum quaestio 4^a (*in marg.* cropped). Utrum beatitudo sit actus intellectus vel voluntatis et primo arguitur quod sit actus intellectus quia in eadem potentia est beatitudo.... aut ne adipiscatur non autem metuit ergo non cupit haec ista potentia tunc metus.
    Folio 113v and the five following folios, 113*-113*****, are blank.

* * *

MS 5, ff. 114-119***:** Parchment. *Gathering*: xi^{11} (114-119*****). The text is copied by Robert Law in a "mixed *Anglicana*-Secretary" script (Hanna), 1 col., 146 x 90 mm, 31-32 lines per col.

8) PETRUS THOMAE, *Medulla formalitatum* (fragmentum), f. 114r:
    ....primo modo est vera secundo modo. Vera falsa est maior.... et ita non facit dici realiter sed per paternitatem differt a filio realiter. (*Litt. notab.*): Explicit medulla fomalitatum Petri Thomae secundum Hardyng.
    As Hanna observes, since this text was copied by Robert Law, the signature "Hardyng" must be the name of the scribe of the exemplar of this manuscript.

9) ANONYMUS, *Bona quaestio metaphysicalis de ente*, ff. 114v-119v:
    Bona quaestio metaphysicalis (*in marg. sup.*). Utrum scientia metaphysicalis quae est theologia philosophorum omnium tradatis notitiam sub ente.... patet responsio ad illud et ad alia argumenta adducta contra quaestionem. Laus Deo. (*Litt. notab.*): Explicit Bona quaestio de Ente.
    Folios 119*-119***** are blank.

* * *

MS 6, ff. 120-145: Parchment and paper sheets. *Gatherings*: xii^{12} (120-131), xiii^{14} (132-145); the rectos in the first-half of each gathering are signed with arabic numerals; copied by Robert Law in 1 col., 147 x 90 mm, 35-38 lines per col.

10) ANONYMUS, *Quaestio optima metaphysicalis*, ff. 120r-145v:
   Quaestio optima metaphysicalis (*litt. notab.*). Utrum metaphysica omnium scientiarum Deo principium similiter principii et omnium rerum creatarum.... non ab intellectu operante circa extrema in comparatione ergo conclusio falsa quae dicit etc.

* * *

MS 7, ff. 146-203: Parchment with some paper leaves. *Gatherings*: 1 (inserted leaf, 146), xiv^{10} (147-156), xv^{12} (157-168), xvi^{12} (169-180, stubs of 2 missing leaves), xvii^{16} (181-196), xviii^{7} (197-203, stubs of 4 missing leaves; a last leaf is probably lost). Copied by Robert Law in 1 col., 154 x 90 mm, 38-40 lines per col. Folio 146r is blank; f. 146v bears the rubric: "Incipiunt tituli quaestionum distinctionum alias formalitatum Petri Thomae. Sequitur titulus primae quaestionis"; no table of questions follows the rubric.

11) PETRUS THOMAE, *Tractatus distinctionum alias formalitatum*, ff. 147r-200r:
   Tractatus distinctionum alias formalitatum Petri Thomae (*litt. notab. in marg. sup.*). Quoniam secundum sententiam contrariis 10. Metaphysicae distinctio est propria passio entis.... a qua ponitur distinctum etc. in realitate generis et differentiae respectu speciei et materiae et formae respectu compositi. (*Litt. notab.*): Expliciunt quaestiones de distinctione formalitatum determinatae a Petro Thome de ordine fratrum minorum de provincia S. Jacobi quod Lawe.
   Cf. MS **N**, ff. 37ra-63rb.

6. *Oxford, Magdalen College Library, Ms. lat. 80* [= **N**].

English (Oxford, Magdalen College?), first-quarter of the 15th c.; parchment, 290 x 195 mm, iii + 256 ff. (numbered ff. 1-233 but including formerly unnumbered ff. 160, 160*-160** and rear pastedown).[12] *Gatherings*: iii + i-iii^{12} (1-36, followed by 8 stubs of a missing gathering), iv-v^{12} (37-60), vi^{7} (61-67, 5 stubs of missing leaves, followed by 12 stubs of a missing gathering), vii-xiii^{12} (68-151), xiv^{11} (152-160**; a leaf is torn out between 160* and 160**), xv-xx^{12} (161-232) + 1 (233). Catchwords are written at the bottom of the last verso of each gathering (the catchwords in gatherings vii-xx are boxed); the rectos of the first-half of each gathering are numbered; gatherings iv-v are signed a-b, indicating that the book binds together booklets that originally were written separately. Otherwise, the whole Folio manuscript was written by a single scribe (save ff. 31vb-36vb, probably by a second hand) in "mixed *Anglicana*-Secretary" script "of university mien" (Hanna); frame-ruled in brown crayon for 2 cols., 203 x 63-65 mm (centerspace: 14 mm), 52-60 lines per col. Five-line blue initials, infilled in red, with red flourishing that runs up and down the margin begin each text; the flourishing on f. 1r frames the writing-space, running down the left side, the centerspace and the top and bottom margins; 3-line blue initials of the same design begin the questions; generally the texts are not divided further by paraphs. There are no text-headings, and colophons are written by the scribe "in text ink in bastard Secretary" (Hanna). The decoration and rubrication in this manuscript are very similar to that in MS **O** (see below).

The name Magister Bentley appears twice on the rear pastedown and after the colophon of the *Quaestiones De anima* (f. 177rb), where an annotator writes: "etiam Magister Bentley."

---

[12]Coxe, *Catalogus* II.10, 45-46. Again, Kent Emery thanks Ralph Hanna for giving him a copy of his description of this manuscript. Hanna's description will appear in his forthcoming catalogue of Latin manuscripts in Magdalen College Library.

Bentley was evidently the owner of the manuscript rather than the copyist; the tag "etiam Magister Bentley" might be a note to the binder indicating that this booklet along with the others is to be bound in the codex. John Bentley (†1486) of the Worcester diocese was the Chaplain of Magdalen College in 1477-78, Precentor of the College in 1483-86 and Principal of the grammar hall in 1485-86.[13] Evidently the manuscript has stayed in the library of Magdalen College since the Middle Ages. The manuscript contains texts suitable for a (largely 'Scotistic') pedagogy in the Arts. A table of contents is written on the front pastedown:

> Haec sunt contenta huius libri:
> Primus est Petrus Thomas de ente
> 2 Formalitates Petri Thomae
> 3 Burleus de memoria et reminiscentia
> 4 Alexander de anima
> 5 Quaestiones doctoris subtilis de anima
> 6 Expositio Burlei de motu animalium
> 7 Idem de longitudine et brevitate vitae
> 8 Quaestiones super 4 libros meteororum

1) PETRUS THOMAE, *Liber de ente*, ff. 1ra-36vb:
   Sicut dicit Philosophus primo Physicorum capitulo primo Primum est secundum naturam communia discere.... (1ra) Ad primum sic proceditur et videtur quod conceptus entis sit cognoscibilis.... aliquorum si quodlibet istorum ab isto 3° abstrahatur manet causa....
   The last gathering of the text is missing.

2) PETRUS THOMAE, *Formalitates*, ff. 37ra-63rb:
   Ad evidentiam distinctionis praedicamentorum sic intendo procedere primo enim praemittam neccessaria.... sicut in realitate generis et differentie respectu speciei et in materia et forma respectu compositi et [est] finis. Expliciunt formalitates fratris Petri Thomae.
   Cf. MS **M**, ff. 147r-200r.

3) GUALTERUS BURLAEUS, *Expositio in librum de memoria et reminiscentia*, ff. 63va-67vb:
   De memoria autem et memorari etc. In prohemio huius libri quod durat usque ibi.... (63va) Primum quid haec est pars executiva in qua Philosophus exequitur.... in eis quapropter figuratur in aspectu earum et propter hoc de difficili amittit eas. Explicit expositio Magistri Walteri Burley de memoria et reminiscentia.

4) ALEXANDER [BONINI DE ALEXANDRIA?] [*Quaestiones*] *de anima*, ff. 68ra-160*rb.
   Interrogasti me honoret te Deus illustrissime fili Philippe de Melduno de optimo quod est in nobis scilicet anima... Ubi non est scientiae animae non est bonum Proverbiorum 19. Augustinus De Trinitate 4°. capitulo primo: Scientiam terrestrium caelestiumque rerum.... (68rb) ....'Bonorum honorabilium'. Liber iste cuius expositioni intendimus dividitur in duas partes.... (88va) Secundus de anima (*in marg. sup.*). Quoniam quid a prioribus postquam Philosophus dixit de anima secundum operum aliorum.... (134ra) Tertius de anima (*in marg. sup.*). De parte ante animae postquam Philosophus

---
[13]Emden, *BRUO* I (1957), 170.

determinavit de parte anima sensitiva.... (160*rb) ....aliquid alteri et hoc modo animalia multas habent operationes et virtutes ad bene esse determinatas Explicit sententia Alexandri (*al. man. add.*): super tertio de anima.

This commentary on *De anima* is probably by Alexander Bonini de Alexandria, OFM. The work contains a short preface to Philippus de Melduno (identified on f. 68*ra*), an introduction, and the text of the questions on the three Books. This work, without the introduction and prefatory material, is also contained in MS **D**, ff. 95*r*-134*v*, and there it is explicitly and wrongly attributed to Alexander of Hales. Folios 160*v*-160** are blank.

5) IOANNES DUNS SCOTUS, *Quaestiones super secundum et tertium De anima*, ff. 161*ra*-177*rb*: Quaeritur utrum sensus tactus sit unus vel plures. Videtur quod unus quia si esset plures.... species obiecti et ratio sibi intelligendi per quam est in actu ergo etc. Expliciunt quaestiones doctoris subtilis super secundum et tertium de anima. (*Al. man.*): etiam Magister Bentley.

The *Quaestiones* are contained in two Folio gatherings, xv[12] (161-172) and xvi[12] (173-184), containing also two small treatises by Walter Burley, the three works forming one manuscript unit. The text contains the 23 questions of the collection but in the following order: qq. 1- 4, q. 5 to n. 11, q. 9 starting at n. 13, qq. 10-12, q. 13 to n. 6, q. 5 starting at n. 11, qq. 6-8, q. 9 to n. 13, q. 13 starting at n. 6, qq. 14-23. The first disruption of the text occurs in q. 5: the first part of that text (nn. 1-11) is written in ff. 163*ra*, lin. 5-163*rb*, lin. 12; at that point the scribe picks up the text of q. 9 *in medias res* (at n. 13), which he copies to the end of that question in ff. 163*rb*, lin. 13-163*va*, lin. 3. A later user (Bentley?) of the book realized the error in the order of the text; in the margin of f. 163*rb*, lin. 12 (at q. 5 n. 11), he directs the reader to the rest of q. 5 further on in the manuscript: "Quere residuum huius questionis in principio quarti ab hinc folij ad tale signum §§"; that sign is found at f. 166*ra*, lin. 3, in the middle of q. 13 (to n. 6), where the rest of q. 5 (at n. 11) resumes. At the transition from q. 13 to q. 5 at f. 166*ra*, lin. 3, the ink becomes much darker. None of the other disruptions in the text are cross-noted by the annotator. The copyist of the text does not number the questions, as neither does the copyist of the *Quaestiones* in MS **O** (see below); this indicates that the questions were not numbered in their common model, Epsilon, and that they were not numbered in Beta, another model to which the copyist of this manuscript took recourse (see the note to MS **M**, item 5, above). It is the scribe himself who has written the Explicit to the *Quaestiones* in a "bastard Secretary" script slightly different from the script in which he copied the text.

6) GUALTERUS BURLAEUS, *Expositio de motu animalium*, ff. 177*va*-180*va*: De motu autem eo qui est animalium secundum Philosophum 3° Physicorum volentem considerare de natura necessarium est considerare motu.... in eo in uno tempore et non in alio. Postea recapitulat et patet finis. Explicit expositio Magistri Walteri Burley super libro de motu animalium.

The text is edited by F. Scott and H. Shapiro, "Walter Burley's Commentary on Aristotle's *De motu animalium*," *Traditio* 25 (1969): 171-90. This text is also copied in MS **K**, ff. 122*r*-134*r*, where it is anonymous.

7) GUALTERUS BURLAEUS, *Sententia libri De longitudine et brevitate vitae*, ff. 180*va*-184*vb*: De eo autem quod est causa rem longae vitae etc. Intentio Philosophi in hoc tractatu est determinare de causis longitudinis et brevitatis.... est causa secundum speciem longitudinis vitae in aliis et aliis viventibus. Explicit sententia libri de longitudine et brevitate vitae secundum Magistrum Walterum Burley.

This text is copied in MS **K**, ff. 104*v*-114*r*, where it is anonymous.

8) 'SCOTULUS', *Quaestionaria sententia super tres libros Meteororum*, ff. 185ra-223vb:
Quaeritur utrum de impressionibus meteororum sit scientia tamquam de subiectis. Arguitur quod non.... (222va) ....distarent circulo dato. Ad responsiones dicitur quod solutae sunt ex praecedentibus. Explicit quaestionaria sententia super tres libros Meteororum secundum Scotulum. (222vb) Quaeritur circa quartum utrum putrefactio sit possibilis vel possibile sic fieri putrefactionem.... ad generationem alterius sicut putrefactio bovis est pepansis ad generationem apum.

This copy contains all four Books of this text, which is often attributed wrongly to Scotus, as it is in Wadding's edition (IV:1-208). The name *Scotulus* sometimes refers to Antonius Andreae. For these questions, see also MS **H**, ff. 109ra-169rb; MS **L**, ff. 121r-215r; MS **O**, ff. 86ra-134rb.

7. *Oxford, Oriel College Library, Ms. 35* [= **O**].

English (Oxford, House of Blessed Mary, i.e., Oriel College), first decade of the 15th c., certainly before 1414; parchment, 318 x 200 mm, 259 ff (f. 259 is the soft back cover).[14] This codex binds together three separate manuscripts, ff. 1-5, 6-151, 152-258. The book was bound before 1414. On f. 257v are a number of pledge or "caution" notes that are either partly or wholly effaced or scraped. Towards the bottom of the side one finds this note: "Magister [scraped out] exposita in cista Rowthbury in vigilia Sancte Cecilie virginis Anno domini millesimo cccc^{mo} xxxij° etc." Beneath this is another illegible inscription, and beneath that, entirely effaced and visible only under ultra-violet light, is a note recording that the book was pledged as security for a supplemental loan in 1414: "anno domini m cccc^{mo} xijii supplementum."[15] At the top of the same f. 257v an ownership-note indicates that in 1414 as today the book belonged to Oriel College: "Iste liber est domus beate Mariae Oxoniensis."[16] In the middle of f. 258r is written the signature of a "Magister Carysdeall," who seemingly was the owner of the book. "Magister Carysdeall" is probably Richard Garsdale (aka: Carsdale, Cartisdale, Cartysdale) of the York diocese, who was a fellow of Oriel College ca. 1404-1413, M.A., Sch. Th. by 1411, B.Th. by 1413, D.Th. by 1417. Garsdale was a member of the University commission that drew up a list of 267 errors in the works of John Wycliffe, which was submitted to the Archbishop of Canterbury.[17] The codex contains writings by three Oxford Masters who flourished in the last decade of the fourteenth century or at the turn of

---

[14]Coxe, *Catalogus* I.5, 12-13. See also C. Balić, "Segnia e note critiche nelle opere di Giovanni Duns Scoto," *Studi e Testi* 126 (1946): 316 nn. 36-37; W. Seńko, "Un traité inconnu *De ente et essentia*," AHDLMA 27 (1960): 239; James A. Weisheipl, "Ockham and some Mertonians," *Mediaeval Studies* 30 (1968): 178. Kent Emery profoundly thanks Jeremy Catto, Oriel College, Oxford, for his assistance in studying this manuscript, and especially for pointing out the pledge notes, one of which is invisible and which Catto first discovered by ultra-violet light.

[15]By means of the pledge system in Oxford, scholars could "pawn" a book or books as a security to one of the University chests for a loan of cash to meet various expenses or for the purchase or use of another book. The colleges also lent money to their members against the security of a book. Moreover, a scholar could deposit as a pledge one of his own books at another College library in order to borrow a book from that library; when a loan remained unredeemed, the pledged book remained with the library of the College that had issued the loan. The Robury or "Rothbury" Chest mentioned on f. 257v of this manuscript had become a chest of the University by 1321; the Selton Chest (see the Description of MS **K**, nr. 3, above) had become a chest of the University by 1360. Concerning the pledge and caution system at Oxford, see Parkes, "The Provision of Books," 409-12, and T.H. Aston and R. Faith, "The Endowments of the University and Colleges to circa 1348," in *The History of the University of Oxford I: The Early Oxford Schools*, ed. J.I. Catto (Oxford, 1984), 274-87.

[16]The House of Blessed Mary or Oriel College was founded in 1326; Magdalen College, which came to own MSS **M** and **N**, was founded in 1458. Thomas Wyche, Fellow of Oriel College, donated MS **M** along with several other books, possibly as pledges, to Magdalen (see Description nr. 5, above); evidently he did so shortly after Magdalen was founded.

[17]Emden, *BRUO* III, 744.

the new century. Robert Alington was a fellow of Queen's College (1379-86) and became Chancellor of the University in 1393-95; John Sharpe, a master from Prague who then taught at Oxford, was elected as a fellow of Queen's in 1391; less is known concerning William Milverley, who is thought to have flourished ca. 1400.[18] Because of the positive dates yielded by the codex and because of its contents, we judge that the manuscripts in the book were copied between 1400 and 1414, although it is possible that any one of the manuscripts was copied shortly before, in the last decade of the fourteenth century. As its contents and ownership suggest, this Folio volume was prepared for a student ("Gratiasque Deo et meis doctoribus," f. 151va) and/or teacher in the Arts at Oxford, following disputes and lectures immediately contemporary with the manuscript.

MS 1, ff. 1-5: *Gathering:* i⁵ (1-5); frame-ruled for 2 cols., 215 x 155 mm (centerspace: 69 mm), 44 lines per col. The title-heading and the colophon are written by the scribe of the text. There is no rubrication; spaces for initials are left blank with guide letters. Folios 1-2r are blank.

1) GUILLELMUS MILVERLEY, *Compendium de quinque universalibus,*[19] ff. 2va-5vb:
   Universalia magistri Mylverley (*in marg. sup.*). Pro superficiali notitia universalium primo notandum quod triplex est universale quantum spectat ad propositum.... equaliter praedicatur de homine puncto et albedine et sic de singulis aliis speciebus specialissimis etc. Explicit compendium de quinque universalibus secundum magistrum William Mylverley.

* * *

MS 2, ff. 6-151: *Gatherings:* ii¹² (6-17), iii¹² (18-29), iv¹⁴ (30-43), v-xiii¹² (44-151). The scribe writes catchwords at the foot of col. b on every verso; catchwords on the last versos of gatherings are boxed. Pricked and frame- and line-ruled for 2 cols., 225 x 155 mm (centerspace: 12 mm), 51-55 lines per col. (the writing-space for the *Quaestiones De anima* is ruled for 55 lines throughout). The copyist signs his initial, M, at the end of the last work in this manuscript (f. 151va). M. writes a mixed *Anglicana*-Secretary script; he writes the opening lines of questions in slightly enlarged letters in a bastard Secretary script; he uses the same script for writing title-headings, colophons, etc. The works begin with divided red and blue initials, infilled and flourished in the margins with red penwork (8-line Q on f. 6ra, 5-line Q on f. 44ra, 5-line Q on f. 61ra, 3-line C on f. 86ra and 4-line F on f. 134va); 2- and 3-line blue initials, infilled and flourished in the margins with red penwork, mark the beginnings of questions; further text-divisions are signaled by alternating red and blue paraphs. The style of decoration and rubrication is similar to that in MS **N**, except that the latter manuscript does not display divided initials and lacks paraphs.

2) ROBERTUS ALINGTON, *Litteralis sententia super Praedicamenta Aristotelis,*[20] ff. 6ra-43vb:
   Antepraedicamenta Alyngtōn (*in marg. sup.*). Quoniam logica ad omnium scientiarum principia viam habet.... De istis tamen et aliis dubiis in hac parte plenius Deo favente

---

[18]Emden, *BRUO* I, 30-31, and Dobson, "The Religious Orders," 227-28 (Alington); Emden, *BRUO* III, 1660 (Sharpe); Emden, *BRUO* II (1958), 1284, and E.J. Ashworth and P.V. Spade, "Logic in Late Medieval Oxford," in *The History of the University of Oxford* II, ed. Catto and Evans, 50 (Milverley).

[19]Cf. Charles H. Lohr, "Medieval Latin Aristotle Commentaries," *Traditio* 24 (1968): 203; G.E. Mohan, "Incipits of Logical Writings in Latin (XIII-XVth. cent.)," *Franciscan Studies* 12 (1952): 435. Excerpts of Milverley's *Compendium* and Alington's *Sententia* have been edited and published by Alessandro D. Conti, *Iohannes Sharpe: Quaestio super Universalia* (Firenze, 1990), 159-64, 149-58.

[20]Cf. C.H. Lohr, "Medieval Latin Aristotle Commentaries," *Traditio* 29 (1973): 96-97.

dicetus in libro sexti principiorum. Ista igitur ad praesens dicta sufficiant in compendio pro litterali sententia huius libri. Explicit litteralis sententia super praedicamenta Aristotelis secundum expositionem Magistri Roberti Alyngtoni veritatis theologicae professoris cuius animae propicietur Deus. Amen.

3) IOANNES DUNS SCOTUS, [*Quaestiones super secundum et tertium*] *De anima*, ff. 44ra-60vb:
Doctor Subtilis De anima (*in marg. sup.*). Quaeritur utrum sensus tactus sit unus vel plures. Videtur quod unus quia si essent plures tunc essent sex sensus.... circumstantiando eam ut dictum est supra. Explicit Doctor Subtilis De anima.

The attribution of the *Quaestiones* to Scotus in the title-heading and the Explicit is made by the copyist in his bastard Secretary display script. The text contains qq. 1-22 of the collection, omitting q. 23, in the same disorder as MS **N**: qq. 1-4, q. 5 to n. 11, q. 9 starting at n. 13, qq. 10-12, q. 13 to n. 6, q. 5 starting at n. 11, qq. 6-8, q. 9 to n. 13, q. 13 starting at n. 6, qq. 14-22. The scribe does not number the questions in his copy. He writes catchwords at the bottom of every verso; catchwords are missing, however, on ff. 45vb and 51vb, which are in sections of the work where the text is disrupted (in q. 5 melded with the last part of q. 9, and in q. 9 melded with the last part of q. 13). The text ends on f. 60vb, lin. 30; the scribe leaves a 13-line space between the end of the text and the colophon; we know that q. 23, omitted here, was in the manuscript that was the model of this one; the scribe's placement of the Explicit probably was meant only to occupy empty space in the column, but perhaps the space between text and colophon bespeaks his indecision as to whether to copy the last question in his model (see Introduction § 2.N, below).

4) IOANNES SHARPE, [*Quaestiones super libros Physicorum I-II*],[21] ff. 61ra-86ra.
Scharpe (*in marg. sup.*). Utrum tantum tria sunt intrinsecum rerum naturalium principia.... consequenter in eis dictum extiterat imputetur memoriae labilitati et periatur aetati etc. Deo gratias.

5) IOANNES SCOTUS IUNIOR, *Quaestiones in libro Meteorum*, ff. 86ra-134rb:
Hic incipiunt quaestiones libri Meteorum per M.J. Scotum Iuniorem (*al. man.*). Circa primum Meteorum quaeritur utrum impressionibus meteoricis sit scientiam tanquam de subiectis. Arguitur quod non.... Ad rationes dicitur quod solutae sunt ex praecedentibus etc. etc. Expliciunt quaestiones in libri [sic] Meteorum secundum Scotum. *Al. man.*: Iuniorem *add. in marg.* secundum exemplar Parisius. Ffinito libro. Sit laus et gloria Christo.

The *Hic incipiunt*.... is written by an annotator different from the copyist of the text in a space that had been left blank; the same annotator adds the information *Iuniorem* (over effaced text) *secundum exemplar Parisius* to the colophon written by the scribe. Scotus Iunior is probably Ioannes de Lythona Scotus, licensed at Paris in 1345, or Ioannes Rede Scotus, who determined at Paris in 1348; see L. Meier, OFM, "Nicolas de Gorham, O.P., Author of the Commentary on the Apocalypse Erroneously Attributed to John Duns Scotus," *Dominican Studies* 3 (1950): 359-62, at 359-60 n. 3. For these questions, often attributed to Scotus, see MS **H**, ff. 109ra-169rb; MS **L**, ff. 121r-215r; MS **N**, ff. 185ra-223vb.

6) [GUILLELMUS MILVERLEY], *De sex principiis*,[22] ff. 134va-151va:
Sex principia (*in marg. sup.*). Forma est compositum continens. Intentio auctoris in hoc libello est diffusius tractare de sex principiis respectivis.... verborum infallibiliter perscrutari. Gratiasque Deo et meis doctoribus in saecula saeculorum etc. quod M.

---

[21]Cf. C.H. Lohr, "Medieval Latin Aristotle Commentaries," *Traditio* 27 (1971): 279; *Iohannes Sharpe: Quaestio super Universalia*, ed. A. Conti, 213, 218-20.
[22]Cf. C.H. Lohr, "Medieval Latin Aristotle Commentaries," *Traditio* 24 (1968): 203.

MS 3, ff. 152-258: *Gatherings*: xiv-xxii[12] (152-258); boxed catchwords on the last versos of the gatherings; gatherings xx-xxii are signed a-c. Pricked, frame- and line-ruled for 2 cols., 228 x 158 mm (centerspace: 12 mm), 51 lines per col. The script is similar to that in MS 2, above, but is more spikey and angular. There are running headers in an alternating red and blue pattern (L | I, L | II, etc.) that indicate the book numbers on facing openings of the first four Books. The writing-space on the first sides of Books I-III (ff. 152r, 170r, 178v) are box-framed by a bar-border with red and blue bands. The text-marking is similar to that in MS 2, above; 6- and 8-line red and blue divided initials, infilled and flourished with red penwork, begin each Book; other text-divisions are signaled by 4-line blue initials, infilled and flourished with red penwork; further text-divisions are marked by alternating red and blue paraphs.

7) IOANNES DUNS SCOTUS, *Quaestiones super Metaphysicam*,[23] ff. 152ra-255vb:

(151vb, al. man.): Doctor subtilis super Metaphysicam. (152ra) Omnes homines naturaliter scire desiderant. In principio Metaphysicae quam prae manibus habemus permittit Philosophus hanc propositionem.... Tunc ad argumentum equivocat potentiam quia maior est vera de potentia obiectiva patet ex prima quaestione et in minore accipit potentiam.

The title *Doctor Subtilis super Metaphysicam* is written by a later hand in blank space of col. b on the folio before the *Quaestiones* (f. 151vb); the text of the *Quaestiones* is incomplete, concluding towards the end of q. 7 n. 20 of Book IX. Folio 256r is blank, as is f. 256v except for an inscription at the top edge: "aue maria gracia plena dominus tecum"; f. 257r bears pen jottings, and on f. 257v are a number of pledge notes (see above); at the top of f. 258r is an inscription, "Inspice verte lege bene conspice claude recede 333," and in the middle is the signature, "Magister Carysdeall" (see above).

8. *Roma, Biblioteca Angelica, Ms. 953 (R.5.4)* [= **Q**].

English, 14th c. (catalogue description: "XIV ineuntis"); parchment, 191 x 132 mm, 84 ff.[24] This Octavo manuscript was copied by at least five hands; changes of hand occur at ff. 57r, 74r, 80r, 82v and 84v. Folios 1r-79v and 83v-84r are written in 1 col. of 36 lines, while ff. 80r-82v are written in 2 cols., 47 lines per col. The collection of texts served as a handbook for a curriculum in the Arts.

1) ANONYMUS, [*Quaestiones logicales*], ff. 1r-25r:

(f. 1r): Circa primum principium complexivum negotiando. Quaeritur utrum 'de quolibet affirmatio vel negatio et de nullo ambo simul' sit primum principium. Et videtur quod sic....

(f. 2r): Secundo fuit quaesitum utrum ens sit adaequatum subiectum primi principii complexi quoad nos....

(f. 3v): Tertio fuit quaesitum utrum subiectum primi principii complexi quoad nos quod fuit positum conveniat(?) secundum eandem rationem formaliter omnibus ad quae se extendit veritas(?) istius principii. Et videtur quod non....

---

[23]Scotus, *OPh* III: xvi.
[24]H. Narducci, *Catalogus codicum manuscriptorum praeter graecos et orientales in Biblioteca Angelica olim coenobii Sancti Augustini de Urbe* (Roma, 1862), 402-3.

(f. 9v): Quarto fuit quaesitum utrum unitas rationis formalis quae posita est entitatis creatae et increatae sit unitas ex natura rei....

(f. 10v): Quinto fuit quaesitum utrum unitas entitatis creatae et increatae sit unitas realis. Et videtur quod sic....

(f. 11v): Sexto fuit quaesitum utrum subiectum istius includatur quiditative in alia inferiori. Et videtur quod sic....

(f. 12v): Septimo fuit quaesitum utrum subiectum istius principii dicatur denominative de omnibus. Et videtur quod non....

(f. 13r): Octavo quaesitum fuit utrum ratio entis se habet per omnimodum indifferentiam ad omnes alias rationes. Et videtur quod sic....

(f. 14r): Nono fuit quaesitum utrum aliqua ratio sit communior ratione subiecti principii primi. Et videtur quod sic....

(f. 14v): Decimo quaesitum fuit utrum istud principium de quo fit sermo habet esse in anima vel rerum natura. Videtur quod tantum in anima....

(f. 15r): Undecimo fuit quaesitum utrum istud principium complexum de quo fit sermo sit demonstrabilis. Et videtur quod sic....

(f. 16r): Duodecimo fuit quaesitum utrum istud principium sit demonstratum omnium veritatum cognoscendum(?) a nostro intellectu. Et videtur quod sic....

(f. 17r): Tertio decimo fuit quaesitum utrum istud principium possit in aliquo pati calumniam. Et videtur quod sic....

(f. 17v): Quarto decimo fuit quaesitum utrum principium istud quod immediate sequitur istud et ponitur secunda pars totius primi principii scilicet de nullo ambo simul possit infringi. Et videtur quod sic....

(f. 19r): Quinto decimo fuit quaesitum utrum subiectum istius principii habet plures passiones de ipso demonstrabilis. Et videtur quod non....

(f. 21r): Sexto decimo fuit quaesitum utrum subiectum primi principii complexi sit subiectum in metaphysica. Et videtur quod non....

(f. 21v): Decimo septimo fuit quaesitum utrum subiectum primi principii complexi sit adaequatum obiectum potentiae intellectivae. Et videtur quod non....

(f. 22v): Decimo octavo fuit quaesitum utrum subiectum istius principii primi complexi dividatur per differentias oppositas formaliter distinctivas. Et videtur quod non.... (f. 25r).... Sed principium sine principio de quo formatur ut patuit prima complexio. Vitam carentem det termino scriptorum horum miserimo. Amen.

Another anonymous question follows on ff. 25v-27v:

Utrum aliquis conceptus simpliciter simplex primae intentionis possit esse conveniens univoce Deo et creaturae. Arguitur quod non.... Scilicet de veritate univocationis potuisset plura dici sed quantum ad propositum spectat sufficit istud breve verbum.

2) [IOANNES DUNS SCOTUS, *Quaestiones super secundum et tertium De anima*], ff. 28r-54r, [cum quaestione *De ente*, ff. 48r-50r]:

De sensu et intellectu. Quaeritur utrum sensus tactus sit unus vel plures.... circumstantiando eam ut dictum est supra. Amen.

The text contains qq. 1-6, 8-15, 17-22 (ff. 28r-45v, 50r-54r), omitting qq. 7, 16 and 23. On f. 45v, q. 20 breaks off before the end, and is tagged with an aborted *Explicit*: "....est obiectum intellectus ut visum est. Deo gratias Deo gratias amen. Explicit liber de...." Folios 46r-47v are blank; in ff. 48r-50r is an extra question: "De ente. Quaeritur utrum ens dicatur univoce de omnibus. Et videtur quod sic...." Questions 21-22 of Scotus' *Quaestiones* follow in ff. 50r-54r. The question *De ente* may belong to the Scotist, Petrus Thomae. The *Quaestiones* in this manuscript bear the short-hand title *De sensu et intellectu* and are *sine nomine*; cf. MS **B**, ff. 26r-37v (Description nr. 14, item 2).

3) ANONYMUS, *Quaestio*, ff. 54r-56v:
Utrum actio et passio constituunt diversa praedicamenta vel unum....

4) ANONYMUS, [*Quaestio de Categoriis*], ff. 57r-57v:
Utrum superiora praedicarentur de inferioribus ut superiora vel sub ratione communi vel contracta.... Sed est quaedam res relata nulla intellectu existentem vel apprehen....
The text ends abruptly and is incomplete.

5) ANONYMUS, [*De propositionibus, etc.*],[25] ff. 58r-69r:
Cum de propositionibus intendamus.... Unde dicimus quod terminus ille simpliciter tenetur quod nec tantum pro pluribus nec tantum pro non tenetur sed communiter ad hoc.

6) PORPHYRIUS, *Institutiones ad Chrysaorium* [*Isagoge*], ff. 69v-73v.
Cum sit necessarium Crissorori et ad ea quae est apud Aristotelem praedicamentorum doctrinam nosse quid sit genus....

7) ARISTOTELES, *Praedicamenta* [*Categoriae*], ff. 74v-79v.
Praedicamenta Aristotelis (*al. man.*). Equivoca dicuntur quorum nomen est solum commune....

8) ARISTOTELES, *Perihermenias* [*De interpretatione*], ff. 80r-82r (f. 82v is blank).
....[uni]versale vel non universale universaliter vel non universaliter ut omnis homo albus est non est omnis homo albus.... Explicit Peryermenias. Deo gratias.

9) ANONYMUS, [*Fragmenta grammaticales*], ff. 83r-84v.

9. *Città del Vaticano, Biblioteca Apostolica Vaticana, Cod. Urbinas latinus 1406* [= **U**].

Copied in England by a German scribe? second half of the 15th c.; parchment, 224 x 160 mm, 94 ff.[26] This composite codex comprises four manuscripts written by four different hands: ff. 1-31, ff. 33-35, ff. 36-90, ff. 91-93. The first manuscript (ff. 1r-31v), containing the *Quaestiones De anima*, is written in a *bastarda libraria* script, typical in Germany and the Netherlands, in 1 col. of 37-39 lines. Other sections of the book are written in two columns. The initials and the text-marking are also typical of Germanic manuscripts. The border decoration on the first folio, however, is Italian, and was possibly penned later, perhaps in Italy. Also, the copyist sometimes uses the English abbreviation for *patet per*. Our critical examination of the text reveals that the *Quaestiones De anima* were copied from the same model in Oxford from which John Saunder, fellow of All Souls, copied the *Quaestiones* in MS **K** (see Description nr. 3). In the mid-fifteenth century foreign professional scribes, notably from Germany and the Low Countries, worked in Oxford and were commissioned to copy books for the masters and

---

[25]G.E. Mohan, *Incipits of Philosophical Writings of the 13th-15th Centuries* (*pro manuscripto* in the Franciscan Institute Library of St. Bonaventure University), 178, has identified other manuscripts containing this work.
[26]C. Stornajolo, *Codices Urbinates latini III: Codices 1001-1779* (Città del Vaticano, 1921), 310-11.

students there (including works by Scotus). Moreover, from the late thirteenth century onwards many friars from the continent, especially from Italy and Germany, were sent to study in Oxford and copied books there. Some like Petrus Pauli of Nyköping, who copied the *Quaestiones* in MS **L** (Description nr. 4), left what they had copied in Oxford. Others, like the friar Nicholas Comparini of Assisi, a student in the Oxford *studium* in the mid-fourteenth century, carried their books with them from Oxford when they returned to convents on the continent,[27] as seemingly did the copyist of Scotus' *Quaestiones* in this manuscript. In sum, the present manuscript presents the problem for localizing caused by the reality of traveling scribes and bookmen, from convent to convent and from university to university, and of the eclectic usages that they might have picked up in their travels.

1) IOANNES DUNS SCOTUS, *Quaestiones super duos libros De anima*, ff. 1r-31v:
   Utrum sensus tactus sit unus vel plures.... Expliciunt quaestiones secundum doctorem subtilem super duos libros de anima.

   The text contains 22 of the 23 questions in the collection, omitting q. 14, in the following order: qq. 1-4, q. 5 to n. 7.3, q. 10 starting at n. 26.5, qq. 11-12, qq. 7-9, q. 6, q. 13, qq. 15-23. Furthermore, q. 5 breaks off before the end ("aliud ab agente pure corporali...."), q. 10 lacks the beginning of its text ("....sensus particularis quia ab illo actu"), q. 13 breaks off before the end ("non cognitis extremis...."), and q. 15 lacks its beginning ("....Item si distinctio animarum").

2) THOMAS STAKKYS, *Tractatus de animae essentia, officio et retributione*, ff. 33r-35v:
   Qui possessor est mentis diligit animam suam.... utriusque in retributione quoad congressum.

3) ANONYMUS, *Ars grammatica per interrogationes de responsiones*, ff. 36r-87r:
   Quid est quod unusquisque homo naturaliter scire desiderat. Scientiam. Unde habes hoc. Ex philosopho.... cum vero quaeritur quanta debet responderi perfecta vel imperfecta. Et sic est finis huius operis.

4) IOANNES DE EVERISDEN, *Legum medulla versibus hexaemetris*, ff. 87v-90v:
   Iste(?) quod humanum ius divinum quae vocatur.... dilige decretum si iustis canonicari.

5) ANONYMUS, *Casus papales, episcopales et abbaciales*, ff. 91r-93v:
   Primus casus papalis est in illo, qui percutit enormiter clericum.... Finiunt casus papales episcopales et abbatiales.

10. *Città del Vaticano, Biblioteca Apostolica Vaticana, Cod. Vaticanus latinus 890* [=**W**].

Italian, first quarter of the 14th c.; parchment, 289 x 224 mm, 42 ff., written in 2 cols.[28] At the top of f. 31r, the first side of the *Quaestiones De anima*, is a note of ownership: "nota quod solum iste questiones de anima sunt magistri ludouivi de montecorone de...." (two words erased); below the erased line, the note continues, "tabula vero tota precedens est ad usum mei magistri francisci," and then another hand writes the purchase price of the book: "dedi pro eo boll[endinos]." This manuscript is possibly the earliest surviving witness of Scotus' *Quaestiones De anima*.

---
[27] Parkes, "The Provision of Books," 413-17, 438-39; Dobson, "The Religious Orders," 558-59.
[28] A. Pelzer, *Codices vaticani latini* II.1 (Città del Vaticano, 1931), 274-77.

1) GUILLELMUS DE MISSALI, *Abbrevatio et dearticulatio operum Ioannis Duns Scoti*, ff. 1ra-30r:
Tabula super primo Scoti de Reportatione. Utrum Deus sub propria ratione deitatis possit esse subiectum alicuius scientiae.... an distantia que est inter extrema contradictionis sit realiter infinita. Explicit abreviatio et dearticulatio quaestionum super 4^{or} libros Sententiarum magistri Iohannis Scoti et super Quodlibet et super quaestiones Metaphysicae quam composuit frater Guillelmus de missali de prouincia acquitaniae ambo de ordine minorum. Deo gratias amen.

Guillelmus' *Tabulae* contain abbreviations of questions in the *Reportatio* of Scotus' Parisian Commentary on Book I of the *Sentences* (ff. 1r-3r), of the *Quaestiones De anima* and of various questions by Scotus (ff. 3r-5r), of Books I-IV of Scotus' Oxford Commentary on the *Sentences* (ff. 5v-25v), of the *Quodlibet* (ff. 25v-27v), and of Scotus' questions on the *Metaphysics* (ff. 27v-30r). The *Tabulae* are recopied from this manuscript in MS **Y**, ff. 183ra-280vb.[29] The table of the *Quaestiones De anima* is written here in ff. 3rb-4va:

Incipit tabula super quaestiones de anima et super aliquas cedulas. Utrum sensus tactus sit unus sensus.... Utrum singulare sit a nobis intelligibile per se.... quando loquitur de hoc.

Guillelmus lists and abbreviates qq. 1-22, omitting q. 23. Standing in the place of that question, in f. 4ra-va, is the abbreviation of a long question, consisting of four articles, each subdivided into *declarationes* and *conclusiones*:

Utrum intellectivam esse formam corporis humani possit demonstrari. In primo articulo exponit quid intelligit per animam intellectivam et quid per formam. In secundo articulo tractat opinionem Commentatoris in qua sic procedit.... forma praecedit compositum.

2) IOANNES DUNS SCOTUS, *Quaestiones super secundum et tertium De anima*, ff. 31ra-40vb:
Quaeritur utrum sensus tactus sit unus sensus.... (*Al. man.*): Expliciunt quaestiones venerabilis doctoris magistri Johannis scoti de ordine fratrum minorum super 2^m et 3^m de anima amen.

The text contains qq. 1-23 in the order established by the edition. The copyist of the *Quaestiones* does not identify their author; the colophon ("Expliciunt quaestiones....") is written in a later *cursiva formata* script. After a ten-line space running to the foot of the column and immediately at the top of the next folio, we find on ff. 41ra-42vb, written by the same copyist, the six questions that Wadding (V:318-37), using this manuscript, attributed to Scotus and printed under the title *De cognitione Dei*:

3) ANONYMUS, [*Quaestiones de cognitione Dei*], ff. 41ra-42vb:
Quaestio est utrum de Deo possit haberi cognitio media inter cognitionem fidei et patriae....
Quaeritur utrum cognitio abstractiva possit dici cognitio scientalis....
Utrum cognitio abtractiva proprietatum personalium possit habere rationem scientiae....
Utrum talis cognitio abstractiva que ponitur media possit haberi de Deo per aliquod commune representativum limitatum....
Utrum cognitio intuitiva et abstractiva possibilis haberi de Deo sint eiusdem speciei....

---

[29] A different redaction of Guillelmus' *Abbrevatio et dearticulatio*, containing abbreviations of Scotus' commentaries on the *Sentences*, *Quodlibet* and questions on the *Metaphysics* but lacking his abbreviations *super Quaestiones de anima et super aliquas cedulas*, is preserved in at least two other manuscripts: Bologna, Biblioteca Comunale dell'Archiginnasio, Ms. A.162, ff. 1-74 (1463), and Biblioteca Apostolica Vaticana, Cod. Vat. lat. 889, ff. 1-45 (14th c.); see G. Mazzatinti, *Inventari dei manuscritti delle bibliotheche d'Italia* 30 (Firenze, 1924), 76, and Pelzer, *Codices vaticani latini* II.1, 273-74.

Utrum cognitio abstractiva possibilis haberi de Deo et intuitiva de eodem simul possint stare in intellectu.... quia utraque scientifica.

Question 6 is incomplete in this manuscript and hence in Wadding who used it. The first five of these questions are appended to Scotus' *Quaestiones De anima* in MS **F**, ff. 184*vb*-189*va*, and the six questions are incorporated, with five other questions concerning the same topic, within the *Quaestiones De anima* in MS **C**, ff. 139*ra*-148*va*. All eleven questions are listed as pertaining to Scotus in the register in MS **Z**² (items 77-87). Duns Scotus almost certainly was not the author of these questions; concerning their authorship and their relationship to the *Quaestiones De anima*, see the comments on MS **C**, item 2 (Description nr. 15, below), and also on MS **V**, item 4 (Description nr. 24, below).

11. *Città del Vaticano, Biblioteca Apostolica Vaticana, Cod. Vaticanus latinus 3092* [= **X**].

English (or script in the English style), mid-14th c.; paper, 290 x 220 mm, ii + 148 + i ff., written in 2 cols., 57-59 lines per col.[30] This is a large, miscellaneous codex comprising many separate manuscripts of philosophical and theological texts, many written by Franciscan authors (e.g. Scotus, Gerardus Odonis, Walter Burley, William of Alnwick, Franciscus de Marchia, Francis of Meyronnes, William of Ockham), and other anonymous questions.

The manuscripts bound within the codex were copied by twelve different hands. The copyist of the *Quaestiones super secundum et tertium De anima* (hand 5) was a later user of the book. Besides copying his own gatherings, he filled in the empty space at the end of gatherings in other manuscripts. He is the copyist of ff. 53*va-vb*, 54*vb*-72*rb*, and 95*vb*-124*rb*. Besides copying the *Quaestiones De anima*, he also copied Francis of Meyronnes' disputed questions concerning the Divine Word (ff. 100*ra*-101*rb*), an anonymous question *de continuo* (f. 108*ra-rb*), an anonymous treatise *super artem veterem* (ff. 108*va*-109*rb*), William of Alnwick's questions *de distinctione a parte rei* (ff. 110*rb*-111*ra*), questions concerning adequate objects of the intellect, beatific fruition and the augmentation of charity (ff. 111*ra*-113*rb*), and Gedeon of Paris, *Tractatus de continuo* (ff. 113*va*-124*rb*). The writer, who was a scholar copying texts and treatises for his own use, writes in a *cursiva currens* hand with distinctive letterforms of the *Anglicana* script. He writes so rapidly, with a knowledge of what the text is saying, that he often repeats the same words at different places in the line, omits words and phrases, and moreover, intentionally omits whole arguments and parts of arguments. His paleographical abbreviations are reduced as much as possible, and are sometimes equivocal; otherwise, they are sometimes redundant. He uses some characteristic English abbreviations (e.g., for *patet per*). When all of these features of the writer's style and intention are taken into account, the copies otherwise evince an "intelligent text."

The writer copies the *Quaestiones De anima* in three different sections of the codex in the following order: qq. 22 (ff. 53*vb* and 61*rb*), 23 (59*va*), 12 (ff. 59*va*-60*rb*), 14-15 (ff. 60*rb*-61*ra-b*), 17 (ff. 61*va*-62*ra*), 16 (f. 62*ra-va*), 19-20 (ff. 62*va*-63*rb*), 13 (f. 63*rb-va*), 21 (f. 63*va-b*), 11 (f. 64*ra-b*), 18 (f. 64*rb*), 1-5 (ff. 97*rb*-98*va*), 7-10 (ff. 98*va*-99*vb*); only q. 6 is missing. At every place throughout the codex where the *Quaestiones* are copied they are anonymous and without title. Furthermore, they are copied in three distinct bunches. On f. 53*va*, anonymous questions *in I-II De anima*, copied by hand four, end; in the remaining space of col. a and in the empty col. b, our writer copies three questions:

(f. 53*ra-va*): Utrum voluntas movendo intellectum et alias potentias inferiores imprimat

---

[30]Girard J. Etzkorn, *Iter Vaticanum Franciscanum* (Leiden-New York, 1996), 19-23.

sive causat aliquid res in eis....
(f. 53va): Utrum potentiae animae sint idem cum ipsa anima....[31]
(f. 53vb): Utrum singulare sit per se intelligibile ab intellectu nostro....

This last question, q. 22 of the *Quaestiones De anima*, is written in the same format and with no indication of separation in the text. The scribe, looking at the length of the question and the one column of space, severely abbreviates the text of the question and omits arguments. Even so, he needed more space, unavailable on the filled next folio, so that at the end of the column he instructs the reader: "Quare articulus (paraph sign?) ante ad sex folia" (f. 53vb). The next folio presents questions *de ente mobili* and concerning the common sense, written by two different hands (f. 54ra-b, hands 6a-6b). Thereafter follow folios written again by our scribe, containing a question concerning Book III of *De anima*: "Quaeritur utrum virtus sensitiva et intellectiva differant...." (ff. 54vb-56vb), questions on matter and form in composites, *de ente et essentia*, and excerpts *ex Correctorio Coruptorii 'Quare'* (ff. 57ra-59ra).

On f. 59va of the manuscript, where one might expect q. 22 to resume, one instead finds *Quaestiones De anima* q. 23, followed by qq. 12-15 (ff. 59va-61ra). At the top of f. 61rb, at the paraph sign, we find the rest of q. 22. To allow space for it, the copyist needed to finish q. 15 on the bottom seven lines of col. b, clearly marking-off the continuation from the close of q. 22. When he resumes q. 22, although he still omits arguments, he rejoins the text of his model, which he does not so severely abbreviate, presumably because he now has the space. Immediately thereafter follow *Quaestiones De anima* qq. 17, 16, 19-20, 13, 21, 11, 18 (ff. 61va-64rb). Following these are three more anonymous questions: "Quaeritur utrum materia dicat aliquam entitatem positivam...." (ff. 64-67rb); a logical question, ff. 67va-68rb; "Quaeritur utrum formae aliquid preexistant ante generationem formae...." (ff. 68va-72rb).

Manuscripts written by two other hands (6a and 7), containing works by Gerardus Odonis and Walter Burley (ff. 72vb-95va) intervene before our scholar-copyist resumes with another anonymous question concerning the soul: "Quaeritur circa lectionem 'Primum autem necessarium'...." (ff. 95vb-97rb). Immediately follows another block of *Quaestiones De anima*, in the order qq. 1-5, 7-10 (ff. 97rb-99vb). After a question by Francis of Meyronnes (ff. 100ra-101rb), unidentified in the manuscript, the copyist adds yet another question on the soul: "Quaeritur utrum anima sit actus corporis dans esse corporereum ipsi corpori...." (ff. 101va-107vb).

The haphazard sequence of the *Quaestiones De anima*, scattered in three places throughout the codex, bundled with other questions concerning the soul that might well be attributable to Scotus, written in empty spaces in the existing book on sheets and in separate gatherings, and copied for personal use without any identification, does not suggest that the scholar-scribe reordered the questions from the collection in what he judged to be some more satisfactory way.

12. Wien, Österreichische Nationalbibliothek, Cod. lat. 1447 [= **Z**].

Origin: Italian? Provenance: Austria (Vienna), late 14th c. (possibly early 15th c.); parchment, 280 x 196 mm, 167 ff., written in 2 cols., ca. 49 lines per col.[32] The scripts in the

---

[31] Etzkorn, *Iter Vaticanum Franciscanum*, 27-28.
[32] Michael Denis, *Codices manuscripti theologici Bibliothecae Palatinae Vindobonensis latini* II.2 (Wien, 1800), 1299-1302 (DLXXIX); *Tabulae codicum manu scriptorum... in Bibliotheca Palatina Vindobonensi asservatorum* I (Wien, 1864; reprt. Graz, 1965), 239.

book appear to us to be Italian or at least 'Italianate'. The manuscript comprises several separate manuscripts of different origin. The book was bequeathed to the Dominicans in Vienna by an eminent professor at the University of Vienna, as an inscription on the front pastedown, written in a fifteenth-century *bastarda* hand, attests:

> Hunc(?) liber testatus est ad librarium domus collegii ducalis wienne apud fratres praedicatores venerabilis pater et domnus olim magister jodicus weiler de hailprunna arcium et sacrae theologiae professor egregius Ecclesiaeque collegiatae Sancti Stephani ibidem canonicus potestatus cuius animam Deo devotis precibus recommendent qui praesentis voluminis studio usum haberent ut illa pace perfruatur eterna amen.

Iodicus Weiler of Heilbronn (†1457) at the University of Vienna became a Master of Arts in 1419 and taught in the Arts faculty until 1440. As a Master of Arts, he composed a commentary on the *Ethics* ("Circa inicium Ethicorum Buridanus in prologo talem innuit...."). Iodicus was also a student in the Theology faculty, matriculating as a *Cursor biblicus* in 1427, becoming a *Baccalaureus formatus* in 1433, receiving his Licentiate in 1439 and becoming a Doctor of Theology in 1441. As a student in theology, he composed cursory commentaries on the Gospels of Matthew and Mark. In 1440, he became a Canon at St. Stephen's in Vienna, and was a renowned preacher there and in the Dominican convent. Like many other fifteenth-century theologians, he wrote many treatises of pastoral theology. Perhaps significantly, Iodicus was especially renowned as a student and teacher of rhetoric (*ars dictandi*), composing many treatises on the subject; that possibly explains how he came to possess what we judge to be a book from Italy.[33]

1) IACOBUS DE AESCULI, *Quodlibet*, ff. 1ra-33ra:
    Quodlibetum magistri Iacobi de Aesculo ordinis minoris. Quia teste beato Ioanne Apocalypsi primo capitulo.... concedo quia concludit verum.
      A running table at the header on each *verso* folio introduces Q[*uodlibet*], while each *recto* folio contains the headers *Jaco*[*bi*]; f. 33ra-b contains a table of questions in the *Quodlibet*.

2) IOANNES DUNS SCOTUS, *Quodlibet*, ff. 33va-95vb:
    'Cunctae res difficiles' ait Salomon.... ex hoc tamen nihil novum ponimus in Deo ut dictum est. Et sic patet ad rationes. Explicit quodlibet Magistri Ioannis Duns Scoti de Ordine Minorum (f. 96r-v is blank).
      A running title at the header introduces Q[*uodlibet*] S[*coti*] on each *verso* folio while each *recto* folio enumerates the questions; the set includes 21 questions as printed in Vivès-Wadding XXV:1-586 and XXVI:1-345.

3) ALEXANDER [BONINI DE ALEXANDRIA], *Quodlibet*, 97ra-137ra:
    Primo utrum in una et eadem re simplici possint includi diversae formalitates sive diversa esse quiditativa. Et videtur quod non... sed secundum partem hominis et ideo proprio non verificatur nisi per synodochem.
      A running title reads Q[*uodlibet*] A[*lexandri*] on each *verso* folio while each *recto* folio gives the number of the question. On f. 137va is a table of the 21 questions in the *Quodlibet*. The first question of the *Quodlibet* ("Primo utrum in una et eadem....") is copied in MS Z^2, ff. 93rb-94va.

---

[33]F.J. Worstbrock and A. Hausmann, "Weiler, Jodocus, von Heilbronn (Jodocus de Hailprunna)," in *Die deutsche Literatur des Mittelalters: Verfasserlexikon* 10, ed. B. Wachinger et al., 2nd ed. (Berlin-New York, 1999), 794-801; see also Friedrich Stegmüller, *Repertorium biblicum medii aevi* 3 (Madrid, 1951), 247-48.

4) ANONYMUS, *Quaestio*, ff. 133rb-142rb:

   Queritur utrum aliqua essentia alia ab essentia prima sit ab eterno aliquid secundum aliquam differentiam esse vel entis ex intellectu.... (ff. 142rb-144vb are blank).

5) IOANNES DUNS SCOTUS, *Quaestiones* [*super secundum et tertium*] *De anima*, ff. 145ra-162vb:

   Quaestiones Scoti de anima (*in marg. sup.*). Utrum sensus tactus sit unus vel plures.... circumstantiando ipsum ut dictum est supra.

   The text contains qq. 1-22 in the order established by the edition, omitting q. 23. Attribution of the questions to Scotus is ambiguous. The text as copied here was originally anonymous and without title, but on f. 145r a later medieval hand has written "q. Scoti de anima" at the left and center of the top of the page. A *tabula quaestionum*, written in a different but contemporary hand, follows the text on f. 162vb:

   Utrum anima sit
   Utrum intellectus agens sit aliquid animae nostrae
   Utrum corpora caelestia possunt agere in in intellectum nostrum
   Utrum caro sit organum tactus
   Utrum sensus tactus sit unus
   Utrum ad tactum requiratur medium extrinsecum
   Utrum sensibile positum super sensum faciat sensum
   Utrum sensus sit receptivus specierum sine materia
   Utrum sint tantum quinque sensus
   Utrum actio et passio sint idem motus
   Utrum sensus patricularis possit simul recipere contraria
   Utrum necesse est ponere sensum communem
   Utrum sensus communis sit unus vel plures
   Utrum potentia animae intellectiva vel sensitiva sit potentiae passivae
   Utrum species maneant cessante actu intelligendi
   Utrum intellectus noster sit immaterialis
   Utrum magis universale prius intelligatur
   Utrum in intellectu nostro sint species intelligibiles priores naturaliter actu intelligendi
   Utrum possimus intelligere sine phantasmate
   Utrum quidditas rei sensibilis sit obiectum tantum
   Utrum verum sub ratione veri sit obiectum intellectus
   Utrum ens sit primum obiectum intellectus
   Utrum singulare sit per se intelligibile

   The order of questions in the *tabula* does not agree with the order in the text. Moreover, the first question in the table "Utrum anima sit" is not in the *Quaestiones De anima* at all. The order of questions in the table is: qq. 13, 11, 2, 1, 3-10, 12, 14-22. A later hand in the right hand margin has renumbered some of the questions to make them correspond with the text.

6) ANONYMUS, *Quaestio*, ff. 163ra-167rb:

   Utrum theologia sit scientia proprie dicta. Arguitur quod sic sicut se habet lumen universale sentitur ad lumen universale intellectus operans illa lumen fidei ad lumen intelligentiae.... quod non est de illo lumine quod ponunt et sic apparet quod nullus est contrarie exitis.

   This question is written by the same hand and in the same format as the *Quaestiones De anima*.

B. The Manuscripts Not Selected for the Edition

By means of test-collation, we have determined that the following manuscripts, most belonging to the family of Gamma (see below) or otherwise badly contaminated, cannot contribute significantly to the constitution of the text, and thus we have eliminated them from the edition.

13. *Avignon, Bibliothèque Municipale, Ms. 328* [= **A**].

The provenance of this manuscript is probably Burgundian; it was once owned by the Dominicans of Avignon. 15th c.; paper with some parchment folios, 219 x 140 mm, 98 ff.[34] The texts are written by four different fifteenth-century hands, for the most part in *bastarda* scripts; changes of hand occur at ff. 12r, 13r, 33r, 39r (at the beginning of q. 1 of the *Quaestiones De anima*) and 60v (in the middle of q. 10). Scotus' *De primo principio* (ff. 1r-31r) is written in 1 col., but the other texts are written in 2 cols., alternating between 27, 29 and 38 lines per col. (f. 92r contains only 1 col. of 47 lines). The contents of the book are written at the beginning of the manuscript in a fifteenth-century hand:

> In isto volumine continentur libri qui sequuntur:
> Primo tractatus a primo principio doctoris subtilis
> Item quaestiones eiusdem supra secundum et tertium de anima
> Item tractatus samuelis israelitae de fide et adventu Christi
> Item tractatus francisci maraonis de signis naturae
> The two latter treatises have become detached and no longer circulate with the manuscript.

1) IOANNES DUNS SCOTUS, *De primo principio*, ff. 1r-31r:
Primum rerum principium mihi ea credere sapere ac proferre concedat.... sed tu es unus naturaliter Deus verus ex quo omnia in quo omnia per quem omnia. Tu es benedictus in saecula amen. Explicit primum principium magistri Ioannis Duns natione Scoti qui apud totum orbem nomen Subtilis adimplevit cuius memoria et fama in benedictione manet. Incipit tabula eiusdem tractatus....
The *tabula quaestionum* for *De primo principio* is copied in ff. 31r-32r. Following the *tabula* is a short poem lamenting the premature death of Scotus (f. 31r-v):

> Scotia, plange, quia periit tua gloria cara,
> Funde precem, confunde necem, tibi cum sit amara;
> Quam fera, quam neque sit mors, tribuens tibi legem
> Cum relinquis equam, rapiens ex ordine regem.
> Caelum, terra, mare nequeuent similem reparare.
> Si quaeras quare probat hec editio clare,
> Troia luit florem de viribus Hectora fisum:
> Sic luo doctorem, iuveli flore recisum.
> Ergo, legens, plora, quia non huic subfuit hora,
> Sed ruit absque mora: pro quo studens, precor, ora,

---

[34] M.L.H. Labande, *Catalogue générale des manuscripts des bibliothèques de France 27: Avignon* (Paris, 1894), 238-39.

Christum implora salvantem te sine mora,
Matrem adora, ut sibi succurat in hora. Amen.[35]

2) IOANNES DUNS SCOTUS, *Quaestiones super secundum et tertium libros De anima*, ff. 39ra-92rb, [cum aliis *Quaestionibus de luce, de intellectu*, etc.], ff. 33ra-39ra, 92va-98r.

The manuscript presents a collection of 27 questions identified in the colophon as "quaestiones supra secundum et tertium libros De anima secundum Doctorem subtilem" (f. 98r). The collection can be divided into three groups. The first group, copied in ff. 33ra-39ra, contains two questions which, as established by our edition, do not belong to the *Quaestiones De anima*:

(ff. 33ra-36rb): Circa librum de anima aliqua quaerentur et primo utrum lumen sit actus dyaphani. Sed circa hoc videndum est quid sit lumen.... non habent opinionem suam vel saltem non expectatur actio earum.

This question also appears at the beginning of MS **E**, f. 2rb.

(ff. 36va-39ra): Quaeritur utrum lux sit vetus in initio(?). Ut patet inseparatis a materia....

Following these initial questions, in ff. 39ra-92rb, are qq. 1-22 of the *Quaestiones De anima*, omitting q. 23, in the order established by the edition:

(ff. 39ra-92r): Utrum sensus tactus sit unus vel plures.... circumstando eum ut dictum est supra.

The first nine and one-half questions are written in a hand different from the previous two. Another hand begins in the middle of q. 10 and completes the rest of the questions. The *Quaestiones De anima* qq. 1-22 are followed in this collection, in ff. 92va-98r, by three additional questions:

(f. 92va): Utrum substantia intelligatur a nobis per propriam speciem substantiae. Videtur quod non aut illa species causant immediate a quiditate substantiae aut a quiditate accidentis....

This question is also copied in Paris, Bibliothèque Mazarine, Ms. 853 (1022), n° 3, f. 14, and is cited in the register of questions pertaining to Scotus in MS **Z²** (item 57).

(f. 95va): Utrum necesse sit ponere species impressas in intellectum. Videtur quod sic quia nulla potentia videtur potest producere actum determinatum nisi determinatur....

This question may correspond with item 48 in the register of questions pertaining to Scotus in MS **Z²** (see Description nr. 27, below).

(f. 96v): Utrum ad eundem effectum concurative(?) possunt esse diversi ordinis. Videtur quod sic.... (98r) ....licet separatio secundum rem sufficiat. Expliciunt quaestiones supra secundum et tertium libros De anima secundum Doctorem Subtilem.

14. Basel, Universitätsbibliothek (Öffentliche Bibliothek der Universität Basel), B.V.31 [= **B**].

The manuscript belonged to the Dominicans in Basel; late 14th or early 15th c. (ca. 1400);

---

[35] Redactions of this poem are found also in Schlägl, Prämonstratenser-Stiftsbibliothek, Cod. 140, f. 14rb, and Cambridge, University Library, Ms. 1234 (III.26), f. 131ra-b. Cf. *Ioannis Duns Scoti Opera omnia* I (*Ordinatio: Prologus*), ed. C. Balić (Città del Vaticano, 1950), 68*, 105*.

parchment, 215/220 x 150/155 mm, 49 ff.[36] The book binds together three manuscripts, all written in Germanic scripts: ff. 1r-23r, written in 2 cols., 57 lines per col.; ff. 26r-37v (containing Scotus' *Quaestiones De anima*), written in 1 col. of 60 lines; ff. 39r-49v, written in 2 cols., 55-56 lines per col. Although the scripts are Germanic, a note on the blank f. 38r is written in French: "Jeu hoy me... par fare desposar Jeu ne say pa plus." The codex contains Aristotelian commentaries, texts relevant to an Arts curriculum, and brief *notae sermonum*.

1) ANONYMUS, *Quaestiones super libros De generatione et corruptione*, ff. 1ra-23rb:
   Quaeritur de ratione Empedoclis: posuit enim Empedocles elementa esse intransmutabilia. Et ideo quaeratur utrum sit intransmutabilia.... accessus et recessus et per hoc patet ad rationes. Terminantur quaestiones super libros de generatione.
   A *tabula quaestionum* follows the text of the questions on f. 24va-b. Folio 25 is blank.

2) [IOANNES DUNS SCOTUS], *Quaestiones* [*super secundum et tertium*] *De anima*, ff. 26r-37v:
   Prima quaestio de spiritu et sensato vel de anima (*in marg. sup.*). Quaeritur utrum sensus tactus sit unus vel plures.... ut dictum est prius cognita natura circumstantiando ipsam ut dictum est supra.
   The *Quaestiones* in this manuscript bear the descriptive title *de spiritu et sensato vel de anima* and their author is not identified; cf. MS **Q**, ff. 28r-54r (Description nr. 8, item 2). The text contains qq. 1-22, omitting q. 23, in the order established by the edition.

3) ANONYMUS, [*Expositio super Libellum de sex principiis*], ff. 39ra-46rb:
   Lectura super praedicamenta Aristotelis (*in marg. sup.*). Plato scribit in Timaeo quod inter initia fieri decet.... ad cuius evidentiam dubitatur utrum actio sit principium. Et videtur.

4) ANONYMUS, [*Sermones et notae sermonum*], ff. 46va-49rb:
   (f. 46va): Elevata est gloria domini.... (Ezech. 10:4)....
   (f. 47ra): Nota quod Beata Virgo est et fuit elevata....
   (f. 47ra): Multi enim sunt vocati.... (Matt. 22:14)....
   (f. 47ra): Conside filia fides tua....
   (f. 47rb): Nunc enim proprior est nostra salus....
   (f. 47va): Revertantur(?) ei peccata multa quam dilexit intellectum....
   (f. 47vb): Mundum servari animam meam a iuventute mea....
   (f. 48ra): Est puer unus hic qui habet V panes ordrateos(?)...
   (f. 48rb): Non quiescat donec egrediaturus splendor iustus....
   (f. 48rb): In me omnes spes....
   (f. 48va): Beati qui persecutionem patiuntur propter iustitiam....
   (f. 48vb): Nota dicentem ut patientia vestra preciosior sit auro quod per ignem probatur....
   (f. 49ra): In Domini Dominum Iesum Christum. Nota quod Christus....
   (f. 49ra): Fiat mihi secundum voluntatem tuum....
   (f. 49rb): Quia facit voluntatem patris mei, qui in coelum est....
   (f. 49rb): [Notae de timore et de caritate].

---

[36]Gustav Meyer and Max Burckhardt, *Die mittelalterlichen Handschriften der Universitätsbibliothek Basel. Abteilung B: Theologische Pergamenthandschriften I* (Basel, 1960), 538-42.

15. *Cambridge, Gonville and Caius College Library, Ms. 335 [= C].*

English, 15th c.; parchment, 275 x 190 mm, ii + 148 ff., written in 2 cols. of 43 lines.[37] The codex is copied by at least three hands, with changes at ff. 83ra and 115ra. A *tabula quaestionum* of the *Quaestiones super Metaphysicam* by Antonius Andreae appears on the flyleaf.

1) ANTONIUS ANDREAE, *Scriptum super Metaphysicam*, ff. 1ra-112vb:
   Girum caeli circuivi sola.... regnum super universam creaturam per infinita sec. sec. Amen. Explicit scriptum super metaphysicam Aristotelis secundum novam translationem compilatum a Fratre Antonio Andreae ordinis minorum provinciae Aragoniae Amen.

2) [IOANNES DUNS SCOTUS, *Quaestiones super secundum et tertium De anima*], ff. 115ra-139ra (ff. 113-114 are blank), [cum *Quaestionibus de cognitione Dei*], ff. 139ra-148va:
   This section of the manuscript, ff. 115r-148v, contains a collection of 31 questions (actually 32 questions), *sine nomine et sine titulo*. The first 21 questions are from Scotus' *Quaestiones De anima*:

   (f. 115ra) Utrum sensus tactus sit unus vel plures.... (139ra) ....aut loco aut tempore et sic de aliis accidentibus. Ad aliud dicendum est | *quod simpliciter est verum*. Ad minorum dico quod falsum est. Ad probationem cum dicitur quod cognitio abstractive abstrahit ab esse....

   The text contains qq. 1-20, 22, omitting qq. 21 and 23, but otherwise in the order established by the edition. The text breaks-off in q. 22 at n. 31.3-4 ("....et sic de aliis accidentibus"); the scribe then jumps to the first words of n. 33: "Ad aliud dicendum est." After these words, a reader has inserted a dividing-line | after which follow the words "quod simpliciter est verum" (italicized above). These seem to be transitional words devised by the scribe, who thence, without any break, melds Scotus' q. 22 *de anima* with the last part (*in medias res*) of q. 1 in the collection *De cognitione Dei*, which Wadding published and attributed to Duns Scotus (cf. Vivès-Wadding V: 321a, lin. 10-323a):

   (f. 139ra-139va): ....Ad minorem dico quod falsum est. Ad probationem cum dicitur quod cognitio abstractiva abstrahit ab esse.... nec sunt istae duae nisi secundum rationem secundum istos.

   Hereafter follow ten more questions *De cognitione Dei*:

   (ff. 139va-141ra): Utrum cognitio abstractiva possit dici cognitio scientialis.... accidit scientiae inquantum scientia est et demonstrationi quod sumuntur(?) ex causis in essendo.
   (f. 141ra-vb): Utrum cognitio abstractiva proprietatum personalium possit habere rationem scientiae.... concedo quod verum est de subiecto limitato cuiusmodi [non] est essentia divina ideo non valet.
   (ff. 141vb-142va): Utrum talis cognitio quae ponitur intellectu possit habere de Deo per aliquod commune repraesentativum limitatum.... si Deus non suppleat requiritur species et ut sic ponenda est.

---

[37]M.R. James, *A Descriptive Catalogue of the Manuscripts in the Library of Gonville and Caius College* I (Cambridge, 1907), 377-78.

(ff. 142*va*-143*va*): Utrum cognitio intuitiva et abstractiva possibilis haberi de Deo sint eiusdem speciei.... Modo dico quod cognitionem fidei non sequitur visio immediate ex natura rei sed secundum rationem praemii et meriti ergo etc.

(ff. 143*va*-144*vb*): Utrum cognitio abstractiva possibilis haberi de Deo et intuitiva de eodem simul possunt stare in intellectu.... Ad aliud (*spat. vac.*) de matutina et vespertina dictum est.

(ff. 144*vb*-146*ra*): Utrum intellectus videtur pro statu viae ex puris universalibus possit de aliquo obiecto habere cognitionem intuitivum.... ideo de sensu exteriori non potest dici quod cognoscit aliquid aliud.

(f. 146*ra-rb*): Utrum cognitio intuitiva possit habere per speciem de obiecto creato.... per illud idem ad secundum patet.

(f. 146*rb-vb*): Utrum intellectus noster pro statu isto possit habere cognitionem intuitivam secundo modo dictarum et cognitionem certam experimentalem concernentem praesentiam rerum ut est in effectu de habitibus acquisitis vel infusis.... Non tamen causae ut est causa notior est non sui effectus ut effectus est ergo etc.

(ff. 146*vb*-147*vb*): Utrum intellectus noster separatus ex puris suis naturalibus possit habere (*scr.* haberi) de re sensibili cognitionem intuitivam primo modo dictarum.... Ad tertium nulla operatio partis est operatione totius verum est per se loquendo sed per accidens potest.

(ff. 147*vb*-148*va*): Utrum de eodem obiecto cognitio intuitiva sit prior abstractiva.... non tamen est simpliciter primum nisi pro statu isto et sic ad quaestionem dictum est.

The first six of these questions (ff. 139*ra*-144*vb*) are published in Vivès-Wadding (V: 321a-337) under the title *De cognitione Dei* and are attributed to Scotus. The first five of these questions are appended to Scotus' *Quaestiones De anima* in MS **F**, ff. 184*vb*-189*va*, and the first six are appended to the *Quaestiones De anima* in MS **W**, ff. 41*ra*-42*vb* (the manuscript used by Wadding). In both of those manuscripts the questions are anonymous. All eleven questions *De cognitione Dei* are listed in the register of questions pertaining to Scotus in MS **Z²** (items 77-87).

The questions *De cognitione Dei* are almost certainly not by Scotus; indeed, although he wields noetic distinctions famously employed by Scotus in the *Quaestiones De anima* and in his major writings (between abstractive and intuitive cognition, between knowledge *in statu isto et in patria*), the author of these questions is at several points critical of Scotus' doctrines. This manuscript bears a precious if ambiguous note. At the bottom of col. b on f. 148r an annotator has written: "finis commentarii Dionysii de Borgo(?) in librum dicti Scoti (*forsan* Aristotelis?) libri de Anima." "Dionysius de Borgo" is most likely the Augustinian Hermit (OESA) Dionysius de Burgo Sancti Sepulchri, who commented on the *Sentences* at Paris in 1317 and who was a critic of Scotus.[38] The note in this manuscript is too obscure to be construed as an indication of authorship; nonetheless, it would be worth investigating whether the questions *De cognitione Dei* are extracted from Dionysius' commentary on the *Sentences*, and whether Dionysius there criticizes arguments from Scotus' *Quaestiones De anima*. In any event, medieval scholars and scribes from an early date (cf. MSS **W** and **Z²**) evidently perceived the *Quaestiones De anima* and the questions *De cognitione Dei* to be dialectically related in the same "discursive formation." (Concerning authorship, see also the comment on MS **V**, item 4, Description nr. 24, below.)

Immediately following the last question, on f. 148*va-b*, is a table of all 31 questions in the collection. Questions 7 and 8 are transposed in the table but not in the text; q. 21 in the table corresponds with q. 22 in the *Quaestiones De anima* (q. 21 being absent in the manuscript), and its title in the table embraces part of the first question *De cognitione Dei*, as we have indicated:

---

[38] Cf. Friedrich Stegmüller, *Repertorium commentariorum in Sententias Petri Lombardi* I (Würzburg, 1947), 78-79 n° 181; Damasus Trapp, "Augustinian Theology of the 14th Century," *Augustiniana* 6 (1956), 156-60; Adolar Zumkeller, OSA, *Manuskripte von Werken der Autoren des Augustiner-Eremitenordens in mitteleuropäischen Bibliotheken* (Würzburg, 1966), 108-9 n°ˢ 233-234a. None of these authorities mentions any questions *De cognitione Dei*.

1. Utrum sensus tactus sit unus vel plures
2. Utrum caro sit organum tactus
3. Utrum ad tactum requiritur medium extrinsecum in quo fiat
4. Utrum sensibile positum super organum sensum sentiatur
5. Utrum sensus sit receptivus specierum sine materia
6. Utrum sint tantum quinque sensus
7. Utrum sensus particularis possit simul contraria sentit
8. Utrum actio et passio sint unus actus vel unus motus
9. Utrum sit ponere sensum communem
10. Utrum sensus communis sit unus vel plures
11. Utrum corpora caelestia possunt agere in intellectum nostrum vel voluntatem
12. Utrum potentiae animae sensitivae et intellectivae sunt tantum passiva
13. Utrum de intentione Philosophi fuit ponere intellectum agentem
14. Utrum species maneat in intellectu cessante actu intelligendi
15. Utrum intellectus noster sit immaterialis
16. Utrum magis universale prius intelligitur a nobis quam minus universale
17. Utrum in intellectu nostro sunt species intelligibiles priores naturaliter actu intelligendi
18. Utrum intellectus noster possit intelligere sine phantasmate
19. Utrum quiditas sensibilis tantum sit obiectum intellectus
20. Utrum ens sub ratione veri sit primum obiectum intellectus
21. Utrum singulare ab intellecto nostro sit per se intelligibile
22. Utrum cognitio abstractiva possit dici cognitio scientialis
23. Utrum cognitio abstractiva proprietatum personalium possit habere rationem scientiae
24. Utrum talis cognitio quae ponitur intellectu possit habere de Deo per aliquod commune repraesentativum limitatum
25. Utrum cognitio intuitiva et abstractiva possibilis haberi sint eiusdem speciei
26. Utrum cognitio abstractiva potest haberi de Deo et intuitiva de eodem simul possunt stare in intellectu
27. Utrum intellectus videtur pro statu viae ex puris universalibus possit de aliquo obiecto habere cognitionem intuitivum
28. Utrum cognitio intuitiva possit habere per speciem de obiecto creato
29. Utrum intellectus videtur pro statu isto habere cognitionem intuitivam 2 De anima et cognitionem certam experimentalem concernens
30. Utrum intellectus videtur separabilis ex puris suis universalibus possit haberi de re sensibili
31. Utrum de eodem obiecto cognitio intuitiva sit prior abstractiva

16. *Cambridge, Peterhouse Library, Ms. 239* [= **D**].

English, 15th c.; paper, 227 x 152 mm, 94 + 59 ff.[39] The book binds together two separate volumes: ff. 1-94 (item 1, ff. 1r-88r) are copied in 1 col., 42-45 lines per col.; ff. 95-152 (containing Scotus' *Quaestiones De anima*) are copied in 1 col., 48-50 lines per col. In the second manuscript, a hand change occurs at f. 143r, in the text of Scotus' *Quaestiones*. A table

---

[39] M.R. James, *A Descriptive Catalogue of the Manuscripts in the Library of Peterhouse* (Cambridge, 1907), 290-91.

of contents is written by a later hand on the front flyleaf:

> In isto libello continentur subscripta videlicet:
> In primis Antonius Andree super metaphysica (*add.* exc. Parisii 1495)
> Item quaestiones Alexandri Halys de anima (*add.* sepultus Parisii 1245 Anglus)
> Item quaestiones doctoris subtilis de anima
> Item dyalogus Guillelmi de Conchis (*add.* Vixit sub Ricardo I hunc librum Baleus omittit)
> (*add.* Item Imago Mundi)

1) ANTONIUS ANDREAE, *Quaestiones super Metaphysicam*, ff. 1r-88r:
    Antonii quaestiones super metaphysicam (*in marg. sup.*). Girum caeli circiui sola. Eccl. 24. Secundum doctrinam Aristotelis.... Unde ergo est princeps totius universi qui est Deus benedictus universos et regnans super universalem creatam a saeculo et usque in saeculum. Amen.
    The title "Antonii quaestiones super metaphysicam" is written across the top of f. 1r; a table of the *Quaestiones super Metaphysicam* appears on ff. 88r-89r. Folios 90v-94r are blank.

2) [PS.-]ALEXANDER HALENSIS [ALEXANDER BONINI DE ALEXANDRIA?] *Quaestiones de anima*, ff. 95r(1v)- 134v(40v):
    'Bonorum honorabilium notitiam opinantes' etc.... Laus Deo per omnia. Expliciunt quaestiones Alexandri Halys de anima.
    The questions are wrongly attributed to Alexander of Hales; they probably were composed by Alexander Bonini de Alexandria. These *Quaestiones de anima* were also copied in MS **N**, ff. 68ra-160*rb; note that these questions concern all three Books, and thus in this manuscript supply questions on Book I missing in Scotus' *Quaestiones*. A *tabula quaestionum* for the work appears on f. 134v.

3) IOANNES DUNS SCOTUS, *Quaestiones [super secundum et tertium] De anima*, ff. 135r-152v:
    Quaeritur utrum sensus tactus sit unus vel plures. Videtur quod unus quia si esset plures tunc essent sex sensus.... est tamen univocum logice loquendo....
    The text contains qq. 1-8, 10-21, omitting qq. 9, 22-23, but are otherwise in the order established by the edition. The text breaks-off in q. 21 n. 33.5. The copyist does not title the questions or name the author; the only attribution of the *Quaestiones* to Scotus in the manuscript is in the table of contents written on the flyleaf by a later hand. The rear pastedown contains a question presumably on Aristotle's *De sensu et sensato* written in a fifteenth-century hand: "....commentare et ex hoc quod homines dormiunt quando audiunt...."

17. *Milano, Biblioteca Ambrosiana, C.62 sup.* [= **E**].

Italian, second half of the 15th c.; parchment, 380 x 260 mm, 99 ff.[40] The manuscript is copied by one hand in 2 cols., 34 lines per col. On the inside front cover, written in a later hand, is the inscription: "In isto libro continentur quaestiones Scoti De anima et quaedam annotationes in eius metaphysicam." The flyleaf (also numbered f. 1ra) contains two columns of text, which extend over to f. 2rb, where Scotus' *Quaestiones De anima* begin. The first parchment leaf (f. 2ra-b) contains the fragment of a question written in two columns:

---

[40]Louis Jordan and Susan Wool, *Inventory of Western Manuscripts in the Biblioteca Ambrosiana* II (Notre Dame, IN, 1986), 90-91.

"signandum tamen denominationem quae est a colore reali.... non habent opinionem suam vel saltem non expectatur actio earum." This turns out to be the question "Utrum lumen sit actus dyaphani sed circa hoc videndum est quid sit lumen," which is added to the *Quaestiones De anima* at the beginning (as q. 1) in the expanded collection in MS **A**, ff. 33ra-36rb. At the bottom of the flyleaf, a later hand has written "Quaestiones Scoti de anima et in metaphysicam." This indicates that the question "Utrum lumen sit actus dyaphoni" once began this collection as well and that its first folio became detached.

1) IOANNES DUNS SCOTUS, *Quaestiones super librum De anima*, ff. 2rb-50vb:
   Utrum sensus tactus sit unus vel plures.... circumstantiando eam ut dictum est supra. Expliciunt quaestiones Scoti supra librum De anima. Deo gratias. Incipiunt notabilia eiusdem supra metaphysicam.
   The text contains qq. 1-22, omitting q. 23, in the order established by the edition.

2) IOANNES DUNS SCOTUS, *Notabilia super Metaphysicam*,[41] ff. 51ra- 98rb:
   Nota quod Philosophus dicit in fine secundi quod infinitum additione non cognoscuntur.... simplicia et postea componendo. Expliciunt notabilia Scoti super metaphysicam.
   The title of this work is written in the colophon of the previous work. On ff. 98v-99v, a later hand has written a partial list of questions. The first question listed (f. 98v) is again "Utrum lumen sit actus dyaphoni"; other questions recorded, which are also written on the flyleaf, are q. 11, "Utrum corpora coelestia possint agere in intellectum nostrum" (f. 99r), and q. 2, "Utrum caro sit organum sensus tactus" (f. 99r). Folio 99v bears the words "Lumen sit actus dyaphoni" and a few other notes.

18. *Oxford, All Souls College Library, Ms. 87 [= **G**]*.

English (Oxford, All Souls College), later 15th c. (1473-1474); paper, 217 x 150 mm, i + 239 + I-IV (parchment) ff.[42] Gatherings: i-iii^{10} (flyleaf + 1-30), iv-xv^{12} (31-174), xvi^{14} (175-188), xvii-xviii^{12} (189-212), xix^{13} (213-226, wants last leaf), xx^{14} (226-239) + I (= 240)-IV; catchwords are written on the last versos of the gatherings. The main copyist of the manuscript signs his work J. de D. and gives the date 1473 (f. 188v); he copied the first two texts of the book and most of the third in a Secretary script; another more angular Secretary hand takes over at f. 230r, lin. 14, and finishes the copy of *De potentiis animae* (to f. 239v) that J. de D. had begun. The pages are frame-ruled in crayon for 1 col., 150-157 x 110-115 mm, 33-40 lines per col. There is no rubrication; 3-line spaces with guide letters are left for initials.

A note on the bottom margin of f. 2r, written in a late fifteenth- or early sixteenth-century hand, states that the book belongs to All Souls: "Liber Collegij animarum omnium fidelium defunctorum." The book is cited in the Vellum Inventory of the College in a list of Books from Unknown Donors or by Purchase.[43] Watson estimates that the book came to the College ca. 1501, the date of a list of Fellows on f. 226r and of names mentioned elsewhere in the manuscript. There is another possibility. According to Emden, John Saunder, the one-

---

[41]Giorgio Pini, "*Notabilia Scoti super Metaphysicam*: Una testimonianza ritrovata dell'insegnamento di Duns Scotus sulla Metafisica," *Archivum Franciscanum Historicum* 89 (1996): 137-80.

[42]Coxe, *Catalogus* II.1, 27; Watson, *A Descriptive Catalogue of the Medieval Manuscripts of All Souls College Oxford*, 183-85.

[43]N.R. Ker, *Records of All Souls College Library 1437-1600* (Oxford, 1971), 222 (List XXVIB): "(4a) Johannes Canonicus, Quaestiones in Physica Aristotelis etc."

time owner and copyist of MS **K** (see Description nr. 3, above), gave another manuscript to All Souls, "ex propria manu," that contains precisely the three main works in this manuscript, in order.[44] This book is cited in the Vellum Inventory of All Souls in the list of Gifts of Known Donors, 1438-1592.[45] The hand in the present manuscript does not match well the hand in MS **K**, and it is doubtful that the signature J. de D. could somehow refer to Saunder. Curiously, the concluding formula in the colophons of items 1-2 below, "....cuius anima propicietur Deus. Amen" (ff. 186v, 225v), matches the formula in Saunder's donation note in MS **K** (f. 3r). Possibly the manuscript containing these three texts copied by Saunder himself is now lost, but Saunder's manuscript may have served as the model of this one.

1) IOANNES CANONICUS, *Quaestiones super octos libros Physicorum*, ff. 1r-188v:

    Primus liber johannis canonicus (*in marg. sup.*). Quaeritur hic primo utrum substantia facta in suo conceptu communi in quantum natuarlis sit primum subiectum et adequatum substantiae naturalis. Et videtur quod non.... (186v) ....primitas est tantum secundum rationem nec est aliquid dare in re etc. Finitur liber octavus Johannis canonicae cuius anima propicietur Deus. Amen. [Tabula quaestionum].... (188v) .... Expliciunt quaestiones Johannis canonici super 8 libros Physicorum per manum J. de D. et finiuntur in die Sancti Hilarii Anno domini 1473. Deo gratias.

    This commentary by Ioannes Canonicus is also found in MS **H**, ff. 2va-108vb; see the comment in Description nr. 2, item 1 (MS **H**). The text in this manuscript is followed by a table of questions written in ff. 186v-188v, which is followed by a colophon for the whole.

2) IOANNES DUNS SCOTUS, *Quaestiones super libros De anima*, ff. 189r-225r:

    In nomine Trino hoc opus incipio (*in marg. sup.*). Utrum sensus tactus sit unus vel plures. Videtur quod unus quia si esset plures tunc essent plures sensus quam quinque sensus.... (225r) ....ut dictum est prius cognita natura circumstantiando eam ut dictum est supra. Et sic finiuntur quaestiones doctoris subtilis super libros de anima cuius animae propicietur Deus. Amen.

    The text contains qq. 1-22, omitting q. 23, in the order established by the edition. The *Quaestiones De anima* are copied by the same scibes who copied the questions on the *Physics* by Ioannes Canonicus. A table of *Quaestiones De anima* follows on f. 225v:

Utrum sensus tactus sit unus vel plures
Utrum caro sit obiectum tactus
Utrum ad tactum requiritur medium extrinsecum
Utrum sensibile positum super organum sensus facit sensum
Utrum sensus sit receptivus specierum sine materia
Utrum sint tamen quinque sensus
Utrum actio et passio sint idem actus
Utrum sensus particularis possit sit sentire contraria
Utrum necesse sit ponere sensum communem
Utrum sensus communis sit unus vel plures
Utrum corpora supercelestia possunt agere in intellectum nostrum et voluntatem
Utrum potentiae animae sunt tamen passivae

---

[44] See Emden, *BRUO* III, 1643: "Io. Canonicus, *Questiones in Aristotelis physicorum libros viii*; *Questiones in Aristotelis de Anima libros iii*; *De potentiis animae secundum Aristotelem*."

[45] Ker, *Records of All Souls College*, 108 (List XXVIA): "librum dictum Io. Canonici ex propria manu." Saunder bequeathed this book to All Souls in his will registered at Eton College, 3 June 1485 and proved 21 October 1485.

Utrum fuit de intentione Philosophi ponere intellectum agentem
Utrum species manent in intellectu cessante actu intelligendi
Utrum intellectus noster sit immaterialis
Utrum magis universale prius intelligitur a nobis quam minus universale
Utrum in intellectu nostro neccesario sunt species priores naturaliter actu intelligendi
Utrum intellectus noster posset intelligere sine phantasmate
Utrum quiditas sensibilis tantum sit obiectum intellectus
Utrum verum vel ens sub ratione veri sit obiectum primum intellectus
Utrum ens sit primum obiectum intellectus nostri
Utrum singulare sit ab intellectu nostro per se intelligibile. Et sic finitur tabula quaestionum De anima

On f. 226r is List of Fellows of All Souls, 1501; f. 226v is blank.

3) [GUALTERUS BURLAEUS], *De potentiis animae*, ff. 227r-239v:

Ut dicit Aristoteles 2° de anima potentiarum animae et animatis quibusdam insunt omnes.... secundum illud possimus dicere quod potentia motiva dividitur in secundo membra sicut appetitus etc. Explicit tractatus de pontentijs animae secundum D.

This treatise is edited by M.J. Kitchel, who identifies Burley as the author, in *Mediaeval Studies* 33 (1971): 84-113. The treatise is anonymous in the manuscript.

4) ANONYMUS, *Quaestio*, f. I (= 240)r:

Utrum privatio sit existens extra animam.... Etiam sic arguitur quod sit entitas portia(?) quia de essentia entis port^i(?).

This question is written on a paper leaf pasted over a parchment leaf by a third hand in an *Anglicana* script. Folios Iv-IVv are leaves from a fourteenth-century manuscript containing theological questions.

19. *Oxford, Bodleian Library, Ms. Canon Misc. 402* [= **J**].

Italian (Venice), mid-15th c. (1442); paper, 292 x 215 mm, i + 131 + i ff.[46] *Gatherings*: i + i-xiii^{10} (1-130) + 1 (131); the catchwords on the last versos of the gatherings are decorated. All of the treatises were written by one scribe in Venice in 1442 in a spindly, thin-stroked, small *currens* script; frame-ruled in lead or with a dull-point instrument for 2 cols., 170 x 116 mm, 30-40 lines per col. (for Scotus' *Quaestiones*, 2 cols., 180 x 128 mm, centerspace: 18 mm, 31-34 lines per col.). In items 1-5, the rubrication follows the same design. Initials throughout the manuscript were meant to be rubricated but none were, so that the large spaces left for initials are empty except for guide letters. Each treatise was to begin with an 8- to 10-line capital the full width of the column, and 3-line spaces are left for capitals beginning each chapter or question. Rubricated title-headings, written in a thin *textualis* display script, which summarize the following question or chapter, sit a-top the space left for the capital; at the foot of the empty space, the first line of the text is written in capital letters, stroked in red; likewise, at the ends of the text the scribe leaves several lines of empty space before the colophons, which

---

[46]H.O. Coxe, *Catalogi Codicum Manuscriptorum Bibliothecae Bodleianae Pars tertia Codices Graecos et Latinos Canonicianos complectens*. Official Annotated Copy (Oxford, 1854), col. 740; F. Madan, *A Summary Catalogue of Western Mss. in the Bodleian Library at Oxford* IV.2 (Oxford, 1897), 407 nr. 19878; Winfried Fauser S.J., *Codices manuscripti operum Alberti Magni pars 1 Opera genuina* (München, 1982), 54, 106, 163, 203.

are written in the same script as the title-headings; chapter headings and other text-division headings are rubricated by the scribe in the current script of the text; thin red paraphs mark other internal text-divisions. In the first treatise copied in the manuscript, rubrication instructions written by the scribe himself survive uncropped at the bottom edge of the folios; there is no reason to believe that it was not the scribe who rubricated the manuscript. Scotus' *Quaestiones De anima* (item 6, ff. 111ra-131rb) are not so heavily rubricated as items 1-5. Question-titles are not rubricated and there is no space between the end of the text and the rubricated colophon.

This book was part of the large collection formed by the Venetian Jesuit, Matheo Luigi Canonici (1727-1805), which was purchased by the Bodleian in 1817. Canonici acquired most of his books, including this one, in Venice. The Canonici collections are divided into several fonds; the Miscellaneous Manuscripts (576 volumes) comprise works of medicine, philosophy and science, theology and *belle lettres*.[47] The front flyleaf (f. Ir) of the book bears an old shelf-mark, "Ms. 1442," written by a sixteenth-century hand; on the same page is a table of contents for the book in the same hand:

> Magni Commentatoris Alberti de Generatione et corruptione
> Eiusdem de Natura et origine animae
> Eiusdem de Intellectu et intelligibili
> Eiusdem de Diversitate Animarum post mortem
> Tractatus de Anima Intellectiva
> Ioannis Scoti ordinis Minorum quaestiones super libro de Anima

1) ALBERTUS MAGNUS, *De generatione et corruptione*, ff. 1ra-36va:
   Magni commentatoris Alberti de generatione liber primus incipit primus tratatus est de generatione et corruptione in communi simpliciter dictis. Capitulum primum de Prohemio in quo declaratur intentio libri (*rubr.*) ....Cum duae sint considerationes de mobili simplici.... dicta sunt in tertio et in quarto [De] caeli etc. (*Rubr.*): Magni commentatoris Alberti de generatione et corruptione liber secundus explicit feliciter.

   The first three leaves have been torn vertically down the middle, so that only one column of text, now pasted on paper leaves, exists on ff. 1ra-3vb. Folios 37r-40v are blank.

2) ALBERTUS MAGNUS, *De natura et origine animae*, ff. 41ra-59va:
   De natura et origine animae liber incipit (*rubr. in marg. sup.*). Magni commentatoris Alberti liber de natura et origine animae incipit Tractatus primus de origine animae in corpore et natura (*rubr.*)... De anima quidem secundum quod est perfectio corporis et de partibus eius secundum quas est actus corporis.... et incorruptione et opere tantum dictum sit a nobis. (*Rubr.*): Amen Deo gratias. Magni commentatoris Alberti de origine animae et natura et statu eius post mortem tractatus explicit. Ex Venetiis 17° Kalendas Aprillis 1443.

   The number 2 is written at the top center of f. 41r, probably signifying that this is the second text to be bound in the volume. Folios 59v-60v are blank.

3) ALBERTUS MAGNUS, *De intellectu et intelligibili*, ff. 61ra-73va:
   Magni commentatoris Alberti liber de intellectu et intelligibili incipit Tractatus primus est de natura intellectus. Capitulum primum de quo est intensio et quis dicendorum ordo

---

[47]See W.D. Macray, *Annals of the Bodleian Library Oxford with a Notice of the Earlier Library of the University* (Oxford, 1890), 299-302.

etc. Sicut a principio istius operis diximus scientia de anima non satis complete habetur ex hoc quod de anima secundum se ipsam in libro De anima determinatum est.... altissimum enim est huiusmodi negotium et primae philosophiae indigens inquisitione etc. (*Rubr.*): Finis. Deo gratias. Amen. Magni commentatoris Alberti de intellectu et intelligibili secundus et ultimus liber explicit. Ex Venetiis octavo Kalendas Junii 1442. Deo gratias infinitas.

Folios 73v-74v are blank.

4) ALBERTUS MAGNUS, *De diversitate animarum post mortem*,[48] ff. 75ra-89va:
Magni commentatoris Alberti de diversitate animarum post mortem resolutis corporibus contra Averroim et eum sequentes unam in omnibus dicentes liber incipit. Capitulum primum de modo procedendi distinctione (*rubr.*). Quia apud non nullos eorum qui philosophiam profitentur scire dubium est de animae separatione a corpore.... Hic igitur sit finis quaestionis ubi est finis dubitationis. (*Rubr.*): Finis Magni commentatoris Alberti contra Averroim et eius de anima intellectiva disciplinam sequentes. Quaestio Romae disputata explicit in qua non nisi secundum Peripateticarum philosophiam erga eos obiecta formavit eorum rationes contra opinionem solvens. Ex Venetiis Idibus Junii 1442.

5) [IOANNES DE RUPELLA], *Tractatus de anima intellectiva*, ff. 90ra-105vb:
Si ignoras es O pulcherrima mulierum. Vade et abi post greges caprarum. Tibi anima rationalis proponetur istud verbum quae es pulcherrima mulierum.... quod ad minus de intellectuali anima constat esse venum etc. (*Rubr.*): Finis tractatus de anima intellectiva explicit quem 10° Kalendas Augusti complevi ex Venetiis 1442.

The author is identified in the Official Annotated Copy of Coxe, *Catalogi Codicum... Pars tertia*, col. 740. Folios 106r-110v are blank.

6) IOANNES DUNS SCOTUS, *Quaestiones super libro De anima*, ff. 111ra-131rb:
Incipiunt quaestiones Johannis Scoti ordinis Minorum super libro De anima (*rubr.*). Utrum sensus tactus sit unus vel plures. Et videtur quod unus quia si essent plures tunc essent 6 sensus.... Ad aliud dicendum quod artifex post intelligit naturam domus in individuo vago.... Vel aliter est dicendum quod artifex cognitione universali per intellectum intelligit singulare signatum et hoc sentat de istis etc. Finis. (*Rubr.*): Expliciunt quaestiones Johannis Scoti super libro De anima feliciter.

The text contains qq. 1-15, 18, 20-22, omitting qq. 16, 17 and 23, in the order established by the edition. The text of q. 22 in the manuscript is incomplete, ending at n. 41.15-17; one should note that the text of this question is also incomplete in MSS **CJ**, and under different circumstances in MS **X**. A table of the *Quaestiones* follows the text on f. 131rb; in the table qq. 16 and 17 have been crossed out, as they are also missing in the text; qq. 18-22 are thus renumbered in the table as qq. 16-20:

prima Utrum sensus tactus sit unus vel plures
2ª Utrum caro organum sensus tactus
3ª Utrum ad tactum requiratur medium extrinsecum
4ª Utrum sensibile positum supra sensum vel organum sentiatur
5ª Utrum sensus sit receptivus specie sine materia
6ª Utrum sint tantum quinque sensus

---

[48] Fauser, *Codices manuscripti*, 202 nr. 9 (under title *De unitate intellectus*).

7ª Utrum actio et passio sint idem actus
8ª Utrum sensus particularis possit simul percipere contraria
9ª Utrum necessum sit ponere sensum communem propter illos duos actus positos secundo De anima
10ª Utrum sensus communis sit unus vel plures
11ª Utrum corpora supercelestia possint agere in intellectum nostrum vel voluntatem
12ª Utrum potentiae, id est, intellectiva et sensitiva sint tantum passivae
13ª Utrum de intentione Philosophi fuerit ponere intellectum agentem aliquid animae nostrae
14ª Utrum species maneat in intellectu cessante actu intelligendi
15ª Utrum intellectus noster sit immaterialis
16ª Utrum magis est universale prius intelligitur a nobis quam minus universale (*del.*)
17ª Utrum in intellectu nostro sint plures species intelligibiles priores actu intelligendi (*del.*)
18ª (16) Utrum intellectus noster possit intelligere sine phantasmate
19ª (17) Utrum quiditas sensibilis tantum sit obiectum intellectus nostri
20ª (18) Utrum ens sub ratione veri sit tantum obiectum intellectus nostri
21ª (19) Utrum ens sit primum obiectum intellectus nostri
22ª (20) Utrum singulare sit nobis primo et per se intelligibile

20. *Padova, Biblioteca Antoniana, Ms. 173 Scaff. IX* [= **P**].

Italian, later 14th c.; parchment, 335 x 245 mm, ii + 206 + i ff.[49] The manuscript is written by one hand throughout in a *libraria minutissima* script in 2 cols., 72-73 lines per col. Whereas in most manuscripts the *Quaestiones De anima* are accompanied by other treatises and questions suitable for instruction in the Arts, in this manuscript the *Quaestiones* are tucked in among Scotus' major theological writings. The manuscript also contains many questions by Franciscan authors, most of whom were students or followers of Duns Scotus. Our test-collation proves that the *Quaestiones De anima* in this manuscript were copied directly from MS **V**.

1) IOANNES DUNS SCOTUS, *Quodlibet*, ff. 1ra-25ra, [cum aliis *Quaestionibus*], ff. 25ra-28va: 'Cunctae est res difficiles' ait Salomon.... Utrum in divinis essentialia sint.... Require ubi est finis Quodlibeti.

   The text contains the 21 questions of Scotus' *Quodlibet* but the last question is incomplete. The colophon for these questions does not appear until f. 36vb (see below). Two questions without any indication of their author but perhaps by Scotus follow immediately in the manuscript:

   (ff. 25ra-27rb): Utrum auferens vel detinens alienum iniuste possit vere paenitere nisi resituat.... nec ad aliquam restitutionem teneretur.
   (ff. 27rb-28va): Quaestio extra. Utrum confessi fratribus praedicatoribus vel minoribus teneatur iterato eadem peccata confiteri.... Patet in isto argumento quod non commutatum in quocum sive in quale iterationis. Finis.
   This question is found in MS **V**, ff. 125r-128r.

---

[49]See the analysis of this manuscript by C. Balić in *Ioannis Duns Scoti Opera omnia* I (*Ordinatio*), 97*-104*; see also the complete description by Giuseppe Abate and Giovanni M. Luisetto, *Codici e manoscritti della Biblioteca Antoniana* I (Vicenza, 1975), 202-3.

2) IOANNES DUNS SCOTUS, *Quaestiones* [*super secundum et tertium*] *De anima*, ff. 28va-34va, cum aliis *Quaestionibus*, ff. 35ra-36vb:

> Quaestiones de anima. Quaeritur sensus tactus sit unus vel plures.... (35ra) circumstantiando eam ut dictum est supra.

The text contains qq. 1-22, omitting q. 23, in the order established by the edition. A colophon attributing the *Quaestiones* to Scotus does not appear until f. 36vb, after intervening materials. At the end of q. 22, with no break or change in the format of the text, immediately follow three questions which in this collection seem to replace the missing q. 23. Since q. 23 of the *Quaestiones* was included in the model (MS **V**) for this copy, one wonders why the copyist of this manuscript omitted the question and replaced it with others, similar to the way in which q. 23 is omitted and replaced with another in Guillelmus de Missali's *Tabulae*.

(ff. 35ra-36ra): Utrum praelati ecclesiae possint dimittere poenam debitam pro peccatis secundum suam voluntatem. Hoc est quare utrum indulgentiae tantum valeant quantum sonant.... ideo non valet.

This question is printed in Vivès-Wadding as q. 4 of a set which Wadding titled *Quaestiones miscellaneae de formalitatibus* (V:370-84). The copyist of this manuscript found the question in his model, MS **V**, ff. 140v-143v. P. Glorieux attributes this question to Nicholas of Lyre but the evidence is weak;[50] see the comment at Description nr. 24, item 6.

(f. 36ra): Iuxta hoc quaeritur qui praelati possunt dare indulgentias.... nisi sit sacerdos.

(f. 36ra-vb): Iuxta hoc quaeritur quibus valeant ut cum dicitur visitantibus talem ecclesiam concedimus 40 dies.... ex hoc tamen aliquid novum non ponimus in Deo ut dictum est. Et per hoc solutae sunt ratione(!) principales. Finis totius negotii.

Filling in the remaining half-column on f. 36vb is a list of "less probable opinions" of Peter Lombard that is found as a filler-text in many Scholastic manuscripts.[51]

(f. 36vb): Istae sunt opiniones minus probabiles quas ponit Magister Sententiarum quas non sustinent nunc doctores.... notitia nostra super accidens quam super substantiam.

After this list of the Lombard's opinions another anonymous question follows on f. 36vb. The colophon for both Scotus' *Quodlibet* and the *Quaestiones De anima* appears only after this question:

(f. 36vb): Utrum substantiam sit prior accidente notitia sicut dicit Philosophus.... Explicit quodlibet cum quaestionibus de anima doctoris subtilis Magistri Joannis Scoti de ordine fratrum Minorum.

This clear attribution to Scotus of the *Quaestiones De anima*, made by a scholar-scribe in a manuscript that contains Scotus' most important works, seems especially credible.

3) IOANNES DUNS SCOTUS, *Quaestiones super Metaphysicam* [*Prologus et Liber I quaestio 1*], ff. 37ra-37vb:

> Omnes homines natura scire desiderant. In principio Metaphysicae quam prae manibus habemus.... Item quomodo est circa altissimas causas si tantum est circa.

The question breaks-off in the middle of Book I q. 1 n. 55.

---

[50] Palémon Glorieux, *La littérature quodlibétique* II (Paris, 1935), 200-1.
[51] For this list, cf. *Doctoris seraphici S. Bonaventurae... Opera omnia* 1 (Quarrachi, 1882), LXX.

4) [ALDOBRANDINUS DE TUSCANELLA, OP], *Tractatus de articulis fidei seu scala fidei*, ff. 38ra-45vb:
   Funiculus triplex difficile rumpitur. Funiculus ille quo a terra trahimur ad caelum est fides spes et caritas.... quod nobis concedat princeps gloriosus Iesus Christus Dei filius in saecula saeculorum Amen. (*Al. man. rub.*): Explicit tractatus qui dicitur scala fidei.

5) PETRUS AUREOLUS, *Quaestio*, ff. 45vb-47rb:
   Utrum ens dicat unum conceptum unius rationis sub quo contineatur Deus.... Praeterea omne scibile est quid et ens et aliquid. Explicit. (*Al. man.*): Quod hic est omilia Petri Aureoli.

6) GUILLELMUS DE ALNWICK, *Quaestio de tempore*, ff. 47rb-50rb:
   Utrum tempus sit quantitas continua vel discreta.... et in tempore non movetur per se sed per accidens ad motum alterius ut dictum est. (*Rubr.*): Explicit quaestio de tempore fratris Guilielmi Almoych.

7) 'MONACHUS' [IOANNES DE MERCURIA], *Quaestio de mobilitate*, ff. 50rb-51va:
   Utrum mobilitas sit formalis ratio subiectiva primi subiecti physicae naturalis.... quod alterabile maneat immobile secundum locum. Et sic patet quaestio Monachi.

8) ANONYMUS et AUCTORES VARII, [*Quaestiones logicales, de animalibus, physicales et metaphysicales, etc.*], ff. 51va-59va:
   (ff. 51va-53ra): Utrum continuum componatur ex indivisibilibus et resolvatur in indivisibilia....
   (ff. 53rb): Utrum visus sit simpliciter nobilior omni sensu....
   (ff. 53va-vb): Utrum quodlibet animal habeat omnes sensus....
   (f. 53vb): Quaeritur utrum quodlibet animal habeat memoriam....
   (ff. 53vb-54ra): Consequenter quaeritur utrum bruta animalia habeant aliquam imaginationem seu aestimationem....
   (ff. 54ra-rb): Quarto quaeritur utrum in brutis sit prudentia....
   (ff. 54rb-va): Quinto quaeritur utrum aliquod animal carens auditu sit disciplinabile....
   (f. 54va): Sexto quaeritur utrum bruta habeat experientiam....
   (f. 54va): Unde quaeritur utrum experientiam sit causa artis....
   (ff. 54va-vb): Utrum ars sit praecise circa universalia....
   (f. 54vb): Iuxta hoc quaeritur utrum experientia sit efficacior in operando quam ars....
   (f. 54vb): Quaeritur utrum in sensu sit compositio et divisio....
   (ff. 54vb-55ra): Utrum sensus erit circa proprium obiectum....
   (ff. 55ra-rb): Quaeritur utrum magnitudo sit tanta quanta videtur a remotis....
   (ff. 55rb-va): Utrum inter contradictoria sit aliquod medium....
   (ff. 55va-56ra): Utrum finis sit per se causa....
   (ff. 56ra-rb): Quaero utrum logica sit scientia....
   (ff. 56rb-va): Item utrum quidquid est sive definitio rei sit demonstabilis de ipsa re....
   (f. 56va): Ad hoc quaeritur utrum astrologica perpectiva musica et huiusmodi sint de genere scientarum mathematicarum....
   (f. 56va): Et similiter quaeritur utrum scientia cuius subiectum se habet per additionem ad subiectum alterius scientiae....
   (f. 56vb): Utrum divisio scientiae per speculativam per practicum sit divisio essentialis vel accidentalis....

(ff. 56vb-57ra): Quaeritur utrum forma resolvatur in materia....
(f. 57ra-rb): Aureolus (rubr.). Utrum accidentia proprie definiantur.... sic est in proposito de accidente et sic patet haec quaestio Aureoli.
(ff. 57rb-58ra): Ocham (rubr.). Quaero utrum universale sit res extra animam.... et species quae tamen sunt verae qualitates.
(f. 58ra-rb): Utrum ultimum mobile sive prima sphaera sit per se in loco....
(ff. 58rb-va): Quaero utrum elementa maneant in mixto tantum in potentia passiva....
(f. 58va): Item utrum elementum sit tantum in actu virtuali....
(f. 58va): Geraldus (Odonis? rubr.). Et iterum utrum elementum sit tantum in actu perfectibili....
(ff. 58va-59ra): Quaero utrum aliquid a Deo sit vel possit esse actu infinitum....
(ff. 59ra-rb): Utrum anima intellectiva sit tota in toto vel tota in quaelibet parte....
(ff. 59rb-va): Utrum in universitate omnium sit dare aliquod ens universaliter perfectum....

9) IOANNES DUNS SCOTUS? *Super XII^{um} Metaphisicae*, ff. 59va-60vb:
Quaerat primo aliquis utrum privatio sit principium substantiae mutabilis.... Deo gratias. Amen. Explicit his est de quaestionibus super Metaphysicam magistri Ioannis Scoti cum quibusdam additionibus extraneis.

This collection contains 18 questions, the titles of which are given by Balić, 101*. Although the colophon attributes the questions to Scotus, they have not yet been verified as authentic.

10) IOANNES DUNS SCOTUS, *Summa quaestionum super libros I-III Sententiarum* [*Ordinatio*], ff. 61ra-175ra, cum *Additionibus* RICHARDI [DE NORHAUTONIA] et ALEXANDRI [BONINI DE ALEXANDRIA], ff. 175rb-186vb:
Cupientes aliquit(!) etc. Circa prologum primi libri quaeruntur quinque.... (112vb).... Explicit quaestionum summa super primo Sententiarum edita a reverendo magistro Ioanne Dino(!) de Scotia Ordinis Fratrum Minorum. (113ra) Creationem rerum. Postquam Magister determinavit in primo libro de Deo.... (150va) ....Explicit summa quaestionum super secundo Sententiarum edita a reverendo doctore magistro Ioanne de Scotia. (150vb) Cum igitur venit plenitudo. Circa primam distinctionem tertii libri.... (175ra) ....Expliciunt quaestiones magistri Ioannis Scoti Ordinis Minorum super tertio Sententiarum.

Hereafter in ff. 175rb-186vb, without title or the names of the authors (who however are indicated in the colophon), follow *Additiones* by Richardus de Norhautonia and Alexander Bonini de Alexandria. Balić gives the question-titles in his description (*102-103*):

Utrum omnis actio procedens ab homine per voluntatem sit actus liberi arbitrii.... Expliciunt quaestiones Scoti super tertium Sententiarum cum quibusdam additionibus Richardi et Alexandri doctorum.

11) IOANNES DUNS SCOTUS, *Super libro IV Sententiarum* [*Ordinatio* q. 1 dd. 1-13], ff. 187ra-205va:
Samaritanus ille piissimus videns hominem sauciatum ab Ierusalem in Iericho descendentem in latrones impios incidisse.... Circa distinctionem istam 13^{am} quaero utrum quilibet sacerdos possit confitere [q. 1 d. 13] ....talem poenitentiam sibi inflictam.

21. *Roma, Biblioteca Angelica, Ms. 1034 (R.7.15)* [= **R**].

Italian, 15th c.; paper, 230 x 160 mm, 93 ff., written in 2 cols., 32-38 lines per col.[52] The book seems to be the product of two hands, with the change occuring at f. 37ra.

1) PAULUS NICCOLETTI VENETUS, *Summa naturalia*, ff. 1ra-2vb:
   [P]lurimo astrictus pretibus quorum pridem meae introductionis in facultate logicae.... per aliquam causam eius minor.
   The text is incomplete.

2) IOANNES DUNS SCOTUS, *Quaestiones super secundum et tertium De anima*, ff. 3r-33va:
   Quaeritur utrum sensus tactus sit unus vel plures.... per quam est in actu etc. Expliciunt quaestiones venerabilis doctoris subtilis Magistri Ioannis Scoti de ordine Minorum super secundo et tertio De anima.
   The text contains qq. 1-23 in the order established by the edition. Folios 34r-36v are blank.

3) [ANTONIUS ANDREAE, *De tribus principiis naturalibus*], ff. 37ra-91ra:
   Cum secundum doctrinam Aristotelis.... Sic igitur terminatur tractatus quaestionum de principiis naturae. Deo gratias. Laus sit Deo et Beatae Mariae genetrici eius et Beato Francisco. Attende igitur lector qui legis quod si quidem bene dictum est in quibus supra dictis ab arte doctrinae scoti[sti]cae procesit cuius vestigia quantum potui et quantum ipsum capio sum secutus. Si autem aliquid male dictum vel doctrinae dictae reperires vel repugnans meae imperitiae ascribatur quod vere aliquid tale ibi continetur nunc pro tunc revoco tamquam dictum fuerit ignoranter puta quod ignoraveram mentem Scoti. Deo gratias.
   At the end of his text, Antonius indicates that he is more of a compiler of Scotus' teaching than he is an author. It is this character of Antonius' writings, besides the attribution to *Scotulus* in MS **M**, that led Balić to suspect that Antonius was the *compilator* of the *Quaestiones De anima*. Bérubé, in turn, argues that Antonius is simply the author of the *Quaestiones* (see § 3: Authenticity, below). A table of the questions follows the text on f. 91ra-b; f. 91v is blank.

4) [ANTONIUS ANDREAE, *Quaestiones de sex principiis*], ff. 92ra-93vb:
   [Q]uia notitia subiecti in scientia praesupponitur....

22. *Torino, Biblioteca Nazionale Universitaria, Ms. 1046 (G.IV.16)* [= **S**].

Italian, 15th c.; paper, 283 x 204 mm, ii + 131 ff., written in 2 cols., 43 lines per col.[53] This manuscript seems to be the work of one scribe. A note written by a later hand on the top of f. 1r names the author and title of the *Quaestiones De anima* to be found in the volume: "Scotus super secundum et tertium de anima." The codex has been severely water-damaged, and portions of it are illegible. On the flyleaf, the same scribe who has copied the rest of the manuscript has again copied (in two columns) part of q. 4 and of q. 5 of Scotus' *Quaestiones De anima*. For our edition, we have treated the text on the flyleaf as a separate manuscript, and therefore have assigned the fragment a separate *siglum* **Z**³ (see Description nr. 28, below).

---

[52]Narducci, *Catalogus*, 426-27.
[53]G. Mazzatinti, *Inventari dei manoscritti delle bibliothece d'Italia* 28 (Firenze, 1922), 108.

1) ANTONIUS ANDREAE, *Quaestiones super Metaphysicam*, ff. 1r-101v:
Quia secundum doctrinam Aristotelis et communiter eum sequentium....
This copy lacks its scriptural incipit: "Gyrum caeli circuivi sola. Eccl. 24"; see MS **C**, item 1, MS **D**, item 1 (Descriptions nrs. 15-16, above), and M. Gensler, "Catalogue of Works By or Ascribed to Antonius Andreae," *Mediaevalia Philosophica Polonorum* 31 (1992): 149. The ending of the text is illegible because of heavy water damage. A table of questions for the work, written by a different hand, begins on f. 102r; f. 102vb is blank.

2) IOANNES DUNS SCOTUS, *Quaestiones super secundum et tertium De anima*, ff. 103ra-131rb:
Quaeritur utrum sensus tactus sit unus vel plures.... per quam est in actu etc. Expliciunt quaestiones venerabilis doctoris subtilis magistri Ioannis Scoti de ordine Minorum super 2 et 3 de Anima.
The text contains qq. 1-23 in the order established by the edition. The text of the *Quaestiones* is heavily annotated and corrected by another writer; the annotator seems to have drawn his corrections from the copy of the *Quaestiones* in MS **R**.

23. *Torino, Biblioteca Nazionale Universitaria, Ms. 1260 (H.III.43)* [= **T**].

Italian, late 15th c. (1482); paper, 287 x 194 mm, 22 ff., written in 2 cols., 39 lines per col.[54] The only work contained in the manuscript is Scotus' *Quaestiones De anima*. The *Quaestiones* were copied by two scribes: the first scribe wrote ff. 1ra-18vb; the second scribe took over at the beginning of q. 15 on f. 19r. A different but contemporary hand writes on the top of f. 1ra: "Quaestiones Scoti super libros De anima."

1) IOANNES DUNS SCOTUS, *Quaestiones super secundum et tertium De anima*, ff. 1ra-21rb:
Quaeritur utrum sensus tactus sit unus vel plures.... per quam est in actu etc. Expliciunt quaestiones doctoris subtilis super secundum et tertium De anima. 1482. 13 Sept. Iacobus de Praeto scripsit.
The text contains qq. 1-23 in the order established by the edition. On f. 22v, a different hand records the table of contents:

1. Utrum sensus tactus sit unus vel plures.
2. Utrum caro sit organum sensus tactus.
3. Utrum ad tactum requiritur medium extrinsecum in quo fiat.
4. Utrum sensibile positum supra sensum vel organum sensus sentiatur.
5. Utrum sensus sit receptivus specierum sine materia.
6. Utrum tantum sint quinque sensus.
7. Utrum actio et passio sint idem.
8. Utrum sensus particularis possit simul sentire contraria.
9. Utrum necesse sit ponere sensum communem propter illos duos actus positos 2 De anima.
10. Utrum sensus communis sit unus vel plures.
11. Utrum copora celestia possint agere in intellectum nostrum vel voluntatem.
12. Utrum potentiae animae scilicet intellectivae et sensitivae sint tantum passiva.
13. Utrum de intentione Philosophi fuerit ponere intellectum agentem.
14. Utrum species maneat in intellectu cessante actu intelligendi.

---

[54]Mazzatinti, *Inventari* 28, 130.

15. Utrum intellectus noster sit immaterialis.
16. Utrum magis universale prius intelligitur a nobis quam minus universale.
17. Utrum in intellectu nostro sunt species intelligibiles priores naturaliter actu intelligendi.
18. Utrum intellectus noster possit intelligere sine phantasmate.
19. Utrum quiditas rei sensibilis tantum sit obiectum intellectus.
20. Utrum verum vel ens sub ratione veri tantum sit primum obiectum intellectus.
21. Utrum ens sit obiectum primum intellectus nostri.
22. Utrum singulare sit ab intellectu modo per se intelligibile.
23. Utrum in elicitione actus intelligendi intellectus sit movens motu ab obiecto.

24. *Città del Vaticano, Biblioteca Apostolica Vaticana, Cod. Vaticanus latinus 869* [= **V**].

Italian? English (or consciously copied in the English style)? mid-14th c.; parchment, 250 x 195 mm, 245 ff.[55] This large codex, containing a miscellany of Scholastic texts, binds together many *libelli* and is copied (in 2 cols.) and annotated by many hands. Since Pelzer has fully recorded all of the items in the volume, we shall record only those items in the first manuscript bound in the book (ff. 1r-152v), which besides the *Quaestiones De anima* contains other writings by Scotus and various questions that have been attributed to him, and questions by other Franciscan authors (see below). S.D. Dumont states that the works listed in items 3-4 below "can be dated confidently to the years 1312-1316."[56] The writing of the copyist of the *Quaestiones De anima* presents something of an anomaly. His letterforms are those that distinctively characterize the *Anglicana formata* script; indeed, the distinctive forms seem exaggerated. At the same time, he regularly misreads and mistranscribes distinctive English abbreviations. Possibly, the scribe was not English but was trying to reproduce the writing in his model, which was English. There are other medieval examples of such "graphic piety." Usually, the scribe makes such an attempt when he knows or thinks that his model is "original" or especially valuable, and thus worthy of preservation in its visual as well as textual details.

1) IOANNES DUNS SCOTUS, *Tractatus de primo principio*, ff. 1ra-9vb:
Incipit tractatus reverendi magistri fratris Iohannis scoti sacrae theologiae Doctoris De primo principio et Quaestiones subtiles et alia pulchra (*rubr.*). Primum rerum principium mihi ea credere sapere ac proferre concedat que.... (f. 8r) ....Explicit primus tractatus de primo principio (*rubr.*). Amen. (*Al. man.*) : Omne excessum habet causam extrinsecam.... (f. 9v) ....compositum generetur et cetera. (*Al. man.*[2]): Explicit tractatus magistri fratris Iohannis scoti sacrae theologiae doctoris de primo principio. (*Al. man.*[3]): Deinde quaestiones super libros de anima....

Extracts from question 2 of the *Tractatus* ("Omne excessum habet causam extrinsecam....") are appended at the end of its text in ff. 8r-9v. As indicated, a table of Scotus' *Quaestiones De anima* is appended immediately to the *Tractatus de primo principio*. This suggests that the *Quaestiones De anima*, in the minds of at least the rubricator and annotator of the manuscript, constitute the "Quaestiones subtiles et alia pulchra" referred to in the incipit of the *Tractatus*. Folio 10r-v is

---

[55] Pelzer, *Codices vaticani latini* II.1, 242-53; cf. A. Pelzer, *Appendix ad tomi II partem priorem, qua codices 679-1134 enarraverat* (Città del Vaticano, 1933), xxv-xxvi; see also the partial description of the manuscript in Ephrem Longpré, "Le *Quolibet* de Nicolas de Lyre, O.F.M.," *Archivum Franciscanum Historicum* 23 (1930): 42-45.
[56] Stephen D. Dumont, "The Scotist of Vat. Lat. 869," *Archivum Franciscanum Historicum* 81 (1988): 277, 283.

blank.

2) IOANNES DUNS SCOTUS, *Quaestiones in libros De anima*, ff. 11ra-28va:
Quaestiones in libros de anima scoti de ordine minorum fratrum sacrae theologiae doctoris (*in marg. sup.*). Utrum sensus tactus sit unus vel plures.... est in actu (*al. man.*): hic finiuntur quaestiones libri de anima magistri Iohannis scoti de or- (*al. man.²*): -dine minorum solempnis Purificationis(?).

The text contains qq. 1-23 in the order established by the edition. The copyist of the *Quaestiones* does not title the work or name the author. The title (f. 11r) is written in a hand different from, but contemporary with, the hand of the text. The name of the author that follows the title ("scoti... doctoris") is noted by another writer. At the top of the last column of the text (f. 28va), a later hand has written "hic finiuntur questiones de anima"; immediately beneath, a third hand continues: "Magistri iohannis scoti de or-" finishing on the bottom line of the column "-dine minorum solempnis Purificationis."

3) ANONYMUS, [*Duae quaestiones ordinariae de conceptibus transcendentibus* et *Quaestiones miscellaneae de formalitatibus*], ff. 29ra-51va:
(ff. *29ra-39rb*): Utrum aliquis conceptus simpliciter simplex primae intentionis possit esse communis univoce Deo et creaturae.... Si occurrant plura solvas per ista.
(ff. *39rb-44rb*): Utrum sit aliquis conceptus simpliciter simplex praeter conceptum entis.... quod ens et unum sint una natura sola ratione differentia.
(ff. *44rb-48rb*): Quoniam in sacra scriptura traditur notitia de Deo modo quodam supernaturali ut videamus secundum quem conceptum cognoscitur primo videndum est usque ad quem conceptum de Deo potest attingere lumen rationis naturalis erit quaestio.... implicior prior et perfectior et cetera.
(ff. *48rb-51va*): Utrum scientia naturalis sit scientia una.... quaedam moveri et cetera.

The first two questions have been edited from this manuscript by S.D. Dumont and S.F. Brown under the first title given above.[57] The last two questions are attributed to Scotus and printed in Vivès-Wadding as qq. 5 and 7 of the *Quaestiones miscellaneae de formalitatibus* (V:384-404, 417-32). In Wadding's edition, the title of the first question in the manuscript ("Quoniam in sacra scriptura... erit quaestio") is worded "Utrum perfectissimus conceptus possibilis haberi de Deo a viatore ex puris naturalibus sit conceptus entis infiniti." Dumont argues that all four of the questions as well as the questions on Books I-II of *De anima* that follow in the manuscript were composed by the same author and that the most likely candidates are Hugh of Newcastle and Aufredus Gonteri.[58] For further questions from the collection *de formalitatibus* as printed by Wadding, see item 6 below.

4) ANONYMUS, *Quaestiones in libros I et II De anima*, ff. 51vb-101rb:
Quoniam in scientia naturali cuius quidem pars est scientia libri de anima contingit quatuor causas asignare.... ab aliquo determinato ex quo quantum (*add. al. man.*): est de se indiferens(!) est ad illa duo.

Longpré opines that these questions were composed by either William of Alnwick or John of Reading.[59] P. Stella, who has partially edited the questions, attributes them and the *Duae*

---

[57]Stephen F. Brown and Stephen D. Dumont, "Univocity of the Concept of Being in the Fourteenth Century: III: An Early Scotist," *Mediaeval Studies* 51 (1991): 39-123. These questions are now said to be "Cuiusdam Scotistae" active in Paris in the early fourteenth century.
[58]Dumont, "The Scotist of Vat. Lat. 869," 254-83.
[59]Longpré, "Le *Quolibet*," 44.

quaestiones ordinariae de conceptibus in item 3 above to Petrus Thomae.⁶⁰ Dumont, however, disproves the attributions of Longpré and Stella, and judges that these questions on *De anima* were probably written by either Hugh of Newcastle or Aufredus Gonteri. Dumont shows further that extracts from the questions *De cognitione Dei*, which Wadding printed under Scotus' name, are incorporated in the elaborate first question of the exordium to these *Quaestiones De anima*, ff. 51*vb*-55*rb*. Because the author of the questions on *De anima* incorporates extracts from the questions *De cognitione Dei* in his text, and because he otherwise has the habit of citing his own writings, Dumont conjectured that the author of the two works might be the same; in light of further evidence, he has since withdrawn that conjecture (see the comment at Description nr. 15, item 2, MS **C**).⁶¹ As we have recorded, Alexander Bonini's questions on Books I-III of *De anima* accompany Scotus' *Quaestiones De anima* in two surviving manuscripts (MSS **D** and **N**); it would seem that some of those who were compiling Scotistic materials for instruction in the Arts perceived a need to supply a lacuna in the Master's writings: questions concerning Book I of *De anima*.

5) ANONYMUS, *Quaestiones*, ff. 102*r*-125*r*:

Quaeritur utrum notitia quam habet anima de se sit abstractiva.... accipitur unitas passionis quare et cetera ad primum exemplum quod adducitur.

In his description, Pelzer lists the titles of the twelve questions copied in this section, which he judges to have been written by the same author and which he relates to Books I-II of the *Sentences*. These questions are followed in ff. 125*r*-128*r* by an anonymous theological question:

(ff. 125*r*-128*r*): Utrum confessi praedicatoribus et minoribus tenentur iterato eadem peccata confiteri vel etiam eodem anno confiteri propriis sacerdotibus.... non commutatur (quantum *in marg.*) in quotum(!) sive in quale iterationis.

This question also appears in MS **P** (copied from this manuscript), ff. 27*rb*-28*va*, where it is appended to Scotus' *Quodlibet*.

6) ANONYMI ET AUCTORES FRANCISCANI [NICOLAUS DE LYRA, PS.-IOANNES DUNS SCOTUS, RICHARDUS DE MEDIAVILLA], *Quaestiones miscellaneae*, ff. 130*ra*-152*vb*:

(f. 130*ra-b*): Quaeritur utrum Iudaei cognoverunt Iesum Nazarenum esse Christum sibi promissum.... multae aliae auctoritates consimiles in sequenti quaestione adducuntur.

(ff. 130*rb*-138*rb*): Quaeritur ex Scripturis receptis a Iudaeis possit efficaciter probari Salvatorem nostrum fuisse Deum et hominem.... et plures iam baptizati ad vomitum revertuntur.

(ff. 138*rb*-140*vb*): Quaeritur utrum per sacram scripturam possit eficaciter(!) probari finalis salus Salomonis.... quae ad veram vitam ducit gignitur defenditur et roboratur.

(ff. 140*vb*-143*va*): Utrum praelati ecclesiae possi[n]t dimittere poenam debitam pro peccatis secundum suam voluntatem hoc est quaerere et utrum indulgentiae tantum valeant quantum sonant.... ideo non possunt conferre indulgentias ergo etc.

(ff. 143*vb*-146*ra*): Quaeritur utrum sacerdos in peccato mortale actus ecclesiasticos exercens peccet mortaliter in quolibet actu.... et insuper animae imprimitur indelibilis character.

Pelzer identifies the author of the second question (ff. 130*rb*-138*rb*) as Nicholas of Lyre. P.

---

⁶⁰See P.T. Stella, "*Res generabilis simplex est*: Il radicalismo antiilemorfico di Tommaso Barneby et di Giacomo di Carseto nella recensione si Pietro Tomás (Thomae)," *Salesianum* 38 (1976): 780-803 (ff. 70*va*-75*va*) and "*Erronea et horrenda*.... Antropologie in conorrenza nel *Com. In I-II De anima* di Pietro Tomás," *Aquinas* 21 (1978): 400-38.

⁶¹Dumont, "The Scotist of Vat. Lat. 869," 254-63, 268-72. Longpré, "Le *Quolibet*," 44 had already observed the incorporation of extracts from the questions *De cognitione Dei* but, giving no reasons, Pelzer, *Appendix*, xxv, asserted that Longpré's statement is "false."

Glorieux asserts that the first three questions (*Probatio adventus Christi*) constituted the first three questions of a *Quodlibet* that Nicholas of Lyre reportedly disputed at Paris in 1309. He conjectures further, on the basis of proximity, that the next two questions were also part of that *Quodlibet*. Glorieux's only evidence, then, for attributing all of these questions to Nicholas of Lyre is none other than this manuscript, wherein they are anonymous.[62] The last three questions in the set (ff. 138rb-146ra), in fact, correspond respectively to qq. 6, 4 and 3 of the *Quaestiones miscellaneae de formalitatibus* attributed to Scotus in Vivès-Wadding (V:357-84, 404-17; cf. item 4 above). The second question recorded here (q. 4 in Vivès-Wadding, V:370-84) is bundled together with the *Quaestiones De anima* in MS **P**, ff. 35ra-36ra. Question 2 of the *Quaestiones miscellaneae de formalitatibus* attributed to Scotus by Wadding is found below at f. 150vb.

(ff. 146ra-148va): Quaeritur utrum clerici possint cogi ad solutionem exactionum factarum in civitate propter utilitatem boni communis.... et si aliquid minus bene dictum est a melius intelligentibus corrigatur.
(f. 148va): Quaeritur utrum praedicator verbi Domini ratione sui officii teneatur omnia illa facere quae docet et praedicat.... et sic de similibus et ex iis patet argumentum.
(f. 148va-vb): Utrum magister teneatur recipere quaestionem per quam incurret malevolentiam quam tamen quaestionem est utile scire.... dissimulando malitiae et falsitati.
The author of these questions is Richard of Middleton, *Quodlibet II* qq. 30-31 and *Quodlibet III* q. 22.

(ff. 148vb-149vb): Utrum vovens paupertatem evangelicam teneatur ad usum pauperem quoad ea quibus uti licet vel quantum ad qualitatem puta quod sint vilia vel quantum ad quantitatem puta quod sint pauca et necessaria.... et etiam idem concludit contra omnem religionem.
The author of this question is Nicholas of Lyre; Longpré has edited the question.[63]

(ff. 149vb-150ra): Utrum saecularis non audiens missam die dominico peccet mortaliter.... qui istam consuetudinem consequuntur.
(f. 150ra-va): Utrum qui lucratur per ludos prohibitos teneatur ad restitutionem.... et haec sine praeiudicio sententiae melioris dicta sunt.
The author of these questions is Richard of Middleton, *Quodlibet I* q. 19 and *Quodlibet II* q. 29.

(ff. 150vb-151rb): Utrum intellectus et voluntas in Deo qui dicunt perfectiones absolutas sint idem totaliter vel distingua[n]tur aliqualiter.... patet ad utr[a]mque rationem.
This is q. 2 of the *Quaestiones miscellaneae de formalitatibus* attributed to Scotus by Wadding (V:353-57).

(ff. 151rb-152rb): Utrum medium in demonstratione sit definitio obiecti vel passionis.... quod quid est autem prius eo cuius quod quid est ergo etc.
(f. 152rb-vb): Utrum intellectus humanus intelligat singularia.... per instrumentalia agentur. Explicit quaestio et....
The first twelve questions in this collection are copied by the same writer; the last question is written by a later hand.

---

[62]Glorieux, *La littérature quodlibétique* II, 200-1.
[63]Longpré, "Le Quolibet," 51-56.

25. *Venezia, Biblioteca Nazionale Marciana, Cod. lat. III.230* [= **Y**].

Italian (but evidently written by an English scribe, John Aston), later 15th c. (1468); parchment, 290 x 215 mm, 282 ff., written in 2 cols., 35 lines per col.[64] This manucript was copied in Rome directly from MS **W**. The text of the *Quaestiones* is copied with extreme accuracy by an experienced scribe, writing in a beautiful "proto-humanist" script. The copyist worked in tandem with a corrector, and both compared their text with that in another manuscript, which evidently comes from the "English tradition." The teammates corrected from their other manucript only in the cases of obvious mistakes and large omissions, as well as small omissions crucial to sense. The system of correcting is precise and ingenious. When the scribe encounters doubtful readings in MS **W** in comparison with those in the other manuscript, he leaves a lacuna but connects the successive words with an underline of the open space. He leaves it to the corrector to decide what the reading should be and whether to emend from the other manuscript. Sometimes the corrector writes the chosen reading on the line; other times he must write it in the margin. Sometimes he leaves the space blank if he decides that the reading of MS **W** should stand. Further, the corrector indicates small insertions by sub-linear "quotation marks," writing the inserted word above the line at the place marked. This manuscript, which compares manuscripts from the continental and English traditions of the *Quaestiones De anima*, in respect of the whole transmission of Scotus' texts provides valuable analogical evidence: it opens a window to the medieval practice of editing a text from two manuscripts. Our collation and stemmatic analysis of the text of the *Quaestiones* demonstrates that at crucial junctures in its manuscript transmission other editor-scribes adopted the same practice (see § 2.K, below). The codex also contains the *Abbreviationes* of Scotus' works compiled by Guillelmus de Missali and contained in MS **W**, ff. 1ra-30r; see the comment in Description nr. 10, item 1.

1) IOANNES DUNS SCOTUS, *Reportatio super primum librum Sententiarum*,[65] ff. 1ra-150va:
   Utrum Deus sub propria ratione deitatis possit esse subiectum alicuius scientiae....
   Explicit reportatio Scoti super primum.

2) IOANNES DUNS SCOTUS, *Quaestiones super secundum et tertium De anima*, ff. 151ra-181vb:
   Quaeritur utrum sensus tactus sit unus vel plures.... Expliciunt quaestiones super 2^m et 3^m de anima.

   The text contains qq. 1-23 in the order established by the edition. The author is not named here but is named in the colophon to the *Abbreviationes* of Guillelmus de Missali, which follow in the manuscript.

3) GUILLELMUS DE MISSALI, *Abbreviatio super primum Reportationum*, ff. 183ra-191vb; *Abbreviatio super Quaestiones De anima*, ff. 192ra-198vb; *Abbreviationes super Ordinationes*, ff. 199ra-262va; *Abbreviatio super Quodlibet*, ff. 264ra-271vb; *Abbreviatio super Quaestiones metaphysicales*, ff. 272ra-280vb.

   On ff. 280vb-281ra, the scribe and corrector jointly copy and modify the colophon for these *Abbreviationes* that they found in their model, MS **W**, f. 30r:

---

[64] Pietro Zorzanello, *Catalogo dei Codici Latini della Biblioteca Nazionale Marciana di Venezia* I (Venezia, 1980), 200-2.
[65] Actually this work is Scotus' *Additiones magnae in I Sent.*; see C. Balić in *Ioannis Duns Scoti Op. om.* I (*Ordinatio*), 145*.

Explicit abbreviatio et dearticulatio quaestionum super primum Reportationum super Quaestiones de anima et collationes super 4^{or} libros Sententiarum magistri Johannis Scoti et super Quodlibet et super quaestiones Metaphysicae (*corrector*): quam composuit frater Guillelmus de Missali de provincia Acquitaniae ordinis minorum (f. 281*ra*; *scriptor*): Finitum et completum per me Johannem Aston anno domini 1468 die 23 novembris. Deo gratias. Amen.

26. *Tortosa, Biblioteca de la Catedral y del Cabildo de la Santísima Iglesia Catedral (Archivo Capitular de Tortosa), Cód. 201* [= **Z¹**].

French, mid-14th c. (ca. 1350); parchment, 310 x 220 mm, 87 ff.[66] The manuscript is written in 2 cols., 235 x 150 mm, 58 lines per col. The script, initial decoration and pen-flourishing, alternating red and blue initials and paraphs for purposes of text-division, running-header Book numbers in red and blue, are all characteristic of the Parisian Scholastic style. The parchment flyleaves at the beginning and end of the manuscript contain fragments of papal bulls from the pontificate of the antipope Benedict XIII (†23 May 1423).

The manuscript contains two works by Scotus, the *Quaestiones super Metaphysicam* (ff. 1*ra*-85*rb*) and qq. 7-12 of the *Quaestiones in librum Porphyrii Isagoge* (f. 86*ra-vb*). The text of the *Quaestiones super Metaphysicam* is in a confused order: parts of Book 7 q. 14 are interspersed with Book 1 q. 5, while all of Book 7 q. 14 is copied in its proper place and then again after the last question of Book 9; qq. 2-3 of Book 8 are written between qq. 17-18 of Book 7, and Book 7 q. 19 is located after Book 7 q. 20. Curiously, without any sign of transition or disturbance in the manuscript, the text of what is q. 23 in Scotus' *Quaestiones De anima* is inserted at f. 70*ra-b* between Book 7 q. 19 of his questions on the *Metaphysics* ("Utrum conceptus generis sit alius a conceptu differentiae") and Book 8 q. 4 ("Utrum ex materia et forma fiat per se unum"). This seems to be the only manuscript involved in the transmission of the *Quaestiones De anima* that originated in Paris, in anomalous circumstances, wherein q. 23 is detached from the rest of the collection.

27. *München, Bayerische Staatsbibliothek, Clm 8717* [= **Z²**].

Italian, early-14th c. (before 1320); parchment, 300 x 225 mm, 104 ff., written in 2 cols. in a semicursive hand.[67] This manuscript does not contain Scotus' *Quaestiones De anima*; its interest for the edition is a register of questions pertaining to Scotus discussed below. Otherwise, the manuscript contains major theological works by Scotus.

1) IOANNES DUNS SCOTUS, [*Ordinatio* II], ff. 1*ra*-60*va*:
   Circa creationem etc. In hoc secundo ubi tractat Magister de Deo quantum ad causalitatem eius primariam.... (60*rb*) ....ita est a Deo quoniam ex ipso et [in] ipso et per ipsum sunt omnia ipsi honor et gloria in saecula saeculorum. Amen.
   A table of questions follows in f. 60*rb-va*. This copy lacks dd. 15-25 of Book II. Questions drawn from Scotus' *Super Metaphysicam* and the *Additiones magnae* of William of Alnwick are

---

[66]Cf. E. Bayerri y Bertomeu, *Los códices medievales de la Catedral de Tortosa* (Barcelona, 1962), 356-57; Scotus, *OPh* I:xii.
[67]Franz Pelster, "Eine Münchner Handschrift des beginnenden vierzehnten Jahrhunderts mit einem Verzeichnis des Duns Scotus und Herveus Natalis (Cod. lat. Monac. 8717)," *Franziskanische Studien* 17 (1930): 252-72; *B. Ioannis Duns Scoti... Opera omnia* VIII (*Ordinatio Liber II dd. 4-44*), ed. Commissio Scotistica (Città del Vaticano, 2001), 6*-8*.

interspersed in the text.

2) IOANNES DUNS SCOTUS, *Quodlibet* [cum aliis *Quaestionibus*], ff. 61ra-100ra:
Incipit Quodlibet Ioannis Duns Scoti de Ordine Minore Fratrum Minorum, determinatur Parisiis. (61ra) 'Cunctae res difficiles' ait Salomon (Ecc. 1).... Explicit Quodlibet determinatum Parisiis per venerabilem doctorem fratrem Ioannem Scotum de Ordine Minorum.

Questions 1-10 of the *Quodlibet* are contained in ff. 61ra-78rb; qq. 16-21 follow in ff. 78rb-85vb; qq. 11, 15 and 12 are copied in ff. 86ra-89va. After five folios of questions by diverse authors, qq. 13-14 of the *Quodlibet* are copied in ff. 95ra-100ra. The following questions, which intervene between qq. 12 and 13, are found in ff. 89va-94vb:

(f. 89va-91ra): Utrum idem corpus numero simul et semel posit esse in diversis locis localiter per divinam potentiam. Et videtur quod non.... Ad ultimum argumentum dico quod omnis actus immanens non esset sibi in quocumque ubi licet non infieret sibi ut in isto ubi. Ave Maria.

The author of this question has not been identified; f. 91rb contain portions of Scotus' *Quodlibet* q. 1 omitted on f. 61rb.

(f. 91rb-va): Utrum quando caritas augetur prima caritas corrumpatur. Videtur quod sic.... Quaero a quo aut a frigido aut a nullo? Si a frigido tunc frigidum per se calefaceret.
(f. 91va): Utrum aliquid terminet relationem in quantum relativum vel in quantum absolutum.... Non a Deo quia cum in Deo sit nova termination ibi esset novum intelligere et per consequens mutatio.
(ff. 91va-92va): Utrum prima causa sit infinita. Et videtur quod non.... Quae agit necessitate naturae agit melior modo quo potest igitur omne illud quod melius posset fieri contingeret ergo nullum monstrum vel peccatum in natura esset ut videtur. Ave Maria.

The name Richard of Conington is written in the margin of f. 91va.

(ff. 92va-93rb): Utrum in divines sit aliqua pluralitas numeralis. Quod sit.... Opinio Thomae de numero quaere prima parte q. 30 a. 1 ad ultimum argumentum illius quaestionis tenet illud idem quod dicitur hic de numero.

This question corresponds with Aufredus Gonteri, *In I Sent.* d. 24 q. 3.

(ff. 93rb-94va): Utrum in una et eadem re simplici possint includi diversae formalitates sive diversa esse quiditativa. Et videtur quod non.... Ista variatur et multiplicatur secundum plura esse et secundum plures conceptibilitates vel modos reales eiusdem rei. Et sic patet solutio ad argumenta.

The name "Frater Alexander" is written in the margin of f. 93rb; this is Alexander Bonini de Alexandria, *Quodlibet* q. 1.

(ff. 94va-94vb): Utrum aliquis posit scire certitudinaliter se esse in caritate pro statu viae. Quod sic.... Paulus scivit se esse in caritate et etiam alios unde pluraliter dixit non separabit nos tamen si Paulus per revaltionem specialem hoc scivit non oportet verificari de allis.

The question corresponds with Aufredus Gonteri, *In I Sent.* d. 17 q. 8. As indicated above, qq. 11, 15, 12-14 of Scotus' *Quodlibet* resume in ff. 95ra-100ra.

Folios 100*ra*-102*ra-b* contain three tables: an *Index alphabeticus* to the *Quodlibet* of Scotus (ff. 100*ra*-101*vb*), a table of questions in the *Quodlibet* (f. 101*vb*), and a register of 87 questions and four sermons by Hervaeus Natalis and Duns Scotus (or attributed to him), none of which are contained in the present manuscript.[68] The entries in the register indicate folio numbers and place-finder alphabetical letters within the folios (e.g., 9 a, 9 b, 9 e, 20 b, 20 c, etc.); this indicates that the register was once attached to a particular manuscript. Pelster thinks that the register was attached to the Munich codex but that a second part of the book is now lost; the register, however, could just as easily have been detached from another manuscript and bound with this one. The references with folio numbers and alphabetical letters indicate that the compiler of the register employed a common system of indexing found in many other later medieval manuscripts. According to this method, the text in an opening (verso-recto) of the book would be divided into, say, quadrants, and each of the divided sections of the text would be indicated by alphabetically ordered letters in the margins.[69] This enabled readers to find specific texts more easily. Interestingly, when once such an indexing system had been devised for one manuscript, the alphabetical text-divisions sometimes became standard and thence were transmitted in other copies of the text and referred to by medieval authors.

The first 33 items in the register cite questions by Hervaeus Natalis. Item 34 mentions Scotus: "Conclusiones de duplici cognicione et de modo intelligendi 28 b c d. Scotus." From this marker, Pelster infers that all of the subsequent questions in the register (items 35-87) pertain to Scotus and indeed he identifies many of them in Scotus' writings. At items 66-77 one finds the titles of Scotus' *Quaestiones De anima*, qq. 1-5, 7-8, 15, 18, 22. Separate from these, in item 61, may be q. 19: "Utrum quidditas substancie materialis sit primum obiectum intellectus nostri 46 a." Not cited in the register, then, are qq. 6, 9-14, 16-17, 20-21, 23. Immediately following the block of *Quaestiones De anima* are the first six questions Wadding published under the title *De cognitione Dei* (items 77-82). The next five questions in the register, all concerning intuitive and abstractive knowledge *in statu isto* and *in patria* (items 83-87), are the rest of the questions in this sequence as found in MS **C** (see Description nr. 15, item 2, above). Moreover, many other questions cited in the register concern the soul, the relationship between the intellect and will, problems of knowledge, etc. (items 46-49, 53-55, 57, 62-63). In sum, some of the *Quaestiones De anima* appear in this early witness amidst a multitude of other questions perhaps in Scotus' repertoire, and later attached to him, and are immediately associated with the questions *De cognitione Dei*, as they are in MSS **C**, **F** and **W**.

Following the index, table and register, the manuscript in ff. 102*rb*-104*r* bears questions by Peter Aureoli, from Scotus' *Quaestiones in Metaphysicam*, and by Albert of Metz.

28. *Torino, Biblioteca Nazionale Universitaria, Ms. 1046* [= **Z³**].

The flyleaf of MS **S** (Description nr. 23, above), which otherwise contains a full copy of Scotus' *Quaestiones De anima*, contains part of q. 4 and of q. 5. The fragment on the flyleaf is

---

[68] Pelster has transcribed the register of questions in "Eine Münchener Handschrift," 260-64.
[69] Examination of such indexes in other manuscripts suggests that medieval bookmen numbered openings (versos-rectos) and not leaves (rectos and their versos) as is the modern practice.

copied by the same writer who otherwise copied the *Quaestiones De anima* in MS **S**. We have treated the text on the flyleaf as a separate manuscript, and have thus assigned it a separate *siglum*.

* * *

C. Balić and C. Lohr cite a copy of Scotus' *Quaestiones De anima* in Uppsala, Universitetsbibliotek, Cod. C.627.[70] Andrew Traver has shown that the manuscript in fact does not contain a copy of the *Quaestiones De anima*.[71]

C. Printed Editions

Pavia = *Quaestiones super libris De anima Aristotelis* (Pavia: A. de Caracano, ca. 1490) bound with Gometius Hispanus, *Quaestio de cuiuscumque scientiae subiecto* (Pavia: A. de Caracano, ca. 1490). The book is listed in Frederick R. Goff, *Incunabula in American Libraries: A Third Census of Fifteenth Century Books Recorded in North American Collections* (Millwood, N.Y.: Kraus Reprint, 1973), 269, G-320.

Selectae = *Questiones Selectae* (Venezia: Wendelin von Speyer, 1476-1477). This volume is listed in Goff, *Incunabula in American Libraries*, 222, D-384.

Quaestiones magistrales = *Quaestiones magistrales in divina subtilissimi Scoti volumina: Sententiarum, Quolibetorum, Metaphysices, De anima, Posteriorum, etc.* (Colonia: Johannes de Colonia, 1510). This printing contains only a single question of the *Quaestiones super libros Aristotelis De anima*.

Vivès-Wadding = *Quaestiones super libros Aristotelis De anima* in *Joannis Duns Scoti, doctoris subtilis, Opera omnia* III, juxta editionem Waddingi (Parisiis: apud Ludovicum Vivès, 1891), 472-642b. This edition is a reprint of, and is taken to be identical with, the version in the Wadding edition of 1639 (Lyons).

---

[70]Balić in *Ioannis Duns Scoti Op. om.* I (*Ordinatio*), 152*-53*; Lohr, "Medieval Latin Aristotle Commentaries," *Traditio* 26 (1970): 197.
[71]Andrew G. Traver, "An Anonymous Fifteenth-Century Commentary on *De anima* in Uppsala, Universitetsbibliotek, Cod. C 627," *Manuscripta* 2001-2002 (45-46): 151-68.

§ 2: MANUSCRIPT TRADITION

The twenty-eight complete or partial extant manuscripts of Scotus' *Quaestiones De anima* descend from a common autograph Alpha written by Scotus probably at Oxford in the early to mid-1290s. We completed soundings on nine of the twenty-three questions and have determined that the surviving manuscripts can be grouped into four families: Beta, consisting of MSS **HLM**; Delta, consisting of MSS **KU**; Epsilon, consisting of MSS **NO**; and Gamma, consisting of MSS **CFGPQRSTVWXYZZ^{1}Z^3**. Manuscript **Z^2** is simply a list of questions and thus its family cannot be identified. Manuscripts **ABDE** and **J** are anomalous and hybrids of several traditions. In the following edition we have not used the manuscripts **VP**, **RSTY**, and **CG** of Gamma since they are either late or better represented by a close relative (e.g., **X** in the case of MS **V**). This edition consists of all of the Beta manuscripts (**HLM**), all of the Delta manuscripts (**KU**), all of the Epsilon manuscripts (**NO**), and five manuscripts of the Gamma tradition (**FW Q X Z**) that allow us to construct their common ancestor Gamma successfully.

Apart from shared variants, homeoteleutic errors, corrections and additions, the most basic material accident that permits us to reconstruct the four families lies in the order which each tradition presents the questions. The original twenty-three question set of Scotus' *Quaestiones De anima* remained unbound at the time of his death. After his death, his students and confreres collected his works and many other texts and/or *quaestiones* that were not by him, as can be seen by the various anonymous *quaestiones* that circulate with his own *Quaestiones De anima*, and then proceeded to edit and circulate them. Thus the extant manuscript tradition of the *Quaestiones De anima* does not reflect an official text proofread and made ready for publication by Scotus; rather, the work is an assemblage of questions most likely, as with many lecture notes, a "work in progress" loosely based on Aristotle's *De anima* that Scotus used in a lecture course within the Franciscan *studium* at Oxford.

However, at some point after his death, when his students began copying his works, the folia of the autograph copy of the *Quaestiones De anima* were accidentally rearranged. The autograph of Scotus' *Quaestiones De anima* either had misplaced gatherings or was itself misbound; as a result, the gatherings containing the portions of the text from question 5 n. 11 to mid-way through question 9 n. 13 were placed after the gatherings containing the remainder of question 9 n. 13 to question 13 n. 6. Therefore, the sequence of questions in the misbound autograph was 1,2,3,4, first part of 5, last part of 9, 10, 11, 12, first part of 13, remainder of 5, 6, 7, 8, the first part of 9, followed by the remaining portion of 13, 14-23. Simply put, sections of three of the *Quaestiones De anima* (qq. 5,9,13) were split in the autograph due to the transposition of folia. The four parents of the manuscript families each attempted to address the problem in different ways.

Sequence of questions in the manuscripts of the Beta family
H: qq. 1-5, 10-12, 7-9, 6, 13-23
L: qq. 1-5, 10-12, 7-9, 6, 13-23
M: qq. 1-5, 10-12, 7-9, 6, 13-23

Sequence of questions in the manuscripts of the Delta Family
K: qq. 1-5, 10-12, 7-9, 6, 13-23
U: qq. 1-4 to q. 5 n. 7, q. 10 n. 26 to qq. 11-12, 7-9, 6, 13, 15-23. (**U** omits q. 14)

Sequence of questions in the manuscripts of the Epsilon Family:

N: qq. 1- 4, q. 5 to n. 11, q. 9 nn. 13-18, qq. 10-12 to q. 13 n. 6, q. 5 nn. 11-47, qq. 6-8, q. 9 to n. 13, q. 13 n. 6-13, qq. 14-23.

O: qq. 1- 4 to q. 5 n. 11, q. 9 nn. 13-18, qq. 10-12 to q. 13 n. 6, q. 5 n. 11-47, qq. 6-8, q. 9 to n. 13, q. 13 n. 6-13, qq. 14-22 (**O** omits q. 23).

Sequence of questions in the manuscripts of the Gamma Family:
F: qq. 1-23
W: qq. 1-23
Q: qq. 1-6, 8-15, 17-22 (**Q** omits qq. 7, 16, 23).
X: qq. 22, 23, 12, 14-15, 17, 16, 19-20, 13, 21, 11, 18, 1-5, 7-10 (**X** omits q. 6).
Z: qq. 1-22 (**Z** omits q. 23).

The sequence of questions found in Epsilon bears witness to this very basic material accident and best represents the series of questions as found in Alpha. All of the families, as we can see above, attempted to correct the error in various ways. Beta's scribe copied the first gathering of folia up to q. 5 to n. 11 and then jumped to the misplaced third quire or gathering of folia to complete question five. He then proceeded to copy questions qq. 10-12 from the mislaid second gathering of folia. He next returned to the third section of gatherings and copied the questions from 7-9 and then question 6. After question six, Beta's scribe jumped back to the second gathering, began copying question 13 and then continued to the remaining gatherings by completing q. 13 in its entirety and then qq. 14-23.

The copyist of Delta attempted to correct the questions in a manner similar to Beta by likewise jumping to the third gathering to finish copying question five. This can be seen most clearly in Delta's best representative, MS **K**. Delta's scribe then proceeded to copy qq. 10-12 from the misplaced second gathering of folia. He then, like the scribe of Beta, copied the questions in the order 7, 8, 9, and 6 from the third gathering of folia. After completing q. 6, he returned to the second gathering, copied the first portion of q. 13 and finished the question from the fourth gathering. After q. 13, Delta proceeded to copy the questions in the order 14-23.[72]

The two manuscripts of Epsilon copied the error as it appeared in the autograph. Their scribes transcribed qq. 1-4 and 5 to n. 11 and then began the latter portion of q. 9 at n. 13, followed by qq. 10-12 and the first part of q. 13 to n. 6. Next follows the missed portion of q. 5 starting from n. 11, qq. 6-8 and then the first part of q. 9 until n. 13, proceeded by the second portion of q. 13 beginning at n. 6. Questions 14-23 then follow. A user of MS **N**, however, realized this error and included a marginal referent at q. 5 n. 11 to redirect the reader to the appropriate gathering. On f. 163rb, a later hand has noted:

Quaere residuum huius quaestionis in principio quarti abhinc folii ad tale signum

MS **N**, however, contains no further marginal guides to help readers locate the misplaced portions of questions 9 and 13. MS **O** contains no referents whatsoever to help a potential reader find the misplaced portions of questions 5, 9, and 13. As we shall see, O's scribe was extremely passive, copying the questions exactly as they appeared before him and making no attempt to repair the problem caused by the transposition of folia if he had even noticed it.

The Gamma editor has himself fixed the error and corrected the sequence of questions. Thus the twenty-three question set one finds in Vivès-Wadding has been reconstructed through the

---

[72] Although **U** has omitted large sections of qq. 5 and 10, and q. 14 altogether.

Gamma corrector. Not only did the Gamma editor restore the order of the questions, he also prepared an early edition of the text that became the continental tradition of Scotus' *Quaestiones De anima*. He added phrases, smoothed the text over, tried to repair and correct disturbed passages, and created what was for all practical purposes, a revised edition of Scotus' text.

The unusual sequence of questions contained in MS **X** of Gamma, although interesting in itself, reveals little about the manuscript tradition. MS **X** did not sire any further copies of the *Quaestiones De anima*. Rather, we assume that the sequence of questions contained in **X** indicates that they were perhaps copied by a student, along with many other types of *quaestiones* probably intended for personal use. With respect to its contents, MS **X** resembles, judging from its *tabulae*, the lost items in MS Z^2, as both manuscripts formed amorphous collections of questions.

A. Existence and Independence of the Four Manuscript Traditions

The existence and relative independence of the four manuscript traditions of the *Quaestiones De anima* can best be seen by comparing the frequency of textual accidents amongst the individual families as well as examining the uniqueness of each manuscript tradition. The following table of the frequency of textual accidents lists the occurrence of readings peculiar to each group in selected questions. The discussion below examines the four manuscript groups and provides extensive examples of the peculiarities and problems encountered in determining the value of each single reading.

Table of Textual Accidents of Each Group against the Other Ones

	Beta	Delta	Epsilon	Gamma
Question 1	16	19	x	20
Question 3	0	16	x	14
Question 5	10	12	11	5
Question 7	9	39	45	10
Question 9	5	30	31	7
Question 15	20	37	58	20
Question 21	35	69	x	27

B. The Families of Manuscripts: Beta

The three manuscripts **HLM** remain the surviving witnesses of their common ancestor Beta. Beta is probably the earliest copy of the *Quaestiones* made or edited from Alpha. The scholar-scribe of this manuscript examined and edited the text in Alpha in order to prepare an exemplar for publication of the work. To perform his task, he accessed other materials surrounding the course for which Scotus wrote the text, in order to clarify *passus* that were otherwise too cryptic, obscure or indecipherable as they stood in Alpha. Furthermore, the editor of Beta corrected what he judged to be lapses of the author, regularized usages (e.g., *item-praeterea*), perhaps according to what he remembered as the Master's more common locutions, smoothed-out grammatical usage (e.g., introducing subjunctives where they are correct but which the author, in haste, overlooked). The evidence suggests, however, that the editor for the most part, insofar as legibility and intelligibility allowed, stuck to the text in Alpha as his authoritative model. Strictly speaking, this edition is not "contaminated," that is, conflated with another redaction of the text. Beta represents, in terms of its medieval perception, the "official exemplar" of the text, examined and edited, however, not by the author himself but by a student or later disciple familiar with the author's idiom. It itself spawned at least three manuscripts although more than likely many more were generated that now have been lost.

If not to the very last word, one can reconstruct the text of Beta in its integrity, at least more so than the text of any other model. Because of its historical priority in the transmission of the text, the circumstances and intention of its composition, not least because it consistently yields the best or most intelligent reading in vexed *loci* in the text, we judge Beta to be the best and most consistent copy of Alpha. Since no copy is without error, we have corrected obvious errors in Beta, for the most part, from Alpha via Epsilon, when we are sure that we can know Alpha through Epsilon.

As noted, the line of transmission represented by manuscripts **H**, **L**, and **M** bears witness to a direct copy of the master's autograph, and presents a text prepared for a circulation of Scotus' lectures on the *De anima* within the educational system of the *studia*. As a supposedly early example of a working edition, the Beta tradition has its own faults. Its rearrangement of the order of the questions, due to the occasional correction of the faulty gathering of the autograph's quires, breaks the organization of the topics concerning human knowledge. In fact, Scotus' *Quaestiones* 1-8 discuss the external senses, qq. 9-10 the common sense, while qq. 11-23 focus on intellectual knowledge, following the progression of Aristotle's text. The order of the questions followed in Beta and Delta obscures this sequence. In spite of this shortcoming, the Beta tradition has turned out to be the most useful version for the critical reconstruction of the text. As for all the four groups, the quantitative analysis of the textual accidents proper to the Beta group reveals the independence of its line of transmission. A qualitative analysis must focus mainly on additions, omissions and variants of the text, since in this type of literature simple textual inversions are not really telling and often reflect the personal preferences of the copyists. One of the most striking qualities of the Beta tradition is the completeness of its text; there are far fewer omissions due to homeoteleuta than in the other three branches of the transmission. These are four main omissions of text in the Beta group, all noted below:

q. 11 n. 8-9 igitur corpora caelestia non possunt in eas directe agere. Praeterea secundum praedicta potest sic probari propositum corpora caelestia non possunt immediate agere in animam nostram] igitur corpora caelestia non possunt immediate agere in animam nostram HL (*hom.*)

q. 14 n. 16 est liberum per participationem a sua causalitate ut scilicet producat effectum igitur non est causa necessaria producendi effectum intelligimus enim cum volumus ut dicitur II De anima potest enim liberum per essentiam scilicet voluntas impedire liberum per participationem a sua causalitate ne producat effectum suum] est liberum per participationem a sua causalitate ut (ne M *adnotavit in mg.* ut M) scilicet producat (producit H) effectum suum HLM (*hom. rest. marg.* M)

> q. 17 n. 29 secundum illud quo agit est perfectius illo quo intellectus possibilis patitur omne autem illud quod est in phantasmate est corporale et omne illud quod est in intellectu possibili est spirituale] secundum illud (id M) quo agit est (*add.* nobilius et L) perfectius illo quo intellectus possibilis patitur omne autem illud quod est in intellectu possibili est spirituale HLM (*hom.*)

> q. 21 n. 21 igitur quod est causa entitatis aliis est maxime ens si tamen ens dicatur de eis univoce et non aliter cum igitur Deus sit causa entitatis creaturae] igitur quod est causa entitatis (entis H) creaturae N HLM (*hom.*)

Note that all four of these omissions can be attributed to homeoteleutic error. Even if the Beta copyist had access to primitive material that was oral in origin, he is clearly copying a written document, and not taking dictation or even necessarily copying a *reportatio* exclusively. The Beta scribe is most likely combining two traditions: the Alpha codex of Scotus' *Quaestiones De anima* along with a *reportatio* of the text or perhaps a memory of a past lecture. The Beta copyist therefore, as we shall detail below, has access to something independent of the Alpha codex and draws upon this source when the text of Alpha fails to make sense or is difficult to read. Through these examples, it is worth mentioning the textual coincidence of MSS **M** and **N**. While MS **N** is part of the Beta group in questions one and twenty-one, there are numerous instances of contamination between the text in **M** and that of **N** in all the questions where **M** and **N** cannot be considered part of the same textual tradition.

There are several readings that suggest that the Beta scribe reported the oral delivery of Scotus' lectures, or else could make sensitive conjectures where the entire manuscript tradition shows signs of textual corruption, originating probably from a poorly written autograph. Just to illustrate a few examples, the Beta group accurately reports passages where the proximity of two similar words tends to cause omissions in the rest of the tradition:

> q. 1 n. 14 quod non potest superiorem diversificare diversitas] quod non potest diversificare superiorem diversitas L   quod non potest superiorem diversitas O KU FW Q X Z

This following passage from Avicenna is correctly quoted in Beta, whereas the remaining manuscript traditions erroneously omit the opening word of the quotation as an unnecessary repetition.[73]

> q. 15 n. 30 est eiusdem rationis materia materia inquit] est eiusdem rationis materia inquit (in qua N inest F *om.* Q) NO KU FW Q X Z

The Beta group is also distinctively precise regarding cases of grammar and textual division, as can be seen in places where the whole tradition struggles to cope with the abbreviations of conjunctions and word endings in the autograph:

> q. 1 n. 12 Cum ergo ex datis principiis separatis disparatis inordinatis ad invicem] = N H
> Cum ergo ex datis principiis separatis disparatis, et inordinatis (*lin.* M) ad (ab L)

---

[73]Cf. **Avicenna**, *Liber primus naturalium* c. 3 (AviL 36): "Fortassis autem ponitur materia subiecti formae quae non corrumpitur, et subiecti formae quae corrumpitur, materia una in se apta recipere omnem formam."

invicem LM   Cum ergo ex duc (*add. spat. vac.*) principiis separatum disparatis inordinatis ad invicem O   Et cum ex duobus principiis non ordinatis sed disparatis ab invicem KU   Cum ergo ex duobus (*add.* et Z) principiis separatis disparatis non ordinatis ad invicem FW Q X Z

Confronted with an abbreviation that could lead to uncertain readings, the scribes attempted to solve the ambiguity of the sign in different manners. Thus, this example illustrates the case of an abbreviation of short word beginning with 'd'. Two families read it as 'duobus', with a reference to the ongoing argument concerning the sensible species of wetness and coldness in the sense perception of water. Here, however, the progression of the argument requires the exposition of a general rule, which is precisely the doctrine that concurrent causes which are not essentially ordered do not produce a specifically determined effect. The Beta family reads the abbreviation as 'datis', which given the doctrinal context seems to fit better in the arrangement of the argument, and represents a *lectio difficilior* than 'duobus'. The whole passage shows evidence of corrections and reworking in the Alpha model which affected all four manuscript families. Other selected examples in which Beta reads against the other families when trying to decipher unclear or uncertain readings in the autograph are listed below:

q. 4 n. 13 Si autem sit immutatio animalis in organo tactus vel aliorum bene facit sensum non autem naturalis quia immutatio naturalis in organo non facit sensum] Sic (Si N) igitur immutatio animalis in organo tactus vel aliquorum bene facit sensum non autem naturalis sed immutatio naturalis in organo non facit sensum NO   Sic immutatio animalis in organo tactus (*om.* U) vel aliorum bene facit sensum non autem naturalis quia (*om.* U) immutatio naturalis (*om.* U) in organo non (*spat. vac.* U) facit sensum KU   Sic igitur immutatio animalis in organo tactus vel aliorum bene facit sensum non autem naturalis sed immutatio naturalis in organo non facit sensum FW Q X Z

q. 7 n. 22 esse enim a quo est aliud]   esse autem a quo est aliud NO FW X   esse a quo est aliquid KU

q. 9 n. 18 non sequitur quod relatio sit sensibile per se]   non sequitur quod relatio sit (sic N) sensibilis per se NO KU FW X Z

q. 10 n. 12 vult quod primum membrum animalis est ex corde]   vult quod primum membrum animalis est cor O FW Q X Z

q. 19 n. 23 ut natura haec vel essentia]   ut vera haec vel essentia L   ut natura haec vel essentia est (haec etc. N) NO   ut vera (vere Q) haec essentia est KU FW Q X Z

q. 21 n. 31 scilicet generis vel differentiae et ceterorum]   scilicet generis speciei vel differentiae et ceterorum L   scilicet generis vel O   scilicet (ut K) generis vel differentiae KU FW Q X Z

Given the peculiar status of the Beta group, a careful assessment of Beta-only readings is required for the critical establishment of the text. These readings should be considered as textual variants occurring in the transmission of the Alpha text to the Beta tradition, according to a general editorial rule. In many cases, however, the nature of these readings may shed light on the process of progressive refinement that the Alpha text underwent in the course of its reproduction.

Some Beta readings may reinforce the hypothesis of the chronological anteriority of Beta in respect of the rest of the tradition or perhaps support the suggestion that part of the source of Beta is some unrevised *reportatio* of Scotus' own lectures:

> q. 10 n. 6 tunc sequitur quod eadem ratione duae potentiae insubordinatae] tunc sequitur (sequeretur L) quod duae potentiae insubordinatae HLM
>
> n. 7 organum est unum unitate aggregationis tantum] = N   organum est unum unitate aggregationis tantum (*ins. mg.*) O   organum est unum unitate aggregationis HLM   organum est unum tantum unitate aggregationis K   organum est tantum unum unitate aggregationis FW Q X Z
>
> n. 8 se habet organum sensus communis ad alia ut centrum ad lineas] se habet organum sensus communis ut centrum ad lineas HLM
>
> q. 19 n. 17 sed sufficit quantum ad actum intelligendi ut scilicet similitudinem scilicet speciem obiecti recipiat vel actum ipsum] sed sufficit quantum ad actum intelligendi ut scilicet (*om.* L) similem (similitudinem M) scilicet speciem obiecti realis recipiat vel actum illum HLM

These examples testify to the likely marginal insertion in the autograph of words, phrases or interlinear corrections, intended to complete the sentence and give a more precise expression. The copyist of Beta relied on a state of the text that in these passages omitted terms, or presented a choice of phrasing inadequate for greater accuracy. The following phrase is indicative of the complexity of the text transmission and the likely existence of multiple redactions of some sentences:

> q. 10 n. 7 est enim (etiam O) sensus communis potentia una unitate ordinationis (ordinis *dub.* O) NO
> est etiam (autem L) sensus communis unus unitate ordinationis (coordinationis L) HLM
> est etiam sensus communis una potentia unitate organi K
> est etiam (autem F enim X) una potentia sensus communis unitate organi FW X Z
> est etiam sensus communis unitate organi Q

This particular case reveals that a marginal correction 'potentia una' for 'unus' was made in such a way to affect all the groups except Beta. Following the evidence attesting to the independence of the four groups, this correction should have been written in the autograph. Furthermore, the difficult transmission was compounded with the confusion arising from an abbreviation which could be expanded as 'organi', 'ordinis' or 'ordinationis', with the agreement Beta-Epsilon, which is particularly authoritative for question ten, for an abbreviation for a word beginning with 'ord-'.

The Beta group, as mentioned, also displays hints of the inclusion of some reporting of the oral delivery of Scotus' lectures. Some examples of this are noted below:

> q. 11 n. 14 cum dicit quod si unus actus est liber et alius eiusdem rationis est liber quod verum est] cum dicit quod (*ant.* cum L) si unus actus est liber et alius (actus M) eiusdem rationis est liber dico quod verum est HLM conceditur quod si unus sit liber et alius eiusdem rationis erit liber quod verum est KU

q. 19 n. 16 sed dices quod potentia activa] sed (si U) dicit (diceres K Q dicens U diceret FW Z) quod (*om.* Z) potentia activa NO KU FW Q Z

C. Manuscript Epsilon

MSS **NO** remain the sole surviving witnesses of the Epsilon tradition and the conjunction of these two manuscripts allows us to reconstruct their common ancestor. The sequence of questions presented in both manuscripts, in addition to their common accidents, shared errors and homeoteleuta, all establish Epsilon as a separate and distinct tradition.

The intention of the Epsilon manuscript was to copy Alpha "exactly as it is" as can be seen by its failure to correct the misplaced gatherings of the Alpha codex. In principle, such a manuscript copy should yield a direct gaze on Alpha; even though afflicted with the many sight-errors as such copies of autographs usually are, we should be able, through such a manuscript, to recover many readings in Alpha, assisted of course by the evidence in other copies deriving from the autograph. The problems posed by Epsilon, as we shall see below, concern 1) the relationship between MS **O** and Gamma and 2) the relationship between MS **N** and Beta. When MSS N and O divide, O most often shares its reading with Gamma, and N most often shares its reading with Beta. Moreover, N frequently shares a distinct common accident with M. (Concerning these phenomena, see § 2.K-N, below.) Thus, Epsilon readings can be determined only when we have distinct agreement between N and O. When MSS **N** and **O** diverge, **N** may represent the Epsilon tradition, but it may also provide corrected and/or corrupted text not found in Epsilon, or it may in fact present readings found in Beta. We can therefore be sure that we have a distinctive, singular reading of Epsilon, and via Epsilon a reading of Alpha, lost in all other families, only in strictly limited conditions: (a) when MSS **NO** have a reading distinct from Beta-Delta, and (b) when that reading, according to sense, is as good as or superior to the reading in Beta-Delta.

Among the textual accidents which help set the Epsilon group apart as an independent family, four large omissions stand out in question nine in manuscripts **N** and **O**, representing a serious corruption in the transmission of this question in Epsilon:

q. 9 nn. 9-10 ex praedictis quod hoc pertinet ad aliquem sensum communem. Secunda via sic patet experimur nos sensibiliter sentire. Item probatur ratione posito effectu ponitur eius causa sed perceptio] ex praedictis perceptio NO

n. 10 per aliquam potentiam sensitivam non autem per sensum particularem quia secundum Philosophum nulla virtus organica vel corporalis est supra se vel supra suum actum reflexiva potentia autem sensitiva] per aliquam potentiam sensus NO (*hom.?*)

n. 15 ad aliud etiam dicendum quod sensus communis sentit et visionem et colorem ad improbationem dicendum quod impossibile] Ad aliud etiam dicendum quod impossibile NO (*hom.*)

n. 17 cogitando tempus medium est enim praeteriti ut praeteritum est sed sensus communis sic confert unum sensibile alteri quod simul sentit ipsa sensibilia et sentit ipsa differre sine intermedio aliquo] cogitando cuius medium in remoto (remedio O) aliquo cognito NO

These omissions occur in the proximity of a quire transition in the apograph of the *Quaestiones*, as attested by the scribe of Epsilon, who did not notice the misplacement of the second and third gatherings of his model. He copied continuously from the *folium versum* containing the text of q. 5, n. 11 (*Sed contra potentia…*) to the next *rectum* with q. 9 n. 13 and remaining (*non requiritur saltem in visu…*) (f. 163rb, *lin.* 12 **N**, with repetition of the lemma 'contra potentia' due possibly to the iteration of the catch words in the model *in imo folio verso*; f. 46ra, *lin.* 42 **O**). He then continued through the other two following transitions of the misplaced quire—again without realizing that the text he was copying was not coherent. The second quire transition in the model of Epsilon occurred at the *versum* containing the text of q. 13, up to n. 6 (*requiritur intellectus agens* **N**; *Praeterea agens et materia* **O**) and the following *rectum* with q. 5 n. 11 and remaining (*sensitiva non est separabilis…*) (f. 166ra, *lin.* 3 **N**; f. 48vb, *lin.* 7 *ab imo* **O**); and the third one at the *versum* containing the text of. q. 9, up to n. 13 (*medium inhaerens vel coniunctum…*) and the following *rectum* with q. 13 n. 7 and remaining (*numquam coincidunt intellectus agens…*) (f. 168va *lin.* 18 **N**; f. 51va *lin.* 10 *ab imo* **O**).

Perhaps not surprisingly, question thirteen also witnesses two large omissions in manuscripts **N** and **O**, corresponding to portions of the text which in the model of Epsilon were placed before and after the change of quire:

q. 13 nn. 2-3 non sunt eiusdem naturae sed intellectus agens et possibilis non sunt univoca secundum Philosophum quia agens est incorruptibilis passivus intellectus est corruptibilis igitur etc. Item nunquam ars et materia vel lumen et color sunt eiusdem naturae sed intellectus agens comparatur] non sunt eiusdem natura sed intellectus agens comparatur NO (*hom.*)

n. 12 differunt secundum eum et ideo si intellectus possibilis est aliquid animae nostrae oportet ponere intellectum agentem esse quandam substantiam separatam secundum ipsum] differunt secundum (sed O) ipsum NO Q

Such accidents are evidence of the original independence of Epsilon with respect to the rest of the manuscript tradition. They also are an indication of the poor state of the apograph with respect to the transitions between the second and third quire, quite possibly the result of the wear and tear of the external *folia* of each gathering, and reinforce the hypothesis that the model of Epsilon may not have been bound at the time of its copying.

In fact, one of the most striking characters of the Epsilon tradition is its proclivity to omit portions of the text, mainly as a result of homeoteleuta, but also, as we have seen in the examples from questions nine and thirteen, sometimes in correspondence with sections where the text transmission in the whole tradition is disturbed in all witnesses. Moreover, in question fifteen two arguments listed before the solution are missing. We have noted below a list of such omissions in Epsilon:

q. 8 n. 1 simul moveri motibus contrariis sed si sensus particularis simul sentiret contraria simul moveretur in contraria probatio prius enim ordine movetur sensus a sensibili] simul moveri motibus contrariis sensus a sensibili NO

n. 21 quando unus actus est ita intensus indivisus quod adaequat sibi potentiam tunc evacuat totaliter alium actum eiusdem potentiae si autem sit minus intensus et citra terminum potentiae] quando unus actus est ita intensus quod ad terminum potentiae NO (*hom.*)

q. 12 n. 13 quia potentia cognitiva est tantum receptiva speciei ideo est tantum receptiva actus] quia potentia cognitiva est tantum receptiva actus (alicuius N) NO (*hom.*)

q. 14 n. 5 quando potentia est de se cognoscitiva non requiritur in ea species nisi praesente obiecto sicut quia organum de se non est cognoscitivum ideo est in eo species etiam absente sensibili sed intellectus noster est potentia de se cognitiva et non indiget specie nisi praesente intellecto scibili existente] quando potentia est (*post* se N) de se cognoscitiva non requiritur species in ea nisi praesente intellecto scibili existente NO (*hom.*)

n. 16 sed species intelligibilis est causa prior actu intelligendi nec est causa necessaria quia quod est formale principium intelligendi quo elicitur actus intelligendi sive sit intelligere sive species est liberum per participationem a sua causalitate ut scilicet producat effectum igitur non est causa necessaria producendi effectum] sed species intelligibilis est prior actu intelligendi non est causa necessaria producendi effectum NO

n. 18 sed perfectionis est in imaginativa potentia habere obiectum praesens in sua sensatione absente obiecto reali extrinseco hoc patet quia in hoc excedit potentias sensitivas particulares et exteriores igitur potentia intellectiva potest habere obiectum praesens in specie remota eius actuali consideratione] sed perfectionis est in imaginativa (*post* potentia N) potentia habere obiectum praesens id est specie remota eius actuali consideratione NO (*hom.*)

n. 20 quia si species sit formale principium intelligendi in intelligente concurrit ad substantiam actus habitus autem scientiae vel alius ibidem nominatus non concurrit ad substantiam actus sed tantum ad modum] quia si species sit formale principium intelligendi in intelligente concurrit (concipit N) ad substantiam actus sed tantum ad modum NO (*hom.*)

q. 15 n. 2 Item oportet intellectum ad hoc quod intelligat recipere formas universales et absolutas sed si esset materialis reciperet eas particulariter tantum et ut particulares igitur etc. *om.* NO

n. 15 Item si distinctio animarum est ex parte corporum tantum Deus non posset creare duas animas sine corporibus si per corpora distinguerentur, nec etiam per inclinationem ad illa igitur etc. *om.* NO

q. 16 n. 11 in quod potest quia terminat actionem perfectissimam quam habere potest] in quod potest NO (*hom.*)

n. 24 quae fortius movent sensum est perfectior quia quae fortius movent sensum fortius movent intellectum] quae fortius movent sensum fortius movent intellectum NO (*hom.*)

q. 17 n. 6 omne quod reducitur de potentia essentiali ad accidentalem oportet quod hoc sit per aliquod sibi impressum formaliter intellectus noster ante addiscere vel invenire cognitionem intellectualem est in potentia essentiali ad actum intelligendi a qua postea reducitur ad potentiam accidentalem] omne quod reducitur de potentia essentiali ad actum intelligendi a qua postea reducitur ad potentiam accidentalem NO (*hom.*)

n. 6-7 per aliquid sibi formaliter impressum quod voco speciem igitur etc. responsio una opinio communis est quod intellectus habet speciem sibi impressam] per aliquid sibi impressum NO (*hom.*)

n. 8 maior patet quia sicut obiectum est prius actu intelligendi ordine naturae sic ratio obiecti probatio minoris quia non potest aliter esse praesens nisi per speciem in phantasmate exsistentem, non sed non per illam probo quia una species] maior patet (probatur N) quia sicut obiectum est prius actu intelligendi ordine naturae sic ratio obiecti probo quia una species NO (*hom.*)

n. 16 species repraesentat obiectum in illa ratione agendi sub qua nata est imprimi hoc autem est sub ratione naturae absolute consideratae non autem sub ratione agentis quod est particulare] species repraesentat obiectum (oppositum O) in illa ratione agentis quod est particulare NO (*hom.*)

n. 31 aut intellectus est in potentia essentiali ad actum intelligendi aut accidentali tantum non in potentia essentiali quia habens habitum intellectualem potest eo uti cum voluerit est igitur in potentia accidentali sine specie sed propter aliud non ponit speciem necessariam ad actum intelligendi nisi ut reducat] aut intellectus est in potentia essentiali ad actum intelligendi nisi ut reducat NO (*hom.*)

n. 32 aut ratione libertatis si primo modo eadem ratione repugnat intellectui quia aeque immaterialis est non autem ratione libertatis quia illa non obstante] aut ratione libertatis quia illa non obstante NO (*hom.*)

n. 35 hoc autem ideo dicit quia in phantasmate obiectum eius repraesentatur sufficienter quod patet quia dicit ibidem] hoc autem ideo dicit ibidem NO (*hom.*)

q. 18 n. 5-6 propter actum intelligendi propter istam rationem dicunt aliqui quod non est necessaria species impressa intellectui ad actum intelligendi quia ad solam conversionem] propter actum intelligendi quia ad solam conversionem NO *sed rest. mg.*

q. 20 n. 7 nulla potentia potest attingere obiectum suum sine ratione formali obiecti sed intellectus potest attingere quodcumque absolutum] nulla potentia potest attingere quodcumque (quod tenet N) absolutum NO L (*hom.*)

n. 13-14 ut patet per inquisitionem Philosophi dicendum ergo ad quaestionem quod verum non est primum obiectum intellectus sub ratione veri probo quia quod secundum propriam rationem intelligi potest ut distinguitur] unde patet per propriam (*post* rationem N) rationem intelligi potest (*om.* N) ut distinguitur NO (*hom.*)

The determination of the Epsilon group as an independent line of tradition is based on the number of textual accidents common only to **N** and **O**. It should be remembered, however, that while **O** was the production of a passive copyist, who tried to make a replica of the material in front of him, the scribe of **N** had access to another model of Scotus' *Quaestiones* belonging to the Beta tradition, evidently Beta itself. Thus, in questions one, three, twenty-one and twenty-two, there are no significant textual accidents common to **N** and **O**, and instead **N** seems to be a copy of a Beta-group manuscript. For the relationship between N and Beta, and between M and N, see § 2. K-N below.

D. Manuscript Delta

MSS **KU** remain the only extant witnesses of the Delta tradition and the conjunction of these two manuscripts allows us to reconstruct their common ancestor. The two manuscript copies of codex Delta reveal their independence vis-à-vis the rest of the tradition by a relatively large number of textual accidents. The following table lists the main omissions and variants evinced in **K** and **U**:

q. 1 n. 3 aeque perfecte sentit] ita perfecte sentit O   aeque (haec U) apprehendit vel sentit KU aeque sentit X

n. 17 per aliam qualitatem et aliam est gustabilis et tangibilis] secundum aliam et aliam qualitatem est gustabile et tangibile KU

q. 3 n. 1 denudata a qualitatibus tangibilibus] denudata a sensibilibus qualitatibus K denudata a sensibilibus qualitatibus tactus U

n. 13 medio alio a corpore cui adhaeret sed immediate] alio medio a corpore immediate KU

q. 4 n. 13 nisi naturaliter] nisi materialiter NO   nisi KU

q. 5 n. 4 terminatio quantitatis] quantitas vel terminatio quantitatis K   quantitas vel quantitatis terminus U

n. 6 quo est forma in agente vel quo modo materia agentis est disposita ad eam et illud] que (quomodo U) est in agente et istud KU

q. 7 n. 20 sed sunt actiones actae vel productae per actiones intellectus et voluntatis quae sunt de genere actionis] *om.* KU (*hom.*)

n. 22 pater et filius respectu eiusdem pater enim est a quo est filius et filius qui est a patre] pater et filius filius enim est qui est (*om.* U) a patre pater est a quo est (*om.* U) filius KU

q. 9 n. 10 ponitur eius causa sed perceptio coniunctionis] ponitur causa eius sed perfectio cognitionis KU

n. 10 et cognoscit actum cuiuslibet sensus particularis, et ulterius cognoscit] et cognoscit KU X Z

q. 10 n. 2 sensus autem sunt in actu per sensibilia quae sunt plura et diversa in actu] sensus communis est in actu per plura quae sunt sensibilia in actu diversa K

n. 12 Item alibi vult quod primum membrum animalis est ex corde *om.* K

n. 18 quod potest dici tangibile in communi ad diversas qualitates sensibiles tangibiles quod non est nominatum] potest etiam dici tangibile in communi quod non est nominatum ad diversas qualitates K

n. 23 sensus proprius perfectissime immutetur a suo obiecto et sic sensus communis perfectissime omnia obiecta sentiet simul] sensus proprius perfectissime omnia obiecta sentiet simul K (*hom.*)

n. 26 ab illo actu immediate immutatur sensus communis] ab illo actu immediate immutatur KU

q. 11 n. 7 motus corporis inferioris sine superiori non tamen diuturnus secundum omnes sed organum phantasiae] motus corporis inferioris sine superiori sed organum phantasiae KU *ins. mg.* tamen non diu duraret U#2

n. 9 movet de necessitate si moveatur de necessitate sed voluntas] movet de necessitate sed voluntas KU

n. 9 alio enim movente de necessitate cum non sit liberum non enim est in potestate nostra quibus visis tangamur secundum Augustinum] alio eam (*ant.* alio U) movente igitur sequitur quod non erit libera non enim erit in libertate nostra vel potestate KU

q. 12 n. 30 Sed contra prudentia est habitus directivus in agibilibus directionem rationis eliciens si autem illa intellectio causatur immediate ab obiecto non requireretur habitus prudentiae quod est falsum *om.* KU

q. 14 n. 5 sicut quia organum de se non est cognoscitivum ideo est in eo species etiam absente sensibili sed intellectus noster est potentia de se cognitiva] sed in organo est species absente sensibili cum non sit de se cognoscitivum sed intellectus noster est de se potentia cognitiva K

n. 9 non autem propter esse eius quia potest esse sine corpore] non propter se K

n. 14 illuminat de necessitate naturae animas nostras se ad eam convertentes suae lucis speciem imprimendo praesente actu animae et obiecto] illuminat de necessitate naturae animas nostras obiecto K

q. 15 n. 27 unius lineae sunt duo termini tantum quorum quilibet est unus tantum sed termini lineae praedicamentalis et contentorum in ea sunt actus primus et materia prima] unius lineae praedicamentalis et contentorum sunt duo termini tantum quorum quilibet est unus tantum KU

n. 28 cum nobiliori perfectibili perfectione essentiali respondeat perfectio nobilior] et perfectior forma KU

n. 34 formae et contrarietati naturali quia nihil corrumpitur naturaliter quod non alteretur] formae quae subicitur contrarietati naturali quia nihil corrumpitur naturaliter nisi a contrario KU

n. 38 sua habeat quod possit recipere illam perfectionem ad quam habet] sua habet KU (*hom.*)

q. 16 n. 15 *Inversion of the two paragraphs 15 and 16 position in KU*

q. 17 n. 14 singulare autem est determinatum et etiam universale ut in singulari non est universale ut universale sed determinatum sed phantasma] singulare autem est terminatum sed phantasma KU

n. 16 hoc autem est sub ratione naturae absolute consideratae *om.* KU

n. 18 cuius phantasma fortius movet intelligentem ad actum primum intelligendi ut patet cum homo excitatur a somno tunc intelligit necessario illud quod prius occurrit vel cuius phantasma fortius movet sed post illum actum intelligit illud] cuius phantasma fortius movet phantasma fortius movet sed post illum (ipsum U) actum tunc illud (idem U) intelligit KU (*hom.*)

n. 35 XII Super Genesim dicit quod anima a corporali nihil facit in se et in eodem dicit quod anima rerum imagines in se de se facit] VII Super Genesim dicens quod anima rerum quiditates in se et de se facit KU

n. 43 talis autem potentia est intellectus ut dictum est in alia quaestione de hoc facta] ut dictum est in alia quaestione de hoc facta talis potentia est (erit U) intellectus KU

q. 19 n. 5 obiectum proportionatur potentiae cognitivae] obiectum debet esse proportionatum potentiae cognitivae KU

n. 17 sic intellectus idem potest multo fortius intelligere sensibile et non sensibile *om.* KU

q. 21 n. 34 sic in proposito est de ente respectu unius quia dicendo ens unitas est nugatio sic ergo illud additum enti effugit rationem entis quod significatur modo differentiae quae est idem generi identice tantum et non formaliter *om.* KU

q. 22 n. 9 Item proprium motivum intellectus est phantasma quod est singulare sed quod movet intellectum est eius obiectum igitur etc. *om.* KU

n. 23 cognoscit differentiam universalis a singulari] cognoscit differentiam inter universale et singulare KU

n. 36 unam a subiecto quia est in subiecto singulari] unam a subiecto quia (*ins. in marg.* quia est intellectus in quo U#2) singulari KU

q. 23 n. 7 Item ad idem motus denominatur a termino a quo et magis quam a termino ad quem igitur actus intelligendi quo attingitur ipsum obiectum magis assimilatur termino a quo quam termino ad quem et praecipue in proposito ab obiecto cum ipsum sit terminus a quo et non ad quem] Item (*add.* magis K) denominatur a termino a quo magis quam a termino ad quem igitur actus intelligendi quo attingitur ipsum obiectum magis assimilatur (*add.* a U) termino a quo quam (*add.* a U) termino ad quem primae K (*precise* U) etiam in proposito ab obiecto cum ipsum sit terminus a quo et non ad quem KU   Item ad idem motus denominatur (determinatur L) a termino a quo et (*om.* L) magis quam a termino ad quem igitur actus intelligendi quo attingitur ipsum obiectum magis assimilatur (*add.* a N M FW X) termino ad quem et praecipue (*precise* L) in proposito ab obiecto cum ipsum (*om.* H) sit terminus a quo et ad quem N HLM FW X

The Delta tradition sporadically introduces corrections, ameliorations and alternate readings into the text of Alpha; its readings and "improvements" of Alpha are not always felicitous, and moreover the alterations appear to be *ad libitum*. Furthermore, MS **U** was contaminated by the Gamma tradition and in its own sequence of questions omits most of qq. 5 and 10, and all of q. 14. The source of the contamination—either MS **U**'s scribe himself or more probably his exemplar's scribe—made no attempt to repair the damage in qq. 5 and 10—nor did he seek to reinstate the lost question fourteen.

Nevertheless, the model Delta did generate a family, and it also resolved the difficulty posed by the misplaced gatherings of the folios of the *Quaestiones* in a manner similar to Beta. Although the scribe of MS **K** is both competent and resourceful, Delta overall offers little help in the constitution of the text. Its main usefulness is that it can provide some corroborative evidence in deciding readings between Beta and Epsilon. In respect of Alpha, however, the number of cases when Delta offers clear testimony, even in corroboration, is few.

E. Manuscript Gamma

The editor or supervisor of this manuscript prepared a wholesale revision of Alpha; his main concern was readability in terms of expression and style, to make the text more assimilable to more young men in the *studia*. But this redaction not only alters the express words of Alpha considerably, it also often loses the sense or botches arguments in its stylistic revisions. The main merit of this edition, which had a wider circulation on the continent than any other, is that it discovered and restored the correct order of the twenty-three questions. This edition uses manuscripts **FW Q X Z** to reconstruct the Gamma text.

In a transmission such as this one, already confused and sometimes inscrutable *in fonte*, edited at first instance by someone else besides the author, then contaminated in each other "head-of-family," and then again contaminated in individual surviving copies, it is inevitable that some readings of the text were lost to the transmission at the very beginning, and that copyists and editors were simply constrained to conjecture or impose, whatever their intentions in respect of fidelity. In such conditions, yielded also because of the loss or destruction of all the key models, each was on his own, and the hierarchy of families lends little help in resolving the reading.

Judging by the number of extant manuscripts, the Gamma tradition of the *Quaestiones De anima* was by far the most widely disseminated. However, many of the Gamma manuscripts are late and provide unique readings or additional matter that separate them from their Gamma ancestors. Below we have provided examples for shared readings in some of Gamma's subgroups in selected questions.

Subgroups of Gamma

Table of Question 1:

CG: 10 unique readings
RST: 5 in combination with **C** or **F**
FW: 3 unique readings
PV: 6 unique readings, but 17 in combination with **D,E** or **J**

Table of Question 5:

CG: 7 unique readings
RST: 2 unique readings; 9 in combination with **F** or $\mathbf{Z}^2$
FW: 1 unique reading; 4 in combination with **Z** or $\mathbf{Z}^2$
PV: 6 unique readings; 2 additional readings in combination with **X**

Table of Question 9:

CG: 1 unique reading; 2 in combination with **J**
RST: 4 unique readings; 11 in combination with **C** or **F**
FW: 1 unique reading; 20 in combination, singly or conjointly, with **RS** or **T**
PV: 15 unique readings

Table of Question 10:

CG: 11 unique readings
RST: 5 unique readings
FW: 1 unique reading; 4 in combination with **RS** or **T**
PV: 10 unique readings

Table of Question 12:

CG: 37 unique readings
RST: 5 unique readings; 37 in combination with either **F** or **W**
FW: 3 unique readings; 34 in combination with **R, S,** or **T**
PV: 29 unique readings

Variants and Omissions in Gamma

The following table lists the main omissions and variants affecting the manuscripts of the Gamma group, with the occasional addition of MS **U**:

q. 1 n. 1 essent sex sensus] essent plures quam quinque sensus FW Q Z essent sensus X

    n. 3 Non sunt igitur solum numero differentia] Non sunt igitur eiusdem speciei U FW Q X Z

    n. 13 est respectu unius generis determinati] est tantum unius generis physici U FW Q X Z

MANUSCRIPT TRADITION 71*

n. 13 de ista univocatione habet maior sua veritatem] de ista veritate habet sua maior veritatem O de ista secunda unitate habet sua maior U de ista veritatem habet sua maior FW Q X Z

q. 3 n. 10 in aestate quando est aqua calefacta et in hieme quando est aer frigidus non sunt illa elementa pura] in hieme frigefacta et in aestate calefacta et aer similiter non erunt illa pura elementa U in hieme quando est aqua calefacta et in hieme aer frigefactus non sunt elementa pura FW Z   in hieme quando est aqua calefacta et aer frigidus (frigescens X) non sunt illa (in hieme Q) elementa pura Q X

q. 4 n. 10 non sentitur quia color non videtur sine lumine] non facit sensum (*ant.* non U) quia (*add. mg.* mediate W#2) color (calor Z) non videtur nisi in (mediante F) lumine U FW Q X Z

q. 6 n. 15 humido et sicco] humido insinuando FW humido in faciendo Q humido sinuando Z

q. 7 n. 9 et hic motus est actio *om.* FW X Z

q. 8 illud minoris non sentitur] illud esse sentiunt FW illud sentiunt X illud commune sentiunt Z

q. 11 n. 14 actus videndi] actus volendi U FW Q X

n. 17 haec est delectatio] hoc (haec W X) est delectatio (dilectio X *add.* conclusio X) ergo (*om.* Q) cum (*om.* X) delectatio (dilectio X) sit passio realis aliquid imprimitur voluntati ab obiecto et (*add. ult.* ita est FW *add. ult.* ita X) non erit (est FW) mere activa etc. (*om.* W Q) FW Q X

q. 12 n. 2 sequitur quod sensus posset sentire] sequeretur quod posset sensus (*ant.* posset Q Z) se sentire et (*add.* quod Q X) posset (*add.* sentire et posset Z) sentire FW Q X Z

n. 3 ab eodem activo] manente eodem activo FW Q X Z

n. 7 *Adnotatio interpolata*: sed (*om.* FW Q X) potentiae praedictae sunt in potentia essentiali ad actum cognoscendi igitur (igitur—cognoscendi *om.* F) si (*om.* Z) reducuntur ad potentiam accidentalem (*add.* hoc non erit nisi W) per speciem eis impressam igitur ista (illa W Q) species est ratio eliciendi actum cognoscendi FW Q X Z

The preceding example shows a text present only in the Gamma tradition. The text seems to be relevant to the conclusion of the outline of Thomas Aquinas' position concerning the agent of the soul's acquisition of scientific knowledge. Scotus makes use of the Aristotelian principle that the intellect possesses an essential potency to its acts before the acquisition of knowledge, and possesses an accidental potency to exercise science after this acquisition. The portion of the text preserved in Gamma concludes the presentation of the argument in a rather sophisticated way, in identifying the intelligible species as the formal first agent of the acquisition of knowledge, acting instrumentarily (secondarily) in the exercise of knowledge. We chose to leave this text as an *additio interpolata*, since even without it the reasoning should be familiar to anyone acquainted with the exegesis of Aristotle's psychological literature.[74]

> n. 8 indeterminatum ad plura non potest determinari] indeterminatum ad plura non determinatur FW Q X Z
>
> n. 10 possunt manere sine subiecto quod possunt intelligere] possint (possunt Z) esse (*om.* Z) sine (sub Z) subiecto quod est potentia possent (posset F Z) intelligere FW Q Z
>
> n. 23 igitur quaecumque forma accidentalis esset nobilior anima intellectiva] igitur esset (*om.* X) forma accidentalis sensibilis (pos. quaecumque Z) quaecumque nobilior anima FW Q X Z
>
> n. 34 contra modum positionis] contra modum positionis passionis KU contra modum rationis FW Q X Z
>
> q. 14 n. 1 sequitur actum intelligendi non autem praecedit sed habitus praecedit] sequitur actum intelligendi habitus (si Q X Z) autem praecedit FW   *add.* habitus alius praecedit Z
>
> n. 9 et frustra uniretur corpori] et uniretur corpori FW Q X Z
>
> n. 16 sed species intelligibilis est causa prior actu intelligendi nec est causa necessaria quia quod est formale principium intelligendi quo elicitur actus intelligendi sive sit intelligere sive species est liberum per participationem a sua causalitate ut scilicet

---

[74]The texts that provide the background to this discussion are: *Lectura* I dist. 3 pars 3 q. 1 (Vat. 16, p. 327 n 255): "Intellectus quandoque est in potentia essentiali et quandoque in potentia accidentali ad actum intelligendi, ex VIII Physicorum et II De anima; sed transitus de potentia essentiali ad actum non est nisi per aliquid quod prius non habetur quando est in potentia essentiali; igitur cum intellectus reducatur de potentia essentiali ad actum intelligendi, oportet quod prius transmutetur ad formam aliquam per quam habet actum intelligendi." (Vat. 5 p. 144, par 13): "Item, secundum Philosophum VIII Physicorum et II De anima, anima ante scientiam est in potentia essentiali, habens autem scientiam est in potentia accidentali. Quod autem reducit de potentia essentiali ad accidentalem respectu operationis, videtur esse principium activum respectu eius, quia est quo habens operatur: unde Philosophus vult II De anima, quod sicut scientia est (quo scimus), ita anima est (quo vivimus et sentimus) etc., et per consequens sicut anima est quo agimus actus vitales, ita scientia est quo active speculamur." (Vat. 5 p. 183, par 90): "Ad aliud, de scientia, dico quod scientia, per quam anima reducitur de potentia essentiali ad accidentalem, est species intelligibilis ipsius obiecti, et de illa concedo quod ipsa est principium activum respectu considerationis. Sed illa species non est habitus de quo loquimur, qui est quaedam qualitas, relicta ex actibus frequenter elicitis; ipsa enim species praecedit naturaliter primum actum elicitum circa obiectum circa quod est, et licet ista species posset esse radicata in intellectu et - cum fuerit radicata - posset dici habitus, non tamen est ille habitus qui generatur ex actibus frequenter elicitis, ut dictum est." Cf. Averroes, *In VIII Phys.*, c. 32 (Iunt. IV, 370D-E) "Exemplum verum potentiae, quae est accidentaliter, est potentia, quae est in ipso igne, quando impeditur a moto ad superius: et potentia, quae est in ipsa terra, ut moveatur ad inferius, quando impeditur. Et ista potentia est similis potentiae, quae est in sciente, quando non scit, id est non utitur sua scientia, et est violenta. Et, quia altera istarum est essentialis, et altera accidentalis, assimilavit essentialem potentiae, quae est in addiscente, ut fiat sciens, et potentiam accidentalem ei, quae est in sciente, quando non utitur scientia, propter aliquod impedimentum. Et hoc intendebat, cum dixit 'Et addiscens est in potentia, etc.' id est et addiscens, antequam addiscat, dicitur esse sciens in potentia alio modo ab eo, quo dicitur in eo, quod habet scientiam in tempore, quo non utitur sua scientia, quod ipsum est sciens in potentia. prima enim est de genere potentiae essentialis. secunda vero de genere potentiae accidentalis. Et ideo potentia essentialis indiget in hoc, quod exeat in actum, agente essentialiter. secunda autem non indiget agente in hoc, quod exeat in actum, nisi per accidens. quoniam non est in potentia, nisi propter impediens, aut propter defectum subiecti, in quo agit."

producat effectum igitur non est causa necessaria producendi effectum] sed species intelligibilis est causa prior actu intelligendi (intelligentia X) nec est causa necessaria quia (*add.* quod Q) est formale principium intelligendi id est quo elicitur actus intelligendi (actus intelligendi] intellectio Q) sive sit intellectus sive species est liberum per participationem ergo non est causa necessaria producendi effectum FW Q X   sed species intelligibilis est causa prior actu intelligendi nec est causa necessaria producendi effectum Z (*hom.*)

n. 17 quia actus primus potest impediri] quia potest impediri (imperari Q impedire X) actus primus (secundus Z) FW Q X Z

q. 15 n. 4 ratione unius partis non] ratione unius (*mg.* F#1 *om.* W) partis tantum et (*om.* Q) non alterius non (*om.* X) FW Q X Z

n. 5 secundo sic si informare corpus convenit ratione formae et non ratione materiae X   sic ideo si informare corpus convenit animae ratione formae et non ratione materiae Q   tamen (et N FW Z *om.* L) non (*lin.* W#1 *om.* O K) ratione materiae (materiale K) NO HLM K FW Z

The preceding example is one of the most remarkable accidents in the entire textual transmission: two members of Gamma seem to retain the premise of an argument that no other manuscript preserves. Two other Gamma manuscripts, **F** and **W**, show signs that these words are also in front of them when they anticipate by writing a line above 'nisi ratione formae…'. It is very likely that no manuscript is an actual witness of the text in its entirety, since the whole argument seems to miss the element of the premise stating that a form that is not primarily united to a matter cannot be the first act of that matter. In terms of explaining the origin of this omission, it can be conjectured that somehow there was a *cedula* for this part of the argument or that it was at the turn of a folium in Alpha, or else the text present in **Q** and **X** is just a provision of an intelligent scribe along the line of Gamma transmission. At any rate, we decided to retain this text as integral part of the argument, if not Scotus' own words.

q. 15 n. 20 *Adnotatio interpolata*: Sed (Si Q) ad hoc diceret Philosophus quod angelus non est in genere aliquo sed extra ideo (rationem F *om.* X) etc. (*om.* X) FW Q X Z Sed ad hoc aliquis dicit LM KU *om.* NO H

This text is found in its most extensive form in Gamma only, but something of it is also found in Beta and Delta. Doctrinally viewed, the material reported for the 'adnotatio' is reacting to the third and fourth arguments because they depend on principles that bear upon ontological genera. From a literary standpoint, however, the material could only be included if the copyist wanted to write an ellipsis in the text because there is no continuation of the sentence. What is noteworthy about the material is that it is just the sort of topic that might come up spontaneously in a classroom environment and be included in a report but not finally incorporated into the text.

q. 17 n. 21 non autem de instrumentali] non autem de agente (*add.* in virtute X) instrumentali FW Q X Z

n. 24 sed potest talis responsio] sed potest talis sensus (sensio Q Z sensitio (?) X) FW Q X Z

n. 25 intellectus agens agit in intellectum possibilem] intellectus agens agit in intellectum possibilem illam (istam Q X *om.* Z) speciem FW Q X Z

n. 42 anima est omnia intelligibilia per actum intelligendi] anima est (*lin.* X *add.* anima Q) intellectiva (intelligibilia Z) per actum sciendi (speculandi Q *add.* sicut sensibilia (sensitiva FW) per actum sentiendi FW X Z) FW Q X Z

This last example testifies to the inferiority of the Gamma tradition at this point, since the text clearly refers to the quotation from *De anima* III t. 37 as occurs at n. 5 of the question. The variant in Gamma seems to be the result of a series of copying errors of a heavily abbreviated sentence, combined with the repetition of Aristotle's passage in its entirety, which is not necessary for the sake of the reasoning.

q. 19 n. 2 actus igitur isti essent eiusdem rationis] actus isti essent eiusdem rationis FW Q X Z

n. 4 felicitas autem potest a nobis adipisci] felicitas autem potest (*post* nobis X *add.* a Z) nobis advenire FW Q X Z

n. 6 sed contra conclusionem] sed contra consequentiam (rationem Q) FW Q X Z

n. 8 excederet etiam potentiam illam] excederet etiam potentiam FW Q X Z

n. 19 cognitione cuiuscumque creaturae distincte cognitae] cognitione cuiuscumque creaturae FW X cognitione cuiuscumque creaturae distincte create Q cognitione cuiuscumque distincte creaturae Z

n. 24 nec est omnino simplex nec primus sed resolubilis in alios] nec est omnino simpliciter ut primus sed compositus et resolubilis FW nec est omnino simplex ut primus sed compositus et resolubilis in alios X Z ut est omnino supra primus sed resolubilis in alios Q

n. 26 sic eum cognoscere perfectius] sic eum cognoscere componendo perfectius U FW Q X Z

q. 20 n. 5 Ad hoc dicunt quidam quod intellectus] Ad hoc dicunt quidam quod (*om.* X Z) scilicet Henricus quod intellectus FW X Z   Ad illam questionem dicit quidam scilicet Henricus quod intellectus Q

n. 18 visibile praedicatur de colore per se secundo modo] visibile (sensibile Z) praedicatur de colore secundo modo FW Q X Z

n. 22 quoad cognitionem nostram obiecta quam actus et actus quam potentiae] quoad cognitionem nostram et (*om.* FW) actus <*add.* et X> quam potentiae FW Q X Z

q. 21 n. 17 cum dicatur de ente increato] cum dicatur de ente (*om.* FW) increato nec ens increatum tantum cum dicatur de ente (*om.* FW) creato FW Q Z

n. 18 nugatio dicendo ens unum et e converso] magis dicere ens unum (*add.* quam e converso *sed exp.* W) vel e converso FW Q Z

n. 24 nullum conceptum perfectiorem conceptu creaturae possumus habere pro statu viae nec de Deo] nullum conceptum in via possumus habere pro statu viae nec de Deo F nullum conceptum perfectiorem creaturae (crearetur Z) possumus habere pro statu viae (*om.* Z) quia nullum conceptum in via (eis Z) possumus habere pro statu viae nec de Deo W Q Z

n. 30 per aliquid sed per non ens] per aliquid FW Q X Z

n. 33 peccat secundum accidens sive *om.* FW Q X Z

q. 22 n. 1 quia quod quid est est obiectum] quia (*om.* X) quod (*lin.* Z#2) quid est est (*mg.* U#2 *om.* Q Z) obiectum proprium (*ant.* obiectum *mg.* U#2 *om.* Q) U FW X Z

n. 1 de ipso posset haberi scientia] de ipso posset haberi scientia per consequens FW Z de ipso per consequens posset haberi scientia Q

n. 20 conclusionem intelligimus sive cognoscimus in syllogismo] conclusiones cognoscimus in (*om.* Q Z) syllogismo FW Q Z

n. 21 unde in I Canonica Ioannis] unde I (*post* Ioannis F Q) Ioannis (Ioanne Q) FW Q Z

n. 34 signatas ad ipsam] signatas et ipsam FW Q Z

F. Table of the Agreements of Two Groups

The following table lists the frequency of occurrences in readings shared by the two groups Beta and Epsilon against the readings of Beta and Delta. In general, the readings shared by the Beta group with Epsilon or Delta retain authority. In this table, the variants on terms such as praeterea/item or igitur/ergo are not listed. Note that the distribution of variants occurring in two groups is not uniform in the questions. In qq. 1-5 we find a predominant Beta and Epsilon grouping, question five witnesses the prevalent Beta-Epsilon grouping up to paragraph nine, while from paragraph ten of question five up to question nine the main agreement is between Beta and Delta and there are no readings exclusively common to Beta and Epsilon. Question ten reveals readings only common to Beta and Epsilon. Question eleven also follow this pattern, save for two Beta + Delta readings at paragraph one and three. Questions twelve to fourteen reverse the pattern and see almost exclusively Beta and Delta readings. Question fifteen shows the predominance of Beta and Delta readings, although there are a number of Beta + Epsilon readings. Question sixteen reveals a complex transmission; we find all the Beta-Epsilon readings before paragraph nineteen, while the Beta-Delta readings are concentrated for the most part in the second half of the question. Questions seventeen to twenty-two show a great deal of contamination, which reflects on the almost even number of Beta-Delta vs. Beta-Epsilon readings. Question twenty-three does not occur in manuscripts O, Q, and Z and bears witness to only Beta + Delta agreements. In questions one and twenty-two the agreements of the Beta group with Epsilon are determined by the common reading of Beta + N + O, when O differs from Gamma and Delta.

	Beta + Epsilon	Beta + Delta
Question 1	20	0
Question 2	12	3
Question 3	7	1
Question 4	8	1
Question 5	9	10
Question 6	0	33
Question 7	0	48
Question 8	0	17
Question 9	0	32
Question 10	19	0
Question 11	15	2
Question 12	2	33
Question 13	2	15
Question 14	0	27
Question 15	8	22
Question 16	15	19
Question 17	21	19
Question 18	8	6
Question 19	15	16
Question 20	7	6
Question 21	16	21
Question 22	9	11
Question 23	0	16

Since we have highlighted the relative independence of the four lines of transmission with respect of their origin in the previous section of the Introduction, we should say something about the phenomenon of the many variants and textual accidents in which the Beta manuscripts share the same readings with either Delta or Epsilon.

The evidence previously discussed points to an initial transmission of the text whereas the autograph, or less probably the apograph, was copied by four scribes, working independently at approximately the same time. They did not have in front of them a thoroughly revised version of the text; the *Quaestiones* were school material that Scotus in all probability did not intend to publish in the form in which they were left. One of the scribes, that at the origin of the Beta line of text transmission, had probably heard the lectures given by Scotus, or had access to notes of those lectures. His transcription shows some hints of reporting oral deliveries of several sentences. Thus, the Beta tradition may be considered a revised and slightly edited version of the material left by Scotus, to be used as an authoritative text when the reputation of the Subtle Doctor had spread among the schools of the Franciscan Order. In fact, all the four lines of transmission provide a text where editorial interventions by the scribes were at times necessary. The distinctive character of each line of transmission helps us to understand the implications of a common occurrence among medieval textual transmissions, that is, contamination or horizontal transmission, in the text preserved in manuscripts of the *Quaestiones*. While the evidence shown above points to a native independence of the manuscripts at the beginning of the four lines of transmission, all the extant manuscripts of the *Quaestiones* witness a text with some degrees of contamination. The institutional setting of the manuscript reproduction—for the most part Franciscan houses—made possible the copying of the text from two or more models; in fact, manuscript **N** had as a model for some questions a codex of the Beta group. The use of the *Quaestiones* in the schools facilitated marginal interventions by masters and students, with the diffusion of these *marginalia* to other manuscripts of this work. Furthermore, the unfinished state of the *Quaestiones* promoted an activity of editorial intrusions which quickly spread throughout the entire textual transmission. These reasons may well account for the textual coincidences and common readings of manuscripts belonging to different groups. The horizontal transmission explains the common readings of either Beta and Delta or Beta and Epsilon by the hypothesis that the interventions of a single scribe, which in the case of the Beta line of transmission might well have been a restoration of authoritative readings, was quickly picked up by other scribes or users of manuscripts from other lines of transmission, and spread throughout the tradition. Finally, we should note that Beta-Delta agreements indicated in these tables imply corresponding agreements of Epsilon-Gamma (or O-Gamma); we treat this phenomenon in § 2.M below.

G. Readings Common to the Beta and Epsilon Groups: Some Examples

q. 1 n. 18 sicut unus] = NO HLM   scilicet ille KU FW Q   scilicet X Z

n. 19 sunt ambo sensus tactus] = NO HLM   conveniunt ambo sensus tactus KU FW Q Z

q. 2 n. 2 quia talis est anima intellectiva] = N HLM   anima est intellectiva O   quia (quae X) illa (huiusmodi Q *om.* FW X Z) est intellectiva KU FW Q X Z

n. 5 sensibile positum supra carnem sentimus] = N HM   positum sensibile supra carnem sentimus O   sensibile positum supra carnem sentitur L   positum tangibile supra carnem facit sensum (tactum sive sensum K) KU X Z   posito tangibili supra carnem facit carnem sensum FW   tangibile positum supra carnem facit carnem sensum Q

q. 3 n. 13 sentitur vehementer] = NO HLM   sentitur immediate sine corpore alio vehementer KU   sentitur valde vehementer F X Z   sentitur bene vehementer Q   sentitur immediate valde vehementer W

q. 4 n. 11 De aliis sensibus non est conclusio Philosophi vera modo dicto] = *coni. cum* M   De aliis sensibus non est conclusio (*mg.* Philosophi vera) modo dicto M   De aliis sensibus non est conclusio Philosophi modo dicta (dicto H) *deinde reliquerunt spat. vac.* HL   De aliis sensibus non est conclusio Philosophi modo dicto N   De aliis sensibus est ut conclusio Philosophi modo dicto O   De aliis autem sensibus secundum Philosophum est dicendum KU   De aliis autem sensibus est ut conclusio Philosophi probat FW   De aliis sensibus est tertio Philosophi non modo dicendo Q   De aliis autem sensibus est ut conclusio Philosophi modo dicendo X Z

The reading of this passage is based on MS **M** only, although it is itself ambiguous, since the words 'Philosophi vera' are in the margin. No other manuscript has 'vera', while **H** and **L** have an empty space. In this example, it is almost impossible to acquire a reading with some paleographic support. **N** and Beta seem to have a consistent reading with the words 'De aliis sensibus non est conclusio Philosophi modo dicto' which may require also the predicative 'vera', to be found only in **M**. MS **O** also seems to support this reading, if we take the 'ut' as a mis-expansion of 'vera'. Significantly, MS **O** differs from the readings of Gamma, which uncharacteristically does not express a coherent tradition. In sum, we have a relatively consistent Beta and Epsilon reading; in the Delta and Gamma groups the 'non' is dropped, which may explain the various efforts to give the sentence a consistent meaning. Note that this 'non' is important, because it introduces Scotus' own solution to the problem of direct perception, which differs from Aristotle's and from the other solutions common during his time.

q. 5 n. 6 realem formam vel materialem] = NO HLM   formam realiter vel materialiter KU   formam realem sive (vel Q Z) materialem FW Q Z   formam materialem vel realem X

q. 10 n. 6 nulla potentia discernit aliqua quae non cognoscit utrumque illorum] = HLM N   nulla potentia discernit aliqua quae non cognoscit quodlibet eorum O   nulla potentia discernit inter aliqua quae non cognoscat (cognoscit K) quodlibet (quolibet Q quam X) eorum (illorum K) sed hoc (non K) est impossibile de duabus potentiis (*add. scilicet* K) non sub invicem ordinatis igitur (*om.* X) etc. (et Z *om.* Q X) K FW Q X Z

n. 25 sensus superioris quam inferioris quia superius est quasi ligamentum sensibus propriis] = HLM sensus superioris quia superius est quasi ligatum sensibus propriis N   sensus (*dub.* O) superioris quam inferioris quia superius est quasi (*dub.* O) signa sensibus propriis O   potentiae superioris (superiori Z) quam inferioris quia superius est communius K FW Q X Z

q. 15 n. 29 ad hoc est auctoritas Commentatoris II Metaphysicae super illud] = HLM   item Commentator II Metaphysicae N item Commentator II Metaphysicae super illud O   ad hoc est auctoritas Commentatoris II (III Z) Metaphysicae super illud (idem U) capitulum secundum (super KU) antiquam translationem KU FW X Z   ad hoc est auctoritas Commentatoris II Metaphysicae super illud antiquae translationis Q

n. 33 corporalibus materia] = HLM NO   inferioribus (*add*. sic Z) materia (est eadem K) KU FW Q X Z

n. 46 de ipso] = NO HLM   de primo modo KU   de primo FW Q X Z

q. 16 n. 3 cum igitur magis universale est medium] = HLM N   cum igitur magis universalis est media O   cognitio (cognitum F) magis universalis (universale X) est media KU FW X

q. 17 n. 8 maior patet quia sicut obiectum est prius (praesens K) actu intelligendi ordine naturae (*om*. X) sic ratio obiecti probatio minoris quia non potest aliter (aliud Z) esse praesens nisi per speciem in phantasmate exsistentem sed non per (*om*. F) illam (istam Z *om*. FW)] = KU FW Q X Z   minor patet (probatur N) quia sicut obiectum est prius actu intelligendi ordine naturae sic ratio (ideo (*dub*.) O) obiecti NO   minor (maior H) patet quia sicut obiectum est prius actu intelligendi ordine naturae sic ratio obiecti probatio quia (*om*. H) non potest aliter esse praesens nisi per speciem in phantasmate exsistente, non autem per illam HLM

At the beginning of the sentence, 'maior' must be correct both because of its content and because the 'minor' cannot both be clear enough and require proof. What is difficult to understand is why Beta does not write 'minoris', but perhaps the word could be understood; noteworthy too is the parallel of 'sed non' and 'non autem' in the Beta group. In light of these considerations, we have decided to retain the text as consistently handed over by the Delta and Gamma groups.

n. 30 vel ipso coadiuvante non poterit (possit N) speciem intelligibilem producere] = NO HLM Q   vel (*om*. Z) ipso (illo Q) coadiuvante (adiuvante K coadunante U X) poterit speciem intelligibilem producere KU FW X Z

q. 19 n. 17 non (et X) enim oportet quod intellectus sit similis in natura vel quantum ad modum essendi obiecto sed sufficit quantum (*om*. Z) ad actum intelligendi] = HLM Q X Z non enim oportet quod intellectus sit similis in natura vel quantum in (*om*. O) omni modo essendi obiecto (obiective N) sed sufficit quantum ad actum intelligendi NO   non enim oportet quod intellectus (*om*. KU) sit similis in natura vel quantum ad modum essendi obiecto sed sufficit quantum ad actum intelligendi non tantum (enim FW *om*. K) oportet quod intellectus noster (sit similis FW) KU FW

q. 20 n. 4 quia ratio veri est ratio intellecti vel intelligibilis] = LM NO   quia ratio veri est intellecti et intelligibilis H   quia ratio veri est ratio (in U) intellectu (*om*. K) ipsius vel intelligibilis KU quia ratio veri est ratio intellecti vel ipsius (*ant*. intellecti Q) intelligibilis FW Q X Z

q. 21 n. 16 quando aliquid praedicatur] = NO HLM   quando unum per se praedicatur K quando unum praedicatur per se U   quando (quod non X) unum FW Q X Z praedicatur

n. 19 propter diversitatem rationum] = NO HLM propter diversitatem rationum scilicet (*om*. Z) quod impeditur praedicatio (*add*. entis FW Q Z) vel (et U) e converso KU FW Q Z

H. READINGS COMMON TO THE BETA AND DELTA GROUPS: SOME EXAMPLES

q. 5 n. 1 est in actu] = HL KU   est ens (*lin.* M *ante* est F) in (*om.* FW Q Z) actu NO M FW Q X Z

n. 11 est separabilis a corpore] = HL   est separabilis scilicet humana] = NO FW Q X Z   est separabilis a corpore igitur etc. M   est separabilis a corpore ut anima humana K *add. mg.* ergo non est eadem cum anima N#2

n. 13 est in proposito de sensu] = HLM K X   est in proposito de sensibili NO FW Q Z

q. 6 n. 2 alia debet esse respectu figurae] = HLM KU alia debeat (debet Q) esse figurae NO FW Q Z

n. 7 secundum esse reale] = HL KU   secundum illud (idem N id M) esse reale NO M FW Q

As a theoretical observation, there is only one 'esse reale' not 'this' or 'that' 'esse reale'. This passage expresses the notion that in natural change the form acting on the patient does so according to the same mode of existence found in the agent.

n. 10 qualis ille sapor est] = HLM KU   qualis est NO FW Q Z

n. 10 si passivum sit extrinsecum] = HLM K Z   si passum sit extrinsecum NO U FW   si passum extrinsecum sit Q

n. 14 diversum gradum] = HLM KU   distinctum gradum NO F Q Z   diversum gradum distinctum W

q. 7 n. 5 quia non est in genere quantitatis] = LM KU   quia est in genere quantitatis (qualitatis FW X) NO H FW X

The subject of the sentence is 'talis actio', and the expressed idea is that every continuous being cannot be measured, according to the principles of Aristotle's *Physics*. If that is true, the 'non' is necessary for the completion of the reasoning. Note that the Gamma group has 'quia est in genere qualitatis', which supports the notion, if not the reading, 'non est in genere quantitatis'. That leaves only the Epsilon group with a truly different reading.

n. 11 a subiecto et fundamento] = HLM KU   subito a fundamento NO   subiecto a fundamento FW X Z

n. 11 Aliqua autem (*om.* H) relativa ut de secundo modo fundantur] = HLM KU   Aliqua est relatio ut dicitur que fundatur secundo modo N   Aliqua autem relatio (re O) ut de secundo modo fundatur O FW X Z

n. 14 cum secundum] = HLM KU   et secundum NO Z secundum FW X

n. 18 vel aliquid aliud temporale] = LM KU   vel aliquid temporale NO Z   ad temporale H FW   vel tempus ad temporale X

n. 20 factio facta] = LM KU   actio facta H   facta NO X Z   factio FW

n. 22 actio praedicamentum nisi quae] = HLM KU actio quae (quia O) est praedicamentum quae NO actio praedicamentum quae FW X Z

q. 8 simul contraria sentire] = HLM KU   simul sentire contraria NO Q   sentire omnia F'   sentire contraria (*mg.*) F#2   sentire (*mg.* W#2) simul contraria W   simul contraria X   recipere contraria Z

n. 2 quod sensus movetur simul] = HM K   quod sensus moveretur simul L   quod sensus simul movetur U   quod sensus moveretur (*add. quod sed del.*) simul F   sensus moveretur simul (*om.* X) NO W Q X Z

n. 9 Praeterea a diversis motoribus sunt diversi motus; diversa sensibilia sunt moventia diversa; igitur etc.] = NO FW Q X Z   *om.* HML KU

n. 21 tamen semper obfuscat ideo possunt simul esse etc.] = H   tamen semper obfuscat ideo potest simul esse L   tamen semper obfuscat et ideo possunt simul ens M   tamen obfuscat semper ideo possunt simul esse etc. K   tamen semper obfuscat ideo possunt esse simul U   tamen obfuscat NO   tamen semper (propter F) obfuscat FW Q X Z

q. 9 n. 1 propter secundum actum] = HLM K   propter actum secundum U   propter actum N   propter primum actum O FW Q X Z

n. 9 albi et dulcis] albi et nigri HLM KU X

Throughout the text the example is always white and sweet, as it is in the pertinent literature. Interestingly enough, the examples 'white and black' could have some basis here. In this instance, the discussion is on the qualities as objects of sense opposed to intelligibles, not on the different genera of qualities. Following this passage is the example of an animal without reason, and yet capable of choosing objects of sense.

n. 15 obiectum proprium] = LM KU   subiectum proprium H   obiectum primum NO FW Q X Z

These expressions convey a difference in meaning. Scotus discusses what is primarily the object for particular and common sense ('obiectum aeque primo utriusque'). They are not the same object, because what is the 'proper object' of a particular sense is not the object 'per se' of the common sense.

n. 17 non repugnat ei sicut non repugnat sensui] = NO Q Z non repugnat ei sicut nec (*om.* X) repugnat sensui F X non repugnat sensui HLM KU W' *sed rest. mg.* W

This omission occurs in the Beta and Delta groups. It can be considered either a homeoteleuton or a refinement posterior to a given text. By stemmatic hypothesis Beta and Delta do not have an intermediate common model; on the other hand, the sentence is needed as it is in Epsilon and Gamma. We have retained this reading in the text, as a homeoteleutic error which very easily could have occurred independently in different manuscripts; it concerns only three words. As can be seen above, it also occurred in MS **W** of the Gamma group.

> q. 12 n. 13 ab actu cognoscendi nisi secundum rationem tantum] = HLM KU   ab actu cognoscendi secundum rem sed secundum rationem tantum (*ant.* secundum O) NO   ab actu cognoscendi re (rem F Q) sed tantum ratione FW Q X Z
>
> n. 28 in potentiis subiective quam in potentiis elicitive (*add. ult.* sive L) effective] = HLM KU   in potentiis subiective (sensitivis X) quam a potentiis effective NO FW Q X
>
> n. 34 sed dicitur formaliter libera per te in quantum passiva] = LM K   sed dicitur formaliter per te in quantum passiva H   *om.* U   sed dicitur formaliter (formale NO) volens per te in quantum passiva NO FW Q X Z
>
> n. 37 vel quia a principio elicitivo libere scilicet voluntate] = Z   vel quia (quasi NO) a principio elicitivo (electivo O) libero (libere NO) scilicet (*add.* a NO) voluntate NO FW Q X   *om.* HLM KU

This omission occurs in the Beta and Delta groups. The sentence seems to be required to illustrate the senses by which an act of will may be defined as free. Its omission in the key witnesses of the text is possibly the result of a marginal correction in the autograph overlooked by the copyists originating the Beta and Delta manuscript groups.

> q. 13 n. 12 quod actio mobilis ad actum primum quod est generans rem differt a motu] = HLM K   mobilis ad actum primum quod est generans rem differt a motu U   quod movens (motus N) ad (*om.* Q) actum primum (unum X) quod (*om.* F) est generans realiter (*post* differt N) differt (differunt Q) a (*om.* F) moto NO FW Q X
>
> q. 14 n. 15 species influxae non valerent ad intelligendum singularia] = HLM K   speciei (species Q X Z) influxae non valerent (valet Z) ad intelligendum inferiora NO FW Q X Z
>
> n. 16 ut scilicet producat effectum igitur non est causa necessaria producendi effectum intelligimus enim cum volumus ut dicitur II De anima potest enim liberum per essentiam scilicet voluntas impedire liberum per participationem a sua causalitate ne scilicet producat effectum suum] *conj. cum codd.*   non est causa necessaria producendi effectum intelligimus enim cum volumus ut dicitur II De anima potest enim liberum per essentiam scilicet voluntas impedire (impedi N) liberum per participationem a sua causalitate naturae scilicet producat effectum suum NO   ut (ne M' *mg.* ut M) scilicet producat (producit H) effectum suum HLM K (*sed rest. mg.* M#2)   ergo non est causa necessaria producendi effectum intelligimus enim cum volumus (volimus Q) ut dicitur II De anima potest enim liberum per essentiam scilicet voluntas impedire liberum per participationem a sua causalitate ne (ut X) scilicet *om.* FW) producat (producant FW) effectum (*post.* suum Q) suum FW Q X   producendi effectum intelligimus enim cum volumus ut dicitur II De anima potest enim liberum per essentiam scilicet voluntas impedire liberum per participationem a sua causalitate ne producat effectum suum Z

This is a large omission, due to homeoteleuton at the word 'producat', occurring in the Beta and Delta group. The whole passage shows evident signs of a troublesome transmission, since all the manuscripts omit portions of the text. The accidents in the transmission probably originated from poorly written notes of Scotus' own lectures.

> q. 19 n. 25 abstrahere (*om.* H) ab omnibus huiusmodi] = HLM abstrahere ab omnibus NO abstrahere huiusmodi figuras KU abstrahere ab omnibus figuris FW Q X Z

> q. 23 n. 3 maior patet per Philosophum II De anima quia in hoc distinguitur potentia accidentalis a potentia essentiali minor etiam tenet per Philosophum III De anima] *conj. cum* F   maior (minor L) patet per Philosophum III De anima N HLM KU Maior patet per Philosophum II De anima quia in hoc distinguitur potentia accidentalis a potentia (*om.* X) essentiali minor etiam patet per Philosophum W X *add.* III De anima W

We have clear evidence here that MS **N** is either copying Beta or one of the Beta witnesses, while Delta is likewise either copying Beta or one of the Beta witnesses, though Delta does not do so consistently and so may combine traditions (or be contaminated if one prefers). Because the skip involves homeoteleuton, it is likely safe to take this text as primitive.

I. THE MANUSCRIPT TRADITION AND WADDING

Neither Alpha nor any of the constituent parents (Beta, Delta, Epsilon, Gamma) of the four manuscript traditions survive. In fact, most of the extant manuscripts of these questions are found in fifteenth-century codices. We can attribute the massive destruction of early manuscripts of these questions, along with Scotus' other works, to a deliberate domestic policy carried out by King Henry's VIII's secretary, Thomas Cromwell, in the sixteenth century. During Henry's reign (1535), Cromwell commissioned a Cambridge priest, Richard Layton, "to destroy all documents and books pertaining to Scotus and to proscribe his teachings, though they were not a foreign imposition, but had been brought to flower on the fertile soil of his fatherland." In a letter to Cromwell reporting the successful completion of his mission, Layton said:

> We have set Duns in Bocardo [Oxford prison], and have utterly banished him from Oxford for ever, with all his blind glosses; and is now made a common servant to every man, fast nailed upon posts at all common houses of easement: that I have seen with mine own eyes. And now the second time we came to New College, after we had declared your injunctions, we found all the great quadrant court full of leaves of Duns, the wind blowing them into every quarter.[75]

Almost certainly more manuscripts containing Scotus' writings—and many of the most precious ones—are lost than survive. Included amongst these lost manuscripts are more than likely other members of the Beta and Delta tradition (and perhaps Epsilon as well) as all three of these families

---

[75]Quoted in Allan B. Wolter, O.F.M., "Reflections on the Life and Works of Scotus," *The American Philosophical Quarterly* 68 (1993): 1-36, at 29 n. 101; the text of the quotation is taken from a letter of Dr. Layton to Thomas Cromwell dated 12 Sept. 1535 published in G. H. Cook, *Letters to Cromwell and Others on the Suppression of the Monasteries* (London, 1965), 48. A second mass destruction of books was carried out in 1550.

represent, in various degrees, the insular and superior manuscript tradition of Scotus' *Quaestiones De anima*.

As we have seen, the most popular tradition of Scotus' questions, judging by the extant manuscript evidence, is the Gamma family. Roughly one-half of the manuscripts derive from the common exemplar Gamma. The Gamma tradition remained the standard continental edition of Scotus' *Quaestiones De anima* and the base text for all of the early modern printed editions of the work. In the seventeenth century, Hugo Cavellus and Lucas Wadding used one of these early modern printings, **Pavia**, as their base text for their edition of the questions. However, Cavellus and Wadding claimed that they also used the MSS **W**, **V**, and **X**, all members of the Gamma family, for their edition.[76] Wadding and his fellow editors presumably chose these manuscripts because of their apparent antiquity, as they were all early copies of the questions (fourteenth-century manuscripts), and their location, as all were housed at the Vatican Library. The editors may well have chosen **W** to correct their printed base text because of its age; MS **W**, however, has many homeoteleuta, other omissions, and faulty readings. The editors repaired these omissions and obvious faults from the other two manuscripts. They did more: if their statements about the manuscripts they used are true, for some inscrutable reason they seem to have alternated their use of them, so that the text of their edition now follows one and then another manuscript. Why the editors made such use of MS **X** is a mystery, for it is extremely difficult to read, omits arguments, and abbreviates and paraphrases the text in many places. Moreover, in respect of the text the editors presented, the order of questions in **X** is completely random. Furthermore, it appears as if the three manuscripts Cavellus and Wadding used come from different stages of descent from Gamma, forming two separate subgroupings within the Gamma tradition, ζ and π, as will be shown in the *stemma codicum* below. The result of the editors' procedures is probably the most contaminated redaction of the *Quaestiones De anima* in the whole textual tradition. That is not all: Wadding throughout introduced his own stylistic preferences into the text, which appear as hundreds of isolated accidents within the history of its transmission. In some questions the editors were, furthermore, careless, introducing their own homeoteleuta, omissions and faulty readings into the text. As a final touch, Wadding imposed heavy, obtrusive, and occasionally faulty punctuation. This is the current text of Scotus' questions available to most researchers. If scholars have been skeptical about the authenticity and merit of the *Quaestiones De anima*, the edition they have had at their disposal could certainly not help improve their opinion of the work.

Despite the fact that three of the Gamma MSS, **V**, **W** and **X**, are of demonstrable antiquity—in fact MS **W** is probably the oldest extant manuscript of these questions, having been copied within a generation of Scotus' death—the Gamma tradition overall is the latest and most edited of all the four families. The Gamma editor, as is apparent throughout the edition, presents a reordered text. Gamma has corrected the order of the twenty-three questions, he has modified the text significantly in many locations, he has added much material, and he has deliberately altered and emended Scotus' text in order to smooth it over and clarify the meaning. Rather than present a faithful copy of the autograph, Gamma has instead constructed an early edition of the text. This modified form of the *Quaestiones* rapidly gained a success that resulted in a proliferation of manuscripts of the Gamma version in the fifteenth century.

J. Nature of the Ur-manuscript Alpha

The evidence of the extant manuscript tradition indicates that Alpha was heavily

---

[76]*Opera omnia* ed. Vivès III:474.

abbreviated in a compact Anglicana hand, probably rapidly scribbled by Scotus himself, with many corrections both interlinear and marginal. As we have seen, the folia in Alpha were transposed so that the third gathering of folia, containing *Quaestiones De anima* q. 9 n. 13 to q. 13 n. 6 was placed before those containing q. 5 n. 11 to q. 9 n. 13. The nature of the work indicates that it was a series of questions designed for a course on Aristotle's *De anima* within the Oxford Franciscan *studium*.

Alpha was the original draft of a text intended for a course in the *studium*, which Scotus himself never revised or examined further with an eye to publication. Because of its elliptical, cryptic sense ("notes" of thoughts and arguments that the author understood), lapses of grammar and diction resulting from speed, the difficulty of the handwriting (doubtless illegible in spots), and subsequent wear in the unbound gatherings, the text in this manuscript was unsuited for providing an intelligible model for use by many readers. Only an immediate student of Scotus, or at least one who had access to supplementary materials associated with the very course (i.e, classroom notes and reports), would be able to scrutinize the manuscript text intelligently. Indeed, we know this was a common phenomenon surrounding Scotus' writings in general, most of which he never finished for publication. It fell upon his students and disciples to prepare his writings for publication. And from what we know of Alpha, only a student of Scotus (if at second and not first remove) could construe correctly the intended meaning in such a difficult manuscript text.

Even when autograph manuscripts or direct copies of them do survive, editors seldom decide to present such texts in their integrity, because they are rough drafts that do not represent the final thoughts and intentions of their authors. Many medieval authors extensively revised and "authorized" or "examined" or "ordered" or "edited" their texts for publication, which they moreover, often personally supervised. That "authoritative" text is what editors seek to recover, when the surviving evidence allows. For Scotus, however, this point is moot; Alpha does not survive, nor, because of the immediate editorial work (Beta and later Gamma) performed on Alpha's text, and even more because of the massive contamination in the other witnesses, could one ever recover the text of Alpha in its integrity. Yet, what one can recover of Alpha has great importance, for every autograph bears decisive readings that are lost in the immediate next stage of transmission (even in corrected manuscripts supervised by the author himself); moreover, as the primitive source of the whole transmission, Alpha, when we can infer it with probability, plays an overall governing role in adjudicating variants among the other most privileged witnesses.

Unlike the *Ordinatio* and his *Questions on the Metaphysics*, the work itself does not contain many interpolated texts and large marginal annotations that would seem to stem from a series of lecture notes used repeatedly and at various stages in his career. Since the *Quaestiones De anima* is largely devoid of the additional matter and *cedulae* found in his other works, we have concluded that the *Quaestiones* represent a lecture course that Scotus taught probably only once, as a student-teacher while probably enrolled in the theological faculty at Oxford, and one that he never revised or otherwise authorized for publication.

The extant manuscripts provide windows into the nature and quality of the autograph that demonstrate problems in the autograph with regard to abbreviations, marginal insertions, and occasionally *lapsus mentis* by Scotus himself. Problems in Alpha are most evident when we encounter a breakdown amongst all the families; when, for example, an error passed from Alpha to its four descendants was fixed in various ways throughout the manuscript tradition.

Several textual accidents throughout the *Quaestiones* reveal the problems faced by scribes when confronted with what must surely have been an unfinished and heavily annotated model. Particularly critical were the portions of text in which marginal corrections did not have a clear indication of their insertion points; moreover, many scribes took alternative readings either as substitutions or additions to the prior text. The peculiar abbreviations of the *Anglicana cursiva* script also gave rise to confusion. These particular accidents allow us a glimpse of the nature of the autograph and a window on Alpha. Some examples have already been discussed in the section covering the Beta-only readings. Here are some other examples.

> q. 1 n. 3 aeque perfecte sentit unam contrarietatem sicut et aliam] = N M Q Z aeque (ita O) perfecte sentit unam contrarietatem sicut aliam O HL FW aeque (haec U) apprehendit vel sentit unam contrarietatem sicut et (om. U) aliam (add. ergo etc. K) KU aeque sentit unam contrarietatem sicut et aliam X

What is noteworthy in this instance is the confusion of the Delta scribe who wrote 'apprehendit', whereas the entire tradition has 'perfecte', and interpreted it as an alternative reading. Furthermore, some scribes may have felt that the 'et' was not necessary and that the sentence read well without it.

> n. 8 unum genus obiectum tactui univoce praedicatum de illis] = L Z unum genus obiectum tactui univoce praedicati de illis NO HM K unum genus obiectum tactui univoce (unitate FW Q X om. U) praedicatum (praedicationis FW praedicatur X) de ipsis (add. qualitatibus X) U FW Q X Z

Here the reading 'praedicati' occurs in Epsilon, the majority of Beta and MS **K**. 'Praedicati' would be grammatically problematic, and the manuscript tradition reflects attempts to write a more coherent text. The sentence stresses the genus as predicated univocally of something; therefore the concordance should be in the accusative. Here the test as it is found in Epsilon and MSS **H** and **M** is probably an attraction of a preceding 'univoce praedicati'.

> n. 10 sed tactus simul sentit] = LM item (mg. K#2) tactus simul sentit N H K#2 praeterea tactus simul perfectissime sentit O probatio tactus simul sentit U FW Q X Z

The model had in this passage, with all probability, only a simple symbol signaling the introduction of the particular minor premise in opposition to the major 'impossibile est unum sensum tactum habere simul et semel duos perfectissimos actus'. The need for an adversative sentence is understandable because the preceding sentence states that the sense of touch cannot have two most perfect acts at once, while here Scotus says that the sense of touch detects the water to be cold and wet at the same time, not with the same act but with two acts, and goes on to prove that these two acts are most perfect. The majority of the copyists took it as a 'Praeterea/Item' sign.

> n. 13 obiectum debet correspondere potentiae vel esse determinativum potentiae et est eiusdem generis determinati] = H obiectum debet correspondere potentiae vel determinatum (est determinata O) potentiae et est eiusdem generis determinati NO M obiectum debet correspondere potentiae si ergo est determinate potentiae debet habere obiectum generis determinati vel esse determinate potentiae et est eiusdem generis determinati L obiectum debet correspondere potentiae si ergo est potentia determinata debet habere obiectum generis determinati vel esse determinatum potentiae et est eiusdem generis determinati K obiectum debet correspondere potentiae si ergo determinata potentia debet habere obiectum determinati generis U obiectum debet correspondere potentiae (ant. correspondere X) si ergo est determinata debet habere obiectum generis determinati (add. sicut X) FW Q X Z

In this instance, Scotus is listing several arguments proving that the sense of touch is not formally one. This argument proceeds in the following manner: one particular sensitive power acts over one determinate genus. This is evident by reasoning. Major premise: an object of sense should correspond to the power, or be determined for the power, and be of one determinate genus; Minor premise: the sense of touch does not regard an object of one determined genus. The middle term is 'object of one determined genus'. The Major premise occurs in the tradition in two different forms:

MSS **NO HM** read: 'obiectum debet correspondere potentiae vel esse (est O *om.* N M) determinativum (determinatum N M determinata O) potentiae et est eiusdem generis determinati'

MSS **U FW Q X Z** read: 'obiectum debet correspondere potentiae si ergo est determinata potentia debet habere obiectum generis determinati'

MSS **L** and **K** have both readings: 'obiectum debet correspondere potentiae si ergo est determinate potentiae (potentia determinata K) debet habere obiectum generis determinati vel esse determinate (determinatum K) potentiae et est eiusdem generis determinati'.

We have chosen the reading of MSS **NO HM**. All indications point to a 'primitive contamination', where MSS **K** and **L** are witnesses of a double redaction of the argument in their models. Note the similarity between MSS **M** and **N** and the consistent reading in Gamma.

> n. 14 adduci potest argumentum] = N M   adhuc potest argui O FW Q X Z   potest adduci argumentum HL   potest sic argui K   potest sic argui adhuc U

> n. 15 Declaratio secundae partis conclusionis principalis est ista] *coni.* Declaratio secundae partis conclusionis (quaestionis H *om.* N M) est ista principalis (*ant.* est M principali N principales HL) N HLM   Declaratio secundae partis (*mg.* U#2) quaestionis principalis est ista KU   Declaratio secundae conclusionis principalis est (per O) ista (illa FW Q) O FW Q Z X

In this passage, one can clearly detect a pattern of variants typical of a marginal correction copied from the Alpha codex imperfectly. The text had originally in all probability 'Declaratio 2^e conclusionis principalis' and the words 'partis' and 'est i^{ta}' were inserted in the margin. Confusion about exactly where to insert the marginalia affected the later manuscript tradition.

> q. 2 n. 11 inquisivit per rationem et investigavit naturam et (ut L) probat (probavit O) II *De anima*] = NO HLM   inquisivit per eundem et investigavit et probavit per rationem II *De anima* K   inquisivit per rationem et invenit et probavit per rationem II *De anima* U   autem inquisivit et pertractavit sive probavit II *De anima* FW   autem inquisivit per rationem et intellexit naturam (*om.* X) et probavit II *De anima* Q X   autem inquisivit et probavit II *De anima* Z

In this example, some variants reflect attempts to refine a text which in origin was in all probability left in the form of hastily written notes.

> q. 3 n. 4 quia si potentia immutatur] = HL   si potentia immutetur N M K   quia potentia immutatur O   quaecumque (quae Z) potentia immutatur FW Z   potentia quae immutatur Q   quod potentia immutatur X

MSS **HL** have 'quia si potentia immutatur', which may be a problematic expression, since the division of the readings between 'immutetur' (N M K) and 'immutatur' (all the rest) seems to reflect the change of the hypothetical into a 'quia' clause, or vice versa. It is difficult to surmise exactly what Alpha contained in the first place, the hypothetical or the 'quia' clause. The ongoing discussion does require the hypothetical: if we put 'quia', it is taken for granted in the major that a sensitive power needs a medium, and the argument would conclude that the sense of touch is not a sensitive power. This variant reflects in all probability an authorial correction of a 'quia' into a 'si', which did not pass to codex **O** and the Gamma group, so that the scribes of the Gamma group had to intervene in various ways to give the argument some sense, confusing the abbreviation for 'quia' into the abreviation for a pronoun. Or else, the 'quia' in MSS **HL** (and in the other manuscripts lacking 'si') is quite possibly an example of an oral expression transmigrating into the written tradition.

> n. 10 aqua pura aut mixta si pura igitur non requiritur ad sui alterationem ... si sit mixta igitur] = H   aqua pura si pura igitur non requiritur ad sui alterationem ... si sit mixta igitur N M'   aqua pura aut non si pura igitur non requiritur ad sui alterationem ... si sit mixta igitur LM (*ins. lin.* 'aut non' M)   aqua pura aut (vel KU) quid (aliquid O F) mixtum si pura igitur non requiritur ad suam alterationem ... si quid (*add. sit mg.* U#2) mixtum (admixtum F) igitur O KU FW Q X Z

MS **H** has 'aut mixta' in the first part of the disjunction, which can perhaps be misread by a distracted eye as 'aut non' as in manuscripts **L** and **M**. The single accident in manuscript **N** is very telling, because in codex **M** the expression omitted by **N** (i.e., the two words 'aut non') is inserted above the line by seemingly the same hand of the main text. There is only a slight doctrinal issue at stake, namely the fact that 'aqua mixta' is not really water, but something else, a fact acknowledged by the reading 'quid mixtum' of all the manuscripts which do not belong to the Beta group. The impression is that 'quid mixtum' and 'sit mixta' could be a case of orality versus a written tradition.

> n. 13 sed fluido ut est aer vel aqua, quorum qualitates immediate tanguntur sine corpore medio alio a propriis subiectis. Si autem qualitas adhaerens sit in corpore terminato non-fluido, aut extrema] seu fluido ut est aer vel aqua, (*add. mg.* signaliter sensibilis sit id est quod corpore terminato et non fluxo H#2) aut extrema H   seu fluido aut extrema L   sed termini vel extrema N M

Here the problem lies in a large omission within the body of the question in the Beta group and in MS **N**, seemingly by homeoteleuton. In this example, Scotus is listing the various solutions of the question according to different kinds of bodies: fluid, wet, and dry. Manuscript **H** retains part of the text omitted by the other witnesses of its group, an indication that the common model may have contained some corrections difficult to construe and thus copy.

> q. 4 n. 6 protensum sive parum] = L   et (*lin.*) protensum parum N   vel protensum sive parum H   protensum vel (*lin.*) parum M   vel parum protensum O FW Q X Z   parvum K   parvum vel extensum vel protensum U

We have chosen the reading attested to in manuscript **L**, postulating an original reading 'nimis protensum' with the linear addition 'sive/vel parum' which was variously misread and inserted in the groups. MSS **H** and **L** have 'sive parum', MSS **M** and **N** seems to have only 'parum' with two different line additions, the Gamma group (**F W Q X Z**) + MS **O** have 'vel parum', while MSS **K** and **U** have singular readings.

> n. 12 igitur verissime ibi poterit esse una sine alia] = N   igitur verissime (verissima W Q Z) poterit ibi esse una sine alia O F W Q Z   igitur ibi verissime poterit una esse sine alia H L   igitur verissime ibi poterit una esse sine alia M K   poterit tamen igitur ibi esse una sine alia U   *om.* X

The position of 'ibi' in this passage is attested only in manuscripts **N M K**. It is a pattern of variants compatible with some marginal addition in the autograph variously interpreted by different scribes.

> n. 13 Naturalis etiam potest esse in inanimatis quae non sentiunt aliquid tangere in quantum huiusmodi et est naturaliter immutare quia tactus potest esse in inanimatis quae tantum naturaliter immutantur] *coni. cum HM sed in codicibus HM exhibetur* Naturalis etiam potest esse in inanimatis quae non sentiunt aliquid (aliquod H) tangere in quantum huiusmodi et est naturaliter immutare quia tactus (*add. lin.* non H#2) potest esse in inanimatis (animatis M) quae tantum naturaliter immutantur (immutatur M) HM   Naturalis etiam potest in animatis quae non sentiunt tangere aliquid (aliquod O) in quantum huiusmodi et (*add.* sic O) est materialiter immutare quia tactus potest esse in animatis quae tantum naturaliter immutantur (mutantur O) NO   Naturalis etiam potest esse in inanimatis quae tantum naturaliter immutatur L   Naturalis etiam potest esse in inanimatis quae non sentiunt aliquid tangere in quantum huiusmodi et est naturaliter immutare quia tactus potest esse in inanimatis K   Naturalis etiam potest esse (*lin.* U#2) in animatis quae non sentiunt tangere in quantum huiusmodi est naturaliter immutare quia tangere in quantum huiusmodi est naturaliter immutare quia tactus potest esse in inanimatis U   Naturalis etiam esse (*ant.* etiam Q) potest in animatis (inanimatis F (*lin.*) W#2) quae non sentiunt tangere (*add.* autem Q) in quantum huiusmodi (*add.* autem X) est materialiter immutare quia tactus potest esse in animatis (inanimatis F) quae tantum naturaliter (immaterialiter Q) immutantur F W Q X

This is an extremely corrupted passage, due to repetitions of terms and several omissions by homeoteleutic error in crucial manuscripts. According to the Aristotelian principle of perception, as it was interpreted in commentaries on the *De anima* in the thirteenth and fourteenth centuries, while the sense organ is affected by natural and intentional immutation, intentional immutation alone causes sensitive perception, whereas natural or material immutation can cause modification and corruption of its subject but not sensation in the organ. We have the situation of the damned, where the intentional immutation occurs without a natural immutation. Then the opposite case, the lifeless creatures (the mineral world), in which the immutations are only natural ones. In this passage there arose confusion between 'in inanimatis' (reading of the groups Beta + Delta) and 'in animatis' (readings of the groups Epsilon and Gamma), between 'naturaliter' and 'materialiter', and there is also the linear addition of 'non' by a corrector of MS **H**. The sentence could be read both with 'animatis' and 'inanimatis'. In the first case, we have "the natural immutation can also occur in living creatures ('animatis'), which do not sense the contact of something as such (because it is the intentional immutation that causes sense, not the natural: hence this 'non sentiunt aliquid tangere in quantum huiusmodi'); and this is to change naturally, because the sense of touch can be in the living creatures which change only naturally." Note that the following example is right on this line of reasoning, with the object of touch in direct contact with the sense organ, causing natural immutation and not sense perception. In the second case, we should read: "Therefore the intentional immutation causes sensitive perception, but not the natural one, since intentional immutation can occur in the damned without the natural one. Also, the natural immutation can occur in lifeless creatures ('inanimatis'), which do not sense the contact of something as such [this time, this 'in quantum huiusmodi' should refer to: 'lifeless creatures, as such, do not have sense perception']; and this is to change naturally, because there can be a sense organ of touch in the lifeless creatures, which change only naturally". In manuscript **H** a corrector added a 'non' to avoid the apparent absurdity of admitting a sensitivity of lifeless things, but the meaning of 'tactus' here is not 'sensitivity' but rather the capability of being changed through contact. The variants 'naturaliter' and 'materialiter' can be explained in terms of similar abbreviations, and doctrine: natural immutation is the one according to the mode of being of the sensible "in re extra sive materiali".

   n. 13 sed species tangibilis recepta in eo intentionaliter facit sensum tactus] = M KU FW Q Z *spat. vac.* O *om.* (*hom.*) NO HL X

The accident reported here occurs in a passage just a line below the text reported in the previous entry. It appears as an omission affecting the Epsilon and the majority of the Beta groups. The preceding sentence, ending with the same wording 'facit sensum tactum', also shows signs of troublesome transmission. Since this passage occurred at the conclusion of a sentence, it may have well been a marginal addition in the autograph. See the discussion on the Beta group readings above, where variants occurring in the following sentence of the paragraph are considered.

   q. 5 n. 7 recipere aliquid ab agente pure naturali corporali] = N aliquid recipere (*om.* M) ab agente pure (puro M) naturali corporali HM aliquid ab agente pure naturali recipere L aliquid recipere ab agente pure corporali KU recipere aliquid ab agente pure corporali O FW Q X aliquid recipere ab agente pure naturali Z

This passage shows signs of corrections in the autograph affecting the position of 'recipere' and regarding also the two words 'naturali corporali'.

   n. 10 essendi vel subsistendi] *coni.* spirandi NO fiendi K Q X sentiendi HLM FW Z

This passage is the result of an emendation, based on the progression of the argument. The corruption in all witnesses was probably due to confusion of abbreviations.

   q. 6 n. 3 sed tactus est] = M K sed tactus est sensus HL U sensus autem tactus est NO sensus tactus est FW Q Z

This case is a textual variant occurring between the Beta and Delta groups on the one side, and the Epsilon and Gamma on the other. The abbreviation for 'sed' is easily confused with that for 'sensus'; it is a also a strong possibility that the word 'sensus' came into the main text in MSS **HL** and **U** from a marginal annotation.

   q. 7 n. 12 realiter refertur ad aliud] = M refertur ad aliud H refertur N L realiter refertur O FW X Z refertur ad ipsum KU

In this passage, the reading of manuscript **M** was retained, since it maintains elements common to the whole tradition. Scotus is giving here the well-known definition of real relation, as opposed to rational relation. The extended definition requires all the terms of the text in codex **M**, but even a text such as that in MSS **N** and **L** is understandable to a competent audience, 'realiter' being already supposed by the earlier 'respectus realis', 'ad aliud' being the constituting character of relations. The two terms 'realiter refertur' occur in MSS **M O** and Gamma; for this expression one could simply assume that two words with similar abbreviations may have been taken by some scribes as a case of repetition.

> n. 12 per opinionem Commentatoris dicit] = M F per opinionem (comparationem N) contrariorum dicimus (dicit O) NO per opinionem Commentatoris dicentis HL per opinionem Commentatoris dicentem KU per opinionem (*spat. vac.* Z) contrariorum (Commentatoris *rest.* W) dicit W X Z

This passage shows the different attitudes of the scribes when facing two ambiguous abbreviations.

> n. 12 a quo est actio est actio] = LM a quo est est actio O a quo est actio N H KU FW X

Two manuscripts of the Beta group witness a redaction of this quotation which report the same wording of a passage from the *Liber sex principiorum*. Such an expression could not have been likely added by chance, while its corruption could easily be seen as the result of the scribes' attempt to take out an apparent repetition.

> n. 15 creantis actio est] = HL KU creatio activa est N M creatio actio (*post* est Z) O FW Z creatio X

> n. 15 sicut creatio-passio quae non differt a creatura] = O M FW X sicut in creatio passio quae non differuntur (*dub.*) a creatura Z sicut creatio passiva quae non differt a creatura N HL U sicut creatio quae est passio K

> n. 15 tunc creatio-actio non] = NO M FW X Z tunc creatio activa non HL creatio que K tunc causatio actio U

This passage was variously understood by different scribes, probably due to some expressions proper to lecturing. Scotus is here considering action as the accident of two agents, the Creator and the creature. Different subjects requires a twofold categorical view of action. Note the text of MS **K**: '...si esset in creatura, sicut creatio quae est passio, tunc creatio quae esset...' which tries to give a running interpretation of the reasoning.

> n. 17 quae sumitur secundum quod fundatur super multitudinem vel unum] = H quae sumitur secundum numerum (multitudinem Z) vel unum NO FW Z quae sumitur *lacuna* X quae fundatur super multitudinem vel (*add.* super KU) unum LM KU *sed rest.* M

The tradition presents here several omissions. The evidence in the Beta group: MS **M** adds this portion of the text ('sumitur secundum quod') in the margin, while MS **L** omits it and **H** retains it. Here is the text in MS **K**: 'in primo modo relationis, quae fundatur super multitudinem, vel super unum'. The edited text is found therefore only in MSS **H** and **M** (*mg.*). The evidence points to a marginal insertion: 'sumitur secundum quod' which was taken as substitution for 'fundatur super'.

> q. 9 n. 4 si alius sensus] = HL KU FW X   si alius proprius M   si autem sensus alius N   si autem sensus O Q Z¹ *pos. corr.* Z   Sed alius sensus est et X

Some scribes introduced an adversative conjunction in place of the reading 'alius'.

> n. 9 oportet omnes animae operationes ad aliquam potentiam reduci] = HM Q   sed omnes animae operationes possunt ad aliquam potentiam reduci L   sed omnes animae operationes ad aliquam (aliam O) potentiam reducuntur NO   et (sed U) omnes animae operationes ad aliam (aliquam U) potentiam habent reduci KU   omnes oportet operationes animae ad aliam F (*sed corr. et rest. mg.* F#2) potentiam reduci F   omnes oportet animae operationes ad aliam potentiam reduci W   oportet omnes operationes animae ad aliquam potentiam reduci Z   operationes ad aliquam potentiam reduci X

This is another disturbance of the text transmission due to a hastily written abbreviation for 'oportet' doubled by another similar abbreviation for 'omnes'. The Delta and Epsilon groups, together with MS **L**, took it for a conjunction, and then they were forced to fix up the sentence in their own way: MS **L** with 'possunt ...reduci', Delta with 'habent reduci', Epsilon with 'reducuntur'.

> q. 10 n. 17 sed sensus communis magnitudine (magna O) deficiente (definite L NO) cognoscit igitur etc. HLM NO   sed sensus communis magis distincte cognoscit igitur etc. K Q Z   sed sensus communis minus FW (magis X) distincte (*om.* X) cognoscit igitur (*om.* X) etc. FW X

In this passage, Scotus adds a short argument against the position that the common sensible is the object of the common sense. He notes that no sense is deceived about its own object, much less the common sense, even when magnitude is not present. Confusion arose around the abbreviation of the expression 'magnitudine deficiente'.

> q. 12 n. 38 Una autem tantum a quo sit motum ab obiecto] = M   Una autem (*om.* K) tantum (tamen H est L) a quo (actio qua L) sit (fit HL) motum (iudicium L) ab (de L) obiecto HL KU   Una autem tantum a quo (actio O) sit (scilicet O) iudicium de obiecto NO   Una autem (*om.* Q) tantum actum (actio Q X) scilicet (secundum Z) iudicium (indifferentia X) de (ab Q) obiecto FW Q X Z

In this instance, confusion arises from a poorly understood abbreviation for 'a quo', thereby affecting all four groups variously.

> q. 14 n. 5 nisi praesente intellecto scibili existente] = NO nisi praesente intelligente (obiecto L) scibilis (scibili H) existente HLM K   nisi praesente intellecto (intellectio (*mg.* W) FW) scibilis (scieretur FW scitur Z) existente FW Q X Z

> n. 16 est liberum per participationem a sua causalitate ut scilicet producat effectum igitur non est causa necessaria producendi effectum intelligimus enim cum volumus ut dicitur II De anima potest enim liberum per essentiam scilicet voluntas impedire

liberum per participationem a sua causalitate ne scilicet producat effectum suum igitur species potest esse sine actu] *coni. cum M#2* non est causa necessaria producendi effectum intelligimus enim cum volumus ut dicitur II De anima potest enim liberum per essentiam scilicet voluntas, impedire (impedi *scripsit* impediter (?) N' *sed corr.* N) liberum per participationem a sua causalitate naturae scilicet producat effectum suum igitur species potest esse sine actu NO est liberum per participationem a sua causalitate ut (ne *adnotavit in mg.* ut M) scilicet (*ins. in mg.* producat effectum igitur non est causa necessaria producendi effectum intelligimus enim cum volumus ut dicitur II De anima potest enim liberum per essentiam scilicet voluntas impedire liberum per participationem a sua causalitate ne M#2) producat (producit H) effectum suum igitur species potest esse sine actu HLM K est liberum per participationem ergo non est causa necessaria producendi effectum intelligimus enim cum volumus (volimus Q) ut dicitur II De anima potest enim liberum per essentiam scilicet voluntas impedire liberum per participationem a sua causalitate ne scilicet (*om.* FW) producat (producant FW) effectum (post suum Q) suum ergo species potest esse sine actu (add. intelligendi Q) FW Q X producendi effectum intelligimus enim cum volumus ut dicitur II De anima potest enim liberum per essentiam scilicet voluntas impedire liberum per participationem a sua causalitate ne scilicet producat effectum suum ergo species potest esse sine actu Z

This last example illustrates a passage in question fourteen where the whole tradition witnesses omissions of different parts of the text. The variety of the omissions points to a series of corrections in the autograph, ruling out the likelihood of a single lacuna. A later corrector inserted a marginal addition in codex **M**, thus restoring the text in its entirety.

q. 15 n. 3 eius est materia] HM W X Z est eius materia NO K F Q est materia eius L

This variant points to a case of primitive contamination—the interlinear insertion of 'eius'. The 'nihil eius est materia' is required by the preceding predicative 'secundum se totam'.

n. 3 illud autem dicimus animam et aliud scilicet quod non est forma] = M illud (idem H) autem dicimus animam et aliud quod scilicet (*om.* L) non est forma HL illud autem dicimus animam secundum (sed N) quae non (*om.* N) est forma NO illud autem dicimus animam et alia scilicet quae non est forma K illud autem dicimus animam et alia secundum (scilicet F) quod (quam Q) non (*om.* Z) est forma FW Q X Z

The phrase 'et aliud' is clearly preferable to 'et alia' because it is the accusative subject of the complementary predicate 'animatum'. That is to say, the sentence reads, in English translation: 'We call that [namely, that which functions, at least partially, as the form of the body] the soul, and the other part, namely, that which is not the form but rather receives the form, we call besouled.' There are two correlative neuter words in this reading, 'illud' and 'aliud'. Confusion in this passage led to the use of 'quae' instead of 'quod' in the following relative clause.

n. 16 forma respectiva] = HLM FW Q X Z forma absoluta O KU forma quae N

This accident is probably due to a primitive double redaction, corrected in the margin of the autograph.

n. 17 et per consequens distinguitur una ab alia sine inclinatione] = L et per consequens distinguitur (*add.* anima H) una ab alia (*add. mg.* essentialiter M) sine (sua KU) inclinatione HM KU   et per consequens distinguitur una denominatur ab alia et anima esse sine inclinatione N et per consequens distinguitur una essentialiter ab alia anima sine inclinatione O   et per consequens distinguitur essentialiter (essentiae X) una ab alia sine inclinatione FW Q X Z

The accidents occurring in this passage are the result of a late insertion of the adverb 'essentialiter', affecting the Gamma group and MS **O**.

n. 21 et bona sicut boni angeli] = HM X   et bona et mala sicut boni angeli et animae patiuntur et bona sicut boni angeli L   bona sicut boni (bona(!) O) angeli NO   et sicut boni angeli KU FW Q Z

The reading is well attested in the Beta and Epsilon groups and maintains the integrity of the text.

n. 22 non habent materiam generabilem si aliquam habent aliam] = M   non habent materiam generalem si (sed N) aliquae (aliae N)   habent aliam NO   non habent materiam generalem si (sed L) habent (*om.* L) aliquam aliam HL   non habent materiam generabilem si habent aliquam aliam KU   non habent materiam generalem (generabilem Q) sed aliquam habent si habent (*om.* Q) aliquam FW Q   non habent materiam generalem sed aliquam habent X   non habent materiam generalem sed habent aliquam Z

The first variant concerns the words 'generabilem' and 'generalem', with the latter providing little sense in the context. Regarding the second variant, the words 'sed' and 'si' are often confused for each other and hence this variant should probably be decided on the sense more than anything. Because these two words 'si' and 'sed' are so similar in abbreviated written Latin, there is also the possibility that the text should read 'sed si', because scribes were trained to ignore the second occurrence of a word whenever a seemingly identical word came next. Finally, the apparent inversion in the expression 'si aliquam habent aliam' may suggest that the MSS **H** and Delta reading want the text, as a whole, to say: 'si habent aliquam, aliam' (a reading that comes quite close to the sense of the reading 'sed si').

n. 26 esset perfectior] = N HM#1 X   esset imperfectio materia L   esset imperfectior O M' KU Z   perfectior FW   esset materia perfectior Q

Here 'perfectior' is probably correct, because the absurdity seems to involve the matter of the angels initially being part of prime matter yet somehow being more perfect.

n. 28 sed materia corporalis corruptibilium aliquorum perficitur anima rationali igitur multo fortius materia corporum coelestium perficitur anima rationali] = M Z   sed materia corporalis corruptibilium aliquorum perficitur anima rationali L sed materia corporalis corporalium aliquorum perficitur anima rationali igitur multo fortius materia corporum supracelestium perficitur anima rationali H   sed materia corporum inferiorum perficitur anima rationali N   sed materia corporalis correspondentorum aliquorum perficitur anima rationali O   sed materia corporum corruptibilium inferiorum (corporalium U) aliquorum perficitur anima rationali (*add. mg.* igitur multo fortius materia corporum superiorum perficitur anima rationali K) KU   sed

> materia corporalis corruptibilium aliquorum perficitur anima rationali igitur multo magis materia corporum coelestium perficitur anima rationali FW Q

This passage brings evidence of the omission by homeoteleuton of the concluding clause of the reasoning in the Epsilon and Delta groups and in MS **L**. The omission should then have occurred in the model of the four groups, where a marginal note probably pointed out the accident.

> n. 38 ex natura propria potentia cuiuscumque creaturae non potest ad hoc] *coni.* cum HLM KU F Q Z   ex natura propria (*add.* nec K) potentia cuiuscumque creaturae potest ad hoc HLM K   ex natura propria cuique est (add. creatum O) potest ad hoc NO   ex (*om.* Q) puris (*om.* FW) potentiis (*om.* X) propriis sibi vel creaturae (creare Q) cuiuscumque non (*om.* W *del.* X#1) potest ad hoc FW Q X Z   ex puris naturalibus potentiis propriis non potest ad hoc U

The expression 'non potest ad hoc' is needed in this phrase. Most manuscripts omit the 'non' and give an unintelligible reply to the argument.

> n. 43 primo id est non per accidens sicut rationale convenit homini primo isto modo sumpto et tamen convenit sibi ratione partis] = *coni. cum* HLM   primo id est non per accidens sicut rationale competit homini primo id est non per accidens et tamen convenit sibi ratione partis H   primo et (id est L) non per accidens sicut rationale convenit homini primo (*add.* modo L) isto modo sumpto et tamen convenit sibi ratione partis LM   primo non per accidens sicut rationale convenit homini primo illo (primo N) modo sumpto et tamen convenit sibi (*om.* O) ratione partis NO   primo ratione partis KU   primo id (illo Q) est (*om.* Q) non per accidens sicut rationale convenit homini primo illo (isto Z) modo sumpto et tamen convenit sibi (*om.* FW) ratione partis FW Q Z   primo illo (isto X) modo sumpto et tamen convenit sibi ratione partis X

This is another passage in which the numerous omissions render the text barely understandable. The entire tradition shows evidence of corrections in the autograph.

> q. 16 n. 9 cognoscere quid est quod dicitur per nomen] = L KU   cognoscere quid est per nomen H   cognoscere quid est quod (*post* dicitur O) per nomen dicitur NO   cognoscere quid dicitur per nomen M FW Z

This variant indicates two different versions of a sentence about the Aristotelian principle that the definition of a substance expresses its essence. We have the MSS **NO L KU** with all the elements of the phrasing, while MSS **HM** and Gamma all lack something. This is probably the result of primitive contamination.

K. "Contamination" and the Medieval Edition of Texts

From what we know from the critical editions of his writings published to date, it is a striking fact that John Duns Scotus never achieved what in medieval terms was called an *edition* of any of his works; that is, he never achieved a final draft of any work that he himself had reworked and supervised from beginning to end, until he authorized it as a model for subsequent copying. Scotus' writings rather survived his death in multiple stages of revision; as he moved from one teaching assignment to another he typically continued to rework his expression, transfer materials from one work into another, rearrange parts of the text and arguments, devise new or *extra* arguments perhaps meant to be interpolated into a final version and which were written in the margins of surviving manuscripts, etc. The work of *editing* Scotus' writings and preparing them for publication fell largely into the hands of his disciples and *socii*, who ordered and disposed the remains of the Master's writings available to them, often revised their phrasing, and in many instances provided *additiones* to fill in lacunae in the unfinished compositions, which they compiled from texts scattered elsewhere in his writings or themselves composed *ad mentem Scoti*. In comparison, the *Quaestiones De anima* occupy a unique status among Scotus' writings. Scotus never intended these hastily written questions for publication, and having penned them (in MS Alpha), he never returned to his text in order significantly to revise it. Scotus' autograph manuscript, in other words, was a "rough draft," which however yields an integral text without further reworking by the author.[77]

Thus, since the source of the text was a single draft and since copyist-editors did not need to grapple with extensive and complicated reworkings of the text made by Scotus himself (in multiple layers of revision and correction), preparing the *Quaestiones De anima* for dissemination was in some ways an easier task than the preparation of his other writings for publication. On the other hand, as our investigation shows, the autograph manuscript of the *Quaestiones*, MS Alpha, was extremely difficult to read and use and needed to be "edited," that is, authorial errors needed to be corrected, ambiguities in sense and handwriting needed to be resolved, phrasing and style perhaps improved; most of all a clearer copy needed to be produced as a model for any further copying of the text. The peril of attempting to copy such a manuscript as Alpha without recourse to any other manuscript is exhibited by the text of Epsilon (as witnessed by MSS **NO**), which, whatever its copyist's intention, copied Scotus' autograph exactly as he saw it, not only faithfully reproducing the large material accidents caused by the reversal of two gatherings in Alpha but also omitting text at the transition of folia and otherwise garbling the sense of the text in many places. In the face of such a manuscript as Alpha, on the other hand, it made good sense for a medieval copyist (no less than it would for a modern editor) to consult another, preferably "authoritative" manuscript, if possible.

For their convenience, modern editors typically wish that medieval scribes had stuck with only one model, as did the copyist of Epsilon—with lamentable results. But a practice that may be inconvenient for the modern editor was simply prudent for a medieval copyist who wished above all to produce an intelligble text suitable for further transmission. As we have shown, other exemplars at the head of the transmission of the *Quaestiones De anima* were "contaminated" by another manuscript or by other material, that is, their texts are "conflated" with texts in other manuscripts. So the copyist of Beta evidently consulted other material (perhaps a report of the original course) in constructing his text, and the copyist of Delta in turn consulted Beta to assist him in construing Alpha. In medieval terms, Beta and Delta are *editions* of the *Quaestiones De anima*, intended as such from the beginning.[78] It is possible that the copyist-editor of Gamma also consulted some other manuscript, but our collations do not make that fact evident, mainly because Gamma was a wholesale revision of the text

---

[77]The transmission of Scotus' writings contrasts sharply, for example, with the transmission of the writings of Henry of Ghent (however complicated that textual transmission might otherwise be), which was tightly controlled by the author from the autograph to the first Exemplar and which proceeded via a single channel, the Stationer's at the University of Paris, and thus via the *pecia* system; see the introductions in the volumes of *Henrici de Gandavo Opera omnia*, ed. Raymond Macken et al., Leuven, 1979-. Moreover, Franciscan friars seem to have taken a strikingly pragmatic attitute towards the manuscript texts that they copied, most of which were made for personal use. In contrast, the Dominicans in general seem to have taken greater pains to control the transmission of authoritative texts.

[78]For a fascinating example of a systematic medieval edition of Scotus' *Quaestiones De anima* (late fifteenth-century), knowingly constructed from a witness of the "English tradition" of the text and a witness of the "continental tradition," see the Description of MS **Y**, nr. 25, above.

in its model Alpha, a revision so thoroughgoing that the text of Gamma comes close to constituting a separate redaction of the *Quaestiones De anima*. Finally, as we shall demonstrate presently, two surviving manuscripts that are crucial for the critical constitution of the text of the *Quaestiones De anima*, MSS **M** and **N**, were likewise not simply copies but intelligent medieval editions of the text.[79] By a certain "cunning of reason," then, it is precisely the intelligent work of medieval forebears that has made the constitution of the text of Scotus' *Quaestiones De anima* so difficult.

The actual circumstances of the editing and transmission of the *Quaestiones* may be inferred, with some probability, from what is known—or reasonably can be inferred—about the medieval locations of the key manuscripts, lost or surviving. These are salient facts that directly or indirectly shed light on the history and locations of the key manuscripts in the transmission: the *Quaestiones De anima* were not copied and thus did not circulate until after Scotus' death (1308); the transmission of the text originated in Oxford; there is no evidence that the text was transmitted from Paris or from Cologne during Scotus' lifetime; the "continental" transmission of the *Quaestiones* derived from a manuscript, Gamma, which even if it were prepared in Oxford came to be located in Italy. Indeed, the majority of surviving manuscripts containing the *Quaestiones* are either English or Italian. The last-stated facts are not surprising. By 1293 political circumstances made it very difficult for English scholars to maintain their traditional contacts with Paris; the events of 1307 that forced Scotus to flee Paris set the pattern for the rest of the century. By the second decade of the fourteenth century (when the text of the *Quaestiones* began most to circulate) traffic between English and Parisian scholars was slight. Contacts between English and Italian friars and students, on the other hand, correspondingly increased. As a result there developed a steady intellectual commerce and exchange of writings between scholars of the two nations. Fourteenth-century English thinkers thus enjoyed their greatest influence, outside England, in Italy.[80] (This pattern is confirmed by the history of Scotus' influence in general.)

Almost certainly, Scotus' autograph of the *Quaestiones*, MS Alpha, came to rest in Greyfriars, the Franciscan convent in Oxford, and continued to stay there until it was destroyed. Scotus either left the gatherings of his script in the convent when he went to Paris (and thence to Cologne) in 1302, or, as seems more likely, he took them with him (wrapped in a parchment folder, as was common practice) for possible use in disputes in which he might participate or for use in the composition of other writings.[81] Now, various Franciscan statutes and regulations pertaining to the use of books stipulated that, except in rare cases, the books of a friar after his death were to be returned to his home convent or to the convent whence the book was issued, or otherwise to the friar's Custody or Province.[82] When, as seems most likely, Scotus' autograph was returned to the

---

[79] As our *Stemma codicum* indicates, "contamination" affected other single manuscripts, which however are not so important as **M** and **N** for the critical reconstruction of the text.

[80] See William J. Courtenay, *Schools and Scholars in Fourteenth-Century England* (Princeton, 1987), 147-67, and the bibliography cited there.

[81] We know that when he went to Paris in 1302, Scotus assisted his Master, Gonsalvus Hispanus, in some of his disputes. That Scotus had his script of the *Quaestiones* with him when he went to Paris, then, might well explain why some of the arguments from that text appear in the text of Gonsalvus' disputed questions of 1302-1303; see *Fr. Gonsalvi Hispani, O.F.M. Quaestiones disputatae et de Quodlibet*, ed. L. Amorós (Firenze, 1935), LXXVI, 196, 214, 216, 219-20, 262, 265. For a detailed treatment of the problem, see § 3 Authenticity, below. (These similarities may be explained otherwise, with equal probability; see the section Chronology, below.) That Scotus used materials from the *Quaestiones* in other of his works composed or worked on in Paris would seem to be proved by the tables in section § 3.B: Parallels to Other Scotistic Works, below.

[82] K.W. Humphreys, *The Book Provisions of the Medieval Friars, 1215-1400* (Amsterdam: Erasmus Bookseller, 1964), 50-52, 59.

convent in Oxford, it was misbound there with two gatherings in the wrong order.[83] The books in Greyfriars were divided into two collections, the *libraria conventus in armario* ("cupboard") and the *libraria studencium*. In the former were kept more precious books, at first consulted with permission, such as the collection of Robert Grosseteste's books, which he himself had bequeathed to the convent at his death and which had constituted the convent's collection in its beginning. The students' library contained books regularly accessible to the friars and visitors of the convent. The Greyfriars also preserved collections of the writings of the members of their Order, especially of those who had taught at Oxford. These manuscripts presumably were also kept *in armario*. In the mid-fourteenth century, Adam Wodeham reported that Scotus' autograph of the *Ordinatio*, the famous *Liber Scoti* from which the extensive notes in the margins of **Assisi, Biblioteca del Sacro Convento di S. Francesco, Ms. 137** (MS A of the critical edition) were copied, was preserved in the Franciscan convent in Oxford[84] (intriguingly, a copy of Scotus' *Quaestiones De anima* was shelved right next to that volume in the medieval library at Assisi; see below). We may presume, then, that Scotus' autograph of the *Quaestiones De anima* was kept there together with the *Ordinatio* and perhaps other "original" writings by him.

Evidently MS Beta (witnessed by the Oxford MSS **HL** and for the most part by **M**) also belonged to the Greyfriars' library: MS **L**, a consistent witness of Beta, was copied in the Oxford Franciscan convent by a Swedish friar in the 1470s.[85] In medieval book culture, it was common to preserve an author's autograph manuscript and the apograph or "fair-copy," intended to serve as the model for transmission, together in the same library; this was so because autographs were notoriously difficult to read and librarians moreover did not wish them to be damaged by too much use. According to the twofold division of collections at Greyfriars, it is likely that Beta was kept among the books in the students' library. That the manuscripts Alpha and Beta are no longer extant is not surprising: when he was commissioned by Thomas Cromwell to destroy all of the manuscripts of Scotus' works that he could find, to what library would Richard Layton have gone first?[86]

MSS Alpha and Beta were not accessible only to friars. As Malcolm Parkes points out, at Oxford "copying from manuscripts in the collections was not confined to members of their orders"; by the system of pledges and loans, common throughout the colleges and convents in Oxford, whereby readers would temporarily deposit a book (or books) with a library while they made use of a manuscript housed there, members succeeded in borrowing books or consulting them in various libraries.[87] The copyist of Delta (witnessed by MSS **KU**) used both Alpha and Beta in confecting his

---

[83]It seems implausible that Scotus himself possessed a bound book with disordered gatherings and would not have made some indication in the book that they were out of order. Likewise it seems implausible that the gatherings were loose when Beta, Delta and Epsilon copied them, and that at least one of those copyists—especially the copyist of Beta who discovered the textual misplacement within some questions—would not have shuffled the gatherings into the right order. Scotus obviously did not number the questions in Alpha (else one of the copyists of Alpha would have noted it); one can understand why, however, once they were bound and someone had numbered the disordered questions sequentially (as they are in various witnesses), scribes would have been reluctant to alter the sequence of questions (a certain piety attends "the book of the Master himself"). Only the editor of Gamma perceived the source of the problem of misplaced texts and repaired it in his copy.

[84]Parkes, "The Provision of Books," 435-41. Parkes, 439, points out the the books kept *in armario* eventually came to treated in the same way as books in the students' library and were even lent to readers from outside the convent, with the result that many of the precious books, including those of Grosseteste, were lost or stolen.

[85]See manuscript Description nr. 4 and the notes there.

[86]See section § 2.I, above.

[87]Parkes, "The Provision of Books," 468, 412.

text. The medieval location of Delta in Oxford is unknown; the manuscript was copied in the 1470s by John Saunder, then a Fellow of All Soul's College.[88]

Nor do we know the medieval location in Oxford of Epsilon, the "photographic" copy of Alpha. The earliest surviving witness of Epsilon is MS **O**, which was copied in the first decade of the fifteenth century and has belonged to the House of Blessed Mary (i.e., Oriel College) from that time until today (the manuscript belonged to Master Richard Garsdale, Fellow of Oriel ca. 1404-1413).[89] MS **O**'s companion witness to Epsilon, MS **N**, was copied somewhat later in the first quarter of the fifteenth century; the manuscript was bound in a book once owned by Master John Bentley, Chaplain and Precentor in the years 1477-1486 at Magdalen College, where the codex still resides today.[90] We have noted the relationship between the text of the *Quaestiones De anima* in MS **N** and in MS **M**, which for the most part follows Beta but which frequently shares Epsilon readings with **NO** and at other times shares distinct common accidents with **N** alone (see below). The *Quaestiones* in **M** were copied by Thomas Wyche, Fellow of Oriel College, who yet deposited this and other books in Magdalen College (where the manuscript resides today), perhaps as an unredeemed pledge for books from that College library that he had used (including seemingly MS **N**). The nexus of key manuscripts (**MNO** and indirectly Epsilon) involving Oriel and Magdalen Colleges is suggestive; it is sure, in any event, that members of the colleges at Oxford no less than the friars themselves desired copies of Scotus' *Quaestiones De anima* based on what they knew to be authoritative models and that they consulted other manuscripts when they deemed that their model was illegible or faulty.

The editor of Gamma (witnessed in our edition by **FWQXZ**) most likely prepared his thoroughgoing revision of the text, based directly however on the autograph MS Alpha, in the Oxford convent where the manuscript was kept. This edition evidently was accomplished quite early-on, since witnesses of Gamma are the earliest surviving copies of the text.[91] If prepared in Oxford, Gamma was taken to Italy, where it served as the exemplar of the "continental" transmission of the text. Circumstantial evidence suggests that Gamma may have been kept at the Motherhouse of the Order in Assisi, a likely place for preserving an official exemplar of an eminent Doctor within the Order. An inventory of the library in Assisi dated 1381 records a manuscript which at the time contained a copy of Scotus' *Quaestiones*:

> (item 96): ¶ Questiones dicti magistri Iohannis [scoti] De anima. Et de primo principio. Ac colibeta eiusdem. Et magistrorum Petri aurioli ordinis minorum. ac henrici de candago. Et quam plura [alia]. Cum postibus et cathena. ¶ Cuius principium est: Utrum sensus tactus. Finis vero: Includantur parentis. Explicit. ¶ In quo libro omnes quaterni sunt: xx.G. Est intus.[92]

---

[88]See manuscript Description nr. 3, above (MS **K**), and also Description nr. 9 (MS **U**). As we have pointed out, MS **U** was itself "contaminated" by a copy from the Gamma family.

[89]See manuscript Description nr. 7, above.

[90]See manuscript Description nr. 6, above.

[91]All of the surviving fourteenth-century manuscripts of the *Quaestiones* belong to the extended Gamma family. The English manuscripts witnessing to the "English text," which we present as the most authentic in our edition, are all from the fifteenth century. Fourteenth-century copies of the text in Oxford (including Beta, Delta and Epsilon), upon which the survivors depend, seem all or mostly to have been destroyed by Layton, who evidently performed his assigned task well. Our edition confirms the principle that later manuscripts are not necessarily inferior witnesses to the original text.

[92]Cesare Cenci, *Bibliotheca manuscripta ad Sacrum Conventum Assiensem* (Assisi: Casa editrice francescana, 1981), 128-29 nr. 96.

Parts of this codex today exist separately in **Assisi, Biblioteca del Sacro Convento di S. Francesco, Ms. 136** and in the **Biblioteca Apostolica Vaticana, Cod. Vat. lat. 12995**. The table of the original contents appears in the Vatican manuscript on f. 1v:

> In isto volumine continentur questiones questiones scoti super de anima. Item de primo principio. Item quodlibet eiusdem scoti. Item quodlibet iacobi de viterbio. Item excepta de quindecim quodlibet mag. henrici de gandavo et prima et secunda parte summae eiusdem. Item excepta de x quolibet godifridi et tribus quolibetis de exculo. Item tabula Scoti pulcra et completa.

The copies of the writings of Henry of Ghent and the *Quodlibeta* of Godfrey of Fontaines and James of Viterbo survive today in the Vatican manuscript, and the *Quodlibeta* of Duns Scotus and Peter Auriol survive today in the Assisi manuscript. An eighteenth-century note in the Assisi manuscript states that (unfortunately) the first three gatherings of the book, containing Scotus' *Quaestiones De anima* and *De primo principio*, by then had been ripped out.[93] Suggestively, in the fourteenth century as today the codex that contained the *Quaestiones* (now Assisi, Ms. 136), sat on the shelf next to the famous codex of Scotus' *Ordinatio* (now Assisi, Ms. 137), the extensive *marginalia* of which, as we have indicated, were copied directly from the *Liber Scoti* preserved in the Franciscan convent in Oxford. Were the lost quires containing Scotus' *Quaestiones* none other than MS Gamma itself? No conjecture concerning this authoritative exemplar seems more probable.[94]

These surmises concerning the histories and medieval locations of the key manuscripts in the transmission of the *Quaestiones De anima* are based only on circumstantial evidence; inasmuch as they propose the simplest hypotheses accounting for the surviving evidence they at least meet the criterion of Ockham's Razor.[95] Yet the general point is clear: the key, authoritative manuscripts of Duns Scotus' *Quaestiones De anima* existed in close proximity in Oxford; this made medieval editions (typically composed from two manuscripts) of the writing logistically easy, which in turn explains the phenomenon of "contamination" or "conflation" that is so evident in the *apparatus criticus* of this edition.

L. THE MOVEMENTS OF MANUSCRIPTS M AND N IN QUESTIONS 20-22

The text of the *Quaestiones De anima* becomes especially turbulent in the last questions in the collection, Questions 20-23 (Question 23 presents a special case, which will be treated separately below). One can imagine several reasons for the increased disturbance of the text in these questions. First, these questions treat the most difficult and urgently disputed topics concerning the soul, so that copyists may well have struggled with their sense; reciprocally, copyists may have been especially

---

[93] Giovanni Mercati, "Codici di S. Francesco in Assisi nella Biblioteca Vatican," in *Miscellanea Francesco Ehrle* 5 (Studi e Testi 24; Roma, 1924), 113-14; Raymond Macken, *Bibliotheca manuscripta Henrici de Gandavo* 2 (Leuven: Leuven University Press, 1979), 827-30.

[94] Despite the lack of any decisive evidence, modern scholars have persistently implicated Antonius Andreae in the divulgation of the *Quaestiones De anima*, some even claiming that he was their author; see § 3: Authenticity, below. Certainly Antonius was a zealous promoter of Scotus' writings and teachings, which he wished to serve as the foundation of an Arts curriculum in the Franciscan *studia*. It would not be surprising, then, if Antonius were the editor of Gamma, which presents a studied revision of the abrupt and cryptic text of the *Quaestiones* in Alpha, designed to make the work suitable for teaching young students.

[95] As the late Paul Oskar Kristeller was wont to say, it is wise to be a "realist" in philosophy but a "nominalist" in historical analysis.

motivated to capture the sense of these questions, so that they were inclined to consult another manuscript when their usual model was difficult to read or understand. We shall show that precisely this happened. Second, because of the importance of these questions, it would not be surprising if Scotus had introduced more corrections *in via* in this part of the text, e.g., insertions between lines, deletions, marginal texts for inclusion; again, our collation indicates that this was so. Finally, it is possible that some folia in the final gatherings of the text had become damaged or soiled, as our collation likewise suggests.

In theory, Epsilon, the "photographic" copy of Alpha witnessed by only two surviving manuscripts, **NO**, should have been the most important witness to the authorial text of the *Quaestiones De anima*. Regrettably, the copyist of this manuscript did a botched job. This is especially made evident by the performance of the copyist of MS **O**, who otherwise was a scholarly scribe[96] and who with considerable discipline strove to copy exactly what he saw and who struggled mightily with his model. If the copyist of MS **O** was completely passive, the copyist of MS **N**, in contrast, was highly active and interventionist. Throughout the text he makes his own divinations of the sense of the text where it is obscure; particularly revealing is his habit of spelling out in full words that must have been abbreviated obscurely in the original manuscript Alpha, as the whole transmission of the text shows (the copyist of **O**, in contrast, often reproduces ambiguous abbreviations graphically). Moreover, when the copyist of **N** becomes dissatisfied or impatient with Epsilon he frequently turns to Beta and adopts its reading; in the later questions, he abandons nearly altogether his first model for stretches at a time and simply copies Beta. One should note that in the *passus* where **N** copies Beta it is the oldest surviving witness of that manuscript.[97]

MS **N** intermittently abandons Epsilon to copy Beta early in the text, as is evident throughout Questions 2-5:

QUESTION 2

n. 0.3 Utrum HLMN] *praem.* Quaeritur secundo K *praem.* Quaeritur U O FWQXZ

n. 5.6 sentitur HLMN] facit sensum KU O FWQZ

n. 6.11 coextensum L KU O FWQXZ] extensum HMN

n. 7.12 responsionis HKLMN] conclusionis U O FWQXZ

n. 7.15 caro HLMN] *add.* autem KU O FWXZ *add.* enim Q

n. 8.7 venis et nervis HLMN] nervis et venis KU O FWQXZ

n. 9.1 sicut aliqui ramusculi nervorum coextenduntur HMN] sicut aliqui ramusculi nervi extenduntur L sunt (*om.* O) aliqui ramusculi nervorum qui extenduntur KU O FWQXZ

n. 11.8 instrumentum et organum HMN] instrumentum vel organum L etiam (*lin.*) organum K organum U O FWQXZ

n. 12.10-11 corpori extenso HLMN] corpori carni coextenso K carni coextenso U FW carni corpori coextenso Q corpori coextenso Z

QUESTION 3

n. 0.4 Utrum HLMN] *praem.* Quaeritur tertio K *praem.* Quaeritur U O FWQXZ

n. 4.6 In oppositum est Philosophus et Commentator *om.* HLMN

n. 7.6 in altero HLMN] ab alio KU (*deinde sequitur spat. vac.* U) O FWQZ

---

[96] See the manuscript Description nr. 7, p. 16* above. At first, we judged that the copyist of **O** was a "pious scribe," perhaps a Brother performing some task of obedience. That may have been the character of the copyist of Epsilon itself.

[97] As stated, **N** was copied in the first quarter of the fifteenth century; the integral witnesses to Beta were copied later: **H** in the mid-fifteenth century, **M** in the 1450s, and **L** in the late-fifteenth century. See manuscript Descriptions nrs. 2, 4-6, above.

n. 7.7 secundum extremitates HLN (*sed corr.* N)] sensui extremitates M in suis extremitatibus K in suis relationibus U secundum suas extremitates O X super suas extremitates FW Z super extremitates Q

n. 7.8 talium corporum] *inv.* HMN

n. 10.3 sui HLMN] suam KU O FWQXZ

n. 12.11 animalis progressivus HLMN Q] processivus animalis K aliquis (*in mg.* U#2) motus processivus animalis U animalis processivus O FWZ

n. 12.13 sensum tactus HLMN] tactum KU O FWQZ

QUESTION 4
n. 0.4 Utrum HLMN] *praem.* quarto K *praem.* Quaeritur U O FWQXZ

n. 2.15 organo HLMN] obiecto KU O FWQXZ

n. 2.18 immediate positum super HN] immediate positum supra LM positum immediate supra K positum supra immediate U positum super O positum immediate super FWQXZ

n. 5.9-10 omnes rationes in tantum quod aliqui dicunt HMN] omnes quaestionistae in tantum quod aliqui dicunt L omnes communiter loquentes in tantum quod concedunt vel dicunt K omnes communiter loquentes concedunt in tantum quod dicunt aliqui U omnes conclusiones hic concedunt in tantum quod dicunt aliqui O omnes communiter (*add.* omnes X) concedunt in tantum quod dicunt aliqui F X omnes communiter concedunt intellectum (in tali Z) tantum quod dicunt aliqui W Z omnes communiter concedunt in tantum quod dicitur ab aliquibus Q

n. 7.5-6 immediatus vel propinquus HLMN] propinquus KU O FWQXZ

n. 10.4-5 per medium HLMN] medium KU O FWQXZ

n. 11.2 autem] enim HLMN

n. 12.1 hoc patet] patet HLMN

n. 14.15 positam HLMN] tactam KU O FWQXZ

QUESTION 5
n. 7.4 sed HLMN] sed tantum K O FWQXZ

n. 9.6 est principalis HLMN] est causa principalis K O FWQXZ

n. 10.9-10 naturaliter sine alio potest agere sine alio HMN] sine alio potest agere sine alio L naturaliter (naturale X) sine alio potest agere K O FWQXZ

n. 11.18 anima HLMN] anima autem K O FWQZ

The copyist of MS **M**, Thomas Wyche, likewise sometimes abandons his model. For the most part, MS **M** is a witness of Beta; in instances throughout the text, however, the manuscript shares a reading with **NO**, deriving from Epsilon, or it shares a reading that otherwise would be singular in **N**. The occasional coincidence of readings in **MN** is exemplified by the following accidents in Questions 1-4:

QUESTION 1
n. 2.1 unam *om.* MN

n. 3.6 verum *om.* MN

n. 10.14-15 sed non eodem actu] sed non eodem tactu M (*lin.* K#2) sed non eodem eodem tactu N

n. 10.16. respectu *om.* MN

n. 13.19 rationem] *add.* patet MN

n. 13.9 uniuntur HL K#2 (mg.) U FWQZ] univocantur MN conveniunt X

n. 15.10 conclusionis O L FWQXZ] quaestionis H KU om. MN

n. 16.3 dicendum] dicendum est MN

n. 18.7 discretio perfectioris contrarietatis HL] perfectioris contratietatis discretio MN (*mg.* K#2) discretivus perfectioris (perfectionis W) contrarietatis (qualitatis Q) KU O FWQXZ
n. 18.9 dicendum] dicendum est MN
n. 19.1 dicendum] dicendum est MN K
n. 19.4 tactus] *om.* MN sensus QZ
n. 20.8 dicendum] dicendum est MN

QUESTION 2
n. 6.9 dicendum] dicendum est MN U F
n. 6.11 coextensum] extensum MN H
n. 11.19 dicendum] dicendum est MN
n. 13.17 dicendum est MN H] dicendum L KU O FWZ om. X
n. 14.19 dicendum HL U O QWX] dicendum est MN K F

QUESTION 3
n. 1.7 aer] sed aer MN KU (*lin.* U#2)
n. 2.12 aeris immediate] *inv.* L MN
n. 8.10-11 in actu tale MN U Z] actu tale L K O FWX in actuale H in actu talis Q
n. 14.1 dicendum] dicendum est MN
n. 14.5 sic sunt] sic MN
n. 15.7 dicendum] dicendum est MN K F
n. 15.8 possit L U O FWQXZ] potest H K posset MN
n. 15.9 calor] caloris MN et praecipue calore K et ideo calor U#2 color Z
n. 15.9 qualitatum] qualitatum et MN K *om.* L
n. 15.11 autem] est MN
n. 16.13 dicendum] dicendum est MN K F
n. 16.17 per ipsa] per ipsam MN X
n. 17.1 dicendum] dicendum est MN *om.* X
n. 18.5 dicendum] dicendum est MN F *om.* X
n. 18.9 primo medium] primo a medio medium MN prius medio Q
n. 18.13-14 etiam in aliqua] in aliqua MN
n. 18.5^2 aqua vel aere MN] vel aqua O aere vel aqua FWQZ
n. 18.10^2 tactiva] activa MN Q

QUESTION 4
n. 6.13 ad obiectum] in obiectum MN
n. 10.6 ipsum] visum MN ipsum visum K
n. 11.8 sciendum est MN F] sciendum HL O WQXZ est sciendum KU
n. 11.42 igitur est passivum] passivum igitur est MN

The shifting allegiances of MSS **M** and **N** become more pronounced in the last four questions of the text, where, as the other manuscripts show, the text had become very difficult in Alpha and hence in its copies Beta and Epsilon. The movement of the two manuscripts is crosswise: MS **N** for stretches of text abandons Epsilon for Beta; MS **M**, in turn, frequently abandons Beta and adopts a reading coming from Epsilon (witnessed in **NO**) or shares what otherwise would be a singular reading in **N**. The shifting alignments of the manuscripts in Questions 20-22 are charted in the following tables. In them, we first indicate the paragraph and line numbers in the question where the variant occurs in the edition (e.g., n. 13.2); within the square bracket are the *sigla* of the manuscripts sharing the reading adopted in the edition; on the other side of the square bracket are the *sigla* of the manuscripts that read against the reading adopted in the edition. In order to highlight their movement, we record the *sigla* of the individual manuscripts in group Beta (**HLM**) and in group Epsilon (**NO**); the key manuscripts **MNO** are recorded in bold. When the manuscripts in Delta (**KU**) read together and the manuscripts in Gamma (**FWQXZ**) read together, we give the Greek family names; when the manuscripts in either group divide in their readings, we indicate the *sigla* of the individual manuscripts. Groups that share the same reading are linked by hyphens; on the variant side of the square bracket, groups or individual manuscripts that do not share the same reading but agree in reading against the reading adopted in the edition are linked by plus signs. To save space, only in instances especially telling for our analysis do we record the readings involved in the variant.

Question 20, nn. 0-16

NO ± other MSS vs. Beta ± other MSS
In the following instances, **N** follows Epsilon with **O** or reads against Beta with **O**:

n. 0.4 HLM] **N**-Delta-Gamma+**O**
n. 0.4 HLM-Delta-FWXZ] **N**Q+**O**
n. 0.5 HLM-Gamma] Delta+**N**+ **O**
n. 1.7 HLM-Delta-Gamma] **NO**
n. 1.9 HLM-Delta-Gamma] **NO**
n. 2.11 Item HLM] Praeterea Delta-**NO**-Gamma
n. 2.13 HLM-K] **NO**+U-Gamma
n. 4.19 Item HLM] Praeterea Delta-**NO**-Gamma
n. 5.5 HLM] Delta-**NO**-Gamma
n. 5.7 HLM-Delta-Gamma] **NO**
n. 5.8 HLM-Delta] **NO**-Gamma
n. 5.11 LM-U] H-Gamma+K+**N**+**O**
n. 5.14 HM-Gamma] L+Delta+**NO**
n. 7.7 HLM-Delta-QXZ] **NO**+FW
n. 7.7 HLM-Delta-Gamma] **NO**
n. 7.10 HM-Delta-Gamma] L-**NO**
n. 8.15 Item HLM] Praeterea Delta-**NO**-Gamma
n. 9.19 Item HLM] Praeterea Delta-**NO**-Gamma
n. 10.2 HLM-Delta-FWQ] **NO**+XZ
n. 10.3 HLM-Delta-FWZ] **NO**+Q+X
n. 11.7 LM-Delta-Z] H-**NO**-FWQ+X
n. 11.7 HLM-Delta] **NO**-FWXZ+Q
n. 11.7 HLM-Delta-FWZ] **N**+**O**+Q+X
n. 12.14 Item HLM] Praeterea Delta-**NO**-Gamma
n. 12.17 HLM-Delta-QXZ] **NO**+FW
n. 13.3 Item HLM] Praeterea Delta-**NO**-Gamma
n. 13.3 Delta-**NO**-Gamma] HLM
n. 13.4 HLM-Delta-Gamma] **NO**
n. 13.5 LM-X] H+Delta-**NO**-FWQZ
n. 13.6 HLM-FWZ] Delta-**NO**+Q+X
n. 13.7 HLM-Delta-Gamma] **NO**
n. 13.7 inquisitionem... secundum HLM-Delta-Gamma] *om.* **NO**

n. 14.12 HLM-Delta-FWQX] **NO**+Z
n. 14.19 HLM] Delta-Gamma+**NO**
n. 15.20 Item HLM] Praeterea Delta-**NO**-Gamma
n. 15.3 HLM-U-Gamma] K-**NO**

N + Beta ± other MSS vs. O + other MSS
In the following instances in the same stretch of text, **N** and **O** split and **N** reads with Beta:

n. 1.9 **M**-Delta-**O**-Gamma] HL**N**
n. 2.11 HLM**N**-X] Delta+**O**+FW+QZ
n. 7.8 L-**O**-Delta-Gamma] HM**N**
n. 10.1 ista LM**N**-Delta-Z] illa H-**O**-FWQX
n. 11.8 tunc HLM**N**-Delta] *om.* **O**-Gamma
n. 15.20 ratione HLM**N**-K] *om.* U-**O**-Gamma

MN ± other MSS vs. Beta ± other MSS
In the following instances in the same stretch of text, **M** splits from Beta and adopts the Epsilon reading with **NO**:

n. 12.1 in comparatione HL-Delta] per comparationem **MNO**-Gamma
n. 13.6 nec **MNO**-Delta-Gamma] non HL (ibid.)
n. 14.9 primum obiectum **MNO**-Delta-Gamma] *inv.* HL (ibid.)
n. 14.15 Ergo...intellectus L-Delta-FWXZ] *om.* H-**MNO**-Q
n. 14.18 **MNO**-Delta-FWXZ] HL-Q (ibid.)

* * *

Question 20, nn. 17-25

At precisely n. 17 of Question 20, **N** evidently abandons Epsilon and follows Beta, leaving **O** as Epsilon's only witness (**O** here reads with other families, especially Gamma).[98] One should note that from this point onwards through Question 22, **N** adopts the distinctive Beta *Item* instead of the *Praeterea* that it exhibits (from its model Epsilon, with Delta and Gamma) throughout most of the text of the *Quaestiones*. In the following instances, **M** seems to be following its normal model Beta:

N + Beta vs. O + MSS
n. 17.9 Item **HLMN**-XZ] Praeterea Delta-**O**-FWQ
n. 17.14 LM**N**-Delta-QZ] H-**O**-FWX
n. 18.15 Item HLM**N**] Praeterea Delta-**O**-Gamma
n. 18.15 HM**N**-Delta-X] L+**O**+FWQZ
n. 19.4 fuit HLM**N**] sit Delta-**O**-Gamma
n. 19.5 igitur non HM**N**] ergo non L non igitur Delta-**O**-Z non ergo FWQ non X
n. 20.10 sint HLM**N**-Delta] sunt **O**-FWQX sit Z
n. 20.21 sint HLM**N**-Delta] sunt **O**-Gamma

---

[98] The transition occurs in MS **N** at f. 174*ra*, line 15. In the preceding column, f. 173*vb*, the copyist of **N** is clearly struggling with his model Epsilon; see, for example, the omission, shared with **O** at n. 13.7-n. 14.10 in our edition. This omission occurs at f. 173*vb*, line -3.

n. 20.23 HLMN] K-**O**-Gamma
n. 20.23 sint HLMN-U] sunt K-**O**-Gamma
n. 21.7 HLN-Delta] **M**-**O**-Gamma
n. 22.13 sint HLMN-U] sunt K-**O**-Gamma
n. 22.14 sint HLMN-U-Z] K-**O**-FWQX
n. 22.15 sint HLMN-Delta] sunt **O**-Gamma
n. 22.15 HLMN-Delta] **O**-Gamma
n. 22.16 HLMN-Delta] **O**-Gamma
n. 22.19 sint HLMN-Delta-Z] **O**-FWQX
n. 23.2 **LMN**-F] H-Delta-**O**-WQXZ
n. 24.6 H**MN**-U-X] K-L-**O**-FWQZ
n. 25.14 HLMN] Delta-**O**-Gamma
n. 25.15 HMN] LWQ+Delta+**O**+F+X+Z
n. 25.19 HLMN] Delta+**O**+Gamma

Beta ± other MSS vs. NO ± other MSS
In only three instances does **N** read with **O** against Beta; the variants are not decisive enough to prove that **N** sought out these readings in Epsilon:

n. 20.9 sint HLM-Delta] sunt **NO**-Gamma
n. 21.6 distinguuntur HLM-Delta-Gamma] distinguitur **NO**
n. 22.18 distinguuntur HM-Delta-FQ] distinguitur L-**NO**-Gamma

MN ± other MSS vs. Beta ± other MSS
In the following instances in the same stretch of text, **M** and **N** share a distinct common accident; the variants reflect stylistic preference:

n. 20.6 Dicendum HL-Delta-**O**-WQXZ] dicendum est **MN**-F
n. 20.7 istarum **MN**-Delta-WXZ] illarum H-**O**-FQ *add.* potentiarum L
n. 22.8 Dicendum HL-Delta-**O**-QXZ] dicendum est **MN** dicitur F dicit W
n. 25.8 Dicendum HL-Delta-**O**-Gamma] dicendum est **MN**
n. 25.19 igitur **MN**-Delta-QZ] H+L-**O**-FWX

* * *

Question 21

In this question, MS **N** evidently had two models before him, Beta and Epsilon (see below); for the most part, however, as in the last part of the previous question, **N** continues to follow Beta, agreeing with Beta 78 times against its Epsilon companion, MS **O**:

N + Beta ± other MSS vs. O + other MSS
n. 0.4 HLMN-Z] Delta-**O**-FWQX
n. 1.9 HLMN-FWX] Delta-**O**-QZ
n. 1.14 LMN-Z] H+Delta-X+**O**+FW
n. 1.16 HLMN] Delta-**O**-Gamma
n. 2.19 Item HLMN] Praeterea Delta-**O**-Gamma
n. 3.5 Item HLMN] Praeterea Delta-**O**-Gamma

n. 3.5 HLMN-U] K+O-FWQZ+X
n. 3.6 HLMN-Delta] O-Gamma
n. 5.13 Item HLMN] Praeterea Delta-O-Gamma
n. 6.18 istam LMN-Q] illam H-FWXZ primam O
n. 6.20 HLMN-Delta] O-Gamma
n. 6.1: H-O-Delta-WQXZ] LMN-F
n. 7.14 HLMN-QXZ] Delta-O-FW
n. 10.10 HLMN-U] K+O-Q+FW+X+Z
n. 11.14 Item HLMN] Praeterea Delta-O-Gamma
n. 12.3: HLMN] Delta-O-Gamma
n. 12.7 Delta-O-FWQX] HMN-Z
n. 12.10 HLMN-Delta] O-Gamma
n. 14.4 illorum HLMN] istorum Delta eorum O-Gamma
n. 15.13 Item HLMN] Praeterea Delta-O-Gamma
n. 15.18 HLMN] Delta-O-Gamma
n. 16.2 Item HLMN] Praeterea Delta-O-Gamma
n. 16.2 HLMN] K-FWQXZ+U-O
n. 16.4 HLMN] Delta-O-Gamma
n. 17.5 HLMN-QZ] Delta-O-FWX
n. 18.11 Item HLMN] Praeterea Delta-O-Gamma
n. 18.14 HLMN-Delta-X] O-FWQZ
n. 20.11 HLMN] Delta-O-Gamma
n. 20.19 HLMN] Delta-O-Gamma
n. 21.21 HLMN-W] Delta+O+FQZ
n. 21.9 HLMN-Delta] O-Gamma
n. 21.12 aliis... entitatis Delta-O-Gamma] *om.* HLMN
n. 21.14 Delta-O-Gamma] HLMN
n. 21.2 LMN-Z] H-Delta-O-FWQ
n. 21.3 HLMN-F] Delta-O-WQZ
n. 21.7 Item HLMN] Praeterea Delta-O-Gamma
n. 22.7 HLMN] Delta-O-FW+Q+Z
n. 22.12 HLMN-K] U+O+FWZ+Q
n. 22.13 HLMN-Delta] O-Gamma
n. 23.19 Item HLMN-O] Praeterea Delta-Gamma (a rare Beta-O agreement on this reading)
n. 23.1 LMN] H-W+Delta-O+F+Q
n. 24.7 Item HLMN] Praeterea Delta-O-Gamma
n. 24.7 HLMN] Delta-O-FWZ+Q
n. 24.7 HLMN] Delta-O-Gamma
n. 25.3 HLMN] Delta-O-Gamma
n. 25.5 HLMN-Delta] O-Gamma
n. 25.14 HLMN-Delta] O-QZ+FW
n. 25.15 HLMN-Q] Delta-O-FWZ
n. 26.22 Item HLMN] Praeterea Delta-O-Gamma
n. 26.1 HLMN-K-FW] U-O-Z+Q
n. 26.2 LMN-Delta-Q] H+O-FWX+Z
n. 27.9 Item HLMN] Praeterea Delta-O-Gamma
n. 27.9 HLMN] Delta-O-Gamma
n. 28.15 Item HLMN] Praeterea Delta-O-Gamma

n. 30.14 Item HLMN] Praeterea Delta-O-Gamma
n. 30.19 HLMN-FWQ] Delta-X+O+Z
n. 30.21 LMN] H+K+U+O-FWQX+Z
n. 30.1 HLMN] Delta-O-FWQX+Z
n. 31.3 Item HLMN-U] Praeterea K-O-Gamma
n. 31.5 HLMN] Delta-O-Gamma
n. 32.13 Item HLMN] Praeterea Delta-O-Gamma
n. 33.16 L-O-Gamma] HMN-Delta
n. 33.2 HLMN] Delta-QXZ+O+FW
n. 33.4 H-Delta-O-Gamma] LMN
n. 33.5 HMN-Delta] L-O-FWQZ+X
n. 34.11 HLMN-Delta] O-Gamma
n. 36.11 sint HMN-K-QZ] sunt O-FWXQZ
n. 36.1 HLMN] Delta-O-Gamma
n. 36.3 sunt HLN-Delta] sint M-O-Gamma
n. 37.7 O+FWQX] HLMN+Delta-Z
n. 37.7 HLMN] Delta-O-Gamma
n. 38.3 HLMN] Delta-O-Gamma
n. 38.7 HLMN] Delta-O-Gamma
n. 38.9 L-Delta-O-FWXZ] HMN-Q
n. 39.12 HMN] L+Delta-O-Gamma
n. 39.14 HLMN-X] Delta-O-FWQZ
n. 39.20 HLMN-Gamma] Delta-O

NO ± other MSS vs. Beta ± other MSS
In Question 21, **N** shares a distinct common accident with **O** only six times; since all of these variants reflect stylistic preference—a stylistic preference that **N** might have carried with him from copying Epsilon—these instances do not suggest that **N** sought out the readings in Epsilon. By the same principle, that **M** splits with **N** in these instances does not seem especially significant (see the next table).

n. 10.11 convenit HLM-Delta-FWX] contingit **NO**-QZ
n. 12.19 possit **NO**-U-Gamma] potest HL-K posset **M**
n. 22.10 probo HLM] probatur Delta-FW probatio **NO**-Q-Z
n. 31.6 est HLM-Delta-FXZ] esset **NO**-WQ
n. 33.2 ergo HLM-FWX] igitur K-**NO**-QZ *om.* U
n. 34.22 ergo LM-Delta-FWQX] igitur H-**NO**-Z

MN ± other MSS vs. Beta ± other MSS
In Question 21, **N** shares with **O** what apparently is the Epsilon reading 18 times, and **M** joins them in this reading against Beta. Moreover, in 27 instances **M** and **N** share a distinct common accident, and in two more instances **M** and **N** share a reading with some other manuscripts against both Beta and **O**:

n. 3.9 ens commune HL-Delta] in communi **MNO**-Gamma
n. 6.3 obiectum adaequatum potentiae **MNO**-Gamma] potentiae obiectum adaequatum HL-Delta
n. 7.16 magis posset **MN**-FWQZ] *inv.* L-O-X magis potest H magis possit Delta
n. 12.19 *inv.* HL-Delta] primum obiectum **MNO**-Gamma

n. 12.19 probo HL-Delta] probatio **MNO**-Gamma

n. 13.14 illud primum **MNO**-Gamma] eius primum HL primum illud K primum idem U

n. 14.1 Minor probatur L-U-X] Et minor probatur H-K Minorem probo quia **MN** Probatio minoris quia **O**-FWQZ

n. 14.5 Probatio **MNO**-Gamma] Probo HL Probatur Delta

n. 15.15 praedicatur per se HL-U-Q] per se praedicatur **MN**-FWXZ praedicatur per se conversim **O**

n. 15.1 per HL-Delta-XZ] secundum **MNO**-FWQ

n. 17.6 subdividitur Delta-**MNO**-FWXZ] dividitur HL-Q

n. 18.11 tunc **MNO**-Gamma] *om.* HL-Delta

n. 18.15 Si HL-Delta-X] Si autem **MNO**-FWQZ

n. 18.15 aliquid addit HL-U-FX] *inv.* **MN**-K-WQZ addidit aliquid **O**

n. 18.16 essentialiter ens HL-Delta-**O**-X] *inv.* **MN**-FWQZ

n. 18.19 includat **MN**-Delta-X] sit H includit L-**O**-FWQZ

n. 20.3 Dicendum L-**O**-Delta-Gamma] Dicendum tamen H Dicendum est **MN**

n. 20.4 ita disparatae **MNO**-Gamma] *inv.* HL-Delta

n. 20.6 essentialem K-**MN**] essentialiter HL-U-**O**-Q-Z essentialem aliam F essentiale W

n. 20.8 scilicet HL-**O**-FWZ] licet Delta sed **MN**-Q

n. 20.8 prout Delta-**MNO**-Gamma] ut HL

n. 21.4 Philosophi II Metaphysicae L-Delta-**O**-Gamma] Philosophum II Metaphysicae L Philosophi in II Metaphysicae **MN**

n. 21.10 sequitur HL-Delta] sequeretur **MN** sequeretur ut dictum est **O**-Gamma

n. 21.11 sic HL-**O**-QZ] sic se habent K ita **MN**-FW

n. 22.8 quia HL-Delta-**O**-Gamma] quod **MN**

n. 23.20 conceptus proprius Dei HL-FW] conceptus Dei proprius K proprius conceptus Dei U-Q proprius Dei **MNO**-Z

n. 24.18 perfectior est **MNO**-Gamma] *inv.* HL-Delta

n. 24.20 nec HL-Delta-**O**-QZ] non **MN** non est FW

n. 26.4 autem utrum **MN**-FWZ] an H-Delta tamen an L utrum autem **O** autem quod Q et utrum X

n. 29.4 potest sic argui H-Delta-Z] potest argui sic L potest argui **MNO**-FWX sic argui potest Q

n. 30.20 in substantiam HL-Delta-**O**-Gamma] *om.* **MN**

n. 31.7 Quia HL-Delta-FWXZ] Quia tunc **MN** Quod **O**-Q

n. 32.14 ad unum **MNO**-Gamma] *om.* HL-Delta

n. 33.18 ibidem **MNO**-Gamma] ibi HL-Delta

n. 33.20 ad **MNO**-Gamma] in HL-Delta

n. 33.2 Dicendum HL-Delta-**O**-WQXZ] Dicendum est **MN**-F

n. 33.3 determinative HL-FWZ] determinate Delta-**MN**-QX determinare **O**

n. 33.7 vel HL-Delta-**O**-Gamma] *om.* **MN**

n. 33.8 univocum **MN**-Delta-Gamma] univocum locutum HL unicum **O**

n. 34.19 quod HL-**O**-FQX] quia Delta-**MN**-WZ

n. 35.3 dicendum quod duplex est HL-Delta-**O**-Gamma] dicendum est quod duplex **MN**-F

n. 37.4 Dicendum HL-Delta-**O**-Gamma] Dicendum est **MN**-F

n. 37.13 logice loquendo HL-Delta-**O**-Gamma] loquendo **M** loquendo logice **N**

n. 38.16 dicendum HL-Delta-**O**-WQXZ] dicendum est **MN**-F

n. 38.16 primum obiectum HL-Delta-**O**-Gamma] *inv.* **MN**

n. 39.11 dicendum HL-Delta-**O**-FWQZ] dicendum est **MN** *om.* Q dicendum quod X

n. 38.14 communem conceptum **MN**-QX] *inv.* H-**O** conceptum L verum conceptum Delta conceptum univocum FW communem Z

Summary Conclusion: As stated above, when copying Question 21 **N** evidently had both Epsilon and Beta before him, for the most part following Beta as he had done in the last part (nn. 17-25) of Question 20 (**N** agrees with Beta 78 times, with **O** and Epsilon 24 times). The behavior of **M** at first appears more confusing, as it agrees with Beta and **N** 78 times (q. 21, first table), with **N** and **O** 18 times, shares a distinct common accident with **N** 27 times, and in three other instances reads with **N** and some other manuscripts against both Beta and **O**. One need not posit unnecessary intervening entities when a simpler explanation accounts for the appearances: the simplest explanation of **M**'s behavior is that for the whole question, its scribe (Thomas Wyche) simply copied **N**, following it when it followed Beta then Epsilon and introduced its own singular readings. No accident in the above tables requires a different explanation.

***

Question 22

The same pattern continues throughout Question 22. Here **N** reads with Beta against **O** 70 times:

N + Beta vs. O + other MSS
n. 0.4 HL**MN**-X] Delta-**O**-FWQZ
n. 1.6 HL**MN**] U-**O**-Q+FWXZ
n. 1.9 HL**MN**-Delta-QXZ] **O**+FW
n. 2.12 Item HL**MN**] Praeterea **O**-Gamma
n. 2.12 H**MN**-FWQZ] L-Delta-**O**+X
n. 3.14 Item HL**MN**-U] Praeterea K-**O**-Gamma
n. 4.17 Item HL**MN**] Praeterea Delta-**O**-Gamma
n. 4.17 HL**MN**-Gamma] **O**-Delta
n. 4.1 L**MN**-U-Gamma] H-K-**O**
n. 4.3 HL**MN**-QXZ] Delta-FW+**O**
n. 5.7 Item HL**MN**-U] Praeterea K-**O**-Gamma
n. 5.15 H**MN**-Delta-Q] L+**O**+FWZ
n. 8.3 Item HL**MN**] Praeterea Delta-**O**-Gamma
n. 9.6 Item HL**MN**-Delta] *om.* **O** Praeterea Gamma
n. 11.18 HL**MN**-Delta] **O**-Gamma
n. 13.7 Item HL**MN**] Praeterea Delta-**O**-Gamma
n. 14.13 Item HL**MN**] Praeterea Delta-**O**-Gamma
n. 14.16 HL**MN**-K-Q] U-**O**-FWZ
n. 15.18 Item HL**MN**-Delta] Praeterea **O**-Gamma
n. 15.3: HL**MN**-Gamma] Delta-**O**
n. 16.5 Item HL**MN**-Delta] Praeterea **O**-Gamma
n. 16.8 HL**MN**-FWZ] Delta-**O**-Q
n. 17.15 H**MN**-Gamma] L-Delta-**O**
n. 17.16 HL**MN**-FWZ] Delta-**O**-Q
n. 18.19 Item HL**MN**] Praeterea Delta-**O**-Gamma
n. 19.3 Item HL**MN**-Delta] Praeterea **O**-Gamma
n. 19.5 HL**MN**-FWZ] K+U+**O**-Q
n. 20.10 HL**MN**] Delta-Gamma+**O**
n. 20.10 H**MN**] L+**O**+Gamma
n. 20.11 HL**MN**-K-FW] U-**O**-QZ

n. 20.11 inductive HLMN] inductione Delta-O-Gamma
n. 20.11 Delta-O-Gamma] HLMN
n. 21.14 Item HLMN-U] Praeterea U-O-Gamma
n. 21.17 HLMN-Delta] O-Gamma
n. 23.6 Item HLMN] Praeterea Delta-O-Gamma
n. 24.9 Item HLMN-Delta] Praeterea O-Gamma
n. 25.13 Item HLMN] Praeterea Delta-O-Gamma
n. 25.16 HMN-Delta-Z] L+O+FWQ
n. 25.18 HLMN-U-Q] K-O-FWZ
n. 26.2 HLMN] Delta-O-FWQ+Z
n. 26.2 HLMN-Delta] O-Gamma
n. 26.11 Delta-O-Gamma] HLMN
n. 29.12 Item HLMN] Praeterea Delta-O-Gamma
n. 29.13 HMN-K-FWZ] L+U+O-Q
n. 30.15 Item HLMN-U] Praeterea K-O-Gamma
n. 31.1: LMN-Delta-Gamma] H-O
n. 32.5 HLMN-Delta] O-Gamma
n. 34.18 HLN-Delta] M-O-Gamma
n. 34.22 HLMN-Delta] O-Gamma
n. 34.10: HLMN-K-FWZ] U+OQ
n. 35.14 HMN-Delta] L+O-Gamma
n. 35.23 HLMN-Delta-Q] O-FWZ
n. 36.7 HLMN] Delta-O-Gamma
n. 37.13 HLMN-Delta-Z] O-FWQ
n. 37.15 HLMN-Delta-FWZ] O-Q
n. 37.16 HLMN-Delta-QZ] O-FW
n. 38.1: HMN-Delta] O-Gamma
n. 38.2 HLMN-Delta] O-Gamma
n. 38.3 HLMN-Delta] O-Gamma
n. 39.7 HLMN-Q] Delta-O-FWZ
n. 39.8 LMN-QZ] H-O-FW+Delta
n. 41.19 NHLM] Delta-O-Gamma
n. 42.25 H-Delta-O-Gamma] LMN
n. 42.25 H-Delta-O-Gamma] LMN
n. 42.2 HLMN-Delta-FWZ] O-Q
n. 42.3 HLMN-Delta-FWZ] O-Q
n. 43.8 HLMN-Delta] O-Gamma
n. 43.9 postea Delta-O-Gamma] praterita H praeterea LMN
n. 44.11 Item HLMN-Delta] Prima O Praeterea Gamma

NO ± other MSS vs. Beta (with M) ± other MSS
Only twice in Question 22 does **N** read with **O** against Beta manuscripts, and even then **N** and **O** share the reading with one Beta manuscript, **L**:

n. 16.5 scilicet HM-Delta-FWZ] *om.* L-NO-Q
n. 35.16 singulare L-NO-U-Gamma] universale HM-K

MN ± other MSS vs. Beta ± other MSS
In Question 22, **M** joins **NO** in reading against Beta 19 times; moreover, **M** shares a distinct common accident with **N** or reads with **N** against Beta and **O** 13 times:

n. 1.9 quia Delta-**MNO**-FWQZ] quia tunc HL quia sic X
n. 2.13 sic... auctoritatibus **MNO**FWXZ] sic de multis auctoritatibus H-U sic de multis auctoritatibus aliis L multis aliis auctoritatibus K sic multae auctoritates aliae Q
n. 5.7 intelligerentur **MNO**-Gamma] intelligentur H intelliguntur L intellegeretur KU
n. 10.12 nihil Delta-**MNO**-FWZ] non HL-Q
n. 10.15 tantum universale est HL-Delta-**O**-QZ] universale est tantum **MN**-FW
n. 11.16 cognoscere Delta-**MNO**-Gamma] intelligere HL
n. 14.13 ponunt HL-Delta-**O**-FWZ] ponunt arguitur **MN**-Q
n. 15.1 phantasmata HL-(lin.U^2)-Gamma] phantasma K-**MNO**
n. 17.13 Dicendum HL-Delta-**O**-WZ] Dicendum est **MN**-F Responsio dicendum est Q
n. 17.15 de ratione U-**O**-FQZ] rationem HL a ratione K-**MN**-W
n. 18.1 K-**MNO**-Gamma] HL-U
n. 27.15 quae Delta-**MNO**-FWZ] *om.* HL-Q
n. 27.15 essent HL-Delta-**O**-Gamma] sunt **MN**
n. 27.1 Cuius causa HL-Delta] Causa huius **MNO** Causa huius autem Gamma
n. 27.2 specialiter est HL-Delta] *inv.* **MNO**-FWZ specialiter Q
n. 31.18 est Delta-**MNO**-F] *om.* HL-WQZ
n. 31.3 vel^2 H-FWZ] et L-Q *om.* Delta-**MNO**
n. 32.7 repraesentare species genita HL-Delta-**O**-Gamma] species generata repraesentare **MN**
n. 33.14 actualem Delta-**MN**-Gamma] accidentalem HL accidentem O
n. 34.1 sunt falsa HL-Delta] *inv.* **MNO**-Gamma
n. 34.6 est HL-Delta] sit **MNO**-Gamma
n. 36.2 Dicendum HL-Delta-**O**-Gamma] Dicendum est **MN**
n. 36.7 se primo U-**MNO**-QZ] *inv.* HL-K-FW
n. 36.10 propria ratione HL-Delta] *inv.* **MNO**-Gamma
n. 38.20 Dicendum HL-U-**O**-QWZ] Dicendum est K-**MN**-F
n. 38.1 intellectus HL-Delta-**O**-QZ] intellectus nostri **MN** intellectus prius FW (*add. in mg.* K)
n. 39.8 est cognoscitivus Delta-**MNO**-WQZ] est cognitivus HL *inv.* F
n. 40.9 Dicendum HL-Delta-**O**-WQZ] Dicendum est **MN**-F
n. 40.12 primum Delta-**MNO**-Gamma] primo HL
n. 42.20 Dicendum HL-Delta-**O**-WQZ] Dicendum est **MN**-F
n. 43.5 Dicendum HL-Delta-**O**-WQZ] Dicendum est **MN**-F
n. 44.11 dato quod HL-Delta-**O**-Gamma] dico quod licet **MN**
n. 44.15 circumstantiando Delta-**MNO**-Gamma] circumstando HL

Conclusion, Questions 20-22: Beginning at n. 17 in Question 20, MS **N** leaves his normal model Epsilon, probably because it was becoming difficult to read and anyway defective in sense, to copy the model Beta. The copyist of **N** continues to rely mostly on Beta through Question 22, although he clearly had Epsilon also before him, which he sometimes consulted for a reading. In the preceding questions, **N** often switched from Epsilon to Beta, if not so thoroughly as here; it would now seem clear that **N** intended to use and consult both manuscripts from the beginning of his project. If Beta in Questions 20-22 was less difficult to construe, apparently it was only relatively so. For in these questions MS **M** abandoned his usual model, Beta, and simply copied **N**, "whithersoever it goeth." Again, **M** and **N** share distinct common accidents throughout the *Quaestiones*; the copyist of **M**,

Thomas Wyche, seemingly had no compunction in using **N** to assist him in construing Beta when it seemed useful or necessary.

M. AFFINITIES BETWEEN EPSILON AND GAMMA

We have already tabulated and exemplified agreements between Beta and Delta against the other manuscripts (§ 2.F-G, above). Conversely, throughout the text there are many agreements between Epsilon and Gamma against readings shared by Beta and Delta. Such agreements are exposed in the tables in the preceding section that chart the movements of manuscripts in qq. 20-22. Common accidents between Epsilon and Gamma occur in three configurations:

1) **NO**-Gamma, when **N** and **O** both follow Epsilon; see q. 20 (4 instances): nn. 2.13, 5.8, 11.7, 20.10. In this question, MS **M** is still copying Beta.

2) **MNO**-Gamma, when **M** abandons Beta to copy **N**, thus joining in Epsilon readings; see q. 20 (1 instance): nn. 12.1; q. 21 (15 instances): nn. 3.9, 6.3, 12.17 (twice), 13.13, 14.20, 14.3, 18.9, 18.12, 18.15, 20.6, 24,17, 32.7,33.11, 33.13; q. 22 (5 instances): nn. 5.7, 27.3, 34.1, 34.6, 36.10.

3) **O**-Gamma, when **N** switches to Beta (sometimes followed by **M**), leaving **O** as the only witness of Epsilon; see q. 20 (8 instances): nn. 11.8, 15.1, 20.12, 20.21, 22.16 (twice), 22.17, 22.20; q. 21 (8 instances): nn. 3.6, 6.20, 12.8, 21.7, 22.12, 25.2, 25.11, 34.13; q. 22 (13 instances): nn. 2.12, 11.19, 15.19, 19.3, 21.15, 24.9, 26.2, 32.5, 34.22, 38.1, 38.2 (twice), 43.7.

To account for Epsilon-Gamma or **O**-Gamma agreements, we have entertained the following hypotheses:

1) Epsilon was "contaminated" by a Gamma manuscript, i.e., the copyist of Epsilon consulted some Gamma manuscript in constructing his text. This hypothesis is implausible, for even if the copyist of Epsilon intended to copy "exactly what he saw," it is difficult to conceive that he was so perverse as to preserve perfectly the huge material accidents in Alpha when he had another model at hand in which they had been repaired. And if the copyist of Epsilon had a copy of Gamma at hand, why did he not use it more often, to provide the many words he could not read or the abbreviations he could not resolve, and in general to improve his often senseless text? Finally, no surviving copy, at least, of Gamma existed in medieval Oxford, where the copyist of **O** would have needed to find it.

2) Not the copyist of Epsilon himself but the copyist of MS **O** consulted some Gamma manuscript. This hypothesis simply moves the question down to another level in the *Stemma*. The same reasons that make hypothesis 1) implausible make this one implausible.

3) At some point, someone imposed a layer of corrections coming from Gamma on MS Epsilon, which might account for **O**-Gamma readings that are not shared by the other copy of Epsilon, MS **N**. This hypothesis is impossible, because **O** was copied before **N**. Moreover, in any case it seems inconceivable that someone would take the pains carefully to impose many corrections on Epsilon and would not somewhere leave some note, like the one found

in MS **N**, indicating that the texts of some questions were misplaced in other questions, or indeed that many of the questions were in the wrong order, as comparison with Gamma proves. Further, supposing that such a note had been written somewhere in Epsilon, we would need then to suppose that both the passive scribe of **O** as well as the intelligent, active scribe of **N** ignored it.

4) It was the editor-copyist of Gamma who consulted Epsilon. For it is not inconceivable that the "photographic" copy of Alpha, MS Epsilon, was intended precisely to be a working instrument made to assist the editor of Gamma in his edition of the difficult-to-read MS Alpha. According to this hypothesis, Epsilon would have been another very early copy of the *Quaestiones De anima*, for as we have indicated, Gamma itself was such. Further, according to this hypothesis, when Gamma was taken to Italy, Epsilon was left behind in Oxford, where MSS **O** and **N** were able to copy it a century or so later (in the early fifteenth century).

The last hypothesis is at least logical, whereas the others are not, and it is consistent with the characters of MSS Epsilon and Gamma, the one completely passive and the other a stylistic revision of the whole Alpha text, which puts all things in order. Furthermore, this hypothesis satisfies the criterion of sense, as we have exercised it in our edition: when the editor of Gamma (most likely from the continent) could not read what was in Alpha, he took recourse to Epsilon and more often than not was misled, whereas the editor of Beta (probably an Englishman) reading Alpha more often than not got it right. Even so, we do not have one piece of external evidence that corroborates or implies such a relationship between the two manuscripts. Thus, the textual fact alone remains: Epsilon and Gamma, each copied (or revised) from Alpha, share many common readings against common readings shared by Beta and Delta, each copied from Alpha. In Beta-Delta agreements, Beta was the pivotal manuscript, since we know that Delta consulted Beta; the pivotal manuscript in agreements between Epsilon and Gamma cannot be determined, although we suspect that the pivotal manuscript was Epsilon.

N. The Anomalous Question 23: More Disturbance *in fonte*

By means of this critical edition we have established that the *Quaestiones De anima* disputed and originally drafted by John Duns Scotus comprised 23 questions in an order loosely hinged on a sequence of selected topics in Books II-III of Aristotle's *De anima*. The order of questions established in our edition verifies the order presented in the old Vivès-Wadding edition. Yet another salient anomaly in the transmission of the *Quaestiones*, which calls into question the original constitution of the collection, is this: eleven of the twenty-five surviving manuscripts that contain all or most of the questions in the collection—nearly half of them—omit Question 23, the final question in the sequence. Moreover, four of the six surviving manuscripts that were certainly copied in the fourteenth century omit q. 23 (**BPQZ**). MSS **BZ** (14th c.) and MSS **CEGO** (15th c.) contain qq. 1-22 (**C** appends questions *De cognitione Dei* to the collection of 22 questions); MS **P** (14th c.) contains qq. 1-22 and in place of q. 23 substitutes another question; MS **Q** (14th c.) contains qq. 1-15, 17-22 (omitting q. 16 besides q. 23 and inserting an extra question after q. 20 and before qq. 21-22); MS **D** (15th c.) contains qq. 1-21; MS **J** (15th c.) contains qq. 1-15, 18-22; MS **A** (15th c.), finally, contains qq. 1-22, omits q. 23, but otherwise expands the collection of *Quaestiones De anima* by adding five other questions to it.

Doubts about the status of q. 23 are strengthened by further, indirect evidence. In his *Tabula super Quaestiones De anima et super aliquas cedulas*, which was meant to serve as a bibliographical register of questions by Scotus, Guillelmus de Missali omits q. 23; instead of q. 23 after his abbreviations of qq. 1-22 of the *Quaestiones De anima*, Guillelmus supplies an abbreviation of another question: "Utrum intellectivam esse formam corporis humani possit demonstrari." Nor is q. 23 found in the list of questions by Scotus in MS Z^2, written before 1320, which otherwise cites qq. 1-5, 7-8, 15, 18 and 22 of the *Quaestiones De anima*. (Besides q. 23, the list also omits qq. 6, 9-14, 16-17, 20-21.) On the other hand, q. 23 strangely is inserted into a fourteenth-century copy of Scotus' *Quaestiones super Metaphysicam* (MS Z^1), which probably was copied in Paris, without any indication that it was imported from another work. This anomalous fact suggests that q. 23 might have circulated separately and detached from the collection of *Quaestiones De anima*.[99]

Indeed, in its content and style q. 23 seems somewhat different from the other 22 questions in the collection. The question discussed is not so clearly linked to the other 22 questions as they are linked among themselves, and the topic does not hang on a topic in Aristotle's *De anima* so clearly and sequentially as do the topics of the other questions. Here Scotus offers no clear solution: the solution proposed (introduced by *dicitur*) favors the idea that in some sense the intellect is a moved mover, but that conclusion is immediately subjected to criticism. By the end, one has the impression that the author meant to acquaint his listeners with the first solution as a received opinion, and that he himself favors the alternative solution, whereby the intellect and its object operate as co-causes. Even so, the author does not state any position decisively. This pattern of argumentation is similar to that in Scotus' *Collationes*, wherein typically he introduces an opinion close to his own, subjects it to criticism, proposes another solution, examines it, etc., but in the end does not indicate any firm resolution. Question 23 might well be the record of a dispute of the *collatio* type, which was not strictly a part of Scotus' course on *De anima* but was associated with it.

Whatever the ambiguity of the status of this question in relation to the others, there can be no doubt that it was bound with the other 22 questions and held the last place in the sequence of *Quaestiones De anima* in MS Alpha, however it came to be there. The question existed in Beta, as witnessed by its inclusion in MSS **HL** (for **M**, see below); it existed in Delta, as witnessed by MSS **KU**; it apparently existed in Epsilon, as witnessed by MS **N** (see below); and it existed in Gamma, as witnessed by MSS **FRSVWXY**. Even so, examination and edition of the text of q. 23 suggests that there was also something materially different about this question as it existed in MS Alpha. Overall, the condition of the text of q. 23 is far more disturbed and confused than the text in any other question; fluctuations among the groups of manuscripts and individual manuscripts that are evident throughout the *Quaestiones* become yet more pronounced; heretofore fairly reliable witnesses break down.

In qq. 20-22, when **N** largely abandons Epsilon for Beta and thus splits with MS **O**, it is difficult any longer to determine surely readings peculiar to Epsilon. In those questions **O** anyway most often reads with Gamma and its isolated accidents more often than not are mistakes. Since **O** did not copy the question, it would seem possible that in q. 23 Epsilon might disappear altogether, or perhaps that it did not exist in that manuscript. Yet that q. 23 existed in Epsilon can be proved indirectly. Analysis of the pattern of variants indicates that, having turned largely to Beta for qq. 20-

---

[99]The overlap of topics *de anima et de metaphysica* is well-known in Scholastic literature. Antonius Andreae, for example, refers often to Scotus' *Quaestiones De anima* (notably q. 22), especially concerning the question of individuation, in his own *Quaestiones super Metaphysicam*. This makes one wonder why, if someone judged it appropriate to insert one question from the *Quaestiones De anima* in a copy of Scotus' *Quaestiones super Metaphysicam* (as evinced in MS Z^1), he did not insert other questions from the same collection concerning the soul that are even more pertinent to metaphysical issues. That the inserter did not suggests that he had at his disposal only a stray copy of q. 23, not the whole set of *Quaestiones De anima*.

22, for q. 23 the copyist of MS **N** returned to his original model, Epsilon;[100] likewise, in q. 23 the copyist of MS **M** continued to copy **N**, as he did in qq. 21-22. In 19 instances in q. 23 MSS **MN** read together against Beta, often agreeing with Gamma (as often did **O** in qq. 21-22). We may presume that in these instances **N** supplies the reading of Epsilon (**N** needed to copy some manuscript, and it was not Beta), since **M** and **N** do not share any distinct common accidents in this question, which would have been produced by a singular reading in **N** that **M** copied.

Question 23: MN ± other MSS vs. Beta ± other MSS
n. 1.17 est magis HL-Delta] *inv.* **MN**-Gamma
n. 1.19 actionibus Delta-**MN**-Gamma] accidentibus H actionibus est L
n. 1.20 subordinatae HL-Delta] sub ordine **MN**-Gamma
n. 1.22 generatur HL-Delta] generatus **MN**-Gamma
n. 1.22 autem HL-Delta] *om.* **MN**-Gamma
n. 2.7 quia HL-Delta] quia illa **MN**-Gamma
n. 2.8 ponitur Delta-**MN**-Gamma] ponatur HL
n. 5.6 dicendum HL-Delta] dicendum est **MN**-FW dicitur est X
n. 5.8 perfectus U-**MN**-Gamma] perfectius HL-K
n. 5.9 nec HL-Delta] non **MN**-Gamma
n. 5.9 per...illa K-**MN**-Gamma] H+L+U
n. 6.14 sic **MN**-Gamma] *om.* HL-Delta
n. 6.15 in **MN**-Gamma] ad HL-Delta
n. 6.15 ex **MN**-Gamma] a HL-Delta
n. 6.16 in **MN**-Gamma] *om.* HL-Delta
n. 7.21 assimilatur HL-K] assimilatur a U-**MN**-Gamma
n. 8.8 non HL] *om.* Delta-**MN**-Gamma
n. 12.2 una HL] una est Delta secunda **MN**-Gamma
n. 12.5 sit Delta-**MN**-Gamma] fuit H fit L

In seven other instances MSS **MN** with Gamma read against Delta and one member of the Beta family, either MS **H** or **L** (at 0.10, 2.9, 3.18, 7.18, 7.21, 9.11 and 11.18). Conversely, not once in the entire question do MSS **MN** share a common reading with the Beta witnesses against the Delta and Gamma manuscripts nor against most of the other manuscripts, nor does either MS **M** or MS **N** alone share a reading with the Beta manuscripts against all of the others. At the same time, as we indicated, MSS **M** and **N** do not share any accidents that distinguish them from all of the other manuscripts in any single reading. That their model was not Gamma is proved by the latter's distinct common accidents witnessed by MSS **FWX** (at 0.9, 3.22, 3.25, 4.4). In sum, in q. 23 **N** once more changed his model, this time from Beta back to Epsilon, and **M** continued to follow him.

MSS **M** and **N** had good reason to leave Beta in this question. Throughout the *Quaestiones*, the text of Beta has proved to be the surest, most comprehending guide to the text in Scotus' autograph, MS Alpha; throughout MSS **HL** have provided steady, common testimony to the text of Beta. In q. 23, however, the usually reliable text of Beta and the usual common testimony of MSS **HL** collapse. In q. 23 MSS **HL** part company 54 times. Nor are their common readings especially sound: eight times in q. 23, because of garbled or clearly inferior sense, the editors have needed to reject the common reading of MSS **HL** (at 2.8, 3.22, 4.4, 5.7, 6.14, 6.15, 7.22, 8.8, frequently here joined by the

---

[100]There are a few variants in the question that suggest that **N** from time-to-time consulted Beta, as he did throughout the *Quaestiones*.

Delta manuscripts). Five more times the editors have rejected the readings of both **H** and **L** when they are otherwise divided between themselves (at 5.8, 8.5, 8.7, 12.3, 12.6); only twice have the editors adopted the distinct common reading of MSS **HL** against the other manuscripts (at 8.8 and 12.2).

This does not mean that any other of the chief manuscripts fared much better than Beta in q. 23. The text of Epsilon, though it may have appeared better than Beta to the copyist of **N**, was itself evidently difficult. Perhaps that is why the copyist of MS **O** at this point finally gave up the task. In this state of general confusion one would have hoped for more help from the Delta and Gamma manuscripts in determining divided readings, but that hope is largely disappointed. Nevertheless, in crucial instances Delta (as witnessed by **KU**) and Gamma (as witnessed by **FWX**) come to the rescue. Twice the editors have adopted the distinct common reading of MSS **KU** as the only possible reading (at 7.20, where all the other manuscripts evince an homoioteleuton, and at 7.22), and twice they have adopted the distinct common reading of MSS **FWX** (at 3.22, where all the other manuscripts evince an homoioteleuton, and at 4.4).

In light of this evidence, we conjecture that the handwriting of q. 23 in the autograph manuscript Alpha appeared to be different from that of the preceding 22 questions, either because Scotus jotted down this question even more rapidly and cryptically than he did the others or because in fact it was written by someone else. That the question was written by someone else would plausibly explain the breakdown of Beta in q. 23; according to this hypothesis, the copyist of Beta, having concentrated on deciphering the cursive of Scotus throughout the text, lost his eye for the new script in q. 23. Moreover, we conjecture further that q. 23 may have been *extra* in the manuscript Alpha because unlike the other 22 questions it was not originally disputed in the course on *De anima* but is rather a report of an "extracurricular" dispute, more or less connected with the course itself.

This hypothesis could also explain why so many surviving manuscripts simply omitted q. 23, why it was omitted in Guillemus de Missali's abbreviations of the *Quaestiones De anima*, and why it is not cited in the early register of questions by Scotus in MS **Z**[2]. The *Stemma codicum* of this edition lends support to the hypothesis that q. 23 was something different. According to the *Stemma* that we have established, MSS **BZ**, which omit q. 23, were copied from Theta, which in turn was copied directly from Gamma; likewise, MSS **CG**, which omit q. 23, were copied from Tau, which in turn was copied directly from Gamma; furthermore, MS **Q**, which omits q. 23, was copied directly from Gamma. At the same time, the MSS **VX**, stemming from Zeta, which was copied directly from Gamma, and MSS **WY** and **FRST** all deriving directly or indirectly from Pi, which was copied directly from Gamma, all include q. 23 with the other *Quaestiones De anima*. From this pattern of evidence, it seems plausible that there was some note in Gamma remarking the difference of q. 23 from the other questions in terms of its form, content and appearance in MS Alpha. That note led some copyists of Gamma (MSS **Q**, Tau and Theta) to omit the question while other copyists of Gamma (Zeta and Pi) decided to include it with the other questions. The anomaly in this stemmatic analysis is MS **P**, which omits q. 23 even though it was included in its model, MS **V**. One cannot know why the scholarly scribe of MS **P**, well-acquainted with Scotus' writings, omitted the q. 23 in his model and replaced it with other questions; that fact in itself seems significant, and suggests that doubt about the question circulated in other ways (e.g., in the *Tabulae* of Guillelmus de Missali). Finally, the anomalous insertion of q. 23 in the text of Scotus' *Quaestiones super Metaphysicam* in MS **Z**[1] intimates the separate status of q. 23 of the *Quaestiones De anima* in another way.[101]

In our edition of q. 23 of the *Quaestiones super secundum et tertium De anima* we have striven not to produce a composite text. More than in any other question, however, we have needed to rely

---

[101] The extreme contamination of the text in MSS **ADEJ**, which omit q. 23, precludes stemmatic analysis.

less on the authority of any one family of manuscripts and more on the criterion of sense. We have needed, in other words, to penetrate through the mixed and confused testimonies of the various manuscript families—the reading of one group more sure in one place and the reading of another group more sure in another—in order to achieve the goal of our whole edition: the recovery of the text of Scotus' *Quaestiones De anima* in the autograph manuscript Alpha, insofar as the surviving evidence has enabled us to "see through a glass darkly."

O. Stemma codicum

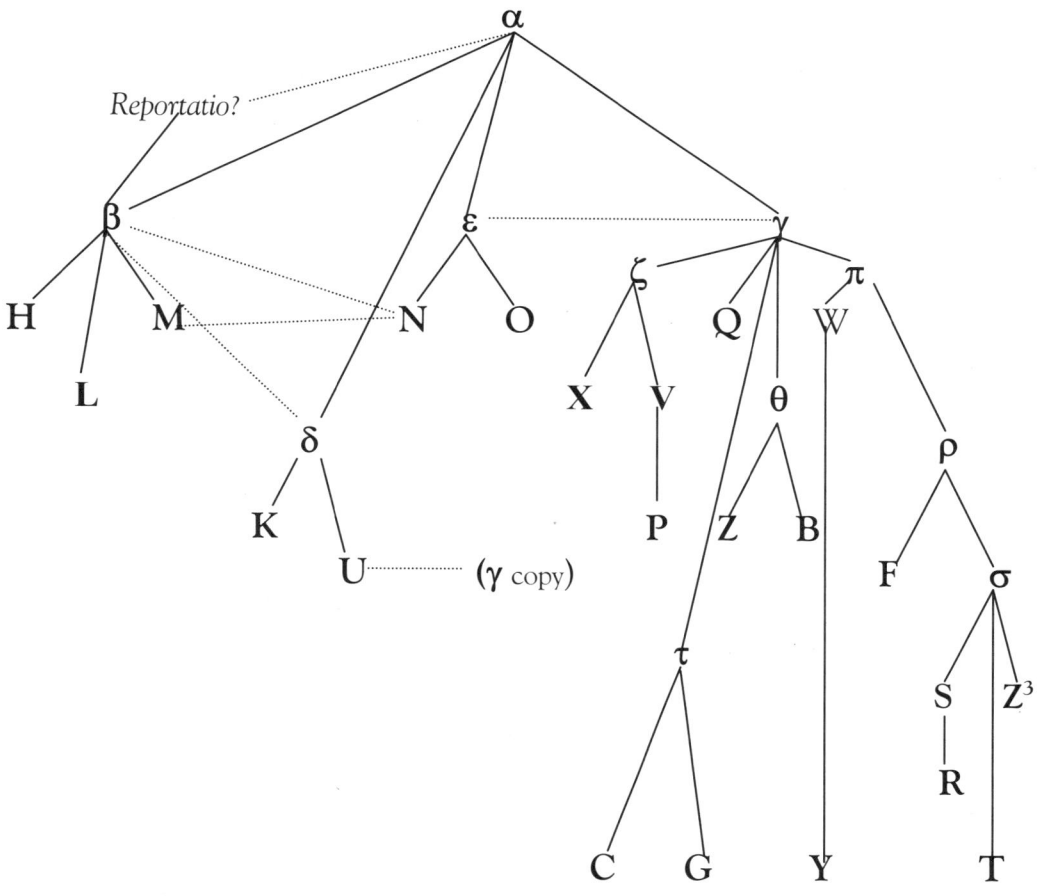

[MSS ADEJ: contaminated]

§ 3: AUTHENTICITY

In articles written in 1923 and 1930, on the basis of ascriptions in manuscripts (**PRWZ²**), Franz Pelster affirmed that Duns Scotus was the author of the *Quaestiones De anima*.[102] In 1926, however, Ephrem Longpré, who was directing the critical edition of Scotus' works begun at Quaracchi, dismissed the authenticity of the *Quaestiones*, on the grounds that the doctrine in some of the questions (e.g., qq. 15, 17-18), i.e., concerning the hylemorphic composition of spiritual substances, the reality of intelligible species, the mind's need to have recourse to phantasms in every act of cognition, flatly contradicts Scotus' teaching in his surely authentic, mature writings. In 1929, Paul Fleig responded to Longpré, arguing that the teaching in qq. 17-18 could be construed in a way consistent with Scotus' positions in later writings. Scholars were not impressed by Fleig's arguments. A reviewer of the dispute judged rightly that "this kind of [doctrinal] discussion is bold speculation as long as a critical edition of Scotus' texts has not established a certain point of comparison."[103] In 1934, in turn, Marianus Müller acknowledged the contradictions between the doctrines concerning the composition of spiritual substances, and the doctrine of intelligible species; he was aware of the ascription of the *Quaestiones* to Scotulus (identified at that time as Antonius Andreae) in MS **M**, but on the basis of other manuscript testimony (including the record of a lost Assisi manuscript), he judged that they were probably authentic. He also noted that the *Quaestiones* were often cited by Antonius Andreae and by Mauritius de Portu (late 15th c.) in his *Annotationes* to Scotus' questions on the *Metaphysics*. He concluded that the doctrinal differences demonstrated by Longpré would not be so surprising were the *Quaestiones* an early writing by Scotus.[104]

The specter of Antonius Andreae in relation to the *Quaestiones* was raised by Martí de Barcelona in 1929, in a bibliographical catalogue of Antonius' writings. Based only on an inquiring attribution of the *Quaestiones* to Antonius in a manuscript catalogue by Montague James (over MS **C**), Martí listed among them Antonius' "dubious" writings.[105] In a superb article in 1942, Charles Balić discussed the way Scotus composed his writings and the ways whereby they were redacted by his disciples. There he addressed the nicknames 'Scotellus' and 'Scotulus' (Antonius Andreae) that appear in the manuscript tradition. In a note, referring to Martí's article and the attribution to Scotulus in MS M, he pronounced apodictically: "Auctor tractatus *De anima* est Scotus; hunc autem tractatum Antonius Andreae compilavit et divulgavit." Balić added that the problem would have to be determined by a critical edition of the *Quaestiones*.[106] In the magisterial first volume of the Scotistic Commission's edition of Scotus' *Opera omnia* (*Ordinatio: Prologus*, 1950), the editors listed manuscripts of the *Quaestiones*, repeated Balić's *dictum* concerning Antonius Andreae, and made this announcement: The *Quaestiones* are attributed to a

---

[102]Franz Pelster, "Handschriftenliches zu Skotus mit neuen Angaben über sein Leben," *Franziskanische Studien* 10 (1923): 1-32, at 27-32; "Eine Münchner Handschrift," 252-72.
[103]Ephrem Longpré, "Pour la défense de Duns Scot," *Rivista di filosofia neoscolastica* 18 (1926): 32-42; Paul Fleig, "Um die Echtheit von Duns Scotus' De anima," *Franziskanische Studien* 16 (1929): 236-42; see the review of D.H.B., *Bulletin de Théologie ancienne et médiévale* 1 (1929-32): 231*-32* no. 422, and the comments by Efrem Bettoni, O.F.M., *Vent'anni di studi Scotisti (1920-1940)* (Milano, 1943), 18.
[104]Marianus Müller, O.F.M., "Stand der Scotus-Forschung 1933. Nach Ephrem Longpré O.F.M. (Referat, gehalten zu Köln am 27. März 1933.)," *Wissenschaft und Weisheit* 1 (1934): 64-65.
[105]Martí de Barcelona, "Fra Antoni Andreu, O.M. 'Doctor Dulcifluus'," *Criterion* (Barcelona) 5 (1929): 321-46, at 344.
[106]C. Balić, "De critica textuali Scholasticorum scriptis accomodata," *Antonianum* 25 (1945): 267-308 at 286 n. 2; revised as "Sermo P. Caroli Balic," in *Relatio Anni III: 1940-1941* (Roma: Commissio Scotistica, 1942), 3-67, at 21-22 n. 4.

certain Iacobus de Turbio in **Biblioteca Apostolica Vaticana, Cod. Ottobonianus latinus 1442**, f. 151*ra*. The editors said that they would determine the question of authorship in their critical edition of the text, which they planned to execute after they finished their edition of the questions on the *Metaphysics*.[107]

The Ottobonianus manuscript (15th c., 160 ff.) contains a series of *compendia* of Aristotelian works (*in logica, de Metaphysica, de Anima, de Generatione, de Caelo et mundo*) by Nicolaus de Orbellis, O.F.M. (d. ca. 1473).[108] In his own exposition of *De anima*,[109] Nicolaus quotes our text, *Quaestiones super secundum et tertium De anima*, concerning the distinction between *immutatio animalis* and *immutatio naturalis* (cf. infra, q. 4 n. 13), and then comments: "Hoc Iacobus de Turbio sequax Scoti in quaestionibus super librum De anima quae quidem a quibusdam dicuntur quaestiones ipsius Scoti, quarum principium est 'Utrum sensus tactus sit unus'. De quo vide vigesima distinctione quarti Sententiarum" (f. 151*ra*). The text in Nicolaus' *Super Sententias compendium perutile* IV contains questions on the pains of the damned and the souls in purgatory; here Nicolaus makes no comments about the authorship of the work. Nicolaus' attribution of the *Quaestiones De anima* to (presumably) Iacobus de Viterbio, O.E.S.A., is late and it is ambivalent: Nicolaus acknowledges that many say that the work is by Scotus himself. Moreover, Nicolaus' attribution is otherwise singular in the whole tradition: the *Quaestiones De anima* are not attributed to Iacobus in any surviving or recorded manuscript of the work, nor evidently has anyone else ever ascribed the work to him.[110] Nicolaus' reference to "Iacobus de Turbio" possibly was based on a quick examination of the manuscript listed in the inventory of Assisi of 1381 (see pp. 99*-100*, above), which then contained copies of Scotus' *Quaestiones De anima* (the gatherings of which are now lost) and Iacobus' *Quodlibet* (the old Assisi gatherings of which are now extant in a Vatican manuscript).

Others have doubted Scotus' authorship of the *Quaestiones De anima*. In the course of his remarkable research on theories concerning knowledge of the individual in the Middle Ages, and thereafter in articles treating Antonius Andreae, Camille Berubé confronted in passing the issue of the authenticity of the *Quaestiones De anima* (1964, 1979). Because Berubé's arguments are historically, hermeneutically and philosophically complex, we can here only sketch their broad lineaments. Berubé focused his attention on q. 22, concerning the soul's knowledge of singulars. He judged that the *Quaestiones* represent an attempted synthesis between old-fashioned (late-thirteenth century) Franciscan theories of knowledge—especially as formulated by Vital du Four—and Scotus' newer ideas expressed in the mature, authentic questions on the *Metaphysics*, *Quodlibet*, and *Ordinatio*. According to Berubé, the text of *Quaestiones De anima* is replete with inner contradictions, searching to reconcile Scotus' sure magisterial teaching that *in statu isto* one may have knowledge of singulars directly only by recourse to phantasms, with the idea that there

---

[107]*Ordinatio* (Città del Vaticano, 1950), I:152*-53*, at 152* n. 1.
[108]On Nicolaus, see Erich Wegerich, O.F.M., "Bio-bibliographische Notizen über Franziskanerlehrer des 15. Jahrhunderts," *Franziskanische Studien* 29 (1942): 174-78. For the manuscript, see Maurus Coster, (handwritten) *Inventarii codicum manuscriptorum latinorum Bibliothecae Vaticanae Ottobonianae*, pt. 1: Ottob. lat. 1-1676 (before 1804), ff. 277*v*-278*r*.
[109]See BAV, Cod. Ottobon. lat. 1442, ff. 146*ra*-155*ra*: "Primus liber De anima. Bonorum honorabilium.... hic incipit liber de anima qui quidem dicitur de anima non quod anima sit subiectum eius sed [MS: secundum] corpus animatum.... (Lib. II: 146*vb*) ....Quae quidem a prioribus. Postquam Philosophus venatus est in primo libro opiniones antiquorum de anima hic in secundo tractat de ipsa anima secundum opinionem propriam.... (Lib. III: 151*vb*) ....De parte autem. In isto tertio libro determinat Aristoteles de parte intellectiva.... (154*vb*) ....Virtus etiam (155*ra*) expulsiva est necessaria ut per eam superfluitas et faex cibi a membris expellatur et sic est finis tertii libri De anima."
[110]Questions on *De anima* are not listed among Iacobus de Viterbio's authentic or dubious works by either Palémon Glorieux, *Répetoire des maîtres en théologie de Paris au XIIIe siècle*, vol. 2 (Études de philosophie médiévale 18: Paris, 1934), 309-12, or David Gutiérrez, O.E.S.A., *De B. Iacobi Viterbiensis, O.E.S.A. Vita, operibus et doctrina theologica* (Roma, 1939), 22-43.

is at least some vague intuition of singulars at the beginning of the process of abstraction and that there exists some kind of intelligible species of the individual. Berubé discovered furthermore that in his *Quaestiones super Metaphysicam* (around questions concerning individuation), Antonius Andreae juxtaposes quotations from the *Quaestiones* with quotations from the *Ordinatio* and elsewhere to the effect of mitigating Scotus' magisterial teaching on the topic, and bringing it back in line with old-fashioned Franciscan tradition. Likewise, Ioannes Canonicus (mid fourteenth-century) employed the same technique in his questions on the eight Books of the *Physics* (in Book 8). Thereafter, the diluted compromise wrought by Antonius and Ioannes, by reference to the *Quaestiones*, became a standard item in at least one Scotistic school in modern times. Concerning the *Quaestiones*, Berubé concludes:

> Le *De anima*, par contre [to Scotus' authentic works], propose une théorie de la connaisance soit sans espèce intellectuale, soit avec espèces intellectuelles singulières. Mais ces théories sont en opposition si radicales avec les enseignements formels du *Commentaire sure les Sentences* et du *Quodlibet* que nous ne croyons pas qu'un même auteur ait pu les écrire. Du point de vue de la connaisance du singulier, le *De anima* nous semble un premier essai de concilier le scotisme avec les théories de la connaisance de franciscains de la fin du XIIIᵉ siècle, notamment de Vital du Four.[111]

Berubé writes with a personal intellectual passion, righteously indignant over the fact that ersatz Scotists have distorted and over-simplified the Master's doctrine for so long. He does not envision another possibility: that the *Quaestiones* are early writings by Scotus, wherein he developed inchoately his own salient ideas about the soul and its knowledge in the context of the traditional pedagogy he had received from his Franciscan teachers. In that case, the *Quaestiones* would represent a synthesis fabricated before the fact of the *Lectura* and later writings, not afterwards by some enthusiastic though reluctant disciple.

Recently, the tide has shifted somewhat again. Leen Spruit judges that the arguments concerning intelligible species in the *Quaestiones De anima* "faithfully represent Duns's thought." His criteria are merely doctrinal. Katherine Tachau, on the other hand, discovered an important fact. In one of his writings, Adam Wodeham cites Scotus and the *Quaestiones* explicitly.[112] More recently, however, Gérard Sondag once more has cast doubt upon the authenticity of the *Quaestiones*, because in at least one of them the author appears to borrow several arguments of Gonsalvus Hispanus nearly verbatim.[113]

A. Consideration of Received Arguments

We need to assess the arguments advanced by scholars denying the authenticity of the *Quaestiones De anima* carefully. Such arguments are of two basic types: 1) historical arguments

---

[111]Camille Berubé, *La connaisance de l'individuel au Moyen Age* (Montréal, 1964), 134-224, at 224. See also Berubé, "Antoine André, temoin et interprète de Scot," *Antonianum* 54 (1979): 386-446, esp. 386-99; "La première école scotiste," *Preuve et raisons à l'Université de Paris. Logique, ontologie et théologie aux XIVe siècle* ed. Z. Kaluza and P. Vignaux (Paris, 1984): 10-24.

[112]Leen Spruit, '*Species intelligibilis*': *From Perception to Knowledge*, 2 vols. (Leiden-New York, 1994), in vol. 1, 259 n. 6; Katherine Tachau, "The Problem of the *Species in medio* at Oxford in the Generation after Ockham," *Mediaeval Studies* 44 (1982): 393-443, at 430-31 n. 127.

[113]Gérard Sondag, *Jean Duns Scot: Prologue de l'Ordinatio*, présentation et traduction annotée (Paris, 1999), 10. Richard Cross, *The Physics of Duns Scotus: The Scientific Context of a Theological Vision* (Oxford, 1998), 10, has accepted them as authentic.

and 2) doctrinal arguments. The historical arguments are not well-developed and none shows acquaintance with the full range of historical evidence to be considered below, but they are rightly construed as textual in nature and claim fundamentally that the *Quaestiones* are a conflation of late thirteenth-century Franciscan philosophical materials with some material or other coming from Duns Scotus' mature writings. The best documented of these arguments is the one advanced by Sondag citing the parallels of sections of the *Quaestiones* with the writings of Gonsalvus Hispanus as evidence that the *Quaestiones* are culled from, and hence dependent upon, the writings of the Spanish Franciscan master. We shall consider the historical arguments first and foremost, holding the doctrinal arguments in abeyance until we have examined the historical arguments.

A few observations regarding the method of study and analysis are warranted at the outset. First, parallels are extremely commonplace among medieval authors who treat similar themes even in quite different literary genres, i.e., the same authorities tend to be adduced and the same opening arguments tend to be recited. Second, in light of the first observation, what will be historically significant and even decisive will be not simply parallels, but *unique* and *close* parallels, that is to say, parallels that cannot be found elsewhere in the relevant literature and ones that have at least a substantial degree of verbal agreement. Should a given parallel be both *unique* and *close*, that parallel would constitute only partial *prima facie* evidence for *influence* or *borrowing*, but not determinative evidence. In addition to being unique and close, parallels that constitute full and proper evidence of borrowing must be clear in terms of directionality. What is at stake in studying the parallels between Gonsalvus and Scotus is whether or not one of these authors has influenced the other and/or whether or not one of these authors has borrowed from the other. To show borrowing, one must be able to point to sections where there are parallels that are unique, close, and unidirectional. As we shall see, it is this last feature that seems to be wanting in the case at hand.

The Case of Gonsalvus Hispanus, *Quaes. disp.* q. 11 'Utrum potentia laudativa qua laudatur Deus si in natura habentis materiam' and Duns Scotus, *Quaes. De anima* q. 15 'Utrum angelus et anima sint compositi ex materia et forma'

Parallel 1

Gonsalvus, *Qq. disp.*, q. 11 (Ed. Amoròs)	Scotus, *De an.* q. 15, n. 44:
Dicitur quod non est inconveniens quod illa forma quae in perficiendo excedit suam materiam, quod perficiat aliam materiam; sicut, e contra, non est inconveniens quod materia, cuius appetitus excedit actualitatem formae, appetit simul aliam formam; talis autem forma quae in perficiendo excedit ipsam materiam est anima intellectiva. Unde perficiens materiam in una parte corporis, idem perficit materiam in alia parte corporis, et ideo non videtur inconveniens quod simul perficiat plures materias.	Ad aliud dicendum est quod non est inconveniens eandem formam perficere plures materias, si in perficiendo excedat suam vel unam materiam; sic est de anima respectu corporis. Videmus enm quod anima per diversas perfectiones unam partem corporis perficit, et aliam et aliter dispositam. Sic in proposito: non videtur inconveniens quod per formam eius perficiat diversas materias non aeque primo, et quae non sunt totaliter unius rationis, quia una est corporalis et alia non.

Parallel 2

Gonsalvus, *Qq. disp.* q. 11 (ed Amoròs, 197):	Scotus, *De an.* q. 15 n. 42:
Dicitur quod non sequitur, si non sit forma adaequata uni materiae, quod propter hoc secundum unum gradum perficit unam materiam, et secundum alium gradum aliam materiam, sicut anima intellectiva non est perfecta adaequata uni parti corporis et tamen non perficit unam partem corporis secundum unum gradum et aliam partem secundum alium gradum; immo ipsa tota secundum totum sui perficit utramque materiam, et secundum totum sui excedit materiam eius.	Ad aliud dicendum est quod sicut secundum ponentes gradus in formis, plures formae possunt unam materiam informare per hoc quod forma praecedens tenet se ex parte materiae et determinat potentialitatem eius, disponendo ipsam ad formam sequentem, sic, econverso, una forma potest plures materias informare per hoc quod altera se tenet ex parte formae, scilicet, illa quae est sibi intimior. Et sic totum compositum ex materia et forma animae informat corpus, non ratione materiae, sed tantum ratione formae principaliter informantis materiam propriam. Ad maiorem ergo rationis dicendum est quod ipsa tota informat corpus, et isto modo potest dici quod secundum se totam, non tamen ratione totius sed ratione partis. Et sic 'secundum se' praedicat rationem informandi, non tamen secundum se totam informat.

Parallel 3

Gonsalvus, *Qq. disp.* q. 11 (Ed. Amoròs, 214):	Scotus, *De an.* q. 15 n. 19:
Primum ostenditur primo sic. Principia debent proportionari principiatis illorum; igitur magis et verius sunt aliqua principia in quibus magis inveniuntur proprietates illorum principiorum; sed proprietates materiae, tum quantum ad fieri tum quantum ad esse, verius inveniuntur in incorporalibus omnibus quam in corporalibus; ergo magis et verius erit materia in incorporalibus quam in corporalibus. Assumpta patet. Quid proprietas materiae quantum ad suum esse, est quod sit ingenerabilis et incorruptibilis; proprietas vero eius quantum ad fieri est quod producitur in esse per creationem a sola potentia creante. Haec autem singulariter conveniunt incorporalibus; ergo materia, quantum ad proprietates sui esse et fieri magis proportionatur incorporalibus quam corporalibus. Ergo etc.	Secunda ratio principalis est: sicut operatio arguit formam, ita proprietas materiae materiam; sed proprietas materiae quantum ad suum esse et fieri suum reperiuntur verius in spiritualibus quam corporalibus. Proprietas enim materiae quantum ad esse est quod est ingenerabilis; sed quantum ad fieri quod tantum producitur per creationem. Haec autem maxime reperiuntur in spiritualibus…

In these parallels, can we say with any degree of confidence who is borrowing from whom? The common material in the first two parallels is introduced in the text of Gonsalvus by 'dicitur', often (though not always) a hint in Scholastic literature that the author is summarizing views garnered from elsewhere. Now it is extremely important to emphasize the point that the historical arguments against authenticity are committed to a dependency of the 'Scotus' text on Gonsalvus' text and not the reverse; indeed, those denying the authenticity of the *Quaestiones* need the latter to be dependent upon Gonsalvus, in order to render plausible their overarching hypothesis that the true author of the *Quaestiones* is a later Francsican writer trying to synthesize the newer teachings of the mature Scotus with the older traditional teaching of the Franciscan school. The nature of these parallels, however, renders it impossible to say with any degree of certainty whether one author was borrowing directly from another. The parallels are themselves best characterized as indeterminate in their directionality and both sets of passages could likewise originate from some third source available to both authors. Moreover, there are possible historical explanations for the resemblance of a few arguments in Scotus' *Quaestiones De anima* and Gonsalvus' disputed questions. As we noted above, Scotus assisted Gonsalvus in disputes in 1302-1303 and may have then introduced arguments from his prior course on *De anima* into his Master's script (see § 2.K n.5, above), or as we argue below (see § 5.B Chronology), the resemblances may be explained by the fact that Gonsalvus and Scotus were together in the Parisian Franciscan *studium* in the late 1280s.

Since the example of the parallels with Gonsalvus of Spain's theological writings represents the only properly historical argument advanced by scholars, we must turn, however briefly, to the doctrinal arguments. The doctrinal arguments point to three main areas of discrepancy between the teaching of the *Quaestiones* and that found in Scotus' other writings: 1) concerning the hylemorphic composition of spiritual substances; 2) the reality of intelligible species; and 3) the mind's need to have recourse to phantasms in every act of cognition. In regard to the latter two doctrinal areas, namely, intelligible species and the necessity of recourse to the phantasm in acts of intellectual cognition, the main point that emerges from a careful reading of the critically established text is that its author does endorse intelligible species, though he resolves certain questions in such a way as to indicate how someone denying intelligible species could answer the same questions. Evidence that the author of the text does endorse intelligible species is readily available from the close of q. 17, which reads: "Teneas quam partem volueris. Prima tamen videtur communior et verior, et 'qui potest capere, capiat.'" Furthermore, the texts on knowledge of the singular in the *Quaestiones super De anima* are generally consistent with the various (and not entirely straightforward) accounts that Scotus gives of intellectual knowledge of the singular in such texts as the *Quaestiones super libros Metaphysicorum* and the *Ordinatio*.[114]

The really problematic area seems to be the first issue, namely, the hylemorphic composition of the spiritual substances, because the opinion that Scotus is taken to propose in the *Quaestiones* seems diametrically opposed to that which he defends in all of his other known writings. To resolve the question of whether or not the opinion expressed by Scotus is actually as opposed to his other writings as it is usually thought to be, however, requires that we examine closely the structure and wording of the pertinent question, q. 15. The title of the question is 'Utrum intellectus noster sit immaterialis', and after the usual opening arguments, there is a response that begins 'Respondeo quod probabiliter potest dici quod in anima est materia, et secundum fundamenta Philosophi et eorum qui ponunt contrarium.' Now Cavellus already in the

---

[114]Scotus, *Quaestiones super libros Metaphysicorum Aristotelis*, ed. R. Andrews, et al. (St. Bonaventure, NY, 1997), II q. 2-3 n.76-122 (OPh III 223-235); ibid., VII q. 15 n. 14-32 (OPh IV 298-306); Scotus, *Ordinatio* IV d. 45 q. 3 [17-19] in Marilyn M. Adams and Allan B. Wolter, "Memory and Intuition: A Focal Debate in Fourteenth Century Cognitive Psychology," *Franciscan Studies* 53 (1993), 205-7.

seventeenth century doubted that this text should be understood to contain Scotus' own solution[115] and, indeed, our historical research on the text and the sources indicates as much: despite the fact that Scotus begins at least one of the principal arguments in this section with the seemingly endorsing phrase 'Quarto, idem sic ostendo..', he is following, apropos of that very paragraph, the views of William de la Mare and others. What he is actually doing in this passage is pointing to an inconsistency between the Thomistic rationale regarding the principle of individuation and the Thomistic denial of hylemorphic composition in individual separated substances. In the actual solution to the question, which begins at n. 25 with the words "Dicendum ad quaestionem quod si in anima et angelo est materia, quod est eiusdem rationis cum materia corporalium.", Scotus is not taking a straightforward position on the question but is instead insisting on the unity of matter as an ontological principle. In this regard, he is siding with such figures as William de la Mare against such thinkers as John Peckham on the nature of matter. The solution to this question, accordingly, does not provide very strong textual grounds for alleging doctrinal inconsistencies between the *Quaestiones* and the rest of Scotus' writings.

B. Manuscript Evidence

The strongest evidence for the authenticity of the *Quaestiones super libros De anima Aristotelis* is to be found within the manuscripts that preserve the work. Certainly, the majority of the manuscripts that contain the work attribute, whether in an explicit or a list of questions or a table of contents, the work to Duns Scotus, as may be readily gathered from the manuscript descriptions above and seen in the following tables:

Manuscripts in which the *Quaestiones super secundum et tertium De anima* are attributed to Duns Scotus:

PVWZ^{1}Z^2 (14th cent.)
ADEFGHJKLMNORSTU (15th cent.)

Manuscripts in which the *Quaestiones super libros De anima Aristotelis* are anonymous:

BQX (14th cent.)
C (15th cent.)

Yet the proper significance of these ascriptions needs to be gauged in light of the quality of the ascriptions and the range of witnesses that attribute the work to Scotus.

Let us start with the quality of ascriptions. Each of the following manuscripts among the collated witnesses attribute the work to Duns Scotus: **F,H,K,L,M,N,O** and **W**. If we examine the wording of the formulae of attribution, we discover a remarkable similarity among the ascriptions:

---

[115] Hugo Cavellus, *Annotationes ad q. 15: conclusio 1* in *Opera omnia*, ed. Vivès III, 559: "....scilicet Divi Thomae I parte quaest. 50, art. 2. Doctor non ponit hanc conclusionem ut suam, sed tantum ait probabiliter deduci ex fundamentis Philosophi, et Divi Thomae.... Videtur ergo, cum Philosophus et Divus Thomas dicant id quod non habet materiam, multiplicari non posse, et simul admittant esse plures individuas animas rationales, ex hoc eorum fundamento, admittendam esse materiam in anima rationali." For a recent study of Hugh of Cavellus' annotations, see P. Alessandro M. Apollonio, FI, *L'intellezione dei singolari materiali nelle "Annotationes" di Hugo Cavellus alle* Quaestiones super libros Aristotelis De anima *attribuite al Beato G. Duns Scoto* (Roma: Pontificia Universitatis Sanctae Crucis: Facultas Philosophiae, 2003).

F= Expliciunt quaestiones venerabilis D. subtilis magistri Ioannis Scoti de ordine minorum super 2 et 3 De anima, etc.

H= Expliciunt quaestiones D. super secundum et tertium de anima.

K= Expliciunt quaestiones doctor[is] subtil[is] super secundum et tertium de anima scriptae domino Ioanne Saundyr

L= Expliciunt quaestiones Doctoris Subtilis super 2 et 3 De anima Oxoniae scriptae per fratrem Petrum Pauli de Nycopia. Lord Ihesu Mercy

M= Expliciunt quaestiones super secundum et tertium libros de anima secundum Scotum, alias doctorem subtilem

N= Expliciunt quaestiones doctoris subtilis super secundum et tertium de anima

Quite clearly this list of ascriptions must arise from a precisely worded original that took pains to specify which books of Aristotle's were the objects of discussion in the work as well as the author of the work. The only qualification to be noted about the manuscripts listed above is that MS **M**, in addition to the explicit listed found at the close of the text, bears a title at the outset, written in the same hand as the explicit given, that reads 'Quaestiones Scotuli super secundum et tertium libros de Anima'. Yet this attribution is entirely without resonance in the manuscripts with which **M** is most closely associated, **H** and **L**, and, indeed, without any correlate in any other known manuscript. Furthermore, as is clear from the Latin 'Scotuli', the meaning of ascription itself is unclear: it may be taken as an attribution to one of several persons known as 'Scotellus' or 'Scotulus,' chief among whom is Antonius Andreae;[116] or, it may be taken as referring to the same person as the explicit with the added note of expressing his youth.

Now, though not all the manuscripts that attribute the work to Scotus word their ascriptions in this precise fashion, we should note the range of witnesses that contain the ascription as well as the wording of their statements. As we have seen above, manuscripts **N** and **O** derive their text from Epsilon; **H**, **L**, and **M** arise from Beta; **K** comes from Delta; and **F** is a copy of Gamma. Yet the wording of the ascriptions of these manuscripts is remarkably similar and consistent. The repeating pattern of wording must originate not from any one of the proximate models mentioned—Epsilon, Beta, Delta, or Gamma—but from their ultimately shared common source, MS Alpha. What this, in turn, implies is that MS Alpha must have had the ascribing formula. Hence, we must conclude that the Urexemplar from which all known copies derive their text carried an ascription to Duns Scotus and that the ascription is not the product of later copyists, librarians or scholars.

C. Parallels to Other Scotistic Works

The parallels to the writings of Duns Scotus known to be authentic are too numerous to list in their entirety here. Let the following examples serve as illustrations.

Illustrative parallels between Scotus' QQ. De anima and the Oxford theological commentaries:

Example #1:

Scotus, *QQ. De anima* q. 12 n. 8:	Scotus, *Lectura*, I d. 3 p. 3 q. 2-3, n. 348 (ed. Vaticana, XVI, 362-3):	Scotus, *Ordinatio*, I d. 3 p. 3 q. 2 n. 458 (ed. Vaticana, III, 277):

---

[116]The ascription was at least at one point taken by Charles Balić to refer to Antonius Andreae. Balić, "Sermo P. Caroli Balić," 21-22.

qui, secundum eos, non est principium activum… Praeterea, indeterminatum ad plura non potest determinari ad unum nisi per aliquid impressum sibi detrmininans; potentiae praedictae sunt indeterminatae, quantum [sunt] de se, ad actus diversos; igitur in eis est species impressa ipsas determinans ad agendum; tale autem sic detrminatum ab alio est tantum in potentia passiva; igitur, etc.	Item, species, ut dicunt, requiritur etiam in intellectu propter determinationem potentiae ad actum, quia quod est indeterminatum ad multa, non determinatur ex nisi per aliquid quod de novo sibi adveniat; igitur cum intellectus antequam intellexit sit indifferens ad intelligendum quodcumque intelligibile, non intelliget antequam determinetur per aliquid; sed illud sic determinans intellectum non potest esse nisi species.	Ad hoc etiam additur quod agens indeterminatum non potest agere actionem determinatam, vel circa obiectum determinatum, nisi determinetur; intellectus de se est indeterminatus ad omne intelligibile et ad omnem intellectionem; ergo ad hoc quod intelligat, requiritur determinatio aliqua; illa non est nisi per speciem aliquam, — ergo species intelligibilis est principium determinativum.

Example #2

Scotus, *QQ. De anima*, q. 12, n. 13: Alii ponunt quod sunt sic passivae, scilicet non distinguendo speciem ab actu cognoscendi nisi secundum rationem tantum, quia species est illud quo aliquid ab obiecto imprimitur in potentia, sed illud idem est actus cognoscendi, causatus ab obiecto tantum effective, Et quia potentia cognitiva est tantum receptiva speciei, ideo est tantum receptiva actus intelligendi, non elicitiva.	Scotus, *Lectura*, I d. 3 p. 3 q. 2-3 n. 349 (ed. Vaticana, XVI, 363): Alia est opinio aliquorum qui sequuntur primam opinionem et dicta eadem opinantur, sed superaddunt quod non solum species requiritur propter actum intelligendi et quod intellectus de se non elicit actum intelligendi, sed species recepta in potentia intellectiva est eadem cum actu suo qui est 'intelligere'. Unde dicunt quod notitia genita est species intelligibilis, si obiectum non sit praesens secundum se nisi in specie; si autem obiectum sit prasens secundum se, tunc actus intelligendi est idem cum obiecto.	Scotus, *Ordinatio*, I d. 3 p. 3 q. 2 n. 460 (ed. Vaticana, III, 277-8): Sexta opinio – quae redit in idem quantum ad conclusionem huius quaestionis – est quod ipsa notitia actualis genita, sive in sensu sive in intellectu, est species; et tunc sicut formalis ratio gignendi 'speciem actualem quae dicitur notitia actualis' est ratio obiecti vel species obiecti in memoria, ita sequitur, quoad propositum, quod ratio formalis gignendi notitiam actualem est ipsum obiectum vel aliqua species in virtute obiecti: et hoc ita, quod quando obiectum est in se praesens, ab eo generatur species quae est intellectio, quando autem non est in se praesens sed per speciem in memoria, tunc ab ista specie vel virtute istius speciei gignetur alia, quae erit intellectio.

Illustrative parallels between Scotus' QQ. De anima, the Oxford theological commentaries, and the Reportatio Parisiensis I-A:

Scotus, *QQ. De anima*, q. 17 n. 9-11:	Scotus, *Lectura*, I d. 3 p. 3 q. 1 [n. 269. 272. 274] (ed. Vaticana, XVI, 332-335):	Scotus, *Ordinatio*, I d. 3 p. 3 q. 1 [n. 353. 355. 359] (ed. Vaticana, III, 212-218):	Scotus, *Reportatio Parisiensis* I-A d. 3 q. 4: (Oxford, Merton College, Ms. 59, f. 36r.)
Sed dices quod hoc verum est eodem lumine, sed luminibus diversis potest eadem species diversa repraesentare, ut patet de noctilucis, quae in die videntur colorata lumine solis sed de nocte lucentia lumine proprio; sic species in phantasmate lumine phantasiae vel virtutis sensitivae potest repraesentare singulare, lumine tamen intellectus agentis penetrante phantasma universale.	Sed dices ad hoc, secundum eos, quod eadem species in alio et alio lumine potest diversa obiecta repraesentare et habere alium modum repraesentandi, sicut patet in exemplo: illud quod lucet de nocte, non est nisi eadem res quae movet ut coloratum de die, et tamen propter diversa lumina – de die et de nocte – movet ut lucens et lucidum de nocte, et ut coloratum de die. Sic haec species in virtute phantastica in ratione phantasmatis repraesentat singulare, et sic tantum ut singulare movet; sed tamen ut est in lumine intellectus agentis, cuius lumine irradiatur, sic movet ut universale.	Responsio: idem repraesentativum in alio et alio lumine, repraesentat obiectum sub alia et alia ratione, sicut nocte-lucentia in lumine diei se repraesentant sub ratione coloratorum, in lumine noctis sub ratione lucentium.	Dicetur quod non est inconveniens eandem speciem repraesentare diversa et opposita repraesentabilia in alio et alio lumine, ut patet in noctilucentibus qui in alio et alio lumine repraesentantur colorata et lucida. Sic in proposito: per lumen intellectus agentis et phantasiae eadem species potest repraesentare opposita in obiecto.
Sed hoc non valet, quia noctilucae repraesentant diversa obiecta de die et de nocte, quia lux et color sunt diversa, et tunc necessario hoc est per diversas species; vel si non sint diversa obiecta,	Aliter etiam dico quod, secundum veritatem, est alia qualitas quae lucet de nocte et alia quae de die, sicut lux et color; et de die etiam movet ut lucidum, sed non percipitur, quia lux minor obumbratur	Nec exemplum aliquid valet ad propositum, immo est ad oppositum, quia vel duae qualitates sunt in tali corpore, ut lux et color, quarum altera multiplicat se in luce maiore praesente, alia in minore, quando	Nec exemplum ad propositum, sed ad oppositum, tum quia vel sunt duae qualitates sensibiles in noctilucentibus, scilicet lux et color, quare altera multiplicat se sensibiliter et

oportet dicere quod huiusmodi habent aliquam qualitatem diversam a luce et colore, virtualiter tamen utrumque continentem; et ideo in die poterit gignere speciem repraesentativam unius, scilicet coloris, et in nocte repraesentativam lucis; sic igitur semper habebit diversas species in quantum repraesentantur in eo diversa. Sic in proposito de universali et singulari.

Praeterea, cuiuslibet potentiae realis activae est actio realis; intellectus agens est potentia activa realis; igitur operatio realis et terminus realis. Sed intelligere non est operatio eius, nec terminus suae operationis saltem propinquus terminus, quia non intelligit, sed operatio eius est facere intelligibilia in potentia actu intelligibilia; fiunt autem aliqua intelligibilia actu per abstractionem speciei; abstrahere igitur speciem est actus eius et species intelligibilis abstracta est terminus eius. Non potest autem talis species in phantasia esse, quae

propter lumen maius; unde multiplicat lumen suum de die sicut de nocte, quemadmodum et stellae; sed ut coloratum non mutat de nocte, quia non est sufficiens lumen in quo posset movere. Et ideo quia species in virtute phantastica est singulare tantum, secundum se habens unam rationem reprasentandi, ideo quocumque lumine posito tantum repraesentabit singulare.

Praeterea, tertio arguitur ex parte luminis. ... Et si non sit [actio intellectus agentis] aeterna, sed quandoque est, quandoque non, quaero quis est terminus istius actionis? Non potest dari aliud quam universale, nec secundum veritatem nec secundum eos. Universale autem nihil est in se nisi in quantum est lucens in aliquo in quo prius non fuit sub aliqua ratione entis realis, quia aliter non est nisi intentio quaedam, et terminus actionis realis debet esse quid reale; sed phantasma non habet aliud quam prius habuit ante

nihil alterum efficacius movet (vel simul utraque multiplicat se in luce maiore, sed efficiacius movens percipitur et minus efficaciter movens non percipitur: sicut stellae multiplicant de die radios suos, nec tamen videntur, quia aliud luminosius efficacius movet visum) – vel si una qualitas sensibilis in tali corpore, ipsa in alio et alio lumine causat diversa repraesentativa, aliud scilicet in maiore, aliud in minore: et ita semper stat quod non est idem repraesentativum obiecti sub diversa ratione repraesentabilis, quantumcumque aliud lumen et aliud concurrat.

Ex secunda via arguo sic: intellectus agens est mere potentia activa, secundum Philosophum III *De anima*, tum quia est 'quo est omnia facere', tum quia comparatur ad possibilem etiam 'ut ars ad materiam'; ergo potest habere actionem realem. Omnis actio realis habet aliquem terminum realem. Ille terminus realis non recipitur in

repraesentat rem illam in luce maiori et alteram in minori, utraque tamen multiplicat se et repraesentat rem in utroque lumine, sed efficacius movens et repraesentans percipitur et minus efficaciter repraesentans non percipitur. Exemplum de stellis, quae ita multiplicant radios suos de die sicut de nocte, licet propter maius lumen non appareant; vel si est una qualitas sensibilis in tali corpore, ipsa virtualiter continet duo repraesentativa. Color enim quodammodo continet lucem cum sit lux in corpore terminato, et ideo in alio et alio lumine causat diversa repraesentativa; aliud in maiori lumine, scilicet de die, et aliud in minori, scilicet de nocte. Et ita semper stat quod non est idem repraesentativum obiecti sub diversa ratione repraesentabilis, quantumcumque aliud et aliud lumen concurrat. Vel si est unum formaliter, diversum tamen virtualiter, quia continet virtualiter

corporalis est et extensa, non autem talis species; igitur oportet eam esse in intellectu possibili.	actionem, quia secundum te nihil actione intellectus agentis causatur in phantasmate, unde concedunt quod phantasma nihil habet quod prius non habuit. Igitur oportet quod universale sit terminus istius actionis secundum quod splendet in specie reali in memoria ante actum intelligendi.	phantasmate, quia ‡illud receptum esset extensum, et ita intellectus agens non transferret ab ordine in ordinem, — nec illud esset magis proportionatum intellectui possibili quam phantasma‡ ; nec etiam intellectus agens causat aliquid in phantasmatibus, quia non est suum passivum, secundum praedictas auctoritates; ergo tantum recipitur in intellectu possibili, quia intellectus agens nullius est receptivus. Illud primum causatum non potest poni actus intelligendi, quia primus terminus actionis intellectus agentis est universale in actu, quia 'transfert de ordine ad ordinem'; universale autem in actu praecedit actum intelligendi (sicut praeassumptum est in antecdente), quia obiectum sub ratione obiecti praecedit actum.…	diversa, et ideo potest causare diversa repraesentativa, scilicet lucem et colorem in alio et alio lumine. Dicetur quod terminus actionis intellectus agentis est obiectum universale sub ratione universalis lucens in phantasmate. Contra: universale obiectum sub ratione universalis non esse nisi deminutum ut cognitum quemadmodum Hercules in statuta non habet esse nisi deminutum, quia repraesentatum in imagine; sed si aliquod esse reale habet, hoc est in quantum est in aliquo ut repraesentante ipsum sub illa ratione, ita scilicet quod intellectus agens facit aliquid repraesentativum universalis de eo quod fuit repraesentativum singularis. Ergo cum terminus actionis realis non sit obiectum habens esse deminutum, ut esse cognitum vel repraesentativum vel cognitum, sed aliquid reale, sequitur quod realis actio intellectus agentis terminatur ad realem formam in

			exsistentia qua formaliter repraesentat universale ut universale, quam formam realem concomitatur terminus intentionalis ut obiectum universale secundum esse repraesentatum quod habet in specie.

In addition to such parallels, which could be multiplied, we find certain references that are likely to be references to Scotus' own *Quaestiones super libros Metaphysicorum Aristotelis* and *Quaestiones in librum Praedicamentorum Aristotelis*, since the doctrinal content they contain are strikingly similar to remarks of Scotus in those works:

QQ. De anima q. 6 n. 12 to *QQ. in lib. Praedic.* qq. 30-36 n.54.n.57-60 (OPh I 487.489).

QQ. De anima q. 6 n. 13 to *QQ. in lib. Praedic.* qq. 30-36 n.54.n.57. 76 (OPh I 487.489.494).

QQ. De anima q. 7 n. 18 to *QQ. in lib. Metaph.* V q. 11 n. 56 (OPh III 585).

D. EXTERNAL EVIDENCE: CITATIONS AND USES

Among the earliest witnesses to Scotus' *Quaestiones De anima* is a list and abbreviation of the questions compiled by Guillelmus de Missali, probably in the late fourteenth century. This list, preserved in MSS **W** and **Y**, cites only the first 22 questions; immediately after q. 22, in the twenty-third position, Guillelmus abbreviates a question different from the q. 23 of our edition; see Guillelmus' list in the appendix to this edition.

The first known explicit citation of the *Quaestiones super libros De anima* in a separate philosophical or theological work is that of Adam Wodeham in his *Lectura secunda*. Here is the citation and the comparable text of the *Quaestiones super libros De anima*:

Adam Wodeham, *Lectura secunda*, I prol. q. 3 n. 9 (ed. Gál-Wood, 81):

> Nec solum decipitur tunc auditus erroribus rectis sed reflexis, quia homo quandoque somniat se somniare et imaginatur se imaginari et syllogizare et discurrere et componere et dividere [et] multa huiusmodi. Cuius causam assignat Scotus super *De anima* quaestione 9, quia actus imaginandi multiplicat speciem suam in organum alterius sensibilis, etc.

Scotus, *QQ. De anima*, q. 9 n. 16 [ad quartum argumentum principale]:

> Ad aliud dicendum quod imaginatio sentit actum proprium: imaginamur enim nos imaginari vel imaginatum fuisse, et memoramur nos memoratum fuisse, et somniamus nos somniare, sicut experimur manifeste.

The importance of this attestation may be garnered from several considerations. First, as one can readily see, Wodeham's citation is explicit and correctly refers to the question by number, something that is telling in terms of the primitive accounting of the number of the questions. Second, Wodeham cites the text as if it should be familiar to his Norwich audience, something that is perhaps even more surprising. Finally, we should note that it is precisely a reference in this same writing of Wodeham that establishes, in combination with the manuscript ascriptions for that work, the authenticity of the *Quaestiones super primum librum Perihermenias*.

Another reference comes from an unexpected source: a commentary composed of short questions, *dubia*, and literal summary preserved in two Prague manuscripts (**Praha, Knihovna Metropolitní Kapituli, Cods. L.51** and **M.89** above). These two witnesses were thought to contain other copies of the *Quaestiones De anima*, but they prove to contain a work that both manuscripts attribute to Antonius Andreae. Furthermore, one concludes from collating the two manuscripts that they are not copies of each other since they each supply text for homeoteleutic omissions found in the other copy. Hence, their attributions must be rooted in the source-text of both and not in any proclivities of the individual scribes. Though both manuscripts are from the fifteenth century, the text they preserve is unlikely to come from after 1340; in the discussion of such controversial topics as the intelligible and sensible species the author does not mention any position that denies such species altogether, though he includes summaries of the positions of both Henry of Ghent and Godfrey of Fontaines. In other words, the writer of the work seems to be entirely unaware of the positions of such authors as William of Ockham and Adam Wodeham.

Throughout the text, the author of the 'Antonine' commentary refers to a 'doctor' whose positions are either being explained, upheld or defended. But it is clear from the material found in the first book that the doctor of the greatest interest is Duns Scotus. Here are some examples:

> His praemissis, est una opinio de ista materia, habens quinque conclusiones. Prima quod impossibile est naturam divinam abstractive concipi primo modo loquendo de notitia abstractiva, scilicet concipiendo ipsam et non suam exsistentiam. Ratio eius: quia exsistentia actualis est de conceptu quidditativo et per se primo modo ipsius essentiae divinae et naturae, ut dicunt. Quod probant. Tum quia essentia divina est ex se formaliter necesse esse, ergo esse. Tum quia alias esset natura possibilis et indifferens ad esse et ad non-esse, quod est impossibile cum sit purus actus. Tum quia ad quaestionem factam de natura divina vel de Deo 'quid est,' communiter respondetur ab omnibus doctoribus quod est ipsum esse. (Hoc dicit Robertus Lincolniensis super principium II Posteriorum et Avicenna et Algazel in sua metaphysica. Hoc etiam dicit Magister Ioannes Scotus Doctor et primi libri quaestione prima. Dicit enim quod qui videret essentiam divinam sicuti est quod in suo conceptu includitur ipsum esse primo modo non secundo modo. Item in suo Quodlibet dicit quod in toto ordine divinorum est accipere unum primum quod est essentia et quae vocatur esse nec est in potentia ad esse. Item septima quaestione sui Quodlibet, utrum per rationem naturalem posset investigari omnipotentia divina, dicit hoc idem, ut videtur.). (Praha, Knihovna Metropolitní Kapituli, Cod. L.51, f. 85*rb*)

> Fundantur autem illae dispositiones per totum corpus, una super aliam sicut est ex parte obiecti contrarietas qualitatum passivarum quae sequitur materiam fundat contrarietatem activarum quae sequitur formam, sicut materia sustentat formam. Aristoteles autem non numeravit hunc sensum pro duobus licet sint duo realiter et specifice distincti, quia in qualibet parte corporis inveniuntur ambo; non sic de gustu qui numeratur cum tactu nec facit aeque distinctos gradus in

entibus seu in animalibus. Uterque enim illorum etiam tactuum in animali reperitur. Ista videtur fuisse intentio huius doctoris de istorum tactuum distinctione. (Praha, Knihovna Metropolitní Kapituli, Cod. L.51, f. 95*va*)

Ad quartum quod ideo in capite est coextensus nervus cum carne, licet videatur dicere Doctor ille quod non secundum quod est ibi aliquid loco nervi, puta cartalago (Praha, Knihovna Metropolitní Kapituli, Cod. L.51, f. 96*vb*; cf. *Quaestiones De anima*, q. 2, n. 6. n. 13)

The key point for the authenticity of the *Quaestiones De anima* occurs in the commentary on the second book, wherein the 'Antonine' author notes, according to the text of both manuscripts:

Ista est opinio huius Doctoris Scoti [add. mg. P^2], et in commento et in quaestionibus istis *De anima*. (Praha, Knihovna Metropolitní Kapituli, Cod. M.89, f. 250*r*)

Ista est opinio huius Doctoris et in commento et in quaestionibus istis *De Anima*. (Praha, Knihovna Metropolitní Kapituli, Cod. L.51, f. 99*va*)

In addition to these references to the text being authored by Duns Scotus, we must note the multiple uses of the text during the first decades of the fourteenth century. As has already been noted by Fr. Berubé, there are multiple early uses of the text in the writings of John the Canon and Antonius Andreae.[117]

Conclusion: Let us summarize the evidence for the authenticity of the *Quaestiones De anima*. The work must have been attributed to Duns Scotus in Alpha, the copy from which all known witnesses derive. The work is ascribed to Scotus explicitly by Adam Wodeham and Guillelmus de Missali; it is known and used by both of them as well as Antonius Andreae and William Alnwick. Furthermore, the work is attributed to Scotus by the author of a commentary on *De anima*, itself ascribed to Antonius Andreae, which likely was written prior to 1340.

Perhaps a comparative note regarding the strength of attestations for authenticity would be in order. The reasons for attributing the *Quaestiones super libros Perihermenias* to Duns Scotus are based primarily on the ascriptions of the surviving manuscripts and secondarily on the attestation provided by early users of the text such as Antonius Andreae and Adam Wodeham. The evidence available for attributing the *Quaestiones De anima* to Duns Scotus is practically the same. If, as is commonly believed among the majority of modern scholars, the attribution of the *Quaestiones in libros Perihermenias* is not subject to any serious doubts, then the attribution of the *Quaestiones De anima* to Scotus should not be either. Speaking as historians, the present editors can see no clear reason to doubt either one of the works, but rather propose that to doubt one work while not questioning the other is a violation of the principle '*De similibus simile fiat iudicium*'. Consequently, based on the preponderance of evidence, internal and external, we conclude that the *Quaestiones super secundum et tertium librum De anima* are the work of Blessed John Duns Scotus.

E. Translation Used by Scotus

Since Duns Scotus' work is not a literal commentary, but rather questions, there has been no need to reconstruct precisely the version that he read. What we have found in checking his occasional quotations, however, is that his text is based upon a Latin version similar to that

---

[117] Berubé, *La connaissance de l'individuel*, 240-41.

accompanying R.-A. Gauthier's edition of St. Thomas Aquinas' *Sentencie libri De anima* in volume XLV[1] of the Leonine edition.

F. SOURCES USED BY SCOTUS

The range of sources employed by Scotus in the *Quaestiones De anima* is practically identical with that used in the writing of the *Lectura*, *Ordinatio* and *Reportatio Parisiensis* I-A. The chief sources throughout the 23 questions are the commentaries upon Aristotle's *De anima* of Averroes, Thomas Aquinas and Giles of Rome, and the sections of Peter John Olivi's *Summa* (a revised commentary on the second book of Peter Lombard's *Sentences*) that deal with sensation and intellection, mainly questions 58 and 72.

The sources, however, become much more similar to those of the theological writings and much more complex once Scotus reaches the questions on intellect and will: q. 11 and following. In fact, the questions themselves undergo a metamorphosis at just that point. They are suddenly transformed from relatively brief questions that occasion few digressions and even fewer discussions of alternative views to questions containing long digressions, interspersed with complicated sequences of arguments and counterarguments on behalf of divergent opinions, a style of approach reminiscent of Scotus' *QQ. in Metaph.* and, doubtless, one pointing to the origins of the work in the classroom. In this second and more philosophically interesting section of the work, Scotus is heavily indebted to the following sources indicated throughout the *apparatus fontium*: Thomas Aquinas' *Summa theologiae* and *Summa contra gentiles*, Giles of Rome's *Quodlibeta* and *Quaestiones disputatae de cognitione angelorum*, Henry of Ghent's *Quodlibeta* and *Summa*, Godfrey of Fontaines' *Quodlibeta* and *Quaestiones disputatae*, Peter John Olivi's *Summa*, Roger Marston's *Quodlibeta*, Matthew of Aquasparta's *Quaestiones disputatae de cognitione*, John Peckham's *Quodlibeta* and *Tractatus de anima*, Richard of Meddleton's *Commentaria in libros Sententiarum*, John of Paris' *Quaestiones in libros Sententiarum*, and possibly the first of James of Viterbo's *Quodlibeta*.

Of these sources, the one that we would like to highlight is Giles of Rome's *De cognitione angelorum*. A little read work, Giles' *De cognitione* is actually a masterful summary of commonly held as well as distinctly Aegidian views on human psychology. Indeed, Giles carefully distinguishes in his text the more common interpretations of Aristotelian psychological principles from his own opinions, even while arguing forcibly for the preferability of the latter. Furthermore, he reviews in considerable detail Henry of Ghent's *Quodlibet V* q. 14 and the related texts by the Flemish master that deny intelligible species. So carefully does Giles do this that, practically speaking, one could gain a complete account of Henry's views just from reading the first two or three questions of the *De cognitione*. One is not surprised, then, to discover that many teachers and scholars at the close of the thirteenth century turned to Giles' work on the angels for aid when preparing their own lectures on human and angelic psychology; indeed, in our readings for the sources of the *Quaestiones De anima*, we have found the following authors exhibiting a considerable degree of dependence upon Giles' *De cognitione angelorum*: in Paris, James of Viterbo, John of Paris, Vital du Four, and Gonsalvus Hispanus; at Oxford, Thomas Sutton and William Ware. To this list, we must add John Duns Scotus.

To show the degree of Scotus' dependence upon Giles of Rome, we present the following comparable, illustrative texts:

Scotus, *QQ. De anima* q. 17 n. 16:	Scotus, *Ordinatio* I d. 3 p. 3 q.1 n. 380 (ed. Vaticana, III, 231):	Giles of Rome, *De cognitione angelorum* q. 5 (ed. Venice, 1503, f. 88ra-b):

Ad primum in oppositum, moderni dicunt quod differt ratio agendi et ratio agentis. Verum est autem quod species repraesentat obiectum in illa ratione agendi sub qua nata est imprimi; hoc autem est sub ratione naturae absolute consideratae, non autem sub ratione agentis, quod est particulare, et ideo species repraesentat universale.	Ideo respondeo quod aliqua potest esse 'ratio agendi', et aliqua 'ratio agentis'. Singularitas est condicio agentis, non ratio agendi, sed ratio agendi est ipsa forma in singulari, secundum quam singulare agit. — Cum ergo accipitur quod 'quaecumque species giginitur ab aliquo, repraesentat ipsum secundum illam rationem secundum quam gignitur ab eo', si intelligatur, de 'ratione gignentis', falsa est, si de 'ratione gignendi' concedi potest, — et tunc non sequitur quod repraesentat ipsum sub ratione singularis, sed sub ratione naturae, quia 'ratio naturae' est ratio gignendi.	Tertia autem via [ostendendi quomodo species intelligibilis possit movere intellectum angelicum] sumitur, prout illa species comparatur ad obiectum quod repraesentat. Nam illa species non agit [ita] quod ei attribuatur actio, sed agit quia est ratio agendi, sicut nec calor calefacit, sed est ratio calefaciendi. Nunc autem inter causas agendi videmus hanc distinctionem quod aliquid principaliter agit et aliquid agit in virtute alterius. Et hanc distinctionem quam videmus inter ipsas rationes actionum, nam aliquid est ratio agendi secundum se, aliquid vero est ratio agendi in virtute alterius. Dupliciter ergo in talibus potest esse defectus: primo, si non agat, sed sit solum ratio agendi; secundo, si non sit ratio agendi secundum se sed sit ratio agendi in virtute alterius. Utrumque defectum habet species intelligibilis. Primo non agit sed solum est ratio agendi…Secundo deficit huiusmodi species intelligibilis quia non solum non est agens, sed est ratio agendi; sed non est ratio agendi secundum se, sed magis est ratio agendi, ut est repraesentativa obiecti.

§ 4: NATURE, FUNCTION AND CHRONOLOGY OF THE *QUAESTIONES SUPER SECUNDUM ET TERTIUM DE ANIMA*

A. Nature and Function of the Work

Scotus' *Quaestiones De anima* are not a commentary on Aristotle's *De anima*. Scotus does not expound Aristotle's text and he seldom engages the actual arguments of Aristotle and his commentators. Indeed, he more frequently addresses the arguments of theologians, Thomas by name and others whom he recites or abbreviates tacitly (e.g., Vital du Four, Gonsalvus Hispanus, Henry of Ghent, Godfrey of Fontaines, Giles of Rome). The writing is only loosely related to Aristotle's work, posing a series of questions in sequence with the order of topics in Books 2-3 of *De anima*. The *Quaestiones* do not constitute a *summula* and were never perceived to be such (else some manuscript would have so-named them). Nor are the questions a *reportatio* of disputes or the cursory jottings of a student's notebook. The questions are exactly what they seem to be: a series of independently disputed questions concerning the soul, written down in connection with some teaching activity in the liberal arts.

The argumentation in the *Quaestiones De anima* suggests that they were designed as teaching materials for introductory courses. The argumentation is not elaborate or complicated. Essentially, the author presents standard contrary opinions on the question and exposes the basic logical outlines of the arguments and solutions. The solutions are not magisterial or determinative. The questions are dialectical strictly speaking, that is, they yield probable opinions that seem *verior* than the alternatives. The *Quaestiones* would serve well in introducing young students to the kinds of questions that they would encounter should they pursue their studies further, and to the basic elements of argument that they would employ in higher theological studies. Indeed, the rather immediate orientation of the questions towards theology is clear. In the questions that concern intellection and cognition, for example, the topics of the knowledge of God *in statu isto* and of the beatific vision *in patria* are repeatedly introduced; this might well reflect the disposition of the lecturer but it also serves to remind young friars of the "relevance" of laboring over the workings of the active and passive intellects, etc. The *Quaestiones* are a good example of philosophy in service as *ancilla theologiae*. In this respect, the *Quaestiones* are well-domesticated for young friars; not by any stretch of the imagination could one educe from them some "autonomous philosophical ethical ideal and theory of natural deification."

B. Chronology

Throughout most of the twentieth century, Scotus scholars have been preoccupied with a possible period of Parisian study for the Subtle Doctor in the 1290s. André Callebaut, basing his argument on the statutes of the theological faculty of the University of Paris, first posited an early period of Parisian training for Scotus in order to synchronize the known chronological facts about his training with the existing statutory requirements at Paris.[118] This view had additional benefits as it could explain seeming known consistencies in Scotus' academic career. As one example, in 1304, Scotus' former master and later Minister General of the Franciscan Order, Gonsalvus

---

[118] André Callebaut, "Le Bienheureux Jean Duns Scot étudiant à Paris vers 1293-1296," *Archivum Franciscan Historicum* 17 (1924): 3-12 and later in "Les séjours du B. Jean Duns Scot à Paris," *La France Franciscaine* 12 (1929):353-374. Allan Wolter has traced much of this controversy in *Scotus and Ockham: Selected Essays* (St. Bonaventure, NY, 2003), 1-24.

Hispanus, recommended that he be promoted to the doctorate at Paris. In his recommendation, Gonsalvus claimed that he had known Scotus by reputation and "long experience."[119] An early period of Parisian training would presumably explain a lengthy association between Gonsalvus and Scotus. Furthermore, a possible intellectual sojourn by Scotus to Paris could also help to explain his familiarity with Parisian sources and opinions both in his *Lectura* and his *Ordinatio*, works demonstrably known to have been written at Oxford. Following Callebaut, this position became standard amongst scholars in the field.[120]

In his seminal article detailing Scotus' early career at Oxford, C.K. Brampton sought to refine Callebaut's hypothesis by examining the statuatory requirements at Oxford.[121] Like Callebaut, however, he also posited an early period of Parisian study for Scotus in the 1290s. In the 1990s, Brampton's modifications were themselves challenged largely on the basis that the university statutes that he used applied to secular rather than mendicant students.[122] The chronology of Scotus' early life and training has since been a topic of much recent revision.

In the latter-half of the twentieth century, scholars began to focus on the differences between the training of secular and non-secular students at the medieval university. Eelcko Ypma detailed the existence of a lectorate system within the Augustinian Order in which the best and brightest students were sent to Paris for a period of theological training and then functioned as lectors within the Order's provincial schools.[123] Michèle Mulchahey has shown that a similar system existed for the Dominicans,[124] while William Courtenay has done the same for the Franciscans.[125] With respect to the lectorate program within the Franciscan Order, in the latter half of the thirteenth century, the Order devised a new pedagogical system in order to meet a growing demand: an increased need for more friar-teachers within the provincial houses. In 1260, the Franciscan general Chapter of Narbonne legislated a four-year period of theological study at Paris (or another *studium generale*) for advanced Franciscan friar-students in the Arts.[126] But the careers of the Salimbene and Gerard of Borgo San Donnino reveal that even before 1260 it had been the policy of the Order to send outstanding students to Paris for a period of further training that may—or more probably may not—have resulted in doctoral studies. Franciscan chapters throughout the thirteenth century legislated that friar-students needed at least two to three years of study in their own custodial *studium* before embarking on the studies within a *studium generale*. Although provincial requirements varied throughout the Order, by the latter-half of the fourteenth century, the Chapter requirements mandated at least three years of preparatory training in logic and two in philosophy before entering a *studium generale*.[127]

---

[119] A.G. Little, "Chronological Notes on the Life of Duns Scotus," *English Historical Review*," 47 (1932): 577-78.

[120] See, for example, C. Balić, "The Life and Works of Duns Scotus," in *Studies in the Philosophy and the History of Philosophy* 3 (1965):10-11.

[121] C.K. Brampton, "Duns Scotus at Oxford, 1288-1301," *Franciscan Studies* 24 (1964): 5-20

[122] William J. Courtenay, "Scotus at Paris," in *Via Scoti: Methodologica ad mentem Ioannis Duns Scoti* (Roma, 1995), I:149-63.

[123] Eelcko Ypma, *La formation des professeurs chez les ermites de Saint-Augustin de 1256 à 1354* (Paris, 1956), 72-73.

[124] Michèle Mulchahey, *"First the Bow is Bent in Study" : Dominican Education before 1350* (Toronto, 1998).

[125] William J. Courtenay, "The Parisian Franciscan Community in 1303," *Franciscan Studies* 53 (1993): 155-65, and "The Instructional Programme of the Mendicant Convents at Paris in the early Fourteenth Century," in *The Medieval Church : Universities, Heresy, and the Religious Life: Essays in Honour of Gordon Leff*, ed. P. Biller and B. Dobson (Suffolk, 1999), 77-92.

[126] "Statuta Generalis Ordinis edita in Capitulis generalibus celebratis Narbonae an. 1260, Assissii an. 1279 atque Parisiis an. 1292 (Editio critica et synoptica)," ed. M. Bihl, *Archivum Franciscan Historicum* 34 (1941): 72; Bert Roest, *A History of Franciscan Education (c. 1210-1517)* (Leiden-Boston, 2000), 91.

[127] Roest, *A History of Franciscan Education*, 90. Before the Constitutions of Narbonne the amount of training received by a friar before the lectorate often varied. Roest notes that some students, notably Salimbene, had much more than five years of training before embarking on the lectorate; Roest, *A History of Franciscan Education*, 88 n. 296.

The Franciscan Chapters of Assisi (1279) and Paris (1292) renewed the Constitutions of Narbonne regarding the lectorate.[128] Both Chapters recognized the privileged place Paris played amongst all the Franciscan *studia*; not only is Paris the only *studium* continually mentioned in the general statutes, it was also the only *studium* where friars from all provinces could go. Thus although there were other Franciscan *studia generalia*, Paris held a place of honor. By the early fourteenth century, the Franciscan practice allowed each province to send two students to Paris *de debito* (at the expense of the Paris convent) and one or two additional students *de gratia* (at the province's expense).[129] Courtenay has shown that in Paris ca. 1303, almost half of the friars residing in the Franciscan house at Paris were students in the lectorate program.[130] Few of these students, however, would actually have the opportunity to begin the theological degree; most were sent to teach within the custodial or provincial houses of the Order which may, as in the cases of Paris, Oxford and Cambridge, have also contained a *studium generale*. After a period of teaching philosophy and theology at the custodial level or theology at the level of the provincial *studium*, the former lector might then be selected by the Order to resume theological studies at a *studium generale* and advance to the rank of *Sententiarius*. Only a small proportion of Franciscan students and teachers could ever hope to obtain a magisterial title. And of those Franciscans who advanced to the rank of *Sententiarius*, Courtenay has shown that in the early fourteenth century they needed to have met the two following criteria: 1) they must have completed the lectorate at Paris or had an equivalent training in another *studium generale* and 2) they must have come to the attention of the Minister General.[131]

The chronology of the young Scotus is not known with any degree of precision.[132] The first certain date in Scotus' academic career is his ordination to the priesthood on 17 March 1291.[133] Since the minimum age for ordination was twenty-five, Scotus was born presumably before 17 March 1266. At the time of his ordination, Scotus would have, following the standard chronologies, already commenced his theological studies at Oxford. The next certain fact of Scotus' career is that he participated in a disputation under Philip of Bridlington at Oxford during Bridlington's year as a regent theologian in 1300-1. Scotus was certainly at Oxford in the summer of 1300 as on 26 July, as Hugh of Hertilpole, the English provincial, presented Scotus, along with twenty-one other candidates to the Bishop of Lincoln, for faculties to hear confessions in the Franciscan church at Oxford.[134]

According to John Major, Scotus was taken from Duns to Oxford as a boy. Although Scotus had already received training in grammar, Scotland had no university for further instruction in the thirteenth century.[135] By Scotus' time, boys could enter a Franciscan convent at the age of twelve. Early on—usually in their first year—they participated in a religious program free

---

[128]Roest, *A History of Franciscan Education*, 92.
[129]Courtenay, "Parisian Franciscan Community," 159; Roest, *A History of Franciscan Education*, 88-89.
[130]Courtenay, "Parisian Franciscan Community," 164; *Parisian Scholars in the Early Fourteenth Century: A Social Portrait* (Cambridge, 1999).
[131]Courtenay, "Parisian Franciscan Community," 160.
[132]For more recent chronologies, see Wolter, "Reflections," 1-36; Thomas Williams, "Introduction: The Life and Works of John Duns the Scot," in *The Cambridge Companion to Duns Scotus* (Cambridge, 2003), 1-13, and Stephen D. Dumont, "John Duns Scotus," in *A Companion to Philosophy in the Middle Ages; Blackwell Companions to Philosophy*, ed. L. Gracia and T.B. Noone (Oxford, 2003), 353-69.
[133]Ephrem Longpré, "L'ordination sacerdotale du bx. Jean Duns Scot: Document du 17 mars 1291," *Archivum Franciscanum Historicum* 22 (1929): 54-62.
[134]Williams, "Introduction," 4.
[135]*A History of Great Britain as well as England and Scotland Compiled from the Ancient Authorities by John Major, by name a Scot, but by profession a Theologian*, trans. A. Constable (Edinburgh, 1892): 206; quoted in Williams, "Introduction," 2, and Wolter, "Reflections," 6.

from studies for one year.[136] If Scotus entered the Franciscan convent around the ages ten to twelve, following the standard *cursus*, he would have studied logic and natural philosophy and probably spent a period of time teaching the material in a regional school either at Oxford or elsewhere. One cannot state with precision at exactly what date Scotus studied or lectured on which text as the Franciscan educational system allowed for much flexibility. Moreover, one cannot say with any degree of certainty when he completed the equivalent of what was for a secular student a degree in Arts.

Bert Roest infers that the typical age of the Franciscan candidate for the lectorship was 21-23.[137] During the lectorship, advanced students were sent to a *studium generale* to begin theological studies. They could attend both cursory and ordinary lectures on the Bible and the *Sentences*, canon law and moral philosophy; although they were not members of the university proper, they nevertheless benefited from its milieu. They would be expected to attend the lectures of the Order's regent master of the University and the bachelors within the house and most certainly attended disputations and heard sermons within the larger academic community. When the lectorship had ended, the lector was probably between 23-28 years of age. The lector then returned home with university training but without a university degree.[138] The provincial chapter then reassigned the *quondam* lector to a period of teaching within a local or provincial school. The former lector would then instruct young friars on courses in logic, natural or moral philosophy, and thus train them in the Arts at a custodial school or theology at the provincial level.

Scholars have traditionally agreed that Scotus' philosophical works were probably written early in his career. Scotus wrote his philosophical works in question-style commentaries that betray an oral flavor (*dices, dicas, possum, possumus*) common in medieval school texts that originated as school exercises.[139] Like Callebaut and Brampton, we would like to posit an early period of Parisian study for Scotus. Unlike them, however, we would like to move the date back to the 1280s, quite possibly 1286-1290, as part of the Franciscan lectorate system. Such a view would be consonant with what we know of Scotus' works, namely his breezy familiarity with Parisian sources and opinions, as seen especially in his questions on *De anima* (Giles of Rome, Henry of Ghent, Peter John Olivi, Godfrey of Fontaines), and could thus account for a period of time in which we have no known information about him. As a lector at Paris and as one of potentially ninety other lectors—and perhaps even more—at the Paris house attending classes, one would not expect Scotus to draw the same type of attention as a doctoral student in Theology. The sources do not mention him during this early period of Parisian study and we should not expect them to. After Scotus returned from the lectorate, he was most likely appointed to teach at the Oxford house before beginning his theological studies there. We believe that most of his philosophical works date from this time. At various points throughout the 1290s, Scotus was most likely assigned to teach introductory logic and philosophy classes both before and after he started his studies in Theology. Such a view would be consistent with what we known of other Franciscan authors; Ockham for example, who taught courses in philosophy in advanced stages of his career. Indeed, those friars who were promoted to *Sententairius* at Paris were only those who had considerable teaching experience.

---

[136]William J. Courtenay, *Adam Wodeham: An Introduction to His Life and Writings* (Leiden-New York, 1978), 45-53, and *Schools and Scholars in Fourteenth-Century England*, 66-69. Roest gives examples as young as eight.

[137]Roest, *A History of Franciscan Education*, 91. Courtenay places the age of the average student in the lectorate in the mid to late twenties. "Instructional Program," 82.

[138]Roest, *A History of Franciscan Education*, 92; Courtenay, "Instructional Programme," 82.

[139]William J. Courtenay, "Programs of Study and Genres of Scolastic Theological Production in the Fourteenth Century," in *Manuels, programme du cours et techniques d'enseignement dans les universités médiévales : actes du Colloque international de Louvain-la-Neuve*, ed. J. Hamesse (Louvain, 1994), 338-49.

Scotus' extant philosophical corpus represents questions that he disputed, as part of longer courses at the Oxford convent and thus provide "windows" into his activities in the early and mid-1290s. Apart from the *Quaestiones super Perihermenias*, which survive as two sets of questions and were thus probably two separate courses, and his *Quaestiones super Metaphysicam*, portions of which were revised over time and some questions (e.g., those on books seven, eight and nine) are late in his career,[140] all of the remainder of Scotus' philosophical corpus—his questions on the *Praedicamenta*, *Sophistici Elenchi* and *De anima*—seems to reflect a series of lectures taught only once, as these latter works do not bear witness to successive stages of corrections and additions that once would expect in a set of questions taught repeatedly.

A dating, therefore, of the *Quaestiones super libros De anima* to the early 1290s solves two problems: Scotus' familiarity with Parisian sources and the claim by Gonsalvus Hispanus that he had known Scotus "from long experience." The association with Gonsalvus, however, raises yet another question, namely the shared matter between the two authors. There are parallels in some of their works, most notably between Scotus' *Quaestiones De anima* q. 15 and Gonsalvus' *Quaestiones disputatae* q. 11; Scotus' *De anima* q. 13 and Gonsalvus' *Quaes. disp.* q. 13; and between Scotus' *QQ. De anima* and Gonsalvus' *Quodlibeta* q. 10. Since each of these texts treats quite different issues of philosophical and theological doctrine (e.g., the possibility of hylemorphic composition in human souls and angels, the identity and status of the possible and agent intellects, and the knowability of singulars), one must examine each of the questions and their respective issues separately and carefully, bearing in mind the history of thirteenth century discussions of these issues. Scholars should not be misled by the tyranny of print, in this case by the fact that the edition of Gonsalvus' disputed questions has appeared before this critical edition Scotus' *Quaestiones super secundum et tertium De anima*. It seems to us evident, as we have said, that the resemblance of some arguments in Gonsalvus' and Scotus' questions can best be explained by the fact that the two friars were twice together in the Parisian *stadium*, in the late 1280s and 1302-1303.

---

[140]Stephen D. Dumont, "The Question of Individuation in Scotus's *Quaestiones super Metaphysicam*," in *Via Scoti: Methodologia ad mentem Joannis Duns Scoti: Atti del Congresso Scotistico Internazionale Roma 9-11 marzo 1993*, ed. L. Sileo (Roma, 1995), I:193-227; Timothy B. Noone, "Scotus's Critique of the Thomistic Theory of Individuation and the Dating of the *Quaestiones in libros Metaphysicorum*: VII q. 13," in *Via Scoti* I:391-406.

§ 5: EDITORIAL PRINCIPLES

The edition presented here is a critical reconstruction *ad fidem codicum* of the autograph of John Duns Scotus' *Quaestiones super secundum et tertium De anima*. All of the evidence points to the fact that the Subtle Doctor never intended to publish this work as such, but rather chose to incorporate parts of the doctrinal results shown here in later works. As the preceding discussion makes clear, there are no clear and unmistakable signs of intervention on the part of the author leading to the preparation of the text for publication. This state of affairs makes the task of a modern editor a daunting one, since the recreation of the author's intention—the first and foremost job of a critical editor—must be to cut through several layers of corruption and contamination brought about through the circulation of the text. The autograph of this work, as well as the parents of the four manuscript traditions, no longer survives. All indications are that Alpha was scribbled, heavily abbreviated and messy. Two of the manuscript traditions—Beta and Gamma—have tried to rectify this situation by creating early "editions" of these questions. The editor of Beta employed other sources pertaining to Scotus' course on Aristotle's *De anima*—either written *reportationes* or oral reports of teaching and doctrine *ad mentem Scoti*. The editor of Gamma, as we have seen, prepared a wholesale revision of Alpha.

In the following edition we have followed mainly the line of tradition offered by the English group Beta (**HLM**), the best and most faithful transmitter of the questions. We have had recourse to the other two English families, Epsilon (**NO**) and Delta (**KU**), when the text in Beta suffered obvious corruption, is in manifest error, or has presented an incoherent arrangement of the text.

We have not collated **Vivès-Wadding** in this text for, as we have seen, it is based on a manuscript from the late Gamma tradition to which Wadding has added a further layer of contamination. We have prepared this edition with a view toward readability and accessibility. We use modern Latin orthography save occasionally in the *apparatus fontium*. Punctuation is in accord with modern practice.

We have produced the titles of the questions as they are found in the manuscript tradition. We have given the reader a text with proper divisions and marginal Wadding number referents. We have added subtitles to the questions, dividing arguments and the corpus of some solutions to show the articulations of Scotus' reasoning and use of sources. We have identified implicit and explicit sources to the best of our abilities. These are indicated in the *apparatus fontium*.

SIGLORUM INTERPRETATIO

Sigla codicum

F   Modena, Biblioteca Estense, Cod. a M.5.29 (Lat. 302)

H   Oxford, Balliol College Library, Ms. 117

K   Oxford, Bodleian Library, Ms. Digby 44

L   Oxford, Corpus Christi College Library, Ms. 227

M   Oxford, Magdalen College Library, Ms. lat. 16

N   Oxford, Magdalen College Library, Ms. lat. 80

O   Oxford, Oriel College Library, Ms. 35

Q   Roma, Biblioteca Angelica, Ms. 953 (R.5.4)

U   Città del Vaticano, Biblioteca Apostolica Vaticana, Cod. Urbinas latinus 1406

W   Città del Vaticano, Biblioteca Apostolica Vaticana, Cod. Vaticanus latinus 890

X   Città del Vaticano, Biblioteca Apostolica Vaticana, Cod. Vaticanus latinus 3092

Z   Wien, Österreichische Nationalebibliothek, Cod. lat. 1447

Alia sigla

AL   Aristoteles latinus. Corpus philosophorum medii aevi, Academiarum consociatarum auspiciis et consilio editum. 1939 sqq.

AMPh   Ancient and Medieval Philosophy. De Wulf-Mansion Centre. Series 2. Leuven 1979 sqq.

AverL   Corpus Commentariorum Averrois in Aristotelem, consilio et auspiciis Academiae Americanae mediaevalis adiuvantibus Academiis consociatis. Cambridge, MA 1953

AviL   Avicenna latinus. Louvain-Leiden 1968 sqq.

BAW   Bayerische Akademie der Wissenschaften. München 1965 sqq.

BFS   Bibliotheca franciscana scholastica medii aevi, cura Patrum Collegii S. Bonaventurae. Ad Claras Aquas-Grottaferrata 1903 sqq.

BGPTM	Beiträge zur Geschichte der Philosophie und Theologie des Mittelalters. Begründet von Clemens Baeumker. Münster i.W. 1891 sqq.	PG	Patrologiae cursus completus, series graeca, accurante J. P. Migne. Parisiis 1857 sqq.
CCL	Corpus christianorum, series latina. Turnhout 1971 sqq.	PhB	Les Philosophes belges. Textes et études. Collection publiée par l'Institut Supérieur de Philosophie de l'Université de Louvain. Leuven 1901 sqq.
CLCAG	Corpus latinum commentariorum in Aristotelem graecorum. De Wulf-Mansion Centre. Leuven 1971 sqq.	PL	Patrologiae cursus completus, series latina, accurante J. P. Migne. Parisiis 1844 sqq.
CSEL	Corpus scriptorum ecclesiasticorum latinorum, ed. Academia Vindobonensis. Wien 1866 sqq.	SB	Spicilegium Bonaventurianum, cura Patrum Collegii S. Bonaventurae. Ad Claras Aquas-Grottaferrata 1963 sqq.
FIP t. s.	Franciscan Institute Publications. Text series. St. Bonaventure, N.Y. 1951 sqq.		
GL	Grammatici latini. Ex recensione Henrici Keilii. Leipzig 1855-1880		

SIGNORUM INTERPRETATIO

IN APPARATU CRITICO

—   (linea) inter duo verba posita, in apparatu critico et in apparatu variantium, lemma intermedium supponit

...   (tria puncta) inter duo verba posita, in apparatu lectionum variantium, lemma intermedium excludunt

...   (tria puncta) in auctorum allegationibus adhibita, verba intermedia, utpote ad propositum non necessaria, excludunt

Numeri $^{2\ 3}$ post verba lemmatum altius positi distinguunt verba in eadem textus linea pluries occurrentia

Numerus ^{1} post sigla codicum lectionem manu ipsiusmet scriptoris inductam significat

Numeri $^{2\ 3}$ post sigla codicum lectionem alia vel ulteriore manu inductam designat

-2, -3   linea et numerus adiuncti verba lemmatis pluries occurrentia in textu, non immediate, sed cetera porro sequentia conferunt

,   post sigla codicum, est tantum signum attentionis, quod remittit ad aliam, correctam lectionem eorumdem codicum, quae legitur immediate post vel ante

ABBREVIATIONUM INTERPRETATIO *

-á	casus ablativus (E.g.: 'forma naturá prior est materiá')	*med.*	medius, in medio
		mg.	margo, in margine
		not.	notavit
add.	addidit	*om.*	omisit
adnot.	adnotavit	*praem.*	praemisit
cap.	caput	*quaest.*	quaestio
cod.	codex	*rell.*	reliqui codices
codd.	codices	*rep.*	repetivit
col.	columna	*rescrip.*	rescripsit
corr.	correxit	*restit.*	restituit
del.	delevit	*scrip.*	scripsit
exp.	expunxit	*seq.*	sequitur
fin.	finis, in fine	*sign.*	signavit
f.	folium	*trp.*	transposuit, transpositio
ff.	folia		
init.	initium, in initio	*spat. vac.*	spatium vacuum
lac.	lacuna	*text.*	textus
lib.	librum		
lin.	linea, in linea, sub linea, supra lineam		

---

* Interpretatio abbreviationum secundum numerum vel casum tempus varietur, contextu adhibito.

QUAESTIONES SUPER SECUNDUM ET TERTIUM DE ANIMA

[QUAESTIO 1]

UTRUM SENSUS TACTUS SIT UNUS VEL PLURES

Quaeritur utrum sensus tactus sit unus vel plures.[1]

[1]   Videtur quod unus:

Quia si esset plures, tunc essent sex sensus,[2] in cuius contrarium est PHILOSOPHUS in fine II *De anima*.[3]

Item, sensus ille est unus cuius organum est unum,[4] quia sensus fundatur in organo; organum tactus est unum, quia est corpus mixtum quod habet unitatem ab una perfectione dominante in eo; igitur, etc.[5] Minor sic: quaecumque pars nervi vel carnis

---

3 Quaeritur *om.* Z *add.* (f. 43vb) Explicit literalis sententia super Praedicamenta Aristotelis secundum expositionem magistri Roberti Alnington veritatis theologiae professoris cuius animae propitietur Deus. Amen O *add.* ult. (*mg.*) Doctor Subtilis De anima O *add.* (*mg.*) Quaestiones Scotuli super secundum et tertium libros De anima M *add.* circa secundum librum De anima K *add.* (*mg.*) Scotus U² *add.* (*mg.* Q) Scoti De anima Q Z 4 Videtur *post* unus X | quod] *add.* sit K | unus] non Q *add.* primo sic K 5 esset] essent O U FW X Z *om.* L | esset — tunc] non esset unus tunc (*mg.*) F² | essent] esset Q | sex] plures quam quinque FW Q Z *om.* X | in *om.* O KU FW Q X Z | contrarium] oppositum Z 6 est] probat K W Q Z dicit (*post* Philosophus) U probatur F X *om.* O | Philosophus *om.* H X | in fine *post* anima KU | De anima] huius (ant. II) Q *om.* X 7 Item] Praeterea O U W Q X Z Postea F | ille *om.* O U FW Q X Z | cuius *om.* O | organum] organum est] *inv.* X | quia] sed Q X Z | sensus²] *add.* tactus X 8 in] *add.* uno X | organum] *add.* autem K | quia] quod X 9 unitatem] unionem H | ab] *add.* perfectione X 10 igitur] quare U | igitur etc. *om.* X | Minor sic] Item probatur minor sic O FW Q Z Item (*om.* U) minor probatur sic U X | nervi vel carnis] carnis vel nervi X

---

[1] **Aristot.**, *De an.* II c. 22 (B c. 11, 422b 19-20).

[2] **Averroës**, *De an.* III com. 128 (AverL 324): "Impossibile est invenire animal habens sex sensus"; **Anonymus**, *Sententia super II et III De anima* II, lect. 24 (ed. Bazán 302): "In hac vero parte intendit ostendere quod non est possibile esse sex sensus. Unde hic ostendit quod impossibile est plures sensus esse quam quinque"; **Avicenna**, *De an.* I c. 5 (AviL I 83): "Apprehendens a foris sunt quinque sensus aut octo"; **Ioannes de Rupella**, *Tractatus De anima* II c. 3-4 (ed. Michaud-Quantin 73 v. 156): "Quinque vel octo."

[3] **Aristot.**, *De an.* II c. 25 (Γ c. 1, 424b 22-24): "Quod autem non sit sensus alter praeter quinque (dico autem hos visum, auditum, olfactum, gustum, tactum) ex hiis credet aliquis"; *Auctoritates Aristotelis* (ed. J. Hamesse 179): "Quinque sunt sensus, scilicet visus, auditus, odoratus, tactus et gustus"; cf. infra q. 6.

[4] **Anonymus (Jacobus de Duaco?)**, *Quaestiones De anima* II q. 30 (ed. Bazán 449): "Ille sensus est unus qui habet unum organum tantum et unum medium tantum; sed sensus tactus habet unum organum et unum medium; ergo est unus sensus."

[5] **Petrus Hispanus**, *Scientia libri de anima* c. 10 (ed. Alonso 241): "Est autem eius organum mixtum, non simplex, ex eo quod ipsum est corpus animalis et quia in elementis sunt qualitates ultimatae, quarum una receptionem alterius impedit; eius autem organum per indifferentiam recipit, et inter sensus quibus organa deserviunt, causa essentialis propter quam animalis corpus est mixtum, est necessitas tactus."

(quodcumque eorum sit organum tactus)⁶ sentit unam contrarietatem, sentit et aliam;⁷ ergo nervus est unum organum tactus, et per consequens est unus sensus.

3   Item, si sint plures, aut differunt specie aut numero:⁸

Non numero, quia sunt in eodem subiecto, quod non esset verum si solum numero differrent. Et similiter alter eorum superflueret, quia quandocumque aliqua duo sunt eiusdem speciei, a quocumque potest pati unum, et aliud; a quacumque igitur contrarietate vel sensibili immutaretur unus tactus, et alius. Non sunt igitur solum numero differentia.

Nec differunt specie,⁹ probatio: quia specie diversi non sunt¹⁰ aequales (nec esse possunt secundum ALIQUOS), igitur unus esset

---

1 quodcumque] quidquid (*lin.* O) O U FW Q X Z | unam *om.* N M   2 sentit *om.* U   3 est *om.* O H FW Q X Z | unus *post* sensus U   4 Item] Praeterea O U FW Q X Z *adnot. mg.* Tertium argumentum U | sint] sunt FW Q X Z | aut *post* differunt K | specie — numero] specifice aut numero H specie vel numero L numero aut specie O U FW Q X Z | numero] *mg.* X   5 in *om.* O | eodem] uno N LM *om.* O | quod] quia Q   6 verum] unus Q *om.* N M | solum] solo O L U FW Q X Z | numero] non X | Et *om.* KU FW Q X Z | alter] alterum U aliqui X | superflueret] superfluum esset U   7 quandocumque] quando O U FW X Z | duo *om.* Z | sunt *post* speciei H   8 pati unum] *inv.* N   9 vel *om.* FW | vel sensibili] *rep.* O | tactus] sensus tactus Q | Non — differentia] = N HM Non sunt igitur numero differentia O Igitur non sunt solum numero differentia L Igitur non differunt solum numero K Non sunt igitur eiusdem speciei U FW Q X Z   11 specie] specifice H | probatio] probo M | specie diversi] = N HL *inv.* K specie universi O M species universi U FW Q X Z   12 nec] neque U | esse *om.* N | esse possunt] *inv.* Q X

⁶Cf. **Aristot.**, *De an.* II c. 22 (B c. 11, 422b 20-23) (caro est medium); *De part. animal.* II c. 8 (B c. 2 653b 20-25) (caro est organum); **Averroës**, *In De an.* II c. 107 (AverL 295): Necesse est ut caro sit quasi medium, et ut non sit quasi instrumentum"; *In De sensu* (ed. Shields 8): "Instrumentum tactus est caro"; cf. etiam *De part. animal.* II c. 1 (ed. Iuntina VI¹ ff. 129G); "Hoc autem oportet etiam quod fateatur ipse Galenus licet opinetur quod membrum, deferens carni sensum tactus, sit ipse nervus. Nihil tamen hoc refert circa id, quod diximus de carne, videlicet ipsam esse proprium instrumentum sensus tactus, sive hoc insit carni per se, sive per nervum." Hanc rationem dat Averroës ad explicandam discrepationem: "Velit Aristoteles (in *De anima*) ... quod caro est quasi id medium. Licet iste sermo sit contrarius sermoni in libro de Animalibus; sed tamen forte ille sermo fuit secundum quod apparuit illic, scilicet quod scivit de membris animalium in illo tempore; tunc enim adhuc nesciebat nervos, et dixit quod instrumentum istius sensus est caro" (*In De an.* II c. 108 (AverL 298); *Auctoritates Aristotelis* (ed. J. Hamesse 182, 218): "Caro non est medium tactus, sed aliqua circa carnem sicut nervus"; "Instrumentum sensus tactus est caro. Dicit tamen postea quod instrumentum tactus non est caro, sed aliqua infra carnem, ut infra dictum est de anima"; cf. **Petrus Hispanus**, *Scientia libri de anima* c. 10 (ed. Alonso 186-187): "Est autem tactus virtus a corde et cerebro originem contrahens in nervis magnis in cute totius corporis insita et in omnibus carnis partibus expansa"; cf. etiam **Anonymus**, *Sententia super II et III De anima* II lect. 19 (ed. Bazán 231 cum adn. 143-144) et II lect. 21 (ed. Bazán 264 cum adn. 140). Cf. infra q. 2 n. 6-10.

⁷**Aristot.**, *De an.* II c. 22 (B c. 11, 422b 23-24): "Omnis et enim sensus unius contrarietatis esse videtur, ut visus albi et nigri, auditus gravis et acuti, gustus amari et dulcis"; cf. **Aegidius Romanus**, *De an.* II com. 108 (f. 50rb).

⁸Cf. **Albertus M.**, *De an.* II tr. 3 c. 30 (VII¹ 142): "Videtur passivum his activis respondens plures esse sensus et non unus specie vel numero vel genere."

⁹Cf. **Ioannes Pecham**, *Tract. De an.* c. 10 (BSF I 35).

¹⁰Subaudi: sensus tactus.

alio perfectior. Sed hoc est falsum, quia tactus aeque perfecte sentit unam contrarietatem sicut et aliam.

[2] Item, sensus tactus facit animal esse animal,[11] quia est primus sensus.[12] Si igitur in animali sunt plures sensus tactus, animal erit plura animalia, quod est falsum. Similiter, animal imperfectum est unum ab unitate unius naturae vel formae; sed non habet formam nec perfectionem ultra sensum tactus;[13] ergo est unus tantum.

Item, sensus tactus est unius contrarietatis; ergo est unus.[14] Probatio antecedentis: quia istae quattuor qualitates tangibiles[15] sic opponuntur quod quaedam sunt activae, quaedam passivae;[16] haec est una contrarietas; ergo, etc.

[3] In oppositum est PHILOSOPHUS:

---

1 alio perfectior] inv. X | est] esse O videtur esse KU Z videmus esse FW X videremus esse Q | quia tactus] tactus enim O K FW Q X Z add. ult. sensus X | aeque perfecte] ita perfecte O aeque K X haec U add. ult. apprehendit vel KU 2 et om. O HL U FW | aliam] add. ergo etc. K 3 Item] Praeterea O U Q W X Z Postea F adnot. mg. Quartum U | est om. U 4 in] add. uno O U FW Q X Z | sunt] sint HM K Q | sensus² om. O U FW X Z | tactus] add. unum U FW Q X add. ergo unum Z | erit] esset HL 5 animalia] alia W | est falsum] inv. O U FW Z | falsum] add. ergo etc. O U FW Q Z | Similiter] Praeterea U FW Q X Z adnot. mg. Quintum U 6 unius] mg. K² huius X om. U Q | unius naturae] inv. O 7 nec perfectionem] neque perfectionem L K² vel perfectionem FW Q X Z perfectiorem U | ergo] igitur N add. tactus L add. sensus tactus U | est om. N HM 8 Item] Praeterea O U FW Q X Z | ergo — unus om. X | est²] et U om. Q 9 Probatio antecedentis] Antecedens patet N HLM | istae] illae O L FW X Z | sic] nunc X 10 quod] quia FW quae X | quaedam sunt] inv. N HLM | sunt — activae] mg. Z² | activae] add. et H U FW | quaedam²] add. sunt Q add. autem Z | passivae] add. sed Z | haec] hoc O X Z hic F add. ult. autem O U FW Q X 11 ergo etc. om. O K FW Q X Z

---

[11]**Aristot.**, *De an.* II c. 3 (B c. 2, 413b 2-6): "Animal autem propter sensum primum. Et namque quae non moventur neque mutantia locum, habentia autem sensum, animalia dicemus, et non vivere solum. Videntur autem et huiusmodi multa esse animalium; manentia autem cum sint natura, habent solum sensum"; *De an.* III c. 12 (Γ c. 13, 435b 17); **Averroës**, *De part. animal.* II c. 1 (ed. Iuntina VI¹ ff. 129D): "Cum definitio animalis sit corpus nutribile sensitivum sensu tactus, cum non detur animal sine hoc sensu ..."; cf. *Auctoritates Aristotelis* (ed. J. Hamesse 178): "Animal est animal propter sensum tactus".

[12]**Aristot.**, *De an.* II c. 3 (B c. 2, 413b 4-5); *De part. animal.* II c. 8 (ed. Iuntina VI¹ f. 73rb B c. 8 653b 23-24); **Avicenna**, *De an.* II c. 3 (AviL II 130); cf. *Auctoritates Aristotelis* (ed. J. Hamesse 189): "Sensus tactus est primus omnium sensum, quia sine eo animal esse non potest."

[13]**Aristot.**, *De an.* III c. 10 (Γ c. 10, 433b 31—434a 1): "Considerandum autem et de imperfectis, quid movens est quibus tactus solum inest sensus."

[14]Cf. **Anonymus, Magister Artium**, *Lectura in librum De anima* II, 20 (ed. Gauthier 391); **Aegidius Romanus**, *De an.* II com. 108 (f. 50rb).

[15]**Averroës**, *De an.* II com. 107 (AverL 295): "v.g. calidum et frigidum, et humidum et siccum, et asperum et lene, et durum et molle"; cf **Aristot.**, *De an.* II c. 22 (B c. 11, 422b 26-27); *De gener. et corrupt.* II c. 2 (329b 18-20).

[16]**Aristot.**, *De gener. et corrupt.* II c. 2 (AL IX¹ 54-8; B c. 2, 3 329b 7—331a 6); **Anonymus, Magister Artium**, *Lectura in librum De anima* II, 20 (ed. Gauthier 391): "Licet sensus tactus sit plurium contrarietatum, reducuntur tamen omnes ad unam, quoniam tangibilia tactus sunt quattuor prime qualitates, haec autem aut sunt activae aut passivae, et sic omnes reducuntur ad contrarietatem activi ad passivum"; **Anonymus**, *Quaestiones in tres libros de anima* II q. 52 (ed. J. Vennebusch 233); **Ps. Petrus Hispanus**, *Expositio libri de anima* (ed. Alonso 234-235).

Quia probat ipsum tactum non esse unum, quia non est tantum unius contrarietatis,[17] et reprobat solutionem apparentem[18] ad rationem suam.[19]

7 Item, omnis potentia una habet obiectum unum sibi adaequatum;[20] non sic autem tactus, quia qua ratione diceres calidum et frigidum, eadem ratione humidum et siccum.

8 Item, omnis potentia una est respectu unius generis univoce praedicati de omnibus quae ab illa potentia cognoscuntur, ut patet de colore respectu albedinis et nigredinis; qualitates autem tangibiles non habent unum genus, obiectum tactui, univoce praedicatum de illis;[21] qualitates autem activae et passivae sunt in tertia specie qualitatis, durum et molle sunt in secunda specie, secundum PHILOSOPHUM in *Praedicamentis*.[22]

---

1 Quia] Qui L KU FW Q X Z | ipsum] sensus Q om. K | tactum] tactus Q | est om. X | tantum om. Z   2 reprobat] improbat X | solutionem] rationem (mg.) L² add. suam FW   4 Item] Praeterea O U FW Q Z om. X | una om. X | obiectum unum] inv. O K F X Z | unum post adaequatum W   5 non] nec FW Q | sic om. Q | autem om. X | diceres] dices FW dicaretur O | calidum et frigidum] frigidum et calidum L | et] vel O U FW Q X Z   6 ratione om. X add. dicaretur O add. diceres U add. dicerem FW Q Z add. dices X | humidum] frigidum K' restit. lin. K² | humidum et siccum] siccum et humidum N | et] vel O FW Q X Z   7 Item] Praeterea O U FW Q X Z | omnis om. U | respectu om. U | generis] add. obiecti FW | univoce] = O KU Z univoci N HLM unitate FW Q X   8 praedicati] praedicationis FW | de] add. illis L | ab illa potentia] ab ipsa ratione H sub illa potentia L ab ipsa potentia F ab alia potentia X   9 albedinis et nigredinis] albi et nigri O U FW Q X Z | autem post tangibiles Q enim K   10 univoce] unitate FW Q X om. U | praedicatum] = L U Q Z praedicati NO HM K praedicationis FW praedicatur X   11 illis] ipsis U FW Q X Z add. ult. qualitatibus X | autem] enim U Z | et] om X   12 durum et molle] dicuntur autem movere FW | et om. X | sunt om. U FW Q X Z add. ult. scilicet H | sunt — Praedicamentis] in secunda (mg.) O | specie om. FW Q X Z add. ult. qualitatis H | secundum — Praedicamentis om. U FW Q X Z   13 Praedicamentis] add. ergo etc. KU FW Q Z

[17] **Aristot.**, *De an.* II c. 22 (B c. 11, 422b 25-26): "'In tangibile autem multae insunt contrarietates."
[18] **Aristot.**, *De an.* II c. 22 (B c. 11, 422b 28): "solutionem quandam."
[19] **Aristot.**, *De an.* II c. 22 (B c. 11, 422b 32-33); cf. **Themistius**, *De an.* IV (CLCAG I 167); **Anonymus, Magister Artium**, *Lectura in librum De anima* II, 20 (ed. Gauthier 389-390): "... istam solutionem improbat ... dicens quod non est similiter de contrarietatibus circa sonum et colorem et circa tangibile ... Non sic autem est manifestum utrum contrarietates plures tangibilium ad unam possint reduci; non enim sic possunt reduci ad unam"; **Anonymus**, *Sententia super II et III De anima* II lect. 21 (ed. Bazán 262-263).
[20] **Thomas**, *De an.* II c. 22 (XLV¹ 160b): "Considerare oportet quod distinctio potentiarum et obiectorum proportionalis est, unde, cum unus sensus sit una potentia, oportet quod sensibile ei corrrespondens sit unum genus."
[21] **Averroës**, *De an.* II com. 108 (AverL 297): "Necesse est enim, si posuerimus quod unus sensus comprehendit multos modos contrarietatis, ut genus subiectum illis modis sit unum; quoniam necesse est aliquid esse commune illi multitudini quod comprehendatur ab illo uno sensu ... Necesse est, si tactus sit una virtus, ut modi contrariorum quos comprehendit sit unum genus subiectum eis quod dicatur de eis univoce, ut sonus, qui dicitur univoce de modis sonorum, et color de modis colorum. Sed contraria tactus non videntur habere genus quod dicatur de eis nisi aequivoce"; II com. 109 (AverL 299): "Quia sensibilia tactus non communicant in eodem genere quod de eis dicatur univoce, necesse est ut sit plus uno."
[22] **Aristot.**, *Praedic.* c. 8 (AL I² 64; c. 8, 9a 25-28): "Similiter autem his et durum et molle se habet ... tertia vero species qualitatis est passibiles qualitates et passiones."

[I. — Responsio ad quaestionem]

[4] Respondeo quod sensus tactus sunt formaliter duo, non tamen ita diversi vel divisi sicut alii ab invicem.[23]

[PROBATIO PRIMAE PARTIS CONCLUSIONIS PRINCIPALIS] Probatio primi:

Quia impossibile est unum sensum tactus habere simul et semel duos perfectissimos actus; hoc autem non conceditur de intellectu, de quo magis videtur. Et ratio huius est quia unus actus perfectissimus adaequat totam virtutem potentiae in illo actu; si igitur secum compareretur alium actum perfectissimum, primus non adaequaret, et sic simul esset adaequatus et non-adaequatus potentiae. Patet ergo maior, scilicet quod tactus non potest habere simul duos actus perfectissimos.

Sed tactus simul sentit aquam humidam et frigidam esse — sed non eodem actu. Probatio: quia impossibile est actum sentiendi esse respectu talis obiecti, quo remoto esset ille actus sentiendi; sed remota frigiditate ab aqua (per impossibile vel potentiam divinam) adhuc tactus sentit humiditatem; igitur actus sentiendi humiditatem aquae non est respectu frigiditatis aquae eius, nec e converso, quia, remota humiditate, adhuc sentit frigiditatem; ergo, etc.

Sunt igitur duo actus perfectissimi, quorum unus ab alio non

---

2 Respondeo] *adnot. mg.* Responsio quaestionis U | sunt] est K Q | formaliter duo] *inv.* U | duo] dua O *add.* et U | non] *add.* sunt U | tamen *om.* N HLM 3 diversi vel] *mg.* Z² | vel] et KU FW | alii] aliqui alteri U | ab invicem] *ant.* alii F Z ad invicem Q 6 Quia *om.* L | tactus] tantum F 7 perfectissimos actus] *inv.* O KU Q X Z *adnot. mg.* Quod tactus habeat perfectissimos actus duos Z² | autem] enim KU FW Q X Z | conceditur] contingit H 8 ratio huius] *inv.* Q | huius *om.* FW | actus *post* perfectissimus FW effectus U *om.* Q X Z 9 adaequat] adaequatur X *add.* sibi L U FW Q X Z | virtutem] realitatem FW rationalitatem Q | illo] primo Q isto X | igitur] autem U | secum compareretur] *inv.* L Q 11 sic *om.* K X | esset] est sed L | esset adaequatus] *inv.* O | adaequatus] adequatio Q | et² *om.* K | non-adaequatus] non adaequatio Q *add.* suae Z 12 scilicet *om.* H | scilicet — non] nec tactus O sed tactus U FW Q X Z | potest — specifice aut numero H specie vel numero L simul] simul potest habere O FW Q potest simul habere LM Z | duos] illos O 14 Sed] = LM Item (*mg.* K²) N H K² Praeterea O Probatio U FW Q X Z | simul] *add.* perfectissime O | humidam et frigidam] frigidam et humidam O U FW Q X Z | sed non] non autem U 15 eodem] *rep.* N | actu] tactu (*lin.* K²) N M K² | Probatio] Probo U Z 16 respectu *om.* N M | remoto] regulato(!) N *spat. vac.* O *add.* nihil minus Q | ille] talis U 17 aqua] una H | per impossibile vel] quod est possibile X | vel] *add.* per O KU F Q X Z 18 humiditatem] *add.* eius KU FW Q X Z | igitur *om.* O | actus] tactus N 19 aquae *om.* N | aquae² *om.* N H | eius *om.* KU | nec] vel H | e converso quia] est actus sentiendi frigiditatem O U FW Q Z est actus sentiendi respectu humiditatis quia X *add.* ult. similiter O U FW Q Z 20 humiditate] *add.* aquae O U FW Q X Z | ergo *om.* Q X | etc *om.* Q 21 Sunt — est *om.* X | actus] *add.* et KU FW Q | quorum] et KU | unus] unum O

[23]**Thomas**, *De an.* II c. 22 (XLV¹ 161a): "Formaliter loquendo et secundum rationem, sensus tactus non est unus, sed plures; subiecto autem est unus"; **Anonymus (Jacobus de Duaco?)**, *Quaestiones De anima* II q. 30 (ed. Bazán 449): "Sed considerando tactum formaliter, sic sunt plures sensus."

dependet, ut visum est.

11   Item, respectu obiectorum formaliter diversorum non est idem actus; sed humidum et frigidum sunt obiecta formaliter diversa; igitur, etc.

12   Item, ab aqua in quantum frigida recipitur una species in organo tactus, et in quantum humida alia species in eodem organo; species enim humiditatis non est species frigiditatis. Sed species in organo est principium actus, vel formale vel inclinativum. Cum ergo ex datis principiis separatis, disparatis, inordinatis ad invicem, non egrediatur unus actus, sequitur quod actus sentiendi humiditatem et frigiditatem aquae sunt diversi.

13   Item, una potentia particularis sensitiva est respectu unius generis determinati, sicut patet per inductionem in aliis sensibus particularibus; et per rationem, quia obiectum debet correspondere potentiae, vel[24] esse determinativum potentiae, et est eiusdem generis determinati — sensus autem communis habet obiectum commune plurium sensuum. Patet igitur maior. Sed tactus non est unius generis physici, quia tale est tantum unius contrarietatis, ut patet per PHILOSOPHUM.[25] Et per rationem, quia quae sunt unius

---

1 est] *add.* ergo etc. O KU FW Q Z   2 Item] Praeterea O U FW Q X Z | respectu *om.* X   4 igitur etc. *om.* X | etc. *om.* Q   5 Item] Praeterea O U FW Q X Z | una species] *inv.* N   6 organo² *om.* X *add.* recipitur K   7 enim *om.* U | humiditatis ... frigiditatis] frigiditatis ... humiditatis O U FW Q X Z   8 actus] activum X | inclinativum] inclinatum FW *add.* cognitionis KU | Cum ergo] Et cum KU   9 datis] duobus KU FW Q X Z duc + *spat. vac.* O *add.* et Z | separatis disparatis] separatum disparatis O sed disparatis (*post* inordinatis) KU | disparatis] *add.* et LM | inordinatis] *lin.* M non ordinatis KU FW Q X Z | ad] ab L KU   10 egrediatur] egreditur Z | unus actus] *inv.* Z | actus *om.* X | humiditatem et frigiditatem] = L KU frigiditatem et humiditatem NO M FW Q X Z humiditatem vel frigiditatem H   11 aquae *om.* KU   12 Item] Praeterea O U FW Q X Z | particularis sensitiva] *inv.* U | respectu] tantum U FW Q X Z   13 determinati] physici U FW Q X Z | rebus sensibilibus L sensibilibus U   14 sensibus] correspondere potentiae] *inv.* X   15 vel — generis determinati] = NO HLM K si (sed X) ergo est (*om.* U) determinata potentia (*om.* FW Q X Z), debet habere obiectum generis (generis determinati] *inv.* U) determinati (*add. sicut* X) U FW Q X Z *add. ult.* si ergo est potentia (potentia determinata] determinatae potentiae L) determinata, debet habere obiectum generis determinati L K | esse determinativum] = H esse determinatum K determinatum N M est determinata O esse determinatae L | potentiae et est eiusdem] he et + *spat. vac.* O   16 autem *om.* U FW X Z | obiectum commune] *inv.* Z   17 plurium] physicum U | sensuum] generum sensibilium (sensuum FW) O FW Q X Z *om.* U | maior] minor K   18 tale] *lin.* K²   19 per] *lin.* U | Et per rationem *om.* FW | Et — Metaphysicae *om.* Z | rationem] *add.* patet N M | quae] *mg.* F² *om.* W

[24]Codices U FW Q X Z textum alterum exhibent; cf apparatum criticum. Codices L K autem tam textum proprium quam alterum exhibent. Utrum Doctor in originali textum proprium in margine seu in schedula scripserit, nescimus.

[25]**Aristot.**, *Physica* I c. 6 (AL VIII[1-2] 26; A c. 6 189b 14): "una contrarietas in omni genere uno"; cf **Averroës**, *In Phys.* I com. 50 (ed. Venetiis 1562, f. 31rb D); **Thomas**, *In Physica* II, 11 (ed. Marietti n. 96); *In De an.* II c. 22 (XLV¹ 160); *Quaest. Disp. De anima* q. 13 (XXIV¹ 115).

generis sunt ad invicem transmutabilia, ut patet X *Metaphysicae*;[26] talia autem sunt contraria aut media, ut ibidem dicitur;[27] similiter, II *De generatione*,[28] quae sunt unius contrarietatis, non sunt transmutabilia per se in alia alterius contrarietatis et per consequens eiusdem generis; certum est autem quod qualitates tangibiles non sunt unius contrarietatis, secundum PHILOSOPHUM expresse,[29] nec ergo unius generis physici, et per consequens nec sunt obiecta unius sensus particularis.[30] Tertia ratio[31] potest esse ratio COMMENTATORIS superius posita,[32] sed illa videtur non valere. Est enim duplex univocatio: una est logica, secundum quam plura conveniunt in uno conceptu communi tantum; alia est naturalis, secundum quam

---

1 generis] *add.* physici KU FW Q X | ad] ab Q | ut — Metaphysicae *om.* X | X] 'V' O   2 aut] vel Q | ibidem dicitur] *inv.* H FW Q X Z | dicitur] habetur L | similiter] scilicet O et KU FW Q X Z | II] 'I' KU FW Q X   3 quae] quia X *add.* ergo O U FW Q Z *add.* ult. non U | unius] unitatis X | sunt *om.* O | sunt — et *om.* U   4 alia] illa H | consequens] *add.* neque L K *add.* non U FW Q Z *add.* nec X   5 certum est autem] ita est U | tangibiles] *add.* quae sunt unius sensus particularis W | unius] eiusdem U   6 contrarietatis] qualitatis X *add.* est inconveniens X | secundum] per FW Q Z | expresse *om.* FW Q Z | expresse — physici] *mg.* H | nec ergo] *inv.* O U FW Q X Z igitur non H   7 sunt *om.* FW | sunt obiecta] *inv.* O KU Q X Z | obiecta] obiectum M   8 potest esse ratio *om.* X   9 sed illa] quae L | sed — non] videtur etiam non X | videtur non] *inv.* O U FW Q   10 est *om.* Q | plura *om.* X   11 conceptu] concepto O | communi tantum] *inv.* Z communi X *om.* U

[26]**Aristot.**, *Metaph.* X c. 4 (I c. 4 1055*a* 5-9); cf **Thomas**, *In Metaph.* X lect 5 (ed. Marietti n. 2024): "In illis autem quae differunt genere non est accipere huiusmodi viam transmutationis unius in alterum"; cf. etiam **Aristot.**, *Metaph.* V c. 28 (Δ c. 28 1024*b* 10-13): "Diversa vero genere dicuntur quorum diversum primum est subiectum et non resolvitur alterum in alterum, nec ambo in idem."
[27]**Aristot.**, *Metaph.* X c. 7 (AL XXV² 198; I c. 7 1057*a* 20-30): "Quoniam vero contrariorum contingit medium esse ... omnia namque media in eodem sunt genere et quorum sunt media. Media namque ea dicimus in quae permutari prius est necesse quod permutatur ... sed permutari vero ex alio genere in aliud genus non est nisi secundum accidens, ut ex colore in figuram"; cf. **Thomas**, *In Metaph.* X lect. 9 (ed. Marietti n. 2100); cf. **Aristot.**, *Metaph.* IV c. 7 (AL XXV² 80; Γ c. 7 1011*b* 33-36): "Non est enim permutatio nisi in contraria vel media"; **Thomas**, *In Metaph.* IV lectio 16 (ed. Marietti n. 723): "Non enim potest esse mutatio nisi inter contraria et media quae sunt unius generis; nec potest esse mutatio ab uno extremo in alterum nisi per medium"; **Aristot.**, *Physica* I c. 6 (AL VII¹ 29; A c. 6 189*b* 25-26): "Semper enim in uno genere contrarietas est, omnes autem contrarietates reduci videntur in unam"; **Thomas**, *Physica* I 11 lect. 11 (II 39*b*); *De an.* II c. 21 (XLV¹ 160*b*): "Quod in uno genere est una prima contrarietas, unde oportet quod circa obiectum unius sensus attendatur tantum una prima contrarietas"; *In II Sent.* dist. 19 q. 1 a. 2 (VI 556): "Ea quae differunt secundum genus, non sunt transmutabilia invicem. Sed corruptibile et incorruptibile sunt huiusmodi, ut in 10 *Metaph.* dicitur."
[28]**Aristot.**, *De gener. et corrupt.* II c. 1 (AL IX¹ 53-54; B c. 1 329*a* 33—*b* 2): "Quapropter primum quidem potentia corpus sensibile principium, secundum autem contrarietates, dico autem verbi gratia caliditas et frigiditas, tertio autem iam ignis et aqua et talia. Haec quidem enim transmutant ad invicem ... , contrarietates autem non transmutant"; cf. *De gener. et corrupt.* II c. 4 (331*a* 13-15): "Generatio quidem enim in contraria et ex contrariis; elementa autem omnia habent contrarietatem ad invicem, quia differentiae contrariae sunt."
[29]Cf. supra, n. 6.
[30]Cf. **Aristot.**, *Metaph.* X c. 4 (I c. 4 1055*a* 30-32): "(contraria sunt) quae sub eadem potentia plurimum differentia"; **Thomas**, *In Metaph.* X lect 5 (ed. Marietti n. 2035).
[31]Scilicet, tertia probatio minoris.
[32]Cf. supra n. 8.

aliqua conveniunt in aliqua natura reali ad extra, ut in specie atoma, de qua loquitur PHILOSOPHUS VII *Physicorum*[33] — illud est univocum secundum quod aliqua sunt comparabilia. Si COMMENTATOR intelligat de prima univocatione, minor[34] est falsa, quia omnes qualitates tangibiles conveniunt in uno conceptu qualitatis. Si de secunda, tunc sua maior[35] est falsa, quia plures species atomae sunt ab uno sensu sensibiles, ut patet de albo et nigro respectu visus. Potest tamen sua ratio sic colorari: quia praeter utramque univocationem est una metaphysicalis, secundum quam aliqua uniuntur in genere propinquo, et est media inter utramque praedictam — est enim maior primā et minor secundā. Et de ista univocatione habet maior sua veritatem, ut patet ratione superius posita pro ista parte ante responsionem.[36]

Sed contra maiorem sic intellectam adduci potest argumentum

---

1 aliqua *post* conveniunt U Z alia K plura U *om.* X | aliqua²] una O U FW Q X Z | aliqua natura] *inv.* L | natura] quantitate U | ad *om.* O U FW Q X Z | extra] exemplum L F X *add.* intentum U 2 Philosophus] Aristoteles Q *om.* X | Physicorum] *add.* dicens KU W Q X Z *add.* dicit F | illud] idem H U aliquid L illa X id Z | est] esse KU FW Q Z | univocum] univoca X unitum(?) O 3 quod] quid Q quae X *add.* ult. secundum X | aliqua] alia K | sunt] dicuntur K dicuntur esse U | comparabilia] compossibilia W | Commentator intelligat] *inv.* O KU FW Q Z loquitur Commentator X 4 minor] *add.* sua KU FW Q X Z | omnes] diversae X | qualitates] quiditates N 5 conveniunt] *ant.* qualitates U FW Q X Z 6 tunc] iterum Q *om.* X | sua *post* maior Q *om.* X | est falsa] *inv.* W Q Z | species *om.* O K | species — sunt] sunt atomae species H atomae species sunt Q 7 et] *lin.* O *add.* de + *spat. vac.* O | Potest — ratio] Praeterea sic sua ratio posset (*om.* X) FW X 8 sua ratio] *inv.* KU | sic] *ant.* sua O Q *om.* FW X Z | colorari] corrobari(!) F | quia] et N | praeter] *post* N HM | utramque] *rep.* N | univocationem] unionem H unitatem U 9 una] univocatio K | metaphysicalis] mathematicalis(!) Q inordinalis(?) X | quam] quid Q | uniuntur] *mg.* K² univocantur N M conveniunt X | in] *add.* suo FW | genere] *mg.* F² *add.* esse FW 10 et est] ratione U | inter] in K | praedictam] praedicamentarum F productam X *om.* U | est — secunda *om.* L 11 prima] falsa Z | et *om.* H | et — secunda] et secunda minor U et minor Z *om.* X | secunda] *add.* univocatione K | ista] illa NO M F Q | univocatione] veritate O secunda U *om.* FW Q X Z | habet] *rep.* N | habet — veritatem] = HM habet maior suam veritatem N L habet sua maior veritatem O habet ista minor veritatem K unitate habet sua maior intelligi U veritatem habet sua maior FW Q X Z 12 patet] *add.* (lin.) in U | superius] prius H | ista] illa NO M F Q | parte ante] *mg.* X² | ante *om.* U 13 responsionem] rationem H 14 contra] *add.* illam O FW Q *add.* istam KU Z | adduci potest argumentum] = N M adhuc potest argui O FW Q X Z potest adduci argumentum HL potest sic argui K potest sic argui adhuc U

---

[33] **Aristot.**, *Physica* VII c. 4 (AL VII¹ 269; H c. 4, 248*b* 6-9): "Sed quaecumque non aequivoca, comparabilia sunt. Ut quare non comparabile utrum acutius stilus aut vinum aut ultima? Quia namque aequivoca sunt, nec comparantur"; Cf. *Physica* VII c. 4 (AL VII¹ 271-2; H c. 4, 249*a* 20-29); **Thomas**, *Physica* VII lect. 4 n. 7 (II 348*b*): "Ita scilicet quod secundum ea quae non aequivoce praedicantur, possint ea de quibus praedicantur, ad invicem comparari"; **Aegidius Romanus**, *De an.* II com. 108 (f. 50*va-b*): "Haec ratio Commentatoris magnam videtur habere calumniam, quia univocatio vera non reperitur nisi in specie specialissima ... sic non est univocatio nisi in specie specialissima"; *Auctoritates Aristotelis* (ed. J. Hamesse 155): "Sola univoca et non aequivoca sunt comparabilia."

[34] Scil. "Sed contraria tactus non videntur habere genus quod dicatur de eis nisi aequivoce" — cf. notam in n. 8 supra.

[35] Scil. "Necesse est enim, si posuerimus quod unus sensus comprehendit multos modos contrarietatis, ut genus subiectum illis modis sit unum" — cf. notam in n. 8 supra.

[36] Cf. supra n. 8.

de sensu communi, qui est unus et non est tantum unius generis talis, tanquam obiecti, nec unius contrarietatis.[37]

Sed dicendum quod aliquid potest diversificare potentiam inferiorem, quod non potest superiorem diversificare. Diversitas igitur generis propinqui sensibilium diversificat potentias sensitivas proprias, vel saltem ostendit earum diversitatem non esse diversitatem sensus communis, qui est superior — immo iudicat de obiectis et actibus sensuum particularium.

[PROBATIO SECUNDAE PARTIS CONCLUSIONIS PRINCIPALIS]

Declaratio secundae partis conclusionis principalis[38] est ista: potentiae cognitivae correspondent ipsis obiectis. Sicut igitur se habent ad invicem obiecta sensus tactus, quae sunt qualitates activae et passivae, ita et potentiae tactivae. Modo ita est quod qualitates activae fundantur in passivis et se invicem concomitantur, sicut forma in materia fundatur, et se concomitantur quia qualitates activae consequuntur compositum ratione formae, et passivae ratione materiae; ergo et potentiae tactivae se invicem consequuntur, ut ubicumque et in quocumque est una potentia, foret et alia. Exemplum de sapore, qui fundatur in tangibilibus qualitatibus ex quibus causatur tanquam qualitas secunda. Ideo gustus, cuius obiectum est sapor, fundatur in tactu — immo est quidam tactus,

---

1 est² *om.* L | tantum] tamen U | generis talis] *inv.* O U FW Q X Z 2 obiecti] subiecti N *om.* L | unius *om.* F *add. spat. vac.* O 3 dicendum] sciendum L *add.* est F | dicendum quod] *lin.* X | aliquid] *mg.* H 4 inferiorem] in superiorem N | non *om.* Q | potest] *add.* potentiam L Z | superiorem diversificare] = N HM *inv.* L superiorem O KU FW Q X Z | Diversitas] Diversitate W Z 5 sensitivas] *rep. post* proprias FW 6 ostendit] apparet N ostendunt O dicit FW concludit Z *om.* X | earum] eorum K | non — diversitatem] *mg.* Z² *om.* O U | esse] autem H 7 communis] communiter O | immo] in illo U *add. (mg.)* ordine U² | iudicat] indicat O U | de — actibus] in actibus et obiectis U de actibus et obiectis X 8 sensuum] sensibilium N 10 partis] *mg.* U² per (*post* principalis) O *om.* FW Q X Z | conclusionis] = O L FW Q X Z quaestionis H KU *om.* N M | principalis est ista] est illa principali N est ista (illa L) principales HL | est *om.* O | ista] illa K FW Q | potentiae cognitivae] contentie(!) O cognitivae L potentiae K FW Q X Z 11 cognitivae] *mg.* U | ipsis] istis X 12 invicem] *add.* ipsa KU | sensus *om.* KU FW Q X Z 13 tactivae] activae N U | Modo] motae(!) Q | activae] *mg.* U 14 fundantur] finiuntur(?) Q fiunt O | concomitantur] comitantur Z | sicut — concomitatur] *mg.* F² 15 fundatur] finitur Q | et] etiam L | se *om.* F² | concomitantur] concomitatur N H X | quia qualitates *post* activae X | qualitates] *add.* sequuntur W | qualitates activae] *inv.* U 16 consequuntur] sequuntur FW Q X Z | compositum] composita KU 17 tactivae] activae L KU X *add.* ult. et passivae K | consequuntur] concomitantur KU | ut] et O KU FW Q X Z 18 et in quocumque *post* alia Q | potentia foret] potentia (*post* alia) K *om.* U FW Q X Z 19 Exemplum] *praem.* Ponitur U FW Q X Z | tangibilibus qualitatibus] *inv.* O KU FW Q X Z 20 quibus] quo Q Z | Ideo] *praem.* Et KU FW Q X Z Ratio N H *om.* L 21 tactu] *add.* quia N | quidam tactus causaliter] quod X

---

[37]Cf. **Ioannes Blund**, *Tractatus de anima* c. 17 (ed. Callus et Hunt ABMA II 62-67).
[38]Scil. 'sensus tactus non sunt ita diversi vel divisi sicut alii ab invicem', cf. supra n. 9.

causaliter loquendo, sicut "gustabile est quoddam tangibile".[39]

[II. — Ad argumenta principalia]

16   Ad primum in oppositum[40] dicendum quod sicut sunt quattuor gradus viventium,[41] tamen sunt quinque genera potentiarum[42] — quia appetitivum non constituit distinctum gradum a sensitivo, quia ubi est appetitivum, et sensitivum;[43] tamen alia est potentia appetitiva et sensitiva —, sic in proposito sunt quinque genera sensitiva, quia illi duo tactus non constituunt diversa genera sensuum — immo ubi est unus, et alius; sunt tamen diversae species tactus, ut probatum est[44].

17   Ad aliud[45] dicendum quod organum non est unum formaliter sed tantum materialiter. Unde in eodem nervo est alia qualitas secundum quam est discretio humidi et sicci, et alia secundum quam est discretio frigidi et calidi. Quia tamen se invicem concomitantur illae qualitates, ideo non est organum ita distinctum, sicut

---

1 causaliter om. O | loquendo] adnot. mg. nota M | est om. Q | quoddam] quiddam W Q quod est X   3 Ad] adnot. mg. Ad primum U | in oppositum om. Z | oppositum] contrarium FW Q | dicendum] add. est N M | sicut] lin U² om. K   4 gradus] generus H | tamen] ita Z   5 quia] mg. F² | non — sensitivum] mg. Z² | constituit] constituunt(!) F | gradum] add. viventium O U FW Q X Z² | sensitivo] sensibilibus F sensibili L   6 ubi est] lin. O | appetitivum et sensitivum] sensitivum et (est K) appetitivum KU FW Q X Z² | tamen — appetitiva] mg. K² | alia] altera Z | appetitiva et sensitiva] sensitiva ab appetitiva O FW X Z   7 et] add. alia H | sic] sicut W Z | proposito] add. (mg.) non U | sunt] add. nisi U | sensitiva²] sensibilium Q   8 illi] illa X isti Z | sensuum] sensibilium Q | immo om. U   9 est] add. nervo U | unus] add. ibi K | et] est K   10 est] lin. X   11 Ad aliud post dicendum U | dicendum] add. est F | non om. X   12 sed tantum] est tamen N | tantum post materialiter K | alia] aliqua O L U FW Q X   13 discretio] = N HM discretivus O KU Q X Z distinctivus FW | discretio — est om. L   14 discretio] discretivus KU FW Q X Z | frigidi et calidi] calidi et frigidi O L KU FW Q X   15 illae] istae O KU X Z

[39]Aristot., De an. II c. 21 (B c. 10, 422a 8): "Gustabile autem est quoddam tangibile"; cf. Thomas, Summa theol. I q. 78 a. 3 ad 3 in opp. (V 254b): "Qui tamen non separantur ab invicem secundum organum, sed per totum corpus se concomitantur; et ideo distinctio non apparet. Gustus autem, qui est perceptivus dulcis et amari, concomitatur tactum in lingua, non autem per totum corpus; et ideo de facili a tactu distinguitur."
[40]Cf. supra n. 1.
[41]Cf. Aristot., De an. II c. 3 (B c. 2, 413a 22-25); Aegidius Romanus, De an. II com. 108 (f. 51ra): "Dicendum quod supra dicebantur esse quattuor genera animatorum videlicet vegetativum, sensitivum et secundum locum motivum et intellectivum."
[42]Cf. Aristot., De an. II c. 5 (B c. 3, 414a 29-32): "Potentias autem diximus vegetativum, sensitivum, appetitivum, motivum secundum locum, intellectivum"; Thomas, In De an. II c. 5 (XLV¹ 88-99); Summa theol. I q. 78 a. 1 (V 250a—251b); Aegidius Romanus, De an. II com. 108 (f. 51ra): "Et tamen dicebantur esse quinque genera potentiarum videlicet sensitivum, vegetativum, appetitivum, secundum locum motivum et intellectivum".
[43]Aegidius Romanus, De an. II com. 108 (f. 51ra): "Appetitivum ergo est distincta potentia ab omnibus animalibus: non tamen facit distinctum gradum animatorum quia numquam separat a sensativo; nec sensativum ab ipso: sic est in proposito."
[44]Cf. supra n. 9-15.
[45]Cf. supra n. 2.

organa aliorum sensuum, si est nervus vel vena. In lingua autem secundum aliam et aliam qualitatem est organum gustus et tactus, et sic humor et potus per aliam qualitatem et aliam est gustabilis et tangibilis.[46]

[9] 5   Ad aliud[47] dicendum quod illi tactus in specie differunt, sicut et obiecta formalia.[48] Ad obiectum dicendum est quod unus est perfectior alio, sicut unus qui est discretio perfectioris contrarietatis, scilicet calidi et frigidi. Et tu dicis quod aeque perfecte sentit unus suum obiectum sicut alius. Dicendum quod hoc est verum secundum aequalitatem proportionis, non tamen secundum aequalitatem adaequationis et perfectionis, quia perfectior est immutatio a calido et frigido quam ab humido et sicco. Ponitur exemplum de visu aquilae respectu solis, et noctuae respectu obiecti sibi proportionalis; utraque enim visio est aeque proportionaliter perfecta, sed absolute una est perfectior alia.[49]

---

1 organa] organum L K | si] sicut X Z | si est] scilicet KU | In] *lin.* Z Sicut FW | autem] enim N *om.* O KU FW Q X Z   2 aliam *om.* X | gustus *om.* N | et³ *om.* U   3 sic] sicut O U FW Z | et²] vel FW Q X *om.* U | potus] potatus U | per — aliam²] secundum (per FW) aliam et aliam qualitatem KU FW *om.* Z | et aliam *om.* O Q X | gustabilis et tangibilis] gustabile et tangibile KU   5 illi] isti KU | in *om.* O KU FW Q X Z | et] *add.* alia KU   6 obiectum] obiectionem K Z oppositum Q | est *om.* O KU W Q X Z | unus] unus ... perfectior] obiectum ... perfectius X | est² *om.* Q | est perfectior] *inv.* F   7 sicut] scilicet KU FW Q X Z | unus] ille KU FW Q *om.* X Z | discretio *post* contrarietatis N M discretivus O KU FW Q X Z | perfectioris] perfectionis W | contrarietatis] qualitatis Q   8 scilicet *om.* Z | Et] Et cum U *om.* Z | tu *om.* U | dicis] dices F | quod *om.* L | aeque] tam O Z | perfecte *om.* X | sentit unus] *inv.* X   9 obiectum] ant. suum Z | sicut] *add.* et U | Dicendum] *add.* est N M | hoc] hic O *om.* F Q   10 tamen] autem O U FW Q X Z | secundum² *om.* H   11 et] vel O L FW Q X   12 ab] a KU | humido et sicco] sicco et humido KU | Ponitur] Probatur X | visu] visione U   13 et] *add.* oculi FW Q Z | noctuae] *mg.* K² *om.* U | proportionalis] proportionabilis H U Q   14 enim] autem FW Q X Z | visio *om.* U | proportionaliter] proportionabiliter H KU X   15 sed] licet U | absolute] absoluta O | una est] *inv.* HL | alia] altera Q

---

[46] **Aristot.**, *De an.* II c. 22 (B c. 11, 423a 17-21): "Plures sunt qui in lingua tactus; omnia enim tangibilia sentit secundum eandem partem et humorem"; cf. **Thomas**, *In De an.* II c. 21 (XLV¹ 155): "Sapor, qui est obiectum gustus, non est aliqua de qualitatibus simplicium corporum ex quibus animal constituitur quae sunt propria obiecta sensus tactus, sed causatur ab eis et fundatur in aliqua earum sicut in materia, scilicet in humido; unde manifestum est quod gustus non est idem quod sensus tactus, sed quodam modo radicatur in eo"; cf. etiam II c. 22 (XLV¹ 162); cf. **Anonymus (Jacobus de Duaco?)**, *Quaestiones De anima* II q. 30 (ed. Bazán 449): "Primum sic confirmo: ille sensus materialiter est unus qui habet unum organum et unum medium; sed sensus tactus est huiusmodi; ergo etc. Tunc confirmo secundum, scilicet quod, considerando sensum tactus formaliter, quod sunt plures."

[47] Cf. supra n. 3.

[48] **Thomas**, *Summa theol.* I q. 78 a. 3 ad 3 (V 256b): "Sensus tactus est unus genere, sed dividitur in multos sensus secundum speciem; et propter hoc est diversarum contrarietatum'; cf. etiam *In De an.* II c. 22 (XLV¹ 161): "Unde formaliter loquendo et secundum rationem, sensus tactus non est unus, sed plures; subiecto autem est unus."

[49] Cf. **Aristot.**, *Metaph.* II c. 1 (AL XXV^{3.2} 43; A c. 1 993b 9-11): "Sicut enim nicticoracum oculi ad lucem diei se habent, sic et animae nostrae intellectus ad ea quae sunt omnium naturae manifestissima"; *Auctoritates Aristotelis* (ed. J. Hamesse 118): "Sicut se habet oculus nicticoracis ad lumen solis vel diei, sic se habet noster intellectus ad manifestissima naturae."

19 Ad aliud[50] dicendum quod ideo tactus facit esse animal quia est communior[51] sensuum et est fundamentum[52] aliorum, sicut anima vegetativa facit corpus esse animatum, non quia sit perfectior anima nec quia tactus sit perfectior sensus. In illa autem communitate sensus sunt ambo sensus tactus, quia in quocumque animali reperitur unus, reperitur alius, et in quacumque parte organi. Ideo non constituunt diversa animalia.

20 Ad aliud[53] dicendum quod non sufficit contrarietas qualitatis activae et passivae, quae non communicant in uno genere naturali, sed tantum logico. Secundum autem genus naturale differunt, ut contrarietas tangibilium qualitatum. Ideo non est unum obiectum.

---

1 Ad aliud — diversa animalia (*fin. par.*) *om.* X | dicendum *om.* Z *add.* est N M K | ideo *om.* U | facit] *add.* animal KU | animal] animalis H   2 communior] *add.* aliorum Q | sensuum] sensus KU | est] sic N M *om.* U Q | fundamentum] finiter(!) Q | aliorum] *add.* sensuum FW Q Z   3 esse *post* animatum Q *om.* K | quia] quod Z | sit] est KU | anima *om.* FW Q Z   4 nec] vel U | nec — perfectior *om.* FW | tactus] sensus Q Z *om.* N M | sensus *om.* Z | illa] ista L anima Q | autem *om.* FW | communitate] qualitate Z   5 sunt] conveniunt KU FW Q Z   6 reperitur²] et KU FW Q Z *add.* unus et O | in *om.* KU Z | parte organi] *inv.* N LM organi O   8 dicendum] *add.* est N M   9 quae] quia K | communicant] convenit FW conveniunt U Q X Z   10 genus *om.* X | ut *om.* U   11 contrarietas] contrarietates KU FW Q X Z | tangibilium *post* qualitatum K X | obiectum] *add.* et (*add.* ideo Q) haec (*add.* dicta Q) sufficiant (*add.* etc. O) O U FW Q Z

[50] Cf. supra n. 4.
[51] **Aristot.**, *De an.* II c. 2 (B c. 2, 413*b* 8-9): "Animalia autem omnia videntur tangendi sensum habentia."
[52] Vox 'fundamentum' apud Aristotelem non invenitur, sed iam invenitur apud Albertum et Thomam; cf. **Thomas**, *In De an.* II c. 19 (XLV¹ 149).
[53] Cf. supra n. 5.

[QUAESTIO 2]

UTRUM CARO SIT ORGANUM TACTUS

Utrum caro sit organum sensus tactus.[1]

[1] Videtur quod sic per PHILOSOPHUM XII *De animalibus*:[2] 1
Dicit quod caro est instrumentum tactus, sicut pupilla visus; pupilla autem est organum visus; igitur, etc.

Item, caro animalis est animata: aut igitur animā organicā aut 2 non-organicā. Non potest dici non-organicā, quia talis est anima intellectiva tantum — multa enim sunt animalia habentia carnem animatam sine anima intellectiva;[3] igitur animā organicā, et per consequens est pars organica animalis.

Item, ubi est sensus tactus, ibi est organum tactus; sed non in 3 omni parte animalis ubi est sensus tactus, ibi est nervus — ibi tamen est caro; ideo caro est magis organum quam nervus.[4] Probatio minoris: in capite est tactus, et non nervus.

---

3 Utrum] *praem.* Quaeritur O U FW Q X Z *praem.* Quaeritur secundo K | sensus *om.* L Z 4 Videtur] *praem.* Et K F Q *om.* X | per *om.* Q | Philosophum] Philosophus Q 5 Dicit] Dico O Dicentem K Dicens U W *om.* Q *add.* ult. enim L | quod *om.* Q X 6 autem *om.* HL Q | igitur *om.* X | etc. *om.* K 7 Item] Praeterea O KU FW Q X Z | est] autem X | igitur *om.* X | anima] animata NO alia(!) X 8 dici] *add.* anima K *add.* quod anima U FW X Z *add.* quod Q | non-organica] organica O | quia — intellectiva] anima est intellectiva O quia (quae X) illa (huiusmodi Q *om.* FW X Z) est intellectiva KU FW Q X Z 9 multa] in multis X | enim] autem O U FW Q X Z | carnem — intellectiva] animam non intellectivam U 10 animatam] animata(!) O | igitur] *add.* est KL | anima] *add. spat. vac.* U 12 Item] Praeterea O KU FW Q X Z | est *om.* L | ibi *om.* X | est[2] *om.* L 13 ubi] in qua KU FW Q X Z | ibi *om.* X 14 ideo] ergo KU FW Q X Z | est magis] *inv.* N M Q X Z | organum] *add.* tactus Z 15 minoris] maioris X | et non] tantum X | nervus] *add.* igitur etc. K

[1] Cf. **Aristot.**, *De an.* II c. 11 (B c. 11 422b 34—423a 6); **Avicenna**, *De an.* pars 2 c. 3 (AviL I 138-140); **Averroës**, *De an.* II com. 109 (AverL 298-300); **Ioannes Blund**, *Tractatus de anima* c. 16 (ed. Callus et Hunt ABMA II 59-60); **Albertus M.**, *De an.* II tr. 3 c. 31 (VII[1] 142b—144a); **Aegidius Romanus**, *De an.* II com. 109 (f. 51ra).
[2] **Aristot.**, *De part. animal.* II c. 8 (ed. Iuntina VI[1] f. 139v; B c. 8 654a 9-11): "... tactus vero sensorium pars eiusmodi est aut prima, ut pupilla visus"; *Auctoritates Aristotelis* (ed. J. Hamesse 218): "Instrumentum sensus tactus est caro. Dicit tamen postea quod instrumentum tactus non est caro sed aliquid infra carnem, ut infra dictum est de anima"; **Themistius**, *De an.* I (CLCAG I 4 170): "Sed quod quidem a principio proponebamus quaerere, non hoc erat, sed si caro ipsa est sensitivum tangabilium, sicut pupilla visibilium, aut sensitivum quidem intus, et caro intermedia organi primi et tangibilium."
[3] Cf. **Aristot.**, *De an.* II c. 3 (B c. 3 414a 29—b 2); *De an.* II c. 3 (B c. 3 415a 1-10); *De an.* II c. 3 (Γ c. 3 429a 5-8); **Avicenna**, *De an.* pars. 4 c. 1 (AviL II 2); *Auctoritates Aristotelis* (ed. J. Hamesse 178): "... et tam secundum locum motiva quam sensitiva possunt esse sine intellectiva, ut patet in animalibus brutis ...".
[4] Cf. **Albertus M.**, *Physic.* V tr. 2 c. 3 (IV[2] 426a).

4   Item, sunt aliqua animalia quae non habent nervos, ut pisces; tamen habent sensum tactus.[5]

5   In oppositum est COMMENTATOR, dicens quod organum tactus est nervus extensus toti corpori, et non caro, sed[6] est medium in tangendo.[7] Hoc etiam probat PHILOSOPHUS[8] a proposito, quia sensibile positum supra sensum non sentitur, sed sensibile positum supra carnem sentimus; igitur, etc.

[I. — Solutio quaestionis]

6   Ad istam quaestionem dicendum quod caro non est organum sensus tactus, sed aliquid infra carnem, scilicet nervus, vel aliquid loco nervi coextensum corpori.[9]

7   Probatio responsionis: quia oportet organum sensuum particularium continuari organo sensus communis, quia sensus communis habet iudicare de speciebus receptis in organis sensuum particularium;[10] caro non continuatur organo sensus communis, quod est in cerebro vel in corde — immo nervi vel venae, derivatae a corde

---

1 Item] Praeterea O KU FW Q Z | sunt aliqua] inv. O KU FW Q X Z | aliqua] quaedam N | nervos] nervum L | pisces] *add.* igitur Q   2 tamen *post* habent N Q X | sensum] sensus Q | tactus] *add.* ergo, etc. O KU W Q Z   3 In *om.* Q | oppositum *om.* Q | dicens] dicit (*ant.* Commentator Q) F Q *om.* X   4 est *om.* Q | extensus] coextensus KU FW Q Z | extensus toti corpori] diffusus toto corpore L | corpori et] corpore U | et *om.* FW Q Z | sed] *add.* caro L   5 etiam *post* probat F *om.* X | quia] quod W   6 positum *post* sensum KU Q posito FW | sentitur] facit sensum O KU FW Q X Z | sensibile positum] *inv.* O posito tangibili FW posito tangibile KU X Z tangibile posito Q   7 sentimus] sentitur L facit tactum sive sensum K facit carnem sensum FW Q facit sensum U X Z | igitur etc. *om.* K X   9 istam] illam O H K | quaestionem *om.* X | dicendum] *add.* est N M U F   10 sensus *om.* O U FW Q X Z | sed] licet L | infra] intra F | scilicet] sicut Q si X vel Z | aliquid²] aliquo O *add.* in K   11 nervi] nervum Q *add.* et H | coextensum] extensum N HM   12 responsionis] conclusionis O U FW Q X Z | organum] organa M | particularium *post* continuari X   13 sensu communis *om.* O   14 habet] *spat. vac.* O | iudicare] cavere O | in] non X | organis] organo F | sensuum] sensus U   15 caro] *add.* (*mg.* U) autem O KU FW X Z *add.* enim Q | caro — communis] *mg.* U | quod — immo] et ipsi O | est *post* cerebro X *mg.* W²   16 immo] *mg.* U | venae] *mg.* U *add.* eius O | derivatae — venae *om.* L

---

[5]Cf. **Aristot.**, *De part. animal.* II c. 8 (ed. Iuntina VI¹ f. 73*va*; B c. 8 653*b* 30—654*a* 2); *De an.* II c. 3 (B c. 3 414*a* 29—*b* 2); **Albertus M.**, *De animalibus* (BGPTH 15 865).
[6]Subaudi: caro.
[7]**Averroës**, *De an.* II com. 116 (AverL 311): "... modo autem, quia videmus quod virtus tangibilis non sentit nisi quando tangibile fuerit positum super carnem, necesse est ut caro sit medium, non instrumentum"; Cf. **Themistius**, *De an.* IV, V (CLCAG I 4 170, 175, 195); **Avicenna**, *De an.* pars 2 c. 3 (AviL I 138-140); **Ioannes Blund**, *Tractatus de anima* c. 16 (ed. Callus et Hunt ABMA II 59).
[8]**Aristot.**, *De an.* II c. 11 (B c. 11, 422*b* 34—423*a* 6); **Averroës**, *De an.* II com. 109 (AverL 299).
[9]**Aristot.**, *De sensu et sensato* [c. 4] (c. 4, 439*a* 1-2); **Thomas**, *De an.* II c. 23 (XLV¹ 160); **Aegidius Romanus**, *De an.* II com. 108 (f. 50*vb*).
[10]Cf. **Aristot.**, *De an.* II c. 25 (Γ c. 1 425*a* 11—*b* 3); *De an.* II c. 26 (Γ c. 2 426*b* 8-29); **Thomas**, *Summa theol.* I q. 78 a. 4 ad 2 (V 256*b*).

secundum PHILOSOPHUM[11] vel a cerebro secundum medicos,[12] continuant organa sensuum particularium organo sensus communis, et ipsi nervi vel venae eius continuantur;[13] igitur, etc.

Item, quaedam sunt virtutes naturales, quaedam animales.[14] Naturales bene fundantur in carne, quae est corpus mixtum[15] in quo sunt qualitates activae et passivae, saltem virtute; virtutes autem animales fundantur in venis et nervis; sed virtus tactiva est virtus animalis; igitur, etc.

Ulterius est sciendum quod quaedam est caro nervosa, quaedam pura; nervosa autem non tantum est medium, sed etiam organum.[16] Illi autem nervi coextenduntur toti carni animalis, non quia sunt in qualibet parte carnis quantumcumque modica nervi — aut quod non sit caro pura in animali — sed quia prope vel iuxta quamlibet

---

1 a] in Q *om.* U FW Z 2 continuant] continuantur Z | communis] *add.* quia F 3 eius] ei U FW Q X Z | igitur etc. *om.* X 4 Item] Primum O Praeterea KU FW Q X Z | quaedam] quod O | naturales] *add.* et HL 5 bene *om.* X | in quo] etiam F 6 saltem] *add.* in K | autem] enim L 7 animales] naturales H | venis et nervis] nervis et venis O KU FW Q X Z | tactiva] activa F 8 igitur etc. *om.* X 9 quod] *add.* est K | quaedam est] *inv.* FW Q X Z | quaedam est caro] est caro quaedam O | nervosa] *add.* et O 10 autem] aut(!) L | tantum *om.* H | est *post* medium Q | etiam *om.* Q | etiam organum] *spat. vac.* H" *add. mg.* tantum sed organum etiam H² 11 Illi] Isti O KU FW | autem] enim K | coextenduntur] extenduntur Q | sunt] sint O FW sit Q sicut Z *om.* U 12 carnis] animalis U W *add.* animalis H *add.* in O | modica] medica M modicum X modum Z *add.* aut FW | nervi] est nervus U | aut] ita KU autem X | non sit *om.* X 13 sit] fuit Q | prope ... iuxta] iuxta (mixta X) ... prope KU FW Q X Z

[11]Cf. **Aristot.**, *De hist. animal.* I c. 4 (ed. Iuntina VI¹ f. 2*rb*; A c. 4 523*a* 30—524*b* 29); *De part. animal.*, II. c. 1 (ed. Iuntina VI¹ f. 68*ra*; B c. 1 647*a* 30-31); *De part. animal.* II. c. 8 (ed. Iuntina VI¹ f. 73*va*; B c. 8 653*b* 30-35); *De part. animal.* II. c. 10 (ed. Iuntina VI¹ f. 74*vb*—75*rb*; B c. 10 656*b* 10-30); **Avicenna**, *De an.* pars. 1 c. 5 (AviL I 88); **Dominicus Gundissal.**, *De immortalitate animae* (BGPTH 2³ 20-1); **Alfredus Anglicus**, *De motu cordis* (BGPTH 23¹ 14-15); **Philippus Cancellarius**, *Quaestiones de anima* q. 29 (ed. Keeler 91); **Guilelmus de Alvernia Parisiensis**, *De immortalitate animae*, (BGPTH 2³ 57); **Ioannes Blund**, *Tractatus de anima* c. 17 (ed. Callus et Hunt ABMA II 63); **Albertus M.**, *De animalibus* (BGPTH 15 864-6).
[12]**Costa Ben Luca**, *De differentia animae et spiritus* c. 3 (ed. Barach et Wrobel 126); **Avicenna**, *De an.* pars 1 c. 5 (AviL I 87); **Thomas**, *Summa theol.* I q. 78 a. 4 in corp (V 256*b*): "... cui medici assignant determinatum organum, scilicet mediam partem capitis ..."; **Constantinus Africanus**, *De nervis* 34-35: "Quorumlibet nervorum fundamentum est cerebrum, cum voluntarii motus atque sensuum sit fundamentum. Omnes autem nervi aut de cerebro procedunt aut de mediatoribus cerebri."
[13]**Averroës**, *De an.* II com. 108 (AverL 298): "Nervi habent introitum in tactu et motu."
[14]**Alcher**, *Liber de spiritu et anima* (PL 40, 794): "Habet quoque anima vires quibus corporis commiscetur: quarum prima est naturalis; secunda, vitalis; tertia, animalis ... Naturalis namque virtus operatur in hepate sanguinem et alios quosque humores, quos per venas ad omnia corporis membra transmittit, ut inde augeantur et nutriantur ... Vis animalis est in cerebro, et inde vigere facit quinque sensus corporis."
[15]**Averroës**, *De an.* II com. 111 (AverL 302): "Contingit ut medium in sensibus tactus esset corpus admixtum super quod habundaret terrestritas; et est caro."
[16]**Avicenna**, *De an.* pars 2 c. 3 (AviL I 138): "Ex proprietatibus autem tactus est quod instrumentum naturale quod est caro nervosa aut caro et nervus ex hoc quod sentit, sentit ex tactu, quamvis non sit ibi medium aliquo modo"; cf. **Ioannes Blund**, *Tractatus de anima* c. 16 (ed. Callus et Hunt ABMA II 59-60).

partem carnis sicut aliqui ramusculi nervorum coextenduntur per corpus ad modum retis, et hoc patet in folio arborum ad sensum. Per istos autem nervos vel ramusculos derivatur virtus tactiva a corde vel a cerebro per totum corpus. Caro autem pura est tantum medium in tangendo, ut probat PHILOSOPHUS, II *De anima*.[17]

Necessitas autem ponendi sensum vel organum tactus esse extensum toti corpori est quia qualitates tangibiles possunt agere in quamcumque partem corporis, cum quaelibet pars sit mixta ex quattuor elementis, in qua reducuntur ad medium, et per consequens est in potentia ad receptionem et passionem naturalem ab excellentiis qualitatum. Si igitur in una parte corporis non esset organum tactus discretivum huiusmodi excellentiarum, tunc illa pars cito posset corrumpi ab eis, et similiter alia in qua esset organum. Ad consequendum igitur convenientia ad conservationem animalis, et fugiendum nociva, est organum tactus ita extensum, et etiam est intrinsecum propter eandem causam, ne de facili corrumpatur ab excellenti tangibili.[18]

[II. — Ad argumenta principalia]

Ad primum[19] dicendum quod, ut COMMENTATOR dicit,[20] ARISTOTELES tunc nescivit naturam nervorum, postea autem inquisivit per

---

1 carnis *om.* X | sicut] sunt KU FW Q X Z *om.* O | nervorum] nervi(!) L | coextenduntur] = N HM qui extenduntur O KU FW Q X Z extenduntur L | per] *add.* totum KU Z 2 ad] per X | hoc *om.* Q | folio] foliis L filio X | arborum] arboris O H 3 istos] illos O H FW Q Z | derivatur] derivantur FW divinantur Z | virtus] *add.* tota K | virtus tactiva] *spat. vac.* tactivum X tactiva(?) Z *om.* F 4 a *om.* O U FW Q X | corpus] *add. mg.* sentimus F² | tantum *post* medium Q tangit (*ant.* est) X 5 in tangendo] tangendi KU 6 autem] enim L | esse *om.* KU 7 extensum] coextensum KU FW Q X Z 8 quamcumque partem] quacumque parte K qualibet parte F quamlibet partem W Q X | ex *om.* U 9 quattuor elementis] *inv.* H | in qua] vel X | reducuntur] reducitur U W Q 10 et] *lin.* U | passionem] *add.* et H 11 Si] *mg.* U | in] *lin.* Q² | corporis] *mg.* U² *om.* O FW Q X Z | non *om.* O 12 discretivum] discretum X | excellentiarum] excellentis F | illa] ista X 13 cito posset] *inv.* L KU potest cito H | et] etiam X est Z | alia] aliud W Z | qua] *add.* non L U 14 convenientia] convenientiam(!) O K 15 fugiendum] frigidum F | extensum] coexsistens Q existens X | et² *om.* KU W Q | est² *om.* F Q X Z 16 intrinsecum] extrinsecum X | propter] per Z | causam *om.* X | corrumpatur] corrumpantur X 17 excellenti] excellente(!) L 19 dicendum] *add.* est N M | quod ut] prout L quod nec X | dicit] *ant.* Commentator U Z *post* Aristoteles X *add.* quod L K | Aristoteles *om.* H 20 tunc] *ant.* Aristoteles L | naturam] naturas Q | autem] enim U | per — et²] et pertractavit sive FW et Z

---

[17] **Aristot.**, *De an.* II c. 11 (B c.11, 423*b* 25-26).
[18] Cf. **Ioannes Blund**, *Tractatus de anima* c. 16 (ed. Callus et Hunt ABMA II 59): "Tactus distenditur per plura membra quam alii sensus, quia tactus tribuitur animali a natura sue complexionis ... Est etiam tactus ad conservationem sui subiecti, et ideo respuit tactus nociva"; **Ioannes de Rupella**, *Summa de anima* q. 94 (ed. Bougerol 238); **Petrus Hispanus**, *Scientia libri de anima* c. 10 (ed. Alonso 243); **Aegidius Romanus**, *De an.* II com. 111 (f. 51*rb*).
[19] Cf. supra n. 1.
[20] **Averroës**, *De an.* II comm. 108 (AverL 298).

rationem et investigavit naturam et probat, II *De anima*, carnem non esse organum; tamen potest curalius dici, excusando Philosophum, quod non contradixit sibi, quia statim post in *De animalibus*[21] subdit quod caro non est primum organum tactus sicut nec pupilla est primum organum visus — immo est intus; est tamen aliqualiter instrumentum; ita etiam caro est instrumentum, scilicet sicut medium. Vel potest dici quod intelligit de carne nervosa, quae non tantum est medium, sed instrumentum et organum.

Ad secundum,[22] dicendum quod caro animalis est animata animâ vegetativâ immediate aut sensitivâ mediate, nervo toti corpori extenso et interius exsistente.

Ad aliud 'ubicumque est tactus in animali, ibi est nervus vel organum':[23] non autem requiritur quod ibi sit nervus formaliter in qualibet parte carnis, sed sufficit quod sit prope vel iuxta realiter vel formaliter, et sic in qualibet parte virtualiter, quia virtute nervi prope exsistentis quaelibet pars potest sentire tangibile. Ad improbationem dicendum quod in cerebro sunt cartilagines loco nervorum.[24]

Ad aliud[25] dicendum quod in piscibus est aliquid proportionale nervis, et hoc sufficit.

---

1 rationem] eundem K | investigavit] intellexit(?) Q X invenit U | naturam *om*. KU X | et²] ut L | probat] probavit O KU FW Q X Z *add*. ult. per rationem KU | non] etiam FW 2 tamen *om*. K | potest] *mg*. U *add*. melius et X | curalius *post* dici Q curiuius HL Z 3 contradixit] contradicit KU | statim *om*. F | in] inde U 4 primum *om*. L | tactus] *mg*. F² *om*. NO M W Q X Z 5 primum] similem(?) X | est tamen aliqualiter] aliud U | aliqualiter] aliquo modo Q X 6 ita] illa M | ita — instrumentum *om*. X | scilicet *om*. KU 7 dici *om*. X | de carne *om*. O 8 tantum *post* est K | medium — est] *mg*. Z² | instrumentum et] etiam (*lin*.) K *om*. O U FW Q X Z | et] vel L 10 vegetativa immediate *om*. Z | aut — nervo] aut sensitiva medi*ante* sensitiva mediate (medi*ante* W) nervo K W anima autem sensitiva nervo mediate U autem anima vegetativa (sensitiva Q) medi*ante* nervo Q X | toti] *add*. carni Q | corpori] carni O U FW X *add*. ult. carni K 11 extenso] coextenso KU FW Q Z | et — exsistente] *spat. vac*. X | interius] intus FW 12 aliud] *add*. quod H KU FW X Z *add*. cum dicitur quod Q | tactus] motus Q | ibi *post* est FW | est² *om*. Z | nervus] *add*. in O | vel organum] in ratione organi U FW Q X Z 13 ibi sit] *inv*. NO M W Q ibi X 14 qualibet] quacumque KU | prope ... iuxta] iuxta ... prope KU W Q X Z | realiter vel formaliter *om*. H 15 et sic] ut est K et sicut est FW Q et est X *add*. ult. est U Z 16 potest *om*. O | improbationem] probationem O L U FW Q X Z *add*. autem H 17 dicendum — aliud *om*. X *add*. est N H M | quod — est *om*. Z | sunt] *lin*. (*post* cartilagines) F² | cartilagines] *add*. in U 19 dicendum] *add*. est N M K F | proportionale] proportionabile H 20 et] *add*. de U | hoc] haec F Q | sufficit] sufficiant F sit quaestio Q *add*. etc. O H

[21]Cf. supra n. 1.
[22]Cf. supra n. 2.
[23]Cf. supra n. 3.
[24]**Avicenna**, *De an*. pars 5 c. 8 (AviL II 181): "Auditus enim fit a nervis cerebri, qui pertingunt ad cartilaginem et expanduntur in superficie eius. Tactus quoque fit a nervis cerebri."
[25]Cf. supra n. 4

[QUAESTIO 3]

UTRUM AD TACTUM REQUIRATUR MEDIUM EXTRINSECUM IN QUO FIET

Utrum ad tactum requiritur medium extrinsecum in quo fiet.[1]

[1]   5   Videtur quod non: 1

Medium debet esse denudatum a sensibilibus illius sensus, cuius est medium, ut patet inductive; aer vel aqua, quae sunt media extrinseca, non sunt denudata a qualitatibus tangibilibus; igitur, etc.[2]

10   Item, si qualitas tangibilis potest immediate sentiri sine medio   2
extrinseco, illud non requiritur;[3] sed in hieme sentimus frigiditatem aeris immediate sine corpore alio ab aere quod sit medium vel obiectum; igitur, etc.

Item, "contigua sunt quorum ultima sunt simul";[4] sed tangens et   3
15   tactum sunt contigua; igitur ultima sunt simul. Quorum autem ultima sunt simul, non est medium extrinsecum, quia eorum ultima

---

4 Utrum] *praem.* Quaeritur O KU FW Q X Z *add.* ult. tertio K | requiritur] requiratur FW Z | in — Videtur *om.* X | fiet] fiat L KU FW Q X Z   5 Videtur] Dicitur FW   6 sensibilibus] *mg.* U² sensibus F | illius] istius F   7 inductive] *add.* (*lin.* U²) sed N M KU² | vel] et K W Q   8 qualitatibus] quantitatibus Q | qualitatibus tangibilibus] sensibilis qualitatibus K sensibilibus qualitatibus sensus tactus U | igitur etc.] igitur L Q *om.* X   10 Item] Praeterea O U FW Q X Z | qualitas] *add.* sensibilis O Q | potest] posset X | sentiri] *add.* et Q   11 extrinseco *om.* O | illud] idem U | illud — requiritur *om.* X | frigiditatem aeris] *inv.* Z   12 aeris immediate] *inv.* N LM | sine] *add.* et Z | corpore alio] *inv.* Z | ab aere] habere Q *om.* Z | ab — etc. *om.* X | vel *om.* KU   13 etc. *om.* Q   14 Item] Prima(!) O Praeterea U FW Q X Z | sunt² *om.* Q   15 sunt] sine(?) X *add.* simul FW Z | igitur] *add.* eorum KU FW Q Z | ultima *om.* X | Quorum — simul *om.* Q | autem *om.* N   16 simul] *spat. vac.* O | est] sunt est(!) F *add.* aliud O *add.* aliquod U FW Q X

[1] **Aristot.**, *De an.* II c. 11 (B c. 11 423a 15-17, 423a 21—423b 7); **Averroës**, *De an.* II com. 113, 114, 115 (AverL 304-9); **Albertus M.**, *De an.*, II tr. 3 c. 32, 33 (VII¹ 144a—146b); **Thomas**, *De an.* II c. 23 (XLV¹ 164a—167b); **Aegidius Romanus**, *De an.* II com. 115-116 (f. 52rb—52vb).
[2] **Averroës**, *De an.* III com. 66 (AverL 542): "Omnes isti sensus, scilicet tres, agunt sensum quia indigent simplicibus instrumentis et medio extrinseco, idest denudatis a sensibilibus, scilicet ut instrumentum in visu et medium non habeant colorem, neque in olfactu odorem, neque in auditu sonum. Et quae denudantur ab istis aut sunt corpora simplicia aut in quo dominantur corpora simplicia. Sed tactus differt ab istis sensibus, quia comprehendit suum sensibile sine medio, et ideo nullo elemento medio utitur in extrinseco"; cf. **Thomas**, *De an.* II c. 23 (XLV¹ 164b): "Oportet enim id quod est medium in aliquo sensu esse denudatum a qualitatibus sensibilibus secundum illum sensum ... manifestum est autem quod aer et aqua habent tangibiles qualitates...".
[3] Cf. **Albertus M.**, *De an.* II tract. 3 c. 32 (VII¹ 145b): "Quae sentiuntur vel sentiri possunt in gustu et tactu, non requirunt medium extrinsecum propter esse sensus."
[4] **Aristot.** *Physica* V c. 5 (AL VII¹ 201; E c. 5, 227a 6-7); *Physica* V c. 5 (AL VII¹ 202; E c. 5, 227a 21-23); *Auctoritates Aristotelis* (ed. J. Hamesse 153): "Contingua sunt quorum ultima sunt simul, ut cutis et camisia."

sunt in eodem loco.

4 Item,[5] quia si potentia immutatur a sensibili mediante alio, prius immutatur a medio quam a sensibili, quia medium est ei propinquius; sed tactus non prius immutatur a medio extrinseco quam ab obiecto, sed simul; igitur, etc.

In oppositum est Philosophus et Commentator.

[I. — Status quaestionis
A. — Opinio Commentatoris]

5 Responsio COMMENTATORIS[6] est quod animal vivens in aere non patitur ab aere, nec animal vivens in aqua patitur ab aqua. Cuius ratio est: quia passio naturalis est a contrario; locus autem non est contrarius, sed conformis locato; igitur, etc.

---

1 loco] *add.* igitur etc. H K *add.* primo ergo etc. O U FW *add.* primo ergo Q 2 Item] Praeterea O FW Q X Z | Item — etc. *om.* U | quia si] = HL si N M K quia O quaecumque FW quae (*post* potentia Q) Q Z quod X | immutatur] immutetur N M K 3 immutatur — prius] *mg.* H² *om.* X | a medio *om.* H² | medio] sensibili O | a sensibili] ab obiecto O H² FW Q *add.* ult. ab ipso alio H² | medium] medius(!) O illud H² | est] enim N | ei sibi H² *om.* F | propinquius] proprius H² 4 non *post* prius L *mg.* W² | extrinseco *om.* X 5 igitur etc.] exemplum Philosophi de clipeo Q *om.* X 6 In — Commentator *om.* N HLM | est] sunt K | Commentator] *add.* vero W 9 Responsio] Ratio Q | est] *add.* talis K | aere — aqua] *spat. vac.* O 10 non] *lin.* U² | nec ... aqua] et ... aqua non U Q vel ... aqua non FW Z | nec — aqua²] et similiter in aqua X | animal *om.* U FW Z | aqua] *add.* non O | ab²] in Q | aqua²] *add.* passio autem non est ab aqua U 11 Cuius] Eius U Q | est *om.* X | a] cum N 12 igitur etc.] igitur O *om.* Q X

[5]Cf. **Aristot.**, *De an.* II c. 23 (B c. 11 423*b* 12-15): "Sed tangibile differt a visibilibus et facientibus sonum. Nos enim sentimus ista ita quod medium agit quoquo modo in nobis, et nos in tangibilibus non a medio sed cum medio"; cf. **Averroës**, *De an.* II com. 115 (AverL 307): "Tangibilia differunt a coloribus et a sonis in hoc quod indigent medio; quia sensibilia in illis tribus primo agunt in medium, deinde medium in nos, tangibilia autem insimul agunt in nos et in medium."
[6]**Averroës**, *De an.* II com. 115 (AverL 308): "Omne enim animal quod innatum est esse in aqua aut in aere non sentit aliquam qualitatem calidi aut frigidi in eis, si fuerint in simplicitate quam debent habere, quia est locus eius naturalis, et locus est similis locato, ut declaratum est in sermonibus universalibus, et iam declaratum est quod sensibile est contrarium ante passionem"; cf. **Thomas**, *De an.* II c. 23 (XLV¹ 164*b*): "Respondet autem ad hoc Averroës quod nos non patimur a puro aere vel aqua: nihil enim patitur nisi a suo contrario secundum principium passionis, aer autem et aqua non contrariantur nobis, sed sunt nobis similia, comparantur enim ad nos sicut locus ad locatum; unde tactus noster non patitur a qualitatibus aeris vel aquae, sed ab extraneis qualitatibus..."; cf. **Albertus M.**, *De an.* II tr. 3 c. 33 (VII¹ 145*b*—146*a*); cf. **Aegidius Romanus**, *De an.* II com. 113 (f. 52*ra*): "Dicendum quod Commentator videtur velle huiusmodi elementata non pati ab elementis huiusmodi: eo quod oportet locum esse locato similem; elementa ergo in quibus naturaliter elementata exsistunt sunt illis similia et non agunt in ea"; cf. **Aristot.**, *De an.* II c. 23 (B c. 11, 423*a* 21—423*b* 1); cf. *Auctoritates Aristotelis* (ed. J. Hamesse 185): "Locus est similis et aequalis locato."

Ulterius dicit⁷ quod si sentirentur talia media, hoc non est ut pura sunt, sed propter admixtionem alicuius vaporis vel alterius corporis cum ipsis.

[2] Contra consequentiam primae rationis⁸ arguo sic: corpora nostra non habent locum naturalem nisi ratione elementi dominantis in eis; sed quando unum elementum locatur in altero, alteratur ab eo: elementa enim alterant se secundum extremitates, secundum quas se invicem locant; igitur, non obstante locatione talium corporum, adhuc poterit animal pati ab eis.⁹

Item, quod est in potentia tale, patitur ab eo quod est in actu tale; corpora nostra sunt in potentia ad excellentias qualitatum tangibilium, cum sint ad medium reducta et comparata.¹⁰

Contra secundum¹¹ sic: generatio potest fieri sine mixtione in simplicibus; sed generatio requirit alterationem; igitur potest fieri

---

1 dicit] dicitur U | quod *om.* L | sentirentur] sentirent HL sentiuntur U FW Q | est] esset Z   2 pura] *rep.* W | propter] oportet(!) O | admixtionem] commixtionem L | vel] *add.* alicuius Q   3 cum ipsis *om.* X   4 consequentiam] conclusionem LM K commentatorem U *add.* ult. (*mg.*) et dicta U² | rationis] responsionis H | arguo] arguitur FW Z   5 in eis] *mg.* Z²   6 unum] primum Z | in altero] ab alio O KU FW Q Z ab eo X *add.* ult. *spat. vac.* U | altero] *add.* et K   7 enim *om.* K | alterant se] *inv.* KU | se *om.* X | secundum extremitates] = N HL secundum suas extremitates O X sensui extremitates M super extremitates Q super suas extremitates FW Z in suis extremitatibus K in suis relationibus U   8 se *om.* L U | invicem locant] *inv.* Q | talium corporum] *inv.* N HM   9 animal *post* eis F Z | eis] eo O *add.* animal W   10 Item] Praeterea O U FW Q X Z | est *om.* O | in *om.* K | tale] talis Q | in²] = N M U Q Z *om.* O HL K FW X | actu tale] actuale H   11 tale] talis Q | ad] *add.* multas U | excellentias qualitatum tangibilium] multas qualitates K   12 tangibilium] *mg.* U² | comparata] temperata U FW Q *add.* ult. ergo etc. O KU FW Z *add.* ult. ergo Q   13 sine] cum FW Q X Z   14 igitur] et X | potest fieri] poterit esse K poterit fieri U

---

⁷**Averroës**, *De an.* II com. 115 (AverL 308): "Et cum ita sit, animal non sentit calorem aut frigus in aere aut in aqua nisi quando cum eis admiscentur corpora calida aut frigida; illa igitur corpora sunt alia ab aqua et ab aere naturali"; melius in **Thomas**, *De an.* II c. 23 (XLV¹ 164*b*—165*a*): "...quod enim sentitur de qualitatibus tangibilibus in aere et aqua est de admixtione extraneorum corporum, ut ipse dicit, quia sicut ignis numquam amittit calorem suum, ita nec aqua amittit suam frigiditatem, sed quod aliquando sentitur calida, hoc est ex permixtione extranei"; cf. **Albertus M.**, *De an.* II tr. 3 c. 33 (VII¹ 146*a*): 'Hoc non fit, ut dicit, nisi per admixtionem corporum calidorum vel frigidorum'; cf. **Aegidius Romanus**, *De an.* II com. 113 (f. 51*vb*): "...animal quod est aptum natum esse in aere vel in aqua non sentit calorem aut frigus in aere aut in aqua nisi quando cum eis admiscerentur corpora calida aut frigida...".

⁸Cf. supra n. 5.

⁹**Thomas**, *De an.* II c. 23 (XLV¹ 165*a*): "Manifestum est enim quod corpora nostra sortiuntur locum naturalem sicut et motum naturalem ex natura elementis praedominantis, non ergo aliter comparantur ad locum et ad corpora continentia corpora nostra quam ipsa elementa locata; elementa autem in suis extremitatibus se alterant"; cf. **Thomas**, *Sent.* I d. 14 q. 1 a. 4 ad 2 (VI² 508*b*): "...sicut in aere et igne, cuius extremitates ex alteratione corporum contingentium diversis proprietatibus disponuntur"; cf. **Albertus M.**, *De gen. et corrupt.* I tr. 6 c. 9 (V² 174*b*—175*a*).

¹⁰**Thomas**, *De an.* II c. 23 (XLV¹ 165*a*): "Item, omne quod est in potentia natum est pati ab eo quod est in actu; corpora autem nostra, cum sint in quadam medietate constituta inter extremitates tangibilium qualitatum quae sunt in elementis, habent se ad qualitates elementares ut potentia ad actum...".

¹¹Cf. supra n. 6.

alteratio in aqua et ab aqua sine admixtione alterius corporis.[12]

10 Item, aut aqua calefacta est aqua pura aut mixta; si pura, igitur non requiritur ad sui alterationem aliquod corpus sibi admixtum, sed ipsamet poterit alterari, et per consequens potest alterare sensum; si sit mixta, igitur in aestate, quando est aqua calefacta, et in hieme, quando est aer frigidus, non sunt illa elementa pura in regione nostra.

11 Item, sequeretur quod qualitates tangibiles non sunt corporum simplicium, sed mixtorum tantum.[13]

12 Item, secundum IPSUM,[14] si esset vacuum, ibi posset esse motus animalis progressivus ubi pes tangeret terram et eius frigiditatem, non autem aerem vel aquam; ideo potest elementum simplex immutare sensum tactus.

[B. — Solutio quaestionis]

13 Respondeo igitur quod tactus potest comparari ad qualitatem aliquam accidentalem inhaerentem vel adhaerentem, id est, non

---

1 alteratio] add. (mg.) ab aere U² | in] ab X | aqua] aquam U | ab] in X | aqua²] add. (mg.) in aerem U² | admixtione] mixtione Q   2 Item] Praeterea O U FW Q X Z | aut mixta] = H aut non (lin. M) LM aut aliquid mixtum O F vel quid mixtum KU aut quid mixtum W Q X Z om. N   3 sui] suam O KU FW Q X Z | aliquod] aliud H quid U | corpus post admixtum Q | corpus sibi om. KU | admixtum] mixtum K   4 ipsamet] ipsam N X ipsaque O ipsum L | poterit alterari] p. alterare N H potest alterare L | potest om. KU FW Q X Z   5 sit mixta] quid (add. mg. sit U²) mixtum (admixtum F) O KU FW Q X Z | igitur] add. (mg.) aqua U² | aestate — frigidus non sunt] = N M aestate quando est (est aqua) a. e. HL) aqua calefacta (calida K) et in hieme quando est (est aer) a. e. L) aer frigidus (frigefactus O) non sunt O HL K hieme frigefacta et in aestate calefacta et aer similiter non erunt U hieme quando est aqua calefacta et in (in hieme om. Q X) hieme aer frigefactus (frigidus Q) non sunt (add. in hieme Q) FW Q X Z   6 illa] ista H om. U FW Q Z | elementa post pura U   7 regione nostra] regionibus nostris Z   8 Item] Praeterea O U FW X Z | sequeretur] sequitur U   9 simplicium om. Q | tantum om. FW Z   10 Item] Praeterea O U FW Z | Item — tactus om. X   11 animalis progressivus] animalis processivus O FW Z processivus animalis K aliquis (mg. U²) motus processivus animalis U | ubi] ergo K F Q quo W Z | pes] res H om. Q   12 autem om. KU | aquam] aliquam U add. quia ponitur vacuum Q | ideo potest] potest igitur KU F Q   13 sensum tactus] tactum O KU FW Q Z   15 Respondeo] Dicendum FW add. est F | igitur] autem X | quod] quando X | comparari] add. vel U FW Q X | qualitatem aliquam] inv. Q   16 aliquam om. U | accidentalem inhaerentem] inv. FW Q X Z | vel] add. ad qualitatem K | id est] et X | non] vel F Q Z

---

[12]**Thomas**, *De an.* II c. 23 (XLV¹ 165b): "...corruptio autem et generatio in elementis potest fieri sine mixtione et sequitur alterationem..."; cf. **Aristot.**, *De gener. et corrupt.* I c. 2 (AL IX¹ 10; A c. 2 315b 20-24); cf. *De gener. et corrupt.* I c. 2 (AL IX¹ 16; A c. 2 317a 31).

[13]**Ps.-Petrus Hispanus**, *Expositio libri de anima* (ed. Alonso 237): "Patet quod medietas in aliis sensibilibus non ponit mixtionem, in tactu autem ponit. Et etiam alia differentia est quod sensitivum tactus est medietas plurium sensibilium non ad unum aliquod reductorum, et propter hoc, mixtio, qua miscetur sensus tactus, non redit ad aliquid unum."

[14]Nequimus invenire ullam allusionem ad hanc doctrinam apud opera Averrois. Cf. **Thomas**, *Physic.* VIII lect. 4 n. 6 (II 378a-b): "Videtur enim quod animal quod prius quiescebat, postmodum moveatur progressivo motu ... forsitan causa huius naturalis mutationis est continens, idest aer ..."

exsistentem in suo proprio subiecto sed in alio sibi coniuncto. Primo modo potest fieri tactus sine corpore medio extrinseco, sicut patet de dolore apostematis, qui sentitur vehementer non nisi per tactum, ut patet inductive;[15] igitur, etc. Loquendo autem de qualitate adhaerente, quodammodo sentitur immediate sine corpore medio, alio a corpore cui adhaeret sed immediate tangente, sicut patet de qualitate exsistente in corpore non-terminato sed fluido ut est aer vel aqua, quorum qualitates immediate tanguntur sine corpore medio alio a propriis subiectis. Si autem qualitas adhaerens sit in corpore terminato non-fluido, aut extrema tangentis vel tacti sunt humida vel sicca. Si humida, tunc sentitur qualitas illius corporis mediante alio corpore, scilicet subiecto humiditatis illius, sive sit aer sive aqua;[16] si autem extrema sunt sicca, tunc immediate sentitur quod illa sunt sicca, et hoc potest esse vel propter caliditatem corporum se tangentium consumentem humiditatem corporum circumstantium, vel propter fortem applicationem eorum ad invicem eam violenter expellentem.

---

1 in *om.* U | suo *om.* O U FW Q X Z | sed] vel O K FW Q X Z | in²] lin. U² | sibi] communi Q | coniuncto] composito X 2 potest fieri] inv. O H | medio extrinseco] inv. KU FW Q X Z 3 sentitur] *add.* immediate sine corpore alio KU *add.* bene Q *add.* immediate valde W *add.* valde F X Z | non] *add.* autem O U FW Q X Z | nisi *om.* Q 4 patet inductive] inv. K | inductive] inductione Q | igitur etc. *om.* X | etc *om.* Q | autem *om.* X 5 adhaerente] non inhaerentem U inhaerente FW X Z | immediate] *add.* et X | corpore medio] inv. X | medio alio] inv. KU 6 alio] aliquo Q aliquo alio FW *om.* L | a *om.* F X | cui adhaeret sed *om.* KU | sed] licet Z 7 qualitate] *add.* tangente F | corpore] cererebro W | sed] seu HL | fluido] finito FW | ut —terminato *om.* N LM 8 est *om.* KU | aer ... aqua] aqua ... aer X | quorum] quarum O quare Q | quorum — fluido] signaliter sensibilis sit id est quod corpore terminato et non fluxo (*mg.*) H² 9 medio alio] inv. KU | adhaerens] adhuc esset X 10 sit] fit Z | terminato] terminato non-fluido] non terminato sed fluido F non terminato fluido W | non-fluido] non termini(!) N M non fluida K *om.* L | aut] vel N M autem X | vel] et H FW Q X Z 11 humida] humecta O KU FW Z *add.* ult. aere vel aqua KU | humida — humida] humidifica(?) X | vel] aut U F | vel sicca *om.* W | humida²] humecta O FW Z | humida — sunt *om.* U 12 mediante] immediate X | alio] illo X | subiecto *om.* FW | humiditatis] humiditas X | sive] cum FW Z 13 aer ... aqua] aqua ... aer O | sive] *add.* sit Z | extrema] exterminata X | sunt] sint N HL scilicet X | tunc] *add.* ex X | tunc — sicca *om.* FW Z | sentitur] *add.* hoc autem U 14 quod] quia HL | illa] extrema U Q autem extrema X | sunt *post* sicca X | et hoc] quia Q *om.* FW X Z 15 consumentem] conservantem W 16 circumstantium] circumstantem FW Q Z 17 eam] *adnot. lin.* aerem U² | violenter] vehementer L | expellentem] excellentem L expolientem U

[15] Cf. **Petrus I. Olivi**, *In II Sent.*, q. 61 (ed. Jansen 574): "Gravedines indigestionum et inflationum et apostemationum ... videmur sensu tactus sentire."
[16] **Averroës**, *De an.* II com. 113 (AverL 304): "Continget ut corpora sicca inter quae est medium corpus humidum impossibile est ut tangant se ad invicem absque eo quod suae superficies sint humefactae ab illo corpore humido, et humiditas impossibile est ut sit extra illud corpus medium; v. g. corpora humectata quoniam impossibile est ut tangant se nisi inter ea sit aqua aut aliquid aquae"; cf. **Aegidius Romanus**, *De an.* II com. 121 f. 53va.

[C. — Ad argumenta Commentatoris]

14 Ad primum in oppositum COMMENTATORIS[17] dicendum quod elementa possunt considerari secundum suas qualitates activas et passivas, et sic non sunt similia sed contraria se invicem alterantia; vel secundum quod unum continet et locat aliud, et sic sunt partes universi.[18]

15 Ad aliud[19] dicendum quod aqua pura potest calefieri cuius contrarium dicit, licet ignis non possit infrigidari, quia ignis inter elementa est maxime activus. Calor respectu aliarum qualitatum habet rationem formae, ut dicitur quarto *Meteororum*,[20] et ideo est minime passivus. Non sic autem aqua, quae est materialior.

[II. — Ad argumenta principalia]

16 Ad primum principale[21] in oppositum dicendum quod medium debet esse denudatum a qualitatibus tangibilibus omnino vel secundum suas excellentias.[22] Ita se habent illa media, aer et aqua, in quantum sunt media: si enim haberent aliquam qualitatem in magna excellentia, tunc magis sentirentur quam alia per ipsa; immo impedirent sentiri alia, sicut patet de aqua congelata vel valde calefacta vel aere valde frigido.

---

2 in oppositum *om.* X | dicendum] *add.* est N M 3 considerari] conscire F *om.* H | suas *post* qualitates K *om.* U 4 passivas] passibiles U | sunt *om.* X | contraria] e converso U | se] *add.* ad X 5 quod *om.* O | continet et locat] l. et c. FW Q Z | et] vel L X | aliud] ant. locat F | et²] *add.* secundum hoc U | sic] hic O hoc FW Q X Z *add.* secundum quod FW Q X Z | sunt *om.* N M 7 aliud] secundum H | dicendum] *add.* est N M K F | aqua pura] *inv.* Q | pura *om.* HL | cuius] per eius KU 8 dicit *om.* KU | possit] posset N M potest H K | inter] *add.* omnia KU 9 Calor] *praem.* Et praecipue K *praem.* Et ideo U² caloris N M calore K color Z | qualitatum *om.* L *add.* et N M K 10 habet rationem formae] *mg.* U² | rationem] causam X | ut — Meteororum *om.* U | Meteororum] Metaphysicorum O Metaphysicae X | et *om.* X | est] *lin.* U² 11 autem] est N M | aqua] *add.* est K | quae] quia K *om.* X 13 in oppositum *om.* Q | dicendum] *add.* est N M K F 14 tangibilibus] *add.* vel KU | vel *om.* Z | secundum] *mg.* W² 15 Ita] *praem.* Et FW *spat. vac.* O | illa *post* media KU FW X Z ista L U W Z *om.* O | media] in alia X | et] *lin.* M 16 haberent] habent X | qualitatem] talitatem U 17 ipsa] ipsam N M X | immo] *mg.* U² *add.* vero U 18 sentiri] = O LM K Z sentire N H U FW Q X | de] extra X | valde] *add.* frigida vel L 19 vel] et O U FW Q X Z *add.* in L | aere] aer Q | valde] vel X

[17] Cf. supra n. 5.
[18] **Thomas**, *De an.* II c. 23 (XLV¹ 165a): "...dicendum est igitur quod elementa possunt dupliciter considerari: uno modo secundum qualitates activas et passivas, et sic contrariantur ad invicem et se invicem immutant in suis extremis"; **Aegidius Romanus**, *De an.* II com. 113 (f. 52ra): "...elementa dupliciter possunt considerari: vel secundum formas substantiales vel secundum qualitates activas et passivas...".
[19] Cf. supra n. 6.
[20] **Aristot.**, *Meteor.* IV c. 4 (Δ c. 4, 379a 16); **Thomas**, *De an.* II c. 23 (XLV¹ 165b).
[21] Cf. supra n. 1.
[22] Cf. **Aegidius Romanus**, *De an.* II com. 118 (f. 53ra).

Ad aliud[23] dicendum quod si duo corpora se tangentia sint sicca in ultimis, tangunt se sine medio et sunt contigua et eorum ultima sunt simul; si autem humida sunt, eorum ultima non tangunt se immediate, sed mediante corpore humido.

[5] Ad aliud[24] dicendum quod aliquid potest esse prius alio vel causalitate vel tempore vel situ.[25] Ita dico quod "potentia prius immutatur per medium extrinsecum quam per obiectum" potest esse verum, et hoc secundum situm et secundum causalitatem in aliis sensibus a tactu, sicut in visu. Immutatur enim primo medium a visibili secundum situm, quod est ei propinquius; etiam secundum causalitatem, quia immutatio medii est causa immutationis organi; licet non prius tempore, quia visio fit in instanti. In auditu etiam est prior immutatio medii et causalitate et situ et tempore — etiam in aliqua sui parte, scilicet in remota ab organo, quia sonus se multiplicat mediante motu locali. Sic etiam in olfactu et gustu, in quo — gustu — medii extrinseci immutatio est causa immutationis organi, licet simul tempore immutetur saliva — quae est medium extrinsecum — et organum. Sed in tactu medium extrinsecum prius quidem secundum situm immutatur, quia est propinquius, non tamen prius tempore, sicut simul tempore percutitur clypeus et clypeatus, non autem prius causalitate (non enim clypeus percussus percutit clypeatum). Nec aer vel aqua in quantum sunt media extrinseca immutant

---

1 dicendum *om.* X *add.* est N M | si *post* tangentia U *lin.* K² | sint] sunt Q X *om.* HL 2 tangunt] tangant Q tangent X | se] *add.* immediate U 3 humida] humecta U FW Q X Z *adnot. mg.* id est humecta M | sunt²] sint HM simpliciter U *om.* K | tangunt] tangent X 4 sed] se(!) NO 5 dicendum *om.* X *add.* est N M F | quod] *add.* (*lin.*) similiter U² | aliquid — potentia] *mg.* Z² | prius alio] *inv.* Z² | vel *om.* L 6 Ita — visu *om.* O | potentia *om.* U 7 immutatur] immutetur U W Q Z | per *om.* U | per — *fin. om.* X | per obiectum] *forsan lapsus pennae apud originale, coniecimus autem cum* H organum N LM U FW Q Z per organum K | potest] *add.* etiam(?) F 8 verum et hoc] et Z *om.* FW | hoc *om.* U Q 9 sensibus] sensibilibus H | a tactu] ac actu(!) Q *om.* F | enim *om.* K | primo] prius Q *add.* a medio N M 10 situm] *add.* quia L | quod] quia O U | est *om.* U | etiam] et U FW Q Z 12 licet] hoc F | non] autem L | quia — fit] sed FW | in instanti *om.* F | etiam. FW | est prior] *inv.* O L 13 causalitate] causa K | et² *om.* U | tempore] *add.* prius Q | etiam *om.* N M 14 sui *post* parte Q *rep.* F 15 locali — gustu] *mg.* Z² | in *om.* O 16 immutatio] *mg.* U² mutatio (*ant. extrinseci*) F 17 licet — organum] *in imo fol.* U² | immutetur] mutetur F 18 Sed — extrinsecum] *rep. ant.* licet K | in] et Z 19 secundum *om.* Z | situm] *add.* prius Z | non tamen] *inv.* U FW 21 autem] tamen K | prius *om.* KU | enim] autem Z *add.* prius KU 22 vel] nec K

[23] Cf. supra n. 3.
[24] Cf. supra n. 4.
[25] **Aegidius Romanus**, *De an.* II com. 115 (f. 52*va*): "Dicendum quod prius et posterius quendam ordinem important ordo autem quantum ad praesens tripliciter potest accipi videlicet secundum situm et secundum tempus et secundum causalitatem...".

organum tactus, licet bene immutant in quantum sunt obiecta.[26] Et hoc ideo, quia medium extrinsecum in tactu est accidentaliter requisitum,[27] propter hoc quod non potest animal vivere sine eis, nec tactus est nisi in aqua vel in aere, ideo non tangit nisi mediante aqua vel aere modo praedicto, non quia de necessitate tangent per aquam vel aerem tanquam per medium essentialiter requisitum, sicut caro, vel sicut requiritur ad alios sensus; immo magis sensibiliter tangerentur tangibilia extrinseca sine talibus mediis quam in ipsis. Licet igitur non prius tempore et causalitate immutatur potentia tactiva a medio extrinseco quam obiecto, prius tamen secundum situm immutatur, et hoc sufficit ad tale medium.

---

1 immutant *post* obiecta W bene immutant (*post* obiecta) F immutent KU Q Z *add.* ult. organum tactus FW | sunt *om.* O FW Q Z 2 hoc] hic O | est *om.* F 3 hoc] *lin.* K *om.* H | animal] ant. non KU Q 4 tactus *post* est Q actus Z | aqua ... aere] aere ... aqua O K Q aere vel aqua U FW Z | ideo non *om.* O | ideo — aqua] *mg.* W² | ideo — aere *om.* HL KU 5 aqua vel aere] = N M vel aqua O aere vel aqua FW² Q Z | modo praedicto] ant. ideo W | non *om.* K | tangent] tangens L tangat Q tangunt U FW Z 6 aquam vel aerem] aquam et aerem O aerem et aquam U FW Q Z | essentialiter] extrinsecum Q 7 alios] aliquos H 8 tangerentur] sentirentur HL | tangibilia] sensibilia Z | mediis] *mg.* L 9 tempore et causalitate] c. et t. L | et] vel O U FW Q Z | immutatur] immutetur O U FW Q Z 10 tactiva] activa N M Q | quam] *add.* ab L KU FW Q Z 11 sufficit] sufficiant Q | medium] *add.* extrinsecum L *add.* etc. M F

[26]**Aristot.**, *De an.* II c. 23 (B c. 11, 423*b* 12-16): "Sed differt tangibile a visibilibus et sonativis, quoniam illa quidem sentimus ex eo quod medium movet aliquid nos, tangibilia vero non a medio, sed simul cum medio, sicut per clipeum percussus: non enim clipeus percussit percussit, sed simul accidit utraque percuti." Cf. **Themistius**, *De an.* I (CLCAG I 4 172); **Aegidius Romanus**, *De an.* II com. 116 (f. 52*vb*).
[27]**Averroës**, *De an.* II com. 115 (AverL 307): "In tactu autem medium et sensus moventur insimul a tangibili, sed medium nihil facit in hoc, sed est aliquod accidens ex necessitate ... istud non est medium quod est necessarium omni sensui in sentiendo; sed medium quod est huiusmodi in hoc sensu est caro, et hoc si dicetur medium, erit secundum accidens. "

[QUAESTIO 4]

UTRUM SENSIBILE POSITUM SUPRA SENSUM VEL ORGANUM SENSUS SENTIATUR

Utrum sensibile positum supra sensum vel organum sensus sentiatur.[1]

[1] Videtur quod sic:

Quia cultellus scindens nervum causat maximum dolorem, maiorem quam si scinderet carnem;[2] nervus autem est organum tactus, qui sentit dolorem; igitur, etc.

Item, aliquis humor potabilis positus supra medium gustus, scilicet super carnem linguae, sentitur; igitur multo magis positus super organum. Antecedens patet. Probatio consequentiae: quia caro, quae est medium in gustu, est corpus mixtum et compactum;[3] potabile autem non est ita mixtum vel compactum, nec materiale; igitur species potabilis materialius recipitur in medio quam in organo, quia unumquodque recipitur secundum modum recipientis.[4] Si igitur species potabilis recepta in medio causat gustum, multo fortius potabile immediate positum super organum causat gustum.

---

4 Utrum] praem. Quaeritur O U FW Q X Z praem. Quaeritur quarto K adnot. mg. Quaestio quarta M | vel — sentiatur] faciat sensum vel sentiatur Q faciat sensum Z 6 Videtur om. X 7 scindens] sciendens W Z 9 igitur etc. om. X | etc om. Q 10 Item] Praeterea O KU FW Q X Z | aliquis humor] inv. X | supra] super HM U W 11 super] supra HLM F Q | carnem — super om. U | sentitur] fuerit X | multo magis om. FW Z | magis] fortius K 12 super] supra L Q | Probatio] Probo O 13 quae] quia X om. L | est post gustu X | gustu] add. et L | compactum] compositum(!) U 14 vel — materiale] vel compactum vel materiale N vel (nec Q) materiale nec (et KU) compactum (compositum U) KU FW Q X Z 15 igitur] ergo W Z | materialius recipitur om. W | recipitur] reperitur N add. in organo F | organo] obiecto O KU FW Q X Z 16 recipitur] reperitur N add. in aliquo Q | secundum] per L Q | modum om. H 17 potabilis om. KU | medio] add. in mixto Z 18 fortius] magis KU | immediate — super] positum super O immediate positum supra L positum immediate super (supra K) K FW Q X Z positum supra immediate U

[1] **Aristot.**, De an. II c. 11 (B c. 11, 423b 20-26); **Aegidius Romanus**, De an. II com. 121 (f. 53vb).
[2] **Albertus M.**, De an. II tr. 3 c. 34 (VII¹ 147a): "Omni temptanti per experimentum constet nervos esse magis sensibiles, quando tanguntur a sensibilibus quam ipsam carnem"; cf. **Aegidius Romanus**, De an. II com. 121 (f. 53vb): "... quia si incidant nervus, fit ibi maior dolor, quod non esset nisi ex applicatione laesivi ad nervum resultaret ibi sensus tactus."
[3] **Albertus M.**, De an. II tr. 3 c. 35 (VII¹ 148a): "Cum oporteat omnes partes animati corporis esse mixtas et tangibilibus differentiis, neccesse est quod organum et medium in tactu aliquo modo habeant istas qualitates."
[4] Cf. Liber de causis prop. 23 [24] n. 180 (ed. A. Pattin 98-9); Auctoritates Aristotelis (ed. J. Hamesse 232): "Quicquid recipitur ab alio recipitur per modum rei accipientis et non receptae."

3   Item, sonus habet esse reale in omni parte medii; sed auris potest audire in omni parte medii exsistente, igitur in parte sibi coniuncta; igitur, etc. Probatio maioris: quia quod habet esse intentionale tantum, non manet absente generante; sed sonus manet in omni parte medii, absente corpore sonativo; igitur habet in omni parte medii esse reale. Minor est manifesta. Igitur, etc.

4   Item, odor in fumali evaporatione habet esse reale;[5] sed si fumalis evaporatio intret nasum, sentitur odor;[6] igitur, etc.

[2]

5   In oppositum est PHILOSOPHUS,[7] et omnes rationes in tantum quod ALIQUI[8] dicunt quod si cultellus scinderet immediate nervum, in quo est sensus tactus, homo non sentiret.

6   Istam autem conclusionem sic probant ALIQUI:[9] oportet sensum habere proportionem non tantum ad obiectum sed ad medium, ad hoc quod exeat in actum suum ita quod sicut ab excellenti sensibili et improportionabili sensui non immutatur sensus — nec etiam a remisso improportionaliter —, ita nec sentit suum obiectum si

---

1 Item] Praeterea O KU FW Q X Z | habet] potest X | reale om. Z | parte] tempore L | sed] et K | sed — medii om. X 2 audire] add. sonum KU | exsistente] exsistens L om. N | igitur] etiam KU FW Q Z om. X | sibi] ibi W 3 igitur] ergo W X Z | quod habet] quodlibet O L K | esse] mg. U² 4 tantum om. H | manet] movet(!) Q 5 absente — medii] secundum U Z om. F | corpore om. Q | corpore — reale] generante in esse reali] igitur] ergo W 6 est manifesta] patet Q | Igitur etc] Ergo etc. W Z. om. X 7 Item] Praeterea O KU FW Q X Z | odor om. W | evaporatione] vaporatione H est vapor et(!) X | habet] rep. Z | si] sicut U FW Q X Z 8 intret] intrat U FW Q Z intrans X | igitur etc. om. X 9 In oppositum] Contra U FW Q X Z | rationes] = N HM conclusiones hic concedunt O quaestionistae L communiter concedent FW Q Z communiter loquentes (omnes X) concedent (om. K) KU X | in tantum] intellectum W in tali Z 10 quod] add. concedunt vel K | aliqui dicunt] inv. O KU FW X Z dicitur ab aliquibus Q | immediate] ant. scinderet U FW Q om. L K 11 sensus om. L | sentiret] add. illud K 12 Istam] Illam O U F Hanc Q | conclusionem] quaestionem Z | sic post aliqui K post probant FW sicut X om. U Q | probant post aliqui X 13 ad] in N M 14 hoc] mg. U² | ab] in F 15 improportionabili] improportionali O U F X Z in proportionato Q | sensui] sensibili HM U | a om. X 16 improportionaliter] improportionabili N improportionali L X | suum post obiectum L eius N

---

[5] **Aristot.**, *De sensu et sensato* [c. 4] (c. 4, 438b 24-25): "Odor vero fumalis evaporatio est"; *Auctoritates Aristotelis* (ed. J. Hamesse 196).
[6] Cf. *Auctoritates Aristotelis* (ed. J. Hamesse 198): "Instrumentum odoratus est aer positus in naso"; **Avicenna**, *De an.* pars 2 c. 4 (AviL I 151): "Quidquid habet partes subtiles et solet diffundi, cum attigerit instrumentum odorandi et offenderit in illud, sive sit vapor sive aer, permutabitur in odorem et per ipsum sentietur odor."
[7] Cf. **Aristot.**, *De an.* II c. 7 (B c. 7, 419a 12-13); II c. 7 (B c. 7, 419a 25-31); *Auctoritates Aristotelis* (ed. J. Hamesse 180): "Sensibile positum extra sensum non facit sensationem."
[8] **Aegidius Romanus**, *De an.* II com. 121 (f. 54ra): "Dicendum quod ex eo quod applicatur cultellus vel aliquid laesivum ad nervum qui est organum sensus non fit sensus."
[9] **Aegidius Romanus**, *De an.* II com. 121 (f. 54ra): "Tertia via sumitur ex parte ipsius sensus. Nam cum ipse sensus habeat rationem cuiusdam medietatis et proportionis, oportet quod quodam modo proportionato immutetur ab obiecto. Quare sicut requiritur ibi debita proportio obiecti, ita et debita proportio medii …"

medium sit nimis protensum sive parum, vel nimis remotum et propinquum; quia igitur, obiecto posito super organum, non servatur medii debita proportio, ideo, etc.

[3] Contra istam rationem arguitur sic: caro immutata ab obiecto tangibili immutat immediate organum tactus. Similiter aer immediatus vel propinquus pupillae immediate immutat illam;[10] haec igitur propinquitas medii non tollit eius immutationem.

Alia ratio eorum est haec: species in organo habet esse ab obiecto; igitur mediante corpore medio in quo habet esse minus materiale quam in obiecto — magis tamen quam in organo —, causatur species ita intentionalis in organo, quia ab extremo in extremum devenitur per medium.[11]

Contra istam rationem arguo sic: caro habet esse materialius quam aer, quia est corpus mixtum,[12] et per consequens calor in carne habet esse materialius quam in aere; tamen calor carnis potest immediate immutare organum tactus, quia est eius medium; igitur calor aeris multo magis.

---

1 protensum sive parum] = L vel protensum sive parum H protensum vel (*lin.*) parum M et (*lin.*) protensum parum N vel parum protensum O FW Q X Z parvum K parvum vel extensum vel protensum U | remotum et propinquum] remotum vel propinquum LM K Z propinquum vel remotum X   2 igitur] *add.* (*mg.*) quando est K | obiecto posito] *inv.* Q obiectum positum K | super] supra HL KU | organum] sensum K | servatur] servitur O   3 medii *post* proportio KU FW Q X Z *om.* O L | ideo etc.] igitur etc. U Q *om.* X   4 istam] illam O HL F Q Z | rationem] responsionem HL K | sic] quia sicut X | immutata — caro (n. 9)] *rep.* X   5 immutat *post* immediate X | Similiter] Sicut W | immediatus vel *om.* O KU FW Q X Z   6 immediate immutat] *inv.* L F | illam] eam O FW Q X Z | haec *post* igitur HL *om.* O U FW Q X Z   8 eorum *om.* X | est *post* haec O U FW X Z | organo] *add.* non KU | esse] *add.* immediate KU   9 corpore] *add.* in X | in quo] non Z | esse minus] *inv.* O   11 causatur] *add.* (*lin.*) enim U[2] | causatur — organo *om.* H | ita] illa L *om.* KU   12 devenitur *post* medium K debetur L devertitur O   13 istam] illam O HL F Q | rationem] responsionem N HLM conclusionem Q | arguo] arguitur N M FW Q X Z | habet esse materialius] m. e. h. U | esse *post* materialius L X   14 quia — mixtum *post* aere (*mg.* W[2]) FW[2] *mg.* U[2] *om.* Z | calor *om.* Z *add.* etiam U   15 habet esse materialius *om.* O U FW Q X Z | quam] extra(!) Q | calor] *rep.* O | potest immediate] *inv.* O U FW Q X   16 est] *lin.* U[2]   17 calor aeris *post* magis Z | magis] fortius (*mg.*) U[2]

[10]Cf. **Thomas**, *De an.* II c. 17 (XLV[1] 141*a*); *Sent.* II d. 13 q. 1 a. 3 in corp. (VI[2] 500*b*).
[11]Cf. **Aegidius Romanus**, *De cognitione angelorum* (ed. 1503 f. 83*vb*—84*ra*): "Est igitur hic modus immutationis sensus quod sensibile primo immutat medium et per medium immutat sensum. Propter quod species sensibilis habet triplex esse: in organo, in medio, et in re sensibili. Sed in re sensibili habet omnino esse materiale, in medio habet esse magis spiritualiter et immaterialiter; in organo vero adhuc magis spiritualiter et immaterialiter. Oportet ergo quod prius fiat species in medio quae habebit esse magis materiale quam species in sensu et minus quam ipsum sensibile. Non enim naturaliter itur ab extremo in extremum sine medio"; **Albertus M.**, *De an.* II tr. 3 c. 34 (VII[1] 147*a*); **Vital du Four**, *Quaest. disput. de cognitione* q. 2 (ed. Delorme 198-199).
[12]**Averroës**, *De an.* II com. 111 (AverL 302): "Animalia enim indigent necessario corpore duro, ex quo contingit ut medium in sensibus tactus esset corpus admixtum super quod abundaret terrestritas; et est caro."

[I. — Solutio quaestionis]

10 Respondeo quod in uno sensu, scilicet visu, est causa specialis, quare sensibile positum supra sensum non sentitur, quia "color non videtur sine lumine",[13] et adhuc requiritur quod videatur per medium illuminatum; si autem color poneretur supra organum visus, obumbraret ipsum, et ideo sequitur quod non potest videri.[14]

11 De aliis sensibus non est conclusio PHILOSOPHI[15] vera modo dicto. Circa quod sciendum est quod duplex est immutatio ipsius sensibilis. Una est naturalis, quando scilicet immutatur sensus a sensibili secundum idem vel tale esse, vel secundum eundem modum essendi, quo est in re extra ut cum sensus tactus calefit vel alius sensus aliqualiter alteretur vel movetur secundum locum. Alia est immutatio animalis secundum quam immutatur[16] intentionaliter vel spiritualiter a sensibili, licet habeat[17] modum essendi extra realem

---

2 Respondeo] *add.* igitur U | scilicet] videlicet H | specialis] spiritualis L X 3 quare] cuius X | supra] super M F Z | non sentitur] sensum non facit U non facit sensum FW Q X Z | quia] *add. mg.* mediate W² | color] calor(!) Z 4 sine] nisi medi*ante* F nisi in U W Q X Z | adhuc] ad hoc (*post* requiritur) K U FW Q X Z | requiritur] requirit FW | quod] ut F Z | videatur] videtur H | per *om.* O KU FW Q X Z 5 supra] super N K W X Z sicut O Q | organum] *add.* sensus L 6 ipsum] visum N M *add.* visum K | et *om.* X | potest] posset O FW Q X Z possit U 7 De — dicto] = M De aliis sensibus non est conclusio Philosophi modo dicta (dicto H) *deinde reliquerunt spat. vac.* HL De aliis sensibus non (ut O) est conclusio Philosophi modo dicto NO De aliis sensibus est tertio Philosophi non modo dicendo Q De aliis autem sensibus est ut conclusio Philosophi probat FW De aliis autem sensibus est ut conclusio Philosophi modo dicendo X Z De aliis autem sensibus secundum Philosophum est dicendum KU | Philosophi vera] *mg.* M 8 sciendum est quod duplex est] = N M F sciendum quod duplex est O W Q X Z sciendum quod est duplex HL est sciendum quod duplex est KU | ipsius *om.* Z 9 a sensibili] convenienti Z 10 idem] illud O L FW Q X Z | tale esse] potest esse tale X 11 in] *lin.* X | tactus] *lin.* K *om.* X | vel] et U ut(!) X 12 aliqualiter] aliter O aequaliter KU *om.* N M W | alteretur] alteratur U FW Q X Z 13 intentionaliter] intentio naturaliter N

[13]Cf. **Aristot.**, *De an.* II c. 15 (B c. 15, 419*a* 8-9).
[14]**Aegidius Romanus**, *De an.* II com. 121 (f. 53*vb*): "Ideo si quis ponat habens colorem supra visum non videbitur: sed haec ratio est specialis in visu"; **Thomas de Sutton**, *Quaest. ordinariae* q. 15 in corp. (ed. Schneider BAW III 440).
[15]Cf. supra n. 5.
[16]Subaudi: sensus.
[17]Subaudi: sensibile.

sive materialem.[18] Modo ita est quod aliquis sensus immutatur spiritualiter tantum, ut visus.[19] Tactus autem utraque immutatione immutatur realiter et naturaliter.[20] Probo: quia organum tactus est corpus mixtum, sicut medium quod est caro, igitur est passivum naturale et receptivum actionis naturalis; qualitates autem tangibiles sunt naturaliter activae; igitur, etc. Similiter, immutatur intentionaliter: quia, si tantum immutaretur naturaliter ratione qua mixtum naturale, non plus sentiret qualitates tangibiles quam lignum vel lapis, quae naturaliter immutantur; quia igitur tactus sentit huiusmodi qualitates; ideo, etc.

---

1 sive materialem] et materialem O U Q X Z *om.* FW | est *om.* Z 2 tantum *om.* L | autem] enim N HLM | immutatione] mutatione Q 3 immutatur] *add.* quod KU FW Q *add.* quia X *add.* scilicet Z | et naturaliter] vel naturaliter (*post* probo Q) KU FW Q X Z | Probo] Probatio Z | tactus *om.* KU FW Q X Z 4 sicut] dicit(!) X | est] *add.* aer L | igitur est passivum] passivum i. est N M 5 naturale] naturaliter KU | receptivum] receptum O receptivus Z | actionis] passionis KU | naturalis] *add.* sive actionis KU 6 naturaliter] similiter W | igitur etc. *om.* L | etc. *om.* Q 7 immutaretur *post* naturaliter FW Q X Z immutetur hac L *om.* U | ratione] scilicet ratio U | qua] quia L *add.* tunc N 8 naturale] materiale H *om.* U | plus *post* sentiret F | qualitates] *add.* sensibiles H | lignum vel lapis] lapis vel lignum U 9 naturaliter *om.* X | tactus] *add.* huius N 10 ideo *om.* X

[18]Cf. **Thomas**, *De an.* II c. 14 (XLV¹ 127b—128a): "Sensus visus est spiritualior ex modo immutationis ... dico autem immutationem naturalem prout qualitas recipitur in patiente secundum esse naturae, sicut cum aliquid infrigidatur vel calefit aut movetur secundum locum; immutatio vero spiritualis est secundum quod species recipitur in organo sensus aut in medio per modum intentionis et non per modum naturalis formae; non enim sic recipitur species in sensu secundum illud esse quod habet in re sensibili"; **Henricus Gand.**, *Quodl. XII* q. 9 in corp. (AMPh s. 2, XVI 48): "In causando dolorem ex actione sensibilis corporalis materialiter concurrit primo laesio in ipso sentiente aut intelligente ex actione materiali ipsius sensibilis, secundo ipsa sensatio aut intellectio ex actione spiritualis immutationis ab eodem, tertio perceptio illius laesionis"; **Aegidius Romanus**, *De an.* II com. 121 (f. 54ra): "Nam in impressione facta in sensu est duplex generatio: una quasi aequivoca, alia quasi univoca. Nam primo ab obiecto in quo habet esse forma et species realiter multiplicantur species intentionaliter, et haec est quasi generatio aequivoca cum ex reali generetur intentionale. Ulterius autem ab illa intentione facta generatur intentio alia, et haec est generatio quasi univoca cum ex intentione generat intentio"; **Petrus I. Olivi**, *Summa* II q. 61 (BFS V 577): 'Formalis actio et immutatio sensus per quam actu sentit suum obiectum est actio et immutatio viva et animalis et cognitiva et intentionalis; unde non est de natura corporalium et naturalium alterationum, quamvis aliquando extrinsecus sint sibi in organo suae annexae.'

[19]Cf. **Aristot.**, *Eth. Nic.* X c. 6 (AL XXVI³ 355; I c. 6, 1176a 1): "Differt autem a tactu, puritate ..."; **Thomas**, *De an.* I c. 10 (XLV¹ 50b); *De an.* II c. 14 (XLV¹ 127a—128a); *Metaph.* I lect. 1 (ed. Parmen. XX 248b); *Sent.* IV d. 48 q. 2 a. 4 ad 1 (VII²·² 1177b): "Inter sensus autem nostros spiritualior est visus et subtilior ..."; *Summa contra gent.* III c. 53 (XIV 147a): "... et praecipue quae pertinent ad visum, qui inter ceteros sensus nobilior est et spiritualiter ..."; *Summa theol.* I q. 83 a. 3 in corp. (V 254a): "Visus autem, quia est absque immutatione naturali et organi et obiecti, est maxime spiritualis, et perfectior inter omnes sensus, et communior"; *Summa theol.* I-II q. 83 a. 4 arg. 3 (VII 103a); **Aegidius Romanus**, *De an.* II com. 121 (f. 54ra).

[20]Potius legendum est : intentionaliter. Omnes codices vero lectionem "naturaliter" perperam tradunt. Utrum lectio ex litteris male intellectis atque obscure scriptis an ex lapsu ipsius Scoti orta sit, nescimus.

12 Item, hoc patet ratione theologica:²¹ in damnatis post resurrectionem generalem erit sensus tactus et omnes sensus in actu suo, et tunc tactus non immutabitur naturaliter (quia illa immutatio est corruptiva); igitur tantum intentionaliter. Tamen illa erit maxime afflictiva: igitur verissime ibi poterit esse una sine alia. Tamen in statu isto non est intentionalis immutatio sine reali et naturali immutatione, quia causatur ab ea.²²

13 Immutatio igitur intentionalis facit sensum, non autem naturalis, cum sine naturali possit esse in damnatis — naturalis etiam potest esse in inanimatis, quae non sentiunt aliquid tangere in quantum huiusmodi; et est naturaliter immutare, quia tactus²³ potest esse in inanimatis quae tantum naturaliter immutantur. Et

---

1 Item] Praeterea O U FW Q X Z | hoc *om.* N HLM   2 erit] quando W *om.* X | et *om.* W | omnes sensus] *inv.* O omnis sensus N M K W | actu] tactu O   3 et *om.* O U FW Q X Z | tunc] autem | tactus *om.* X | immutabitur] immutatur H N | quia *om.* N H | quia — immutatio] illa enim naturalis M | illa *om.* H L X | immutatio est corruptiva] *del. atque substit.* quia immutatio naturalis est corruptiva H²   4 est] erit KU *add.* non O | corruptiva] incorruptiva U | Tamen] Cum O X | illa] ista U *add.* immutatio K | maxime] multum U   5 igitur — una] = N igitur verissime poterit ibi esse una O F igitur ibi verissime poterit una esse HL igitur verissime ibi poterit una esse M K poterit tamen igitur ibi esse una U igitur verissima(!) poterit ibi esse una W Q Z | igitur — alia *om.* X   6 isto] uno N illo F Q | immutatio *om.* U | et] sive N   7 immutatione *om.* U   8 igitur *post* intentionalis U | facit *om.* FW X | sensum] sensus FW | autem] sic H est L FW *add.* realis sive KU   9 cum] *add.* tantum U | naturali] ea *om.* U | possit] posset HM U | esse] fieri KU *add.* scilicet KU FW X | damnatis] *add. mg.* naturali W²   10 esse] *ant.* etiam Q *ant.* potest FW X *lin.* U² *om.* NO | inanimatis] *lin.* W² animatis NO U Q X Z | quae — inanimatis *om.* L | aliquid tangere] = M K Z tangere aliquid N tangere aliquod O aliquod tangere H tangere U FW X tangere autem Q   11 et] autem X *add. sic* O *om.* U FW Q | naturaliter] materialiter NO FW Q X | tactus] *add. lin.* non H²   12 potest] facit M | inanimatis] animatis NO M W Q X Z | quae — Et *om.* KU | naturaliter] immaterialiter Q | immutantur] immutatur LM mutantur O

---

²¹Cf. **Petrus Lombardus**, *Sent.* IV, d. 44 c. 7 (SB V.2 520-521); **Thomas**, *Sent.* IV d. 44 q. 1 a. 3 in corp. (VII²·² 1102*b*): "Quia igitur post resurrectionem, et motu caeli cessante, non poterit aliquod corpus alterari a sua naturali qualitate ... ideo in corporibus damnatorum sensus poenae erit sine mutatione naturalis dispositionis"; **Errores condemnati Parisii** (CUP I 487, n. 432): "Quod anima post mortem separata nullo modo patitur ab igne corporeo"; (ed. Hissette 214-215, ed. Piché 112-113): "Quod anima separata non est alterabilis secundum philosophiam, licet secundum fidem alteretur"; **Henricus Gand.**, *Quodl.* XI q. 8 in corp. (f. 460C-E): "Sciendum secundum aliquos, quod licet duae sint radices doloris praedictae, scilicet immutatio corruptiva et eius apprehensio, sola tamen apprehensio sufficeret si possibile esset eam esse sine illa immutatione talem qualis est cum illa ... et ponunt ... quod tali modo cruciabuntur secundum corpus homines damnati; ... ignis inferni ... immutabit ... secundo genere immutationis per speciem intentionalem caloris ac si arderent ... Sed quomodo hoc possit fieri naturaliter, non video"; ad quem diffusius respondet **Duns Scotus**, *Ordinatio* III d. 15 q. un. in corp. n. [5]-[7] (ed. Vivès XIV 568*a*—570*a*); **Petrus I. Olivi**, *Summa* II q. 61 (BFS V 576-577): "In gloriosis corporibus beatorum erit sensus tactus absque necessitate talis immutationis. Nec mirum, quia nec forte corpora damnatorum sentiendo summos ardores et algores et ictus vel percussiones habebunt tales alterationes ex se materialiter eductas, sicut nunc habent homines vel animalia."

²²Cf. **Henricus Gand.**, *Quodl.* XI q. 8 in corp. (f. 460E): "In nobis autem pro statu vitae praesentis, quia non potest naturaliter sensum sic excessive immutare, nisi calefaciat medium et organum realiter, non solum intentionaliter: et sic corrumpit proportionem, qua impeditur tam excessiva apprehensio; ideo impossibile est in nobis sequi tam excessivum dolorem."

²³Exempli gratia, in angulo muri se tangunt, minime autem sentiunt.

ideo tangibile positum supra organum tactus, cum non immutet nisi naturaliter, ipsum non facit sensum tactus, sed species tangibilis recepta in eo intentionaliter facit sensum tactus. Si autem sit immutatio animalis in organo tactus vel aliorum, bene facit sensum, non autem naturalis; quia immutatio naturalis in organo non facit sensum — immo magis impedit —, quia si sine naturali posset esse intentionalis, magis sentiretur sensibile, sicut patet in damnatis. Tamen immutatio naturalis in carne, quae est medium, bene facit sensum, causando immutationem similem in organo, non de se tantum.

[II. — Ad argumenta principalia]

[5] Rationes autem in oppositum[24] bene probant quod immutatio animalis est simul cum immutatione naturali pro statu viae, nec sine illa potest esse quantum ad illos quattuor sensus de quibus fuit argutum, licet de visu aliter sit propter rationem superius positam.[25] Non tamen probant quod immutatio naturalis, in quantum huiusmodi, facit sensum, quia magis impedit, ut visum est; sed si sentiantur huiusmodi sensibilia tangentia organum, hoc est ratione immutationis animalis per se, quae causatur a naturali immutatione secundum quam tangunt organum. Et ideo secundum hoc, est propositio PHILOSOPHI vera quod sensibilia tangentia sensum non faciunt sensum:[26] quia ratione immutationis naturalis, secundum quam tangunt organum, non faciunt sensum.

---

1 supra] super NO H *add.* sensum Q | cum *om.* N | immutet] immutat N HM Q immutetur O 2 naturaliter] materialiter NO *om.* KU | ipsum] ant. nisi Q | tactus *om.* L | sed — tactus] *spat. vac.* O *om.* N HL X | tangibilis recepta] tangibiles receptae K 3 eo] ea F | facit] faciunt K | Si autem sit ...quia] Si igitur ... sed N Sic ... quia (quia *om.* U) KU Sic igitur ... sed O FW Q X Z 4 tactus *om.* U | tactus — non] *mg.* W² | aliorum] aliquorum NO 5 naturalis² *om.* U | non] *spat. vac.* U 6 immo] sed K | si] *add.* non FW X Z | posset] potest H possit N 7 intentionalis] intentionaliter W Z *om.* N | sentiretur *om.* X | sicut] ut L 8 Tamen] Cum O U | naturalis *om.* L *add.* quae K 9 immutationem] commutationem FW | similem] sensibilem K | in organo *om.* K 10 tantum] *add.* etc. X 12 Rationes] Responsiones U | autem *om.* U Q X | oppositum] obiectum(!) X | bene *om.* Q | immutatio] mutatio O 13 est simul] *inv.* KU est similis HM est animal X | immutatione] mutatione O *om.* KU | viae] mediae(!) F isto X | sine] *rep.* Q 14 illa] *add.* non O | illos] istos N L | sensus] *add.* alios HM K | fuit] fiat M fit N fuerit Z 15 aliter] aliud KU F Q X Z *om.* N *spat. vac.* O | sit] fit W | superius] prius N | positam] tactam O KU FW Q X Z 16 Non *post* tamen H | probant] probat O LM prout N | immutatio] mutatio O | huiusmodi] huius L 17 facit] faciat FW Q X Z | quia] immo KU 18 sentiantur] sentirentur FW Q sentiat Z | sensibilia] *mg.* F² | tangentia] tangibilia FZ 19 immutationis *post* animalis Q | animalis] naturalis N naturalis animalis O | a *om.* Z | immutatione *om.* U 20 quam tangunt] quod intentiones NO quod tangunt U | Et ideo *om.* N *spat. vac.* O | est — quod] scilicet (sunt unus O) propositio plus quam NO est vera (una Q) propositio Philosophi quod (*om.* F) U FW Q X Z 21 sensum *om.* H 23 sensum] *add.* etc. O M U

[24]Cf. supra n. 5. 6. 8.
[25]Cf. supra n. 10.
[26]Cf. supra n. 5.

[QUAESTIO 5]

UTRUM SENSUS SIT RECEPTIVUS SPECIERUM SINE MATERIA

Utrum sensus sit receptivus speciei sine materia.[1]

[1] Videtur quod non:

Quia omne quod recipit aliquid ab agente patitur ab eo secundum quod est in actu; sed agens in sensum est obiectum materiale vel forma exsistens in materia;[2] igitur, etc.

Item, sensus recipit speciem obiecti cum condicionibus materiae quae sunt hic, nunc; igitur cum materia, quia condiciones materiae non separantur ab ea.[3]

Item, tactus est unus sensus, tamen recipit calorem materialiter et realiter, non intentionaliter solum;[4] igitur etc.

Item, exemplum PHILOSOPHI de cera et figura[5] non videtur conveniens, quia si sic, sequitur quod sicut cera configuratur anulo,

---

4 Utrum] *praem.* Quaeritur NO KU FW Q X | sit] *lin.* H U² | speciei] specierum KU Z 5 Videtur] *praem.* Et FW *om.* X 6 Quia *om.* NO M FW X Z | patitur] recipitur KU | secundum *om.* Q 7 est] *add.*(ant. est F *lin.* M) ens NO M FW Q X Z | in *om.* FW Q Z | agens in sensum] accidens NO *add. spat. vac.* O 8 forma *om.* Q | igitur *om.* X 9 Item] Praeterea NO FW Q X Z Propterea U | recipit] *add.* formam et U | obiecti *om.* X | materiae] materialibus X 10 hic] *add.* et KU FW Q X Z | igitur cum materia] igitur etc. cum materia (*lin.* H²) H et caetera L igitur et caetera M 11 ab ea] a materia HLM Q 12 Item] Praeterea N U FW Q X Z Prima O | tamen] cum N Z 13 et] *add.* naturaliter vel Z *om.* X | realiter] *add.* et HL | igitur etc.] igitur HL Q *om.* X 14 Item] Praeterea NO U FW Q Z Positum X | Philosophi] physici Q | et figura *om.* K | videtur *om.* N *add.* esse NO U FW Q X Z 15 si] *lin.* U similitudo Z *om.* F Q X | sic] sint O *add.* ibi Q | quod *om.* Q | configuratur] conformatur N figuratur K *add.* ab F | anulo] aulo O

---

[1] **Aristot.**, *De an.* II c. 12 (B c. 12, 424*a* 17—424*b*2); **Avicenna**, *De anima* II c. 2 (AviL 114); **Averroës**, *De an.* II com. 121-124 (AverL 317-319); **Albertus M.**, *De an.* II tr. 4 c.1 (VII¹ 149*a*—150*a*); **Thomas**, *De an.* II c. 24 (XLV¹ 168*a*—171*b*).

[2] Cf. **Thomas**, *De an.* II c. 24 (XLV¹ 168*b*): "... omne enim patiens recipit aliquid ab agente secundum quod est agens; agens autem agit per suam formam et non per suam materiam; omne igitur patiens recipit formam sine materia"; **Aegidius Romanus**, *De an.* II com. 121 (f. 53 *rb*): "Nam passum non recipit ab agente nisi secundum quod agens agit: agens autem non agit secundum materiam sed secundum formam."

[3] **Thomas**, *De an.* II c. 24 (XLV¹ 169*a*): "... non enim aer recipit ab igne agente materiam eius, sed formam. Non videtur hoc esse proprium sensus, quod sit susceptivus specierum sine materia"; **Aegidius Romanus**, *De an.* II com. 121 (f. 53 *rb*): "... quia non recipit formam modo materiali cum quicquid recipitur in sensu recipiant hic et nunc ..."

[4] **Ps. Petrus Hispanus**, *Expositio libri de anima* c. 11 (ed. Alonso 238): "... dico quod calidum materialiter agit in carnem primo ut materialiter generet ibi suam speciem."

[5] **Aristot.**, *De an.* II c. 12 (B c. 12, 424*a* 18-20): "Sensus quidem est susceptivus specierum sine materia, ut cera anuli sine ferro et auro recipit signum"; cf. *Auctoritates Aristotelis* (ed. J. Hamesse 182): "Omnis sensus est susceptivus omnium specierum sensibilium sine materia, sicut cera suscipit figuram sigilli auri sine auro."

ita sensus obiecto; sed figura non est absolutum aliquid super ceram; igitur species, ratione cuius configuratur obiecto, non est aliquid absolutum super potentiam sensitivam. Hoc est falsum, cum sit aliquale principium sentiendi. Probatio assumpti: quia si figura esset forma absoluta, esset activa magis quam passiva, et sic cera cederet figurae magis quam e converso; quantitas autem, cuius figura est terminus, est magis passiva quam activa, cum sequatur compositum ratione materiae. Item, hoc probo sic: quandocumque aliqua passio sequitur aliquod subiectum, circumscripto omni absoluto a subiecto, illa passio non est forma absoluta; sed figura consequitur quantitatem, circumscripto omni absoluto alio a quantitate, quia, statim posita quantitate finita, ponitur figura, quia figura secundum PHILOSOPHUM[6] non est aliud quam terminatio quantitatis; igitur, etc.

5   In oppositum principalis conclusionis est PHILOSOPHUS II *De anima*.[7]

---

1 sensus] *add.* ab (*mg.* W) FW *add. spat. vac.* O | sed — obiecto] *mg.* W | est] *lin.* K | absolutum aliquid] *inv.* O KU Z res absoluta FW | super] supra H U | ceram] causam F   2 igitur] ergo L FW Q X Z | configuratur] *add.* sensus K FW Q *add.* ult. ab (*mg.* W) K FW | est] erit KU FW Q X Z   3 aliquid *om.* KU | super] supra H KU | est *om.* Q   4 sit *om.* N Q | Probatio] Probo O K | assumpti] assumptae O FW Q X Z | si] *add.* in FW Z   5 esset] est F *add.* aliquid absolutum sive U | sic] si X   6 cederet] caderet O cedet FW | figurae magis] *inv.* X figuram(!) magis K | cuius figura] *rep.* K   7 passiva *om.* Z | passiva ... activa] activa ... passiva X | quam] quod Q | sequatur] sequitur H U X Z   8 compositum] oppositum FW | Item] Praeterea NO U FW Q X Z | hoc] hic O | probo] probatur U | quandocumque] quantumque L quando KU X quandoque Q   9 passio] *add. spat. vac.* O | sequitur] consequitur KU W X Z | omni] ni(!) X *om.* U   10 absoluto] obiecto Z *add.* alio KU FW Q X Z | a subiecto] a quantitate K" *sed del.* K ab illo(?) U subiecto X | illa] ita X Z | est — absoluta] erit absoluta Z   11 consequitur] sequitur L | omni] *post* absoluto K ni(!) X *om.* U *add.* subiecto N | absoluto] obiecto O | quantitate] quanto Z   12 quantitate finita] *inv.* H quantitate aliqua finita KU | finita] figurata L *add.* statim O FW X Z | ponitur] *add.* aliqua U W Q X Z *add.* alia F | figura] finita L   13 secundum Philosophum *om.* Q | Philosophum] Euclidem O U FW Q X Z | aliud] *add.* secundum primum Geometriae Q | terminatio quantitatis] quantitas vel terminatio quantitatis K quantitas vel quantitatis terminus U   14 igitur *om.* X | etc.] *add.* (*mg.* W) contra quantitas circumscripto omni alio consequitur substantiam corpoream et tamen est aliquid absolutum FW Q   15 conclusionis] quaestionis H K | Philosophus] Aristoteles Q   16 anima] *add.* XII(?) L

[6] **Aristot.**, *De an.* II c. 12 (B c. 12, 425a 16-17): "Haec enim omnia motu sentimus, ut magnitudinem motu; quare et figuram: magnitudo enim quaedam et figura est"; (a M. Scoto transl.) "figura enim est aliqua quantitas"; cf. **Averroës**, *De an.* II com. 133 (AverL 332): "Figura enim est quantitas cum aliqua qualitate"; **Euclides**, *Elementa* I def. 14 (ed. H. Busard 31): "Figura est quae termino vel terminis continetur"; **Thomas**, *De an.* II c. 25 (XLV¹ 175b): "Figura est aliquid magnitudinis, quia consistit in terminatione magnitudinis (est enim figura quae 'termino vel terminis continetur', ut dicitur in I Euclidis)."

[7] Cf. supra n. 4.

[I. — Solutio quaestionis]

[2] Respondeo: aliquando patiens recipit formam secundum eundem modum essendi quo est in agente, et hoc est quando est eodem modo dispositum ad formam quo est forma in agente, vel quo modo materia agentis est disposita ad eam;[8] et illud accidit in actione naturali, in qua agens et patiens communicant in materia. Aliquando patiens non est eodem modo dispositum, et tunc recipit sine materia, non quia forma in ipso recepta sit sine materia, vel prius fuerit sine materia, sed quia recipit formam non cum materiali dispositione praecedente,[9] vel non recipiendo dispositionem materiae praecedentis (per oppositum ad alium modum quo patiens recipit realem formam vel materialem, quia cum dispositione materiae praecedente). Modo ita est in proposito, quod sensus non est eodem modo dispositus ad recipiendum speciem vel formam obiecti sensibilis sicut materia prima, et ideo recipit speciem eius

---

2 Respondeo] add. quod F | aliquando] an X | patiens] mg. O² | recipit] recipis Z 3 est³] in H add. in KU" W" sed del. U W² 4 quo est forma] quomodo est forma L U quae est forma K Z om. H | forma om. KU X | vel] in Z | vel — eam om. KU | modo² om. FW 5 materia] ant. modo Z | illud] istud KU W | accidit] accipit X | in om. U 6 materia] anima F" sed restit. mg. F² | Aliquando] an X add. autem KU FW Q X Z 7 modo om. O | dispositum] add. ad eam N | et] add. illud N add. non X 8 materia] add. quod U" FW sed del. U | non] lin. O | forma] formaliter F | ipso] eo N ipsa M K | recepta] ant. in KU | sit] est HLM 9 fuerit] fuit M | materia] add. scilicet tali qualis materia requiritur ad accidens scilicet subiectum quia materia speciei in medio est aer et materia speciei in visu est organum visus quia in hiis hii subiectantur(?) K | materiali post praecedente KU add. naturali KU" sed. del. U² 10 non om. Z 11 oppositum] opposita N 12 realem — materialem] formam realiter vel materialiter KU formam realem sive (vel Q Z) materialem FW Q Z formam materialem vel realem X 13 praecedente] praecedentis U FW | Modo] non FW | quod] quia F 14 est] erit X | modo] lin. U² | vel — speciem om. Z 15 obiecti] subiecti FW Q | materia] add. in X | prima] propria O ipsa L U FW Q X | et om. U | ideo] add. non F | speciem] species L | eius] eiusdem F

[8] **Thomas**, De an. II c. 24 (XLV¹ 169a): "Nam forma quae in patiente recipitur ab agente, quandoque quidem habet eundem modum essendi in patiente quem habet in agente (et hoc quidem contingit quando patiens eandem dispositionem ad formam quam habet et agens; unumquodque enim recipitur in altero secundum modum recipientis, unde si eodem modo disponantur patiens sicut agens, eodem modo recipitur forma in patiente sicut erat in agente) ..."
[9] **Thomas**, De an. II c. 24 (XLV¹ 169a): "Quandoque vero forma recipitur in patiente secundum alium modum essendi quam sit in agente, quia dispositio materialis patientis ad recipiendum non est similis dispositioni materiali quae erat in agente, et ideo forma recipitur in patiente sine materia in quantum patiens assimilatur agenti secundum formam et non secundum materiam"; cf. **Aegidius Romanus**, De an. II com. 121 (f. 53va).

sine materia, id est sine dispositione materiae.[10]

7 Sed contra, potentia sensitiva, ut dictum est, est idem quod essentia animae;[11] sed essentia non potest recipere aliquid ab agente pure naturali corporali, sed[12] ab agente pure spirituali; igitur, cum obiectum sensus sit corporale, potentia sensitiva non poterit ab eo speciem recipere.

8 Dicendum quod anima potest mediante corporeo organo aliquid recipere ab obiecto corporeo, licet anima non posset immediate, ut concludit argumentum. Quia igitur potentia sensitiva propinqua non est anima tantum, immo includit organum, ideo potest ab obiecto speciem recipere, stante identitate reali ipsius potentiae cum animae essentia.[13] Immo, si esset diversa essentia ab anima, sicut

---

1 id est] et N U   2 sensitiva] passiva Q | dictum est] inv. NO Q | est² post idem X   3 essentia animae] inv. X | sed] add. aliqua KU | essentia²] add. animae HLM Q | recipere post naturali L post aliquid H KU Z om. M   4 pure] puro M | naturali om. O KU FW Q X | corporali om. L Z | sed] add. tantum O K FW Q X Z | sed — quam unum ideo etc. (ad finem quaestionis) deest in codice U propter folium deperditum | agente²] obiecto Z | pure² om. FW Q X Z | spirituali] incorporali N superiori W Z add. ita F add. (mg.) spirituali W   5 obiectum post sensus K | sensus] add. pure naturale et L | sit] est (post corporale) LM | non] mg. H nec (ant. potentia) NO FW Q X Z | poterit] potest M K add. et Q   6 speciem] aliquid K   7 Dicendum] add. est M K F X | corporeo organo] inv. K corpore(!) organo F   8 recipere post corporeo O FW Q X Z | corporeo om. K | licet] sed K | anima] ea X | posset] possit NO potest K | immediate] ant. non K   9 Quia om. N | igitur] ergo L FW Q Z | propinqua] add. scilicet ad sentiendum K   10 non est anima K | tantum] ant. est O FW Q X Z | tantum immo] inv. L | ab om. F   11 ipsius] ipsi X | potentiae] add. nude N"O sed del. N add. unde FW Q X Z   12 animae essentia] inv. X | essentia] add. etc. L | essentia²] realiter (ant. diversa Z) O FW Q X Z | anima] spat. vac. Z

[10]Cf. **Duns Scotus**, *Ordinatio* IV d. 12 q. 3 n. [19] (ed. Vivès XVII 594b): "Passum receptivum formae secundum esse reale non est receptivum eiusdem secundum esse intentionale, II *De anima*; oportet enim receptivum soni esse absonum, saltem regulariter receptivum formae isto modo; non est receptivum formae alio modo, maxime in receptivis materialibus; ergo organum et subiectum contrarii non sunt receptiva formae, secundum idem esse, quia unum recipit intentionaliter, aliud realiter, et per consequens cum agens agat in passum secundum potentiam receptivam eius, secundum illud II *De anima*; actus activorum sunt in patiente bene disposito, sequitur quod agens non agat in hoc passum, et illud actione eiusdem rationis."

[11]Cf. **Aristot.**, *De an.* II c. 2 (B c. 2, 412b 17-22); **Averroës**, *De an.* II com. 9 (AverL 144): "Ita est anima de corpore sicut forma in materia (forma enim in corporibus naturalibus magis habet hoc nomen *substantia* quam materia)"; **Thomas**, *De an.* II c. 2 (XLV¹ 75b); *De an.* II c. 24 (XLV¹ 170a): "... potentia enim est quia forma organi, ut supra habitum est." Notandum vero Sanctum Thomam ipsum opinioni favere quae potentias animae realiter distingui ab essentia animae teneat — cf. *Summa theol.* I q. 77 a. 1; ab hinc litigiosa quaestio orta est apud doctores, cf. C. Piana, 'La controversia della distinzione fra anima e potenze ai primordi della Scuola Scotista (1310-1330 c.)' in *Miscellanea del centro di studio medievali*, Milano 1956, 65-168.

[12]Hic codex U terminat ex abrupto, modo tamen alio quam ceteri codices in familia antiqua, quae amplectitur N et O. Codex U autem resumit in q. 10 n. 26.

[13]Cf. **Themistius**, *De an.* IV (CLCAG I 179): "Species autem est sensus et ratio primi sensitivi; potentia enim ipsius est et forma. Et subiecto quidem idem sensus et sensitivum, sicut omnis forma est cum eo quod suscipit eam; esse autem est alterum organi et potentiae: organum quidem enim magnitudo quaedam et corpus est, potentia autem est ratio et species illius"; **Thomas**, *De an.* II c. 24 (XLV¹ 170a): "Organum igitur sensus cum potentia ipsa, utputa oculus, est idem subiecto, sed esse alterum est, quia ratione differt a corpore potentia ..."

qualitas quaedam absoluta, sequeretur quod ipsa cum organo, sine essentia animae, posset sentire, quia posita causa totali, ponitur et eius effectus (potentia sensitiva cum organo est talis causa sentiendi).

Sed forte tu dicis quod potentia sensitiva non possit exire in actum nisi virtute animae, quae est[14] principalis, dato quod sit eius qualitas absoluta.

Contra: quod per se potest habere esse qualitercumque, sive per naturam sive per miraculum, per se naturaliter — sine alio — potest agere sine alio, sicut patet de accidente in sacramento Altaris, quod non habet esse in subiecto, et tamen naturaliter agit. Modus enim essendi vel subsistendi[15] non impedit naturalem actionem, sicut et oculus restitutus per miraculum potest naturaliter videre. Modo ita est quod accidens absolutum potest per miraculum a subiecto absolvi quantum ad inesse actu, et ideo, si potentia sit absoluta qualitas, potest agere sine eius subiecto, quod est anima.[16]

[4] Sed contra: potentia sensitiva non est separabilis a corpore; anima secundum suam essentiam est separabilis a corpore.

---

1 sequeretur] *add.* sequitur O | quod] quia K 2 essentia] esse NO | posset] possit N | causa totali] *inv.* L Q tali causa HM K | ponitur *om.* NO FW Q X Z 3 eius *om.* K | talis] totalis O FW Z | sentiendi] *add.* totalis K 5 forte *post* dicis L | tu *om.* FW Q X Z | dicis] dices K FW Q X Z | possit] = N M posset O L K W Q X Z potest H F 6 nisi] *add.* in K FW Q X Z | quae] quo Z | est] *add.* causa O K FW Q X Z | sit *om.* Z | eius *post* qualitas L K 7 absoluta *om.* X 8 Contra *om.* X | per se *post* potest F | potest] *add.* tamen X 9 naturam] materiam X | per *om.* Q | naturaliter] naturale X *om.* L 10 sine alio *om.* O K FW Q X Z | patet] potest N | accidente — Altaris] sacramenti accidente in Altari L sacramento accidento Altaris M | Altaris *om.* Z 11 et *om.* X | naturaliter agit] *inv.* HLM materialiter agit F | Modus enim] Modum X 12 subsistendi] spirandi NO fiendi K Q X sentiendi HLM FW Z | naturalem] naturaliter HL | actionem] *add.* rei K | et] etiam FW Q X *om.* K 13 restitutus] resolutus NO | potest naturaliter] *inv.* FW Q X Z | naturaliter] materialiter O *om.* N 14 accidens] actus O | potest *post* miraculum X *om.* K | a] *add.* suo N | absolvi] *mg.* W 15 inesse] esse O FW Q X Z | sit — qualitas] sit (est Z) qualitas absoluta O FW Q X Z absoluta sit qualitas K 16 eius subiecto] *inv.* K 17 Sed — anima *om.* F | potentia] *add.* seu rep. contra potentia N *add. mg.* Quaere residuum huius quaestionis in principio quarti ab hinc folii ad talem signum *ins.* florilegium N[2] | potentia — quam unum ideo etc. *(ad finem quaestionis); reliqua pars quaestionis invenitur in fol. 166ra, linea tertia codicis N, atque in fol. 48vb, linea septima ab imo codice* O | separabilis *post* corpore Q 18 anima] *add.* autem O K FW Q Z | a corpore] *scilicet* humana NO FW Q X Z *add.* igitur etc. M *add.* ut anima humana K *add.* ult. *(mg.)* ergo non est eadem cum anima N[2]

---

[14]Subaudi: causa.

[15]Quia omnes codices verba falsa — aut 'spirandi' aut 'fiendi' aut 'sentiendi' — perperam tradunt, ideo verbum 'subsistendi', contextu disceptandi perpenso, scripsimus.

[16]Cf. **Gonsalvus Hispanus**, *Quaest. disputat.* q. 10 (BFS IX 168): "Accidentia perfecta et absoluta, ut quantitatem et qualitatem, potest Deus facere sine suis subiectis; sed si potentiae animae sint accidentia absoluta superaddita essentiae animae, erunt accidentia et formae accidentales maxime perfectae"; **Richardus de Mediav.**, *Quaest. disputat.* q. 9 (cod. Vat. Lat. 868, f. 20ra): "Forma accidentalis, si separetur a forma substantiali, se ipsa agit, ut patet in sacramento Altaris; ergo multo fortius forma substantialis sine omni forma accidentali seipsa agere potest. Substantia ergo animae per suam formam substantialem potest agere ..."

12 Dicendum quod potentia propinqua ad sentiendum quae est totalis causa eliciendi actum, supposito obiecto, non est separabilis, quia talis includit organum corporeum, quod est aliud ab essentia animae, et sic ipsa potentia differt ab anima. Sed potentia sensitiva, praecise quae est remota, talis est separabilis, sicut et essentia, quia idem sunt. Sed causa quare magis dicitur sensitiva inseparabilis quam intellectiva est quia sensitiva dicitur per respectum ad actum sentiendi, quia potentia sensitiva est qua homo potest sentire, et intellectiva per quam homo potest intelligere. Modo ita est quod ad actum sentiendi concurrunt per se duae causae partiales ex parte hominis, scilicet potentia sensitiva et organum, et ideo requiritur utrumque et neutrum sufficit, et potentia sensitiva ut sic est inseparabilis ab organo. Sed potentia intellectiva est totalis causa intelligendi, nec requirit aliam causam per se ex parte hominis, ideo dicitur separabilis; non enim per se utitur organo tanquam instrumento.

[II. — Ad argumenta principalia]

13 Ad primum in oppositum[17] dicendum quod si intelligatur maior quod patiens formam recipiat secundum eandem dispositionem qua est in agente, non est verum, nisi de patiente passione naturali et univoca, non autem de intentionali, sicut est in proposito de sensu.[18] Si autem intelligatur sic quod agens non agit nisi secundum quod est in actu, non secundum quod est in potentia, et per consequens patiens non recipit aliquid ab agente nisi secundum

---

1 Dicendum] add. est M | est om. Q 2 totalis] talis X | eliciendi] eligendi O | non est] inv. FW Q X Z 3 corporeum om. HLM 4 sic] ita K | ipsa] illa HLM ista K | potentia] mg. F² add. animae K | ab anima om. X | potentia²] add. passiva NO 5 praecise] pure N H(?)M | est] add. potentia NO | et] etiam HLM om. X | quia] quae X 6 quare] quia X | magis — sensitiva] dicitur magis sensitiva O sensitiva potentia (om. Z) dicitur magis L Z dicitur sensitiva magis K | inseparabilis quam] mg. F² 7 sensitiva] add. magis K 8 et om. K 9 per quam] qua K Q | quam om. NO M K Z 10 per se om. K | causae om. X 11 requiritur utrumque] utraque requiritur NO K FW Q X Z 12 neutrum] neutra NO FW Q X Z | et²] add. ideo NO FW Q X Z | potentia sensitiva] inv. NO FW Q Z | inseparabilis] separabilis M Q 13 totalis] totaliter K 14 ex parte] respectu L | hominis] add. et X 18 dicendum] add. est (ant. dicendum L) LM F | intelligatur] intelligitur M K 19 quod om. X | recipiat] add. eam F 20 verum] argumentum N | patiente om. L | et om. L 21 univoca] unica O K F Q | de om. FW Z | sicut] sic NO X Z | sensu] sensibili NO FW Q Z 22 intelligatur] intelligitur HM K | intelligatur sic] inv. K FW Q X Z | agit] add. seu rep. sicut est in proposito W 23 in om. X | quod²] lin. O | in² om. X | et] add. sic K | per consequens patiens] patiens et per consequens K 24 ab agente] absolute Z | secundum om. NO Q

[17]Cf. supra n. 1.
[18]**Thomas**, De an. II c. 24 (XLV¹ 169a): "Sensus recipit formam sine materia, quia alterius modi esse habet forma in sensu et in re sensibili; nam in re sensibili habet esse naturale, in sensu autem habet esse intentionale sive spirituale."

quod est in actu, ita quod receptum est procedens ab actualitate agentis, non potentialitate, verum est, sed non concludit propositum sub illo intellectu.

Ad aliud[19] dicendum quod condiciones materiae possunt accipi prout opponuntur universalitati et sunt condiciones singularitatis: et sic verum est quod sensus recipit speciem cum condicionibus materiae. Alio modo pro dispositione reali qua materia recipit formam naturalem et realem, quae dispositiones sunt qualitates activae et passivae;[20] illo modo non est verum quod sensus, in quantum huiusmodi et per se, recipiat speciem.

Ad aliud[21] dicendum quod tactus in quantum sensus non recipit calorem materialiter vel realiter, sed immutatur intentionaliter tantum in quantum sensus (licet illa immutatio non possit separari a naturali immutatione pro statu viae), et ideo recipit speciem sine materia ut sic.

[6] Ad aliud[22] dicendum, concedendo argumentum, quod similitudo non valet quantum ad illud de quo procedit. Quia figura cerae non est forma absoluta sicut species, ut bene probatum est, sed est similitudo ita quod sicut, mediante figura, cera assimilatur anulo et cera figurata est similitudo formae anuli non materiae (quia recipit tantum formam, non materiam), ita, mediante specie, sensus

---

1 est] *lin.* W *om.* Z | quod²] quia Z | receptum] receptio HLM | procedens *post* agentis HLM | ab] in N 2 agentis] *add.* et FW | sed] et NO sic Q si Z | non concludit] includit FW Z | concludit] includit X | propositum] intentum NO 3 illo] isto W Z | intellectu] intentum L intellectum F 4 dicendum] *add.* est M F X | quod *om.* Z 5 opponuntur] opponitur Z | et sunt] secundum HLM | sunt *om.* Z | condiciones] condicionibus Z | singularitatis] signatae N singulares K singulis Q 6 sic *om.* M | sensus] *add.* inquantum huiusmodi HLM | speciem] species N *om.* K | cum] sub N a X 7 pro] per X | qua] quia HM | formam] *add.* materialem F 8 naturalem] materialem NO | et] vel O | et²] vel K 9 illo] isto O FW X Z *add.* autem Q | verum *om.* Z | in — speciem] recipit speciem huiusmodi per se K 10 et — speciem] recipit speciem per se HL K 11 dicendum] *add.* est M 12 calorem] colorem L | materialiter] materialem K X | vel realiter *om.* FW Z | realiter] realem X | immutatur] mutatur Q immutat X 13 sensus *om.* Z | illa] ista Q | immutatio] mutatio X | possit] potest N H posset M X | a naturali immutatione] ab immutatione naturali N 14 naturali] materiali L | ideo *om.* O *add.* non NO | speciem *om.* L 15 sic] *add.* etc. K 16 dicendum] *add.* est M *add.* est quod F *add.* quod W | concedendo] concedo FW Q 17 quantum *om.* Q | illud] idem H id F | quo] *add.* (*lin.*) argumentum tantum N²| cerae] esse Z *om.* K 18 est *om.* Z | sicut] sed HM | probatum est] probatur L | est] fuit K *om.* Q | sed est *om.* Z | est³] erit X 19 ita quod] in hoc quod NO K *om.* L | sicut *om.* Q | cera] causa Q | anulo] a nullo X 20 cera figurata] cera fracta N cerae figura K esse Z | formae anuli] *inv.* H | anuli] *add.* et K *om.* X | recipit] repraesentat NO K 21 formam] *add.* et K | ita] ista Q item X

---

[19]Cf. supra n. 2.
[20]**Thomas**, *De an.* II c. 24 (XLV¹ 171a): "Nam tangibilia sunt qualitates activae et passivae elementorum secundum quas accidit universaliter alteratio in corporibus."
[21]Cf. supra n. 3.
[22]Cf. supra n. 4.

assimilatur obiecto[23] et species tantum repraesentat formam obiectivam, sicut species coloris tantum colorem, non parietem vel superficiem, quia per se non faciunt ad substantiam immutationis, licet magnitudo et figura faciant ad differentiam eius; aliter enim immutat magna quantitas quam parva, quia fortius, et plura alba vel colorata quam unum; ideo, etc.

---

1 tantum] tamen O   2 coloris] colorum FW(?) colore Z | colorem] colorationem Q | parietem] aerem K   3 quia] quae L | ad — ad] a X | substantiam] formam N   4 figura] forma H M figuratur Z | faciant] faciunt HLM | eius *om.* HLM   5 immutat] iniungat(!) K | magna — etc.] magis quam qualitas quam per unum quia fortius et plura vel colorata quam unum ideo etc. X | quantitas] qualitas K FW Z | alba vel colorata] alba K colorata vel alba Z | vel *om.* HLM   6 unum] *add.* tantum HLM *add.* et FW | ideo etc. *om.* N L K

[23]**Thomas**, *De an.* II c. 24 (XLV¹ 169*b*): "... assimilatur enim sensus sensibili secundum formam, sed non secundum dispositionem materiae."

[QUAESTIO 6]

UTRUM SINT TANTUM QUINQUE SENSUS

Utrum¹ sint tantum quinque sensus.²

[1] Videtur quod non: 1

Quia potentiae distinguuntur per obiecta; sed obiecta sensuum sunt accidentia extrinseca, quae non sunt tantum quinque generum, sed plurium;³ igitur, etc.

Item, magnitudo et figura sunt per se sensibilia et differunt a colore plus quam sonus, quia sunt in alio praedicamento, non autem color et sonus; igitur, cum sit alia potentia sensitiva respectu coloris, alia respectu soni, videtur quod alia debet esse respectu figurae et magnitudinis ab aliis sensibus particularibus.⁴ 2

Item, unus sensus est tantum unius contrarietatis; sed tactus est plurium contrarietatum;⁵ igitur non est unus, et per consequens sunt sex sensus.⁶ 3

Item, quod non sunt quinque, probatur: quia inferius non distinguitur a superiori, nec ponit in numerum cum eo; sed "gustus 4

---

3 Utrum] *praem.* Quaeritur NO FW Q Z *praem.* Quaeritur duodecimo K *adnot. mg.* Quaestio duodecima M | sint tantum] *inv.* O FW Z tantum sunt M sunt tantum KU   4 Videtur] *praem.* Et U   5 obiecta] opposita O | obiecta²] opposita O   6 accidentia extrinseca] *inv.* L | tantum *om.* NO | generum] genera N   7 sed plurium *om.* NO | etc. *om.* Q   8 Item] Praeterea NO FW Q Z   9 colore] calore Z | sonus] genere N s + *spat. vac.* O   10 igitur cum] *inv.* NO | sit alia] *inv.* M | alia] aliqua L U   11 alia] et FW | videtur] dicitur F | alia²] aliqua U | debet] debeat NO FW Z | respectu² *om.* NO FW Q Z   12 et magnitudinis] alia magnitudinis N cum magnitudini F | sensibus] speciebus N   13 Item] Praeterea NO FW Q Z | sed] sensus NO FW Q Z *add.* ult. autem NO | est²] *add.*ᵃ sensus HL U   14 unus] unius Q   15 sex] lin. O   16 Item] Praeterea NO FW Q Z | sunt] sint O Q Z | probatur *om.* NO FW Q Z | non distinguitur] cum differt U   17 in *om.* HL K F Q

¹Deest ista quaestio in codice X.
²**Aristot.**, *De an.* II c. 25 (Γ c. 1 424b 22-27); **Albertus M.**, *De an.* II tr. 4 c. 3 (VII¹ 151a—152b); **Thomas**, *De an.* II c. 25 (XLV¹ 173a—176b); *Summa theol.* I q. 78 a. 3 (V 253a—255b); **Aegidius Romanus**, *De an.* II com. 128 (f. 55ra); *Auctoritates Aristotelis* (ed. J. Hamesse 179): "Quinque sunt sensus, scilicet visus, auditus, odoratus, tactus et gustus."
³**Thomas**, *Summa theol.* I q. 78 a. 3 arg. 1 (V 253a): "Sensus enim est cognoscitivus accidentium. Sunt autem multa genera accidentium. Cum ergo potentiae distinguantur per obiecta, videtur quod sensus multiplicentur secundum numerum qui est in generibus accidentibus."
⁴**Thomas**, *Summa theol.* I q. 78 a. 3 arg. 2 (V 253a).
⁵**Aristot.**, *De an.* II c. 11 (B c. 11 422b 23-27): "Omnis et enim sensus unius contrarietatis esse videtur, ut visus albi et nigri, auditus gravis et acuti, gustus amari et dulcis; in tangibili autem multae insunt contrarietates ..."; cf. **Themistius**, *De an.* IV (CLCAG I 166); **Thomas**, *Summa theol.* I q. 78 a. 3 arg. 3 (V 253a).
⁶Cf. supra q. 1 n. 1.

est quidam tactus";⁷ igitur, etc.

5   Contra est PHILOSOPHUS, qui hoc probat ex intentione in hoc capitulo: "Quod autem non sunt sensus praeter quinque".⁸

[I. — Solutio quaestionis]

6   Respondeo: dicendum quod probatio PHILOSOPHI non est a priori, quia probat propositum ex numero organorum;⁹ organa autem sunt propter sensum, non e converso.

7   Procedendum est igitur a priori sic: omnis potentia cognitiva elicit operationem suam per quamdam conformitatem ad obiectum. Quod non potest facere potentia organica nisi per receptionem speciei, in organo, sui obiecti. Quae species est conformis obiecto, et etiam determinativa potentiae ad cognoscendum hoc vel illud obiectum, secundum quod a diversis obiectis imprimitur diversa species in organo per diversas immutationes organi ab obiecto. Est autem duplex immutatio in genere: quaedam naturalis, quaedam animalis.¹⁰ Naturalis est secundum quam vel per quam forma recipitur in paciente secundum esse reale, et secundum dispositionem materiae, consimilem illi quae est in agente. Animalis autem secundum quam recipitur secundum esse intentionale species obiecti

---

2 Contra] Ad oppositum L Ad contrarium N *add.* illud KU | est *om.* Q | qui] quia NO Q | hoc probat] *inv.* Q probat NO L KU | intentione] *add.* oppositum L | in hoc capitulo] in isto (illo O FW Q Z) capitulo NO FW Q Z hoc capitulo Q *om.* K   3 capitulo] *add.* scilicet L | autem *om.* L K | sunt] est K sit F Q sint Z *om.* U | sensus *post* quinque N | praeter] nisi NO Z | quinque] *add.* praedictos K   5 Respondeo] Responsio O L F Z | dicendum] *add.* est M F | Philosophi *om.* H   7 propter] praeter L per Q | non] *add.* autem KU   8 Procedendum] Probandum N FW Q Z Proponendum O | cognitiva] cognoscitiva U Z   9 elicit] efficit Z | suam *om.* U | obiectum] oppositum O   10 nisi] nec Q   11 speciei — obiecti] speciei obiecti in organo NO Q ipsius obiecti in organo FW speciei obiecti in obiecto in organo Z | Quae] quo Z | species *om.* NO FW Q Z | conformis] *add.* suo M | obiecto — diversis *om.* Z   12 et] est FW Q | etiam *om.* N KU | determinativa] indeterminativa N U | hoc *om.* U | vel] et NO | illud] idem U   13 obiectum] oppositum O | secundum] sed Q | obiectis *om.* NO | imprimitur] imprimuntur N | diversa] diversae N   14 organi] immutatur solum N | obiecto] opposito O   15 autem] enim N L Q Z *om.* F | duplex immutatio] *mg.* N² *inv.* K | quaedam] *add.* scilicet H | quaedam²] *add.* et H   16 secundum ... per] per ... secundum N | per] *post* Z   17 secundum] *add.* idem N *add.* illud O FW Q *add.* id M | secundum — agente *om.* Z | et] vel KU   19 secundum²] in H | intentionale] *add.* in anima H

---

⁷**Aristot.**, *De an.* II c. 10 (B c. 10, 422a 8): "Gustus autem est aliquis tactus"; **Albertus M.**, *De an.* II tr. 3 c. 27 (VII¹ 138a): "Cum dicitur gustus esse quidam tactus, intelligitur quidam tactus, qui non simpliciter est tactus ..."; **Thomas**, *Summa theol.* I q. 78 a. 3 arg. 4 (V 253a).
⁸**Aristot.**, *De an.* II c. 25 (Γ c. 1, 424b 22-23): "Quod autem non sit sensus alter praeter quinque"; cf. supra q. 1 n. 1.
⁹**Aristot.**, *De an.* II c. 25 (Γ c. 1, 424b 24—425a 2).
¹⁰Cf. supra q. 4 n. 11.

agentis in potentiam animalem. Ista autem species sic recepta non denominat sensum. Unde visus non dicitur coloratus proprie, sicut paries dicitur coloratus, quia recipit colorem realiter.[11] Sensus autem non tantum immutatur naturaliter ab obiecto, quia tunc inanimata, quae sic naturaliter immutantur, possent sentire.[12]

[3] Si autem immutentur aliqui sensus naturaliter, cum hoc tamen immutantur intentionaliter — immo magis intentionaliter quam naturaliter; immutatio enim naturalis impedit animalem sensationem, ut visum est.[13] Si enim esset immutatio intentionalis sine naturali, sicut est in visu, magis sentiretur et verius quam cum ea.

Ex diversitate ergo immutationis organi ab obiecto et conformationis sumitur sic sufficientia sensuum: quia aliquando sensus immutantur intentionaliter tantum, aliquando cum hoc naturaliter. Si primo modo, sic est visus; si secundo modo, aut est transmutatio naturalis ex parte obiecti, aut ex parte organi.[14] Si ex parte obiecti, aut fit talis immutatio mediante motu locali, et sic est auditus, qui immutatur a sono se multiplicante in aere usque ad auditum mediante motu locali;[15] aut fit mediante motu alterationis, et sic est

---

1 animalem] animalis L | Ista] Illa NO L F | sic recepta] KU 2 sensum] obiectum N subiectum FW Z | Unde] Cum KU Ut N | coloratus proprie] inv. O | sicut] ut N 3 paries] add. sicut F | colorem] colores M | realiter] respectu NO naturaliter Z | autem om. N 4 non] lin. Z² | tantum] tamen NO KU add. seu rep. recipit colorem vel Z | obiecto] opposito O | tunc] sunt NO 5 sic] nec NO | immutantur] add. nec N | possent] possunt NO H posset F Z 6 immutentur] immutantur NO L FW Q (post sensus) Z | cum hoc] non H | tamen immutantur] inv. Q 7 intentionaliter] add. seu rep. quam naturaliter F | immo magis intentionaliter] mg. W | intentionaliter²] intentio Z | quam naturaliter] rep. (mg.) W 8 immutatio — immutatio om. U | animalem sensationem] inv. N animalem et sensationem Q Z 9 esset om. L | immutatio] mutatio K 10 visu] visus U | sentiretur] sentirentur FW Q Z add. obiecta Q | ea] eo U 11 Ex] adnot. mg. quomodo sumitur sufficientia sensuum notetur hic N² | ergo om. H | conformationis] conformitatis N rasura + ationis M conformi FW adnot. ult. mg. sufficientiam quinque sensuum M 12 sumitur] sumatur NO M FW Z | quia] quod F 13 immutantur] immutatur L FW add. solum FW | intentionaliter tantum aliquando] intentionaliter aliquando NO W intentionaliter aliquando tantum F intentionaliter tamen aliquando U tantum intentionaliter aliquando Q Z | cum hoc] tantum (mg.) W om. F | naturaliter] materialiter W Z 14 modo om. N U | est² post naturalis NO fit L | transmutatio] immutatio O 15 naturalis] add. aut L U | obiecti] opposiit O 16 fit post immutatio NO sit sic Z | motu locali] inv. F 18 mediante] movente O | fit om. F | et om. NO Z

---

[11] **Thomas**, *De an.* III c. 1 (XLV¹ 206b).
[12] Cf. supra q. 4 n. 11-13 et infra q. 7 n. 14.
[13] Cf. q. 4 n. 12.
[14] **Thomas**, *Summa theol.* I q. 78 a. 3 in corp. (V 254a): "Sed in quibusdam sensibus invenitur immutatio spiritualis tantum, sicut in visu. In quibusdam autem, cum immutatione spirituali, etiam naturalis; vel ex parte obiecti tantum, vel etiam ex parte organi"; cf. **Duns Scotus**, *Ordinatio* II d. 3 pars 2 q. 1 (VII 541): "Oppositae dispositiones requiruntur in organo sensus: quod debet esse receptivum sensibilis sine materia, et in eo quod debet recipere obiectum secundum esse materiale; ideo igitur oportet organum denudari a forma quam recipit, et per consequens sensum qui est in tali organo."
[15] **Thomas**, *Summa theol.* I q. 78 a. 3 in corp. (V 254a): "Ex parte autem obiecti, invenitur transmutatio naturalis, secundum locum quidem in sono, qui est obiectum auditus."

odoratus, qui sentit odorem procedentem ab odorabili secundum quod est alteratum per calefactionem — unde in hieme male odoratur corpus odorabile, specialiter si sit congelatum.[16] (Non autem accipitur aliquis sensus proprius secundum quod immutatur per motum in quantitate, quia quantitas est sensibile commune, non proprium, et ideo secundum eam non debet assignari sensus proprius.) Si autem immutatio sit naturalis ex parte organi, sic habemus gustum et tactum. Sed differunt, quia organum tactus immutatur a calore et qualitate sensibili quae est eius obiectum immediate, vel saltem potest ab ea immediate immutari; gustus autem non potest immediate immutari a sapore, qui est eius obiectum, sed mediante humore coniuncto linguae.[17]

Probatio secundi istius: quia si immediate immutaretur a sapore, semper iudicaret saporem esse talem qualis ille sapor est; hoc autem est falsum in febricitantibus, quia videtur dulce amarum propter amaritudinem humoris coniuncti; igitur, etc. Probatio primi: quia in quodcumque passum eiusdem rationis potest agere unum activum eiusdem rationis, et aliud eiusdem rationis activum in illud agere potest, specialiter si passivum sit extrinsecum. (Quod dico propter intellectum et voluntatem, quae possunt pati ab obiectis, quae

[4]

---

1 odoratus] olfactus NO ad adoratus (!) Z | sentit] sensis Z | odorabili] adorabilem(!) O adorabili(!) Z   2 est *om.* KU | per] *add.* alterationem W | male] non (*lin.*) F² vix Z *om.* W | odoratur] adoratus Z   3 odorabile] adorabile O Z | specialiter] spiritualiter Q principale Z | autem] tamen L   4 sensus *om.* Z | quod] quem NO FW Q Z | immutatur] immutetur H FW Z immutat K immutet L U   5 motum] modum H | quantitas] quantitatis L | commune] *add.* et HL U | non proprium] proprium O *om.* N   7 immutatio *om.* H | sit] fit L *add.* proprie U | naturalis] naturaliter U | ex parte] respectu KU   8 differunt] *add.* ei F | quia] *add.* (*mg.* W) oportet FW | immutatur] immutari F   9 et] in N Q vel K FW Z | obiectum] oppositum O   10 non *om.* KU | non — immediate *om.* L | potest — medi*ante om.* Z | immediate immutari] *inv.* LM K   13 Probatio secundi istius] Probatio istius secundi NO W Probatio secundi illius L U Probatur hoc secundum Q Probatio illius secundi F Z | si *om.* Z | immediate immutaretur] *inv.* O FW Q Z | sapore] *add.* tunc Q   14 saporem] de sapore ipsum M *add. seu rep.* saporem O | esse talem] *inv.* FW | qualis] qualiter Z | ille sapor *om.* NO FW Q Z | est] *ant.* ille H | autem *om.* U   15 est falsum] *inv.* M non est verum Q *add.* ut FW | febricitantibus] febribus K | quia] quibus O FW Q Z   16 coniuncti] *add.* linguae Q | igitur etc.] quia etc. Z *om.* L | Probatio primi] Probatur primum Q   17 quodcumque] quocumque N Q | eiusdem rationis] cuius ratione KU | potest — rationiis *om.* Z | unum *om.* NO | activum] actum NO F Q   18 eiusdem rationis *om.* L | rationis] *mg.* W | aliud] ad N | activum] actum (*ant.* eiusdem Q) NO F Q | in illud agere potest] potest agere in iillud Q | illud] idem U   19 passivum] passum NO U FW Q | sit extrinsecum] *inv.* Q   20 intellectum et voluntatem] voluntatem et intellectum L | et] vel U | quae] qui N | quae — voluntatem *om.* Z | ab] in F | obiectis] oppositis O *add.* intrinsecis NO FW Q

[16]**Thomas**, *Summa theol.* I q. 78 a. 3 in corp. (V 254a): "Secundum alterationem vero, in odore, qui est obiectum olfactus: oportet enim per calidum alterari aliquo modo corpus, ad hoc quod spiret odorem."

[17]**Thomas**, *Summa theol.* I q. 78 a. 3 in corp. (V 254a): "Ex parte autem organi est immutatio naturalis in tactu et gustu; nam et manus tangens calida calefit, et lingua humectatur per humiditatem saporum."

tamen obiecta moventia intellectum et voluntatem unius hominis non movent propter hoc — nec movere possunt — intellectum et voluntatem alterius; tunc enim diversorum posset esse una intellectio numero.) Modo ita est quod calor in aere, et in alio corpore extrinseco, et calor in carne, quae est medium intrinsecum, sunt eiusdem rationis, quia unus generatur ab alio generatione univoca; igitur, si calor carnis potest immediate agere in organum tactus, ita poterit immediate calor extrinsecus. Item, probo illud primum sic: calor magis materialiter recipitur in carne quam in aere, cum sit materialior; igitur, si calor carnis potest immediate immutare organum tactus, quod est receptivum speciei sine materia, multo magis calor aeris, quia, ut probatum est,[18] immutatio materialior magis impedit, et spiritualior est sensibilior.

[5]

Ex praedictis patet ordo potentiarum, quia visus, cum immutetur tantum intentionaliter, est sensus nobilior[19] et certior; post hunc autem auditus, qui minus materialiter immutatur, quia mediante motu locali tantum qui est primus motuum; post hunc olfactus, qui immutatur materialiter ex parte obiecti, quod est remotius a potentia quam organum;[20] post hunc gustus, qui immutatur materialiter ex parte organi, sed non immediate cum suo obiecto,

11

---

1 obiecta] opposita O | moventia] movent Q | et] vel N *om.* O | unius hominis] *inv.* F 2 movent] moverent NO | nec] non Z | movere possunt] *inv.* NO FW Q Z 3 alterius *om.* K *add.* hominis NO Q | tunc] et sic H aliter O | una] *add.* immutatio Q 4 in] et Z | et in] vel NO FW Q Z vel in M | alio] aliquo U | corpore *om.* L 5 quae] qui K | sunt] sint U 6 unus] unum NO | ab] ex KU 7 carnis *om.* H | immediate agere] *inv.* NO FW Q Z 8 poterit immediate] *inv.* H immediate potest KU | immediate calor] *inv.* N | Item] Praeterea NO FW Q Z | probo — sic *om.* NO FW Z | illud] idem U 9 materialiter] naturaliter K | cum] in O 10 potest immediate] *inv.* FW Q 11 est] *add.* per rationem F | receptivum speciei] specierum receptivum F | magis] minus (*lin.* F) FW Z 12 aeris] aere U | quia *om.* L | est *om.* N | materialior] immaterialior H | magis impedit et spiritualior] spirituraliori Z 13 est] et KU | sensibilior] sensatio NO 14 quia] quod Z | cum] *add.* spiritualiter NO | immutetur] *add.* quia NO Q 15 sensus nobilior] *inv.* NO FW Q Z *adnot. mg.* nota ordinem potentiarum M | certior] interior N | hunc autem] *inv.* NO 16 qui minus] primus KU | materialiter] immaterialiter FW | quia *om.* L 17 tantum qui] *inv.* U Z | motuum] *add.* nam N *add.* non O | hunc] *add.* autem K | olfactus] effectus O | qui] quae O quia W Z 18 parte] *add.* organi U | obiecti — parte *om.* W | quod est] *rep.* F | a] et O 19 quam *om.* NO | organum] organi N | hunc] hoc O | qui] quia Z 20 non *om.* U | obiecto] subiecto O L Q Z

[18]Cf. supra n. 8.
[19]**Thomas**, *De an.* II c. 14 (XLV 127*b*—128*a*): "Sensus visus est spiritualior ex modo immutationis: nam in quolibet alio sensu non est immutatio spiritualis sine naturali ... immutatio vero spiritualis est secundum quod species recipitur in organo sensus aut in medio per modum intentioni et non per modum naturalis formae: non enim sic recipitur species in sensu secundum illud esse quod habet in re sensibili ... sed immutatio visus est sola immutatio spirituali"; cf. **Thomas**, *Summa theol.* I q. 78 a. 3 in corp. (V 254*a*); cf. supra q. 4 n. 10-11.
[20]**Thomas**, *Summa theol.* I q. 78 a. 3 in corp. (V 254*a*): "Et post hunc auditus et deinde olfactus, qui habent immutationem naturalem ex parte obiecti. Motus tamen localis est perfectior et naturaliter prior quam motus alterationis ..."

sed mediante humore intrinseco;[21] ultimus autem quantum ad cognitionis nobilitatem est tactus, qui ab obiecto suo immediate immutatur; est tamen prius ordine generationis vel imperfectionis vel communitatis, quia est fundamentum aliorum[22] et communis omnibus habentibus sensum, etiam imperfectis.

[II. — Ad argumenta principalia]

Ad primum in oppositum[23] dicendum quod obiectum sensus est tantum accidens de tertia specie qualitatis. Unde VII *Physicorum* dicitur[24] quod illa secundum quae fit alteratio, non differunt a sensibilibus; certum est autem per PHILOSOPHUM, ibidem,[25] quod alteratio est tantum in tertia specie qualitatis. Similiter, in *Praedicamentis* dicitur[26] quod in tertia specie qualitatis est passio et passibilis qualitas, quae dicuntur passiones, quia passiones inferunt sensibus; illae autem qualitates differunt formaliter quantum ad immutationem sensuum, et ideo secundum hoc accipiuntur diversi sensus, non autem secundum genera accidentium, ut supponit argumentum.

---

1 sed] *add.* etiam HLM | ultimus] alterius Q | autem] notandum est N est O | quantum] quo Z   2 cognitionis nobilitatem] *inv.* NO W Q Z *add.* ult. quod nobilior N | tactus *om.* NO | qui] quae N | suo] *add.* materialiter (ant. suo O) NO FW Q Z | immediate] ant. ab NO FW Q Z   3 tamen] enim Q | prius] primus W Z | vel imperfectionis] et imperfectionis N perfectionis K | imperfectionis] in perfectione U   4 vel] et NO | fundamentum] finitudinem obiectum Z | aliorum] aliquorum KU   5 habentibus] animalibus N | sensum *om.* NO | etiam] et L U | imperfectis] imperfectionis M imperfectum F imperfectionem(?) W Z *add.* ult. cuiusmodi est tactus N   7 in oppositum *om.* KU | dicendum] *add.* est M F | obiectum] omnibus F   8 accidens] *add.* commune N   9 dicitur *om.* Q | fit *om.* Z | non — alteratio *om.* L   10 sensibilibus] sensibus F *add.* illud KU | autem *om.* N   11 est tantum] *inv.* FW sunt tantum L | tantum *om.* Z | Similiter] Sicut H   12 passibilis qualitas] passibiles qualitates K   13 quae] *add.* et NO Q *add.* etiam FW Z | quia] et N | passiones inferunt] *inv.* K passiones inferunt passionem NO F Z inferunt passionem U | sensibus] sensibilibus U FW   14 illae] istae O FW | differunt] dicuntur KU differuntur Q | immutationem] mutationem FW Q Z   15 sensuum *om.* L | sensus] *mg.* W   16 supponit] supponis Z

---

[21]**Thomas**, *Summa theol.* I q. 78 a. 3 ad 4 (V 254*b*): "Gustus autem organum non immutatur de necessitate naturali immutatione secundum qualitatem quae ei proprie obiicitur, ut scilicet lingua fuit dulce vel amara; sed secundum praeambulam qualitatem, in qua fundatur sapor, scilicet secundum humorem, qui est obiectum tactus."

[22]Cf. **Petrus I. Olivi**, *Summa* II q. 60 (BFS V 573): "Tactus propter sui primitatem et materialitatem potest esse fundamentalis [*sed in codice Borgh. 54 habetur* fundamentum et] dispositio ad alterum sensum naturaliter posteriorem et immaterialiorem in materia vel materialiori organo suscipiendum."

[23]Cf. supra n. 1.

[24]**Aristot.**, *Physica* VII c. 3 (AL VII¹ 268; H c. 3 248*b* 27-8); **Albertus M.**, *Physic.* VII tr. 1 c. 4 (IV² 526*b*).

[25]*Auctoritates Aristotelis* (ed. J. Hamesse 155): "Alteratio solum est in tertia specie qualitatis"; cf. **Thomas**, *Summa theol.* I q. 78 a. 3 ad 1 (V 254*a*).

[26]**Aristot.**, *Praedic.* c. 8 (AL I¹ 64-65; c. 8 9*a* 29—*b* 7): "Tertia vero species qualitatis est passibiles qualitates et passiones ... passibiles vero qualitates et passiones dicuntur ... quoniam singulum eorum quae dicta sunt secundum sensus qualitatum passionis perfectiva sunt"; cf. **Duns Scotus**, *Praedic.* qq. 30-36 n. 54. n. 57-60 (OPh I 487, 489).

Ad secundum:[27] quod magnitudo et figura non differunt a propriis sensibilibus secundum rationem obiectivam formalem et propriam quae requiritur ad distinctionem potentiae sensitivae propriae, licet absolute, quantum ad suam entitatem realem, distinguantur ab eis magis quam ipsa inter se.[28] Circa quod sciendum quod sensibilia communia sunt quasi media inter sensibilia propria, quae immutant sensus proprios per se et proprie, et sensibilia per accidens, quae nec per se nec primo immutant sensus, quia sensibilia communia immutant per se sensus proprios quia faciunt ad differentiam immutationis; aliter enim immutat magnitudo magna et parva, et unum quam multa, et circulare et triangulare, et quiescens et motum; sed non faciunt ad substantiam immutationis sensus proprii nisi mediante sensibili proprio, et ideo secundum illa non debet sumi aliqua potentia sensitiva propria.[29]

[7] Ad aliud[30] dicendum quod tactus est plures sensus secundum speciem, non autem secundum genus; ideo sunt tantum quinque genera sensuum, sicut sunt quinque genera potentiarum, licet non sint nisi quattuor gradus viventium.[31] Ita in proposito, quia unus sensus tactus super alium non constituit diversum gradum tangentium. Vel sic potest dici: quod tactus est tantum unius

---

1 secundum] *add.* dicitur NO *add.* dicendum L W Q Z *add.* dicendum est F | magnitudo et figura] figura et magnitudo HL 2 sensibilibus] sensibus N U | obiectivam] subiectivam N 4 licet absolute] *inv.* F | distinguantur] = H distinguitur N L distinguatur O M KU FW Q Z 5 magis] *ant.* ab M | ipsa *om.* F | sciendum] *add.* est M U 6 communia] *add.* quae NO | sunt *post* media Q *om.* Z | media] medium K | propria] *add.* per se K 7 quae immutant *om.* Z | proprie] primo N | et²] vel U 8 nec² *om.* NO | sensus] sensum KU *add. seu rep.* sensus Z | quia — sensus *om.* NO | quia — proprios *om.* Q 9 communia] propria FW *om.* Z | immutat *post* se KU | proprios] *add. seu rep.* per se et proprie et sensibilia per O | quia] nec N *add.* faciunt differentiam ad immutationem N 10 differentiam immutationis] *inv.* U | aliter] *lin.* N | immutat] immutant Q | magna et parva] parva et magna NO FW Q Z 11 et] quam L | et² *om.* H | et⁴] quam N H KU Z 12 et] quam KU | motum] movens KU | ad — immutationis] differentiam ad immutationem N | substantiam] differentiam O *add.* motus L | immutationis *om.* Q 13 nisi] non O | illa] ista NO Q 14 non *om.* U | non — aliqua] debet sumi nulla K | aliqua] alia L aliqualis N | propria] proprie N *om.* L 15 dicendum] *add.* est M | plures sensus] *inv.* U sensus L | sensus secundum speciem] species secundum sensum Q 16 autem] tamen H KU *om.* L Q | genus] *add.* et K | ideo] *add.* non H | sunt tantum] *inv.* L 17 genera sensuum] *inv.* KU | sunt] *add.* tantum Q | non *om.* L 18 sint] sunt H KU | viventium] *add.* tangentium Q 19 super alium *post* constituit KU | diversum] distinctum NO F Q Z | gradum] *add.* distinctum W 20 tangentium *om.* H KU | Vel] Et H | sic *om.* KU Z | quod — dici *om.* Q | tactus] *add.* non K

[27]Cf. supra n. 2; cf. **Duns Scotus**, *Praedic.* q. 30-36 n. 54 (OPh I 487); n. 57 (OPh I 489); n. 76 (OPh I 494).
[28]**Albertus M.**, *De an.* II tr. 4 c. 1 (VII¹ 149b): "Magnitudo enim materialis subiecta sensibus non est illud quod sentitur, secundum quod sensatum actus est sensus, quia esse sensitivum est esse intentionale."
[29]Cf. **Aristot.**, *De an.* II c. 25 (Γ c. 1 425a 13-21); **Albertus M.**, *De an.* II tr. 4 c. 6 (VII¹ 154b—156b); **Thomas**, *Summa theol.* I q. 78 a. 3 ad 2 (V 254ab).
[30]Cf. supra n. 3.
[31]**Thomas**, *Summa theol.* I q. 78 a. 3 ad 3 (V 254b); cf. supra q. 1. n. 19.

generis physici;³² talia autem non solum sunt illa quorum unum transmutatur in alterum per se, sed etiam illa quae transmutantur in tertium; omnes autem qualitates tangibiles sunt transmutabiles in mixtum vel eius qualitates. Vel potest dici quod habent unum genus propinquum innominatum, quod potest dici qualitas tangibilis, sicut omnes sensus habent unum genus innominatum, quod potest dici sensus in communi.³³

15 Ad aliud³⁴ dicendum quod quantum ad modum immutandi, qui est realis in utroque, gustus est tactus, quia gustabile tangit realiter, vel medium gustus gustatur tangendo; tamen, quantum ad obiecta formalia, sunt diversi sensus; sapor enim est obiectum gustus, qui sapor est qualitas secunda causata a primis, sed obiecta tactus sunt qualitates primae. Aliter etiam potest dici quod gustus est quidam tactus ratione medii requisiti utrobique, quia idem est re, scilicet corpus aliquod humidum; gustus enim sapit saporem mediante humido et sicco coniuncto; tactus etiam est sic mediante aere, vel aqua quando extrema tangentium se non sunt sicca, ut dictum est supra;³⁵ tamen illud medium in tactu est accidentale, non autem in gustu, ut dictum fuit supra.³⁶

---

1 solum sunt] inv. M sunt NO F solum K | unum] add. per se Z   2 in — tangibiles om. Z | per se] ant. transmutatur N ant. in O M FW   3 omnes] uniens H | sunt] mg. W om. LM U | transmutabiles] mg. W   4 qualitates] qualitatem O M FW Z | potest] posset Z | habent] habet K om. U | genus] illius Z   5 propinquum] proprie Q | innominatum] non nominatum NO | quod] add. seu rep. genus quod genus H add. autem FW Q   6 genus] add. propinquum Z   7 sensus] sensibile N sensum Z   8 dicendum] add. est M | quod om. NO Q Z   9 est²] et N | gustabile] add. est H | tangit] tangitur Q om. KU F | realiter om. F   10 vel om. FW | gustus] add. et NO FW Q Z | gustatur] statur N | tamen om. U   11 sapor — qualitas] mg. W | est om. F | gustus] sensus U | qui] quae quidem qualitas O add. quidem N FW Q Z   12 a om. K | obiecta] obiectum N FW Q Z oppositum O   13 Aliter etiam] Ad rationem KU | etiam] autem N F om. H | potest dici] inv. Q posset dici Z | quod gustus] mg. W | quidam] ant. gustus L   14 tactus] mg. K sensus U | quia idem est] quod est idem NO FW Z quod idem est Q | est] add. in KU Q | re] res N H medium L | scilicet om. H   15 corpus aliquod] inv. L corpus FW Z | mediante] immediate U   16 et sicco] insinuando FW in faciendo Q sinuando Z | etiam post sic U autem L | est] lin. W om. NO F Q Z | sic om. F   17 aqua] add. vel L | tangentium] tangentia H tangunt KU   18 tamen illud] inv. NO cum illud U illud Z | in tactu] in actu Z om. N | accidentale] active Z | autem] est NO add. est Z | in²] mg. Z²   19 fuit] est N H | supra om. U

³²Cf. supra q. 1 n. 14. Cf. **Averroës**, *De an.* II com. 108 (AverL 297): "Necesse est enim, si posuerimus quod unus sensus comprehendit multos modos contrarietatis, ut genus subiectum illis modis sit unum; quoniam necesse est aliquid esse commune illi multitudini quod comprehendatur ab illo uno sensu."
³³**Thomas**, *Summa theol.* I q. 78 a. 3 ad 3 (V 254b): "Illae contrarietates et singulae conveniunt in uno genere proximo, et omnes in uno genere communi, quod est obiectum tactus secundum rationem communem. Sed illud genus commune est innominatum ..."
³⁴Cf. supra n. 4.
³⁵Cf. supra q. 3 n. 17.
³⁶Cf. supra q. 3 n. 18.

[QUAESTIO 7]

UTRUM RATIONE HUIUS QUOD DICITUR IN LITTERA QUOD 'IDEM EST ACTUS SENSIBILIS ET SENSITIVI', ACTIO ET PASSIO SINT IDEM ACTUS SIVE MOTUS

Quaeritur[1] de ratione huius quod dicitur in littera quod "idem est actus sensibilis et sensitivi," utrum actio et passio sint idem actus vel idem motus.[2]

[1] Arguitur quod sic:

Secundum PHILOSOPHUM, idem est actus motivi et mobilis; actus activi est actio, mobilis actus est passio;[3] igitur, etc. 1

Item, actio est in patiente; sed si actio non esset idem quod passio, esset contraria sibi — sed sic non esset in patiente, cum contraria non possunt esse in eodem; igitur est idem quod passio. Probatio maioris: quia si actio esset in agente, cum fundetur in motu, tunc omne agens et movens in quantum huiusmodi moveretur, quia illud movetur in quo est motus;[4] consequens est falsum; 2

---

5 Quaeritur] add. utrum U X adnot. mg. Quaestio nona M K | de om. FW X Z | de — huius om. NO 6 sensitivi] sensui H sensus L X sensibile KU | sint] sunt O M KU | idem om. FW | idem — vel om. X | actus ... motus] motus ... actus N K 7 vel] ut O et U sive Z | idem om. Z | motus] mod(!) O 8 Arguitur] Videtur L om. X | quod sic om. U 9 idem] eidem O | motivi] moti H U | mobilis] add. sed K 10 activi] motivi L | actio post mobilis U | mobilis actus] inv. NO L immobilis actus Z | mobilis — passio] et actus passivi est passio scilicet mobilis K | igitur etc.] ergo etc. FW Z om. X 11 Item] Praeterea NO FW X Z | esset post idem O | esset — cum om. Z 12 esset] essent K W | sibi] add. invicem K | sed] et NO K FW X | non om. X | cum] quia NO 13 possunt] possint FW X Z om. U | esse in eodem] inesse eidem L | eodem] add. subiecto simul K | igitur] ergo FW X Z 14 Probatio maioris] Probatur maior NO Probo maiorem L Probatio minoris KU | cum] et X | cum fundetur] confundetur F | fundetur] fundatur N L 15 tunc] add. esset U | omne om. Z | et] vel L | et movens om. Z | huiusmodi] movens FW agens Z 16 quia] spat. vac. U | illud] idem H id M om. Z | movetur] moveretur U | consequens] sequens X | est[2] om. H K

---

[1]Deest q. 7 in codice Q.
[2]**Aristot.**, De an. II c. 26 (Γ c. 2, 425b 25-26), ubi in translatione "vetere" sive "Jacobi" legitur: "Sensibilis autem actus et sensus idem quidem est et unus, esse autem ipsorum non idem" (in **Thomas**, De an. III c. 2 (XLV[1] 177)).
[3]Cf. **Aristot.**, Physica III c. 3 (AL VII[1.2] 105; Γ c. 3 202a 13-25): "Et dubium autem manifestum est, quod est motus in mobili; actus enim est huius et ab hoc; et motivi autem actus non aliud est ... haec enim unum quidem sunt, ratio tamen non una; similiter autem est in movente et moto ... necessarium est enim fortassis esse quendam actum activi et passivi; hoc quidem enim actio, illud vero passio."
[4]Cf. **Aristot.**, De an. III c. 2 (Γ c. 2, 426a 4-6); Physica III c. 3 (AL VII[1.2] 105-7; Γ c. 3, 202a 21-32); **Averroës**, De an. II com. 139 (AverL 342); Physica III com. 19 (ed. Iuntina IV f. 93vL): "Ex hoc, quod ponimus, quod agere est motus exsistens in agente per se, non ex agente in patiens, sequitur alterum duorum, scilicet aut ut omne, quod movet, moveatur, aut ponere possibile esse aliquid habere motum et non moveri, scilicet motorem, quod est valde inopinabile."

igitur et antecedens.

3 Item, PHILOSOPHUS probat V *Physicorum*,[5] quod ad actionem et passionem non est motus, quia ad motum non est motus; sed illa probatio non valeret, si actio et passio non essent motus; igitur, etc.

4 Item, actio est duplex ut dicitur IX *Metaphysicae*:[6] una transiens in materiam exteriorem et alia immanens.

5 Item, actio cum motu est continua, et per consequens successiva; sed omne successivum est tempus vel tempore mensuratum; igitur et talis actio. Sed non potest esse tempus, quia non est in genere quantitatis; igitur est tempore mensuratum. Sed omne mensuratum tempore est motus; igitur, etc.

6 Contra:[7]

Potentia activa et passiva sunt essentialiter distincta; sed potentiarum diversarum sunt diversi actus distincti essentialiter; igitur et actus talium potentiarum sunt essentialiter diversi actus — potentiae activae est actio et passivae passio; igitur, etc.

7 Item, ignis agens in duo ligna aut agit unica actione aut duabus. Si una, aut illa erit in agente, et sic habetur propositum; si in passo — in duobus lignis — sic sequitur quod idem accidens numero sit in diversis subiectis, quod est inconveniens. Si autem duabus

---

1 igitur] ergo N FW Z | et *om.* X | antecedens] cetera KU 2 Item] Praeterea NO FW X Z | Physicorum] phi O | et *om.* Z 3 illa] ita H ista M U W 4 probatio *post* valeret X | valeret] valet U valeres Z | igitur etc.] ergo etc. FW Z etc. X *om.* L 5 Item] Praeterea NO FW Z | Item — immanens *om.* X | IX] quinto KU | IX Metaphysicae] cum medi*ante* Z 6 immanens] immutatio N 7 Item] Praeterea NO FW X Z 8 sed] et L | omne] esse X | successivum] *add.* quod est aut F *add.* (*mg.* W) aut NO M W X Z | vel] aut (*mg.* W) NO M FW Z aut est X | mensuratum — tempore *om.* Z 9 igitur] ergo L FW X | et *om.* X | talis actio] inv. H | Sed *om.* L | non *om.* NO H FW X 10 quantitatis] qualitatis FW X | igitur] ergo W X | tempore] ipsum FW | mensuratum] mensuratus Z | omne *om.* K 11 mensuratum tempore] inv. N | igitur etc.] ergo etc. L FW Z *om.* X 13 Potentia *om.* N | passiva] passio X | distincta] distincte FW X Z 14 distincti *om.* FW Z | distincti — actus[2] *om.* X | igitur] ergo L FW Z 15 sunt] *add.* actus O | sunt essentialiter] inv. K 16 est actio *post* passivae X | et *om.* KU *add.* (*post* passivae Z) potentiae NO FW Z | passivae] *rep.* H *add.* est M K Z | passio *om.* F X | igitur] ergo L FW Z *om.* N X 17 Item] Praeterea NO FW X Z | aut *om.* N | unica] eadem N | aut[2]] vel KU 18 una] unica HL | illa — passo *om.* X | erit *post* agente K | agente] agentis O | et *om.* O Z | sic *om.* N K | habetur] habeo NO FW Z | propositum] *add.* et H | si in passo] si passio U *om.* NO | passo] *add.* aut (tunc FW X Z) erit NO FW X Z *add.* scilicet L K 19 lignis] *add.* et NO FW X Z | sic] erit L tunc X | sequitur] sequetur(!) F | idem] unum NO FW X Z | accidens] *add.* in N | sit] erit N X Z 20 diversis] duobus W X Z | subiectis] obiectis O

[5] **Aristot.**, *Physica* V c. 2 (AL VII[1.2] 196; E c. 2, 225b 10-15): "Secundum substantiam autem non est motus ... neque agentis patientis, neque omnis quod movetur aut moventis, quia non est motus motus, neque generationis generatio neque omnino mutatio mutationis."

[6] **Aristot.**, *Metaph.* IX c. 8 (AL XXV[3.2] 189-90; T c. 8, 1050a 30—b 1); *Auctoritates Aristotelis* (ed. J. Hamesse 134): "Duplex est actio: quaedam est transiens in materiam extra ut aedificatio et illa dicitur factio vel operatio factiva, quaedam est immanens sive intra manens in operante et est visio vel intellectio et illa dicitur actio activa."

[7] Hic intromittuntur a Scoto rationes in oppositum.

actionibus agit, puta calefactionibus, tunc idem agens numero habebit plures actiones numero differentes et eiusdem speciei.

Item, si actio sit in passo ita quod actio et passio sint idem motus, sequuntur illa tria inconvenientia posita III *Physicorum*:[8] scilicet quod diversorum specie sit idem actus specie et numero, quia activum et passivum specie differunt; similiter doctio erit doctrina; et actio erit passio, et ulterius agere erit pati.

Item, si actio et passio sint idem motus, accipiamus unum motum singularem. Verum est quod hic motus est passio, et hic motus est actio; igitur actio est passio; quod est inconveniens; igitur, etc.

[I. — Solutio quaestionis]

[3] Respondeo. Dico duo: primo, quod actio, secundum quod est praedicamentum, est in agente; secundo, quod aliquo modo actio et passio sunt in patiente.

[A. — Articulus primus: Actio secundum quod est praedicamentum est in agente]

Probatio primi sic: relatio non separatur a subiecto et fundamento suo vel a ratione fundandi. Aliqua autem relativa, ut de secundo modo,[9] fundantur super actionem et passionem, scilicet

---

1 agit *om*. NO | puta] *add*. duabus FW   2 actiones] actus N accidens(?) O | eiusdem] *add*. rationis sive N   3 Item] Praeterea NO FW X Z | si actio] *rep*. X | sit] est NO FW X Z | in] et Z | passo] passione X | et passio *om*. N | sint] sunt M Z | idem] eidem M   4 sequuntur] sequerentur N sequeretur O sequetur(?) FW consequuntur Z | illa] ista N L haec(?) U | tria *om*. H | posita *om*. NO *add*. in KU | III] scilicet H   5 scilicet *om*. Z | quod *om*. U | diversorum specie] diversarum specie O diversarum specierum H KU | specie²] sensitive(?) O *om*. X | et *om*. U   6 quia *om*. NO | passivum] passum O | similiter] *praem*. sicut K sed N scilicet(?) O | erit] et U X   7 et *om*. NO H X | erit] et F X Z *om*. NO W | ulterius *om*. X *add*. igitur N *add*. quod O FW Z | agere] *add*. a(!) U | erit²] est O et X   8 Item] Praeterea NO FW X Z | sint] sit H sunt M K X Z | motus] actus F   9 est] erit FW | passio] actio N | et — actio *om*. FW X Z   10 actio] passio N | igitur] ergo FW X Z | est²] et U | quod] hoc NO M X sed hoc FW hoc autem Z | igitur²] ergo L FW Z *om*. O X   12 Respondeo] Responsio L *adnot. mg.* Responsio propria L *add*. et K | duo *om*. NO | primo] primum FW | actio *om*. KU | secundum quod] quae L ut N | est *om*. U   13 secundo] secundum FW *add*. modo U | quod *om*. X | aliquo modo *post* passio HL U *post* patiente K   17 Probatio] Probo U *om*. X | primi] primo U | a — et] subito a NO subiecto a FW X Z   18 ratione] relatione X | fundandi] fundanti X | autem] est N *om*. H | relativa ... fundantur] relatio ... fundatur N FW X Z re ... fundatur O | de] dicitur N *add*. quae N   19 fundantur] *ant*. secundo N | scilicet] sicut NO FW X Z

[8] **Aristot.**, *Physica* III c. 3 (AL VII^{1.2} 106-107; Γ c. 3, 202*b* 1-6): "Sed irrationale est duum alterorum specie eundem et unum esse actum; et erit, si quidem doctrina et doctio idem sunt passio et actio, et docere cum addiscere idem et agere cum pati, quare docentem necesse erit addiscere et agenti pati."
[9] Cf. **Aristot.**, *Metaph.* V c. 15 (AL XXV³ 112; Δ c. 15 1020*b* 28-30): "Alia ut calefactivum ad calefactibile et sectivum ad secabile, et omne activum ad passivum"; cf. **Duns Scotus**, *Metaph.* V q. 11 n. 51-61 (OPh III 584-587).

relatio calefacientis ad calefactum, patris ad filium; vel saltem rationes fundandi illas relationes sunt actio et passio: vel secundum suum esse, sicut in patre et filio, vel secundum fieri, ut in calefaciente et calefacto, vel secundum factivum ad faciendum, ut calefactivum ad calefactibile, ut patet V *Metaphysicae*.[10] Igitur talis relatio non potest separari ab actione et passione in subiecto; sed talis relatio est in agente quae est agentis ad patiens, vel in patiente quae est patientis ad agens — paternitas enim est in patre, filiatio in filio; igitur et actio est in agente.

Item, omnis respectus realis est in eo quod realiter refertur ad aliud per illum, licet hoc non oportet de respectu rationis, sicut patet de scibili quod non refertur ad scientiam, sed scientia ad scibile;[11] actio autem est quidam respectus realis agentis ad patiens; igitur est in agente sicut relatio. Probatio minoris per BOETHIUM *De Trinitate*:[12] dicit quod septem praedicamenta non dicunt absolutas res, sed tantum respectus. Probari etiam potest per opinionem

---

1 calefacientis] calefactibilis H calefactivitatis M | calefactum] calefactivum N KU calefactionem X add. et L 2 rationes] relationes Z | fundandi] fundanti X | illas] tales N istas M FW Z huiusmodi K istae X | et] vel X | vel] et KU 3 suum om. X Z | et] add. in F | ut] vel U | in²] lin. O 4 et] add. in NO | vel] ut NO | secundum factivum] aptitudinem H | factivum] factum NO KU Z | ad] aliud NO add. secundum N | faciendum] factibile L | ut] sicut L 5 calefactivum] calefactum NO Z | Igitur] Ergo L FW X Z 6 relatio om. X | in om. NO FW X Z 7 quae] ut NO FW Z nec X | vel] et KU 8 quae est] ut N | enim om. X | patre] add. et F | filiatio] filio U 9 igitur et] ideo NO ergo et FW X Z | et om. U | agente] agento(!) O add. etc. L 10 Item] Praeterea NO FW X Z | est — realis] *post* tantum respectus NO | eo] ea U | realiter refertur ad aliud] = M refertur N L realiter refertur O FW X Z refertur ad aliud H refertur ad ipsum KU 11 illum] ipsum F eum Z | hoc om. X | oportet] oporteat NO FW X Z 12 scibili] factibili O | sed] add. in Z | scientia om. X 13 quidam] quaedam O quidem U om. FW Z | respectus] ant. est Z 14 igitur] ergo L FW X Z | in agente] materia gente(!) O | sicut] sic W X | relatio] relato W Z | minoris] huius KU | per] pro O | Boethium] *spat. vac.* L 15 De Trinitate] add. capitulo septimo NO | De Trinitate dicit] in praedicamentis KU | quod] add. alii N add. a O | septem] si Z om. L | praedicamenta] prima menta(!) NO | absolutas res] inv. NO FW X Z 16 sed — respectus om. Z | respectus] rep. N add. seu rep. agentis ad patiens NO | Probari] Probans(?) X | etiam om. N | potest] post X | opinionem] comparationem N *spat. vac.* Z

---

[10] **Aristot.**, *Metaph.* V c. 15 (AL XXV² 103-104; Δ c. 15, 1020*b* 26—1021*a* 25): in translatione "arabica" legitur (ed. Ponzalli c. 13 168-170): "Quaedam relativa dicuntur, sicut duplum ad dimidium ... Et quoddam dicitur, sicut calefaciens ad calefactum, et abscindens ad abscissum, et omne agens ad patiens. Et quaedam, sicut mensuratum ad mensuram ... Passiva autem et activa per potentiam activam et passivam, et actiones potentiarum, sicut calefaciens quod calefacit, quia potest; et etiam calefaciens ad illud, quod calefacit ... Et dicuntur relativa illa, quae sunt secundum tempus, ut agens ad patiens; et illud, quod aget, ad illud quod patietur, et sic dicitur pater est pater filii."

[11] **Aristot.**, *Praedic.* c. 7 (AL I² 61; c. 7, 7*b* 27-28); *Auctoritates Aristotelis* (ed. J. Hamesse 303): "Multa sunt scibilia de quibus non est scientia."

[12] **Boethius**, *De Trin.* c. 4 (ed. R. Peiper 159; PL 64, 1353C): "Iamne patet quae sit differentia praedicationum? Quod aliae quidem quasi rem monstrant, aliae vero quasi circumstantias rei; quodque illa quae ita praedicantur, ut esse aliquid rem ostendant, illa vero ut non esse, sed potius extrinsecus aliquid quodam modo adfigant?"

COMMENTATORIS:[13] dicit quod motus, ut refertur ad agens sicut a quo est actio, est actio; igitur formaliter importat respectum realem; certum est autem quod illo respectu refertur agens ad patiens; igitur, etc.

[4]   Item, impossibile est aliquod creatum fieri de non-agente agens nisi mutetur ad aliquam formam in eo exsistentem — forma enim secundum quam est mutatio est in eo quod mutatur; sed illa mutatio non est ad formam absolutam, quia de non-agente non fit aliquid agens per aliquid exsistens in eo absolutum; sed certum est quod non fit agens formaliter nisi per actionem; igitur actio est forma respectiva exsistens in agente.

Item, novem genera accidentium habent esse in subiecto — et in hoc differunt a substantia; sed relatio habet esse in subiecto, licet in respectu ad terminum; actio est de illis; igitur habet esse in subiecto, et secundum suam rationem formalem est in subiecto. Non autem potest dici quod sit formaliter in patiente, quia accidens exsistens formaliter in subiecto denominat ipsum, et ideo si esset actio formaliter in patiente, patiens diceretur agens, sicut paries dicitur coloratus in quo est color formaliter. Hoc autem est falsum, quia solum agens denominatur ab actione. Igitur est in eo,[14] sicut in subiecto.

---

1 Commentatoris] contrariorum NO X Z | dicit] dicimus N dicentis HL dicentem KU | motus] *add. (mg.* W) est FW | sicut — agens *om.* Z 2 actio est actio] = LM actio N H KU FW X est actio O | igitur] ergo FW X | formaliter] forma NO 3 illo] isto O M W | ad] et Z | patiens] patienter *seu* patitum O | igitur etc.] ergo etc. FW Z *om.* NO X 5 Item] Praeterea NO FW X Z | aliquod] aliquid HLM | creatum] tantum N causatum O | agens *om.* NO 6 nisi] *add.* agens H | mutetur] immutetur M mutatur F 7 quam] quod Z | mutatio] mutatur U | est² *post* eo U | quod] *lin.* W | sed] si NO | illa] ista KU 8 de] esse NO 9 aliquid] aliquod N H KU X Z | agens] accidens O | agens — aliquid *om.* U | aliquid²] aliquod K | absolutum] *ant. in* K | certum] H *om.* X | est *om.* O 10 fit] *lin.* K sic X *om.* U *add.* aliquod N | igitur] ergo FW X Z 11 forma] formaliter NO | exsistens *post* agente F existente O 12 Item] Praeterea NO FW X Z | esse] se N | et — subiecto² *om.* X 13 sed] sicut L scilicet FW | esse *post* subiecto NO FW Z | in²] *lin.* F 14 ad terminum] termini K | de] in K | igitur] ergo FW Z 15 et] = NO Z tamen HM K cum L U *om.* FW X | suam rationem formalem] rationem suam formalem H suam formalem rationem M | autem] enim L 16 sit] si X | quia] cum N *spat. vac.* O quod X | quia — formaliter *om.* U | quia — patiente *om.* F | accidens] actionis Z | exsistens formaliter] = LM K formaliter inexsistens NO formaliter exsistens H W X Z 17 in — patiente] *mg.* U | esset actio] *inv.* L detur actio N 18 patiens *om.* KU | diceretur] differetur O | coloratus] colorata NO 19 autem] consequentem(?) (*ant. hoc*) U enim FW *om.* Z | quia] sed NO FW X Z 20 denominatur] denominatus Z | Igitur] Ergo FW X Z | eo] se N | sicut] tamquam H

[13] **Averroës**, *Physica* III com. 3 (ed. Iuntina IV f. 86vI): "Motus est actio motoris in moto". Cf. etiam **Averroës**, *Physica* III com. 19 (ed. Iuntina IV f. 93vL): "Agere est motus exsistens in agente per se, non ex agente in patiens"; cf. *Liber sex principiorum* c. 2 n. 20 (AL I⁷ 39): "Scire autem oportet quoniam omne quod in motu est actio est; moveri etenim actio est; si quid igitur movetur agit necessario; omnis igitur actio in motu omnisque motus in actione firmabitur; proprium igitur actionis est in motu esse, sicut proprium motus in actione esse"; *Auctoritates Aristotelis* (ed. J. Hamesse 152): "Omnis motus recipit denominationem a termino ad quem."
[14] Scilicet, in agente.

15 Item, creantis actio est in creante, igitur similiter actio agentis creati est in agente. Probatio antecedentis: quia si esset in creatura, sicut creatio-passio quae non differt a creatura, tunc creatio-actio non esset prior naturaliter creatura; hoc autem est falsum, quia eius causa est. Consequentia patet: quia sicut se habet agens increatum ad actionem suam, ita agens creatum ad actionem suam.

16 Item, per auctoritatem AVICENNAE[15] dicentis quod secundum ALIQUOS movere, motio et motus sunt idem secundum essentiam, sed secundum veritatem hoc est falsum, quia movere non dicit respectum motus ad movens, ut DICUNT, sed moventis ad motum vel passum; nec motio dicit respectum moventis ad passum, sed passi ad motum; movere autem est agere; igitur agere est respectus agentis ad passum, non e converso, ut dicunt ALII.

17 Dicendum igitur est secundum praedicta quod actio est respectus agentis ad passum in agente exsistens, et passio respectus patientis ad agens in patiente exsistens; motus autem est forma fluens media inter utrumque vel est fluxus formae secundum quod ponit istos duos modos intelligendi motum COMMENTATOR III

---

1 Item] Praeterea NO FW X Z | creantis actio] creatio activa N M creatio actio (*post* est Z) O FW Z creatio X | est] *rep.* W | in *om.* O | igitur] ergo FW X Z *om.* O | similiter] aliqua N substantia O | actio²] creatus(?) F 2 Probatur antecedentis] Probatur antecedens NO | creatura] causatur O 3 sicut] *add.* in(!) Z | creatio-passio] creatio passiva N HL U | passio — creatura] quae est passio K | differt] dentur(!) Z | creatura] *add.* et H | tunc] ut X | creatio-actio] creatio activa HL creatio quae K causatio actio U 4 non *om.* K | non — prior *om.* U | naturaliter] *add.* quam K | creatura] causa NO creaturatur(?) Z | autem *om.* NO 5 est] ant. eius NO K FW Z | quia *om.* Z 6 actionem suam] inv. NO W X Z actionem KU | actionem — actionem *om.* F | ita] *add.* se habet N *add. seu rep.* se habet agens increatum ad suam actionem ita se habet O | actionem² *om.* NO W X Z 7 Item] Probatur N Praeterea O X *om.* W Z | per — dicentis] Avicenna dicit HL secundum Avicennam dicentem (dicit U) KU | quod *om.* K | secundum aliquos *om.* NO 8 motio et motus] motus et motio L 9 sed] et KU | *add.* hoc] *mg.* antecedens N *add.*(ant. hoc X) autem O W X Z 10 motus] moti L | motus — sed *om.* Z | moventis — respectum *om.* U | motum vel passum] passum vel motum HL 12 est *om.* N | igitur] ergo L FW X Z | respectus] illius N 13 passum] passus(!) X | alii] aliqui HL *adnot. mg.* Nota in quibus sunt actio et passio K 14 Dicendum] *adnot. mg.* Via sua propria L | igitur *post* est H U *post* praedicta K ergo (*post* est FW Z) L FW X Z | est *om.* NO L X | respectus] *add.* quidam NO FW X Z 15 agentis] *rep.* Z | respectus²] *add.* (ant. respectus F) quidam NO FW X Z 17 media] mediativa(?) U 18 istos] illos HL F | motum *om.* N | Commentator] Commentatoris N | III] est X

[15]Cf. **Avicenna**, *Sufficientia* II c. 1 (f. 24*v*B): "Post haec autem verisimile est quod motus et movere et motio sunt una essentia. Sed cum accipitur in respectu sui ipsius est motus. Cum autem accipitur in respectu eius in quo est nominatur motio. Cum autem accipitur in comparatione eius a quo est vocatur movere; et nos oportet istud certificare hic et distinguere consideratione subtiliori quam sit illis verisimile. Ergo dicemus quod veritas est contra hanc formam scilicet quia motio dispositio est mobilis et hoc quod motus confertur mobili secundum quod in eo est. Dispositio est motus non mobilis, quia comparatio motus ad subiectum est alia ab intellectu comparationis subiecti ad motum, quamvis se comitentur in esse. Similiter movere dispositio est moventis non motus. Et comparatio motus ad moventem dispositio est motus non moventis. Ergo quandoquidem hoc sic est; motio erit comparatio subiecti ad motum non motus comparatus ad subiectum. Unde non est motio ipse motus qui est propter subiectum, sicut nec movere est ipse motus qui est in subiecto."

Physicorum;[16] dicit quod "iste secundus modus est famosior, sed primus est verior." Secundum primum modum, motus est in genere sui termini vel formae secundum quam est motus; secundum autem alium modum est in genere "ad aliquid", in primo modo relationis, quae sumitur secundum quod fundatur super multitudinem vel unum, quia respectu termini 'a quo' importat talis fluxus multitudinem, respectu termini "ad quem" unitatem.

Est autem intelligendum, propter conclusionem principalem, quod respectus quoad praesens est in duplici differentia. Est enim quidam respectus intrinsecus adveniens, qui de necessitate advenit, positis extremis, et talis est tantum de genere relationis, sicut, positis duobus albis, de necessitate sequitur similitudo.[17] Similiter, posita activa et passiva generatione in facto esse, de necessitate ponitur paternitas et filiatio.[18] Alius est respectus importatus extrinsecus adveniens, qui non ponitur de necessitate, positis extremis. Talis est respectus importatus in sex aliis praedicamentis relativis; posita enim re quandali vel temporali et tempore, non de necessitate ponitur "quando", sed requiritur adiacentia temporis vel aliquid

---

1 dicit quod] et dicit ibi quod NO M FW Z sunt X | iste] ille H FW X Z *om.* K | modus] motus O | est *om.* N 2 modum *om.* N | est²] igitur O 3 secundum — est *om.* FW Z | autem] sed (ant. secundum) N *om.* O FW X Z 5 sumitur — quod] *mg.* M *om.* L KU | secundum — unum] *spat. vac.* X | quod — super *om.* NO FW Z | multitudinem] numerum NO FW | vel] *add.* super KU 6 importat *post* fluxus K importatur Z | multitudinem] multiplicitatem N FW X Z 7 ad quem] ad quam F *om.* Z *add.* capit H 8 conclusionem] quaestionem N condicionem FW 9 respectus] *adnot. mg.* Respectus duplex K X | est *om.* N *add.* duplex sive M | in *om.* F | duplici] triplici NO | differentia] residet genere(!) N 10 quidam *om.* X | qui] ubi(?) X 11 est tantum *inv.* O FW X Z | de] in NO | sicut] similiter H | positis duobus *inv.* NO 12 albis *om.* NO X | sequitur *ant.* de N | Similiter] Sicut N | posita] positis L KU 13 esse *om.* X Z 14 importatus] importaret U *om.* NO FW X Z | extrinsecus] extrinsece H KU 15 qui] quae O H KU | qui — est *om.* X | extremis] *add.* et K 16 importatus] imparatus *vel* imperatus O *om.* X | sex] = O LM quinque N H FW U X haec K quibuslibet Z | aliis] *add.* et NO | praedicamentis] praedictis NO | posita] posito N | re *om.* N | quandali] quandalitate (*post* vel) KU quanli FW quando X | vel] et N L | temporali] *ant.* vel KU 18 sed] similiter F | requiritur] *add.* vel Z | adiacentia] *add. mg.* stude M | temporis *om.* X | vel aliquid aliud] vel aliquid NO Z ad H FW vel tempus ad X

[16] **Averroës**, *Physica* III com. 4 (ed. Iuntina IV f. 87rD).

[17] *Liber sex principiorum* c. 1 n. 14 (AL I⁷ 38): "Eorum vero quae exsistenti contingunt singulum aut extrinsecus advenit aut intra substantiam simpliciter consideratur..."; cf. **Duns Scotus**, *Metaph.* V q. 11 n. 56 (OPh III 585); cf. *Ordinatio* III d. 1 q. 1 a. 1 (ed. Vivès XIV 40b—41a); **Henricus Gand.**, *Summa* a. 32 q. 5 in corp. (AMPh s. 2, XXVII 95): "Propter huiusmodi rationem accidentalitatis in istis sex diversam, contractam ab illo super quod fundatur eorum respectus ab accidentalitate in praedicamento relationis, contracta ab illo super quod fundatur eius respectus, in *Sex principiis* dicuntur ista sex accidentia "extrinsecus advenientia", cum tamen proprie dicta relatio dicatur esse de accidentibus intrinsecus advenientibus"; cf. *Quodl.* V q. 6 in corp. (f. 161I—163V).

[18] *Liber sex principiorum* c. 1 n. 13 (AL I⁷ 38): "Quaedam vero difficile erit assignare, ut scientia et paternitas et filiatio, nisi forte in generantium et componentium complexione."

aliud temporale.[19]

19 Hoc viso, sciendum est quod agens potest comparari vel ad terminum productum vel ad passum. Si comparetur ad terminum productum — sive sit in fieri sive in facto esse — ut calefaciens ad calefactionem sive ad calorem (quod est idem quantum ad hoc), tunc sic includit relationem vel refertur ad ipsum productum relatione, quae est de genere "ad aliquid", quae advenit, positis extremis, de necessitate; positis enim agente et patiente et producto, necessario est relatio agentis ad effectum. Si comparetur ad patiens, ille respectus quem includit non est de genere "ad aliquid"; non enim, posito igne agente absolute et lignis, de necessitate sequitur calefactio vel talis relatio, sed requiritur appropinquatio extremorum; non est igitur de genere "ad aliquid,' sed de genere actionis; talis ergo respectus extrinsecus adveniens, qui est agentis ad patiens, in agente exsistens est actio quae est praedicamentum, et simile est de passione.

[B. — Articulus secundus: Actio et passio sunt aliquo modo in patiente]

20 Quantum ad secundum articulum, est sciendum quod est actio quaedam de genere actionis et illa est proprie dicta actio, de qua dictum est immediate, et est quaedam actio acta seu producta, quae

---

2 Hoc viso *om.* K | sciendum] dicendum L | est *om.* NO KU Z | vel *om.* X   3 productum] proiectum N | vel] *adnot. mg.* agens potest dupliciter comparari K | ad *om.* X | passum] passivum X | comparetur *om.* X   4 productum] proiectum N | sive] sine Z | in² *om.* U | ut] vel O   5 sive] sine(!) Z | sive ad calorem *om.* X | calorem] colorem O | est idem] *inv.* N   6 tunc *om.* H | sic] sicut X *add.* vel L | vel] ut K | productum] proiectum N | relatione] relationi N   7 ad — agente *om.* Z | quae²] qui X | extremis *om.* L   8 de *om.* X | positis] posito (*post* enim N) NO positionis M | enim. K X | et²] etiam M | producto] probatio N productione H KU | necessario] necessaria Z   9 est] esse O ponitur L | Si] *add.* autem NO FW Z | ad²] a Z | ille *om.* KU Z   10 quem] qui F | aliquid] aliud Z   11 agente *om.* U *add.* et X | lignis] linguis Z | necessitate] *add. lin.* non K   12 sed] si X | appropinquatio] approximatio H U   13 igitur] ergo FW Z *om.* X | ergo] = L FW X Z autem NO est H K igitur M etiam U   14 in *om.* U   15 actio] duo(!) X | praedicamentum] praedicamentio(!) O | est³ *post* passione X   19 Quantum] *adnot. mg.* Secundus articulus actio 2x K | secundum] tertium NO | actio] passio L   20 quaedam] *add.* quae est NO M FW X Z | illa] ista O Z   21 acta] acte O | seu] vel NO W X Z sive K id est F | producta] proiecta N

[19]Cf. **Duns Scotus**, *Ordinatio* III d. 1 q. 1 a. 1 [n. 15] (ed. Vivès XIV 41*a-b*): "Tunc ad Philosophum concedo quod non est motus nec mutatio ad relationem primo vel secundo modo se habentem ... Illa enim est relatio intrinsecus adveniens, id est, necessario consequens fundamentum, puta, quantitatem vel qualitatem vel substantiam; quae intrinsecus inest non absoluta necessitate, sed posito termino ad quem est relatio ... Sed ad relationem tertio modo se habentem, quia illa est extrinsecus adveniens, id est, non necessario consequens fundamentum, puta, qualitatem vel quantitatem vel substantiam, sed absque novitate alicuius absoluti in illo in quo est, vel in termino contingenter consequitur; bene potest esse mutatio et aliquae tales relationes forte pertinent ad illa sex principia, quae dicuntur extrinsecus advenientia."

non est de genere actionis, sicut intelligere et velle sunt quaedam formae absolutae non de genere actionis; sed sunt actiones actae vel productae per actiones intellectus et voluntatis, quae sunt de genere actionis. Istam divisionem ponit SIMPLICIUS *Super Praedicamenta*, quaerens quare "facere ponitur praedicamentum" et "non factio."[20] Et respondet quod ideo est quia factio dicitur de actione et de effectu actionis; utrumque enim dicitur factio, et actio et effectus eius. Certum est enim quod effectus actionis est actio, non quae est praedicamentum, sed factio facta. COMMENTATOR etiam III *Physicorum* dicit[21] quod agens et patiens, et actio et passio, differunt, sed 'actio facta inter illa est eadem' secundum auctoritates; igitur illa est quaedam actio facta in patiente, quae differt ab actione, quae est praedicamentum, et de hac actione facta loquitur PHILOSOPHUS II *De anima*:[22] dicit quod illud quod imprimitur a sensibili in sensum est actio; certum est autem quod non imprimitur in illo aliquid de genere actionis, sed est eius effectus quod in sensu imprimitur; igitur est aliqua actio acta praeter illam quae est de genere actionis.

[8] Sed hic potest quaeri, quare sic nominatur. Respondeo quod actio, quae est de genere actionis, est respectus in agente tantum. Et quia latet nos, quantum est in se, manifestatur per effectum qui est actio acta; et quia sic res intelligimus et nominamus, sicut per

---

1 velle] *add.* quae U   2 de — sunt² *om.* K | sed — actionis *om.* U | sunt actiones] finis actionis L   3 productae] proiectae N | actiones] operationes L | intellectus] intelligibiles X   4 Istam] Illam O   5 quare] quia Z | facere ponitur] *inv.* X | praedicamentum] *add.* unum U   6 Et] *add.* ideo F | respondet] *add.* ad hoc N *add.* est F | quod] *add.* (*post* ideo F) hoc O FW X Z | ideo] causa KU | factio] actio NO | dicitur *post* actionis (*lin.*) U est K | actione] agente N | et] *rep.* F | de² *om.* X Z   7 factio et actio] a. et f. F Z | et] tam L | et²] quam L | effectus] effectio O   8 enim] autem (ant. est X) NO FW X Z | quod] quid O   9 factio facta LM KU facta NO X Z actio facta H factio FW | III] 2 Z   10 et actio] actio H KU *om.* X | differunt *om.* NO   11 actio facta] factio U | illa] ista X | auctoritates] auctores L K FW auctoritatem U | igitur] ergo L FW Z *om.* U | illa²] ista O W X Z   12 actio *om.* X   13 II] et Z   14 dicit] dicens N U | illud] idem H id W | imprimitur] primitur(!) Z | a] alii(?) Z | sensum] sensu X   15 certum] dictum X | autem] igitur H enim L | non *om.* K | in illo] in ipso NO M FW Z *om.* X | de] in N *om.* O   16 sed — actionis *om.* N   17 igitur] ergo L FW X Z | est] erit KU | illam] istam X | de] in X | actionis] *add.* etc. K   18 Sed] Si Z | hic *om.* NO K FW X Z | Respondeo] Responsio H Respondetur U | quod *om.* H   19 est *om.* L | de] in H KU | actionis] agentis Z | Et *om.* NO FW X Z   20 quia] quod L | latet] latens NO X Z latent F | nos] *add.* in H | quantum] qualiter K quantumcumque F X Z | est *om.* FW X Z | in] de NO FW Z ex U dicitur X | manifestatur] *add.* autem NO FW X | effectum] *add.* eius NO | qui] quae NO L   21 et] *lin.* K | sic res] *inv.* H sicut res L U | res *om.* X | intelligimus et] in aliis reales (*mg.* W) FW in aliis (*post* nominamus) Z

[20]**Simplicius**, *In Praedicamenta*, praed. "De facere et pati" (CLCAG V² 414): "Horum autem rursum facere ante factionem praehonoravit, quia dupliciter dicitur factio; nam et actio dicitur factio et effectus actionis, sicut dicimus 'Homeri poesim' (id est factionem); opportunitas autem non effectus, sed actionis erat, quam agere significat uno modo."
[21]Cf. **Averroës**, *Physica* III com. 18 (ed. Iuntina IV f. 92*v*L).
[22]**Aristot.**, *De an.* II c. 24 et c. 27 (B c. 12, 424*a* 17-20; Γ c. 2, 426 *a* 9-10).

sensum apprehendimus ut communiter, igitur, etc. Ponitur exemplum de caritate quae, licet sit habitus nobilis quia tamen latens est in anima, nominatur per effectum, qui est dilectio.

[C. — Summarium amborum articulorum]

22 Est igitur duplex actio secundum iam dicta; sed actio acta est illa quae est in patiente, quae est effectus actionis proprie dictae, et ideo non est actio praedicamentum nisi quae est in agente; nihil enim est causa sui ipsius. Et differunt in hoc quod actio, quae est praedicamentum, est secundum quam vel per quam ab aliquo est aliud; actio autem acta est secundum quam aliquid est ab alio; esse enim a quo est aliud et quod est ab alio sunt rationes oppositae, nec eidem possunt convenire, sicut idem per se non potest esse producens et productum: pater et filius respectu eiusdem — pater enim est a quo est filius, et filius qui est a patre. Non igitur est verum quod dicunt ALIQUI, scilicet quod motus, ut ab agente, est actio nisi intelligitur de actione acta quae est effectus actionis — hoc enim est proprium producto, ut productum est per actionem: esse ab alio —, sed potius potest dici e converso quod actio est a qua vel per quam ab aliquo est aliud.

[II. — Ad argumenta principalia]

23 Ad primum,[23] dicendum quod verum est quod idem est actus motivi effective, qui actus est passivi vel mobilis formaliter; sed ille

---

1 sensum] assensum O | communiter] add. dicitur NO | igitur etc.] ideo etc. NO FW Z om. L X | Ponitur] Ponatur N HL 2 quae] qui X 3 latens est] inv. NO K FW Z | est²] adnot. mg. actio 2x K | dilectio] delectatio H 5 igitur] autem NO ergo FW Z | actio] actus O | iam] istam N | sed actio] scilicet acta N | acta om. K 6 quae²] quia NO FW X Z | est² om. L | dictae] dictus L 7 actio] add. quae (quia O) est NO | nisi om. NO FW X Z | nihil] non Z 8 Et] Etiam F add. ideo NO | quod] quia FW | est²] add. in Z 9 vel per quam om. N | aliquo] alio KU | aliud] lin. X aliquid KU | actio — aliud om. Z 10 est om. NO | est² post alio N | alio] aliquo N H X | enim] autem NO FW X om. KU 11 aliud] aliquid KU | alio] aliquo N | rationes] res NO 12 producens] productivum N productius(!) O 13 respectu eiusdem om. KU | respectu — filius² om. X | pater — filius post patre KU | enim] autem N om. KU 14 est om. U | et filius] filius enim NO KU add. ult. est K | qui est] inv. U | igitur est] inv. NO H ergo est L est ergo FW X Z | quod] non M 15 aliqui] alii F | scilicet] secundum Z | ut] add. est NO KU | est] et X | nisi] non X | intelligitur] intelligatur NO FW X Z 16 proprium producto] proprie productum KU proprie producto X producto Z 18 potest] debet NO FW Z | e converso om. U | actio] add. spat. vac. K | qua] aliqua O 21 Ad — agente² om. X | dicendum] add. est LM F | verum — est² om. L | idem est om. KU | actus] mg. F² 22 effective] active Z | actus est] inv. NO K FW Z | formaliter] add. est idem actui mobilis L

[23] Cf. supra n. 1.

actus non est actio quae est praedicamentum quae est in agente formaliter, sed est actio producta effective ab agente.

Ad secundum,[24] dicendum quod actio acta est in paciente, ut dictum est, non autem illa quae est praedicamentum. Ad probationem: dicendum quod actio illa quae est in agente non est motus, et ideo non sequitur quod omne agens in quantum huiusmodi moveatur, sed potius quod sit motivum.

Ad aliud,[25] dicendum quod consequentia PHILOSOPHI non tenet per illud medium quod actio sit motus, sed tenet per simile sic: "si ad motum non est motus, igitur" — a simili — "ad actionem non est actio"; ex qua consequentia ulterius sequitur "ad actionem non est actio, igitur ad actionem non est motus", quia actio est causa motus effectiva vel formalis, qua agens agit, vel dicitur agens. Ulterius dicitur per hoc[26] quod esset processus in infinitum in actionibus, quia si ad actionem esset motus, cum illius motus aliqua actio esset causa, oporteret supponi aliquam actionem aliam ad quam esset ille motus; sed tunc quaeratur de illa actione quae est causa illius motus, utrum ad illam sit motus vel non; si non, eadem ratione nec ad primam; si sic, erit processus in infinitum.

[10] Item, tenet — per locum a minori — consequentia PHILOSOPHI, quia cum motus sit actus potentiae passivae vel mobilis, si ipsa potest exire in actum suum, qui est motus sine motu praecedente, multo fortius potentia activa potest in actum suum, qui est actio sine motu praecedente.

Ad aliud,[27] dicendum quod PHILOSOPHUS non intendit

---

1 quae — actio om. Z | est³ om. K 2 est] lin. F 3 secundum] aliud X | dicendum] add. est HM F | acta] actus W Z 4 est om. O | est²] de Z 5 dicendum] add. est M F | actio om. X | agente] agendo X | et om. FW Z 6 moveatur] movetur KU 7 quod om. L 8 aliud om. O | dicendum] add. est M 9 simile] assimile K assimilem U | sic om. X | si] scilicet N 10 igitur] ergo FW X | igitur — motus om. Z | actionem] activam(?) F 11 ex] extra F | ex — actio om. H | qua] quam F | consequentia] mg. F | est] esse KU 12 igitur] ergo L FW X | igitur — motus om. KU | quia om. NO 13 vel] et KU | formalis] forma X formaliter Z | qua] quia KU 14 dicitur] tenet NO dicatur H debet Z om. L 15 ad actionem] actio X | actionem] add. non K | cum — motus om. X | illius] istius W | aliqua actio] inv. FW X Z om. N | esset²] = HL U est K sit NO M FW X Z 16 oporteret] oportet L | supponi] praesupponi NO M FW X Z F | aliquam] rep. U aliam M Z | aliam] ant. actionem KU add. ab illa N FW X Z add. ab ista O | quam] quem(!) U | esset om. M | ille] iste O X 17 sed] et NO FW X Z | quaeratur] quaeram NO FW X quaeretur K 18 illam] istam X | sit] rep. X | vel non om. L | si non om. Z 19 erit] est H esset X 20 Item] Praeterea NO FW X Z | locum] locus Z | minori] = O KU FW X maiori N HLM Z | consequentia] consequens FW 21 actus] actio NO | vel mobilis] spat. vac. X om. Z | si] add. in K 23 qui] quae U | actio] motus KU Z 25 dicendum] add. est M F om. H | Philosophus] Philosophi(!) O | intendit] add. ibi NO FW X Z

---

[24] Cf. supra n. 2.
[25] Cf. supra n. 3.
[26] Cf. **Aristot.**, *Physica* V c. 2 (AL VII[1.2] 197; E c. 2, 225b 34—226a 7).
[27] Cf. supra n. 4.

distinguere actionem quae est praedicamentum in illos duos modos ita quod uterque sit de genere actionis, immo uterque modus, ibi positus, est extra genus actionis; utraque enim actio tam manens in agente, sicut intelligere et velle, quam transiens est actio producta. Sed differentia est quantum ad hoc: quod talium actionum quaedam est perfectio agentis — licet non secundum quod agens est sed secundum quod perfectibile est — ita quod idem secundum diversas rationes sit agens et recipiens; quaedam est perfectio extrinseci operati, sicut transiens.

28. Ad aliud,[28] dicendum quod actio quae est praedicamentum, quae est respectus adveniens extrinsecus manens in agente, non est successiva quia mensuratur tempore vel quia sit tempus, sed tantum quia coexsistit tempori; ex consequenti tamen, quia coexsistit motui, cuius est causa et manet cum motu — non tamen est motus, quia nihil est causa sui ipsius — et motus mensuratur tempore, non tamen oportet propter hoc quod illa actio mensuretur a tempore — sicut angelus coexsistit tempori, non tamen mensuratur a tempore, ut patet.

---

1 quae] qui(!) U | in] inter K | illos] istos NO KU X | duos *om.* X | modos *om.* FW Z 2 immo — actionis *om.* NO | modus] motus K 3 manens] immanens H movens Z 4 et *om.* L | transiens] transciens(!) O 5 differentia — hoc] dicendum est F | est] *ant.* differentia L | hoc] haec O 6 est² *om.* X 8 sit] est NO sicut X | recipiens] patiens KU | quaedam] *add.* autem NO M FW X Z | est *om.* X Z | extrinseci operati] extrinseca operati NO K extrinsece operati Z 9 transiens] transciens(!) O 10 dicendum] *add.* est M F 11 quae] qui *om.* N | adveniens extrinsecus] *inv.* NO L K FW Z 12 mensuratur] mensuretur O FW X Z | quia² *om.* FW X Z 13 tempori] *add.* tamen H | consequenti] consequente KU | tamen] tum U *om.* FW Z | coexsistit²] exsistit Z *om.* L 14 cuius est causa] cum est H | cuius — motus *om.* L | est *post* causa KU 15 et] vel K 16 oportet *post* hoc K *add.* quod H U X | hoc] haec O | quod] *ant.* propter FW Z | mensuretur] mensuratur NO U X | a *om.* NO K FW X Z 17 tempori] tempore N Z | mensuratur] commensuratur L transmutatur X | a *om.* O FW X Z | tempore] tempori X 18 ut patet] sicut patet K *om.* NO FW X Z *add.* plane L | patet] *add.* igitur etc. H *add.* etc. X

[28]Cf. supra n. 5.

[QUAESTIO 8]

UTRUM SENSUS PARTICULARIS POSSIT SIMUL SENTIRE CONTRARIA

Utrum sensus particularis possit simul contraria sentire.[1]

[1]   5   Videtur quod non: 1

"Impossibile est idem simul moveri motibus contrariis";[2] sed si sensus particularis simul sentiret contraria, simul moveretur in contraria. Probatio: prius enim ordine movetur sensus a sensibili quam sentiat, et ideo si simul sentit contraria, simul movetur a
10   contrariis et ad contraria.

Item, si ita esset, ut dictum est, quod sensus movetur simul a   2
duobus contrariis: aut igitur sunt aequalis virtutis illa contraria, et tunc impediunt se ne utrumque sentiatur; aut alterum est maioris virtutis, et tunc illud minoris non sentitur, quia maior motus depel-
15   lit minorem, secundum PHILOSOPHUM.[3]

In oppositum est PHILOSOPHUS.[4]   3

---

4 Utrum] praem. Quaeritur NO U FW Q Z praem. Quaeritur decimo K praem. spat. vac. X adnot. mg. Quaestio 10a M | possit] potest H | simul contraria sentire] simul sentire contraria NO Q sentire omnia F" sentire contraria (mg.) F² sentire (mg. W²) simul contraria W simul contraria X recipere contraria Z   5 Videtur] praem Et M FW om. X   6 simul moveri] inv. HM Q | sed] quia X | sed — movetur om. NO | si om. Z   7 simul post contraria LM post sentiret Z om. KU X | simul moveretur] inv. Z | in contraria] motibus contrariis Q   8 Probatio] add. minoris Q | prius] primo U | enim] add. in KU | moveretur Q   9 sentit] sentiat KU Q sentiret L | movetur] moveretur N Q | a om. Z   10 et om. L F Q | ad] a X   11 Item] Praeterea NO FW Q X Z | quod om. NO W Q X Z | movetur post simul U moveretur NO L FW Q X Z | simul om. X | a om. Z   12 duobus om. L | igitur] ergo FW Q X | aequalis] aequales Z | illa] ista X   13 se — sentiatur] spat. vac. X | sentiatur] videatur N | est] erit K   14 et om. Q | illud om. N | minoris non sentitur] minor non sentitur N minoris virtutis non sentitur H U esse sentiunt FW sentiunt X commune sentiunt Z | motus] virtus N | depellit] depressit FW impedit Q deprimit X   15 secundum Philosophum om. H   16 In — est] Contrarium vult Q

[1]**Aristot.**, De an. II c. 27 (Γ c. 2-3 426b 29—427a 14); **Aristot.**, De sensu et sensato [c. 8] (c. 8, 447b 6-30, 448b 17—449a 31); **Albertus M.**, De an. II tr. 4 c. 11 (VII¹ 163a—164b); **Thomas**, De an. II c. 27 (XLV¹ 184b—185a); **Thomas**, De sensu et sensato tr. I c. 18 (XLV² 99a—100a).
[2]**Aristot.**, De an. II c. 27 (B c. 27 426b 29-31); cf. **Aristot.**, De sensu et sensato [c. 8] (c. 8, 448a 1-19).
[3]**Aristot.**, De sensu et sensato [c. 8] (c. 8, 447a 21-22); cf. Auctoritates Aristotelis (ed. J. Hamesse 198): "Motus maiores expellunt minores."
[4]**Aristot.**, De an. II c. 27 (B c. 27 427a 9-14); **Aristot.**, De sensu et sensato [c. 8] (c. 8, 449a 10-31); cf. **Thomas**, De an. II c. 27 (XLV¹ 184b—185a).

[I. — Solutio quaestionis]

4 Respondeo quod hoc est possibile, quia possibile est duo sensibilia contraria simul offerri sensui. Aut igitur utrumque sensus sentit, et sic habeo propositum; si alterum, igitur eadem ratione et alterum, quia suppono quod sint aeque propinqua et aequalis virtutis ad movendum.

5 Item, experimur ad sensum quod per unam manum sentimus calidum, et frigidum per aliam. Si dicatur quod sensus tactus non est unus, non valet — saltem respectu unius contrarietatis, quia est unus respectu eius; calidum et frigidum sunt unius contrarietatis; igitur, etc.

6 Item, potentia, discernens inter duo et cognoscens eorum differentiam, necessario cognoscit utrumque; sed visus cognoscit differentiam albi et nigri; igitur, etc.

[II. — Obiecta contra solutionem propositam]

7 Contra hoc arguitur sic:

Si sentit album et nigrum, aut una sensatione aut pluribus:

Non una, quia intellectus est potentior sensu, et tamen non potest simul plura intelligere — immo si intelligat magnitudinem, oportet eam esse unam in actu; igitur, etc.

8 Item, diversitas actuum consequitur diversitatem obiectorum; obiecta sunt plura; igitur et actus.

9 Praeterea, a diversis motoribus sunt diversi motus; diversa

---

2 Respondeo] Dicendum L | hoc] *mg.* O | est² *om.* N | sensibilia contraria] *inv.* NO 3 igitur] ergo FW Q X | utrumque sensus] *inv.* NO FW Q X Z 4 habeo] habetur U Q | igitur] ergo FW Q X | et²] *ant.* eadem L 5 quod *om.* O Q | sint] sunt H K X fit O *om.* Q | aeque propinqua et *om.* M | propinqua] propinquae HL KU W 6 movendum] modum(!) O F Q X Z 7 Item] Praeterea NO FW Q X Z | experimur] *add. in nobis* Q | quod] quia N | manum] *spat. vac.* F 8 et — aliam] et aliam frigidum N per aliam frigidum O M FW Q Z et per aliam frigidum X | Si] Sed si (*lin.* W) FW | dicatur] dicas NO dicam FW dices Z | quod *om.* NO Z 9 valet] videt(!) Z | saltem *post* contrarietatis O *om.* N | unius *om.* X 10 eius] unius contrarietatis FW eiusdem NO X *om.* K | calidum — frigidum] calidi et frigidi et ita K | unius contrarietatis] *inv.* H | igitur etc.] ergo etc. FW Q *om.* X 12 Item] Praeterea NO FW Q X Z | potentia *om.* N 13 necessario] naturaliter L | utrumque] *rep. lin.* K | sed] si U X | cognoscit²] agat U cognoscis(!) Z *om.* X 14 et nigri] a nigro NO | igitur etc.] ergo etc. FW Q *om.* X | etc. *om.* Q 17 Si *om.* X | et] aut KU | aut] ergo Q | una] sentit illa unica KU 18 Non] Sicut X | sensu] *add.* quia X *om.* H 19 potest — intelligere] = HM plura simul intelligere potest NO potest plura intelligere simul L K plura potest simul intelligere U potest plura simul intelligere FW Z possit plura simul intelligere X plura intelligere Q | intelligat] intelligas(!) Z 20 eam] causa (*post* esse) X *om.* Z | unam] una X | in *om.* NO FW Q X Z | igitur etc.] ergo etc. FW Z ergo Q *om.* X 21 Item] Praeterea NO FW Q X Z | obiectorum] oppositorum(!) O *add. sed* NO 22 obiecta] opposita(!) O | igitur et actus] igitur etc. NO ergo et actus FW Q Z *om.* X 23 Praeterea — etc. *om.* HLM KU | a *om.* FW Q X Z | motoribus] motibus Q | sunt diversi] *inv.* N

sensibilia sunt moventia diversa; igitur, etc.

[3] Item, in *De sensu et sensato*[5] dicitur quod unum sensum sentire diversa obiecta una sensatione est simile et unam lineam terminari ad diversa puncta; sed hoc est inconveniens; igitur, etc.

Similiter, non pluribus sensationibus, probatio. Quia si ab eadem potentia possunt egredi plures operationes simul, pari ratione et infinitae; sed hoc est inconveniens; igitur et primum. Probatio consequentiae per PHILOSOPHUM, IV *Physicorum*:[6] si duo corpora possunt esse simul, pari ratione et infinita, quia sicut dimensiones infinitorum corporum simul se compati non possunt, ita nec duorum.

Item, impossibile est idem corpus simul figurari diversis figuris;[7] igitur nec idem sensus diversis sensationibus simul. Probatio consequentiae: quia species in organo assimilatur figurae in cera secundum PHILOSOPHUM.[8]

---

1 sunt moventia] inv. N | moventia diversa] inv. FW | igitur etc.] = O ergo etc. FW Q Z om. N X   2 Item] Praeterea NO FW Q X Z | in] etiam F om. L | sensato] de sensato F   3 obiecta] opposita(!) sub(?) O | sensatione] sensitiva(!) O | est] et N | et] sicut KU om. Q | unam om. K   4 sed om. NO FW Q X Z | igitur etc.] ergo etc. FW Q om. X   5 Similiter] Sed NO FW Q X Z add. ult. quod NO | non] add. in O | sensationibus] sub actionibus(!) X | probatio] probo U FW | si ab] sub X   6 possunt] possint W | egredi] progredi N | operationes om. U | simul om. N   7 et infinitae] centum N om. O | sed] autem (*post* hoc) N | est om. N | igitur et primum] igitur etc. O ergo primum KU ergo et primum FW Q X om. N | Probatio consequentiae] Probatur consequentia K Probo conclusionem L   9 possunt] possent L | esse simul] inv. H | et om. L FW Z | sicut om. Q | dimensiones] divisibiles(?) Z   10 infinitorum] infinito X | simul se] simul H X se in simul Q se Z om. KU | non possunt] nequeunt Q | ita] sic Z   12 Item] Praeterea NO FW Q X Z | corpus] corpore L | simul om. N L Z | figurari] add. a LM   13 igitur] ergo FW Q X | nec] et FW | sensationibus] sensibus H sensibilibus L   14 assimilatur] assimilantur O M U Z similantur N | in cera] *spat. vac.* X   15 secundum] per N

[5] Cf. **Thomas**, *De sensu* tr. 1 c. 18 (XLV² 98b—99a); cf. **Aristot.**, *De sensu et sensato* [c. 7] (c. 7, 449a 10-20); cf. *De an.* II c. 27 (Γ c. 2, 427a 10-14).
[6] **Aristot.**, *Physica* IV c. 6 (AL VII¹ 155; Δ c. 6, 213b 7-8): "Si vero recipiat, et sunt duo in eodem, continget utique et quotlibet simul esse corpora"; IV c. 8 (AL VII¹ 165; Δ c. 8, 216b 10-12): "Et si duo huiusmodi sunt, propter quid et non quotlibet in eodem erunt?"; cf. III c. 5 (AL VII¹ 117; Γ c. 5, 204b 20-23): "Unumquodque autem infinitum esse impossibile est; corpus enim est penitus habens dimensionem, infinitum autem interminate distans est, quare infinitum corpus ubique erit distans in infinitum"; *De an.* II c. 13 (B c. 7, 418b 17). Cf. **Averroës**, *Physica* IV com. 76 (ed. Iuntina IV f. 166va): "Si fuerit possibile ut duo corpora penetrentur secundum dimensiones, ita quod subiiciantur in uno loco, quid prohibet ut in eodem loco subiiciantur multa corpora infinita?"; *Auctoritates Aristotelis* (ed. J. Hamesse 180, 307): "Impossibile est duo corpora esse in eodem loco"; "Duo corpora non possunt esse simul in uno loco, nec unum corpus in diversis locis"; **Thomas**, *Summa theol.* I q. 86 a. 2 arg. 3: "Si unum corpus non impediret aliud ad existendo in uno et eodem loco, nihil prohiberet infinita corpora in uno loco esse."
[7] **Thomas**, *Summa theol.* I q. 58 a. 2 arg. 2 (V 81a): "Sed unum corpus non potest formari diversis figuris"; *Summa theol.* I q. 85 a. 4 in corp. (V 339b): "... sicut impossibile est quod idem corpus secundum idem simul coloretur diversis coloribus, vel figuretur diversis figuris."
[8] Cf. **Aristot.**, *De an.* II c. 24 (B c. 12, 424a 19-20).

[III. — Resolutio obiectorum]

13 Dicendum quod aliquando una sensatione sentitur utrumque, sicut quando cognoscit[9] unum in aliqua habitudine ad alterum, scilicet ut differentia vel contraria vel similia, si sint similia; aliquando autem pluribus, scilicet quando sentit utrumque absolute et secundum se.

14 Ad primum in contrarium[10] dicendum quod intellectus noster unica intellectione non potest plura obiecta intelligere si sint disparata, sed hoc tamen potest sub una ratione obiectiva; sicut etiam visus potest album et nigrum cognoscere simul secundum quod conveniunt in quadam differentia vel contrarietate, quae est una ratio obiectiva cognoscendi simul utrumque.

15 Per idem ad secundum et tertium,[11] quia ut simul cognoscuntur, habent rationem unius obiecti et unius motoris.[12]

16 Ad argumenta alterius partis: dicendum ad primum[13] quod consequentia non valet. Ad probationem PHILOSOPHI dicendum quod non est simile, quia non est maioris potentiae facere infinita corpora esse simul, et duo; tantam enim repugnantiam habent dimensiones duorum corporum ad invicem, quantam dimensiones

---

2 Dicendum] *add. est* M | aliquando una] unica N amica(!) O | una] unica FW Q Z | sentitur] sentit NO FW Q X Z *add. ult. sensus* Q   3 cognoscit] contingit N continet(?) O | aliqua] aliquo O alia HL quadam KU *om.* Z | ad alterum *om.* K   4 scilicet ut] *inv.* Z | vel *om.* N | sint] sunt O FW Q X Z | aliquando] alteri(!) Z   5 autem] aut O H Z a M | pluribus] *add.* quando(!) K | scilicet *om.* L X | absolute et *post* se L   7 dicendum] *add. est* M F   8 unica] univoca(?) Q | intellectione] intentione(!) O | non] nec Z | potest] ponit(!) O | intelligere] *ant.* plura KU | sint] sunt FW Q X Z *add. ult.* plura F   9 sed hoc tamen] sed tamen hoc K et hoc tantum NO sed hoc tantum FW Q Z | potest] ponit NO | sub] super(!) Z | obiectiva *om.* U | sicut] sic FW si Q X sed Z | etiam] enim(!) L et U | visus] sensus M *add.* non(!) K   10 potest] ponit(!) O *add.* simul FW *add.* etiam X | et nigrum *om.* X | conveniunt] conveniant U   11 quadam] unicam FW | differentia] differentiam W | ratio *om.* NO   12 utrumque] *add.* per idem K   13 Per — tertium] Per illud ad secundum et tertium M Per ad secundum et tertium idem K Praeterea idem ad secundum et tertium FW Z Praeterea ad secundum et tertium X | quia *om.* Z | simul *om.* U X | cognoscuntur] cognoscantur K cognoscere X   15 argumenta] obiecta X *add.* ulterius H X | dicendum ad primum] dicendum primum O dicendum est ad primum M F ad primum dicendum K | ad — consequentia] quod primum L   16 consequentia] contraria X | Philosophi *om.* X | dicendum] exemplariter N essentialiter(!) O *om.* FW Z *add. ult. est* M   17 quod *om.* N | est *om.* Q | est² *om.* U | potentiae] potentia Q | facere] *mg.* M | infinita — esse] infinitam contrarietatem X   18 esse simul *om.* N | simul *om.* L | et] quam N KU F | repugnantiam habent dimensiones] h. d. et (*om.* L) r. HL   19 ad invicem] simul K esse simul U | quantam] *mg.* F² | dimensiones²] dimensionem(!) O

---

[9] Subintellige: sensus.
[10] Cf. supra n. 7.
[11] Cf. supra n. 8. 9.
[12] **Thomas**, *Summa theol.* I q. 58 a. 2 in corp. (V 81a): "... sicut ad unitatem motus requiritur unitas termini, ita ad unitatem operationis requiritur unitas obiecti."
[13] Cf. supra n. 11.

infinitorum, sed maior virtus requiritur ad sciendum simul plura quam unum, et infinita quam duo.

Ad aliud[14] quod similitudo quantum ad hoc erit quod sicut cera per figuram assimilatur anulo, sic sensus per speciem obiecto; sed non quantum ad propositum, ut ratio concludebat, quia figura est terminus intrinsecus quantitatis, et ideo unius quantitatis corporeae est tantum una figura; species autem non est forma ex sensu intrinsece procedens, sed ab obiecto extrinseco in sensum.

[IV. — Ad argumenta principalia]

Ad primum principale in oppositum[15] dicendum quod sensus non movetur propter hoc contrariis motibus, quia motus contrariorum in sensu non sunt contrarii, sicut nec in medio (immo minus quam in medio, et tamen in eodem puncto medii potest esse species albi et nigri), et hoc ideo est quia species sensibilium non recipiuntur materialiter in sensu sicut in re extra, ubi tantum sunt contraria.

Ad secundum[16] dicendum quod illi motus possunt esse aequales si obiecta sint aequaliter immutantia, vel inaequales si inaequaliter. Ad improbationem dicendum quod duo motus reales corporales se impediunt, non autem intentionales sicut in proposito.

Sed contra:

Hoc videmus etiam in spiritualibus, sicut intelligere unum obiectum impedit intellectum ab intelligendo aliud vel sensum a sentiendo, et e converso.

---

1 sciendum] fiendum FW Z sentiendum NO phantasiandum Q   3 aliud] *add.* dicendum X | erit] est HL U dicit M currit(?) W X Z | quod²] erit H | sicut] *add.* secundum H   4 per figuram *om.* U | assimilatur] ant. per Q | sensus] *add.* etiam NO FW Q Z   5 ut] et N | concludebat] concludit L | est *om.* Q   6 terminus] terminis Q | et ideo] ut ratio Z   7 tantum *post* figura L   8 extrinseco] intrinseco U Q X | in] scilicet X   10 primum] *rep.* U | principale] principium N | dicendum] *add.* (ant. dicendum H) est HM F   11 non] si X | movetur] moveretur FW Q moverentur Z | contrariis motibus] *inv.* N K diversis motibus L   12 non] *lin.* K | in² *om.* N | medio] medius(?) Z | immo — medio *om.* K   13 quam *post* medio X | et *om.* NO FW Q X Z | tamen] cum FW *om.* X | species] ant. potest Z   14 et²] *add.* secundum FW Q Z | ideo] non(!) KU | recipiuntur] recipitur Q   15 ubi] *add.* tamen U | sunt *om.* U   16 dicendum] *add.* est M F | illi] isti L   17 si] sicut Z | sint] sunt FW Q X Z | aequaliter] aequanimiter N aequalia U *add.* moventia et Q | si²] sive N X | inaequaliter] aequaliter X   18 improbationem] probationem FW Q X | dicendum] *add.* est M | reales] *add.* et FW Q   19 sicut *om.* X   20 Sed *om.* H   21 Hoc *om.* Q | videmus etiam] *inv.* Z | etiam *om.* N | sicut] quod NO sic M   22 ab *om.* NO *add.* alio Z | vel] sic NO et H | a sentiendo] ad sensibile NO assignando H   23 et e converso] vel e converso X *om.* M Q *add. seu rep.* tamen non totaliter depellit O

[14] Cf. supra n. 12.
[15] Cf. supra n. 1.
[16] Cf. supra n. 2.

21 Dicendum ergo quod quando unus actus est ita intensus, indivisus quod adaequat sibi potentiam, tunc evacuat totaliter alium actum eiusdem potentiae; si autem sit minus intensus et citra terminum potentiae, licet aliqualiter impediat alium et e converso, tamen non totaliter depellit, sed secum compatitur. Unus actus sentiendi unum obiectum obtenebrat alium, non tamen semper obfuscat; ideo possunt simul esse etc.

---

1 ergo] *add.* (ant. ergo F) est M F | intensus] perfectus Z *om.* X 2 indivisus *om.* NO K FW Q Z | adaequat — intensus *om.* NO | totaliter] *add.* et F 3 actum *om.* FW Z | eiusdem] eidem FW Z | sit] sic X | et citra] ad NO 4 aliqualiter] qualiter(!) L | tamen non] *inv.* H KU FW 5 totaliter depellit] *inv.* K | depellit] repellit X depellet Z | Unus] *praem.* Unde NO U *add.* ergo Z | actus] actum X 6 obiectum] oppositum(!) O | obtenebrat] obtenebat N obtenebatur F | alium] aliud K | semper *post* obfuscat K propter F *om.* NO | obfuscat] *add.* et M 7 ideo — etc. *om.* NO FW Q X Z | possunt] potest L | simul esse etc.] = H K simul esse L simul ens M esse simul U

[QUAESTIO 9]

UTRUM SIT PONERE SENSUM COMMUNEM

Utrum sit ponere sensum communem propter istos duos actus positos II *De anima*,[1] scilicet propter distinctionem sensibilium propriorum et propter cognitionem sensationis propriorum sensuum.

[1] Quod non propter secundum actum probo:

Quia sensus particularis sufficit ad cognoscendum actum proprium; igitur ad hoc non requiritur sensus communis. Consequentia patet. Probatio antecedentis: cum actus proprius sit medium inter sensum et obiectum,[2] oportet quod sit propinquius sensui quam obiectum; cum igitur sensus proprius percipiat obiectum proprium, quod tamen est remotius, sequitur quod multo magis proprium actum.

Item, operatio sensus proprii non est sensibile per se; igitur a nullo sensu potest sentiri, nec proprio nec communi. Consequentia

---

3 Utrum] *praem.* Quaeritur NO FW Q X Z *praem.* Quaeritur undecimo K *add.* (*post* sit X) necesse NO FW Q X Z *adnot. mg.* Quaestio 11 M | istos] illos O H FW Q Z | duos] illos(!) O | actus] *mg.* F 4 positos] ponentes NO | II] *lin.* W | distinctionem] discretionem NO FW Q Z 5 propriorum sensuum] plurium sensuum W *om.* F | sensuum] sensibilium N H 7 secundum actum] *inv.* U actum N primum actum O FW Q X Z | probo] probatur Q 8 particularis] *add.* non X 9 igitur] ergo F Q Z *add. spat. vac.* H 10 Probatio antecedentis] Probatur antecedens K Probo antecedens F | medium] medius Z 11 sensum] subiectum HM medium Z | propinquius] propinquum O X propinquior K F | sensui] sensibili H sensum X 12 obiectum] oppositum O | igitur] ergo L F Q Z | sensus] *add.* particularis X | percipiat] participat KU percipit X | obiectum²] oppositum F 13 est] erit X | magis] fortius NO citius Q minime X *add.* percipiet N | proprium actum] *inv.* NO FW Q Z 15 Item] Praeterea N FW Q X Z Prima(?) O | sensibile] sensibilis KU | igitur] ergo F Q Z 16 sensu] sensus O | sentiri] sentire H separari Q | Consequentia patet *om.* NO

---

[1] **Aristot.**, *De an.* III c. 27 (Γ c. 2, 426b 8-29); **Averroës**, *De an.* II com. 144-147 (AverL 348-354); cf. **Themistius**, *De an.* V (CLCAG I 195-197); **Albertus M.**, *De an.* II tr. 4 c. 7-11 (VII 157b—164b); **Petrus Hispanus**, *Scientia libri De anima* tr. VII c. 1 (ed. Alonso II ed. 253); **Thomas**, *De an.* II c. 26-27 (XLV¹ 178a—186b); *Summa theol.* I q. 78 a. 4 ad 2; **Anonymus, Magister Artium**, *Lectura in librum De anima* II, 24 (ed. Gauthier 412): '... ostendit et probat ipsum esse per rationes sumptas penes hanc operationem ipsius que est cognoscere apprehensionem sensuum particularium ... idem probat per secundam operationem eius que est discernere et distinguere obiecta sensuum particularium'; **Ioannes de Rupella**, *Tractatus De anima (de divisione multiplici potentiarum animae)*, II c. 6 (ed. Michaud-Quantin 75); **Ioannes de Rupella**, *Summa de anima*, c. 97 (ed. Bougerol 241); **Anonymus (Iacobus de Duaco?)**, *Quaestiones De anima* II q. 39 (ed. Bazán 461-464); **Anonymus**, *Quaestiones in tres libros De anima* II q. 55 (ed. J. Vennebusch 245-249).

[2] Cf. *Auctoritates Aristotelis* (ed. J. Hamesse 185): "Sensus non decipitur circa suum sensibile proprium servatis tribus conditionibus quae sunt debita dispositio medii, debita dispositio organi et debita obiecti distantia"; cf. **Themistius**, *De an.* III (CLCAG I 132).

patet. Antecedens probatur: sensibilia per se sunt qualitates primae vel secundae, vel aliquae qualitates; sed actus sensus proprii neutrum eorum est; igitur, etc.

3   Item, si ponatur sensus communis ad sentiendum nos videre, cum videre non sit nisi respectu coloris, oportet ipsum sentire colorem; sed hoc est inconveniens, ut videtur, quia tunc eiusdem obiecti essent duae potentiae cognitivae, scilicet visus et sensus communis.[3]

4   Item, sensus communis aut sentit actum proprium, aut requiritur alius sensus illum actum cognoscens. Si sentit actum proprium, igitur et eadem ratione sensus proprius, quia uterque est potentia organica. Si sensus alius requiritur ad sentiendum actum sensus communis, quaeratur de illo utrum sentiat actum proprium, et tunc erit processus in infinitum in sensibus, vel erit standum in aliquo sentiente actum proprium.[4]

5   Item, quod non requiritur ad cognoscendum differentiam sensibilium propriorum probo: potentia cognoscens differentiam aliquorum comparat ea, quia differentia est quaedam comparatio; sed solus intellectus, vel saltem cogitativa, sunt potentiae collativae,

---

1 Antecedens probatur] Probatio antecedentis NO M W Q X Z Probo(?) antecedentis F | qualitates] quantitates(?) Q   2 aliquae] aliae KU Q | qualitates] quantitates L Q W | sensus proprii] inv. O   3 eorum] horum X | igitur] ergo L F Q Z *om.* X   4 Item] Praeterea NO FW Q X Z | ponatur] ponitur L | sentiendum] sciendum H KU   5 cum videre] est(?) videre Q *om.* Z | sit] sic Z | nisi] *lin.* N | coloris] colorum X | oportet] oportebit O FW Q X Z   6 est — videtur] videtur inconveniens NO | quia] quod Z   7 essent] esset Z | duae] plures N | scilicet *om.* X   9 Item] Praeterea NO FW Q X Z | sentit] sensit U | proprium] propinquum X   10 alius] aliquis(?) O *add.* aliquis Q | illum actum] seipsum N istum actum L U ipsum actum M | cognoscens] cognoscentes Z | actum[2]] *rep.* Z   11 igitur] ergo F Q Z *om.* L | et *post* ratione O FW Q X Z *exp.* X[2] *om.* N KU | eadem ratione] pari ratione N eodem modo X | quia] ut U | uterque] utrumque F | est] *add.* in H   12 Si] Sed X | sensus alius] autem sensus alius N autem sensus O Q Z alius proprius(!) M | alius] *add.* est et X | requiritur] requiratur FW Z | ad] alio Z   13 quaeratur] quaero F Z quaeram Q W quidem(!) X | de] ab O | utrum] ute(!) Z | et tunc] si non N | tunc] sic M   14 vel] aut F ut K | erit[2]] est H | standum] instandum HM U   15 sentiente] sentit(?) F quod sentiat NO | actum proprium] inv. NO   16 Item] Praeterea NO KU Q X Z | requiritur] requiratur FW Q   17 sensibilium] sensuum Q | probo] Probatio L Z Probatur KU Probatum Q *add.* quia H   18 quia] quae O quod Z | quaedam comparatio] inv. H | comparatio] operatio Q   19 solus] solum M KU Q sole O *add. ult. spat. vac.* O | cogitativa] cognitiva N H KU F

[3]Cf. **Aristot.**, *De an.* III t. 136 (Γ c. 2, 425b 12-15); **Averroës**, *De an.* II com. 136 (AverL 337); **Albertus M.**, *De an.* II tr. 4 c. 8 (VII 158b); **Thomas**, *De an.* II c. 26 (XLV[1] 178a—b).
[4]Cf. **Aristot.**, *De an.* III t. 136 (Γ c. 2, 425b 15-16); **Anonymus, Magister Artium**, *Lectura in librum De anima* II, 24 (ed. Gauthier 410): "Et si dicatur quod erit stare in aliquo, convenientius erit dicere quod primus sentiat apprehensionem suam quam alius"; **Aegidius Romanus**, *De an.* II com. 136 (f. 57vb): "Aut ergo in infinitum procedet aut erit aliquis sensus ipse sui ipsius iudex, id est erit aliquis sensus qui sentiat se sentire et quia quotienscumque itur in infinitum standum est in primis ..."

non autem sensus communis;⁵ igitur, etc.

Item, habitudo differentiae est quaedam relatio; relatio autem non est sensibile per se; igitur a nullo sensu potest differentia sentiri.

In oppositum omnium praedictorum est PHILOSOPHUS II *De anima*⁶.

[I. — Solutio quaestionis
A. — Solutio secundum Aristotelem]

[3]   Respondeo. Secundum PHILOSOPHUM⁷ habentur duae viae ad investigandum necessitatem sensus communis per duas operationes praedictas. Et possunt ad hoc sic formari rationes:

Prima sic: cum potentia sit proprium principium operationum animae, oportet omnes animae operationes ad aliquam potentiam reduci. Cognoscere differentiam albi et dulcis est operatio animae. Hoc autem non reducitur ad potentiam intellectivam, quae tantum habet de rebus intelligibilibus et differentiis eorum, ut intelligibilia sunt, iudicare; differentia autem albi et dulcis⁸ cognoscitur ab

---

1 igitur etc.] igitur L ergo etc. F Q *om*. Z   2 Item] Praeterea NO FW Q X Z   3 non] *add. seu rep. lative* non autem sensus communis, igitur etc. U | est *om*. U | sensibile] sensibilis FW Q | igitur] ergo L F Q Z   5 omnium *om*. L   9 Respondeo] *adnot. mg*. Responsio U² | habentur — viae] sunt duae viae (*post* communis) N habet duas vias X | duae viae] *inv*. L | viae] *lin*. F²   10 investigandum] vestigandum X | communis] *add. scilicet* NO FW Q X Z   11 hoc] = O KU adhuc N HM FW Q Z ad haec L *om*. X | sic *om*. H Q | rationes *om*. H   12 Prima] Primo N Praeterea O *adnot. mg*. Prima via Aristotelis L | cum *om*. Z | proprium] primum N*om*. Z   13 oportet *post* omnes FW *sed* NO L U et K | oportet — animae *om*. X | animae² *post* operationes F Z | operationes] *add*. possunt L | aliquam] aliam O K F"W *sed corr. mg*. F² | potentiam] *add*. habent KU   14 reduci] reducuntur NO | Cognoscere] Praem. Et hoc U *add*. autem LM *add*. tunc H U | animae] *adnot. mg*. Necessitas ponendi communem M   15 Hoc] Haec Q | quae] quia X | tantum habet] est tantum U tamen habet Q   16 habet] *add*. considerare K *add*. potentiam notitiam FW *add*. cognoscere Q Z | de rebus intelligibilibus] res intelligibiles Q | rebus *om*. N | intelligibilibus] intentionalibus N | differentiis] differentia NO" *sed rest*. O differentiam Q | differentiis eorum] *inv*. Z differentiis earum L KU | ut] inquantum L | intelligibilia *post* sunt L intentionalia N   17 iudicare *om*. NO FW Q X Z | autem] enim L | dulcis] = NO FW Q Z nigri HLM KU X | ab anima] albanima(!) F

---

⁵Cf. **Averroës**, *De an*. III com. 6 (AverL 415): "Virtus enim cogitativa apud Aristotelem est virtus distinctiva individualis, scilicet quod non distinguit aliquid nisi individualiter, non universaliter. Declaratum est enim illic quod virtus cogitativa non est nisi virtus quae distinguit intentionem rei sensibilis a suo idolo imaginato; et ista virtus est illa cuius proportio ad has duas intentiones, scilicet ad idolum rei et ad intentionem sui idoli, est sicut proportio sensus communis ad intentiones quinque sensuum. Virtus igitur cogitativa est de genere virtutum existentium in corporibus."
⁶**Aristot.**, *De an*. III c. 27 (Γ c. 2, 426*b* 12-15).
⁷Cf. n. 1.
⁸Quia meliores codices, qui et textum pristinum exhibent, nobis verbum "nigri" porrigunt, ideo Scotum illud scripsisse seu dixisse, lapsum forsan commitendo, nobis videtur. Attamen verbum multo convenientius "dulcis", sequendo alios codices, scripsimus.

anima non tantum ut differunt per suas quiditates, quod pertinet ad intellectum, sed etiam ut sensibilia sunt⁹ (quod patet, quia brutum, in quo non est intellectus,¹⁰ cognoscit eorum differentiam, ut unum sensibile alteri praeeligat vel praeacceptet); igitur hanc differentiam cognoscere pertinet ad animam sensitivam. Sed hoc non pertinet ad sensum particularem, quia ad hoc, quod aliqua potentia sensitiva cognoscat differentiam aliquorum, oportet eam prius ordine naturae utrumque absolute cognoscere; sed nullus sensus particularis cognoscit sensibile alterius sensus, sed tantum proprium (non autem per se potest cognoscere duo sensibilia propria) nec potest inter illa cognoscere differentiam. Igitur sequitur ex praedictis quod hoc pertinet ad aliquem sensum communem.

Secunda via sic patet: experimur nos sensibiliter sentire. Item, probatur ratione: posito effectu ponitur eius causa; sed perceptio coniunctionis convenientis cum convenienti est causa delectationis secundum AVICENNAM;¹¹ delectatio autem in actu sentiendi est, tam in nobis quam in brutis; est igitur in nobis et ipsis perceptio actus sentiendi nobis convenientis. Manifestum est autem quod brutum non percipit se sentire nisi per sensum, quia non habet intellectum; igitur per aliquam potentiam sensitivam. Non autem per sensum

[4]

---

1 tantum ut] inv. F tantum quod KU | differunt] dicunt O | quiditates] quantitates NO 2 etiam] ad U om. K | ut] lin. Q² | quod patet] ut patet L quaedam U quia patet Q | quod — quia] spat. vac. O om. N 3 non om. O L | eorum] eandem KU | differentiam] add. (lin.) ita F | ut] et X 4 alteri] altero KU | praeeligat] praeelegat H Q | praeacceptet] praeacce patet O praeacceptat X praeaccipiat N KU | igitur] ergo FW Q X Z 5 pertinet] partem O | animam] potentiam FW Q X Z | Sed om. H 6 sensus particularem] inv. F | particularem] particulare W | hoc] haec O 7 aliquorum] aliorum Q | ordine naturae om. N 8 absolute cognoscere] inv. Q 9 sensus om. X | per se post potest KU 10 propria] add. igitur NO add. ergo FW Q Z | nec] non Q | potest² post illa N | illa] ea H K alia X 11 Igitur] Ergo L FW Q Z | quod — sed om. NO 12 pertinet] pertineat FW Q | sensum] suum(?) X 13 Secunda — sentire om. K adnot. mg. secunda via L | patet om. U add. sic X | nos sensibiliter] inv. FW | Item] Id X add. hoc Q W Z 14 eius causa] inv. KU | perceptio] perfectio H KU 15 coniunctionis] cognitionis N KU om. Q Z | cum] et W | convenienti] add. sed X 16 actu] sensu H | est] ant. in Z | tam] causa Q Z 17 quam] et Z | est igitur] igitur est NO ergo est FW Q X Z | et] add. in K Q Z om. FW 18 nobis convenientis] inv. N | convenientis] conveniens Z | Manifestum] in quantum F" sed rest. mg. F² | autem] add. modo N add. uno(?) O 19 nisi] nec NO non F | sensum] del. et scripsit lin. intellectum F² add. proprium nec per intellectum N 20 igitur] ergo L FW Q Z | aliquam] aliam Z | sensitivam — autem² om. NO | autem] enim L

⁹**Thomas**, *De an.* II c. 27 (XLV¹ 183*ab*): "Cognoscimus enim differentiam albi et dulcis non solum quantum ad quod quid est utriusque, quod pertinet ad intellectum, sed etiam quantum ad diversam immutationem sensus, et hoc non potest fieri nisi per sensum …"; cf. *Sent.* III d. 22 q. 1 a. 2 in corp. (VII¹ 241*a*).
¹⁰**Avicenna**, *De an.* pars 4 c. 1 (AviL II 2): "In imaginatione animalium quae carent intellectu …"
¹¹**Avicenna**, *Metaph.* VIII c. 7 (AviL 432): "Delectatio non est nisi apprehensio convenientis secundum quod est conveniens; unde sensibilis delectatio est sensibilitas convenientis."

particularem, quia secundum philosophum[12] nulla virtus organica vel corporalis est supra se vel supra suum actum reflexiva; potentia autem sensitiva est organica; igitur sensus particularis non est propriae operationis perceptivus. Igitur sensus communis tantum est cognoscitivus operationis sensus particularis. Hoc autem habet fieri per hunc modum: primo enim sensus proprius a sensibili proprio immutatur; immutatio cuiuslibet sensus proprii ad sensum communem terminatur,[13] sicut plures lineae ductae a circumferentia ad idem centrum terminantur; sensus autem communis sic immutatus a diversis sensationibus vel immutationibus particularibus iudicat et cognoscit actum cuiuslibet sensus particularis, et ulterius cognoscit

---

1 philosophum] Proclum FW X Z *spat. vac.* Q | organica vel corporalis] organica vel corporis X corporalis vel organica Z 2 vel — reflexiva] *mg.* W | est] *adnot. mg.* Notabilia M | supra] super FW Q X Z | supra²] super M FW Q X Z | suum actum] *inv.* FW Q X Z | reflexiva] reflectiva (*ant.* supra) F 3 sensitiva] sensus NO virtus F | est *om.* N F | organica] organici N | igitur] ergo L F Q Z | sensus] *lin.* F *add.* vero(?) Q 4 operationis] *add.* perceptionis X | Igitur] Ergo L Q Z | Igitur — enim *om.* N | sensus communis] *inv.* FW Q X | communis] conveniunt(!) (*ant.* sensus) Z | tantum est] *inv.* O F Z 5 cognoscitivus] cognitivus KU F Q *adnot. in imo fol.:* p 3 M² | sensus particularis] *inv.* HL | sensus — enim *om.* O | Hoc] Haec Q | fieri] *add.* proprie L 6 primo] prius L | enim] autem Q | proprius *om.* U | sensibili] sensu (*post* proprio) U 7 immutatio] immediate N *add.* autem NO FW Q X Z | sensus] *add. (mg.)* particularis Z | proprii *om.* FW Z 8 a] ad O F Q *om.* Z | circumferentia] circumferentiam F Q concircumferentia Z 9 idem] id O | centrum] punctum N *om.* O | terminantur] terminatur X | sic] sibi U 10 vel] sive N | iudicat] iudicas Z 11 cognoscit — ulterius *om.* KU X Z | cuiuslibet] cuiuscumque N | sensus particularis] *inv.* L | ulterius] ulteri(!) O | cognoscit] continet O

[12]**Proclus**, *Elementatio theologica* prop. 15 (ed. Boese 11): "Omne quod a se ipsum conversivum est incorporeum est. Nullum enim corporeum ad se ipsum natum est converti"; cf. **Avicenna**, *De an.* pars 5 c. 2 (AviL 93-94); **Thomas**, *In I Sent.* d. 17 q. 1 a. 5 ad 3m (VI 141): "In potentiis materialibus hoc contingit quod potentia non reflectitur super suum actum, propter hoc quod determinata est secundum compilationem organi"; *In II Sent.* d. 19 q. 1 a. 1 (VI 553-556); **Thomas de Sutton**, *Quaest. ordinariae* q. 2 (ed. Schneider BAW III 39): "Ad hoc dicebat quod ratio philosophi bene tenet de motu corporali, qui est in corporalibus quantis, ubi mobile non potest reflecti supra se, sed in rebus immaterialibus non habet locum, quia res immaterialis potest convertere se supra se ipsam, et ideo potest movere se ipsam"; **Henricus Gand.**, *Quod.* X q. 9 in corp. (AMPh s. 2, XIV 233): "Loquendo autem de tertio modo motus, voluntas movetur a se, et hoc conversione quadam spirituali ad se ipsam, secundum illam 17am propositionem Procli: 'Omne se ipsum movens primo ad se ipsum est conversum'."

[13]**Albertus M.**, *De an.* II tr. 4 c. 11 (VII 163b): "Sensus communis est sicut terminus sensuum particularium."

differentiam sensibilium propriorum.[14]

[B. — Solutio secundum Avicennam]

11   Praedictae viae sumuntur a PHILOSOPHO, sed consequentes ab AVICENNA:

Prima sic: 'natura non deficit in necessariis';[15] sed ad vitam animalis perfectam necessario requiritur conservatio specierum sensibilium,[16] etiam in eorum absentia, quia aliter non possent moveri progressive ad sensibile distans et absens. Et mediantibus speciebus sic reservatis, fit apprehensio sensibilis absentis per aliquam potentiam sensitivam; non autem est particularis, quia talis sentit praesente sensibili tantum;[17] igitur vel illa est communis sensus, vel saltem praesupponit ipsum, sicut imaginativa,

---

1 sensibilium propriorum] propriorum sensuum N inv. L om. Z   3 viae om. Z | sed om. Q | consequentes] = L consequenter(!) H KU viae sequuntur N sequentes O FW Q X Z sequentis M add. ult. vero Q   5 Prima sic] inv. F Sic primo NO W Primo sic H Sic KU Z Prima est haec Q Prima X adnot. mg. Primum via Avicennae L   6 animalis om. Z | perfectam] perfecti NO FW Q X Z | specierum om. U   7 sensibilium om. Q | etiam] et L KU | eorum] rerum Q | absentia] absentiam F | quia om. X | possent] possunt N H U posset Z   8 moveri] movere K | progressive] progressibile U pro genere(?) X add. ult. sive X | Et] Nisi KU om. F | mediantibus] mediis N medium(!) F   9 reservatis] conservatis H | fit] sit U sed illa K | apprehensio] comprehensio F" sed exp. et restit.. mg. F² | absentis om. NO add. fit K   10 autem est] inv. NO K | est om. X   11 sentit] sensibilis N sentitur H | praesente] praesenti H U mediante N | sensibili] sensibile U | igitur vel] inv. N ergo vel FW Q X Z ergo tunc vel L | illa] ita L ipsa Z | communis sensus] inv. N K Q communis tantum(?) sensus W   12 saltem om. U | sicut] add. potentia N | imaginativa] imaginativam O HM K X add. vel NO FW Q X Z

---

[14] **Aristot.**, *De an.* III c. 1 (Γ c. 2 429a 9-10): "Sed sicut quod vocant quidam punctum aut unum aut duo, sic et divisibile"; **Themistius**, *De an.* V (CLCAG I 198): "Illud utique magis rationabilius exsistimabit assimilari potentiam sensitivam puncto, magis autem centro circuli, ad quem omnes ex circumferentia lineae terminantur"; **Averroës**, *De an.* com. 149 (AverL 356): "Ista virtus est una et multa ut punctus qui est centrum circuli quando ab eo fuerint extractae multae lineae a centro ad circumferentiam"; **Albertus M.**, *De an.* II tr. 4 c. 11 (VII 164a): "Per hoc autem quod ipsum substantialiter est medium circuli, est ipsum principium aequalitatis linearum protractarum ab ipso ad circumferentiam, et sic uno et unum et multa discernuntur"; **Thomas**, *De an.* II c. 27 (XLV¹ 185a): "Et solutio ista sumitur ex similitudine puncti; punctum enim quod est inter duas partes lineae potest accipi ut unum aut duo; ut unum quidem secundum quod continuat partes lineae ut communis terminus, ut duo autem secundum quod bis utimur puncto, scilicet ut principio unius lineae et ut fine alterius"; **Petrus Hispanus**, *Scientia libri De anima* tr. 7 c. 1 (ed. Alonso II ed 249): "Comparatur igitur centro circuli et puncto a quo multa lineae emanant ..."

[15] **Aristot.**, *De an.* III c. 8 (Γ c. 9, 432b 21-22): "Si igitur natura non facit frustra nihil neque deficit in necessariis ..."; *Politica* I c. 2 (AL XXIX¹ 5; c. 2 1253a 9); *Auctoritates Aristotelis* (ed. J. Hamesse 188, 252): "Natura nihil facit frustra, unde non deficit in necessariis, nec abundat in superfluis"; cf. **Thomas**, *Summa theol.* I q. 78 a. 4 in corp. (V 255b): "Cum natura non deficiat in necessariis, oportet esse tot actiones animae sensitivae, quot sufficiant ad vitam animalis perfecti"; *Summa contra gent.* III c. 85 (XIV 255a): "Natura enim non deficit nisi in paucioribus"; **Aegidius Romanus**, *De an.* II com. 128 (f. 55ra-b).

[16] **Avicenna**, *De an.* IV, 1 (AviL 2): "Si autem non esset in animalibus virtus in qua coniungerentur formae sensatorum, difficilis esset ei vita ..."

[17] **Avicenna**, *De an.* pars 4 c. 1 (AviL 4-5); cf. **Thomas**, *Summa theol.* I q. 78 a. 4 in corp. (V 255b—256a).

rememorativa.

Alia autem via AVICENNAE[18] accipitur ex eo quod ad sensum videmus, scilicet quod si attendamus ad guttas pluviae sibi mutuo succedentes, apparebit nobis una linea de omnibus illis guttis quasi continua. Similiter, si moveatur circulariter aliqua virga in cuius summitate est aliquis color, apparebit nobis circulus quidam in summitate eius propter motum circularem summitatis vel coni illius virgae. Ex hoc potest sic argui: impossibile est sensum particularem percipere suum sensibile ubi non est; sed summitas virgae motae non est semper in eodem loco in quo apparet circulus, quia circulus apparet quasi immobilis, illa autem semper movetur. Simile est de guttis. Igitur ille circulus vel illa linea non percipitur a sensu particulari:[19] igitur a communi. Simile est de homine exsistente in navi mota, qui iudicat ad sensum ripam moveri.

[II. — Ad argumenta principalia]

[6] Ad primum[20] in oppositum dicendum quod antecedens est falsum. Ad probationem dicendum quod non quaecumque medietas vel propinquitas facit ad hoc quod propinquum sentiatur, sed

---

1 rememorativa] = M U FW Q memorativa N K rememorativam H remorativam(!) O L X remorativa Z 2 autem om. NO FW Q X Z | accipitur] sumitur Q 3 scilicet quod] inv. H | si om. KU Q | ad om. Q | sibi] sic NO H | mutuo] nutuo(!) U 4 succedentes] succedente H | illis om. Q | quasi om. X 5 aliqua] alia N | in cuius] rep. Z | cuius summitate] inv. N 6 est aliquis color] sit color aliquis NO M FW Q Z sit aliquis color X | circulus quidam] inv. L K quidem circulus U | quidam] qui X 7 eius] esse Z | motum circularem] inv. NO M FW Q X Z | coni] coloris(!) FW causa(?) X | illius] ipsius F 8 hoc] add. quod H | potest sic] inv. NO M FW Q Z | est] add. aliquem N add. ad O 9 suum post sensibile Q om. X 10 semper om. KU | apparet — apparet] del.(?) Z 11 quasi om. KU | quasi — circulus om. Z | illa] alia N ille M om. HL KU | autem semper] semper tamen HL U tamen semper K semper FW X | Simile] Sic L Similiter U 12 guttis] guttulis L | Igitur] Ergo U F Q | ille] iste LM U | illa] ista U | non] lin. O | percipitur] percipetur O W Q perciperetur X percipetur Z 13 igitur] ergo L FW Q X Z | a] add. sensu NO 14 qui] quae M X | ad sensum] assensum Q 16 Ad primum] Argumentum Z | in oppositum] modum FW om. X Z | dicendum] dicitur Z add. est M 17 dicendum] dico Q add. est M | medietas vel om. Z 18 propinquum] aliquid melius N propinquius O propri nunc Q | sentiatur] sensus natura Q | sed om. N

[18]**Avicenna**, *De an.* pars 1 c. 5 (AviL 88): "Cum autem volueris scire differentiam inter opus sensus exterioris et opus sensus communis et opus formantis, attende dispositionem unius guttae cadentis de pluvia, et videbis rectam lineam, et attende dispositionem alicuius recti cuius summitas movetur in circuito, et videbitur circulus"; pars 3 c. 7 (AviL 255): "Similiter imaginatio cadentis guttae videtur linea, et gutta quae movetur circulariter, circulus aliquis"; cf. pars 4 c. 1 (AviL 3, ll. 36-41 cum adnotatione); cf. **Ioannes Blund**, *Tractatus de anima* c. 17 (ed. Callus et Hunt ABMA 64); **Ioannes de Rupella**, *Summa de anima*, c. 97 (ed. Bougerol 241).
[19]**Avicenna**, *De an.* pars 4 c. 1 (AviL 3): "Sicut videmus quod ei qui in circuitu volvitur videtur quicquid est in circuitu moveri ..."
[20]Cf. supra n. 1.

tantum proportionalis, quia nec nimis propinqua nec nimis remota. Unde medium inhaerens vel coniunctum non requiritur, saltem in visu. Modo ita est quod actus sentiendi sensibile proprium est medium inhaerens, quia est in sentiente, ideo non sentitur quia non est potentia reflexiva super se, nec sentit aliquid in se exsistens.

14   Ad aliud[21] dicendum quod organum est aliqualiter coloratum per speciem et per visionem, quae multum assimilatur colorato a quo est primo genita, et per consequens potest dici sensibile; potest igitur dici quod non tantum est sensibile per se qualitas prima aut secunda, sed etiam aliquid causatum a qualitate prima vel secunda, ut sensatio vel visio.

15   Ad aliud[22] etiam dicendum quod sensus communis sentit et visionem et colorem. Ad improbationem dicendum quod impossibile est duas potentias disparatas esse respectu eiusdem obiecti, sed duas ordinatas quarum una est superior vel communior alia — non est inconveniens —, sicut se habent sensus communis et sensus proprius; ideo etc. Verum est tamen quod idem non est obiectum aeque primo utriusque, sed obiectum proprium sensus proprii et cuiuslibet potentiae est illud quod adaequat ipsum, ut color visum; illud tamen non adaequat sensum communem, quia potest aliud

---

1 proportionalis] proportionaliter N W X Z proportio Q | quia] quod NO FW Q X Z | nec] ut sic O *mg.* W | nimis] minus(!) KU | propinqua ... remota] remota ... propinqua NO FW Q Z | propinqua nec nimis *om.* X | nec²] vel N | nimis²] minus(!) KU | remota] propinqua X   2 non requiritur —*fin.*] *invenitur in fine q. 5 (in f. 163rb, lin. 12 N; in f. 46ra, lin. 42 O)* NO | requiritur] sentitur H   3 ita] illa Q   4 medium] actus N | quia] quod Z | est] *lin.* H X *add.* medium K | sentiente] sentiendo KU sensibile X | non² *om.* N   5 est] in X | aliquid] aliquod O | se²] eo K | exsistens] *add.* etc. K   6 dicendum] *add.* est (*ant.* dicendum X) M X | aliqualiter] aequaliter L KU | coloratum] complacitum(?) O   7 per² *om.* L K | quae] quo H KU   8 primo genita] primo generata X primogeniter Z | sensibile] *add.* per se NO | potest igitur dici *om.* H K   9 igitur] ergo Q | quod — se] non sensibile per se quod est K | tantum est] *inv.* N tunc est L | est *post* per se U | aut] et NO U FW Q X vel Z   10 secunda] *add.* qualitas NO FW Q | etiam] in N *om.* K | causatum] creatum M | prima vel] *rep.* X | vel secunda] velut prima Q   11 ut — visio] non visio X | vel] et NO FW Q X Z *om.* L   12 etiam] autem O est KU *om.* FW Q X Z *adnot. mg.* Sensus communis K | dicendum] *add.* scilicet H *add.* est M | sensus] sensus — quod *om.* NO | sentit] sentitur Z | et] secundum Z *om.* KU   13 improbationem] probationem U FW X Z | dicendum] dico Q *add.* est M *add.* quando dicitur Z   14 duas potentias *om.* N | respectu *om.* FW *add.* unius et N KU | obiecti] subiecti H *add.* dicendum quod Z | sed duas] si sicut Z   15 duas] *add.* et(?) U *add.* potentias K | ordinatas] subordinatas N X Q ordinatae Z | quarum] ita quod Z | est] sit Z *om.* Q | vel] et N | non] nec NO Q X | non est inconveniens *ant.* sed Z   16 est] *add.* (*post* inconveniens Q) hoc N Q *add.* hic O | sicut] sic LM FW Q X Z | se habent *om.* Q | habent] habet H   17 ideo etc.] igitur etc. O *om.* N W | tamen *om.* Z | quod *om.* L | idem] illud(?) L id M X | est² *om.* O Q | obiectum] oppositum O subiectum H   18 aeque primo] adequatum U | primo] primum K *om.* U X | sed] quia *mg.* K² | obiectum] subiectum H oppositum O | proprium] primum NO FW Q X Z | sensus proprii et *om.* K   19 illud] idem(?) N H U Z id W Q X | visum] *add.* et NO   20 illud] idem(?) N H istud O W | non adaequat] quod adaequat non U

[21] Cf. supra n. 2.
[22] Cf. supra n. 3.

obiectum sentire. Et ideo non est eius obiectum per se.

[7] Ad aliud[23] dicendum quod imaginatio sentit actum proprium; imaginamur enim nos imaginari[24] vel imaginatum fuisse, et memoramur nos memoratum fuisse, et somniamus nos somniare, sicut experimur manifeste. Ita potest dici quod sensus communis sentit actum proprium per aliquem praedictorum. Sed per quem modum est possibile? Dicendum quod sicut ab actu imaginationis defluit quaedam species in organo alicuius sensus, sive exterioris sive interioris,[25] in qua specie est similitudo actus illius, a qua specie potest potentia imaginativa sic immutari; sic est de sensu communi, quod ab eius actu defluit quaedam species in organo sensus particularis interius, a qua specie, retinente similitudinem actus eius, potest sensus communis immutari. Et hoc non est reflecti super actum eius directe, sed mediante specie ab eo defluxa.

[8] Ad aliud[26] dicendum quod sensus communis non est potentia collativa proprie, sicut memorativa vel cogitativa. Memorativa cognoscit suum obiectum ut distans a praesenti nunc, cogitando tempus medium. Est enim praeteriti ut praeteritum est. Sed sensus communis sic confert unum sensibile alteri quod simul sentit ipsa sensibilia, et sentit ipsa differre sine intermedio aliquo, et talis collatio, id est compositio et divisio taliter, non repugnat ei, sicut

---

1 obiectum *om.* N | non *om.* N | obiectum²] oppositum O | per se] propinquum(!) KU 2 dicendum] *add.* est M | sentit *om.* NO | actum] actuum N | proprium] propriorum N 3 enim *post* nos Q *om.* U | imaginari vel] imaginari simul(!) Z | imaginatum] imaginatos Q 4 memoratum] memoratos Q X Z 5 manifeste] mediante (*ant.* experimur) Q | quod] *lin.* F² 6 per *om.* NO FW Q X Z | aliquem] aliquod K aliquam U | Sed per] Secundum X | per²] *spat. vac.* O | quem] *add.* ad O 7 Dicendum] *add.* est M | imaginationis] *adnot. mg.* Stude dicendum M | defluit] O" *sed corr. in* defluunt O fluunt Z 8 quaedam] quaedam — defluit *om.* Z | sive] *mg.* W | exterioris ... interioris] interioris ... exterioris NO FW X interiori ... exteriori Q 9 actus illius] *inv.* NO FW X Z istius actus Q | a] in H U 10 potest] *lin.* M | potentia] *add.* vel X | sic] iterum tamen N iterum tunc O tunc FW X iterum Q *om.* L | immutari] imitari(!) U 11 actu] motu M | quaedam *om.* H 12 qua] *add.* ordine O | retinente] recipiente N *perhaps also* O | eius potest] *inv.* X | potest] ponit O 13 sensus] *add.* aliqua specie O | est reflecti] reflecti O reflectendo L est reflexio X | actum] actus KU ac O | eius] proprium NO FW Q X Z 14 eo] ea L | defluxa] defuxa(!) Q 15 dicendum] *add.* est M 16 collativa] collotiva(?) O | memorativa] memoria NO Q | cogitativa] cognitiva N *add.* proprie HLM X *add.* quia K | Memorativa] Memoria(?) O F Momoria(!) Q *add.* enim NO FW Q X Z | cognoscit] cognovit O 17 suum] *add.* proprium N | obiectum] oppositum O | ut] *add.* est NO | distans] distat Z | nunc] nec O F non Z | cogitando] cognoscendo K Q | tempus] cuius NO tantum(?) Q 18 Est enim] *inv.* X | Est — aliquo] in remoto (remedio(?) O) aliquo cognito NO | enim *om.* KU | praeteriti] praeteritum K 19 communis] *add.* non K | sic] est ut H *add.* sed K | sensibile] sensibiliter X | ipsa] illa K 20 et] etiam LM K X | ipsa] illa Q 21 id est] vel L vel id est Q | et] vel HK FW ut X | taliter] totaliter NO *om.* Z | ei — repugnat] *mg.* W *om.* HLM KU

---

[23]Cf. supra n. 4.
[24]Cf. **Avicenna**, *De an.* pars 5 c. 2 (AviL 96-97, ll. 1-11).
[25]Cf. **Adam de Wodeham**, *Lectura secunda in I Sent.*, prol. q. 3 n. 9 (ed. Wood-Gál 81).
[26]Cf. supra n. 5.

non repugnat sensui proprio affirmare vel negare proprium obiectum de aliquo, ut dicitur II *De anima*.[27]

18   Ad aliud[28] dicendum quod licet sensus communis cognoscat illa quae differunt, et cognoscat album a dulci differre, non tamen cognoscit habitudinem differentiae secundum se, sed tantum in fundamento.[29] Ponitur exemplum: intellectus quidquid intelligit, hoc est sub ratione veri, non tamen quod, intelligendo aliquam qualitatem, intelligat ipsam rationem veri, quia tunc reflexivus esset in quolibet actu suo. Ita, licet sensus communis cognoscat aliqua differre, etiam sub ratione differentiae, non tamen oportet quod patiatur propriam immutationem ab ipsa differentia secundum se, quae est quaedam relatio.[30] Et ideo non sequitur quod relatio sit sensibile per se, licet illa relata sint sensibilia per se.

---

1 non] nec FW *om.* X | sensui] sensum O 2 obiectum] oppositum O *om.* X | dicitur] *add.* in M | II] 'III' NO FW Q X 3 dicendum] *add.* est M | quod licet] *rep.* N | cognoscat] cognoscit M | illa] ea NO 4 quae] quia O | et cognoscat] ut cognoscat KU a cognoscenti X | cognoscat] cognoscit H *adnot. mg.* Nota bene M | a dulci differre] differrre a dulci NO FW Q X et dulce differre U differre ab aliis Z 5 cognoscit] cognoscat Z 6 fundamento] *add.* (ant. fundamento M) suo NO M FW Q X Z | Ponitur] Ponatur N *om.* U F | intellectus] de intellectu Z | quidquid] quidam N quicquid Q *add.* enim Z 7 tamen] *add.* requiritur K | quod] quia X *add.* in HM | aliquam] album(?) N 8 qualitatem] = N H X Z quantitatem O KU Q quiditatem LM FW | intelligat] intelligit Q intelligas(?) Z | rationem] sub ratione KU | reflexivus esset] *inv.* M Q reflexus esset U 9 cognoscat] cognoscit U 10 etiam] et sic N et H KU | tamen *om.* NO FW Q Z 11 ipsa] illa NO Q *add.* forma O 12 sit] sic N 13 sensibile] = HLM sensibilis NO KU FW Q X Z | licet] *add.* in X | illa] ipsa NO M FW Q X Z | se²] *add.* et cetera HL *add.* et igitur de illa quaestione sufficiunt K *add.* et haec de 11 quaestione sufficiunt U

[27]Cf. **Aristot.**, *De an.* III c. 24 (Γ c. 2, 427a 10-14); cf. **Thomas**, *Summa theol.* I q. 78 a. 4 in corp. (V 256a—b).
[28]Cf. supra n. 6.
[29]Cf. **Thomas**, *De an.* II c. 27 (XLV¹ 183a-b).
[30]**Averroës**, *De an.* II com. 146 (AverL 352): "Manifestum est quod, in instante in quo dicit quod alterum eorum est aliud, in illo eodem dicit in altero esse aliud, cum alietas sit aliqua relatio, et relativa insimul exsistunt in actu."

[QUAESTIO 10]

UTRUM SENSUS COMMUNIS SIT UNUS VEL PLURES

Utrum sensus communis sit unus vel plures.[1]

[1] Videtur quod plures:

Quia una potentia est tantum unius organi,[2] sed sensus communis non est tantum unius organi; igitur, etc. Probatio minoris per COMMENTATOREM[3] dicentem quod sensus communis est plura secundum instrumenta. Item, sic per rationem patet minor, quia organum debet esse in media proportione inter sensibilia;[4] sed nulla proportio media una potest reperiri inter omnia sensibilia quae sunt obiecta sensus communis, quia unius contrarietatis tantum est unum medium,[5] sensibilia autem sunt diversarum contrarietatum; igitur, etc.

Item, impossibile est idem esse in actu per plura in actu; sensus autem sunt in actu per sensibilia quae sunt plura et diversa in actu;

---

3 Utrum] *praem.* Quaeritur NO FW Q X Z *praem* Quaeritur sexto K An Q *adnot. lin.* Quaestio sexta M | Utrum — reflexio super actum] *textus huius quaestionis usque ad n. 26 non reperitur in codice U, absciso folio* | unus] *add.* sensus L 4 Videtur quod plures] quod plures X *om.* Z 5 est *om.* Z | tantum] *add.* respectu K | sed — organi *om.* H 6 unius organi] unum organum K FW Q X Z | igitur] ergo L FW Q Z *om.* X | etc. *om.* O Q | Probatio minoris] b probatur X 7 plura] plures K FW Q X Z 8 instrumenta] *add.* igitur etc. K | Item] Praeterea NO FW Q X Z Etiam K | sic — minor] = L sic per rationem minor NO sic per rationem minor patet (probatur Q) H Q sic minor patet per rationem M probatur minor per rationem K sic patet per rationem minor (minoris X) FW X minor pater per rationem sic Z | minor] minorem N(?) O 9 proportione] proptencione(?) O | sed — sensibilia *om.* L 10 media una] *inv.* K medi*ante* una X | una *om.* N | reperiri] inveniri F reperta Z | sensibilia] sensibili O 11 sensus *post* communis FW Q X Z | tantum est] *inv.* K F Z | est *post* unum N 12 medium] *add.* vel Q | autem] *add.* omnia HLM 13 igitur etc.] ergo etc. FW Q Z *om.* X *add. ult.* sicut diversarum contrarietatum diversa media Q 14 Item] Praeterea NO K FW Q X Z | idem *om.* L | esse] essentia X | sensus — actu[2] *om.* Z 15 autem — actu[2]] communis est in actu per plura quae sunt sensibilia in actu diversa K | sunt] *mg.* W est Q | per *om.* X | sensibilia] possibilia X | et diversa *post* actu Q | diversa] distincta (*post* actu) X

---

[1] Cf. **Aristot.**, *De an.* II c. 27 (Γ c. 2, 426b 20-22); **Averroës**, *De an.* com. 146 (AverL 351-2): "Necesse est ut virtus qua idem homo iudicat dulce esse aliud ab albo sit una eadem virtus"; **Petrus Hispanus**, *Scientia libri De anima* tr. VII c. 1 (ed. Alonso II 249); **Thomas**, *De an.* II c. 27 (XLV[1] 184a—185b); **Anonymus (Jacobus de Duaco?)**, *Quaestiones De anima* II q. 40 (ed. Bazán 464-465); **Anonymus**, *Quaestiones in tres libros De anima* II q. 56 [1] (ed. Vennebusch 249-250).
[2] **Averroës**, *De an.* II com. 107 (AverL 294): "Unum instrumentum non est nisi unius virtutis."
[3] **Averroës**, *De an.* II com. 148 (AverL 355): "Haec virtus ... est unica in intellectu et in esse et in actu, et multa secundum instrumenta."
[4] **Aristot.**, *De an.* II c. 23 (B c. 11 424a 4-5); cf. **Anonymus**, *Quaestiones in tres libros De anima* II q. 56 [1] (ed. Vennebusch 249); cf. supra q. 1.
[5] **Aristot.**, *De an.* II c. 22 (B c. 11 422b 23-24); cf. **Anonymus**, *Quaestiones in tres libros De anima* II q. 56 [1] (ed. Vennebusch 249); cf. supra q. 1.

igitur idem sensus non potest esse in actu per plura sensibilia; sed sensus communis reducitur ad actum per plura sensibilia particularia; igitur, etc.

3   Item, unus sensus est tantum unius contrarietatis;[6] sed obiecta sensibilia non sunt tantum unius contrarietatis; igitur sensus communis, qui est respectu omnium, non est unus.

4   In oppositum est PHILOSOPHUS.[7]

[I. — Solutio quaestionis:]
[A. — Conclusio prima]

5   Respondeo quod sensus communis non est unus unitate praedicationis sed unitate singularitatis et causalitatis; est enim radix et causa omnium sensuum particularium.[8] Probatio assumpti: quia quod est unum praedicatione tantum non habet operationem distinctam ab operatione particularium contentorum sub ipso; sed sensus communis habet operationem distinctam ab operationibus sensuum particularium, scilicet distinguere inter sensibilia diversorum

---

1 igitur] ergo L FW Q X Z | potest esse] est H | sed — sensibilia *om.* Q   2 ad actum] in actu K   3 igitur etc.] ergo etc. FW Q Z *om.* X   4 Item] Praeterea NO K FW Q X Z | unus sensus] *inv.* HL sensus iste est unus qui M | tantum *post* unius NO *post* contrarietatis M | sed *om.* K | obiecta] omnia FW Q X   5 sensibilia] sensitiva K *add.* a sensu communi L | tantum *om.* LM | contrarietatis — unus *om.* X | igitur] ergo L FW Q Z   10 quod *om.* FW X   11 sed] et X | singularitatis] simplicitatis FW | radix et causa] causa et (*om.* Z) radix L K Q X Z causa FW   12 sensuum] sensibilium K | assumpti] propositi NO FW K Q X Z   13 praedicatione] unitate praedicationis L   14 operatione] operationibus O K FW Q X | operatione — ab *om.* Z | particularium] singularium M | contentorum] conceptorum K | contentorum sub ipso *om.* L | ipso] subiecto K | sensus *post* operationem O   15 communis] *add.* non X | distinctam] distincte X | ab — particularium] a sensibus particularibus L | sensuum particularium] *inv.* NO particularibus sensuum L   16 scilicet] quia Z | sensibilia] *add.* singularia K FW Z *add.* particularia Q X *add.* ult. et Q

[6]Cf. **Aristot.**, *De an.* II c. 22 (B c. 11, 422b 23-24); **Thomas**, *Summa theol.* I q. 78 a. 3 arg. 3 (V 253a); cf. supra q. 1. n. 2.
[7]**Aristot.**, *De an.* II c. 27 (Γ c. 2, 426b 17-23).
[8]**Thomas**, *Summa theol.* I q. 78 a. 4 ad 1 (V 256a): "Dicendum quod sensus interior non dicitur communis per praedicationem, sicut genus; sed sicut communis radix et principium exteriorum sensus"; cf. **Themistius**, *De an.* V (CLCAG I 199); **Albertus M.**, *De an.* II tr. 4 c. 11 (VII[1] 164a): "... dicimus sensum communem esse principium omnium sensuum particularium et esse formam, a qua est influentia sensus in omnibus propriis sensibus ..."; **Thomas**, *De an.* II c. 27 (XLV[1] 183b): "... ad fontalem radicem omnium sensuum, quae est sensus communis"; *De an.* II c. 27 (XLV[1] 185b): "... videtur quod ibi sit organum huius principii sensitivi communis ubi est prima radix organi tactus ..."; **Ioannes Pecham**, *Tractatus de anima* c. 10 (ed. Melani 35): "... et est sensus communis centrum omnium sensuum, natura, scilicet, in qua omnes sensus radicantur ..."; **Petrus Hispanus**, *Scientia libri De anima* tr. 7 c. 2 (ed. Alonso II 250): "hac virtus ... quae est fons et origo sensuum"; **Pseudo Petrus Hispanus**, *Expositio libri De anima* c. 6 (ed. Alonso 173): "... quia sensus communis est una radix, in quo tamquam in radice fundantur sensus proprii"; cf. **Anonymus (Jacobus de Duaco?)**, *Quaestiones De anima* II q. 40 (ed. Bazán 464).

sensuum; igitur, etc.

[B. — Conclusio secunda]

Est etiam unus unitate actus qui est discernere inter album et dulce, quod est actus eius.[9] Sed dices quod licet eiusdem potentiae sit discernere album a dulci, alterius est discernere album a sono.[10] Contra: si alia potentia discerneret album a dulci quam illa quae discernit album a sono, tunc sequitur quod eadem ratione duae potentiae insubordinatae discernerent sive cognoscerent album, quia nulla potentia discernit aliqua, quae non cognoscit utrumque illorum.[11]

[C. — Conclusio tertia]

Est etiam sensus communis potentia una unitate organi.[12] Dicunt tamen ALIQUI[13] quod eius organum est unum unitate aggregationis tantum. Contra: cum sensus communis sit potentia organica, si organum eius esset unum aggregatione tantum, sequitur quod potentia esset una aggregatione tantum, et per consequens

---

1 sensuum *om.* K | igitur etc.] ergo etc. L FW Z ergo Q *om.* X   3 etiam unus] ergo unus Q *om.* X | actus] *add.* eius L | qui est] quia unus actus est (ant. unus X) K Q X | discernere] distinguere L K Q | inter — dulce] album a dulci NO FW K Q X Z   4 quod — dulci *om.* N | quod² *om.* L   5 dulci] *add.* tamen (ant. dulci O) O K FW Q X Z | alterius] alteri Z | est *om.* X   6 alia] aliqua alia H aliqua L X | discerneret] discernit Z | illa quae discernit] ista quae discernit Q quae discernit X *om.* Z   7 discernit] discerneret FW Q X | tunc *om.* L | sequitur] sequeretur L K Q X Z | eadem ratione] = N FW Q X Z eadem relatio O eaedem K *om.* HLM   8 insubordinatae] subordinatae K non subordinatae FW Q X Z | discernerent sive] discernerunt sive O *om.* K FW Q X Z | sive *om.* O | cognoscerent] cognoscere O   9 discernit] *add.* inter K FW Q X Z | cognoscit] cognoscat FW Q X Z noscit L | utrumque] quodlibet O K FW Z quolibet Q quam X   10 illorum] eorum O FW Q X Z *add.* ult. sed hoc (non K) est impossibile de duabus potentiis (*add.* scilicet K) non sub invicem ordinatis; igitur, (ergo FW Q Z *om.* X) etc. (et Z *om.* Q X) K FW Q X Z   12 etiam] enim N X autem L F | potentia una] inv. (ant. sensus FW X Z) K FW X Z unus HLM. Q | organi] ordinationis N HM coordinationis L ordinis(?) O | aliqui] alii F X quidam Z   14 tantum] *mg.* O ant. unitate K ant. unum FW Q X Z *om.* HLM | cum] si X | communis] *mg.* W² *om.* O K Q X Z   15 si] non X | eius *om.* K | aggregatione] unitate aggregationis H K | sequitur] sequeretur FW Q X Z   16 per *om.* F

[9]Cf. **Aristot.**, *De an.* II c. 27 (Γ c. 2, 426*b* 19-21); cf. **Thomas**, *De an.* II c. 27 (XLV¹ 183*b*); *Summa theol.* I q. 78 a. 4 arg. 2 (V 255*a*).
[10]Cf. **Aristot.**, *De an.* II c. 27 (Γ c. 2, 426*b* 17); **Thomas**, *De an.* II c. 27 (XLV¹ 183*b*).
[11]Cf. **Aristot.**, *De an.* II c. 27 (Γ c. 2, 426*b* 17-19); **Thomas**, *De an.* II c. 27 (XLV¹ 183*b*): "Posset enim aliquis credere quod discernamus album a dulci non quadam una potentia, sed diversis, ut scilicet in quantum gustu cognoscimus dulce et visu album; hoc autem excludit dicens quod non contingit discernere quod dulce sit alterum ab albo separatis potentiis …"
[12]Forsan legendum est "organizationis" pro "organi"; videsis lectiones variantes apud codices NO HLM.
[13]**Avicenna**, *De an.* pars 4 c. 1 (AviL 5); *De an.* pars 4 c.1 (AviL 8-9).

non esset distinctum a particularibus sensibus ex quibus aggregaretur, cuius contrarium est probatum.[14]

8 Dicendum est igitur quod organum eius est unum unitate naturae, non quidem simplicis, sed mixtae et quasi mediae inter naturas aliorum organorum. Sic enim se habet organum sensus communis ad alia ut centrum ad lineas procedentes ab eo ad circumferentiam,[15] vel ad ipsum terminatas quasi sit radix communis organorum sensuum particularium, et potentia sensus communis in eo exsistens est sicut rex sedens in solio,[16] iudicans de actibus particularium sensuum ad ipsum terminatorum repraesentantium sibi propria obiecta.

[D. — Ubinam sit organum sensus communis?]

9 Sed ubi est situatum illud organum? De hoc est controversia

---

1 non] *rep.* H | esset] *add.* simpliciter K FW Q X Z *add.* realiter Q | distinctum] distincta K FW Q X Z *add. seu rep.* simpliciter K | a particularibus sensibus] ab aliis sensibus particularibus K 2 aggregaretur] aggregatur N | est *post* probatum Q | probatum] praesentem F 3 est *om.* Q X Z | igitur] ergo FW Q Z *om.* K X | organum eius] *inv.* L Q | eius *om.* O | est² *om.* X 4 quidem] quae dicitur K *om.* Q | simplicis] simplicitatis N Q Z simplicitatis simplicis FW | sed] *add.* quasi K | mediae] medi*ante* X medio Z 5 Sic] Sicut F Si N | se habet] *inv.* N 6 ad alia *om.* HLM | ut] sicut Z | procedentes] praecedentes(?) K productas FW | ad³] *add.* cuius K 7 terminatas] terminum X | quasi sit] = NO quia sic (*om.* L) est HLM quod K quasi FW Q X Z | communis] *add.* omnium N M 8 organorum *post* particularium K *om.* Q | sensuum *om.* O K FW Q X Z 9 est sicut] *mg.* W sicut H est et sicut W 10 particularium sensuum] *inv.* K | sensuum *om.* X | repraesentantium] recipiens tantum N repraesentantia L 13 est situatum] situatur K | illud] idem H M hoc K | De hoc] Ibi HM *om.* L

[14] Cf. q. 9, n. 10-12.
[15] **Aristot.**, *De an.* II c. 27 (Γ c. 2, 427a 9-10): "Sed sicut quod vocant quidam punctum aut unum aut duo, sic et divisibile"; **Themistius**, *De an.* V (CLCAG I 198): "Sed illud utique magis rationabilius exsistimabit assimilari potentiam sensitivam puncto, magis autem centro circuli, ad quem omnes ex circumferentia lineae terminantur ..."; **Avicenna**, *De an.* pars 4 c. 1 (AviL 3): "... sicut videmus quod ei qui in circuitu volvitur videtur quicquid est in circuitu moveri ..."; **Averroës**, *De an.* II com. 149 (AverL 356): "Id est, sed ista virtus est una et multa ut punctus qui est centrum circuli quando ab eo fuerint extractae multae lineae a centro ad circumferentiam"; **Albertus M.**, *De an.* II tr. 4 c. 11 (VII 164a): "Per hoc autem quod ipsum substantialiter est medium circuli, est ipsum principium aequalitatis linearum protractarum ab ipso ad circumferentiam, et sic uno et unum et multa discernuntur"; **Thomas**, *De an.* II c. 27 (XLV¹ 185a): "Et solutio ista sumitur ex similitudine puncti; punctum enim quod est inter duas partes lineae potest accipi ut unum aut duo; ut unum quidem secundum quod continuat partes lineae ut communis terminus, ut duo autem secundum quod bis utimur puncto, scilicet ut principio unius lineae et ut fine alterius."; **Petrus Hispanus**, *Scientia libri De anima* tr. 7 c. 1 (ed. Alonso II 249): "Est enim virtus una ... est autem in essentia et radice una. ... Comparatur igitur centro circuli et puncto a quo multa lineae emanant et ad quem terminant ..."
[16] **Calcidius**, *Commentarius in Platonis Timaeum* CCXX (Plato Latinus IV 233): "Totaque anima sensus ... velut ramos ex principali parte illa tamquam trabe pandit futuros eorum quae sentiunt nuntios, ipsa de his quae nuntiaverint iudicat ut rex." Cf. Est. 5,1: "Ille sedebat super solium"; 3Rg. 22, 10: "Rex ... sedebat ... in solio suo"; Prv. 20, 8: "Rex qui sedet in solio iudicii."

Q. 10: UTRUM SENSUS COMMUNIS SIT UNUS VEL PLURES

inter medicos et philosophos.[17] Dicunt enim medici quod in capite,[18] quorum ratio est quia sensus communis accipit suam immutationem ex sensibus particularibus, et ideo debet esse situatum eius organum prope organa sensuum particularium; sed organa omnium sensuum particularium sunt in capite; igitur, etc.

[4] Item, expertum est quod per laesionem organi sensus communis laeditur phantasia, quod non esset verum nisi esset prope organum phantasiae, quod est in prima concavitate cerebri;[19] igitur, etc.

Oppositum huius vult PHILOSOPHUS in *De somno et vigilia*,[20] dicens quod primum sensitivum in corde est.

Item, alibi vult quod primum membrum animalis est ex corde,

---

1 philosophos] philosophi O | enim *om.* X | medici] *adnot. mg.* nota ubi medici situant sensum communem K | quod] *add.* est L   2 quia] quod X | suam *post* immutationem K *om.* Q   3 ex] a L K FW X | sensibus] *add.* et Z | debet *post* situatum K | esse *post* organum K   4 eius] *lin.* N illud Q | eius organum] *ant.* debet L | organa] organum K Z *add.* propter X | sensuum particularium] *inv.* O FW Q X Z   5 omnium *om.* K | sensuum *post* particularium Z | igitur etc.] ergo etc. L FW Z igitur Q *om.* X   6 Item] Praeterea NO K FW Q X Z | expertum] experimentum M | quod] propter F | per *om.* Z | organi *post* communis K *om.* Z   7 laeditur] laedatur X | phantasia] phantasma HM X phantasmata Q | verum *om.* F   8 quod] quae L | prima] ipsa N | igitur etc.] secundum Avicennam O K FW Q Z etc. secundum Avicennam X *om.* L   9 huius] eius L *om.* X | in *om.* X *adnot. mg.* nota ubi ponit Philosophus sensum communem K | in — alibi *om.* Z   10 dicens] dicit F *om.* K | sensitivum] sensuum Q | est] *ant.* in L K FW Q X   11 Item] Praeterea NO FW Q X Z | Item — corde *om.* K | vult] velit(?) Z | ex corde] cor O FW Q X Z

[17] **Aristot.** *De iuventute et senectute* III [c.2], (c. 2, 469a 12-13); *De sensu et sensato* [c. 2] (c. 2, 439a 1-5); cf. **Calcidius**, *Commentarius in Platonis Timaeum* CCXIV, CCXVIII-CCXXIV (Plato Latinus IV 220-239); **Thomas**, *De sensu* tr. 1 c. 4 (XLV² 31b—32b); *Ethic.* IV lect. 17 (XLVII² 260a); *Ethic.* VI lect. 6 (XLVII² 352a); **Alfredus Anglicus**, *De motu cordis*, c. 16 (BGPTH 23¹ 88); **Anonymus (Jacobus de Duaco?)**, *Quaestiones De anima* II q. 40 (ed. Bazán 464-465).

[18] **Galienus**, *Opera* I (ed. Lyon 1528, 224); **Hali ibn Abbas**, *Liber regalis disp.* (=*Pantegni*), a **Constantino Africano** translatus, ms. Paris B.N. lat. 14393, f. 17vb: "Virtutes sensibiles et voluntarium motum ... cerebrum facit:"; **Costa Ben Luca**, *De differentia animae et spiritus* c. 3 (ed. Barach et Wrobel 126); **Avicenna**, *De an.* pars 1 c. 5 (AviL 87); **Nemesius**, *De natura hominis* c. V, XI-XII (CLCAG Suppl. 1 72, 86-89); **Averroës**, *De an.* III com. 6 (AverL 415); **Thomas**, *Summa theol.* I q. 78 a. 4 in corp (V 256b): "... cui medici assignant determinatum organum, scilicet mediam partem capitis ..."; **Anonymus (Jacobus de Duaco?)**, *Quaestiones De anima* II q. 40 (ed. Bazán 465).

[19] **Avicenna**, *De an.* pars 1 c. 5 (AviL 87): "... quae est vis ordinata in prima concavitate cerebri, recipiens per seipsam omnes formas quae imprimuntur quinque sensibus"; *De an.* pars 3 c. 8 (AviL I 269): "... qui est repositus in primo ventriculo cerebri ..." *De an.* pars 4 c. 1 (AviL 8): "... cuius locus est anterior pars cerebri ..."; cf. **Ioannes Blund**, *Tractatus de anima* c. 17 (ed. Callus et Hunt 63): "Sed illa vis quae est ordinata in anteriori parte cerebri est sensus communis'; *Tractatus de anima* c. 17 (ABMA ed. Callus et Hunt 64): "... scilicet guttam cuius imago est illa impressio quae est in anteriori parte cerebri; et illa vis dicitur esse sensus communis"; **Albertus M.**, *De an.* II tr. 4 c. 11 (VII 163b): "".. ut in eis discurrat spiritus, qui est vehiculum virtutis sensitivae, diriguntur ad anteriorem cerebri partem ... et ibi est organum sensus communis"; **Ioannes Pecham**, *Tractatus de anima* c. 10 (ed. Melani 35): "... vis ordinata in prima concavitate cerebri ..."; **Anonymus (Jacobus de Duaco?)**, *Quaestiones De anima* II q. 40 (ed. Bazán 464): "Et per hoc vult quod prima pars cerebri ..."; **Petrus Hispanus**, *Scientia libri De anima* tr. 7 c. 1 (ed. Alonso 302): "Haec igitur virtus ortum aliis exhibens, in parte cerebri anteriori colocatur"; **Ioannes de Rupella**, *Summa de anima*, c. 97 (ed. Bougerol 240).

[20] *Auctoritates Aristotelis* (ed. J. Hamesse 202): "Cor est principium sensus et motus in animalibus"; cf. **Aristot.**, *De somno et vig.* [c.3] (c. 3, 456a 1-11).

et ideo residet ibi potentia sensitiva quae est sensus communis.[21]

13 Item, organum sensus communis est radix organi sensus tactus, qui se diffundit per totum corpus;[22] organum autem tactus contiguatur cordi; igitur organum sensus communis est in corde.[23]

14 Respondeo: potest dici quod sensus communis ab alio habet ortum, ab alio complementum, quia ortum habet a corde organum sensus communis, sicut et alia organa sensuum particularium.[24]

15 Imaginandum est igitur quod a corde ad cerebrum procedunt quaedam venae vel nervi,[25] in quibus originaliter continentur organa omnium sensuum, sed in cerebro faciunt conum; a cerebro autem procedunt quinque nervi ad organa exteriora, facientes basim; et sic organum sensus communis habet ortum a corde, sed in cerebro habet suum complementum. Et hoc videtur ad sensum ex hoc quod homo exsistens in navi mota iudicat res exteriores moveri, quae tamen sunt immobiles; hoc autem non est per sensus exteriores, ut probatum est supra,[26] nec per motum cordis, sed per motum capitis; igitur sensus communis, qui hoc iudicat, est in capite. Hoc etiam patet ex hoc quod homines dolent caput ex studio vehementi in

---

1 ideo *om.* LX | ibi] *ant.* residet L K FW Q X Z | quae] in quo X | est *post* sensus K | sensus *om.* Q 2 Item] Praeterea NO K FW Q X Z *add.* ult. est Z | organum *om.* X | communis K | sensus[2] *om.* O K FW Q X Z 3 qui] quae O | per] in K | totum] unum Z | corpus] *add. seu rep.* organum sensus communis X | autem] *add.* sensus Z | contiguatur] continuatur M *rasura* + iguatur Z 4 igitur] ergo L FW Q X Z | organum *post* communis K | est *post* corde H | corde] *add.* igitur etc. K 5 potest *post* dici K Q | ab — communis *om.* X | alio] aliquo K | habet *ant.* ab K FW Q Z 6 ortum] *add.* et L | complementum] *adnot. mg.*: nota quomodo doctor combinat philosophos et medicos simul K | ortum habet] *inv.* K | organum] organi Z | organum sensus communis] *ant.* habet K 7 et *om.* K X cum Z | alia] obiecta O X omnia FW Q alio Z | organa] organum Z 8 est *om.* Z | igitur] *ant.* est M ergo FW Z enim Q *om.* X | ad *om.* X | procedunt] procedens X 9 vel] non K FW Q et M *om.* X | originaliter] origi O 10 omnium *post* sensuum F | sensuum *om.* K | sed *om.* X | in *om.* Z | conum] unam H coitum FW Z sensum communem M rationem X | autem] enim N M *om.* K X 11 quinque *om.* F Z | facientes] *add.* talem K | basim] bassem F basem W has est X 12 organum *om.* N | habet ortum] *inv.* K FW Q X | a] in K FW Q X | in *om.* Z 13 suum] *ant.* habet F unum X | hoc] hic O sic X | videtur] patet K 14 iudicat] videat L dicit K 15 hoc autem non] sed aliter X | est *om.* N | per] propter M 16 supra] *add.* sed X | per[2]] propter K FW Q Z 17 igitur] ergo L FW Z | hoc] homo H hic O | capite] *add.* pars X | Hoc] Hic O 18 ex hoc *om.* K | dolent] dolentes FW Q X | ex[2] *om.* H | vehementi] excellenti NO K FX X Z excessivo Q

---

[21]**Thomas**, *Ethic.* IV lect. 17 (XLVII[2] 260*a*): "Sedes autem vitae est in corde."
[22]Cf. supra q. 1.
[23]Cf. **Aristot.** *De iuventute et senectute* III [c.2], (c. 2, 469a 12-13); *De partibus animalium* II (c. 10, 656b 22-26): "Omne animal habens cerebrum habent ipsum in anteriori capitis, quoniam ipsum est instrumentum sensus per quod sentitur in anteriori. Et iste sensus debet esse ex corde"; **Anonymus (Jacobus de Duaco?)**, *Quaestiones De anima* II q. 40 (ed. Bazán 464).
[24]Cf. **Thomas**, *Summa theol.* I q. 78 a. 4 ad 3 (V 256*b*).
[25]**Avicenna**, *De an.* pars 5 c. 8 (AviL 181): "Cor est principium primum et ab ipso emanant virtutes ad cerebrum, quarum quaedam ... emanant a cerebro ad alia membra ... De virtutibus autem cerebri, visus perficitur humore crystallideo ... olfactum autem fit a duobus caruncolis ... gustus vero fit a nervis cerebri pertingentibus ad linguam et palatum ... auditus etiam fit a nervis cerebri qui pertingunt ad cartilaginem ... tactus quoque a nervis cerebri et nuchalibus diffusis per totum corpus."
[26]Cf. n. 6.

quo vires sensitivae inferiores multum laborant, non autem ita sentiunt dolorem cordis.

[E. — Utrum obiectum sensus communis sit sensibile communis]

De obiecto autem sensus communis dicunt ALIQUI[27] quod est sensibile commune, quia omne sensibile per se est obiectum alicuius sensus; sensibile autem commune est sensibile per se; non autem est obiectum sensus proprii, quia excellens sensibile proprium corrumpit sensum; excellens autem sensibile commune, ut magnitudo vel figura, non corrumpit sensum proprium; ideo relinquitur quod sit obiectum sensus communis. 16

Contra: nullus sensus decipitur circa proprium obiectum;[28] sed sensus communis, magnitudine deficiente, cognoscit; igitur, etc. 17

Dicendum est igitur quod aliquod sensibile commune communitate praedicationis — non autem sensibile commune ut ait PHILOSOPHUS II *De anima*,[29] sicut magnitudo et figura — potest dici obiectum proprium sensus communis. Illud tamen est innominatum, et potest vocari sensibile in communi, sicut dictum fuit supra de obiecto tactus, quod potest dici tangibile in communi ad diversas qualitates sensibiles tangibiles,[30] quod non est 18

---

1 sensitivae inferiores] exteriores sensitivae K Q interiores sensitivae FW Z interiores sensitivus X | ita] ista N illa X *om.* K   4 autem — est²] *om.* Z | communis *om.* FW | dicunt aliqui] *inv.* H   5 commune — sensibile² *om.* X | per se] particulare FW *om.* K | obiectum] *add.* per se Q   6 commune] obiecto N | per se] *ant.* sensibile O K FW Q X Z | non] *rep.* H | non autem est] nam omne NO | non — sensibile *om.* F X *add. mg.* autem sensibile excellens F² | est² *om.* Z   7 sensus *om.* Z | quia *om.* NO | proprium *post* sensum Z   8 excellens] excens(!) O | autem *post* sensibile X   9 non — proprium] *ant.* ut Z | corrumpit] eorum potest(?) Z | sensum proprium] *inv.* K | ideo] igitur O K ergo (*post* relinquitur X) FW Q X Z   10 obiectum] oppositum O   11 Contra] Praeterea N | circa] *add.* suum Q | obiectum] oppositum O   12 magnitudine deficiente] = HM magnitudine definite N L magna definite O magis distincte K Q Z minus distincte FW magis X | igitur] ergo L FW Q Z *om.* X   13 est *om.* X Z | igitur] ergo FW Q Z *om.* X | aliquod *om.* FW   14 autem] *spat. vac.* M | sensibile *om.* Z | ait] accipit K FW Q X Z   15 et] vel M *om.* F X Z | figura] *add.* sed O *add.* etc. FW Q Z *add.* etc. sed Q X | dici] *add.* esse O W Q   16 obiectum proprium] *inv.* K | tamen est] quod non in X | innominatum] ignotum K   17 in communi *om.* X Z | sicut] ut N   18 obiecto] opposito O | quod] et FW Z etiam (*post* potest) K | tangibile] sensibile NO   19 sensibiles tangibiles] tangibiles FW Q X Z *om.* K | quod — nominatum] *ant.* ad K

[27]**Avicenna**, *De an.* pars 4 c. 1 (AviL 5-6); **Averroës**, *De an.* II com. 146 (AverL 351-2); cf. **Aegidius Romanus**, *De an.* II com. 135 (f. 57ra-rb).
[28]**Aristot.**, *De an.* II c. 13 (B c. 6, 418a 14-15); *Auctoritates Aristotelis* (ed. J. Hamesse 179): "Sensus non decipitur circa proprium obiectum."
[29]**Aristot.**, *De an.* II c. 25 (Γ c. 1 425a 14-20).
[30]**Aristot.**, *De an.* II c. 23 (B c. 11 424a 10-15).

nominatum.

[II. — Ad argumenta principalia]

19 Ad primum in oppositum[31] dicendum ad minorem quod COMMENTATOR intelligit per ea "plura instrumenta" loqui de organis sensuum particularium, quae sunt continuata organo sensus communis et sunt eius instrumenta in nuntiando sibi immutationes sensuum particularium; non autem loquitur de organo sensus communis nisi quod est unum formaliter, licet sit plura instrumentaliter, ratione praedicta. Et haec est intentio COMMENTATORIS[32] dicentis quod est receptivus a sensibus particularibus, tamen est agens in iudicando de actibus et obiectis eorum. Ad improbationem dicendum quod sicut in organo olfactus alicuius animalis dominatur aer, sicut animalis viventis in aere, in organo autem olfactus piscis dominatur aqua, quia odor sentitur per utrumque. Est autem aliquod animal quod odorat et per aquam et per aerem, et per consequens habet organum proportionatum utrique. Ita organum sensus communis, cum sit radix aliorum, est continens virtualiter omnia organa secundum suam complexionem; est tamen formaliter determinatae complexionis et distinctae a praedictis.

20 Ad aliud,[33] dicendum quod non est inconveniens idem esse in

---

3 primum] primam Z | dicendum] add. est M   4 intelligit om. L | per] quod K | ea] illa sunt K illa FW Q X Z | instrumenta] mysteria(?) Z | loqui] loquendo M K   5 sunt post continuata K | continuata] contiguata L   6 et] ut K FW Q X Z | sunt om. Q | eius om. K | in nuntiando] in (om. Q) immutando N Q ministrando FW   7 sensuum] ministrando FW sensibilium W X Z om. N | particularium] propriorum NO K Q Z particularium propriorum FW priorum X   8 nisi om. O K FW Q X Z | est post est HM mg. W | unum om. Q | sit] sint Q X   9 instrumentaliter om. K | haec] hoc W X Z 10 est post receptivus M | receptivus] receptis N receptus O Q receptum K add. ult. scilicet K 11 tamen] add. non Z | in om. HLM | iudicando] iudicans M | et] add. de Q   12 eorum] ant. et HLM add. etc. X | Ad] add. (mg.) minoris M | improbationem] probationem F add. eorum X | sicut] si Q   13 alicuius animalis] inv. LM | animalis] mg. W | aer] ager Q | viventis] inventis Z   14 autem om. Z | olfactus] olfactos Z | odor] ordor(!) O   15 quod] add. est O | et om. L K X | aquam ... aerem] aerem ... aquam L   16 habet] habens Z   17 utrique om. L | communis om. Z | cum] et X | sit post aliorum H | est continens] rep. K   18 continens virtualiter] sensitivum immo N contius(!) immo O inv. Z | omnia] add. alia HL | complexionem] add. et K   19 tamen om. K | determinatae] determinato Z | complexionis om. L | et om. K W X Z | a praedictis] ab aliis L   21 dicendum] add. est M | non om. H | est om. Q | esse] est M

[31]Cf. supra n. 1.
[32]**Averroës**, *De an.* II com. 148 (AverL 355, ll. 20-25): "Necesse est ut ista virtus non recipiat formas sensibilium contrarias, si ista virtus eadem, scilicet sensitiva, est talis, scilicet unica in subiecto et plures in essentia. Et dixit 'et intelligere' quia intelligere in hac intentione simile est ad sentire, scilicet quia in utroque est virtus recipiens et iudicans, et haec iudicat contraria insimul."
[33]Cf. supra n. 2.

actu accidentali per multa exsistentia in actu; sicut est de sensu respectu obiectorum.

Contra: omnes sensus proprii possunt simul sentire sua sensibilia; sed sensus communis simul immutatur cum sensibus propriis; igitur potest simul sentire omnia sensibilia, quod videtur impossibile.

Dicendum quod sensus communis, dato quod simul sentiat omnia sensibilia, non tamen aeque perfecte sed perfectius sentit illud a quo perfectius immutatur, et hoc non est inconveniens, ut dictum est supra.[34]

Sed dices quod possibile est quod quilibet sensus proprius perfectissime immutetur a suo obiecto, et sic sensus communis perfectissime omnia obiecta sentiet simul.

Dicendum quod non est possibile quod visus ita perfecte immutetur a colore sicut potest, quando simul auditus immutatur perfecte a sono, nec e converso, propter magnam attentionem animae in una perfecta immutatione, et ideo non potest ita perfecte attendere in alia. Et dato quod perfectissime sicut possunt, immutarentur simul a sensibilibus propriis, quia tamen unum sensibile de ratione sua nobilius et fortius imprimit suam speciem quam aliud, sicut color et alii quam sonus, ideo sensus communis perfectius immutatur ab illo quam ab aliis.

---

1 accidentali] actuali K | exsistentia] extrinseca ex natura FW om. X | sicut] sic NO | est om. H | sensu] add. communi HL Q 3 Contra] praem. Ad aliud Q | proprii] ipsi Z 4 sed — sensibilia om. Z | simul post immutatur X | sensibus] sensibilibus N 5 igitur] ergo L FW Q X | simul post sentire FW X om. NO K | omnia] obiecta K add. illa K 7 Dicendum] add. est M | dato] datur Z | simul om. K 8 omnia] obiecta K | non tamen om. Q Z | perfecte om. K 9 illud] id Z | a quo] quod N | perfectius immutatur] immutatur perfectus K | immutatur] immutat N add. ult. cum sensibilibus propriis N | hoc om. K | est om. Q 10 est] fuit O FW Q X Z 11 quod] quem X | quod²] ut Q | quilibet] quidlibet W 12 immutetur — perfectissime om. K 13 omnia — simul] = M obiecta sentiet simul NO alia sentiet simul H sentiat simul L sentit sua obiecta simul K sentiet omnia simul FW Z sentiet omnia sensibilia simul Q sentit simul communia X 14 Dicendum] add. est M | visus] sensus O" corr. in mg. O | ita] aeque L om. X 15 a colore om. W" add. mg. (vide infra) W² | a — perfecte om. X | sicut potest] = N HM sicut potest immutari (ant. a) O K FW Q Z sicut potest quando auditus non immutatur (post sono) L | quando] quam Z | quando — sono] a colore quando simul auditus immutatur perfecte a sono (mg.) W² | simul post auditus HLM | immutatur post perfecte K 16 attentionem] intentionem Z 17 ideo] lin. H ita M | non om. X | ita om. K 18 possunt] posset NO possent LM | immutarentur] immutaretur NO immutare K add. ult. utrumque K | simul om. Z 19 sensibilibus propriis] inv. K sensibus propriis O HL 20 nobilius et] nominabilius et Z om. X | fortius] perfectius K Q | suam speciem] inv. K X | quam aliud om. X Z | aliud] alius Q | sicut] quia HLM | et alii om. Z | et — quam] et aliquando W" sed exp. et restit. mg. W² 21 alii quam om. K | quam] quod O | ideo] igitur X | ab] in O Q

[34] Cf. q. 9 n. 10.

25 Ad aliud,[35] dicendum quod plus requiritur ad diversitatem sensus superioris quam inferioris, quia superius est quasi ligamentum sensibus propriis; unde, licet proprius non sit cognitivus proprie nisi unius contrarietatis, sensus tamen communis potest esse respectu plurium contrarietatum.

26 De ordine autem actuum sensus communis potest dici sic: primus actus eius est reflexio super actum sensus[36] particularis, quia ab illo actu immediate immutatur sensus communis.

27 Secundus est iudicare de obiecto sensus proprii secundum se et absolute, non tantum unius, sed cuiuslibet sensus, et istum actum attribuit sibi AVICENNA, licet non PHILOSOPHUS.[37]

28 Tertius actus eius est cognoscere differentiam plurium sensibilium propriorum ad invicem, et ille actus sequitur alium: prius enim est cognoscere aliquid secundum se quam cognoscere ut differens ab aliis, quia impossibile est cognoscere differentiam aliquorum nisi cognitis extremis.

---

1 dicendum *om.* X *add.* est M | plus] plura X | diversitatem] diversificationem NO Z diversionem Q veritatem X 2 sensus] potentiae K FW Q X Z ieo-e(?) O | superioris] superiori Z | quam inferioris *om.* N | quasi — unde] communius K FW Q X Z | ligamentum] ligatum N signa O 3 unde — proprius *om.* O | licet] *add.* ergo (igitur K *om.* L) sensus L K FW Q X Z | cognitivus] cognoscitivus W Q X Z 4 proprie *om.* L | proprie — contrarietatum *om.* X | sensus — potest] potest tamen K FW Q Z | esse *om.* Z 5 respectu] *lin.* H | contrarietatum] cognitionum NO K cognitivus F cognoscitivus Q W Z *add. ult.* plurium Z 6 ordine] organo Z | autem *om.* N | communis *om.* K | potest dici sic] potest sic dici quod K FW X Z sic dici potest quod Q | sic] *add.* quod O 7 actus *post* eius K | eius *om.* L | reflexio] reflexivus K FW Q Z | ab] sub L 8 illo] isto O | sensus communis *om.* KU 9 Secundus] Etiam FW Sensus communis Q *om.* X *add.* actus KU | *om.* Z *add.* etiam Q *add.* tunc X | de obiecto *om.* X | obiecto] opposito O aliis KU | sensus proprii] sensibus propriis KU 10 sed] secundum X | istum] illum HL K F Q Z 11 Avicenna] ad invicem NO | licet *om.* L | Philosophus *om.* NO 12 Tertius] Cuius K | actus eius] *inv.* NO | eius *post* est Q | cognoscere] ponere (*mg.*) F² | plurium *om.* L 13 sensibilium] sensuum KU | ad invicem *om.* Z | ille] iste LM KU X 14 prius enim] cum prius HL praesens(!) enim Z | cognoscere²] *add. (lin.)* ipsum W² | ut] ipsum non F secundum quod X 15 differens] *mg.* O | est *om.* Q | differentiam *post* aliquorum X 16 nisi] non O FW Q X Z | extremis] *add.* ut patet igitur etc. M *add.* igitur etc. HL Q *add.* etc. X

---

[35]Cf. supra n. 3.
[36]Hic resumit codex U.
[37]Cf. **Aristot.** *De an.* II c. 25 (Γ c. 2, 425a 2-5); **Avicenna**, *De an.* pars 4 c. 1 (AviL 7-8).

[QUAESTIO 11]

UTRUM CORPORA CAELESTIA POSSINT AGERE IN INTELLECTUM VEL VOLUNTATEM NOSTRAM

Utrum[1] corpora caelestia possunt agere in intellectum vel voluntatem nostram.

[1] Videtur quod sic: 1

Astrologi praedicunt multa vera de agibilibus ab homine quae dependent a voluntate et intellectu;[2] hoc autem non est nisi quia cognoscunt virtutes corporum caelestium; igitur, etc.

Item, corpora caelestia possunt movere phantasmata nostra; ipsa 2 autem possunt movere intellectum sicut sensibilia sensum, secundum PHILOSOPHUM;[3] igitur, a primo ad ultimum, saltem mediate possunt corpora caelestia movere intellectum nostrum.

Item, de voluntate probatur sic: si non possunt movere voluntatem, hoc esset specialiter propter libertatem quae tolleretur in tali 3 motu; sed non propter hoc tolleretur; igitur, etc.[4]

Probatio minoris: quando duo actus sunt eiusdem rationis, si

---

4 Utrum] *praem.* Quaeritur N KU FW Q X Z An Q *adnot. mg.* Quaestio septima M | possunt agere] possint agere M FW Q agant (*lin.*) N *om.* Z | in] *mg.* F *lin.* W 5 nostram] nostrum (ant. vel) NO FW Q Z unum (ant. vel) X 6 sic] *add.* nam KU 7 praedicunt] dicunt FW Z praedicant U | vera] vere L Q | agibilibus] agendis X 8 dependent] dependet Z | a — intellectu] ex (ab KU) intellectu et voluntate O KU FW Q X Z | autem *om.* L | est] esset K Z | quia *om.* Z 9 cognoscunt] agnoscunt Z | virtutes *om.* L | caelestium] *add.* actum L | igitur] *rep.* Z ergo L FW Z *om.* N Q X | etc. *om.* K Q 10 Item] Praeterea NO KU FW Q X Z 11 intellectum] *add.* nostrum X | sicut] *add. seu rep.* sicut U | sensibilia] sensibile X | sensum *om.* Z | secundum Philosophum *om.* X 12 igitur] ergo L FW Q X Z | a] de FW 13 corpora caelestia *om.* HLM U | nostrum *om.* X *add.* etc. K 14 Item] Praeterea NO KU FW Q X Z | voluntate] *add.* hic O *add.* hoc KU FW X Z | probatur] probo M *om.* HL | sic] haec N licet(?) O | possunt] possent O W Q X posset KU Z 15 tolleretur] tolleratur F 16 non *om.* Q | tolleretur] tolleratur F | igitur] ergo L FW Q Z *om.* X 17 Probatio minoris] Probo minorem O Q Minor probatur X Probatur H Probo L | quando *om.* NO | si] sed O

---

[1] Cf. **Thomas**, *De an.* II c. 28 (XLV[1] 188b—189a); **Petrus de Trabibus**, *Quodl.* I q. 14 (ed. Simoncioli 230-232); **Matthaeus ab Aquasparta**, *Quaest. disp. de providentia* q. 5 (BFS XVII, ed. Gál 337-364).

[2] **Thomas**, *Summa theol.* I q. 115 a. 4 arg. 3 (V 544a): "Item, astrologi frequenter vera annuntiant de eventibus bellorum, et aliis humanis actibus, quorum principia sunt intellectus et voluntas"; cf. *Summa theol.* I-II q. 9 a. 5 arg. 3 (VI 80a); *Sent.* II d. 15 q. 1 a. 3 arg. 4 (VI[2] 515b); *De an.* c. 28 (XLV[1] 188b).

[3] **Aristot.**, *De an.* II c. 28 (Γ c. 3, 427a 25-26); cf. **Averroës**, *De an.* III com. 4 (AverL 384): "Anima rationalis indiget considerare intentiones quae sunt in virtute imaginativa, sicut sensus indiget inspicere sensibilia."

[4] Cf. **Thomas**, *Summa theol.* I-II q. 9 a. 5 arg. 2 (VI 80a); **Augustinus**, *De Trinitate* III c. 4 (CCL 50 135; PL 42 873).

unus est liber, et alius, quia liberum et non-liberum specie et ratione specifica differunt; sed si actus voluntatis esset a corpore caelesti movente voluntatem, esset eiusdem speciei et rationis cum illo qui est tantum a voluntate, quia esset actus eiusdem potentiae immediate et respectu eiusdem obiecti, et haec duo concurrunt ad unitatem specificam actus;[5] tamen certum est quod actus voluntatis tantum est liber; igitur actus voluntatis motae a corpore caelesti esset liber.

4   Item, idem est dilectio et delectatio; sed delectatio est a corpore caelesti; igitur et dilectio quae est actus voluntatis. Probatio maioris: quia utraque est eiusdem potentiae et respectu eiusdem obiecti, scilicet boni vel convenientis.[6]

5   Item, illi actus sunt idem, qui immediate ab eadem causa causantur; sed isti sunt huiusmodi, quia causantur ab apprehensione boni convenientis secundum quod huiusmodi; igitur, etc.

6   Oppositum praedictorum vult PHILOSOPHUS.[7]

[I. — Ad quaestionem
A. — Status quaestionis]

7   Dicendum quod si sola phantasmata moverent intellectum et voluntatem et per consequens, ita quod intellectus et voluntas

---

1 est] sit K | alius] add. (mg.) non F | non-liberum] liberum X | specie et ratione] ratione et specie H specie Z   2 specifica om. H Q | si om. X | a] in Z   3 movente] moventi L | voluntatem] voluntate N | esset post rationis O | speciei et rationis] rationis et speciei NO M FW Q X Z | illo] isto O | qui] consequens X   4 esset om. Z | actus om. KU F   5 et om. L add. est Z | et²] quia HL | unitatem post specificam X   6 actus] alicuius N | tamen] add. tantum X | tantum post liber KU nostrae HLM | tantum — voluntatis om. N   7 igitur] ergo L FW Q X Z add. ult. et KU FW Q X Z add. ult. seu rep. actus voluntatis tantum est liber ergo et Z | motae] motus Z | a om. X | caelesti] add. tantum X | esset] est L X erit KU | liber²] add. ergo et actus X   8 Item] Praeterea NO KU FW Q X Z | est] lin. U om. X | et — dilectio om. X | sed delectatio om. Z | delectatio²] dilectio N   9 igitur] ergo L FW Q Z | dilectio] delectatio N | quae] qui O | Probatio maioris] Probo maiorem O Q Maior probatur X   10 utraque] uterque actus (om. O) O KU FW Q X Z | est] esset Z om. O   11 vel] = N et HM ut O FW Q X Z om. L KU   12 Item] Praeterea NO KU FW Q X Z | illi] isti KU | qui] quae N   13 isti] ista L add. actus X | quia] qui H | causantur²] causant X | ab] add. eadem KU   14 convenientis] inconvenientis X | secundum quod] inquantum O KU FW X in quibus Q in quolibet Z | igitur etc.] ergo etc. L FW Z ergo Q etc. X om. K   15 Oppositum] praem. Cuius KU | praedictorum] illorum H horum Q om. K | vult om. Q   18 Dicendum] add. est M | phantasmata moverent] phantasmata movent FW phantasia moveret M KU Q X Z   19 et om. K Q X Z | ita] lin. K | quod] et (lin. K) KU

[5]Cf. **Thomas**, *Summa theol.* I-II q. 9 a. 5 arg. 1 (VI 80a); cf. **Aristot.**, *Physica* VIII c. 9 (AL VII¹ 330-331; T c. 9, 265a 22-28); **Thomas**, *Physic.* VIII lect. 19 (XVIII 524ab); *Sent.* II d. 15 q. 1 a. 3 arg. 2 (VI² 515b); *Summa contra gent.* III c. 84 (XIV 248a).
[6]Cf. **Aristot.**, *Eth. Nic.* VII c. 3 (AL XXVI³ 497-8; Z c. 3, 1146b 9-24); *De an.* III c. 28 (Γ c. 3 427b 8-13); **Thomas**, *Summa contra gent.* III c. 85 (XIV 254ab).
[7]**Aristot.**, *De an.* II c. 28 (Γ c. 3, 427b 6-27).

essent potentiae pure passivae, nec moverent seipsas ad actus suos, sequeretur quod corpora caelestia possunt illas potentias directe movere.

Probatio: omne corpus corruptibile movet de necessitate in virtute corporis incorruptibilis, quod est superius (licet posset esse motus corporis inferioris sine superiori, non tamen diuturnus,[8] secundum omnes); sed organum phantasiae est corpus corruptibile et phantasia est potentia organica; igitur, si ipsa sola movet intellectum et non intellectus seipsum et intellectus sic motus movet voluntatem, sequitur directe quod corpus caeleste, in cuius virtute movet, possit utrumque movere, licet mediante phantasmate — et tunc sequitur ulterius quod mala phantasia de necessitate causabit malam voluntatem.

[3] Sed dices quod in potestate voluntatis est causare et formare bonam vel malam phantasiam, et per consequens, licet mala phantasia sic formata moveat voluntatem ad bonum vel ad malum, tamen totum erit voluntarium ratione primae voluntatis phantasiam formantis.[9]

Contra illum circuitum, circa quem impii ambulant,[10] arguitur sic: illud quod movet, motum ab alio tantummodo, movet de

---

1 potentiae pure] inv. KU FW Q X Z | nec] ut N X Z | moverent] moveretur X movent Z | seipsas] seipsos L de ipsas Z | suos] add. tunc Q 2 caelestia om. O | possunt] possent O L K FW Q Z | illas] istas K | directe] ant. illas HL directione (ant. illas) M 4 Probatio] Probo HL U Q X | corruptibile] incorruptibile X | movet] movetur FW 5 superius] add. et KU FW Q X Z | posset] possit O H FW X 6 inferioris] interioris Z | non] ut X | non — omnes] tamen non diu duraret (mg.) U² om. K | tamen] eam(?) X cum Z | diuturnus] diurnus H 7 phantasiae] phantasmate X | est] et X 8 phantasia] phanccus(!) O | est om. KU FW Q X Z | igitur] ergo L FW Q X Z | sola om. KU FW Q X Z 9 et] etiam U | et — seipsum] mg. W | intellectus] intelliget KU Z intelligat FW | seipsum] seipsam FW | intellectus² om. X | movet] mg. U² moveat LM movente X om. O FW Z 10 directe quod] = HLM inv. NO KU FW Q X Z | corpus caeleste] actio sicut X | caeleste] add. directe HM | in — movet om. Z 11 movet om. X | possit] posset HLM | phantasmate] phantasia KU FW Q X Z 12 tunc] sic N KU FW Q X Z | causabit] ant. de K 14 dices] dicit H dicis L | est] ant. voluntatis X | causare et formare] causare vel formare L formare O KU FW Q Z causare X 15 vel] et H U | mala om. KU FW Q X Z | phantasia post formata Q 16 voluntatem — malum] ad bonam voluntatem et malam Q | vel] et NO U FW X Z | ad² om. X 17 totum] non (ant. tamen) Z | voluntarium] bonum Q | phantasiam] add. sic Q 18 formantis] informantis HLM 19 Contra] praem. Sed K | illum] istum W Q X | illum circuitum] illud (istud U) scilicet circulum KU | circa] contra X | quem] quod O Z | arguitur] incursit(?) Z 20 sic] ant. arguitur (mg.) X om. Z | movet om. NO | alio] aliquo N | tantummodo] termino(?) Q | de] ex L

---

[8]**Thomas**, *De an.* II c. 28 (XLV¹ 188*b*—189*a*: "Virtus autem solis est in die, quia in die nobis apparet ... unde et ab astrologis dicitur planeta diurnus."
[9]**Aristot.**, *Eth. Nic.* III c. 5 (AL XXVI⁴ 419-420; Γ c. 5, 1114*a* 32—1114*b* 17).
[10]Cf. Ps. 11, 8: "Tu, Domine, servabis nos et custodies nos a generatione hac in aeternum. In circuitu impii ambulant cum exaltantur sordes inter filios hominum."

necessitate, si[11] moveatur de necessitate; sed voluntas movet phantasiam ad phantasiandum bonum vel malum, quae voluntas movetur tantum ab intellectu vel phantasmate — alio[12] enim movente de necessitate, cum non sit liberum (non enim est in potestate nostra quibus visis tangamur, secundum AUGUSTINUM[13]); igitur voluntas movebit phantasiam de necessitate ad phantasiandum bonum vel malum.

[B. — Solutio quaestionis]

10 Dicendum est igitur ad quaestionem quod corpora caelestia non possunt movere intellectum nostrum nec voluntatem directe, quia pure corporale non potest agere directe in pure spirituale, eo quod agens est nobilius patiente; intellectus autem et voluntas sunt virtutes pure spirituales; igitur corpora caelestia non possunt in eas directe agere.[14]

11 Praeterea, secundum praedicta potest sic probari propositum: corpora caelestia non possunt immediate agere in animam nostram, cum sint ei improportionata, sed mediante phantasmate tantum,

---

1 si — necessitate *om.* KU | moveatur] movetur H FW Q X Z | de] ex Z | voluntas — phantasiandum] = *coni.* cum L voluntas movet phantasiam ad faciendum KU phantasma movet voluntatem ad faciendum H voluntas movet voluntatem ad phantasiandum O M FW Q X Z intellectus movet voluntatem ad phantasiandum N   2 vel] et FW | voluntas *om.* Z | voluntas — tantum] bonitas tantum NO voluntate tantum movens movetur L   3 tantum *om.* H | vel] et M X sed U nostro Z | phantasmate] *add. mg.* scilicet corpore caelesti L *add. seu rep.* vel phantasmate O | enim] eam (*ant.* alio U) KU *om.* H | movente] manente Z   4 de necessitate] *ant.* voluntatem Q | de — liberum] igitur sequitur quod non erit libera KU | non²] sed NO | enim *om.* N | est] erit KU | potestate nostra] libertate nostra vel potestate KU   5 quibus — Augustinum *om.* KU | visis] visum X | tangamur] tangamus N HL tangemur X | Augustinum] alios N | igitur] ergo L FW Q X ideo Z   6 voluntas] *add.* nostra N | phantasiam *post* necessitate KU FW | phantasiandum] facendum H K   7 vel] *rep.* W   9 est igitur] *inv.* X igitur N K Z | igitur *post* quaestionem K ergo FW Q X   10 nec] et X neque Z | directe] *ant.* movere KU FW Q Z *om.* X   11 pure *om.* FW X | corporale] *mg.* W corporales U | potest] possunt K | agere directe] *inv.* Q Z | pure² *om.* KU FW Q X Z   12 est nobilius] *inv.* HL | intellectus] *praem.* ergo X   13 igitur] ergo FW Q X ideo Z | in *om.* X | in — possunt *om.* HL | eas] eis F   14 directe] *ant.* in Z   15 Praeterea] Item M | secundum praedicta *post* sic FW | sic *om.* Z | probari propositum] arguitur(!) Q | propositum] *add.* quod Z   17 improportionata] improportionabilia HLM

[11]Subaudi: aliud
[12]Subaudi: phantasmate
[13]**Augustinus**, *De libero arbitrio* III c. 25 (CCL 29 319, PL 32 1307): "... sed quo viso tangatur nulla potestas est, fatendum est et ex superioribus et ex inferioribus visis animum tangi ut rationalis substantia ex utroque sumat quod voluerit et ex merito sumendi vel miseria vel beatitas subsequatur."
[14]**Thomas**, *De an.* II c. 28 (XLV¹ 188*ab*); *Summa theol.* I q. 115 a. 4 in corp. (V 544*a*); *Summa theol.* I-II q. 9 a. 5 in corp. (VI 80*a*—81*b*); *Sent.* II d. 15 q. 1 a. 3 in corp. (VI² 515*b*); *Summa contra gent.* III c. 84 (XIV 249*b*); *Summa contra gent.* III c. 85 (XIV 254*a*—255*a*).

quod est obiectum animae repraesentativum. Sed phantasma nostrum non potest sufficienter movere intellectum nostrum vel voluntatem, quia praesente phantasmate, adhuc oportet obiectum intellectus ibi exsistens abstrahi antequam intelligatur, quod fiet per conversionem primam intellectus ad phantasma, quae conversio imperatur a voluntate et elicitur ab intellectu agente — praesente enim obiecto intellectui, et ipso praesentato voluntati, potest idem velle vel nolle propter suam ingenitam libertatem. Igitur corpora caelestia non possunt sufficienter et directe agere in intellectum nostrum vel voluntatem.

[II. — Ad argumenta principalia]

Ad primum in oppositum[15] dicendum quod si astrologi, ut in pluribus, verum dicunt, hoc ideo accidit quia homines, ut in pluribus, sequuntur suas phantasias et passiones in quae possunt directe agere corpora caelestia; tamen hoc non est necessarium — immo homines virtuosi sequentes iudicium rationis reprimunt huiusmodi passiones. Unde dicit PTOLEMAEUS in *Almagesti*,[16] quod sapiens dominatur astris, id est, dispositioni causatae a corporibus caelestibus, et hoc per libertatem arbitrii et rectum iudicium rationis passiones refraenantis.

---

1 obiectum] oppositum O | animae *om.* Z | repraesentativum] repraesentatum K repraesentata tantum Z | phantasma nostrum] phantasia nostra O FW Q Z phantasia KU phantasmata nostri X 2 potest] possunt X | nostrum² *om.* KU FW Q X Z | vel] *lin.* X et KU nec F Q Z 4 ibi] ibidem N | exsistens] assistens FW Q X Z | abstrahi] abstrahere NO K FW Q X Z abstrahetur U | intelligatur] intelligitur H KU intelligat Z | fiet] fit K FW Q X Z fuit O sic U 5 phantasma] phantasmata O KU FW Q X Z 7 enim] etiam O KU FW Q X Z | obiecto] opposito O | ipso *add. lin.* scilicet obiecto L | praesentato] praesente Z | idem] illud O KU FW Q X Z 8 propter] per F *om.* U X | suam *om.* X | ingenitam] = *coni. cum* M Q augmentatam NO HL FW X Z *om.* KU *add. ult. mg.* id est ingenitam vel innatam L | Igitur] Ideo HLM Ergo FW Q X 9 et *om.* O | in *om.* Z 10 nostrum vel] et O KU FW Q X Z | voluntatem] *add.* Contra, tunc actus voluntatis praecederet actus intellectus Q X 12 oppositum] obiectum(!) X | dicendum] *add.* est M F | si *om.* FW X Z 13 verum *post* dicunt Q vera KU | dicunt] dicant L | ideo] enim L | accidit *om.* X | quia] quod X 14 sequuntur] sequentur U | suas *om.* X | et passiones *om.* FW Z | quae] quas FW 15 agere *om.* M F X | caelestia *om.* X | tamen] cum Z | est] *add.* verum Q 16 homines] haec O *om.* K | iudicium] iudicia KU | huiusmodi] suas L 17 Ptolemaeus] Porphyrius Q | in] *rep.* F | Almagesti] Almegestis N Almagesto KU alium Q | sapiens] *add.* homo Q 18 dominatur] dominabitur KU Z | id est] et N *om.* X | dispositioni] dispositiones F | a] in X 19 hoc] huiusmodi Q | rectum iudicium rationis] recti iudicii ratione (ratio U) KU 20 passiones] passionis U | refraenantis] resolventis N resotis(?) O refraenantes Z

[15]Cf. supra n. 1.
[16]**Ptolemaeus**, *Almagestum* dictio 5; cf. **Thomas**, *Summa theol.* I q. 115 a. 4 ad 3 (V 544*b*): "Unde et ipsi astrologi dicunt quod 'sapiens homo dominatur astris', inquantum scilicet dominatur suis passionibus"; *Summa theol.* I-II q. 9 a. 5 (VI 81*b*): "Sed tamen ut Ptolomaeus dicit in Centiloquio, 'sapiens dominatur astris': scilicet quia, resistens passionibus, impedit per voluntatem liberam, et nequaquam motui caelesti subiectam, huiusmodi corporum caelestium effectus."

13 Ad aliud[17] dicitur quod phantasia proprie non movet intellectum, nec aliquid in ipso imprimit, sed tantum repraesentat sibi obiectum. Quo praesente, intellectus ex virtute sua activa elicit actum suum, sicut praesente sensibili sensus elicit actum sentiendi, et in hoc est convenientia, non quia phantasmata sunt obiectum intellectus, sicut sensibilia sensus (quae imprimunt, secundum ALIQUOS, speciem sensibilem in sensu); tamen requiritur phantasma ad intelligendum obiectum, quia sicut quidditas absoluta vel universale, quod est directum obiectum intellectus, non habet esse extra nisi in singulari, ut homo in Socrate, ita non potest repraesentari intellectui secundum speciem intelligibilem pro statu viae nisi in repraesentatione similitudinis ipsius singularis, quod fuit in phantasmate.[18]

14 Ad aliud[19] dicendum, concedendo, quod si voluntas moveretur a corpore caelesti, sicut posset moveri a Spiritu Sancto, quod actus eius esset eiusdem rationis cum actu a voluntate tantum elicito, quia quod potest causa prima mediante secunda, illud idem et eiusdem rationis potest sine secunda.[20] Et ideo si voluntas potest elicere actum volendi, cum sit causa secunda, actum eiusdem rationis potest elicere Spiritus Sanctus qui est causa prima; et si corpus

---

1 aliud dicitur] aliud dicendum O F secundum dicendum KU W Q X Z *add.* ult. est F | phantasia] *adnot. mg.* phantasma M | proprie non] *inv.* KU | movet] *add.* nec Z 2 nec] neque Z | ipso] ipsa L ipsum Q | imprimit] in primis Z | repraesentat] praesentat FW Q X parcas(!) Z 3 sibi *om.* KU | elicit] eligit O 4 actum *post* suum Z | sensibili] sensibile U | sensus — actum] actus elicitur Z | sentiendi] eliciendi Q Z 5 et] etiam (*post hoc*) KU *om.* X | non *post* phantasmata NO nam X | quia] qui X | sunt] sint O FW Q X Z | obiectum] obiecta K oppositum O 6 sicut] *add.* sunt KU | sensibilia] sensibilius(?) F *add.* et X | quae] qui F X | imprimunt] imprimit F K | secundum aliquos *om.* FW 7 speciem] species K | sensu] sensum L Q | phantasma] phantasia N X 8 obiectum] *add.* oppositum O | sicut] sic F *adnot. mg.* ecce quia sicut M² | quidditas] quantitas NO | vel] et U in Z 9 est *om.* Q | directum] dictum N du tantum(!) O 10 potest *om.* X 11 intellectui] intra KU in (*lin.*) intellectu W | secundum] sed F 12 repraesentatione] *spat. vac.* + praesentatione L praesentatione NO FW Q X Z | singularis] singularitatis O X | fuit] fit FW Q X Z sit KU 14 aliud] tertium Q | dicendum *om.* FW X | concedendo] concedo O L FW Q X *om.* N | moveretur] movetur Q 15 posset] potest H possit X | quod] quia X 16 eius] *lin.* L est Z | eiusdem] *add.* speciei et Q | rationis *om.* Z | actu] *add.* tantum U | tantum *ant. a* Z *om.* Q | elicito] elicite U elicitatur Q elicita X 17 causa *post* prima L | prima] *add. seu rep. mediante* causa prima O | mediante] *add.* causa NO M | illud] et hoc L | idem *om.* Z | et] vel KU FW Q X Z *add.* ult. aliquid K 18 rationis] *spat. vac.* O | sine — potest² *om.* H | si *om.* K | potest²] posset L | potest — rationis *om.* X | elicere — volendi] volendi actum elicere Q 20 Spiritus Sanctus] = LM (Spiritus *mg.* M) U Q Spiritus O K specie N H alia scilicet FW ibi scilicet X Z | qui] = LM KU X Z quae NO H FW | qui — prima] prima scilicet (*ant.* Spiritus) Q | causa] cum Z

[17]Cf. supra n. 2.
[18]Cf. **Aristot.**, *Metaph.* VII c. 11 (AL XXV[3.2] 155-156, Z c. 11, 1037a 33—b 7); *Metaph.* VIII c. 6 (AL XXV[3.1], 177-178, H c. 6 1045a 36—b 7); **Thomas**, *De an.* III c. 2 (XLV[1] 209b).
[19]Cf. supra n. 3.
[20]Cf. *Liber de causis* prop. 1 (ed. A. Pattin 48-49); *Auctoritates Aristotelis* (ed. J. Hamesse 231): "Quidquid potest causa secunda, potest et causa prima, nobiliori et altiori tamen modo."

caeleste haberet causalitatem supra illam, eliceret actum eiusdem rationis cum ipsa. Et ideo dicendum est ad maiorem, cum dicit quod 'si unus actus est liber, et alius eiusdem rationis est liber', quod verum est, si unus esset liber per essentiam et alius eiusdem rationis, quia liberum per essentiam et non-liberum specie differunt; et illo modo voluntas, quae est libera per essentiam, specie differt ab aliis potentiis quae non sunt liberae per essentiam. Sed liberum per participationem non de necessitate differt specie a non-libero, sicut actus videndi, qui est imperatus a voluntate, est liber per participationem, non tamen differt specie ab actu videndi non-imperato sed necessario: aliquando contingit videre de necessitate, sicut quando oculis apertis praesentatur obiectum. Modo ita est quod actus a voluntate elicitus non est liber per essentiam sed tantum potentia volitiva, et ideo non oportet quod si sit liber participatione quod actus volendi vel causatus a corpore caelesti sit liber, dato quod sit eiusdem rationis — immo esset non-liber quia haberet causam necessariam.

Ad aliud[21] dicendum quod dilectio et delectatio sunt actus diversi. Ad improbationem dicitur quod identitas obiecti non sufficit ad identitatem actus, quia intelligere et velle sunt respectu unius obiecti formalis, scilicet entis in actu in quantum huiusmodi; sed diversitas obiecti bene sufficit ad diversitatem actus.

Sed dicis ultra quod sunt actus eiusdem potentiae cum identitate obiecti. Dicendum quod hoc est diversimode, quia dilectio est in

---

1 haberet] habeat KU Q Z | supra] super O U FW Q X Z | illam] ipsam HLM FW istam Z 2 est *om.* KU X | cum dicit] conceditur KU quando dicitur Z | dicit] dicitur FW Q X 3 quod] ant. cum L | actus *om.* KU | est] sit KU | liber] *add.* per essentiam (*mg.* W) FW | liber — liber] vel X | alius] actus O M Z | est²] erit KU | liber] *add.* dico HLM 4 dico] sit H est L | alius] illius X 5 et non] etiam (et X) si Q X | specie differunt] *inv.* F | differunt] differant Q 6 illo] isto O M U | specie differt] *inv.* N KU Q 7 liberum *om.* L | per² *om.* F 8 non *post* necessitate NO quia Z | differt] ant. de K | differt specie] *inv.* HLM differunt specie (ant. non) X | sicut] sed Q 9 est imperatus] imperatur KU 10 tamen] ant. non X *om.* F *add.* dicit NO | non-imperato] non-importato N 11 necessario] necessitate FW | aliquando — videre] aliquando enim (*lin.* X) accidit videre (*om.* KU) O KU FW Q X Z | contingit videre] accidit KU accidit videre O FW Q X Z 12 oculis apertis] *inv.* O KU FW Q X Z | obiectum] oppositum O | Modo *post* ita F 14 non *om.* Q | si] s non(!) U *om.* K Q X Z *add.* actus volendi a voluntate tantum elicitus FW | participatione] per participationem FW | quod²] quia O Z 15 volendi] videndi NO HLM Z | vel *om.* FW | causatus *post* caelesti X causatur O | caelesti *om.* L | sit] sicut O 16 haberet] habet L 18 dicendum *om.* H | dilectio et delectatio] delectatio et dilectio Z | delectatio] desecratio(!) X 19 improbationem] probationem M KU Q Z | dicitur] dicendum O KU FW Q X Z *add.* ult. est F 20 respectu *om.* K X 21 unius] = O HM eiusdem L KU FW Q X Z *om.* N | obiecti] oppositi O rationis X | in² *om.* Z | huiusmodi] huius H F 22 diversitas] diversitatem X | diversitatem] diversitate N 23 Sed] Si X | dicis] dices Q | sunt] sint Z | actus *om.* Q X 24 Dicendum] *praem.* Ad quod Q *add.* est M | hoc est] *inv.* Q | dilectio] delectatio Z | est² *om.* X

---

[21]Cf. supra n. 4.

voluntate et a voluntate; delectatio est in voluntate, et non a voluntate, sed potius ab obiecto.[22] Probo: quia eorum contraria, scilicet odium et tristitia, non sunt idem, nec sunt ambo a voluntate causata, sed alterum tantum, scilicet odium. Quod patet per hoc quod voluntas complacet sibi in actu proprio ab ipsa causato — voluntas enim non complacet sibi in tristitia, immo est voluntati contraria, et quilibet invite tristatur; sed bene complacet sibi odium; igitur tristitia causatur tantum ab obiecto et non a voluntate, et per consequens nec delectatio. Sed obiectum conveniens cum perceptione, dum tamen sit praesens, causat delectationem, et obiectum contrario modo tristitiam.

17 Ad aliud[23] dicendum quod delectatio non immediate causatur ab apprehensione convenientis, sed mediante actu dilectionis coniungente potentiam volitivam obiecto sibi convenienti. Quae quidem coniunctio est prior origine naturae ipsa delectatione, licet simul sint tempore; eodem enim instanti quo voluntas coniungitur obiecto suo praesenti per actum dilectionis vel fruitionis, stillat quaedam dulcedo ab obiecto in potentia volitiva, et haec est delectatio.

---

1 delectatio] *add.* enim M *add.* autem O KU FW Q X Z | et²] sed KU FW Q X Z | non] *add.* est FW 2 obiecto] opposito O | Probo] Probatio M Z 3 scilicet] quae sunt KU F Q X Z | ambo *om.* K 4 causata] creata F | per] propter H ex K *om.* N 5 quod] quia Q Z | complacet] placeat F complaceat W X placet Q | complacet — non *om.* U | sibi *om.* X | ab ipsa] ab ipso H K Q X in ipsa F *om.* Z 6 voluntas] voluntarius F voluntati W | enim] autem O K FW Q Z | sibi in *om.* FW | in *om.* X | voluntati] a voluntate Q voluntate X 7 et] sed K | quilibet] quidlibet FW quibus U X | invite] in intellectus Z *om.* KU | bene] non KU | sibi *om.* Q | odium *om.* Z 8 igitur] ergo L FW Q X | tristitia] *add.* non K | tantum] *ant.* causatur L X Z | et *om.* L U FW Q X Z | et non] nec K | et² *om.* Q Z 9 delectatio] dilectio X | Sed] Si U | cum] tamen X | perceptione] participatione K praecipue X praeceptione Z 10 dum] cum X *om.* Z | praesens] prius U | delectationem] dilectionem X | obiectum] *add.* disconveniens L 11 modo] *add.* dispositum KU FW X Z *add.* causat Q *add.* ult. causat FW *add.* ult. ad Z | tristitiam] tristitia K 12 dicendum] *add.* est M F | delectatio] dilectio X | non] *rep.* N | causatur] *mg.* Q 13 dilectionis] delectationis N KU FW Q Z 14 volitivam] volititam(!) F *om.* Z | sibi convenienti] vel convenienti X *om.* N 15 origine] ordine KU W | naturae] nec X *om.* N | simul sint] *inv.* KU simul sit O non FW Z simul Q sit X 16 eodem] *praem.* in HLM | enim] *add.* in N | instanti] *mg.* F *add.* in F X | coniungitur] communis Z | obiecto] opposito O 17 suo *om.* K | dilectionis] delectationis KU FW Z | vel] et H | fruitionis] *rep.* Z figurationis NO fractionis X | stillat] stellat N fluit FW *om.* Z 18 obiecto] oculo KU | volitiva] *ant.* potentia L | haec] hoc F Q Z | delectatio] dilectio X *add.* etc. O H *add.* et hoc (haec U) sufficiunt KU *add.* (*mg.* W) conclusio (*om.* FW Q) ergo (*om.* Q) cum (*om.* X) delectatio (dilectio X) sit passio realis aliquid imprimitur voluntati ab obiecto et (*add.* ita est FW *add.* ita X) non erit (est FW) mere activa etc. (*om.* W Q) FW Q X

[22] Cf. **Thomas**, *Sent.* III d. 15 qc. 3 ad 3 (VII¹ 170a).
[23] Cf. supra n. 5.

[QUAESTIO 12]

UTRUM POTENTIAE ANIMAE, SCILICET INTELLECTIVA ET SENSITIVA, SINT TANTUM PASSIVAE

Utrum potentiae animae, scilicet intellectiva et sensitiva, sint tantum passivae.

[1] Videtur quod sic:

II *De anima* dicitur quod sentire est quoddam pati,[1] et idem dicitur III de intelligere;[2] igitur, cum potentiae dicantur ad actum, illae essent passivae tantum.[3]

Item, si essent activae, cum hoc quod sunt passivae, sequitur quod sensus posset sentire sine obiecto exteriori; similiter, intellectus intelligere, quia activum et passivum sufficiunt sine extrinseco ad actum eliciendum; hoc est falsum; igitur, etc. Hanc rationem facit PHILOSOPHUS contra EMPEDOCLEM I *De anima*.[4]

Item, si sic, omnes operationes eiusdem potentiae essent eiusdem speciei, sicut omnes visiones; sed hoc est falsum. Alia enim est albi visio, alia nigri, cum specie differant album et nigrum. Probatio

---

4 Utrum] *praem.* Quaeritur NO FW Q X Z *praem.* Quaeritur octavo K *adnot. mg.* Quaestio octava M | scilicet *om.* NO Q X Z | sint] sunt U X   6 Videtur] *praem.* Et FW *om.* Q   7 II] in X | dicitur *om.* Q | quod *om.* M Q X | idem] illud O similiter X *om.* Q   8 dicitur *om.* Q X *add.* in K Q | III *om.* L X *add.* De anima M FW *add.* scribitur Q | de *om.* Q X | intelligere] *add.* ergo (ideo Z) etc. FW Z *add.* est quoddam pati ergo etc. Q | igitur] ergo L FW et Q X Z | cum *om.* Z | potentiae] potentia O FW Q Z | dicantur] dicatur FW Q ducatur O Z distinguantur L | ad actum] per actus L   9 illae *om.* X | essent] erunt FW Q X Z   10 Item] Praeterea NO FW Q X Z | cum] quod F | sunt] essent KU | sequitur] sequeretur K FW Q X Z   11 sensus posset] *inv.* FW X | posset] poterit N potest H *add.* se sentire et (*add.* quod Q X) posset FW Q X Z *add.* ult. *seu rep.* sentire et posset Z | sine] *lin.* L | obiecto] opposito O | similiter] sicut H | intellectus] *rep.* N *om.* Z   12 intelligere] intellectivae Z | quia] eo quod FW quod X | sufficiunt *om.* Z | extrinseco] exteriori KU intrinseco X   13 eliciendum] *rep.* W eliciendi X Z *add.* sed X | igitur] ergo L FW Q Z *om.* X | etc. *om.* Q   14 Philosophus] Aristoteles FW Q X | I] 'II' NO FW Q Z in X   15 Item] Praeterea NO KU FW Q X Z | essent] erunt FW Q X Z | eiusdem *post* speciei K *mg.* U² unius FW Q   16 sed *om.* N | est *om.* N | enim *post* est X *om.* Q   17 albi visio] *inv.* FW Q X Z *add.* et H X | cum] quia Q | differant] differunt H F Q | et nigrum] a nigro X

---

[1] Cf. **Thomas**, *De an.* III c. 1 (XLV¹ 202b): "... nam sentire, ut supra in II dictum est, non proprie pati est (patitur enim proprie aliquid a contrario), sed habet aliquid simile passioni in quantum sensus est in potentia ad sensibile et est susceptivus sensibilium"; cf. **Aegidius Romanus**, *De an.* II com. 119 (f. 53ra): "Quod sentire est quoddam pati ..."; **Aristot.**, *De an.* II c. 23 (B c. 11, 424a 1): 'sentire enim est aliquod pati quoquomodo'
[2] **Aristot.**, *De an.* III c. 1 (Γ c. 4, 429a 13-14); *Auctoritates Aristotelis* (ed. J. Hamesse 185): "Intellectus est pars animae. Intelligere est pati."
[3] Cf. **Averroës**, *Metaph.* IX com. 2; **Anonymus**, *Quaestiones De anima* III q. 3 (ed. Van Steenberghen 306).
[4] **Aristot.**, *De an.* I c. 5 (A c. 2, 405b 11-15); cf. **Thomas**, *De an.* III c. 1 (XLV¹ 203a).

consequentiae: quia, eodem activo et passivo, manet eadem actio vel idem effectus, ut dicitur V *Metaphysicae*;[5] si autem eadem est potentia activa et passiva, manet idem principium activum sensationis et intellectionis; igitur semper eadem intellectio et sensatio.

4 Item, cognitio fit per assimilationem et conformitatem potentiae cognitivae ad obiectum; sed illa assimilatio fit tantum per impressionem speciei vel similitudinis obiecti in potentiam, quae impressio est causata effective ab obiecto et recepta in potentia; igitur sunt tales potentiae receptivae.

5 In oppositum est COMMENTATOR II *De anima*:[6]
Dicit quod sunt activae et passivae: passivae in recipiendo impressionem ab obiecto, activae in iudicando.

[I. — Ad quaestionem
Opinio aliquorum]

6 Ad istam quaestionem, dicunt ALIQUI quod sunt tantum passivae; diversimode tamen hoc ponitur a diversis.
[OPINIO THOMAE] QUIDAM[7] dicunt illas esse passivas primo respectu speciei impressae ab obiecto; illa autem species informans

---

1 quia] *add. (post* passivo) manentibus N *add.* manente FW Q X Z *add.* ab HLM KU | et] *add.* eodem W Q X | manet] manat L KU   2 V] 'VIII' O FW Q X Z | eadem] eodem Z | est potentia] *inv.* FW X Z potentia K   3 activa et passiva] passiva et activa N | activum] actum Z *om.* L *add.* et passivum N | et intellectionis] vel intellectionis FW Q *om.* Z   4 intellectionis] intentionis NO Q | igitur] ergo LW Q X *add.* est HL *add.* et FW Z | semper eadem] *inv.* U | eadem *om.* Z | intellectio et sensatio] intellectio vel sensatio FW sensatio et intentio N intentio et (vel Q) sensatio O Q   5 Item] Praeterea NO KU FW Q X Z | et] *lin.* Z² | conformitatem] uniformitatem X   6 illa] ista KU X vera Z | assimilatio] applicatio N | per impressionem] pro impressione N impressionem X   7 speciei vel similitudinis] similitudinis vel speciei KU | in] ad M | potentiam] potentia X   8 causata] tantum(!) NO creata F Q X | et *om.* X | igitur] ergo L FW Q X | sunt *post* potentiae L   9 tales *om.* KU   10 In *om.* Q | est *om.* Q   11 Dicit] Ubi dicit L | passivae² *post* obiecto K *om.* U Q X Z | in *om.* FW Q X Z   12 obiecto] opposito(!) O *add.* et O Q X | in *om.* FW Z | iudicando] dividendo(?) X   15 istam] illam L K F Z aliam H *om.* Q | aliqui] quidam Z *add.* secundum X | sunt] est X | tantum *post* passivae Q   16 ponitur] probatur M | a diversis] ad veritatem X   17 Quidam] *add.* autem N *add.* enim FW Q *add. (post* dicunt) autem similiter X *add.* hic Z | illas] istas N Z | esse passivas] *inv.* U   18 illa] ista X Z | informans] in potentias(?) Z

---

[5]Cf. **Aristot.**, *Metaph.* V c. 15 (AL XXV³·² 112-113, Δ c. 15 1020*b* 26—1021*b* 11).
[6]**Averroës**, *De an.* III com. 4 (AverL 384-385): "Et ideo anima rationalis indiget considerare intentiones quae sunt in virtute imaginativa, sicut sensus indiget inspicere sensibilia. Sed cum videtur quod formae rerum extrinsecarum movent hanc virtutem ita quod mens aufertur eas a materiis, et facit eas primo intellecta in actu postquam erant intellecta in potentia, ex hoc modo videtur quod ista anima est activa, non passiva. Secundum igitur quod intellecta movent eam, est passiva, et secundum quod moventur ab ea, est activa."
[7]Cf. **Thomas**, *Summa theol.* I q. 56 a. 1 in corp. (V 62*b*); *Summa theol.* I q. 79 a. 2 in corp. (V 259*a*); *Sent.* I d. 3 q. 5 ad 5 (I 43*b*).

potentiam cognitivam sibi subiectam est principium elicitivum, sicut ratio eliciendi operationem cognoscendi; ipsa autem potentia non est principium eliciendi actum illius cognitionis, sed totum compositum ex potentia et specie, principaliter tamen ratione speciei; potentia autem non habet in actu huiusmodi causando nisi rationem principii passivi primo respectu speciei, et ex consequenti respectu cognitionis causatae, principaliter tanquam a formali principio operandi a specie impressa ab obiecto.

Ponitur exemplum de igne qui, secundum EOS,[8] non est principium activum calefaciendi, sed compositum ex igne et calore, ratione tamen caloris, est principium calefaciendi active sicut ratio formalis calefactionis; ignis autem est ratio materialis tantum. Hanc autem positionem sic probant: quando de potentia essentiali aliquid reducitur ad potentiam accidentalem, illud per quod fit talis reductio habet aliquem actum primum, qui est ratio eliciendi actum secundum.[a]

[3] Item, indeterminatum ad plura non potest determinari ad unum nisi per aliquid impressum sibi determinans; potentiae praedictae sunt indeterminatae, quantum est[9] de se ad actus diversos; igitur in eis est species impressa ipsas determinans ad agendum; tale autem

---

[a] *Sequitur textus interpolatus*: Potentiae praedictae sunt in potentia essentiali ad actum cognoscendi; igitur reducuntur ad potentiam accidentalem per speciem eis impressam; igitur ista species est ratio eliciendi actum cognoscendi.

1 cognitivam] cognoscitivam W | subiectam] subiectatam(!) M   2 operationem] operationis NO | autem] om K   3 actum] activum N actionem X | illius] istius Z   5 non om. KU | habet om. N add. se L | in om. Q | actu] actum O L FW Q X | huiusmodi] huius O F X | causando] creando X add. seu rep. vel non habet in causando huius actum FW | nisi] spat. vac. U | rationem] ratione L K rationi X   6 principii] principali X principium Z | speciei] add. secundo Q | consequenti] add. seu rep. cum "va-cat" (vide supra) sed totum compositum ex potentia et specie O   7 causatae] tantum N tantae O X | tanquam om. F | a om. X | formali] principali Z   8 operandi] add. et F   9 Ponitur post exemplum X | qui] quod Q | est — caloris om. F   10 activum calefaciendi] inv. KU | ex] ab H | calore] add. in Z   11 ratione om. KU | caloris] calor KU add. qui W Q X Z   12 calefactionis] calefaciendi N calefacientis O FW Q X Z | est om. FW Q X Z | materialis post tantum Z   13 autem om. U Q | positionem] rationem Q | probant] probatur Q | aliquid] ant. de Q   14 ad] lin. Q | illud post reductio FW X Z idem H U   15 reductio] add. illud O add. autem X | qui] quae NO KU   16 secundum] secundae X om. Z   17 Item] Praeterea NO U FW Q X Z | indeterminatum] indeterminatur F | potest determinari] potest praeliari(!) K potest terminari U determinatur FW Q X Z   18 per] secundum Q | aliquid] aliquod L aliud KU | impressum sibi] inv. NO FW Q X Z | determinans] add. ipsum FW   19 de] ex L | igitur] ergo FW Q X   20 eis om. F | est] ant. in L | species impressa] inv. KU | ipsas] ipsa X Z | agendum] attendendum L | autem om. N   21 Potentiae — cognoscendi[2]] (praem. Sed Z) FW Q X Z om. rell.   22 igitur] ergo si W Q X | igitur — cognoscendi om. F | accidentalem] add. hoc non erit nisi W   23 igitur] ergo W Q X | ista] illa W Q

---

[8] Cf. **Thomas**, *Summa theol.* I q. 56 a. 1 in corp. (V 62b).
[9] Subaudi: sunt

sic determinatum ab alio est tantum in potentia passiva; igitur, etc.

9 [CONTRA OPINIONEM THOMAE] Contra istum modum ponendi[10] arguitur sic: actio debet magis attribui formali principio agendi quam materiali, secundum COMMENTATOREM VIII *Metaphysicae*,[11] quia non attribuitur materiali nisi propter formale; si igitur species est formale principium eliciendi actum cognoscendi et potentia materiale tantum, sequitur quod actus sentiendi et intelligendi magis debent attribui speciei quam potentiae, quod falsum est; quia species non sentit nec intelligit sicut potentia.

10 Item, sequeretur, cum species illae per potentiam divinam possunt manere sine subiecto, quod possunt intelligere sine potentia intellectiva et sentire sine sensu, quia quod potest per se esse, potest per se agere;[12] hoc est falsum; igitur, etc.

11 Item, ab eodem actus elicitur et intenditur, II *Ethicorum*,[13] ab eodem generatur habitus et augetur, scilicet per actus; sed per solam potentiam intenditur actus cognoscendi, quia, organo, specie, medio, et obiecto stantibus in eadem dispositione in uno actu cognoscendi sicut in alio, sola potentia intensius se ferente ad cognitionem obiecti, et ab aliis attentionibus se retrahente, sequitur intensior actus cognoscendi; igitur, etc.

12 Item, impossibile est idem per se ordinari ad operationem, sicut

---

1 alio] aliquo N obiecto K | tantum — passiva] in (*om*. Z) potentia tantum passiva K Z in potentia tantum est in passiva U in potentia passiva tantum FW Q X | igitur etc.] ergo etc. L FW Z ergo Q *om*. X   2 istum modum] inv. NO W Q illum modum H F Z modum illum F | ponendi *om*. Z *add*. secundum Commentatorem X   3 arguitur] arguo X | debet *post* magis FW Q X Z | agendi] agenti N Z   5 quia] quando U quod X *om*. FW | non] *add*. enim FW X | formale] *add*. principium eliciendi H | si *om*. X | igitur] ergo L FW Q X   6 actum] *add*. octavum(!) O   7 sentiendi et intelligendi] intelligendi et sentiendi X | 8 debent] debet F Q   9 sentit nec intelligit] intelligit neque sentit Q | nec] neque K | sicut] sed Q | sicut — agere (*circa finem paragraphi succedentis*) *om*. X | potentia] potentiae Z   10 Item] Praeterea NO KU FW Q | sequeretur] sequitur KU Z *add*. quod FW Q Z | cum] quod H | illae *om*. Q | potentiam] *add*. et O | possunt] possint (*lin*. O) O FW Q   11 manere] esse O FW Q *om*. Z | sine] sub Z | subiecto] obiecto H | quod] quia O *add*. est potentia FW Q Z | possunt²] possent O W Q possint M posset F Z   12 sentire] sensitiva K | potest² *post* se Z   13 hoc] *praem*. sed K quod X *add*. autem O FW Q Z | est *om*. N | igitur etc.] ergo etc. FW *om*. Q X   14 Item] Praeterea NO KU FW Q X Z | eodem] *add*. a quo FW | actus *post* elicitur Q | II] III Z | Ethicorum] Physicorum H *add*. et Q   15 eodem] eodili(!) U | generatur] generantur (*lin*. O) O FW X Z | et — actus *om*. Z | augetur] augentur O FW | actus] actum X   16 intenditur] *rep*. F | specie] speciei X   17 medio] media FW Q X Z   19 attentionibus] intentionibus KU FW Q Z   20 intensior] intentio U | igitur etc.] ergo etc. L FW Q igitur Q etc. X   21 Item] Praeterea NO KU FW Q X Z | idem] illud O FW Q Z illud idem L *om*. X | ordinari] cedenti(?) X | operationem] ordinationem KU | sicut ad] tanquam FW Q X Z

[10]Cf. supra n. 6-8.
[11]Cf. **Averroës**, *Metaph*. VIII com. 7 (ed. Iuntina VIII, f. 215*va*I—*b*K).
[12]Cf. **Thomas**, *Summa theol*. I q. 14 a. 2 in corp. (IV 168*b*).
[13]**Aristot.**, *Eth. Nic.* II c. 1 (AL XXVI³ 397; **B** c. 1, 1103*b* 21-22); *Auctoritates Aristotelis* (ed. J. Hamesse 234): "Ex actibus multum iteratis fit habitus."

ad principium eius, quod se habet in potentia contradictionis ad principale principium et formale illius operationis — sicut lignum est in potentia contradictionis ad calorem qui est principium formale calefaciendi active, ideo non ordinatur per se ad calefacere; sed potentia cognitiva est in potentia contradictionis ad speciem obiecti cognoscibilis — potest enim illam quandoque habere et quandoque non; si igitur sola species est principium formale eliciendi operationem sive cognitionem et potentia materiale tantum, ipsa per accidens et non per se poterit dici cognoscere, scilicet per rationem speciei quae est sibi accidentalis — sicut lignum calefacit per accidens; hoc autem est inconveniens; igitur, etc.

[5] [OPINIO AEGIDII] Alii ponunt[14] quod sunt sic passivae, scilicet non distinguendo speciem ab actu cognoscendi nisi secundum rationem tantum, quia species est illud quo aliquid ab obiecto imprimitur in potentia, sed per illud idem est actus cognoscendi, causatus ab obiecto tantum effective. Et quia potentia cognitiva est tantum receptiva speciei, ideo est tantum receptiva actus cognoscendi, non

---

1 principium eius] inv. FW Q X Z proprium(!) eius H | quod] add. per X 2 principale principium] inv. NO FW Q X Z | et om. N | illius] ipsius Q om. X | lignum] add. quod FW Q X Z 3 qui est om. NO | principium formale] inv. FW X Z 4 active] effective FW Q Z | se om. X | calefacere] calorem KU Q 6 enim] tamen Q | illam] illud NO istam X Z add. habere Q X add. ult. et X | quandoque habere] inv. KU FW habere Z | quandoque²] quando O U 7 non] add. habere Q | si] sed Z | igitur] ergo L U FW Q X ista Z | est] sit KU | formale eliciendi] inv. K | eliciendi] incipiendi N initiandi O | operationem sive om. FW Q X Z 8 materiale] materia N | ipsa] ipsi O om. N 9 non om. K | per se] potest U | poterit] potest H | dici] dicere X om. L | scilicet] quia L om. H KU 10 accidentalis] accidens N | sicut — accidens] ant. scilicet NO F mg. (ant. et) W om. Z | calefacit] calefacere N 11 est om. W | igitur etc.] ergo etc. L FW Z ergo Q etc. X 12 Alii] add. autem N | sic] sicut NO K FW om. X | scilicet om. X 13 distinguendo] add. ipsam L | nisi — tantum] secundum rem sed secundum rationem tantum (ant. secundum O) NO re (rem F Q) sed tantum ratione FW Q X Z 14 species om. K | quo aliquid] quod aliquid NO quod FW Q X Z | ab] de H om. NO | imprimitur] ant. obiecto K 15 potentia] potentiam Q add. et non (ut X Z) est in potentia FW X Z | per om. NO FW Q X Z | illud] istud KU W X | idem post est Q om. K | actus om. U 16 tantum — est om. NO 17 ideo] non L U | tantum] ant. est K X om. Z | actus] alicuius N | non om. L KU

[14]**Aegidius Romanus**, *De cognitione angelorum* q. 1 (ed. 1503 f. 76*vb*): "Sciendum ergo quod, licet sit idem visio quod species impressa secundum rem, ut ostendimus per Augustinum et per Philosophum et per rationem, non tamen est idem secundum rationem, sed impressio speciei est ex parte agentis sed quod illa species impressa sit visio est ex parte passi ... (f. 77*ra*) Communiter enim loquendo, dicamus quod a specie impressa oculo procedit visio et quod illa species est causa visionis quod ita verificatur acsi diceretur ab actione procedit passio et actio est causa passionis; sed cum hanc materiam specialiter pertractamus, dicemus quod idem est realiter species impressa et visio sicut idem est realiter actio et passio ... Inquires ergo et perquires; non invenies in virtute visiva aliam formam quam [ed.: quod] speciem impressam a visibili. Secundum rationem ergo potest differre et differt visio ab illa specie, realiter tamen est idem quod ipsa species; et non solum in hoc sed universaliter et ubique semper loquendo de actione quae est idem quod passio, actio et passio sunt idem quod forma impressa passo"; cf. etiam **Thomas de Sutton**, *Quaestiones ordin.* q. 15 in corp. (ed. Schneider BAW III 445-446).

elicitiva.

Propositum sic probant: quando aliquid est in ultima dispositione ad actum aliquem, praesente activo, illum recipit; potentiae praedictae sunt huiusmodi respectu actus cognoscendi; igitur, praesente obiecto activo, actum illum cognoscendi recipiunt. Sed ab obiecto recipiunt speciem ipsius; igitur species in potentia cognitiva non est aliud ab actu cognoscendi, et per consequens potentia non elicit actum, sicut nec speciem, sed tantum recipit.

14 Item, II *De anima*,[15] sensibile in actu et sensus in actu idem sunt, sicut sonatio et auditio; sed sonatio non est nisi generatio speciei soni; igitur auditio non est nisi receptio speciei. Sicut igitur respectu speciei est in potentia receptiva tantum, ita respectu actus cognoscendi.

15 Item, AUGUSTINUS V *De Trinitate* dicit[16] quod forma impressa visui ab obiecto dicitur visio.

16 [CONTRA OPINIONEM AEGIDII] Sed contra hoc, et specialiter de sentire, arguitur sic: quia species recepta in sensu est eiusdem rationis cum illa quae recipitur in medio — cum activum et passivum sint eiusdem rationis, scilicet obiectum activum, organum et medium quae sunt passiva, II *De anima*[17] —, igitur, sicut species est visio quando est in organo, ita quando est in medio, quia eadem

---

2 Propositum sic probant] Probant sic propositum FW Q X Z | probant] *add.* quia FW Q | quando] quantum(!) F quia X Z 3 praesente] *add.* obiecto N KU | activo] active KU | illum] aliquando(?) X item(?) Z | potentiae praedictae] *inv.* H F 4 igitur] ergo L FW Q X 5 obiecto] opposito O | actum illum] *inv.* H | actum — recipiunt] illae (istae X) recipiunt actum cognoscendi FW Q X Z | illum *om.* NO | cognoscendi *om.* L | recipiunt] recipit U 6 speciem] sensationem(!) O | ipsius] illius (ant. speciem X) FW Q X Z | igitur] ergo L FW Q X 7 aliud *om.* X | potentia] intellectus K actus U 8 nec] non X *add.* recipit(!) O 9 Item] Praeterea NO KU FW Q X Z | sensibile in actu *om.* FW X Z | et *om.* W X Z | sunt] sibi FW *add.* ult. cum obiectis in actu FW 10 sonatio] sanatio(!) U sensatio X | et *om.* X | auditio] *add.* unde ibidem sensitivum potentia id est potentia sensitiva est quale sensibile in (iam W) actu FW | nisi *om.* N | generatio] genere F 11 igitur] ergo L FW Q X | igitur[2]] ergo L FW Q X nec U 12 est *om.* U | in *om.* K | receptiva] passiva FW Q X Z | tantum] ant. est K | respectu[2]] *lin.* F[2] 14 Item] Praeterea KU | Augustinus V De Trinitate] Commentator N | dicit] ait Q 16 et *om.* W Q X Z 17 arguitur] dicitur K | quia] quod Z | recepta] receptiva O X | sensu] sensum Q 18 cum — rationis *om.* U | illa] ista X Z | quae *om.* Z 19 sint] sunt L K X | scilicet] sed X | obiectum] oppositum O | activum] *add.* et O Q X Z 20 quae] *mg.* W | sunt] est O | passiva] *add.* ut patet NO FW Q X Z | igitur] ergo L FW X 21 quando] quae U | ita] illa Z | quando[2]] quod Z

---

[15] **Aristot.**, *De an.* II c. 26 (Γ c. 2, 425b 26—426a 1).
[16] **Augustinus**, *De Trinitate* XI c. 2 (CCL 50 334-335, PL 42 985): "Quamvis re visibili detracta nulla sit nec ulla omnino esse possit talis visio si corpus non sit quod videri queat, nullo modo tamen eiusdem substantiae est corpus quo formatur sensus oculorum cum idem corpus videtur et ipsa forma quae ab eodem imprimitur sensui, quae visio vocatur"; cf. **Thomas de Sutton**, *Quaest. ordin.* q. 15 arg. 24 (ed. Schneider BAW III 430).
[17] **Aristot.**, *De an.* II c. 23 (B c. 11, 424a 2-7).

causa manente, manet idem effectus; hoc autem est manifeste falsum quod medium posset dici videns sicut visus; igitur, etc.

[6] Item, in organo caeci vel vigilantis ad alia intense distracti vel dormientis oculis apertis sicut leporis imprimitur species visibilis, tamen nullum illorum videt; igitur, etc.

Item, dormiens non audit et tamen excitatur ad sonum, quod non faceret nisi in eius organo imprimeretur species soni; igitur aliud est receptio speciei et auditio.

Isti contradicunt sibi, ut videtur. Dicunt enim quod in patria Deus videtur ab intellectu creato, non tamen per speciem; igitur aliud est species a visione.[18]

Item, Deus potest actum imaginandi et intelligendi sine specie obiectorum causata ab obiectis in potentiis causare, ut patet in visionibus Prophetarum.[19]

[II. — Solutio quaestionis]

[7] Dicendum igitur quod potentiae animae respectu suarum operationum sunt activae; aliter nimis vilescerent, ut patebit. Quod probo primo auctoritate PHILOSOPHI II *De anima*,[20] dicentis et probantis

---

1 manet *post* effectus X | hoc] hac F   2 quod] quia O L FW Q X Z *add.* tunc L | medium] species Z | posset] possit N potest H | igitur etc.] ergo etc. L FW Q Z etc. K *om.* X   3 Item] Propterea N KU FW Q X Z Prima(!) O | organo] organi U | caeci *om.* X   4 oculis apertis] inv. U | leporis] leporum(!) U lepores X | species *post* visibilis Z sensus O | visibilis] *add.* et KU *om.* X   5 tamen *post* istorum K | nullum] neutrum H | illorum] istorum NO KU X Z | igitur etc.] ergo etc. L FW Z *om.* KU Q X   6 Item] Praeterea KU | et *om.* O FW Q X Z | excitatur] exicatur(!) Z   7 faceret] fieret FW Q X Z | igitur] ergo FW Q X   8 et] aliud Q   9 Isti] *praem.* Item FW Q X Z Illi Z *add.* autem K   10 videtur] videbitur FW Q X Z | creato] causato X Z | non *om.* X | igitur] ergo L FW Q X   12 Item] Praeterea KU Ideo X | actum — intelligendi] intelligere et imaginare N | specie ... causata] speciebus ... causatis N M FW X speciebus ... creatis O Q Z   13 obiectorum] oculorum N | obiectis] oculis L | causare] creare M X   14 visionibus] visione X | Prophetarum] *add.* igitur (ergo FW) etc. NO FW Z   16 Dicendum] *add.* est M | igitur] ergo FW Q X Z *add.* ad quaestionem Q | operationum] actionum X   17 aliter] *add.* autem F | nimis vilescerent] inv. KU | vilescerent] in + *spat. vac.* Z | Quod] autem (*post* probo) Z | probo] probatur KU   18 auctoritate — probantis *om.* X | II] 'I' Q tertio Z | dicentis] dicit FW *om.* Q Z | et] quod H *om.* O Q Z | probantis] probat FW

[18]**Aegidius Romanus**, *Quodl.* III q. 13 (f. 37ra) : "Si ergo tota causa quare res aliqua non intelligeretur per seipsam, ut volunt sancti et philosophi, est quia per seipsam non potest esse praesens in anima, patet ergo quod divina essentia non intelligitur ab intellectu per speciem, sed per seipsam."
[19]**Aegidius Romanus**, *Quodl.* III q. 13 (f. 36va): "Respondeo dicendum quod si bene consideramus dicta sanctorum et philosophorum propter hoc requiritur species media ad supplendum vicem obiecti. Si enim obiectum posset esse praesens ipsi intellectui et esset intelligibile in actu per se et causaret intellectionem in intellectu, non requireretur ibi species media. Ubi igitur ponimus praesentiam rei intelligibilis, non ponimus ibi aliquam speciem mediam."
[20]**Aristot.**, *De an.* II c. 2 (B c. 2, 413a 21-25); II c. 4 (B c. 2, 414a 12-13); *Auctoritates Aristotelis* (ed. J. Hamesse 162): "Anima est principium quo primo et principaliter vivimus, intelligimus, sentimus et movemur secundum locum."

quod anima est principium effectivum non solum vegetandi sed etiam sentiendi. Et idem est de actu intelligendi, licet ibi non exprimatur, sed expresse dicit COMMENTATOR[21] quod intelligere et sentire sunt actiones immanentes in agente. Certum est autem quod manent in sentiente et intelligente, non autem in obiecto extrinseco; igitur obiectum non est activum talium, sed potius homo sentiens et intelligens, mediantibus suis potentiis animae.[22]

22 Item, dicit COMMENTATOR super III *De anima*[23] quod dictae potentiae sunt patientes in quantum impressionem obiecti recipiunt, et agentes in quantum de obiectis iudicant.

23 Et hoc patet rationibus sic: agens in quantum huiusmodi nobilius est patiente in quantum huiusmodi, III *De anima*;[24] sed obiectum sensibile ratione formae accidentalis est agens, et potentia animae vel anima patiens cognitionem; per EOS[25] igitur quaecumque forma accidentalis esset nobilior anima intellectiva, quod falsum est.[26]

24 Item, operationes vitales sunt effectivae a principio vitali et intrinseco, si sint naturales; actus sentiendi et intelligendi sunt

---

1 principium effectivum] inv. N LM U | vegetandi] vigilandi U 2 etiam] *lin.* K | Et *om.* N | est] *rep.* X | de *om.* Z | ibi *om.* FW 3 sed] et W Q Z *om.* F X | dicit] dicitur O FW Q Z *om.* X | Commentator] IX Metaphysicae O FW Q X Z commento U | intelligere et sentire] sentire et intelligere Z 4 actiones] actus KU Z | immanentes] manentes FW X Z 5 manent] permanens FW permanet Z *om.* N | et] *add.* in HM K | autem] est FW 6 igitur] ergo L FW Q X Z | obiectum *om.* L | activum] actuum K | homo] hoc Z *om.* L *add.* est H W 7 sentiens et intelligens] intelligens et sentiens K sentiens (*add.* est F) vel intelligens (intellectus X) FW Q X Z 8 Item] Tunc NO Praeterea KU | super] supra U *om.* X | III] 'II' L FW Q X Z | dictae] praedictae KU 9 patientes] passivae L *add.* (*mg.*) id est patientes L² | obiecti] oppositi O obiectum H 10 agentes] agunt X | obiectis] oppositis O 11 Et] Secundo O FW Q X Z | hoc *post* patet X | rationibus] ratione X | huiusmodi] agens K | nobilius est] inv. NO L FW Q Z 12 est] *add.* in X | huiusmodi] huius F Q X Z *add.* ex KU | III De anima] II De anima X *om.* Z 13 accidentalis] aliqualis X 14 vel] *add.* ipsa L | per eos] per eas Q *om.* KU *add.* secundum eos FW | igitur] ergo (*mg.* W) FW Q X | quaecumque — esset] = L K quaeque forma accidentalis esset H U esset forma accidentalis quaecumque NO esset forma accidentalis quoque M esset forma accidentalis sensibilis quaecumque FW Q forma accidentalis sensibilis quaecumque X esset forma accidentalis quaecumque sensibilis Z 15 intellectiva *om.* O FW Q X Z | falsum *post* est H FW Z 17 Item] Praeterea NO KU FW Q X Z | effectivae] activae Z | et *om.* Z 18 sint] sunt FW Q X Z | sentiendi et intelligendi] intelligendi et sentiendi Q

[21] Averroës, *De an.* III com. 4 (AverL 384-385): "Et ideo anima rationalis indiget considerare intentiones quae sunt in virtute imaginativa, sicut sensus indiget inspicere sensibilia. Sed cum videtur quod formae rerum extrinsecarum movent hanc virtutem ita quod mens aufertur eas a materiis, et facit eas primo intellecta in actu postquam erant intellecta in potentia, ex hoc modo videtur quod ista anima est activa, non passiva. Secundum igitur quod intellecta movent eam, est passiva, et secundum quod moventur ab ea, est activa."
[22] Cf. **Henricus de Gandavo**, *Quodl.* XI q. 5 in corp. (f. 451r T).
[23] **Averroës**, *De an.* III com. 4 (AverL 384-5).
[24] **Aristot.**, *De an.* III c. 4 (Γ c. 5, 430a 18-19); *Auctoritates Aristotelis* (ed. J. Hamesse 187): "Agens est nobilius et honorabilius passo et forma materia."
[25] Scilicet, per Thomam et Aegidium.
[26] Cf. **Petrus I. Olivi**, *Summa* II q. 58 (BFS V 465).

operationes vitales, et etiam substantiales sentienti et intelligenti; igitur a principio intrinseco effectivo.²⁷

[8] Item, si sentire sit pati, sentiri est agere; sed agere est nobilius quam pati; si obiectum igitur intelligi est nobilius quam intelligere, per illud inanimata, quae non intelligunt sed intelliguntur, sunt perfectiora quam homo qui intelligit.

Item, differentia nobilior alicuius generis constituit speciem nobiliorem, sicut rationale respectu hominis, irrationale respectu bruti; sed potentia activa est nobilior differentia quam passiva, ut patet V et IX *Metaphysicae*;²⁸ sed vegetativa est potentia activa; si igitur potentia intellectiva et sensitiva sunt tantum passivae, vegetativa erit nobilior, quod falsum est.

[III. — Dubia subnexa]
[A. — Primum dubium: quomodo potentiae cognitivae activae esse possint]

Sed quomodo possunt esse activae cum hoc quod sunt passivae secundum PHILOSOPHUM?

Dicendum quod est una passio realis, quae est abiectio formae a contrario, et a passione tali non patiuntur potentiae huiusmodi, ut

---

1 etiam *om.* KU | substantiales] finales(?) Z | sentienti et intelligenti] sentiendi et intelligendi Q X   2 igitur] ergo L FW Q X Z *add.* sunt L | principio — effectivo] primo effective intrinseco H principio intrinseco effective LM X   3 Item] Propterea NO KU FW Q X Z | sentire] sensibile Z | sit] est NO FW Q X Z | sentiri] sentire U | agere] *add.* et intelligi FW Q X Z | est² *om.* X   4 si obiectum] si oppositum N sibi oppositum O FW Q X Z obiectum K scilicet obiectum U | igitur] ergo L FW Q X | per illud]= H KU per idem LM et per consequens NO FW Q X Z   5 sed intelliguntur] sed intelligitur N sed intelligentur O sed intelligunt X *om.* Z   6 perfectiora quam homo] nobiliora quam homo O nobiliora homine FW Q X Z nobiliora homine FW Q X Z   7 Item] Praeterea NO KU FW Q X Z | nobilior] *ant.* differentia Z nobilioris FW | alicuius *om.* FW Q X Z nobiliorem] meliorem KU | respectu hominis] hominem O FW X Z *om.* Q | respectu bruti] brutum O FW Q X Z   9 activa] *add.* non U | est nobilior differentia] nobilior differentia est H U nobilior est L | differentia] *add.* potentiae Q X Z | ut *om.* Q   10 V et IX] V FW IX Q commento(?) et(*lin.*) 'IX' X in Z | potentia] *add.* passiva O | si] licet KU   11 igitur] ergo L FW Q X | potentia *om.* W X Z | intellectiva et sensitiva] sensitiva et intellectiva L FW Q sensitiva Z | sunt] sint N | tantum] *add.* potentiae Q | vegetativa] vegetalia X *om.* F   12 erit] erunt X | nobilior] nobiliora X *add.* eis FW Q Z | falsum est] *inv.* F Q | est] *add.* ergo (igitur O) etc. (*om.* Q) O FW Q Z   16 quomodo] quandoque X | esse *om.* U | sunt] sint N possunt U   18 Dicendum] *add.* est HM U X | est una] *inv.* H Q *om.* U *adnot. mg.* duplex est passio N *adnot. mg.* est duplex passio Q²   19 contrario] contraria U | a passione] passione Q factione(?) Z | potentiae huiusmodi] *inv.* O FW Q X Z potentiae N huiusmodi L

²⁷Cf. **Petrus I. Olivi**, *Summa* II q. 58 (BFS V 463).
²⁸Cf. **Aristot.**, *Metaph.* V c. 15 (AL XXV³·² 112-113, Δ c. 15 1020*b* 26—1021*b* 11); *Metaph.* IX c. 2 (AL XXV³·² 179-180; T c. 2, 1046*a* 9-11); *Auctoritates Aristotelis* (ed. J. Hamesse 133): "Potentia activa est principium transmutandi aliud in quantum aliud"; cf. **Thomas**, *Summa theol.* I q. 79 a. 2 ad 3 (V 260*b*); **Anonymus** *Quaestiones De anima* III q. 1 (ed. Bazán 466-7).

patet II *De anima*;²⁹ alia est passio quae est perfectio patientis, ut patet ibidem.³⁰ Et illa subdividitur, quia quaedam est perfectio prima, sicut actus primus habilitans et inclinans potentiam ad actum;³¹ alia est perfectio quae est operatio.³²

Et secundum hoc est duplex modus ponendi dictas potentias esse passivas. Unus enim est quod potentia recipit immediate secundum actum evocatum, et determinatur a specie sibi praesentata sui obiecti in organo potentiae sensitivae ad sentiendum vel in phantasmate ad intelligendum, illa tamen specie in potentia nullatenus exsistente. Istum autem secundum actum elicit ipsa potentia ex virtute sua activa, sicut specie sibi praesentata ipsam potentiam evocante et determinante ad cognoscendum illud obiectum cuius est species, non tamen aliqualiter ipsam potentiam informante.³³

---

1 alia est] inv. W Q Z est autem F X   2 Et illa] Sed ista Z | quia] quod Q   3 sicut — actum *om.* Z | actus primus] primus H primo U *om.* K | habilitans] humilitas(!) O habilitatis X | actum] *add.* secundum O FW Q X   4 perfectio] *add.* secunda O FW Q X Z   5 dictas potentias] inv. FW Q X Z   6 enim *post* est L *om.* FW Q X Z | recipit immediate] inv. KU | secundum actum] inv.. FW Q X Z eius obiectum (oppositum O) NO   7 evocatum] evocata Q *om.* NO | et *om.* F | determinatur] determinata NO Q X Z determinatum FW | praesentata] praesentati Q | sui obiecti] obiecti (*ant.* sibi) NO FW Q X Z   8 sensitivae] subiectivae X | sentiendum] sensus N   9 illa] ista LM talia Z | tamen] in X cum Z *om.* H KU | nullatenus] *ant.* in KU   10 Istum] Illum NO FW Q Z | autem *om.* Q | secundum actum] inv. W Q Z duodevigesimum actum O actum F X respectum actum U | elicit] *add.* illa W | ipsa potentia] inv. KU FW   11 sicut] sic Q X | specie] species N F | praesentata] praesentatas F | ipsam] ipsa N   12 evocante] *ant.* ipsam Z evocantem H U | determinante] determinantem H KU | illud] illum O idem H | obiectum] oppositum O subiectum Z   13 non *post* tamen H | aliqualiter] aliter N K | potentiam *om.* L | informante] informantem H KU

²⁹**Aristot.**, *De an.* II c. 11 (B c. 5, 417b 2-3); *Auctoritates Aristotelis* (ed. J. Hamesse 182): "Passio dicitur dupliciter. Uno modo capitur pro transmutatone quadam quae fit cum abiectione contrarii, et illa dicitur passio proprie dicta"; cf. **Thomas**, *De an.* II c. 11 (XLV¹ 111b).

³⁰**Aristot.**, *De an.* II c. 11 (B c. 5, 417b 4-6).

³¹**Thomas**, *Summa theol.* I q. 79 a. 2 in corp. (V 259a): "Uno modo, propriissime, scilicet, quando aliquid removetur ab eo quod convenit sibi secundum naturam, aut secundum propriam inclinationem ..."; cf. **Anonymus (Jacobus de Duaco?)**, *Quaestiones De anima* III q. 1 (ed. Bazán 466-7).

³²**Henricus de Gandavo**, *Quodl.* XI q. 5 in corp. (f. 450v S—451r T): "Est enim unus modus alterationis quae est secundum privativas dispositiones, mutatio quae est a contrario in contrarium ... et dicitur haec mutatio contrarii abiectio. Alius vero modus est alterationis quae est connaturalis dispositionis receptio quae est a potentia in actum deductio absque omni contrario ... et haec duplex est: una qua acquiritur dispositio in re ad suam propriam operationem et est illa qua aliquid intentionaliter mutatur a sensibili aut intelligibili; altera vero est qua elicitur a re sua propria operatio ... Est autem alia alteratio sensitivi principaliter in ipsa vi sensitiva quae in ipsa est inclinatio quaedam ad actum operationis suae eliciendum, et est specie dicta agente in virtute sensibilis extra et hoc est ex parte sensus; ex parte autem intellectus nostri est ab ipso intelligibili universali quod se ipso est praesens intellectui in phantasmate actione intellectus agentis, propter quod se ipso inclinat intellectum ... et est haec inclinatio intellectus initium habitus cognitivi."

³³Cf. **Ioannes Pecham**, *Tractatus de anima* c. 3-4 (ed. Melani 9-17); *Quodl.* I q. 3 (ed. Etzkorn-Delorme 7-11); III q. 9 (ed. Etzkorn-Delorme 150-152).

[B. — Secundum dubium: quare Philosophus actus cognitionis magis pati quam agere vocaverit]

[9] Sed videtur dubium, quare Philosophus vocat dictos actus magis pati quam agere.[34]

Dicendum[35] quod hoc ideo est quia denominant formaliter suas potentias quas informant, in quantum in eis recipiuntur, non autem ut ab eis eliciuntur. Non enim aliquid dicitur formaliter tale, quia illud efficit, sicut sol non dicitur formaliter calidus, licet efficiat calorem, sed quia talem formam recipit ab illa formaliter denominatur. Quia igitur potentia sensitiva vel intellectiva dicitur formaliter sentiens vel intelligens vel homo per eas (et ut sic denominantur ab eis) — loquitur PHILOSOPHUS[36] — et ideo magis attribuit pati talibus potentiis vel recipere quam agere,[37] quia notum est magis tales actus esse in potentiis subiective quam a potentiis effective, sicut de motu gravis, qui magis patet esse in gravi, quam ab ipso effective causatus. Sic igitur res nominamus, sicut cognoscimus, igitur etc.

Dicunt ALIQUI[38] quod licet illa significentur per modum agendi,

---

3 videtur] rep. N | dubium om. X | quare] quod X quem Z | Philosophus] plus O M | dictos] praedictos K FW Q X | magis] ant. dictos KU 5 Dicendum] add. est M F | hoc] hic O om. F Q | ideo] non U om. L K | quia] quod FW X add. actus Q | denominant] denominat Q Z | formaliter post potentias X om. M | suas] suos U 6 quas informant om. K | informant] informat Q | in om. N | in² om. L | recipiuntur] recipitur O Q Z recipere X 7 eliciuntur] elicitur Q | Non] lin. X | aliquid dicitur] inv. Q dicitur K | formaliter] ant. aliquid X formatum Z | quia] quod F X 8 illud] idem HU | efficit] efficiat NO FW Q X Z | dicitur om. X | formaliter om. KU FW Q X Z | licet] ut X | efficiat calorem] inv. NO M FW Q X Z 9 quia] quid L | illa] ea L | formaliter] forma Z 10 igitur] ergo L FW Q X est U om. K | sensitiva vel intellectiva] intellectiva vel sensitiva X | formaliter] forte Z 11 vel²] ut U X | et om. K Z | ut om. N add. homo KU | denominantur] denominatur KU | ab] de NO FW Q X Z 12 et om. FW Q X Z | ideo] add. Philosophus (post magis X) NO M FW Q X Z | attribuit] accipit NO | talibus potentiis] huiusmodi ponentiis(!) (ant. pati) L potentiis Z 13 potentiis post recipere Z | vel] quam N | quam agere] vel agere NO om. L add. ult. tunc N add. item O FW Q X Z | notum est magis] magis notum est O Q est magis notum FW notum est X magis est Z | tales] talis Q Z 14 esse om. Z | subiective] sensitivis X | a] in(!) HLM KU | potentiis²] add. elicitive HLM KU add. ult. sive L | sicut] add. est K add. patet Q 15 gravis] gravi H generis(!) F | qui] quia O FW X Z quae K quod Q | magis] melius N modo est(?) O | patet] apparet L KU potest Z | in] ant. esse HL KU post gravi Z add. illo M | gravi] genere F magna(?) Z add. subiective FW | ipso] eo KU illo Q | effective post causatus FW Q X Z | causatus] causatur X 16 Sic] Sicut Z om. U | igitur] autem O FW Q X ergo L tamen Z | igitur etc.] igitur N ergo O ideo etc. M FW Q X Z om. L 17 Dicunt] add. tamen Q | quod om. KU | illa] illae KU ista O H Z | significentur] significent F | agendi] agentis H

---

[34]Cf. **Aristot.**, *De an.* III c. 1 (Γ c. 4, 429a 10-14).
[35]Cf. **Petrus I. Olivi**, *Summa* II q. 58 (BFS V 413).
[36]**Aristot.**, *De an.* I c. 10 (A c. 4, 408b 13-15; 24-25).
[37]Cf. **Aristot.**, *De an.* III c. 1 (Γ c. 4, 429a 13-17).
[38]Eadem sententia reperitur apud quaestiones Radulphi Britonis: **Radulphus Brito**, *In Aristot. librum III De an.* q. 2 in corp. (ed. Fauser 123); eademque sententia habetur apud Godefridum: **Godefridus de Fontibus**, *Quodl.* VIII q. 1 (PhB IV 32) et *Quodl.* IX q. 19 (PhB IV 277-280). Neque tamen apud Radulphum neque apud Godefridum, locis saltem citatis, exhibentur eadem verba.

tamen res significata est vere passio, sicut e converso honorari et amari significantur per modum patiendi, tamen honoratus vel amatus nihil patitur ab amante vel honorante nisi honorem, qui non est aliquid absolutum in honorato impressum, immo est in honorante secundum PHILOSOPHUM.[39]

30   Sed contra: prudentia est habitus directivus in agibilibus directionem rationis eliciens;[40] si autem illa intellectio causatur immediate ab obiecto, non requireretur habitus prudentiae, quod est falsum.

Si dicas quod habitus ille requiritur tantum ut disponat potentiam ad rectificandum actum prudentiae[41]: quia 'habitus est quo aliquis utitur cum voluerit',[42] uti est agere perficit — etiam agentem et opus eius bonum reddit—, igitur non passio est tantum.

31   Item, intellectus est summe dispositus ad recipiendum intellectum, quia non habet contrarium.

32   Item, actus intelligendi praecedentes habitum prudentiae vel alium sunt eiusdem rationis cum aliis sequentibus; tamen praecedentes non praesupponunt illam dispositionem habitus in intellectu; igitur nec sequentes.

[10]

---

1 significata] signata U | vere] vera NO FW Q X sola Z | e converso om. HL KU | honorari et amari] amari et honorari F X 2 significantur] significant F signantur W | tamen] cum O | vel] et Q 3 patitur] facitur Z | nisi honorem om. X | honorem om. Z 4 est om. Q | aliquid absolutum om. Z | in om. O 5 secundum] per L 6 Sed om. H | Sed — falsum om. KU 7 eliciens] elicitive L | autem illa] inv. Q | causatur immediate] inv. H creatur(?) immediate X | immediate] in movente N   8 obiecto] opposito O aliquo X | non] si FW X sic Z | requireretur] requiretur NO F requiritur H sequeretur(!) L | est falsum] inv. FW Q X Z 9 Si] praem. Sed FW praem. Nec valet Q Z praem. Nec fiet sed X | dicas] dices H dicis X | ille om. FW Z 10 rectificandum] recipiendum O FW Q X Z | quia] contra M contra hoc est quia FW 11 aliquis] aliquid KU quis FW Q X Z | agere] add. virtus Q | etiam] in X om. Q 12 et] quia X | eius] est O Z om. N | igitur non] autem non NO ergo non L non autem FW Q X Z add. dicit H | passio est] = coniec. edd. passionem NO HLM U Q X Z passione K disponit FW 13 Item] Praeterea KU | recipiendum] rectificandum H | intellectum] intentionem NO intellectionem Q 14 quia] qui X 15 Item] Praeterea KU | praecedentes] praecedens N 16 aliis om. O FW Q X Z | tamen] cum Q 17 praesupponunt om. U | habitus om. X | in] lin. X om. U Q Z 18 igitur] lin. O ergo FW Q X

[39]**Aristot.**, *Eth. Nich.* I c. 3 (AL XXVI³ 378-379; A c. 3, 1095b 24-27); *Auctoritates Aristotelis* (ed. J. Hamesse 233): "Honor magis est in honorante quam in honorato."
[40]Cf. *Auctoritates Aristotelis* (ed. J. Hamesse 240): "Prudentia est recta ratio agibilium.'
[41]Supple: contra *cum cod.* M
[42]**Averroës**, *De an.* III com. 18 (AverL 438): "Haec enim est definitio habitus, scilicet ut habens habitum intelligat per ipsum illud quod est sibi proprium ex se et quando voluerit, absque eo quod indigeat in hoc aliquo extrinseco"; *Auctoritates Aristotelis* (ed. J. Hamesse 190): "Habitus est secundum quem habens ipsum potest agere quando vult."

[C. — Tertium dubium: utrum potentiae cognitivae sint vere activae modo praedicto]

Contra conclusionem[43] in se potest sic argui: omne motivum alicuius passivi est motivum omnium passivorum eiusdem rationis, quia omnis potentia habens aliquod commune pro obiecto primo habet omnia inferiora eo pro per se obiectis; potentia motiva habet pro obiecto primo et adaequato potentiam passivam; igitur habet pro obiecto per se quamlibet potentiam passivam eiusdem rationis et speciei. Si igitur per te potentia sensitiva vel intellectiva est motiva sui ipsius ad actum, cum sit eiusdem rationis et speciei cum sensitiva et intellectiva alterius hominis, sequitur quod eadem ratione movere poterit sensitivam vel intellectivam alterius.

[11] Item, contra modum positionis sic: voluntas in quantum volens est libera; sed dicitur formaliter volens per te[44] in quantum passiva vel receptiva suae volitionis; igitur, in quantum passiva est libera. Quod est inconveniens, quia liberum in quantum huiusmodi habet dominium sui actus nec est subditum.

Ad primum[45] istorum dicendum quod maior est vera tantum de motivo cuius motio transit in passum extrinsecum, non autem de illo cuius operatio est immanens. Non enim oportet quod si moveat se, quod posset aliud.

---

3 conclusionem] positionem H hoc dictum KU | sic argui] inv. F argui KU | omne] esse Z | motivum] motum O necessarium X 4 passivi] passionis Z | motivum] motum O Q | passivorum] passionum Z 5 omnis] lin. X | aliquod] aliquid L Z | primo om. F add. et adaequato KU 6 eo om. Q | pro] quod FW X Z | per om. O | obiectis] obiecto O Q X Z subiectis H om. FW | motiva] notitiam U 7 primo post adaequato Q om. KU | et om. K Q Z | adaequato] ad aequam(!) Z add. aliquam FW | passivam om. U | igitur] ergo L FW Q X | habet om. FW 8 obiecto om. L 9 et speciei om. NO FW Q X Z | Si — speciei om. U | igitur] ergo L FW X | per te] patet N per se O | vel intellectiva om. Q 10 motiva — sit om. Z | rationis et] rationis O om. FW Q X | et — hominis om. Z | cum²] add. potentia FW Q X 11 et] vel FW Q X | sequitur] se omnis X 12 movere post sensitivam Q om. U | movere poterit] inv. (lin. F²) H F²W X Z om. K | sensitivam vel intellectivam] sensitiva et intellectiva K | vel] et H om. O | intellectivam] add. et intellectiva H 13 Item] Praeterea KU | positionis] passionis KU rationis FW Q X Z | sic om. U 14 est] rep. FW Q add. sese X | sed — libera om. U | formaliter] formale NO | volens] libera LM K om. H 15 volitionis] voluntatis N | igitur] ergo L FW Q X | passiva — in quantum om. L | est] rep. FW Q 16 huiusmodi] huius U 17 actus] add. recipiens vero non habet dominium recepti FW | nec] sed FW X et non Z 18 istorum] illorum N H Q X | dicendum] add. (ant. dicendum X) est M F X | vera tantum] inv. FW Q X Z tantum U 19 motivo] motiva L Z | transit] transibilis(?) Q | passum] passivum K | extrinsecum] extrinsece KU 20 operatio] actus L | est] lin. W | immanens] intra manens O manens intra (intellectum X) FW Q X Z | Non enim] Ideo non L | moveat se] mortale(!) O movet se FW Q X Z 21 quod om. X | posset] possit NO Q X Z possit movere L moveri possit F possit moveri W | aliud] alio FW

---

[43] Cf. supra n. 21.
[44] Cf. supra q. 11, n. 14.
[45] Cf. supra n. 33.

36   Vel potest aliter dici quod licet potentia motiva in communi habet pro primo obiecto potentiam passivam in communi, non tamen haec potentia motiva, quae est haec sensitiva vel intellectiva, habet pro obiecto nisi habeat seipsam.

37   Ad aliud[46] dicendum quod volitio qua dicitur volens est quaedam qualitas habitualis spiritualis, libera tantum per participationem, vel quia in subiecto libero essentialiter quod est voluntas, vel quia a principio elicitivo libere, scilicet voluntate, sicut alii actus imperati a voluntate dicuntur liberi per participationem. Dicendum igitur quod si ly in quantum teneatur reduplicative, ita quod dicat illud, cui additur, esse causam inhaerentiae praedicati ad subiectum, falsa est maior, quia volitio non est causa quare voluntas est libera, sed e converso. Si autem ly in quantum teneatur specificative, hoc est dupliciter: aut enim specificat voluntatem ad hoc quod sit eliciens volitionem, et sic maior est vera, quia voluntas sub illa ratione determinata qua eliciens volitionem est libera; si autem ut recipiens formaliter volitionem, ut accipitur in minori, tunc maior est falsa, quia necessario, non libere, recipit volitionem elicitam libere a se ipsa.

---

1 potest] possit X | aliter] ant. potest K alio O om. FW Q X Z | dici om. O | quod] quid U | communi] eo Q   2 habet] habeat O FW Q X habeatur Z | pro om. X Z | obiecto] add. primam Z   3 haec] habet Z | haec² post sensitiva Q | vel intellectiva om. Z   4 habet] habeat Z | pro] add. primo O | obiecto] add. aliquid K | habeat] hanc O Q om. N   5 dicendum] add. est M F | qua dicitur] qua aliquis dicitur L quae dicitur FW X quaedam Z | dicitur volens] inv. N   6 habitualis] habitu O om. FW Q X Z | tantum] tamen N Z   7 quia] add. (post libero M) est LM KU | subiecto] obiecto NO | libero om. Z | essentialiter] esset Z   8 vel — voluntate om. HLM KU | quia] = FW Q X Z quasi NO | elicitivo] electivo O | libere] = NO Z libero FW Q X | scilicet] add. a NO   9 imperati] importati N | dicuntur] divini(?) L | liberi om. F | per participationem] participatione NO M Q X Z om. L   10 igitur] ergo FW Q X om. HL KU | quod om. NO FW X | ly] licet Q om. KU Z | in om. N | teneatur om. L | reduplicative] reduplicatur L   11 illud] idem H | esse] add. tamquam NO | causam] = H FW X Z causa N LM KU Q om. O | praedicati] praesenti(!) Q   12 volitio] add. ut dictum est O FW Q X Z | quare] qua O FW Q Z   13 est] sit O FW Q X Z | sed e converso om. N | ly in quantum om. NO M FW Q X Z | teneatur] tenetur KU   14 enim] lin. F² | specificat] rep. O   15 volitionem] volutionis N | sic] tunc O FW Q X Z | est vera om. X | sub illa] a X   16 qua] add. est K | eliciens] eligens NO M U electionem(?) X | volitionem] volutione N add. et X   17 recipiens] accipiens F | formaliter post volitionem Q formalem N fortior(!) O | volitionem] volitione X | accipitur] arguitur O recipitur X | minori] minore H | tunc] sic O FW Q X Z cum U   18 libere] liber Q | elicitam] elicitivam W   19 libere] licite N liberam F | ipsa] propriam Z

[46]Cf. supra n. 34.

[IV. — Ad argumenta principalia]

[12] Ad primum principale[47] dicendum quod pro tanto dicuntur pati, quia huiusmodi potentiae non dicuntur formaliter sentire et intelligere in quantum eliciunt, sed in quantum illos actus recipiunt, vel secundum ALIQUOS[48] propter hoc quod in potentiis sunt duae passiones: una respectu obiecti a quo recipiunt speciem, et haec est prima, et secunda est respectu sui ipsius, ut elicit actum cognoscendi, et haec est receptio cognitionis; una autem tantum[49] a quo sit iudicium de obiecto.

Ad secundum[50] dicendum quod tantum concludit contra EMPEDOCLEM ponentem sensum realiter esse compositum ex sensibilibus, et per consequens sequitur quod posset sentire, cum habeat sensibile realiter praesens. Nos autem ponimus sensum recipientem speciem esse aliud a sensibili.

Ad tertium[51] dicendum quod consequentia non tenet nisi de operationibus transeuntibus extra, ut patet per PHILOSOPHUM ibidem de artifice, ligno et arca; sed operationes immanentes intra possunt diversificari ab obiectis, potentia passiva et activa manente eadem, ut patet de visione albi et nigri, quae diversas dant species, et causa est quia causantur a diversis sensibilibus.

---

2 dicendum *om.* H *add.* est F | dicuntur pati quia] quia O *om.* N | pati] passive(!) L   3 quia] quod H | huiusmodi] huius N U F X | formaliter *om.* H *add.* non KU | et] vel FW Q X Z   4 eliciunt] efficiunt Z | illos] istos U X   5 aliquos] alios K FW Q Z | quod *om.* Z | potentiis] potentia X | duae *om.* K   6 una] unam X | obiecti] oppositi O | est *om.* X   7 et *om.* Q | secunda] natura N | est *om.* NO F | sui *om.* N | elicit] elicientis FW Q X elicitis Z   8 autem *om.* K Q | tantum] tamen H est L | a quo] actio O Q X actio qua L actum FW Z   9 sit] =L U sit NO HM K scilicet FW Q X secundum Z | iudicium de] motum ab HM KU iudicium ab Q indifferentia de X   10 secundum] aliud Z | dicendum] *add.* est M | concludit] includit X   11 sensum *om.* F | realiter] ant. sensum KU *post* esse HLM | esse *post* compositum X | compositum] comparationem Z Q Z | posset] *om.* Q | sentire] possit NO posse Q *add.* se FW   12 quod *om.* Q Z | posset] possit NO posse Q *add.* se FW   *add.* et quod posset sentire sine alio exteriori FW   13 realiter] reale N | autem] enim L *om.* K   14 speciem] sensationem O FW Q X Z   15 dicendum] *add.* est M X | consequentia *post* tenet H quam communia(?) X   16 transeuntibus] transmutabilibus N transcendentibus H   17 ibidem] ibi F | de] *rep.* H | artifice] architectura(?) KU | immanentes] manentes O K FW X Z | intra] ant. manentes FW X Z *om.* Q   18 diversificari] diversificare(!) KU | ab] de K | passiva et activa] activa et passiva H KU FW Q X passiva Z   19 eadem] eodem O | et nigri *om.* U X | quae] qui U quam X | diversas] diversos U diverse Z *om.* NO | dant] differunt NO dicuntur Z | species] specie NO X   20 et causa est] tamen FW Q X tamen (tum O) quia sunt (*add.* ducere(?) O) diversi NO *om.* Z | sensibilibus] specie FW Q X Z

[47]Cf. supra n. 1; cf. **Duns Scotus**, *Metaph.* VII q. 14 n. 29 (OPh IV 290): "Nam potentia cognitiva non tantum habet recipere speciem obiecti, sed etiam tendere per actum suum in obiectum. Et istud secundum est essentialius potentiae, quia primum requiritur propter imperfectionem potentiae. Et obiectum principalius est obiectum quia in ipsum tendit potentia, quam quia imprimit speciem."
[48]Cf. supra n. 6.
[49]Subaudi: illud est.
[50]Cf. supra n. 2.
[51]Cf. supra n. 3.

41 Ad ultimum[52] dicendum quod assimilatio bene requiritur ad cognitionem, sed non sufficit nisi similiter sit iudicium respectu obiecti cuius habetur similitudo impressa vel expressa; illud perficit assimilationem et conformitatem quae constituit cognitionem.

[V. — Confirmatio per auctoritatem Aristotelis]

42 Confirmatio principalis conclusionis per PHILOSOPHUM II *De anima*,[53] quod odorare non est pati ab odorabili, quia est sentire; igitur sentire non tantum est pati ab obiecto.

43 Item, III eiusdem[54] dicit quod sentire non est motus, quia est actus perfectus; perfectum autem per se non est recipiens, sed potius agens; igitur maior[55] est actio.

---

1 dicendum] dico KU *add.* est M | quod *om.* Z 2 nisi] quod X quando Z | similiter] ant. nisi KU simpliciter N ?? O *om.* H FW Q X Z | sit] fiat KU adsit FW Q X assit Z | iudicium] indicium(!) N | respectu obiecti] de obiecto O FW Q X Z 3 cuius habetur] cuiuslibet NO | similitudo] similatio(!) H *add.* vel Q | impressa *om.* Z | illud] idem U istud W Z *add.* enim L 4 assimilationem] ad similitudinem F | quae] ergo L 6 Confirmatio principalis conclusionis] = LM U Confirmatio principalis N Confirmatur conclusio principalis O FW Q X Z Confirmatur principalis conclusio H Confirmatio est principalis conclusionis K 7 odorare] odorari(!) N | non *om.* Z | quia] quod FW | quia — igitur] quia tunc aer posset odorare etiam (et X) odorare est ergo (*om.* Q) Q X | est — igitur *om.* L | sentire] *add.* quia sentire posset odorare FW 8 igitur] ergo FW Z | tantum est pati] = N LM est tantum pati O KU FW Q X est pati tantum H est pati Z | ab] pro X 9 eiusdem] idem H De anima Q | dicit] dicitur Z | quod] quia H *om.* Z | est² *post* actus X 10 perfectus] perfecti NO FW Q X | perfectum] perfectionem Q | autem] *add.* non N | est *om.* L | recipiens] incipiens X | potius *om.* L 11 igitur] ergo U FW Q X | maior] maius M minor KU magis FW Q X Z | actio] *add.* etc. N X *add.* igitur etc. K

[52] Cf. supra n. 4.
[53] **Aristot.**, *De an.* II c. 24 (B c. 12, 424b 3-9).
[54] **Aristot.**, *De an.* III c. 6 (Γ c. 7, 431a 4-7).
[55] Intellige: sentire est potius actio quam passio.

[QUAESTIO 13]

UTRUM DE INTENTIONE PHILOSOPHI FUERIT PONERE INTELLECTUM AGENTEM ALIQUID ANIMAE NOSTRAE VEL POTIUS SUBSTANTIAM SEPARATAM

Utrum de intentione PHILOSOPHI fuit ponere intellectum agentem aliquid animae nostrae vel potius substantiam separatam.[1]

[1] Videtur ALIQUIBUS secundum PHILOSOPHUM[2] esse aliquid animae nostrae, ut patet per rationes THOMAE in II *Contra Gentiles*[3].

[Opiniones variae una cum sententiis Scoti]
[A. — Opinio prima]

Sed contrarium videtur ALIIS[4] esse de intentione PHILOSOPHI:

Quod probant sic: activum et passivum quae non sunt univoca, non sunt eiusdem naturae; sed intellectus agens et possibilis non sunt univoca secundum PHILOSOPHUM,[5] quia agens est incorruptibilis, passivus intellectus est corruptibilis; igitur, etc.

Item, numquam ars et materia vel lumen et color sunt eiusdem naturae; sed intellectus agens comparatur ad possibilem intellectum

---

5 Utrum] *praem.* Quaeritur N FW Q X *praem.* Quaeritur an U *adnot. mg.* Quaestio 13 M *adnot. ult. in imo fol.* pro materia(?) istius quaestionis nota bene Sententias super primum d. 3 q. 5 et 6 M *adnot. mg.* quaestio decima tertia KU | Philosophi *om.* X | fuit] fuerit NO FW Q X sit M Z | agentem] *add. (mg.)* esse Q² 6 substantiam separatam] separatum N 7 nostrae *om.* FW Q X | aliquibus] alibi NO 8 nostrae *om.* FW Q X | per — in] a doctore quodam Q | rationes] rationem H KU | in *om.* O F | in — Gentiles] et secundum Gentiles N | II] *add.* de L U 11 contrarium videtur aliis] aliis videtur contrarium Q | aliis] *add. seu rep.* videtur U | esse *om.* X | Philosophi *om.* NO 12 Quod] Quia H | probant sic] *inv.* Q 13 agens *om.* X | et] etiam X | et — agens² (med. n. 3) *om.* NO 14 quia] *add.* intellectus K | est *om.* L | incorruptibilis] corruptibilis(!) U 15 passivus] potentiae H possibilis KU | intellectus *om.* Q | est *om.* X | corruptibilis] incorruptibilis F | igitur etc.] ergo etc. FW igitur Q *om.* X 16 Item] Praeterea FW Q X | vel *om.* L U 17 possibilem intellectum] *inv.* NO FW Q

[1] **Aristot.**, *De an.* III c. 4 (Γ c. 5, 430a 20-25); **Thomas**, *Summa theol.* I q. 79 a. 3 (V 264a—265b).
[2] **Aristot.**, *De an.* III c. 4 (Γ c. 5, 430a 14).
[3] Cf. **Thomas**, *Summa contra Gent.* II c. 77, 78 (XIII 488a—495b).
[4] **Rogerus Bacon**, *Opus maius* II c. 5 (ed. Bridges III 44-49); **Ioannes Pecham**, *Quodl.* IV q. 4 n. 16 ad 1 (ed. Delorme-Etzkorn 184:73—185:89); **Rogerus Marston**, *Quaest. disp. de anima* q. 3 (BFS VII 258).
[5] **Aristot.**, *De an.* III c. 4 (Γ c. 5, 430a 22-25): "Separatus autem est solus hoc quod vere est. Et hoc solum immortale et perpetuum est. Non reminiscimur autem, quia hoc quidem impassibile, passivus vero intellectus corruptibilis, et sine hoc nihil intelligit."

animae nostrae, sicut ars ad materiam et lumen ad colores⁶; igitur, etc.

4   Item, substantia nobilior habet nobiliorem operationem; intellectus agens est nobilior possibili secundum PHILOSOPHUM;⁷ igitur nobiliorem habet operationem. Sed abstrahere, quod attribuitur agenti, non est ita nobilis operatio sicut intelligere, quod attribuitur possibili; igitur habet nobiliorem operationem quam abstrahere, scilicet intelligere, et per consequens est quaedam intellectualis substantia separata ab intellectu possibili.⁸

5   Item, PHILOSOPHUS dicit⁹ quod "est semper in actu separatus et immixtus", igitur, etc. Certum est autem quod anima nostra non est semper in actu intelligendi; et sic igitur non est aliquid animae nostrae secundum PHILOSOPHUM.

6   Dicunt igitur ILLI¹⁰ quod PHILOSOPHUS per rationem positam III *De anima*¹¹ non intendit probare quod in anima nostra sit aliquis intellectus agens tamquam pars eius, sed quod est in ea sicut movens in moto; non per essentiam, sed per influentiam vel quantum ad eius operationem ad quam concurrit intellectus agens. Et hoc tali ratione: quando potentia reducitur ad actum, ad actum illum concurrunt agens et patiens; sed anima de potentia intelligente fit

---

1 materiam] naturam F | et] *add.* sicut NO FW Q X | colores] *add.* secundum Philosopho FW X | igitur etc.] ergo etc. FW igitur Q X   3 Item] Praeterea NO H FW Q | nobiliorem operationem] *inv.* KU W Q X *add.* sed X   4 est nobilior] *inv.* F | igitur] ergo L FW Q X   5 nobiliorem habet] *inv.* NO FW Q | operationem] actum N   6 operatio] *add.* et O   7 igitur habet] ergo habet L FW Q *om.* X | habet — possibili] agenti attribuetur alia operatio nobilior quam abstrahere scilicet intelligere et per consequens alia substantia separata ab intellectu possibili intelligit N | nobiliorem operationem] *inv.* FW Q   8 scilicet] sicut H | est] igitur O | quaedam] quod F | intellectualis substantia] *inv.* FW Q substantia intelligibilis O   10 Item] Praeterea NO FW Q X | quod] *add.* intellectus agens L | separatus] separabilis NO | et *om.* FW Q   11 immixtus] mixtus X | igitur etc.] ergo etc. L FW etc. ergo Q *om.* NO X | Certum — autem] Certum tamen est N Cum tamen est autem O | quod] quo O | est semper] *inv.* L   12 et sic *om.* L KU FW Q X | igitur] ergo L FW Q X   13 secundum Philosophum *om.* N   14 igitur] ergo L FW Q X *om.* H KU | per rationem *om.* F   15 probare — intellectus *om.* X   16 eius *om.* L | sed — eius] *mg.* U | sicut] tamquam H ut K | movens] motus N X   17 moto] toto U *add.* et H | non *om.* O   18 agens] *add. seu rep.* tamquam pars eius sed quod est in ea O   19 quando potentia] qua posita N | reducitur] deducitur X | ad *om.* W | actum] *add.* secundum KU | actum illum] istum actum N X illum actum FW Q | concurrunt] concurrit et O M X Z   20 sed] licet H | fit] facit H U

---

⁶**Aristot.**, *De an.* III c. 4 (Γ c. 5, 430a 12-14).
⁷**Aristot.**, *De an.* III c. 4 (Γ c. 5, 430a 18-19); *Auctoritates Aristotelis* (ed. J. Hamesse 187): "Agens est nobilius et honorabilius passo et forma materia"; cf. **Thomas**, *Summa theol.* I q. 84 a. 6 in corp. (V 324a).
⁸Cf. **Ioannes Pecham**, *Quaestiones de an.* q. 6 n. 52-53 (ed. Etzkorn, BFS XXVIII 402) ; *Quaestiones de an.* q. 7 n. 11 (ed. Etzkorn, BFS XXVIII 413); cf. etiam **Petrus I. Olivi**, *Summa* II q. 58 (BFS V 458).
⁹**Aristot.**, *De an.* III c. 4 (Γ c. 5, 430a 17-18).
¹⁰Cf. **Rogerus de Marston**, *Quaest. Disp. De anima* q. 3 (BFS VII 258-259).
¹¹**Aristot.**, *De an.* III c. 4 (Γ c. 5, 430a 20).

aliquando actu intelligens; igitur ad actum intelligendi non tantum sufficit intellectus possibilis, sed requiritur intellectus agens.[12]

Item, agens et materia numquam coincidunt; intellectus agens et possibilis sunt sicut agens et materia secundum PHILOSOPHUM;[13] igitur non sunt eiusdem naturae partes secundum essentiam, sed tantummodo secundum influentiam — sicut movens est in moto, ita intellectus agens est in anima.

[B. — Opinio secunda]

[3] ALII[14] dicunt quod est habitus principiorum. Quod sic potest intelligi quod sit 'habitus': 'habitus[15] est quo quis utitur cum voluerit'; ita intellectus agens est quo homo utitur respectu possibilis cum voluerit se et intellectum possibilem ad illum convertere. Vel sic potest intelligi quod sicut unum contrarium, scilicet perfectius, dicitur habitus respectu imperfectioris, quod dicitur privatio,[16] sic intellectus agens, qui est perfectior, dicitur habitus respectu possibilis.

[C. — Quomodo quaedam dicta Aristotelis intelligenda sint]

[DICTUM PRIMUM] — Item, dicit[17] quod lumen facit potentia

---

1 aliquando *om.* N | intelligens] intellectus X | igitur] ergo L FW   2 requiritur intellectus] *inv.* O   3 Item] Praeterea O FW Q X | Item — materia *om.* N | numquam] non H KU | coincidunt] concidunt(!) N   4 sicut] *add.* materia W | et²] *add.* patiens sive L   5 igitur] ergo L FW Q W   6 tantummodo secundum] tantum secundum H tantum ut dictum est per NO FW Q X Z | movens] motus N | est *om.* H | in moto] motor(!) U | ita] sicut H sic X *om.* Q   9 est] sit L *om.* U | est habitus] *inv.* H | principiorum] principii H principium U X | sic] sicut H   10 quod sit habitus] quod sic sit habitus N *om.* L *add.* qui K | quis] quilibet Q aliquis X   11 ita — voluerit *om.* F | homo] quis L U   12 et *om.* N | intellectum] intelligere NO | ad illum] ad istum NO *om.* U Z | Vel] Et X | sic potest] *inv.* H KU   13 unum *om.* L | scilicet] sit NO si scilicet K | perfectius] perfectionis Q   15 dicitur] sicut NO   18 Item] Tunc NO | facit] *add.* colores NO

[12]Hic terminant ex abrupto codices N et O qui textum ex quaestione quinta excerptum interponunt; deinde (f. 168va N; f. 51va O) codices iterum textum quaestionis exhibent. Cf. supra praefatio nostra, §2C, 62-63.
[13]**Aristot.**, *De an.* III c. 4 (Γ c. 4, 430a 10-16).
[14]Opinio Themistii quae recitatur apud **Aegidium Romanum**, *De an.* III com. 18 (71ra); cf. **Thomas**, *De an.* III c. 4 (XLV¹ 219a).
[15]**Averroës**, *De an.* III com. 18 (AverL 438): "Haec enim est definitio habitus, scilicet ut habens habitum intelligat per ipsum illud quod est sibi proprium ex se et quando voluerit, absque eo quod indigeat in hoc aliquo extrinseco"; *Auctoritates Aristotelis* (ed. J. Hamesse 190): "Habitus est secundum quem habens ipsum potest agere quando vult."
[16]Cf. *Auctoritates Aristotelis* (ed. J. Hamesse 136): "Privatio et habitus sunt radices contrariorum"; cf. **Aristot.**, *Metaph.* X c. 4 (AL XXV$^{3.2}$ I c. 4 1055a 33-35).
[17]**Aristot.**, *De an.* III c. 4 (Γ c. 4, 430a 14-16): "... ut lumen; quodam enim modo et lumen facit potentia exsistentes colores actu colores."

colores, actu colores, cuius contrarium videtur Philosophus innuere II *De anima*.[18]

10 Dicendum quod sicut appropinquans agens ad patiens dicitur agere vel disponens materiam ultimate dicitur informare, quia statim sequitur actio vel informatio, sic lumen dicitur facere colores actu, id est actu visibiles, in quantum disponit medium, quo facto, statim color potest movere visum; sic movens visum est actu color, non quidem actu primo tantum sed etiam actu secundo.

11 [Dictum secundum] — Item, ex littera Philosophi[19] in illa parte "quoniam in omni natura,' etc. volunt aliqui[20] dicere quod nihil movet seipsum, quod per rationem Philosophi patet.

12 Dicendum igitur quod movens ad actum primum, quod est generans realiter differt a moto, quia nihil generat seipsum; sed ad actum secundum aliquid potest movere seipsum, sicut grave movet seipsum ad ubi, licet non ad formam substantialem gravis; sic etiam intellectus et voluntas movent se ad actus suos. Modo ita est secundum Philosophum,[21] quod intellectus agens movet intellectum possibilem ad actum primum, non tamen ad actum secundum, ideo realiter differunt secundum eum, et ideo si intellectus possibilis est aliquid animae nostrae, oportet ponere intellectum agentem esse quandam substantiam separatam secundum ipsum. Et ad hoc

---

1 actu colores] inv. L | Philosophus innuere] inv. X   3 Dicendum] add. est M F Z adnot. mg.: Opinio propria L | sicut] sic U | appropinquans] approximans Q | ad] sive NO   4 disponens] disponere N | materiam] naturam X | informare — statim] inferior respectu illius (om. O) quod immediate (statim O) NO   5 sequitur] requiritur O | vel] et N | sic] sicut O | colores] add. in HL U   6 est] add. in H   7 color potest] inv. KU | visum] add. (mg. M²) et color M² FW Q X Z | sic] sicut N | est actu] inv. N   8 quidem] quid U | etiam] in X om. KU Q   9 Item] Tunc NO | in — parte om. N | illa] ista L respectu(!) U   10 quoniam om. X | natura om. Q X | etc. om. M U Q Z | aliqui] quidam KU | dicere] habere FW Q X   11 movet] producit X | seipsum quod] ipsum et F | Philosophi om. K   12 Dicendum] add. est M Z | igitur] ergo FW X om. Q | igitur quod actio om. U | movens] = O FW Q X motus N actio mobilis HLM K Z mobilis U | ad om. Q | primum] unum X | quod² om. FW Q X KU   13 realiter differt] inv. N rem differt HLM KU realiter differunt Q | a om. F | moto] motu HLM KU F Z | nihil om. Q | sed — seipsum om. H   14 secundum] inquantum O | aliquid] aliquis K | potest movere] inv. NO add. se W | sicut] sic U | movet seipsum] movet NO movet se KU ipsum movet FW   15 ubi] materiam W | sic] sicut O H Q | etiam] et F om. H   17 quod] ant. secundum NO FW Q X | movet om. O | intellectum om. Q   18 secundum] add. et N | ideo] non(!) O   19 secundum] sed O | secundum eum] se ipsum X om. FW | eum — secundum om. NO Q | est] sit U add. ad X   20 animae om. K | esse om. L   21 secundum — Scriptura om. X | ipsum] Philosophum F | Et] Etiam H | ad hoc] huic N FW Q hoc O

---

[18]**Aristot.**, *De an.* II c. 15 (B c. 7, 419a 1-4): "Non autem omnia visibilium sunt in lumine, sed solum uniuscuiusque proprius color; quaedam enim in lumine quidem non videntur, in tenebra autem faciunt sensum, ut quae videntur et lucentia."
[19]**Aristot.**, *De an.* III c. 4 (Γ c. 5, 430a 10-11): "Quoniam autem sicut in omni natura ..."
[20]Cf. **Aegidium Romanum**, *De an.* III com. 17 (f. 70vb).
[21]**Aristot.**, *De an.* III c. 4 (Γ c. 5, 430a 10-19); cf. **Thomas**, *De an.*. III c. 4 (XLV¹ 220a); **Rogerus Marston**, *Quaest. disp. de anima*, q. 3 in corp. (BFS VII 258).

concordat Sacra Scriptura,²² quae ponit Deum esse illud lumen quod ARISTOTELES ponit intellectum agentem; unde Ioannes primo²³: "Ipse est qui illuminat omnem hominem venientem in hunc mundum;" et in Psalmo:²⁴ "Multi dicunt quaerendo quis ostendit nobis bona," et respondet: "Signatum est super nos lumen vultus tui, Domine," etc.

[D. — Opinio tertia et probabilior]

ALII²⁵ tamen dicunt, et probabiliter, quod intellectus agens et possibilis idem sunt in re, differunt tamen ratione vel officiis, quia intellectus, ut eliciens actum intelligendi, dicitur agens, ut recipiens autem intellectionem, dicitur possibilis. Dicuntur autem duae differentiae a PHILOSOPHO,²⁶ scilicet scientificum et ratiocinativum dicuntur duae potentiae diversae in genere, quae tamen sunt idem in re, ut dicunt; differunt tamen in ratione, secundum quod eadem potentia considerat necessaria et contingentia, et illae sunt ratio superior et inferior secundum AUGUSTINUM.²⁷

---

1 quae] quod X | Deum] *add.* ipsum (*ant.* Deum M Q Z) NO M FW Q X Z | illud] idem H *om.* Q 2 Aristoteles ponit] *inv.* NO FW Q X | intellectum agentem] esse intellectus agens NO M FW Q X | primo] secundo X 3 Ipse — mundum] Erat lux vera Q | est *om.* NO H | omnem hominem] *inv.* O 4 mundum] etc. N | in Psalmo *post* bona H Psalmo K | dicunt] *rep.* H | quaerendo *om.* K Q *add.* scilicet FW 5 ostendit] ostendet L | bona] etc. H | respondet] respondit L responsio est Q respondent X *add.* est F 6 vultus tui] tuum Q | etc. *om.* LM Q X Z 8 tamen *om.* H | dicunt] *add.* aliter Q *adnot. mg.* Opinio L | et possibilis *om.* X 9 in *om.* NO FW X | tamen *om.* Q *add.* in HM Z | vel] et N 11 autem *om.* L | intellectionem] intentionem NO FW X actum intelligendi Q *om.* K | autem² *om.* X 12 differentiae] *add.* animae Q X | scilicet] sic H sicut FW Q X *add.* in NO | et *om.* O 13 dicuntur duae *om.* K | potentiae diversae] *inv.* N differentiae diversae HL diversae differentiae K | in *om.* NO M FW X | quae tamen sunt] quia cum sint O | sunt idem] *inv.* H K 14 in *om.* NO FW Q X | ut dicunt *om.* X | in² *om.* NO FW Q X | ratione] *add.* quia Q | quod] quid X 15 considerat] concipiat N | necessaria et contingentia] contingentia et necessaria N | illae] illa L K | ratio] *add.* sive potentiae F *add.* sive prior W 16 superior et inferior] inferior et superior Q | Augustinum] *add.* etc. HL X

²²Hic desinit ex abrupto codex U. Deest autem ei tam quaestio 14 quam initium quaestionis 15; deinde f. 16r codex U sic resumit: "Item, si distinctio animarum", q. 15 n. 15.
²³Cf. **Ioh.** 1:9.
²⁴Cf. **Ps.** 4:6.
²⁵Cf. **Ioannes de Rupella**, *Tractatus de anima*, p. II, c. 21 (ed. Michaud-Quantin 91); **Richardus Rufus de Cornubia**, *Abbreviatio*, II, d. 24, q. 6 (Civitas Vaticana, Bibliotheca Apostolica Vaticana cod. 12993, f. 237ra): "Concedatur tamen quod sint in anima ut vult Philosophus poni. Sunt ergo ibi sic distinctae (*cod.* distingui) ut sint unum per essentiam et differant secundum opera et obiecta et ita potentiae diversae dicantur." cf. **Augustinus**, *De Trinitate* XII, c. 4 (PL 42 1000, CCL 50 358).
²⁶**Aristot.**, *De an.* III c. 4 (Γ c. 5, 430*a* 13): "... necesse et in anima esse has differentias ..."; **Aristot.**, *Eth. Nic.* VI c. 2 (AL XXVI¹⁻³ 478-9; Z c. 2 1139*a* 4-15): "Dictum est duas esse partes animae, et rationem habens, et irrationale. Nunc autem de rationem habente ... supponantur duo ... horum hoc quidem scientificum, hoc autem ratiocinativum."
²⁷**Augustinus**, *De Trinitate* XII, c. 4 (PL 42 1000, CCL 50 358).

[QUAESTIO 14]

UTRUM SPECIES MANEANT IN INTELLECTU, CESSANTE ACTU INTELLIGENDI

Utrum[1] species maneant in intellectu, cessante actu intelligendi.

[1] DICITUR[2] quod non:

Quia omnis qualitas mansiva in intellectu disponens eum ad intelligendum est habitus intellectivus per definitionem habitus,[3] qui est de difficili mobilis disponens potentiam ad agendum; sed species disponit intellectum ad intelligendum; si igitur est mansiva, cessante actu, est idem quod habitus intellectivus. Hoc autem patet manifeste esse falsum per inductionem in habitibus intellectivis, qui sunt sapientia, scientia, intellectus, ars, et prudentia.[4] Item, patet per rationem, quia species sequitur actum intelligendi, non autem praecedit, sed habitus praecedit.

Item, si species unius obiecti maneret, cessante actu, eadem ratione species alterius; sed impossibile est plures species manere in eodem subiecto, quia, cum species assimilentur figurae secundum PHILOSOPHUM II *De anima*,[5] sequitur quod idem subiectum posset configurari diversis figuris, et ad diversa obiecta, quod falsum est;

---

4 Utrum] *praem.* Quaeritur NO FW Q X Z *praem.* Quaeritur 14 K *adnot. mg.* Quaestio 14 M K | maneant] manet H Q manent K maneat FW 5 Dicitur] Videtur H FW Q X Z *om.* NO | non] *add.* videtur K 6 mansiva] mensuratur X 7 intellectivus] intellectus L | definitionem] defectum O dispositionem X 8 qui est *om.* K | potentiam] subiectum N | agendum] cognoscendum Q 9 ad intelligendum *om.* NO | intelligendum] agendum X | si] sic X | igitur] ergo FW Q X | est *om.* X | mansiva] mansive H massiva Q 10 intellectivus] intellectus H 11 manifeste *om.* NO FW Q X Z | esse falsum] *inv.* K | intellectivis *om.* X | qui] = NO M quae HL K FW Q X Z 12 scientia *om.* FW Z *add.* et X | prudentia] *add.* 6 Ethicorum Q | Item] Tunc O | patet *post* rationem F *om.* N X 13 per rationem] ratione Q | species] habitus H | non — praecedit²] habitus autem praecedit FW si autem praecedit Q X Z *add. ult.* habitus alius praecedit Z 14 habitus] species H | praecedit²] *add.* (*mg.*) non praecedit M² 15 Item] Praeterea NO FW Q X Z | maneret] manet H manent X manens Z | actu *om.* X 16 species²] *add.* (*ant.* plures O FW) simul NO FW Z 17 subiecto] obiecto H | cum] *lin.* Q | assimilentur] assimilantur N K assimiletur FW Q X | secundum Philosophum *post* De anima FW 18 Philosophum] *add.* in M | sequitur] sequeretur FW Q X Z | posset configurari] configuratur N potest figurari H possit configurari L FW Z 19 et] *lin.* W | ad] a X | diversa obiecta] *inv.* K | obiecta] opposita NO | falsum est] *inv.* K

[1] Q. 14 deest in cod. U.
[2] Cf. **Thomas**, *Summa theol.* I q. 79 a. 6 (V 270a—271b).
[3] Cf. **Aristot.**, *Praedic.* c. 8 (AL I³ 102; c. 8, 9a 8-10): "Quare differt habitus a dispositione eo quod haec quidem facile mobilis sit, hic autem diuturnior et difficilius mobilis."
[4] **Aristot.**, *Eth. Nic.* VI c. 3 (AL XXVI^{1-3} 480; Z c. 3 1139b 14-17).
[5] Cf. **Aristot.**, *De an.* II c. 23-24 (B c. 11-12, 424a 1-24).

igitur, etc.

3   Contra:

Quando aliquid de potentia essentiali reducitur ad potentiam accidentalem, oportet quod hoc sit per aliquid sibi formaliter impressum, quod habet rationem actus primi, quod tamen est in potentia propinqua ad actum secundum; sed, cessante actu intelligendi, intellectus est in potentia accidentali ad intelligendum, non autem essentiali tantum, sicut ante intelligere est; igitur habet speciem sibi impressam, vel saltem sibi expressam.

[I. — Opinio Avicennae apud mentem Thomae]

4   Dicendum quod, secundum ALIQUOS,[6] opinio AVICENNAE VI *Naturalium*[7] est quod species non sit in intellectu nostro nisi quando actu considerat per hunc modum, quia quando intellectus noster convertit se ad intelligentiam separatam, tunc tantum intelligit, quia tunc speciem ab ea recipit.

5   Et ratio huius est quia quando potentia est de se cognoscitiva, non requiritur in ea species nisi praesente obiecto, sicut quia organum de se non est cognoscitivum, ideo est in eo species, etiam absente sensibili; sed intellectus noster est potentia de se cognoscitiva, et non indiget specie nisi praesente intellecto scibili exsistente.

---

1 igitur etc.] ergo etc. FW Q *om.* N L X | etc.] *rep.* O   4 oportet quod] sed O oportet H *om.* N | hoc *om.* O K | sit] esse H | per] propter Z | sibi *om.* X | formaliter] conformaliter K *om.* NO   5 actus] alicuius NO | est] non Q *om.* Z   6 actum *om.* FW Q X Z | secundum] sensum Z   7 autem] *add.* in N K   8 tantum] tamen O | tantum — expressam] cum sic multo intelligeret igitur habet speciem sibi impressam tamen sicut *ante* intelligere est igitur etc. N | ante] autem K Q | est] esse F X omne W Q *om.* M Z | igitur] ergo L FW Q *om.* X | speciem sibi] *inv.* X | sibi impressam] *rep.* O   9 saltem] aliter K | sibi *om.* FW X Z | expressam] *add.* ergo Q   11 Dicendum] *add.* est M F *adnot. mg.* Opinio Avicennae L | quod *post* aliquos K | VI] 'V' N H   12 est *om.* X | sit] est N sint M F sunt W Q X Z | quando] *add.* intellectus K   13 considerat] constituat F | quia quando] quod X quando autem Z   14 convertit — quia *om.* X | intelligentiam] intellectivam Z   16 huius] eius L | quia *om.* X Z | est[2] *post* se N | cognoscitiva] cognitiva L K FW X Z   17 in ea species] species in ea NO | nisi praesente] absente M nisi praesentato K non praesente Z | nisi — specie *om.* NO | sicut] sed K *del.* M *add.* patet F | quia — sensibili] in organo est species absente sensibili cum non sit de se cognoscitivum K   18 de *post* est FW | se *om.* L | est *om.* X | cognoscitivum] cognitivum L W Z | ideo — eo *om.* F | eo] ea W X | etiam] et Z   19 noster] non L | est — se] de se est in potentia X potentia *post* se K Q | se *om.* Z   20 et] ut K *add.* ideo FW Q X Z | et — specie] *rep.* W | specie] species L | intellecto scibili] = NO intelligente scibili H obiecto scibilis L intelligente scibilis M K intellectio sciretur FW intellecto scibilis Q X intellecto scitur Z

[6]**Thomas**, *Summa theol.* I q. 79 a. 6 in corp. (V 270*a*).
[7]**Avicenna**, *De an.* pars 5 c. 6 (AviL 128-131).

Si autem arguitur sic: in anima est aliquis habitus, vel potest esse — habitus est quo quis utitur cum voluerit;⁸ sed praesentiam obiecti non habet cum voluerit; igitur, absente obiecto, adhuc potest manere habitus scientiae; hoc autem non est sine specie intelligibili; igitur, etc.

Item, si praesente obiecto tantum esset species, cum acquirere speciem sit addiscere, homo addisceret cum intelligeret actu; hoc autem est falsum; igitur, etc.

Respondet ad hoc quod, ex frequenti conversione intellectus nostri ad intelligentiam illam, generatur in anima nostra quaedam habilitas vel facilitas ad intelligendum, quae vocatur habitus; non oportet autem quod talis facilitas insit ei per speciem remanentem, absente obiecto.

[II. — Argumenta Thomae contra Avicennam]

[3] Contra ista:⁹

Contra primum istorum:¹⁰ si intellectus recipit speciem ab intelligentia separata, tunc frustra anima uniretur corpori. Quod probatur sic: corpus est propter animam, non autem propter esse eius, quia potest esse sine corpore; igitur propter eius operationem quae est

---

1 autem arguitur] inv. NO | arguitur] arguatur FW | sic] si FW X Z | in anima] manifeste X | esse] add. aliquid H add. aliqui K 2 habitus] rep. K add. autem NO FW Z add. aut X | utitur post voluerit Z | praesentiam] praesentia K FW primam Z 3 non] mg. M om. NO Q | igitur] ergo L FW Q X | adhuc potest] inv. L 4 habitus] lin. F | specie om. X | igitur etc.] igitur L ergo etc. FW Z ergo Q om. X 6 Item] Tunc O | esset] est NO | acquirere] acquirendo H 7 sit] sic Z | addiscere] addicere(!) H add. (mg. M) semper O M FW Q X Z | intelligeret] intelliget H add. aliquid X | actu] add. cum F | hoc autem] inv. F hoc NO L K 8 est falsum] inv. FW falsum X | igitur etc.] igitur (mg.) K ergo L om. NO FW Q X Z 9 Respondet] Respondeo N Respondent K | ex frequenti] est fallacia consequentis N | intellectus nostri] inv. N nostri sensus O 10 intelligentiam illam] illam intellectivam Z | illam] istam X 11 habilitas] humilitas O H F | vel] et X | facilitas] facultas(!) K | quae] quod NO 12 autem] tamen Z om. N H 15 Contra] adnot. mg. Opinio Thomae contra Avicennam et contra aliam opinionem L | ista] illa FW hoc Q add. duo probo N add. et K add. sic (om. M X) arguit (argumentis Z) Thomas (Themistius X) M FW Q X Z add. ult. et primo Q 16 Contra primum istorum] = O K Contra primum illorum L Contra primum sic FW Q X Z Contra primum N Contra primum istorum sic (lin. M) M Contra primum illorum scilicet H | si] lin. W om. X Z | si intellectus] inv. Q | recipit] respicit(!) O | intelligentia] intellectiva Z 17 tunc] cum X | frustra] tristitia in O infrustra FW om. N | probatur] probat NO FW Z 18 est] esse Z | autem] nisi H om. L | autem — esse²] propter se K | esse eius] inv. H essentiam eius X | eius] lin. M alidem(?) N ad O om. L 19 potest] propter H | igitur] ergo L FW Q X | operationem] opinionem Z

---

⁸**Averroës**, *De an.* III com. 18 (AverL 438): "Haec enim est definitio habitus, scilicet ut habens habitum intelligat per ipsum illud quod est sibi proprium ex se et quando voluerit, absque eo quod indigeat in hoc aliquo extrinseco"; *Auctoritates Aristotelis* (ed. J. Hamesse 190): "Habitus est secundum quem habens ipsum potest agere quando vult."
⁹Cf. **Thomas**, *Summa theol.* I q. 79 a. 6 in corp. (V 270a).
¹⁰Cf. supra n. 4.

intelligere; sed si posset anima intelligere per conversionem ad substantiam separatam, non indigeret cognitione sensitiva, quae fit per organa corporea, ad intelligendum, et per consequens frustra daretur sibi talis cognitio quae fit mediante corpore, et frustra uniretur corpori; hoc est inconveniens; igitur, etc.

10   Contra principale sic:[11] receptum est in recipiente per modum recipientis;[12] sed intellectus est potentia receptiva multum nobilior sensitiva, et ad nobilitatem recipientis pertinet recepta reservare; potentia sensitiva reservat species sensibilium etiam in eorum absentia, ut experimento patet in memoria et phantasia; igitur, etc.

[III. — Opinio aliquorum argumenta Thomae contra Avicennam reprobantium]

11   Sed ALIIS[13] videtur quod istae rationes non concludunt:

Prima[14] non valet, quia secundum illam sequeretur quod post resurrectionem anima frustra uniretur corpori, quia intelligeret tunc perfectius quam modo et tamen non oriretur sua intellectio a cognitione sensitiva; non igitur corpus vel cognitio sensitiva est propter intellectionem. Dato igitur quod anima uniretur corpori ut

---

1 sed *om.* NO | si *om.* K | posset anima] *inv.* O anima possit N potest anima H posset vere L | per] propter L | ad substantiam] ad intelligentiam N FW Q ad set(!) O ad intellectivam Z | ad — cognitione *om.* X 2 indigeret] indiget F | sensitiva] sensitivam X sensibilia Z | fit] fuit O 3 organa corporea] *inv.* F organa corporalia Z *add.* sensitiva X | ad *om.* X | intelligendum] faciendum N formandum O intellectum L | frustra *om.* Z 4 sibi] ei N | frustra *om.* FW Q X Z 5 corpori] *add.* sed NO | hoc] ergo X *om.* O | igitur etc.] ergo etc. L FW ergo Q *om.* X 6 Contra] Supra Z | Contra — sic] Principalis substantiae N | principale] *add.* et K *add.* arguitur Q | receptum] receptus F | in recipiente] incipientes X | per — recipientis] secundum infinitum realitatis (recipientis O) NO hoc modum recipientis F secundum modum recipientis W Q X Z 7 est potentia] *rep.* O | multum] multo NO FW Q Z iusta X | nobilior] *add.* potentia K 8 et *om.* Q Z | recipientis pertinet] *inv.* FW X Z | recepta reservare] = HM receptum reservare L recipere et reservare K receptatus conservatus N receptare conservare O recepta conservare FW Q X Z 9 potentia sensitiva] *inv.* NO FW Q X Z | species] speciem F potentia Q | etiam] et K *om.* Q 10 ut] sicut N | experimento] experimentat H | patet] *add.* ut K | phantasia] phantasma O | igitur etc.] ergo L Q ergo etc. FW *om.* X 13 Sed] *adnot. mg.* opinio L | aliis] aliquibus X | videtur] videretur X | istae] illae HL FW Q X Z | concludunt] includunt O concludant FW Q 14 non] nec Z | illam] istam N 15 resurrectionem] rationem X | anima] *ant.* post FW | anima frustra] *inv.* Q | quia intelligeret tunc perfectius] quia intelligeret perfectius tunc N eo quod tunc intelligeret L quia tunc intelligeret perfectius K quia intelligeret X quia intelliges perfectius Z 16 non] *add.* et O *om.* FW Q Z | oriretur] orietur O M FW Q X Z *add.* ult. tunc Q | sua] si a O *om.* N | intellectio] intellectus NO cognitio K intellectiva X *add.* ult. tunc N 17 igitur] ergo L FW Q X | vel cognitio *om.* X 18 intellectionem] intellectum N | igitur] ergo L FW Q X | quod] ut NO | uniretur] unitur NO uniatur FW Z | corpori *om.* Q

---

[11]Cf. supra n. 5.
[12]**Thomas**, *Summa theol.* I q. 79 a. 6 (V 270b): "Quod enim recipitur in aliquo, recipitur in eo secundum modum recipientis."
[13]Non invenimus.
[14]Cf. supra n. 9.

constituat totum perfectius quam esset sola — quia est pars tantum —, non autem corpus sibi unitur propter operationem, ut SUPPO-NUNT; sed propter hoc unitur sibi corpus, ut per sensus corporeos cognoscat singularia, sed per conversionem ad intelligentiam separatam cognoscit universalia, ut dicit AVICENNA.[15]

Ratio autem secunda[16] non valet, quia eadem ratione sequitur quod intellectus est firmior et durabilior quam sensus, igitur intelligere est firmius in intellectu quam sentire in sensu; similiter intellectus est firmior ligno, igitur firmius retinet speciem quam lignum figuram. Quae falsa sunt.

[IV. — Notandum de opinione Avicennae]

Dicendum igitur quod opinio AVICENNAE fuit aliquas species esse in intellectu, etiam cessante actu. DICIT enim quod in intellectu sunt species ipsum decorantes,[17] et SUBDIT quod, cum recipit intellectus aliquam speciem ab imaginibus, non recipit aliam eiusdem speciei.[18]

Sed ad modum positionis suae sciendum quod PONIT duplicem conversionem intellectus: unam ad sensibilia, a quibus recipit species intelligibiles, quae sunt singulares respectu intellectus quem

---

1 constituat] constituitur NO constituatur Z | totum] compositum(?) N | quam] add. si Q | sola] illa N solum Z | quia] quae X 2 corpus] corpori(?) X | propter] patet per(?) X rep. F 3 sed] similiter W Q Z | propter — corpus] unitur propter hoc L | unitur] unius O | corpus] corporis(?) O | ut om. Z | per] propter Q | corporeos] corporales N 4 conversionem om. N | intelligentiam] intellectivam Z 5 cognoscit] continuit vel contingit O cognosceret X | ut] non sit X | dicit] diceret FW X Z 6 Ratio autem secunda] Secunda etiam ratio N Ratio etiam secunda O M Q Z Ratio K Respondeo quod secunda FW Respondeo etiam secunda X | sequitur quod] sequitur NO M sequeretur FW Q X Z 7 intellectus] add. scilicet(?) Z | est — intelligere om. O | firmior] nobilior Z | et — in om. N | igitur] ergo L FW Q X 8 est] add. durabilius et L | est firmius post intellectu Q inv. K | sentire] figurare(?) N | in² om. Z | similiter] sicut H sic FW 9 igitur] sicut O ergo L FW Q X | firmius] firmus Z | speciem] sensibilem O 10 falsa] phantasia(?) N 12 Dicendum] add. est M | igitur] ergo FW Q X Z om. HL K | Avicennae om. K | aliquas om. X 13 in] sub K | etiam cessante] inv. N et cessante K cessante FW | enim om. K 14 recipit intellectus] inv. Z receperit(!) intellectus FW Q 15 aliquam] aliam X | imaginibus] imaginantibus(?) N | recipit] recepit F om. Z | aliam] aliquam HL K X 17 modum] intelligendum Q motivum(?) X | positionis] rationis FW | suae om. Z add. videt N add. videndum O add. modum Q | sciendum] add. est HM K F adnot. mg. conversio intellectus duplex K 18 unam] autem X | ad] a FW | a — singulares om. X | recipit] recepit F 19 sunt] rep. N | singulares] res HL K | intellectus] rep. Z | quem] quae O HL K W om. F

[15] Avicenna, *De an.* pars 5 c. 6 (AviL 126-127).
[16] Cf. supra n. 10.
[17] Avicenna, *De an.* pars 5 cap. 6 (AviL 137): "Concedo autem formas rerum subsistere in anima, decorantes et nobilitantes eam, quarum quasi locus est anima mediante intelllectu materiali."
[18] Avicenna, *De an.* pars 5 cap. 6 (AviL 129): "Cum autem aliquam formam repraesentat sensus imaginationi et imaginatio intellectui, et intellectus excipit ex illa intentionem, si postea repraesentaverit ei aliam formam eiusdem speciei quae non est alia nisi numero, iam non excipiet intellectus ex ea aliam formam praeter quam acceperat ullo modo, nisi secundum accidens ..."

informant, universales respectu singularium quae universaliter repraesentant; aliam conversionem PONIT respectu intelligentiae separatae, a qua etiam recipit species. Sed illae non manent nisi ad praesentiam influentiae illius intelligentiae vel intellectus agentis, quod idem est secundum IPSUM 'quia ipse Deus est lux illa quae illuminat omnem hominem' etc.[19] Sicut igitur lux aerem illuminat, et ad eius praesentiam tantum manet lumen in aere, sic, secundum IPSUM, ipsa lux quae est Deus vel intelligentia separata illuminat de necessitate naturae animas nostras se ad eam convertentes, suae lucis speciem imprimendo, praesente actu animae et obiecto.

Si autem arguitur sic contra EUM: aut illae species influxae ab intelligentia et aliae causatae a sensibilibus sunt eiusdem speciei, aut non; si eiusdem, altera earum superfluit ad intelligendum; si alterius, species influxae non valerent ad intelligendum singularia, nec e converso:

RESPONDET ad hoc: quod utraeque sunt eiusdem speciei, non tamen superfluunt influxae, quia per ipsas vigorantur species aliae ut per ipsas intellectus intensius et clarius possit considerare et intelligere.

---

1 informant] inferunt L K add. et FW Q X Z | universales] add. plures Q | universaliter] virtualiter NO intellectum FW universale X   2 repraesentant] reputant Z | aliam — ponit] alia est conversio intellectus K | intelligentiae] intellectivae O   3 qua] quo FW | etiam om. F | species om. X | illae] istae O | manent] remanent X add. (lin.) ibi Q | nisi om. NO   4 influentiae] mg. W influentiam O | illius intelligentiae] inv. FW | intelligentiae om. Z   5 est om. X | ipse om. W | Deus om. X | illa om. Q   6 illuminat — etc.] illa Deus est X | omnem hominem] hominem venientem FW | etc. om. Q | Sicut] Dicit H K Dicis X | igitur] ergo K FW Q X   7 et om. X | tantum om. NO | lumen in] mg. X | sic] sed HL K | secundum ipsum om. X   8 ipsa] illa Z | lux om. X | est Deus] inv. O FW Q X Z | intelligentia] intellectiva X | separata] separatat(!) Z | illuminat om. L | de om. X   9 naturae om. NO | animas] animam Z add. etiam Q | nostras] nostram Z | se — et om. K | eam] ipsam N eas H ipsum L | convertentes] convertante O convertens X Z | suae lucis] inv. L   10 obiecto] opposito O   11 arguitur] arguatur FW Q X | sic post eum K | aut] mg. M om. HL | illae] istae L | species] add. sit Z | ab intelligentia] ad intelligentiam X | ab — sensibilibus] et ab aliis causatae scilicet sensibiles L   12 aliae] illae N om. FW Q X Z | sensibilibus] sensibus NO H F X | aut] lin. O   13 non] add. superficiunt influxae O | eiusdem] add. aut F | altera] alterum K | earum] illarum N H eorum O K | superfluit] superflueret L | ad] quoad N quod O   14 species] speciei NO FW | valerent] valet Z | singularia] inferiora NO FW Q X Z   15 nec e converso om. K   16 Respondet] Diceret NO X Z Dicunt FW Dicetur Q adnot. mg. Responsio Avicennae L | ad hoc om. N | hoc om. O | utraeque] uterque O Z   17 tamen om. F | superfluunt] superficiunt O | quia] quam X | ipsas] eas NO FW Q X Z | aliae] lin. Q alia X   18 per om. K | ipsas] eas Q | intellectus] add. alias N | intensius et clarius] clarius et intensius Q | possit] posset H K | considerare et] concipere et NO confidare et M confirmare X considerare Z om. FW

[19] Ioh. 1:9: "Erat lux vera quae illuminat omnem hominem venientem in hunc mundum."

[V. — Solutio quaestionis]

[5] Respondeo quod species potest manere, cessante actu. Quod probatur sic: quod est causa alterius et prius naturaliter eo, non tamen necessaria, potest esse sine effectu; sed species intelligibilis est causa prior actu intelligendi nec est causa necessaria — quia quod est formale principium intelligendi quo elicitur actus intelligendi, sive sit intelligere sive species, est liberum per participationem a sua causalitate, ut scilicet producat effectum; igitur non est causa necessaria producendi effectum. Intelligimus enim cum volumus, ut dicitur II *De anima*.[20] Potest enim liberum per essentiam, scilicet voluntas, impedire liberum per participationem a sua causalitate ne scilicet producat effectum suum. Igitur species potest esse sine actu.

Item, principium formale potest esse in activo sine actione, sicut actus primus sine secundo, quia actus secundus potest impediri; species autem est formale principium intelligendi in intelligente; igitur, etc.

Item, quod est perfectionis in potentia inferiori, debet esse in potentia superiori; sed perfectionis est in imaginativa potentia habere obiectum praesens in sua specie, absente obiecto reali extrinseco — hoc patet quia in hoc excedit potentias sensitivas particulares et exteriores; igitur potentia intellectiva potest habere obiectum praesens in specie, remota eius actuali consideratione.

---

2 Respondeo] *adnot. mg.* responsio propria ad illas opiniones L *adnot. mg.* species K | actu] intellectu L *om.* X   3 probatur] probo H M Z | et] etiam F | prius] primus Z | eo *om.* N   4 necessaria] intra O necesse F necessario Q   5 causa] *mg.* M *om.* NO K | intelligendi] intelligentia X | intelligendi — igitur *om.* NO | nec] *add.* tamen K | necessaria *om.* X | quia — necessaria *om.* Z | quod *om.* FW X   6 intelligendi] *add.* id est FW Q X | actus intelligendi] intellectio Q   7 intelligere] intellectus FW Q X | sive²] *add.* sit H K | a — effectum *om.* FW Q X   8 ut] ne M *adnot. mg.* ut M | producat] producit H | effectum — producat] *mg.* M² *om.* HL K | igitur] ergo FW Q X   9 volumus] volimus(!) Q   11 impedire] impedi N | ne] naturae NO ut X | scilicet *om.* M²   12 producat] producant FW | effectum suum] *inv.* Q | Igitur] Ergo L FW Q X Z | actu] *add.* intelligendi Q   13 Item] Praeterea N FW Q X Z *adnot. mg.* secunda ratio ad illud L | principium] *spat. vac.* O principale K X *om.* N | activo] actu N activa F | sine] sive in NO | actione] active F | sicut — impediri] sicut actus primus (*add.* sicut et O) quia potest esse sine (sine eo) *spat. vac.* O) eo actus primus NO   14 primus] principia(!) X | secundus] *mg.* M² primus HL FW Q X | potest impediri] *ant.* actus FW Q X Z   15 formale principium] *inv.* K | in intelligente] *lin.* M² ab intelligente L immediate H K intelligente X   16 igitur etc.] igitur L ergo etc. FW Z *om.* Q X   17 Item] Praeterea NO FW Q X Z *adnot. mg.* tertia ratio L | est] *add.* effectus NO | perfectionis] perfectius L K Q | in *om.* O Z | potentia inferiori] *inv.* NO ipso inferiori W Q X inferiori Z | in potentia superiori] impotentia in superiori potentia N impotentia superiori O superiori potentia Z   18 potentia] ipso Q *om.* K | perfectionis] perfectius L Q | est *post* potentia Z *om.* Q | in *om.* H | imaginativa potentia] *inv.* N H K | potentia² *om.* L *add.* (*mg.*) debet Q   19 obiectum] *add.* (*mg.* W) sibi FW | obiectum — habere *om.* NO | specie] *coni. cum* FW Q X Z sensatione HLM K *add.* pro Z   20 hoc] quod FW Q X Z | quia *om.* X | sensitivas] *add.* et F   21 igitur] ergo L FW Q X   22 praesens *om.* FW Q X Z | in] id est NO

[20] **Aristot.**, *De an.* II c. 12 (B c. 5, 417b 24-25).

19 Item, aliquid potest reduci de potentia essentiali ad accidentalem sine actu; sed per speciem informantem intellectum reducitur[21] de potentia essentiali ad intelligendum ad potentiam accidentalem; igitur, etc.

[VI. — Ad argumenta principalia]

20 Ad primum in oppositum,[22] dicendum quod species potest dici habitus, large sumendo habitum pro forma quae est principium operandi, prout distinguitur habitus a privatione et a dispositione se tenente ex parte materiae, quae est de facili mobilis; non tamen oportet quod sit habitus intellectivus numeratus VI *Ethicorum*[23] ut ratio procedebat, quia si species sit formale principium intelligendi in intelligente, concurrit ad substantiam actus. Habitus autem scientiae vel alius ibidem nominatus non concurrit ad substantiam actus, sed tantum ad modum; habilitat enim potentiam ad bene vel male operandum, ideo non est talis habitus. Si autem sit species tantum repraesentativa obiecti, non autem informans potentiam, nec impressa sed expressa, adhuc non oportet quod sit habitus scientiae vel alius de praedictis, quia species, scilicet talis, non disponit potentiam ad operandum nec ad modum operandi, sicut habitus talis qui est scientia vel alius qui est dispositio perfecti ad

---

1 Item] Praeterea NO FW Q X Z *adnot. mg.* quarta ratio L | potest reduci] reducitur X | ad] in K *om.* O   2 accidentalem] potentiam X | speciem] suppositionem N   3 reducitur] *add.* intellectus M | ad intelligendum *om.* L | ad potentiam accidentalem] de potentia accidentali Z   4 igitur etc.] igitur L Q ergo etc. FW Q etc. X *om.* NO   6 dicendum] *add.* (ant. dicendum Q) est M F Q | potest *om.* X   7 sumendo habitum] loquendo de habitu N | quae] aut Z | quae — operandi] *rep.* O   8 distinguitur] differt N distinguntur K | a² *om.* NO F | se tenente] *inv.* FW existente NO   9 ex] a FW | materiae] naturae X | facili] difficili H K | mobilis] mobili Q   10 quod *om.* X | habitus intellectivus] *inv.* F | intellectivus] intellectus H | numeratus] *add.* in Q | VI] 'V' NO   11 procedebat] procedat K | si *om.* Z | intelligendi] *mg.* W   12 in intelligente] immediate K Q intelligente X | concurrit] concipit N | ad — actus] ad substantiam actus unde non omne quod dat substantiam actus Q quod dat substantiam actus esse potentia X | ad — concurrit *om.* NO | actus] habitus Z *adnot. mg.* distinctione 17 q. 8 M | Habitus] *rep.* H Actus Z   13 scientiae] secundae(?) X | alius] alicuius L | ibidem nominatus] *inv.* K | nominatus] nominatur X   14 habilitat] humilitat O   15 operandum] *add.* et Q | est *om.* F | sit species] *inv.* NO | species *om.* K   16 autem] est N | potentiam] *add.* agendi FW X Z *add.* cognoscendi Q   17 nec] *add.* enim X | sed] nec N Q Z | adhuc] ad hoc F | oportet] oporteret NO   18 alius de praedictis] alicuius praedictorum HL K | quia] *add.* talis Q | scilicet *om.* HL K   19 operandi *om.* N   20 scientia] potentia NO | alius] alicuius HL aliquis K habitus X *add.* ult. habitus talis K

[21]Subaudi: intellectus.
[22]Cf. supra n. 1.
[23]Cf. **Aristot.**, *Eth. Nic.* VI c. 2 (AL XXVI³ 480; Z c. 2 39*b* 15-17): "Sunt utique quibus verum dicit anima affirmando vel negando quinque secundum numerum; haec autem sunt ars, scientia, prudentia, sapientia, intellectus."

optimum, sed tantum est affixa potentiae, loco obiecti repraesentans eum.

Ad aliud,[24] dicendum quod non est simile de specie et figura corporali. Figura enim, cum sit forma realis, non compatitur secum aliam. Species autem et figura spiritualis non habent esse tale in anima, quale habet obiectum in re extra, ut dictum est, et ideo secum compatitur aliam speciem, secundum AUGUSTINUM IX *De Trinitate*[25].

---

1 optimum] operationem(?) N ultimum optimum X | est affixa] a forma FW affixa Z | potentiae] potentia NO FW Z 2 repraesentans] repraesentant X | eum] ipsum NO FW Z illum Q X 3 Ad] Et ad NO | dicendum] *add.* est M *add.* dico X | et] *add.* de HLM 4 realis *om.* X 5 Species] Speciem X | et] in X | spiritualis *om.* NO | habent] habet L Z | esse tale] *inv.* K 6 habet] *add.* esse FW Q X Z | est] *add.* supra FW Q Z 7 secum compatitur] *inv.* NO K | IX] 'XIV' L K FW Q Z 8 De Trinitate] *add.* et ista sufficiant de illa quaestione K

[24] Cf. supra n. 2.
[25] Cf. **Augustinus**, *De Trinitate* IX c. 3 (CCL 50, 296; PL 42, 962); **Aegidius Romanus**, *Quod.* III q. 13 (f. 36ra); **Duns Scotus**, *Lectura* II d. 3 pars 2 q. 1 (XVIII 310-311).

[QUAESTIO 15]

UTRUM INTELLECTUS NOSTER SIT IMMATERIALIS

Utrum[1] intellectus noster sit immaterialis.

[1] Quod sic videtur:

Secundum COMMENTATOREM[2] omne recipiens denudatur a natura recepti, quia, ut IPSE probat, aliter idem reciperet seipsum et esset idem movens et motum; sed intellectus noster intelligit formas exsistentes in materia, recipiendo earum species, ut vult PHILOSOPHUS III *De anima*;[3] igitur, etc.

Item, oportet intellectum, ad hoc quod intelligat, recipere formas universales et absolutas; sed si esset materialis, reciperet eas particulariter tantum et ut particulares; igitur, etc.

Item, anima est forma corporis: aut ergo secundum se totam, et sic nihil eius est materia, quia materia non potest esse forma alterius; aut secundum aliquid sui tantum — illud autem dicimus animam et aliud, scilicet quod non est forma sed formam recipiens, dicimus animatum.[4]

Et hoc sic confirmatur primo: proprietas conveniens toti ratione

---

3 Utrum] *praem.* Quaeritur NO FW Q X Z *praem.* Quaeritur quintodecimo K   4 Quod sic videtur] Quod sic O FW X Arguitur quod sic Z   6 ipse] *add.* idem Q | idem *om.* X | reciperet] recipiet H Z   7 esset idem] *inv.* K Q esset Z | et *om.* X | noster *om.* X   8 exsistentes *om.* K | earum] eorum O Q W | vult Philosophus] *inv.* HM X   9 III] II HLM K | igitur etc.] igitur L ergo etc. FW ergo Q *om.* X   10 Item] Praeterea W Q X Z | Item — etc. *om.* NO | oportet *post* intellectum Q   11 formas] potentias Z | absolutas] abstractas L Q   12 particulariter] *spat. vac.* Z | et *om.* H X | igitur etc.] igitur L ergo etc. FW Q ergo Q *om.* X   13 Item] Praeterea NO FW Q X Z | ergo] igitur NO H K *om.* Z *add.* sensibilem O | totam] ipsam Z   14 nihil] non (*lin.*) F² | eius est materia] est eius materia NO K F Q est materia eius L | quia materia *om.* Z | alterius] communi(!) X   15 illud] idem H   16 et aliud] et alia K FW Q X Z *om.* NO | scilicet quod] = M F *inv.* H sed quae N secundum quae O scilicet quae K secundum quod W X Z scilicet quam Q quod L | non *om.* N Z | formam] potentiam Z   18 hoc *om.* F | sic confirmatur primo] confirmatur sic NO FW Z confirmatur primo sic Q X | primo] *add.* sic L

[1] Codex U deest usque ad par. 15.
[2] **Averroës**, *De an.* III com. 4 (AverL 385-386): "Secunda autem est quod omne recipiens aliquid necesse est ut sit denudatum a natura recepti ...Si enim recipiens esset de natura recepti, tunc res reciperet se, et tunc movens esset motum..."
[3] Aristot., *De an.* III c. 1 (Γ c. 4, 429 *a* 15-23).
[4] Cf. **Thomas**, *Summa theol.* I q. 75 a. 5 in corp. (V 202*a*): "Dicendum quod anima non habet materiam. Et hoc potest considerari dupliciter. Primo quidem, ex ratione animae in communi. Est enim de ratione animae, quod sit forma alicuius corporis. Aut igitur est forma secundum se totam; aut secundum aliquam partem sui. Si secundum se totam, impossibile est quod pars eius sit materia, si dicatur materia aliquod ens in potentia tantum ... Si autem sit forma secundum aliquam partem sui, illam partem dicemus esse animam; et illam materiam cuius primo est actus, dicemus esse primum animatum."

unius partis non convenit toti primo, ut patet V, VII et VIII *Physicorum*[5]. Verbi gratia, motus saltus vel progressivus convenit animali ratione animae tantum, non autem ratione corporis quod quantum est de se movetur tantum deorsum, quia grave est. Similiter, motus deorsum convenit sibi, scilicet animali, ratione corporis tantum. Et ideo neutrum eorum convenit animali primo. Sic ideo: si informare corpus convenit animae ratione formae et non ratione materiae, quod oportet dicere si sit composita ex materia et forma, sequitur quod non sit primus actus corporis, quod est contra definitionem eius.

Deficit hic secunda confirmatio ad argumentum in omnibus codicibus

Item, si sit composita, aut forma animae est adaequata suae materiae et sibi proportionata, aut non. Si sic, igitur non posset corpus informare substantialiter; si non, igitur secundum unum gradum perficit materiam, et secundum alium corpus, scilicet secundum gradum in quo excellit materiam propriam. Cum igitur anima separata nullum corpus perficiat, ille gradus ei superflueret.

Item, operatio correspondet potentiae; sed operatio intellectus nostri est immaterialis, quia est respectu obiecti immaterialis, scilicet universalis, quia ut est obiectum intellectus est immateriale, quia secundum PHILOSOPHUM III *De anima*[6] "sicut res sunt separabiles a materia, sic sunt intelligibiles"; igitur, etc.

---

1 unius] *mg.* F *om.* W | partis *om.* O L K *add.* tantum et (*om.* Q) non alterius FW Q X Z | non *om.* X | toti primo] *inv.* K | patet] habetur L | V] "IX" NO LM K W *om.* Z *add.* et FW Q X Z | et *om.* X | VIII] "VI" Z   2 vel] ut O FW Q Z et (*lin.* X) N X | convenit] sit(!) X   3 autem *om.* L K Q X | quod] quia N   4 est *post* se (*lin.*) X | tantum deorsum] *inv.* NO | est *om.* K Q X   5 sibi scilicet *om.* Z   6 eorum] istorum N *om.* K | animali] *add.* seu antic. nisi ratione formae et sic non FW *add.* ut toti Q | primo *om.* Z | Sic ideo] Secundo sic X | Sic — formae] = Q X *om.* NO HLM K FW Z   7 et] tamen O HM K *om.* L | non] *lin.* W *om.* O K   8 materiae] *add.* et (*om.* O Z) est O W Z | quod] quia N aeque HL K   9 sequitur *om.* N | non *om.* NO F   12 Item] Praeterea NO FW Q X Z | animae] essentiae NO | suae materiae *inv.* Q   13 sibi] commune O | igitur] ergo FW Q | posset] potest H possit K   14 corpus] *ant.* non F | informare] intelligere NO | igitur] ergo FW Q   15 scilicet] id est Z   16 in *om.* HL K | igitur] ergo FW Q | anima *om.* HL K   17 perficiat] perficit N perficiatur(!) X | ille] iste L *om.* X | ei] illi H *om.* NO | superflueret] superfluit Q   18 Item] Praeterea FW Q X Z | correspondet] corporeae N cor animam O | potentiae] *add.* est materialis N   20 quia] quod NO Q W X | ut *om.* N | est²] igitur NO | quia² *om.* H K   21 III *om.* NO | sicut — etc. *om.* Z   22 igitur etc.] ergo etc. FW ergo Q *om.* X *adnot. mg.* contra praedictam arguit iste doctor L

[5]**Aristot.**, *Physica* V c. 1 (AL VII[1.2] 192-3; Φ c. 1, 224a 31-34); VII c. 1 (AL VII[1.2] 256-7; H c. 1, 242a 1-15); VIII c. 4 (AL VII[1.2] 291; Z c. 4, 254b 7-14).
[6]**Aristot.**, *De an.* III c. 2 (Γ c. 4, 429b 21-22).

Contra:

Secundum BOETHIUM[7] forma simplex subiectum esse non potest; anima est subiecta multis accidentibus; igitur, etc.

Item, anima potest pati ab igne infernali et recipere operationem propriam, quod est principium patiendi.

[I. — Responsio de necessitate materiae in angelis animabusque ponendae ad mentem Guilielmi de la Mare]

[3] Respondeo quod probabiliter potest dici quod in anima est materia, et secundum fundamenta PHILOSOPHI et eorum qui ponunt contrarium. Quorum unum est quod pluralitas individuorum in una specie requirit materiam in illis individuis, sicut patet in XII *Metaphysicae*,[8] ubi dicitur "quod non sunt plura moventia caelum in eadem specie, quia primum non habet materiam". Hoc etiam patet per DIVERSOS ponentes materiam esse principium individuationis;[9] sed in specie animae rationalis sunt plura individua, etiam ipsa a corpore separata; igitur, etc.

DICES, sicut CONTRARII[10] dicunt, quod anima bene habet materiam quam perficit vel est apta nata perficere, scilicet corpus. Et ratione aptitudinis ad diversa corpora perfectibilia, ipsa separata

---

2 Secundum Boethium *post* simplex M | forma simplex] forma substantiae NO   3 subiecta] subiectum N | igitur etc.] igitur L ergo etc. FW ergo Q *om.* X   4 Item] Praeterea NO FW Q Z *om.* X | anima] animam(!) L animae FW ipsa X *om.* M | potest] possunt FW   5 quod] quae FW ergo Q | patiendi] faciendi H *add.* igitur etc. N *add.* in ea Q   8 quod *om.* Q | in *post* est X *om.* Q | est] sit Z   9 et *om.* NO | secundum *om.* K | fundamenta] fundamentum K | eorum] aliorum K | qui ponunt contrarium] contrarium qui ponunt O *add.* et X   10 Quorum *om.* K | est *om.* X | pluralitas] multiplicitas NO   11 requirit] requiritur Z | materiam *om.* X | sicut] ut L illud FW X id Q quod Z | in[3] *om.* N L FW Q X | XII] XIII NO   12 ubi] unde Q | caelum] *add.* (ant. plura W ant. moventia X Z) prima W X Z   13 non *om.* W | habet] haberet W   14 diversos] adversarios FW Q Z alios X | esse] est O *om.* FW Q X Z | individuationis] in individuis F   15 animae rationalis] *inv.* N | sunt *om.* K | plura individua] diversae individuae N | etiam] et K FW | ipsa] tempore N *om.* H   16 separata] separatae N separantur K | igitur etc.] igitur L ergo etc. FW Q *om.* X   17 contrarii] contrarium FW adversarii Q | dicunt] dicentes F dicitur (*lin.*) W[2] | bene] vel Q   18 vel] ut Z | est *post* nata K *om.* FW | apta] acta Q | nata *om.* FW Q X | Et ratione] *rep.* N   19 ratione] ad rationem L | diversa *om.* FW | ipsa] *add.* anima N

[7]**Boethius**, *De Trin.* c. 2 (ed. R. Peiper 153-54; PL 64 1250D—1251A): "Forma vero quae est sine materia non poterit esse subiectum nec vero inesse materiae ... Nulla igitur in eo diversitas, nulla ex diversitate pluralitas, nulla ex accidentibus multitudo atque idcirco nec numerus."
[8]**Aristot.**, *Metaph.* XII c. 8 (AL XXV[3.2] 263-64; M c. 8, 1074*a* 32-36): "Sed quaecumque sunt multa, materiam habent (nam una et eadem est ratio multorum, ut hominis, Socrates vero uno); quid autem erat esse non habet materiam primam."
[9]Cf. **Thomas**, *Sent.* IV d. 12 q. 1 a. 1 ad 3 (VII 655*a*); *Summa contra Gent.* II 93 arg. 2 (XIII 563*a*); *Summa theol.* I q. 7 a. 3 in corp. (IV 75*b*); *Summa theol.* I q. 76 a. 2 ad 1 (V 217*a*); **Godefridus de Font.**, *Quodl.* VII q. 5 in corp. (PhB III 324).
[10]Cf. **Thomas**, *Quaest. disp. de anima* q. 3 ad 19-21 (XXIV[1] 30*b*); q. 6 ad 13 (XXIV[1] 52*b*—53*a*).

potest plurificari, non autem habet materiam ex qua fit.

12 Contra EOS:

Anima non est propter corpus, sed potius e converso; igitur nec distinctio nec pluralitas animarum est propter distinctionem corporum, sed potius e converso.[11] Unde COMMENTATOR VII *Metaphysicae*[12] dicit quod membra leonis differunt a membris cervi, quia differunt animae eorum; et non e converso.

13 Item, destructo fundamento vel termino relationis, non est relatio; sed inclinatio illa vel aptitudo ad corpus est quaedam relatio; igitur, destructo corpore post mortem, non est talis inclinatio animae ad corpus.

14 Et confirmatur ratio: quia entis ad non-ens non est relatio realis, relativa enim sunt simul natura; anima separata est, non autem eius corpus quod informavit; igitur, etc.

15 Item,[13] si distinctio animarum est ex parte corporum tantum, Deus non posset creare duas animas sine corporibus; quia per corpora non distinguerentur, nec etiam per inclinationem ad illa; igitur, etc.

16 Item, omnis forma respectiva praesupponit aliquid absolutum prius se in quo fundatur; sed inclinatio illa ad corpus est quaedam forma respectiva fundata in essentia animae quae sic inclinatur; igitur essentia animae est prior illa inclinatione; prius autem non distinguitur per posterius sicut nec constituitur, sed e converso;

---

1 potest *om.* F | autem *post* habet Q sicut FW *om.* X | materiam] *add.* quam perficiat NO 3 potius] magis H | igitur] ergo FW Q *om.* LZ | nec distinctio *om.* L 4 nec] et NO FW Z *om.* Q | pluralitas animarum] diversitas animarum N propter pluralitas animarum O animarum et pluralitas Q | est] *add.* communi Q | propter] semper F 6 dicit] ait Q | leonis] hominis N *add.* non Q | cervi] corvi H K *add.* nisi Q 7 et *om.* Q 8 Item] Praeterea NO FW Q X Z | fundamento vel termino] termino vel fundamento N 9 illa *om.* L | vel] *lin.* Z^2 | ad] *mg.* Z^2 | quaedam relatio] *inv.* L 10 igitur] ergo FW Q | est] erit N 12 Et] Vel Q *om.* H | ratio *om.* FW Q X Z | non-ens] non X | est] *rep.* F 13 enim *om.* X | sunt simul] *inv.* HL *add.* in HLM | simul natura] *inv.* Q | natura] *add.* nulla N | est] *add.* corpus Q | non — informavit] ad eius corpus quod informavit N corpus autem eius quod informavit non est Q | autem] enim (*lin.*) Z^2 *om.* X | eius] *add.* ad Z^2 14 informavit] ibi fundatur X | igitur etc.] etc. H K ergo etc. FW Q igitur Z *om.* L X 15 Item] Praeterea FW Q X Z | Item — etc. *om.* NO | est] esset Z | parte *om.* L | corporum] corpore L | tantum] *ant. ex* FW Q X Z 16 posset] potest H | quia] *coni. cum* FW si HLM KU sed Q X Z 17 non] *coni. cum* FW *om. rell.* | illa] illud L ista Z 18 igitur etc.] ergo etc. FW ergo Q *om.* X 19 Item] Praeterea NO FW Q X Z | respectiva] quae(!) N absoluta O KU | aliquid] aliquod KU *om.* X 20 prius se] est posterius absoluto N post(!) se H | quo] quantum X | fundatur] fundetur O LM FW | illa] ista L | corpus] corpora W Z 21 essentia *post* animae Z essentiam Q | animae *om.* KU 22 igitur] ergo FW Q X | illa *om.* Q | autem] enim L 23 constituitur] cognoscitur Z

[11] **Averroës**, *De an.* II com. 36 (AverL 185).
[12] Potius **Averroës**, *De an.* I com. 53 (AverL 75): "Membra enim leonis non differunt a membris cervi nisi propter diversitatem animae cervi ab anima leonis."
[13] Codex U resumit ex abrupto.

igitur, etc.

[4] Item, illa inclinatio non est de essentia animae, quia anima est natura absoluta in se; igitur potest intelligi intellectu essentiali sine tali inclinatione, et per consequens distinguitur una ab alia sine inclinatione ad diversa corpora.

Item, quia anima est haec, ideo habet talem inclinationem ad hoc corpus, non e converso; igitur, etc.

Secunda ratio principalis est:[14] sicut operatio arguit formam, ita proprietas materiae materiam; sed proprietas materiae quantum ad suum esse et fieri suum reperiuntur verius in spiritualibus quam corporalibus. Proprietas enim materiae, quantum ad esse, est quod est ingenerabilis et incorruptibilis; sed quantum ad fieri, quod tantum producitur per creationem. Haec autem maxime reperiuntur in spiritualibus. Similiter substare accidentibus; sicut enim corpus subest qualitatibus corporalibus, ita anima spiritualibus, sicut habitibus animae. Quod autem haec sit proprietas materiae, patet per inductionem: non enim inest proprietas composito nisi ratione principiorum; nec etiam formae, quia eius est actuare quae est proprietas contraria; igitur ratione materiae inest animae substare accidentibus. Igitur, etc.

---

1 igitur etc.] igitur L ergo etc. FW ergo Q om. X   2 Item] Praeterea NO FW Q X Z | illa inclinatio] inv. K | est²] add. de N add. ex X   3 natura om. Z | igitur] ergo FW Q | intellectu] intellectum Q X | essentiali] esse Q essentiae X   4 distinguitur] add. esse N add. (post ab O post alia (mg. M) M Z) essentialiter O M FW Q Z add. anima H add. essentiae X | una] add. denominatur N | alia] add. et (om. O) anima NO | sine] sua KU   5 corpora om. X add. igitur L   6 Item] Praeterea N FW Q X Z Prima O | quia om. U | est om. Z | haec] hoc K | ideo] quia (om. K) non KU et Q om. NO FW X Z | talem inclinationem] inv. N add. etiam talem X   7 hoc] tale Z | non e converso] nec e converso L KU X et non e converso Q om. Z | igitur etc.] igitur L ergo etc. FW Q om. X   8 est] add. haec NO add. hoc FW Q Z | arguit] operit KU   9 proprietas] add. maxime U | materiae om. X add. operit KU | materiae²] in(!) X   10 et] in Z | et — suum] et quantum ad suum (om. FW X Z) fieri NO FW X Z | et — esse] mg. U | reperiuntur verius] inv. N reperitur verius H reperiuntur videtur(!) scilicet Q | quam] add. in NO KU FW X   11 enim om. NO KU | materiae] maxime H | quantum om. U Z | ad] add. suum KU   12 quantum] inquantum Z | ad] add. suum esse et U | tantum producitur] inv. L tantum producatur N FW Q Z   13 creationem] causationem N | Haec] Hoc W | Haec — substare om. X | autem om. K FW | maxime reperiuntur] inv. NO magis reperiuntur Z   14 Similiter] Sicut O HLM | corpus subest post corporalibus Z   15 subest] lin. W² substantiae H KU X add. substat K | ita] praem. est Z | anima] omnia H | habitibus] habitus Q habentibus X   16 haec] hoc W Z om. Q | sit] rep. U | materiae] animae HLM KU om. X   17 non] nec X | enim om. NO | inest ... composito] est ... compositi NO FW Q X Z om. ... composito U | proprietas] add. animae U | nisi] nec NO   18 principiorum] principali(!) X | nec etiam] inv. NO FW Q X Z | est] mg. O | actuare] actuale X add. materiam KU   19 proprietas contraria] inv. NO | igitur] ergo FW Q add. enim U | ratione] add. si O | animae] alicui FW Q X Z | substare accidentibus] substantiae accidentalis(!) X   20 Igitur etc.] Ergo etc. FW Q Etc. X Igitur Z om. NO L KU

---

[14]Nota: ratio principalis prima in n. 10 reperitur.

20 Tertio sic:[15] angelus habet materiam, igitur anima. Probatio antecedentis: quia in quocumque genere sunt principia communia — non tantum appropriata — et realiter distincta, oportet omnia illius generis esse ex eis composita; materia et forma sunt talia principia in genere substantiae. Probatio: actus et potentia sunt principia communissima in quolibet genere; actus autem in genere substantiae est forma, potentia in eodem genere est materia; igitur materia et forma sunt principia communissima in genere substantiae. Idem patet VIII *Metaphysicae*.[16] Igitur cum angelus sit species substantiae, est ex eis compositus.[a]

21 Quarto,[17] idem sic ostendo:[18] sicut impossibile est aliquod agens secundum agere nisi coagente primo, ita impossibile est aliquid pati nisi in virtute primi passivi. Sed certum est quod angeli et animae patiuntur, et bona sicut boni angeli, et mala, etiam ab igne corporali, sicut mali angeli; igitur, etc.

---

[a] *Adnotatio interpolata* Sed ad hoc diceret Philosophus[19] quod angelus non est in genere aliquo sed extra, ideo etc.

1 igitur] ergo FW Q *add.* et Q | anima] *add.* habet materiam N   2 genere *om.* KU | sunt] *add.* quaedam KU   3 tantum] tamen H | distincta] differentia F Q Z *add.* et differentia N *add.* et K | oportet] sed NO | omnia] enim(!) X   4 esse *post* eis Z | ex eis *om.* X *add.* realiter KU | composita] *ante* ex FW *add.* ex F *add.* et Z | et forma] *rep.* F   5 Probatio] *add.* antecedentis K *add.* consequentiae Q   6 quolibet genere] *inv.* X   7 potentia] *add.* autem KU Q | igitur] ergo FW Q | materia et forma sunt] forma et materia sunt U   8 in *om.* F | Idem] Item F Illud X   9 Igitur] Ergo FW Q | species *om.* N | substantiae *om.* Z | ex eis compositus] compositus ex eis NO   11 Quarto] *add.* ad Q | idem sic] *inv.* H | sic ostendo] ostendo N ostendo sicut O sic Q | sicut] *add.* est N | impossibile] *add.* est N | est *om.* O | aliquod] aliquid O *om.* H   13 in virtute] ratione L virtute X | primi passivi] patientis N | est *om.* U | quod] quia X | angeli] angelus H | et animae *om.* Z   14 et *om.* NO | bona *om.* FW KU Q Z *add.* seu antic. et mala L | boni] bona(!) O | angeli] *add.* seu rep. et animae patiuntur et bona sicut boni angeli L | mala] mali X | etiam] et X *om.* H Q | ab] in H X   15 sicut — angeli] *ant.* etiam NO sicut mali (*ant.* ab) Q | igitur etc.] ergo etc. FW Q etc. X *om.* KU   16 Sed] Si Q | Sed — etc.] = FW Q X Z *om. rell.*   17 ideo etc.] ratio etc. F *om.* X

[15] Ratio principalis tertia.
[16] **Aristot.**, *Metaph* VIII c. 6 (AL XXV³ 177; H c. 6, 1045a 23-25): "Si autem est, ut dicimus, hoc quidem materia illud vero forma, et hoc quidem potentia illud vero actu, non adhuc dubitatio utique videbitur esse quod quaeritur."
[17] Ratio principalis quarta.
[18] **Guillelmus de la Mare**, *Correctorium*, in *Qq. de anima fratris Thomae*, art. 6 (ed. Glorieux 377): "Hoc etiam patet per rationem sic: in omnibus quae ordinate agunt, secundum agens non agit nisi in virtute primi agentis, quod etiam plus influit in causatum quam secundum agens, ut habetur in libro *De causis*. Igitur similiter in patientibus nihil patietur nisi ratione primi passivi. Sicut autem forma est primum principium sive prima ratio agendi, omne enim quod agit per formam suam agit, ita primum principium vel prima ratio patiendi est materia. Igitur sicut illud quod caret omni forma non agit, ita si anima caret omni materia non patietur."
[19] Cf. **Aristot.**, *Metaph* X c. 10 (AL XXV³,² 216; K c. 10, 1058b 26-29); *Auctoritates Aristotelis* (ed. J. Hamesse 121): "Corruptibilium et incorruptibilium non sunt eadem principia."

Ad hoc etiam est auctoritas COMMENTATORIS VIII *Metaphysicae*,[20] ubi dicit quod corpora caelestia non habent materiam generabilem, si aliquam habent aliam, sicut est dispositio in materia intellectus.

Item, BOETHIUS *Super Praedicamenta*[21] dicit quod, relictis extremis, PHILOSOPHUS agit de substantia composita; anima vero est de genere substantiae.

Item, BOETHIUS *De unitate et uno*[22] dicit quod anima et angelus — quodlibet illorum — est unum coniunctione materiae et formae. Possunt enim aliqua esse unum coniunctione, quae tamen non sunt unum continuitate, ut dicit ulterius.

[II. — Solutio quaestionis]

[6] Dicendum est ad quaestionem quod si in anima vel angelo est materia, quod est eiusdem rationis cum materia corporalium. Quod probo sic:

---

1 Metaphysicae] *add.* commento N 3 generabilem] = M K Q generalem NO HL U FW X Z | si] sed N L FW Q X Z | aliquam habent] *inv.* H KU Z aliae (aliquae O) habent NO aliquam L *add.* si habent FW *add.* si Q | aliam] aliquam FW Q *om.* X Z | in materia] et natura N 5 Item] Idem FW | Item — substantiae *om.* L | dicit] ant. Boethius X ait Q | quod *om.* X 6 Philosophus] Aristoteles K | agit] ait Q | anima *om.* X | vero] non(!) X *om.* NO FW Q Z | de²] in N 8 Item] Idem FW Z | et uno] et de uno O | dicit] ait Q | anima] materia(!) X 9 illorum — unum] istorum est unum NO X *om.* L 10 enim *om.* Z | esse unum] *inv.* NO | tamen *om.* L | non *om.* KU 11 continuitate] unitate X *add.* videtur U | dicit] dicitur N 13 Dicendum est] *inv.* H U Dicendum NO FW Q Z Dicit X | ad quaestionem] ant. Dicendum Z | si *om.* Z | in — angelo] angelus vel anima NO | angelo] angelis H K FW | est²] in F 14 materia quod est *om.* O | quod] quae K Z | Quod *om.* L

[20] **Averroës**, *Metaph.* VIII com. 4 (ed. Iuntina VIII f. 211*v*F): "Caelum habet materiam localem, et tamen non habet materiam generabiliem et corrputibilem."

[21] **Boethius**, *Praed.* I cap. "De substantia" (PL 64 184A—B): "Cum autem tres substantiae sint, materia, species, et quae ex utrisque conficitur undique composita et compacta substantia, hic neque de sola specie, neque de sola materia, sed de utrisque mixtis compositisque proposuit. Partes autem substantiae incompositae et simplices sunt, ex quibus ipsa substantia conficitur, species et materia, quas post per transitum nominat dicens, substantiarum partes et ipsas esse substantias, atque haec hactenus. Nunc expositionis cursum ad sequentia convertamus."

[22] Potius **Dominicus Gundissal.**, *De unitate et uno* (ed. P. Corens BGPTM 1 1; PL 63 1077D—1078A): "Unum enim aliud est essentiae simplicitate unum, ut Deus; aliud simplicium cognitione unum, ut angelus et anima, quorum unumquodque est unum coniunctione materiae et formae. Aliud est continuitate unum, ut arbor et petra. Aliud est compositione unum, ut ex multis tabulis una arca, vel ex multis parietibus una domus. Alia dicuntur unum aggregatione, ut populus, grex, congeries lapidum, vel acervus tritici. Alia dicuntur praepositione unum ut rector navis, et gubernator civitatis dicuntur unum, similitudine officii. Alia dicuntur unum accidente, ut diversa subiecta eiusdem qualitatis dicuntur unum in ea qualitate, sicut nix et cygnus unum sunt albedine." Eadem auctoritas apud Guilliemum de la Mare reperitur: **Guillielmus de la Mare**, *Correctorium*, in primam partem *Summae theologiae fratris Thomae*, art. 10 (ed. Glorieux 50): "Dicendum ergo quod angelus est compositus ex materia spirituali et forma. Unde Boethius *De unitate et uno*: 'Aliud est simpliciter unum, ut Deus, aliud simplicium coniunctione, ut angelus et anima, quorum unumquodque est unum coniunctione materiae et formae'."

Quia non DICERES[23] eas diversarum rationum nisi una esset perfectior et nobilior aliā; sed spiritualis est nobilior corporali; aut igitur est nobilior in potentialitate, aut in actualitate. Si in actualitate, igitur non est materia prima, quia nihil actualitatis habet; si in potentialitate, igitur est imperfectior, cuius oppositum supponebat, quia potentialius est imperfectius.

26 Item, AUGUSTINUS XII *Confessionum*:[24] "Duo fecisti Domine, unum prope te, scilicet angelicam naturam, et unum prope nihil, scilicet materiam primam"; sed si alia esset perfectior, scilicet angelorum, non esset prope nihil; igitur, etc.

27 Item, in linea praedicamentali est unus processus a primo ad ultimum, quorum quodlibet est tantum unum, sicut unius lineae sunt duo termini tantum, quorum quilibet est unus tantum; sed termini lineae praedicamentalis et contentorum in ea sunt actus primus et materia prima; igitur, cum sit una linea, erit una materia tantum. Si non, essent duo principia potentialia, et duo ordines entium super illa fundati.

28 Item, si una sit nobilior aliā, cum nobiliori perfectibili perfectione essentiali respondeat perfectio nobilior, sequitur quod materia

---

1 diceres] diceret Q *add.* et X | nisi] *add.* quia H | una esset] *inv.* NO unum esset X   2 sed] sibi F scilicet W X Z | est nobilior] *inv.* HL KU | aut igitur] igitur aut H aut ergo FW Q   3 nobilior] perfectior FW Q X Z | aut] vel Z | in² *om.* O HM X | Si] *add.* est F | in³ *om.* HL F | actualitate] *add.* si X   4 igitur] ergo FW Q | prima] prius Q | quia] quae FW Q Z | actualitatis habet] *inv.* Q | in *om.* NO L FW Q   5 igitur] ergo FW Q | cuius] *add.* scilicet NO | oppositum *om.* N *add.* suppositum L | supponebat] praesupponebat K supponebas FW Z   6 quia] et N | est *om.* L W   7 Item] Praeterea NO FW Q X Z | XII] XI NO | Confessionum] quaestione(?) H De confessionibus KU   8 prope te scilicet] scilicet prope te N | scilicet] id est L *om.* KU *add. seu rep.* aliud prope nihil prope te Q | naturam] materiam NO *om.* X | et unum] et una Z *om.* Q   9 scilicet *om.* Q | alia] aliqua L X talia Q | esset *om.* FW *add.* materia Q | perfectior] *mg.* M imperfectior O KU Z imperfectio materia L | angelorum] *add.* prima X   10 igitur etc.] igitur L Q ergo·etc. FW Q etc. X   11 Item] Praeterea NO FW Q X Z | in *om.* U | processus a primo] aeque X   12 tantum unum] *inv.* K | lineae] *add.* praedicamentalis et contentorum KU   13 sunt duo] *inv.* N Z etiam duo N | tantum] *ant.* duo Q *om.* N H | unus tantum] *inv.* F unius tantum Q | sed — prima *om.* KU   14 contentorum] conceptorum Q | ea] eadem N | sunt] est F | actus primus] *inv.* ·FW   15 igitur] ergo FW | sit una linea] sit linea una KU | erit] est NO Z | una²] dua O | materia²] *add.* (*ant.* materia U) prima KU W X Z   16 Si] Sed H | non] enim KU FW Q X Z *om.* NO | principia] *add.* materialia FW | ordines] *add.* essent FW   17 entium] necesse Q *om.* N *add.* esset Q | super] dicuntur NO | illa] illam H ista Z | fundati] fundari NO *add.* essent KU   18 Item] Praeterea NO U FW Q X Z | una] *add.* materia Q | sit] est N esset KU Z *om.* O FW Q X | cum — respondeat *om.* KU | nobiliori] nobilior H   19 respondeat] correspondeat N respondeo(!) X | perfectio nobilior] et perfectior forma KU

---

[23]Cf. **Guilelmus de la Mare**, *Correctorium*, in primam partem *Summae theologiae fratris Thomae*, art. 10 (ed. Glorieux 51-52); in *Qq. de anima fratris Thomae*, art. 7 (ed. Glorieux 377); *Sent.* I d. 7 p. 2 q. 3 (ed. Kraml 129-131); **Richardus de Mediavilla**, *Quaest. disp.* q. 5 (Vat. lat. 868 f. 13v); **Gonsalvus Hispanus**, *Quaest. disp.* q. 11 (ed. Amorós BFS IX 186-221).

[24]**Augustinus**, *Confess.* XII c. 7 (CCL 27 220; PL 32 828-9): "Tu eras et aliud nihil, unde fecisti caelum et terram, duo quaedam: unum prope te, alterum prope nihil, unum quo superior tu esses, alterum quo inferius nihil esset."

corporum caelestium perficiatur forma nobiliori quam materia corporum inferiorum; sed materia corporalis corruptibilium aliquorum perficitur anima rationali; igitur multo fortius materia corporum caelestium perficitur anima rationali vel perfectione nobiliori, et per consequens corpora caelestia sunt animata.

Ad hoc est auctoritas COMMENTATORIS II *Metaphysicae*[25] super illud: "quoniam in fundamento naturae nihil est distinctum"; et hoc exponit de materia prima, quae de se est indistincta.

Et AVICENNA in *Physica*[26] sua cap. 3 dicit quod in corporibus inferioribus et superioribus est eiusdem rationis materia. "Materia," inquit, "subiecta formae quae non corrumpitur est una et subiecta formae quae corrumpitur, et est apta nata recipere omnem formam"; et ideo si non recipit, hoc est ratione suae formae.

[III. — Obiectiones contra solutionem propositam]

[7] Sed contra praedicta potest sic argui: sequitur quod anima et angelus essent corruptibiles, si essent materiales; hoc est inconveniens; igitur, etc. Probatio consequentiae: 'materia est qua res

---

1 nobiliori] nobilior H U | quam] quod O 2 corporum inferiorum] corporis inferioris L corporalium inferioris O FW Z | inferiorum — corporum *om.* X | corporalis] corporum N KU | corruptibilium aliquorum] inferiorum N correspondentorum aliquorum O corporalium aliquorum H U inferiorum aliquorum K 3 perficitur — caelestium *om.* N | igitur] ergo FW Q | igitur — rationali] *mg.* K *om.* O L U | fortius] magis FW Q 4 caelestium] supracaelestium H superiorum K 5 et] ergo L | consequens *add.* scilicet X | caelestia] supracaelestia H | sunt] essent N erunt Q 6 Ad — Commentatoris] Item Commentator NO | II] III Z | super illud *om.* N 7 illud] illud capitulum K FW X Z idem capitulum U *add.* secundum (super KU *om.* Q) antiquam (antiquae Q) translationem (translationis Q) KU FW Q X Z | quoniam] quod Q | nihil] vel F | nihil — et *om.* Q | est distinctum] etc. N est H distinctum F | distinctum] *mg.* M | hoc exponit] *inv.* NO 8 exponit] exponentis Q reponit U | de se *post* est X | est *om.* H 9 Et *om.* F | dicit] dicens FW *om.* KU Z 10 et superioribus *om.* NO Z | Materia *om.* NO KU FW Q X Z 11 inquit] in qua N inest F *om.* Q | quae] quod X | non *post* quae KU | corrumpitur] *add.* et L | est una *om.* K | est — corrumpitur] *mg.* X | et — est *om.* L | subiecta²] subiectata(?) N 12 quae] et Z | et *om.* KU | est *post* nata K *om.* N *add.* una U | recipere] suscipere N Z 13 ideo *om.* NO KU FW Q Z | non] materia NO | recipit] recipiat KU | hoc est ratione *om.* Q | suae formae] *inv.* LM formae N 15 Sed] Et X | contra] contraria X | praedicta] dicta K | potest sic] *inv.* H | sic argui] *inv.* F | sequitur] sequeretur NO FW Q X Z | anima et angelus] angelus et anima K FW Q Z anima NO 16 essent] esset NO erunt H | corruptibiles] corruptibilis N H | essent²] esset NO *om.* K | materiales] materialis N *add.* sed U 17 igitur etc.] ergo etc. FW ergo L *om.* Q | Probatio consequentiae] Probo consequentiam NO *add.* quia H | qua] quo KU FW Q

---

[25] **Averroës**, *Metaph.* I com. 17 (ed. Iuntina 14r F); cf. **Aristot.**, *Metaph.* I c. 8 (AL XXV³ 33; A c. 8, 989b 6-7) et *Auctoritates Aristotelis* (ed. J. Hamesse 117).

[26] **Avicenna**, *Liber primus naturalium* c. 3 (AviL 36): "Fortassis autem ponitur materia subiecti formae quae non corrumpitur, et subiecti formae quae corrumpitur, materia una in se apta recipere omnem formam."

potest esse et non esse', VII *Metaphysicae* et II *De generatione*.[27]

32 Item, quod convenit alicui essentialiter, convenit sibi semper et in quocumque fuerit; sed materiae convenit essentialiter appetitus formarum generabilium et corruptibilium; si igitur in angelis vel anima est materia, appetet naturaliter illas formas tanquam exsistens ad eas in potentia naturali.

33 Item, cuilibet potentiae naturali passivae correspondet potentia activa in natura, ut patet I *Caeli et mundi*:[28] si igitur est in spiritualibus et corporalibus materia eiusdem rationis, cum materia inferiorum sit in potentia passiva reducibili per agens naturale ad formam naturalem, eadem ratione agens naturale poterit potentiam passivam spiritualium reducere ad actum formarum naturalium, et sic erunt corruptibilia.

[IV. — Responsiones ad obiectiones]

34 Ad primum istorum[29] dicendum quod ista non est definitio materiae secundum se sed ut est annexa formae et contrarietati naturali, quia nihil corrumpitur naturaliter quod non alteretur; et

---

17 potest esse] inv. X   1 et non esse om. X | esse²] add. ex HLM add. et FW | generatione add. igitur etc. HM add. ergo etc. F   2 Item] Praeterea NO U FW Q X Z | quod] quantum F quam W autem(!) X om. U | convenit] contingit N | alicui] mg. L | convenit sibi] inv. F add. et HM | convenit — essentialiter om. NO | et] etiam KU om. Z   3 quocumque] add. tempore KU Z | fuerit om. Z | materiae] naturae(!) X | convenit] competit M K add. seu rep. et in quocumque fuerit sed materia convenit F | essentialiter appetitus] inv. M appetitus Z   4 formarum] formaliter Z | generabilium] lin. X generalium O | igitur] ergo FW Q | angelis vel anima] anima et angelo L | vel] et H X add. in F   5 est] vel Q esset Z | materia] add. prima Z | appetet] lin. F² ͬappetit H appeteret NO W Q X Z add. et FW | illas] istas H Q Z ipsas L | tanquam exsistens] inv. KU   6 ad eas] ad illas (post naturali) KU | potentia naturali] inv. L   7 Item] Praeterea N U FW Q X Z Ipsa(!) O | cuilibet post naturali Q | naturali passivae] inv. NO K | passivae om. X | correspondet] add. una X | potentia om. H   8 Caeli et mundi] De caelo et mundo F | igitur] ergo FW Q | est] materia K   9 et] add. in M Q | corporalibus] inferioribus KU FW Q X Z add. est K add. sic Z | materia] eadem K   10 inferiorum] inferioris N | sit] sint NO | reducibili] reducibile L | agens] accidens KU | naturale om. N   11 formam naturalem] formas naturales Q | poterit] ant. eadem X   12 passivam post spiritualium Z | spiritualium reducere] inv. N | formarum] formarum] formalium LM KU FW Q X Z | naturalium om. NO | et — corruptibilia om. O   13 corruptibilia] corporalia N   15 istorum] illorum H | dicendum] add. est M F | ista] illa N L U FW Z ita H illud Q   16 secundum] per FW | sed om. N | annexa] annexio H | et] quae subicitur KU om. Q   17 nihil om. Q | quod non alteretur] nisi a contrario KU | et de tali] rep. X

[27]**Aristot.**, *Metaph.* VII c. 7 (AL XXV³ 143; Z c. 7 1032a 20-22); *Auctoritates Aristotelis* (ed. J. Hamesse 129): "Materia est ex qua res potest esse et non esse"; **Aristot.**, *De gener. et corrupt.* c. 9 (AL IX¹ 72; B c. 9 335a 32-33): "Ut materia quidam generabilibus est possibile esse et non esse."
[28]Cf. **Averroës**, *De caelo et mundo* I com. 117 (ed. Iuntina V 37vb): "Omnis enim potentia aut est activa, aut passiva. Si activa, terminatur per ultimum finem eius quod agit; si passiva, per minimum eius a quo patitur"; cf. **Aristot.**, *De caelo et mundo* I c. 11 (A c. 11 281a 2-20); *De anima* III c. 4 (Γ c. 5 430a 10-14); *Auctoritates Aristotelis* (ed. J. Hamesse 162): "Virtus activa terminatur ad maximum, virtus autem passiva ad minimum."
[29]Cf. supra n. 31.

de tali forma naturali et materia sibi correspondente loquitur ibi PHILOSOPHUS, ostendendo quae requiruntur ad generationem naturalem; materia autem caeli et spiritualium non est annexa tali formae vel contrarietati; igitur, etc.

Unde AVICENNA,[30] ubi supra,[31] dicit quod caelum est incorruptibile non ratione materiae sed ratione formae, cui non est contrarietas. Ratio autem materiae secundum se est quod nec est quid nec quantum, et caetera, sed est potentia unumquodque.

[8]   Sed contra:

Omnis potentia passiva est potentia contradictionis, IX *Metaphysicae*;[32] potentia materiae, in quocumque sit materia, est potentia passiva; igitur in quibus est materia, est potentia contradictionis, scilicet ad esse et non-esse; igitur omne tale est corruptibile.

Dicunt ALIQUI[33] quod non est inconveniens caelum, quantum est de se, esse corruptibile secundum quid, quia ratione materiae; tamen connexio materiae et formae eius est necessaria ratione formae tantum. Quia igitur talis connexio non est contingens ex parte utriusque extremi sed ratione materiae tantum — quod tamen requiritur ad hoc quod aliquid sit simpliciter corruptibile —, ideo

---

1 sibi correspondente] inv. M | loquitur ibi] inv. H | ibi Philosophus] Philosophus ibidem N   2 quae] quod X | requiruntur] requirentur O   3 caeli] add. est U | et om. X | tali formae] inv. Q   4 vel] et Q Z | igitur] ideo O KU FW Q Z om. X | etc.] non sequitur intentionaliter Q   5 Unde] Ubi U | ubi supra om. X | dicit om. FW Z   6 sed ratione formae] mg. K om. U | cui] cuius L | cui — est om. X | est] inest M KU FW Q Z   7 Ratio] Non FW Ideo O | quod] add. secundum se Z | quod — est] quod et est X quod neque est KU om. Q | est²] lin. F   8 quid — quantum] quantum NO quantum nec quale M quid est neque quantum U quid est nec est quantum FW Q quod nec quantum X | caetera om. X | potentia unumquodque] inv. H   10 potentia passiva] inv. N passiva O | IX] igitur N | Metaphysicae] add. sed K   11 potentia — contradictionis om. U | quocumque] quacumque N | materia] potentia materiae N   12 passiva] rep. Z | passiva — potentia om. FW | igitur] ergo Q | quibus] quocumque N quo O | materia] add. illa X add. seu rep. ibi est potentia materiae in quocumque sit materia Z | contradictionis] add. ibi NO M   13 scilicet om. HL | et] add. ad H FW | igitur] et NO ergo FW Q | omne om. X | est] esse X   14 caelum om. X   15 est de se] de se est O | quid] quaedam(!) X | quia] scilicet KU om. N | ratione] secundum L | materiam L   16 materiae — eius] formae eius et materiae N | formae eius] formae K formae eiusdem FW   17 igitur] ergo FW Q   18 tantum om. M | quod] lin. Q | tamen] non H tamen non LM U FW X Z non tamen Q non H   19 requiritur] sequitur Q | ideo — simpliciter] rep. W | ideo — corruptibile om. L X | ideo — incorruptibile om. NO

[30]Avicenna, *Liber primus naturalium* c. 3 (AviL 36): "... ergo causa quod non generatur et non corrumpitur erit ex parte suae formae quae prohibet eius materiam ab eo quod est in natura eius, non ex parte materiae obedientialis."
[31]Cf. supra n. 30
[32]Aristot., *Metaph.* IX c. 8 (AL XXV³ 190; T c. 8 1050*b* 9): "Omnis potentia simul contradictionis est."
[33]Cf. **Guillelmus de la Mare**, *Sent.* II d. 12 q. 2 (ed. H. Kraml BAW XVIII 169): "Et quod obicitur quod forma non destruit potentiam, dicendum quod non est verum ubi forma totaliter perficit materiam quia tunc destruitur potentia ad oppositum, et talis est forma caeli."

caelum non est simpliciter corruptibile; immo magis incorruptibile ratione partis principalioris. Et illud idem dicitur de angelo et anima. Nec est inconveniens quod aliquid sibi dimissum vel secundum se consideratum sit corruptibile, quod tamen annexum alii est necessarium. Exemplum de anima viatoris et beati vel in gratia confirmati. Sic materia caeli, quantum est de se, est in potentia contradictionis, tamen a forma caeli determinatur ad unam partem tantum.[34]

38 Ad aliud[35] dicendum quod intellectus noster est in potentia naturali, et desiderium naturale habet ad omnia intelligibilia intelligenda et ad beatitudinem consequendam; secundum AUGUSTINUM[36] tamen ex natura propria nec potentia cuiuscumque creaturae potest ad hoc attingere. Non igitur omni potentiae passivae naturali correspondet potentia activa naturalis, quae posset effective ipsam reducere ad actum; sed sufficit potentiae passivae naturali quod ex natura sua habeat quod possit recipere illam perfectionem ad quam habet potentiam naturalem — et hoc sive ab agente naturali sive supernaturali. Sic homo de natura sua habet potentiam ad fidem et caritatem, non tamen habet potentiam qua de natura sua tantum et ex virtute sua propria effective possit eam

---

1 est *om.* Q | immo] hoc F | magis *om.* F 2 principalioris] principalis NO principaliter U | Et] *add.* ad K | illud idem] ideo NO FW Q X ideo idem U Z | illud — confirmati *post* tantum K | dicitur *om.* F | et] in Z *add.* de F Q 3 quod *om.* L | sibi dimissum] dimissum FW Q X *spat. vac.* Z | secundum] per N *om.* K Z 4 corruptibile] destructibile NO defectibile U FW Q X Z | tamen] non Z | annexum *om.* U | alii] alteri Q | est] sit Q 5 beati vel] beati et Q *om.* X 6 confirmati] conformati(!) N | materia caeli] natura(!) caeli W | de se est *om.* L | est² *om.* X Z | in *om.* NO W X 7 contradictionis] *add.* quantum est de se L | determinatur] *add.* quo Z | unam] illam X 9 dicendum *om.* N *add.* est M F | noster est] videtur esse HLM 10 habet *post* intelligenda FW | intelligibilia] *add.* vel F 11 et *om.* H | ad *om.* K *add.* hoc Z | beatitudinem] habitudinem KU | consequendam] quandam quoniam NO quandam H K *om.* L | secundum] *add.* beatum N 12 tamen] cum U | ex — potentia] ex natura propria NO ex (*om.* Q) puris (*om.* FW) naturalibus (*om.* FW Q X Z) potentiis (*om.* X) propriis (*om.* U) vel (*om.* U) U FW Q X Z | nec] non (*post* creaturae) U FW Q Z *del.* X *om.* NO | cuiuscumque creaturae] *inv.* FW Q X Z cuique est N cuique est creatum(?) O cuiuscumque creare Q *om.* U 13 attingere] contingere X | Non — activa *om.* X | igitur] ergo FW Q Z | potentiae passivae] *inv.* N passivae O 14 potentia activa] *inv.* H | activa] active U | posset] possit NO W Q Z potest H F 15 effective ipsam reducere] ipsam effective reducere HL | actum] *add.* naturalem X 16 natura sua] potentia sua naturali N | habeat — quam *om.* KU | possit] potest H 17 habet *post* potentiam Z | ab *om.* HL 18 sive] *add.* a Q | supernaturali] praeternaturali N | Sic] Sicut KU FW X Z | habet potentiam] habet rationem (*mg.*) M est in potentia passiva L 19 tamen *om.* H X | habet potentiam] *inv.* Z 20 sua² *om.* KU FW X Z | propria] proprie Q *om.* U *add.* et X | effective *om.* N KU | possit] potest H posset L | eam habere] *inv.* X

---

[34] Hic deest responsio ad obiectionem secundam, scilicet, n. 32.
[35] Cf. supra n. 33.
[36] **Augustinus**, *De vera relig.* c. 3 n. 3 (CCL 32 189; PL 34 124).

habere, sed a Deo gratiam infundente. Unde AUGUSTINUS *De vera religione*[37] dicit quod posse habere fidem et caritatem est de natura fidelium. Sic in proposito: materia spiritualium, quantum est de se, est in potentia ad omnes formas substantiales tam corporales quam spirituales; sed non est agens naturale quod illam potentiam posset ad actum reducere, quia est coniuncta formae inseparabili, ut visum est; igitur, etc.

[V. — Ad argumenta principalia]

Ad primum principale:[38] quod bene caret forma materiali, materia sensibili, et forma elementari, non tamen oportet quod careat omni forma spirituali perficiente materiam, quia sic careret seipso. Vel aliter dicendum quod receptivum dicitur aliquid recipere: vel secundum esse naturale, et sic oportet illud esse denudatum a natura recepti; vel secundum esse intentionale, et sic si esset receptivum organicum, necessarium est ipsum esse denudatum a natura recepti, non totaliter sed ab excellentia recepti, sicut sensus tactus ab excellentia tangibilium; si autem est receptivum non-organicum, ut intellectus, maior[39] non est vera, quia tunc denudaretur a propria natura, cuius intellectum potest recipere.

Sed quare magis receptivum organicum quam non-organicum? Dicendum quod in corporalibus receptivum habet oppositam

---

1 infundente] infinite N 2 De vera religione] religione FW *om.* K | dicit quod] hominem N *spat. vac.* O *om.* U FW Q X Z | est — fidelium] de natura fidelium est (ant. posse) K 3 spiritualium] supernaturalium H X | est *post* potentia Q 4 est *om.* H 5 est *om.* NO | quod] qui X | illam potentiam *post* posset KU illam H istam potentiam X | posset *post* actum Z possit N L FW potest KU 6 ad actum *post* reducere KU 7 igitur etc.] etc. K *om.* NO L FW Q X Z 9 principale] *add.* dicendum L K FW Q Z | forma materiali] inv. F *add.* et K FW | materia] materiali M 10 et] *add.* etiam N *add.* in O *add.* id est Q | elementari] corporea NO corruptibili U FW Q Z essentiali X | oportet] oporteat U 11 spirituali] speciali H | sic *om.* M | seipso] seipsa N ipso U 12 dicendum] dicitur L *add.* est M F | dicitur aliquid recipere] dupliciter potest recipere aliquid FW 13 naturale] materiale KU | sic *om.* X | illud] idem U 14 esse *om.* H | sic] tunc U FW Q X tale Z | si] sic Q non X | esset] est NO FW Q X Z | esset — ab *om.* U 15 organicum] organum N *add.* tunc FW | est ipsum esse denudatum] denudatum NO est ipsum denudari FW X Z ipsum denudari Q 16 excellentia] essentia X | recepti — excellentia *om.* NO | sensus *om.* FW | tactus] actus(!) Z 17 tangibilium] sensuum N | receptivum] *add.* sensuum N 18 ut] sicut KU | maior] maiora N | non *om.* NO X | quia] sed L | propria] *add.* essentia et N 19 intellectum] intellectivum NO intellectione Q 20 quare] quia X | magis] *add.* est W | quam non organicum *om.* F 21 Dicendum] *add.* est M F | quod] *add.* semper L | receptivum *om.* X | oppositam] contrariam HL

---

[37]Cf. **Augustinus**, *De vera religione* c. 24-25 n. 45-46 (CCL 32 215-216; PL 34 141-42).
[38]Cf. supra n. 1.
[39]Subintellige: omne recepiens denudatur a natura recepti.

dispositionem respectu recepti, sicut recipiens colorem intentionaliter debet esse non-terminatum; sed color materialiter receptus in obiecto habet esse terminatum. Similiter sensus est in medietate,[40] obiectum autem in excellentia; non sic autem est in intellectu; ideo, etc.

41 Ad aliud[41] dicendum est quod minor[42] est simpliciter falsa, quia quod forma aliqua recipiatur particulariter tantum, hoc non est propter materiam tantum eius in quo recipitur sed propter materiam extensam. Unde materia, sub quacumque forma ponatur, recipit aliquid secundum condiciones illius formae. Ut patet: si materia aeris, quae propter formam aeris recipit colorem spiritualiter, fiat sub forma corporis terminati, recipit colorem materialiter, non intentionaliter.

42 Ad aliud[43] dicendum quod sicut secundum ponentes gradus in formis plures formae possunt unam materiam informare — per hoc quod forma praecedens tenet se ex parte materiae et determinat potentialitatem eius, disponendo ipsam ad formam sequentem —, sic e converso una forma potest plures materias informare per hoc quod altera se tenet ex parte formae, scilicet illa quae est sibi intimior, et sic totum compositum ex materia et forma animae informat corpus, non ratione materiae sed tantum ratione formae principaliter informantis materiam propriam. Ad maiorem igitur

---

1 colorem] calorem Z   2 debet] oportet U | non-terminatum] non-determinatum Q | sed — terminatum om. F X | color] calor Z   3 receptus] repertus O M | obiecto] opposito O oculo H   4 obiectum] oppositum O | autem om. H | in] et X | est] esse Z om. NO H F X   5 intellectu] add. et H | ideo] igitur NO KU om. X | etc. om. U X   6 est om. NO H F Q X Z | quod minor est om. U | est simpliciter] inv. X simpliciter Q Z   7 quod om. K Q | forma om. Z | aliqua] alia N add. (lin.) non F | recipiatur] add. in aliquo U | hoc] igitur K   8 tantum eius] inv. NO eius X | quo] qua NO H | recipitur] reperitur H   9 materia om. U | forma ponatur] sed X   10 secundum condiciones] sub condicionibus N sub condicione KU secundum condiciones FW Z secundum consideratione Q | illius] eius Q | si materia] per formam N sed materia O   11 aeris om. KU | quae] est Z | formam] calorem N colorem O | colorem] secundum colorem NO add. intentionaliter N   12 terminati] animati NO animati terminati HLM | recipit] recipiet NO F reciperet W X | colorem] calorem FW Z   14 dicendum] add. est M | sicut om. U Z | secundum] mg. M om. NO KU Q X   15 formae] informare Z | materiam om. X   16 forma praecedens] inv. FW | tenet se] inv. O F | et om. N | determinat] determinatam N   17 potentialitatem] positionem F   18 materias om. X   19 altera] ultra H | est post intimior X   20 compositum] add. est FW | materia et forma] forma et materia F Q Z | forma] add. seu rep. et materia W | animae om. X add. et W   21 sed tantum] inv. L   22 materiam propriam] inv. X | igitur] ergo FW Q

---

[40]Cf. q. 3, n. 16.
[41]Cf. supra n. 2.
[42]Subaudi: si intellectus esset materialis, reciperet formas particulariter tantum et ut particulares.
[43]Cf. supra n. 3.

rationis⁴⁴ dicendum quod ipsa tota informat corpus, et illo modo potest dici quod "secundum se totam", non tamen ratione totius sed ratione partis; et sic ly "secundum se" praedicat rationem informandi, non tamen secundum se totam informat.

[11] Ad primam confirmationem⁴⁵ dicendum quod aequivocat de "primo". Uno enim modo dicitur ut opponitur ei quod est per accidens; alio modo opponitur ei quod est secundum partem. Loquendo de "primo" illo secundo modo, vera est maior,⁴⁶ sed primo modo falsa est, quia quod convenit alicui essentialiter convenit sibi primo, id est non per accidens, sicut rationale convenit homini primo isto modo sumpto, et tamen convenit sibi ratione partis, scilicet animae, non ratione totius. Illo modo anima est actus primus corporis, quia est actus essentialis eius, et ideo non oportet quod hoc conveniat ratione totius, sed sufficit quod ratione suae formae.

Ad aliud⁴⁷ dicendum quod non est inconveniens eandem formam perficere plures materias, si in perficiendo excedat suam vel unam materiam; sic est de anima respectu corporis. Videmus enim quod anima per diversas perfectiones unam partem corporis perficit, et aliam et aliter dispositam. Sic in proposito non videtur inconveniens quod per formam eius perficiat diversas materias non aeque primo, et quae non sunt totaliter unius rationis, quia una est

---

1 rationis *om.* KU | dicendum] *add. est* M FX | illo] isto O M Z *om.* KU 2 dici *om.* U | quod *om.* H | secundum *om.* X | totam] totum N H 3 ratione *om.* KU | sic ly] ly KU sic si ly FW Z sic Q simili(!) X 4 tamen] enim K *om.* NO U FW Q X Z | totam] totum N H 5 confirmationem] rationem U | dicendum *om.* KU *add. est* M F | quod *om.* K 6 enim] ant. Uno X | enim modo] inv. Q modo NO L KU | dicitur *om.* N *add.* quod X | ei *om.* X | quod est *om.* N Z | quod — ei *om.* X | per] secundum L *om.* NO 7 modo] *add.* ut KU FW Q Z 8 primo illo] isto modo primo O | secundo modo] inv. FW | vera est maior] est maior vera N est vera maior H | maior] minor(!) L | sed] si NO 9 falsa est] inv. X | est *om.* N | convenit] contingit O | alicui] *add.* homini primo illo modo L 10 sibi] ei N FW Z | id est] et M illo Q *om.* NO | id — primo *om.* X | id — sibi *om.* KU | convenit²] competit H 11 primo] *add.* modo L | isto modo] primo modo N id est non per accidens H illo modo FW Q | sumpto *om.* H | convenit²] contingit O | sibi] ei N *om.* O FW 12 scilicet *om.* X | Illo] Isto O M KU | anima est] inv. L | actus primus corporis] primus actus corporis H Z actus corporis primus M 13 et *om.* U 14 hoc conveniat] inv. Q *add.* ei FW Q | suae formae] inv. L 16 aliud dicendum] aliam dicendum O aliam X *add. est* M 17 plures] particulares NO | si in perficiendo] licet imperfecte nec N | excedat] excedit NO KU | vel unam] unam Z *om.* N 18 est *om.* H *add.* in proposito Q 19 quod *om.* N | anima] animam N *add.* quod O | per diversas perfectiones] perficiens FW Q X | unam] vitas(?) X | corporis *om.* K | perficit] perficere N 20 et aliam] aliter X | et²] etiam FW Q Z *om.* HL K | Sic] Sicut X | videtur] est FW 21 per *om.* FW *add.* unam KU | formam] forma FW 22 quae] aeque(!) X | sunt] sint Q *om.* U *add.* eiusdem perfectionis et N | unius] eiusdem H K X | est *om.* F

⁴⁴Subaudi: anima est forma corporis.
⁴⁵Cf. supra n. 4.
⁴⁶Subaudi: proprietas conveniens toti ratione unius partis non convenit toti primo.
⁴⁷Cf. supra n. 5

corporalis et alia non.

45 Ad aliud:[48] quod forma animae excedit suam materiam; non tamen est divisibilis nec habens gradus reales sicut forma accidentalis; sed ipsa simplex exsistens tantum informat materiam propriam et corpus, sicut tota essentia animae informat unam partem corporis et aliam.

46 Ad ultimum[49] dicendum quod non concludit, quia angelus intelligit singulare, non tantum universale; igitur sequeretur, secundum hoc, quod sua essentia esset singularis et materialis, quia intelligit materiale.

Item, aut intelligis de omni modo operandi quod correspondeat operanti, falsum assumis, quia operatio habet modum transeuntem — operans autem substantia vel potentia est permanens; aut de modo determinato. Si autem intelligis de alio modo quam de isto de quo assumis in minori, nihil est ad propositum. Si autem de ipso, petis principium, igitur, etc.

---

1 et *om.* FW Q   2 aliud] *add.* dicendum M K W Q X Z *add.* dicendum est F | animae *om.* N | excedit] excedat U *om.* X   3 nec] vel K ut U | habens] habet L | gradus] genus H contradictiones F | reales] realis H   4 tantum] tamen F *om.* L | materiam propriam] *inv.* X | propriam] primam N   6 aliam] *add.* quia quamlibet H   7 dicendum] *add.* est M | quia] quod Q X   8 tantum universale] *inv.* N tamen universale L KU FW X Z | igitur] ergo FW Q Z | sequeretur] sequitur K Z | secundum hoc *om.* L   9 sua essentia] *inv.* F | singularis et materialis] materialis et singularis NO | et] *add.* non H   11 Item] Praeterea NO FW Q X Z | aut] *rep.* K | intelligis] intelligit NO FW | modo] eo X | operandi] operationi Q | correspondeat] respondeat FW Q correspondet X   12 operanti] *add.* et L *add.* et sic F *add.* sic W *add.* et tunc Q | assumis] intelligis L assumitur X *om.* FW   13 autem *om.* N *add.* vel HLM | est] ant. substantia KU   14 determinato] terminato X | intelligis] intelligit N | isto] illo N H W Q *add.* modo HL KU | de³ *om.* L   15 minori] *add.* vel U F | nihil] vel O | ipso] primo modo KU primo FW Q X Z   16 igitur etc.] Et sic patet responsio L etc. Q X *om.* NO K FW Z

[48]Cf. supra n. 6.
[49]Cf. supra n. 7.

[QUAESTIO 16]

UTRUM MAGIS UNIVERSALE PRIUS INTELLIGATUR A NOBIS QUAM MINUS UNIVERSALE

Utrum[1] magis universale prius intelligatur a nobis quam minus universale.

[1] Arguitur quod sic:

1. I *Physicorum*[2] dicitur quod "innata est nobis via a notioribus nobis ad notiora naturae", et subdit:[3] "sunt autem nobis primo nota confusa magis", id est magis universalia; minus autem universalia sunt naturae notiora, quia sunt perfectiora; igitur, etc.

2. Item, quod primo intellectui imprimitur, prius intelligitur; sed secundum AVICENNAM[4] "ens et unum, quae sunt maxime universalia, prius intellectui imprimuntur" quam obiecta alia intelligibilia; igitur, etc.

3. Item, processus naturalis est ab imperfecto ad perfectum per medium. Cum igitur magis universale est medium inter ignorantiam vel potentiam nudam intellectus et cognitionem certam et

---

4 Utrum] *praem.* Quaeritur NO KU FW X Z *adnot. mg.* Quaestio 16 M | prius *post* nobis X | intelligatur] intelligitur HLM U | a nobis *om.* KU 6 Arguitur] Videtur (*post* sic) N *om.* FW | quod *om.* O | sic] *add. ex* LM 7 Physicorum] *add.* ubi L *add.* nam ibi M | quod *om.* NO | innata] innatum L | via] procedere L *om.* N U X *add.* cognoscendi Z 8 et *om.* X Z | sunt *om.* FW | nobis primo] primo NO nobis magis L prius nobis K nobis prius U | nota] nata H 9 id est] et U Z | universalia] universale N | autem *om.* X 10 sunt naturae] *inv.* L | naturae notiora] *inv.* NO | quia sunt] quae sunt L et sunt KU id est FW | igitur etc.] igitur L ergo etc. FW Z *om.* X 11 Item] Praeterea NO KU FW X Z | intellectui imprimitur] *inv.* N | prius] primo FW 12 et unum *om.* KU | quae] natura O | quae — universalia] quod maxime (*post* est U) est universale KU 13 prius] primo FW | imprimuntur] imprimitur KU | obiecta] aliqua KU omnia FW X Z | intelligibilia] intentionalia KU *om.* Z 14 igitur etc.] igitur L ergo etc. FW Z *om.* X 15 Item] Praeterea NO KU FW X | Item — etc. *om.* Z 16 medium] *add.* cognitum W | Cum — medium] Cum igitur magis universalis est media O Cognitio magis universalis est media KU W Cognitum magis universalis est media F Cognitio magis universale est media X | inter] *add.* potentiam K | ignorantiam vel] et ignorantiam (*post* nudam) U ignorantiam et X *om.* N

---

[1] Quaestio 16 deest in cod. Q.
[2] **Aristot.**, *Physica* I c. 1 (AL VII[1] 7-8; A c. 1, 184*a* 16-25): "Innata autem est ex notioribus nobis via et certioribus in certiora naturae et notiora"; melius in *Auctoritates Aristotelis* (ed. J. Hamesse 140): "Innata est nobis via cognoscendi a communioribus ad propria."
[3] **Aristot.**, *Physica* I c. 1 (AL VII[1] 7; A c. 1, 184*a* 21): "Sunt autem nobis primum manifesta et certa, quae confusa magis, posterius autem ex his fiunt nota…"
[4] **Avicenna,**, *Metaph.* I c. 5 (AviL 31): "Dicamus igitur quod res et ens et necesse talia sunt quod statim imprimuntur in anima prima impressione."

determinatam, igitur, etc.⁵

4 Item, illud prius intelligitur cuius singulare prius sentitur; sed singulare magis universalis prius sentitur quam minus universalis, secundum AVICENNAM in *Metaphysica* sua,⁶ et secundum PHILOSOPHUM I *Physicorum*⁷ ubi dicitur quod 'pueri primo appellant omnes viros patres'; et prius a remotis sentitur aliquid esse corpus quam animatum et prius animatum quam homo.

5 Contra:

Composita sunt nobis prius nota secundum COMMENTATOREM I *Physicorum*⁸ exponendo illud: magis confusa sunt nobis prius nota, id est, magis composita; sed minus universalia sunt compositiora, quia se habent per additionem ad magis universalia; igitur, etc.

6 Item, priora secundum naturam sunt nobis posterius nota, ut dicitur I *Physicorum*;⁹ sed universaliora sunt priora natura, quia ab ipsis non convertitur consequentia¹⁰ et patet quia etiam per ipsa

---

1 igitur etc.] igitur L om. X   2 Item] Praeterea N KU FW X Z Prima(!) O | illud] idem U add. universale KU FW X Z | prius om. Z | cuius om. Z   3 sentitur] intelligitur KU | quam] add. singulare FW | minus universalis] inv. X | universalis²] add. igitur N   4 secundum] per H | Metaphysica sua] inv. KU | secundum² om. FW X   5 I om. F | ubi dicitur om. O | ubi — primo] qui N | pueri] spat. vac. Z | primo appellant] inv. O Z appellant K   6 viros patres] inv. X viros fratres N homines patres H KU | et om. H | prius post remotis KU | aliquid esse] aliquod FW | quam om. FW   7 et — animatum om. FW | prius animatum om. X Z   8 Contra om. X Z   9 Composita] Compositiora KU | nobis prius] inv. U prius K | secundum] sed F   10 exponendo] exponenda X | nobis prius] inv. K nobis primo NO nobis notiora vel prius Z   11 id est] et FW Z | compositiora] magis (om. O) composita NO   12 per om. U | ad magis] ad O L KU X Z om. FW | igitur etc.] igitur U etc. X   13 Item] Praeterea NO KU FW X | Item — etc. om. Z | secundum] quantum ad N | nobis] add. per FW | posterius nota] inv. NO | ut] ubi F   14 I] 'V' N 'II' O | universaliora] universalia O X | priora] prius HLM | natura] naturaliter H   15 et patet] ut patet L et KU FW sed X | etiam post ipsa M om. H U FW | ipsa differunt] illa quae distinguuntur NO

⁵Cf. **Thomas**, *Summa theol.* I q. 85 a. 3 in corp. (V 336a): "Secundo oportet considerari quod intellectus noster de potentia in actum procedit. Omne autem quod procedit in potentia in actum, prius pervenit ad actum incompletum, qui est medius inter potentiam et actum, quam ad actum perfectum. Actus autem perfectus ad quem pervenit intellectus, est scientia completa, per quam distincte et determinate res cognoscuntur. Actus autem incompletus est scientia imperfecta, per quam sciuntur res indistincte sub quadam confusione; quod enim sic cognoscitur, secundum quid cognoscitur in actu, et quodammodo in potentia."
⁶Potius **Avicenna**, *Liber primus naturalium* c. 1 (AviL 7-8): "... erit in his forma docendi et discendi rationabiliter haec scilicet ut incipiatur ab eo quod magis commune est et perveniatur ad id quod magis proprium est."
⁷**Aristot.**, *Physica* I c. 1 (AL VII¹ 8; T c. 1, 1084b 12-14): "Et pueri primum appellant omnes viros patres et matres feminas ..."; *Auctoritates Aristotelis* (ed. J. Hamesse 140): "Pueri primo appellant omnes viros patres et omnes mulieres matres ..."
⁸**Averroës**, *Physica* I com. 3 (ed. Iuntina IV f. 7raC-7rbD); **Arist.** *Physica* I t. 4 (AL VII¹ 8: A c. 1 184a 24-25): "Totum enim secundum sensum notius est, universale autem totum quiddam est; multa enim comprehendit ut partes universale."
⁹**Aristot.**, *Physica* I c. 1 (AL VII¹ 7; A c. 1 184a 21): "Sunt autem primum manifesta et certa quae confusa magis."
¹⁰Cf. **Aristot.**, *Praedic.* c. 12 (AL I² 75; c. 12 14a 30-34).

differunt species et minus universalia; igitur, etc.

Item, quae sunt difficillima ad cognoscendum nobis non sunt prius nota; "maxime universalia sunt huiusmodi", ut patet I *Metaphysicae*;[11] igitur, etc.

[I. — Ad quaestionem
A. — Praenotanda]

[2] Dicendum quod aliquid dicitur prius alio tripliciter, scilicet generatione, perfectione et adaequatione. De duobus primis habetur IX *Metaphysicae*;[12] de tertio I *Posteriorum*[13] ubi dicitur quod universale est quod convenit alicui primo. Et vocat universale et primum adaequatione ipsam propriam passionem quae praedicatur convertibiliter de subiecto. De duobus primis modis dicendum est ad praesens.

Ulterius sciendum quod non est idem cognoscere confusum et confuse, nec distinctum et distincte. Nam confusum potest distincte cognosci, sicut "animal" quod est confusum respectu hominis. Similiter distinctum potest confuse cognosci, sicut "homo", cognoscendo animal vel quod sit animal. Illud autem est confusum quod est indistinctum, distinguibile tamen sicut genus. Cognoscere autem confuse est cognoscere quid est quod dicitur per nomen, vel cognoscere in suo universali tantum; sed cognoscere quid distincte

---

1 differunt] definiuntur KU FW X | et *om.* NO | universalia] universalis N | igitur *om.* X 2 Item] Praeterea NO KU FW X Z *add.* ult. sunt O | difficillima] difficiliora N | nobis] ant. ad Z | sunt²] *mg.* L *add.* nobis NO FW X Z 3 huiusmodi] huius O nobis difficillima ad cognoscendum KU FW X Z | patet] dicitur FW *add.* ex HLM | I] 'VI' N scilicet(!) O 4 igitur etc.] igitur L *om.* X 7 Dicendum] *add.* est M F | prius] perfectius(!) O 8 *add.* in M 9 Metaphysicae] *add.* et N | de — Posteriorum *om.* X | tertio] *add.* habetur in (tertio L *om.* H) HLM | ubi *om.* NO 10 convenit] dicitur NO | alicui] *add.* per se et L | et *om.* K 11 ipsam *om.* H | propriam *om.* N 12 de subiecto *om.* N | modis *om.* KU FW X Z | est *om.* NO X Z 14 sciendum] est sciendum NO sciendum est M est notandum FW | cognoscere] post et X | confusum et confuse] confuse et cognoscere confusum KU confusum et X 15 nec] vel N et H | Nam] *rep.* K | potest — confusum] *rep.* O 16 sicut] ut FW *add.* et HM 17 confuse cognosci] *inv.* H confuse concipi K 18 cognoscendo animal] cognito animali KU FW cognoscitur animal X | animal vel *om.* N | sit] est N | Illud] Ille O Id K Idem U 19 indistinctum] distinctum X | distinguibile] indistinguibile O | sicut] ut N | Cognoscere — confuse] Confuse autem cognoscere HL | Cognoscere — vel *om.* X 20 quid — nomen] = L KU quid est quod (*post* dicitur O) per nomen dicitur NO quid est per nomen H quid dicitur per nomen M FW Z 21 cognoscere] *add.* (*mg.*) aliquid M | quid] aliquid KU FW *add.* est H

[11] **Aristot.**, *Metaph.* I c. 2 (AL XXV² 9-10; A c. 2 982*b* 23-24): "... sed fere difficillima sunt hominibus ad cognoscendum quae maxime sunt universalia ..."
[12] **Aristot.**, *Metaph.* IX c. 8 (AL XXV³·² 188-189; T c. 8 1050*a* 2-15).
[13] **Aristot.**, *Anal. post.* I c. 4 (AL IV¹ 14-15; A c. 4 73*b* 40—74*a* 13).

est cognoscere illud per principia propria posita in sua definitione.

[B. — Solutio
Articulus 1: Minus universale est prius notum nobis prioritate temporis et cognitione confusa quam magis universale]

10 Dicendum igitur ad quaestionem primo quod minus universale est prius notum nobis prioritate generationis et cognitione confusa quam magis universale.

11 Probatio: omne agens secundum ultimum suae potentiae producit perfectissimum effectum quem potest producere, quia da oppositum, quod non producat effectum perfectissimum quem potest, sequitur quod agit citra ultimum potentiae suae; sed omne agens naturale est agens secundum ultimum potentiae suae, quia non agit deliberative, determinando sibi quantitatem effectus, sed determinatur ab alio; igitur agit perfectissimum effectum quem potest. Intellectus autem quantum ad primum actum intelligendi et etiam omnia quae concurrunt ad causandum intellectionem effective — sive phantasia sive species intelligibilis — sunt agentia naturalia; igitur intellectus in primo actu intelligendi praecedente omnem actum volendi intelligit perfectissimum intelligibile in quod potest, quia terminat actionem perfectissimam quam habere potest; tale autem intelligibile est species specialissima; igitur, etc.

12 Item, secundum AVICENNAM[14] et COMMENTATOREM VI

---

1 principia propria] inv. L principia FW | posita *om.* KU | sua definitione] definitione sui N
5 Dicendum] *add.* est M F | Dicendum ... ad quaestionem] Ad quaestionem ... dicendum est H | quaestionem] primum NO | primo *om.* HL | minus universale] inv. U 6 est] *add.* quod Z | notum nobis] inv. N K notum est nobis Z | generationis] temporis NO U FW X Z 7 quam magis] inv. N 8 Probatio] Primo O Item HLM | omne] essentia O *om.* N | secundum] sed F | suae potentiae] inv. NO U FW X Z 9 perfectissimum effectum] inv. K *add.* suum NO | quem] quam O | da oppositum] dato opposito N L 10 producat] producit N L KU | effectum perfectissimum] inv. N H F perfectissimum L | perfectissimum quem potest] perfectissimum L etc. K 11 potest] possit U FW X Z *add.* producere N | citra] secundum NO | potentiae suae] inv. HL K | sed] quia H | sed — suae *om.* X 12 agens naturale] inv. NO | est agens] agit L KU FW Z | secundum] *add.* sui L | potentiae suae] inv. H sive producit L 13 determinando] determinans L 15 primum actum] inv. O KU FW X Z 16 etiam] respectu X *om.* Z | intellectionem] intentionem NO Z actum F intellectum W 17 phantasia sive] phantasma sive FW *om.* Z | intelligibilis] intelligibiles N | agentia] agibilia N 18 praecedente] praecedentem F | omnem actum] omni actu N actum Z 19 volendi] ratiocinandi NO voluntatis KU FW X Z | intelligibile *om.* X | in quod] in quantum H KU F et quod Z | potest] *add.* patet X 20 quia] quod KU | quia — potest *om.* NO | terminat] determinat L Z | habere potest] inv. K Z 21 species *om.* U | igitur etc.] igitur L *om.* X 22 Item] Praeterea NO KU FW X Z | secundum] sed F

---

[14] **Avicenna**, *Metaph.* I c. 3 (AviL 20-21): "Ordo vero huius scientiae est ut discatur post scientias naturales et disciplinales."

Metaphysicae,[15] "metaphysica est ultima scientia in ordine doctrinae"; igitur principia aliarum scientiarum prius tempore a nobis cognoscuntur et concipiuntur quam metaphysicae; principia autem aliarum scientiarum sunt minus universalia, quia metaphysica est de universalissimis; igitur, etc.

Item, si semper intelligamus magis universale prius quam singulare aliquod quod subito movet sensum, erit magnum tempus antequam possumus cognoscere eius speciem specialissimam, quia oportet prius cognoscere omnia eius superiora essentialia, quae cum sint multa non possunt in instanti cognosci; hoc autem manifeste patet esse falsum; igitur, etc.

[4] Item, si prius magis universale intelligitur, aut eadem specie cum minus universali aut aliā. Non eādem, quia illud non est proprium repraesentativum alicuius quod aequaliter repraesentat ipsum et oppositum vel disparatum; sed species repraesentans animal, quod est magis universale, aequaliter repraesentat hominem et asinum, et per consequens per illam simul cognosceret utrumque intellectus, si illa sufficeret — quod falsum est; igitur non est eādem. Si aliā, aut tunc erunt tot species in intellectu quot sunt species generis, si illae debent cognosci; vel quot sunt superiora universalia essentialia, antequam species specialissima intelligatur — quod falsum est;

---

1 est] *add.* per X | ultima scientia] *inv.* H scientia summa et ultima L   2 prius — scientiarum *om.* N | a nobis] ant. prius H | cognoscuntur et] cognoscitur et O et F *om.* KU W X Z   3 metaphysicae] metaphysica O X | autem *om.* U | aliarum *om.* M   4 scientiarum *om.* O U FW X Z | de] ex KU | universalissimis] universalioribus N verissimis K diversis F   5 igitur etc.] igitur KU *om.* L X   6 Item] Praeterea NO KU FW X Z | semper *om.* X | intelligamus magis] *inv.* U intelligimus magis NO H FW X Z | prius] ant. intelligamus NO X Z ant. magis FW *om.* L KU | singulare] *add.* vel K *add.* quando singulare FW   7 aliquod] aliquid KU X *om.* F Z | quod *om.* HLM KU FW Q X Z | subito *post* sensum FW | movet] *add.* aliquem F | sensum] *add.* vel K | erit] est F   8 possumus] possimus O K FW X Z | cognoscere *om.* Z | eius *om.* H   9 oportet] oporteret NO FW X Z | prius] primo N primum O | cognoscere] intelligere (*post* essentialia) K *om.* U | omnia] obiecta NO | eius superiora] superiora ei FW *add.* et N   10 multa] *add.* et incerta NO | in instanti *post* cognosci N in intellectu F | cognosci *om.* O | autem *om.* N FW | manifeste patet] *inv.* FW   11 patet esse] patet KU *om.* N | igitur etc. *om.* L X   12 Item] Praeterea NO FW X Z | prius *post* universale K | cum *om.* L   13 aliā] non L | Non] *add.* est Z | illud] ille O ita L   14 quod] quid U | aequaliter repraesentat] essentialiter repraesentat O U representata essentialiter L   15 repraesentans] repraesentativa N representant Z | animal] animalis N | quod] *add.* non Z   16 magis] *add.* id est Z | aequaliter] essentialiter HL U *om.* NO | asinum] *add.* unum(?) Z   17 per² *om.* U | simul cognosceret] *inv.* H Z | utrumque intellectus] *inv.* KU | si] sed O   18 quod — est] sed hoc est falsum L quod est falsum X | est² *om.* NO | alia aut] autem alia NO FW X Z alia autem M   19 tunc *om.* H | erunt] essent NO | in intellectu *om.* N | sunt *om.* H U FW | si] sed NO KU X Z | si — sunt *om.* L | illae] aliae N istae K   20 debent — sunt] sunt in cognitione vel quot N sunt cognosci vel quot O | vel] ut K | sunt *om.* FW *add.* generis HM | universalia] universalius (ant. superiora) N universaliora O FW Z *om.* X | essentialia] *mg.* F²   21 antequam] ante U | specialissima intelligatur] specialissimae intelligantur K | intelligatur] intelligitur M *om.* L | falsum est] *inv.* F

---

[15] **Averroës**, *Metaph.* VI com. 3 (ed. Iuntina VIII 147r): "Ordo addiscendi istam scientiam est posterius, et ideo discimus eam post physicam."

igitur, etc.

15 Item, illud cognoscitur posterius tempore, cuius abstractio est difficilior; sed abstractio coloris, qui est universalior, est difficilior quam albedinis, quia a dissimilibus abstrahitur quiditas coloris, scilicet ab albo et nigro quae sunt opposita — albedinis autem quiditas a duobus albis quae sunt similia; igitur, etc.

16 Item, possibile est intelligere minus commune, ignorando magis commune; igitur non oportet semper universalius prius cognosci ab intellectu. Probatio antecedentis: quia geometer cognoscit lineam et multa de linea probat, et tamen nescit utrum sit substantia vel accidens; igitur, etc.

17 Item, ad hoc etiam est auctoritas PHILOSOPHI I *Physicorum*[16] dicentis quod definitum prius cognoscitur quam partes definitionis; definitum autem est minus universale, cum sit species, quam genus suum, quod est pars suae definitionis; igitur, etc.

[Articulus 2: Prius cognoscitur magis universale a nobis cognitione distincta quam minus universale]

18 Secundo, dico quod prius cognoscitur magis universale a nobis cognitione distincta.

Probatio: prius distincte illud cognoscitur quod intrat definitionem alterius, per quod aliud distincte cognoscitur; sed ens quod est universalissimum intrat definitionem omnium, cum conceptus entis includatur in conceptu cuiuslibet — ipsum autem non habet

---

21 igitur etc.] igitur L U *om.* N X   2 Item] Praeterea NO KU FW X Z | Item — etc.] *post* etc² (*fin.* n. 16) KU | tempore *om.* K   3 difficilior] *add.* quia eius cognitio intellectualis abstractiva est difficilior FW | coloris *om.* Z | qui] quae NO F Z   4 albedinis] albus N | dissimilibus] dissimilioribus M difficultatibus NO difficilibus H FW | quiditas] quantitas NO   5 ab] sub N | albedinis autem quiditas] albedinis autem quantitas NO quiditas autem albedinis KU   6 albis] *add.* abstrahitur K | igitur etc.] igitur ergo L *om.* X   7 Item] Praeterea NO K FW X Z | possibile] impossibile N U | intelligere] cognoscere FW | ignorando] cognoscendo U ignorato FW X ignoto Z | magis] maius U   8 igitur *om.* X | oportet] *add.* quod F | semper universalius] *inv.* K | cognosci] cognoscatur F | ab intellectu *om.* X   9 geometer] geometricus F | et] vel KU   10 et tamen] attamen NO | utrum] an K si U   11 igitur etc.] igitur U *om.* L X   12 Item] Praeterea NO KU *om.* FW X Z | etiam *om.* NO L KU   13 dicentis] dicit N dicens KU | quod *om.* L   14 autem est minus *om.* L Z | quam] *add.* sit N | genus suum] *inv.* NO   15 est pars] *inv.* K | suae definitionis] *inv.* L FW definitionis NO Z | igitur etc.] igitur L etc. X   18 dico] dicitur NO | cognoscitur magis] *inv.* N | a nobis] *ant.* magis KU   19 cognitione distincta] *inv.* L   20 Probatio] Probo H Probatur K | prius — cognoscitur] = O M FW Z prius illud distincte cognoscitur N H U illud prius distincte cognoscitur L K illud cognoscitur prius distincte X   21 alterius] *add.* et HL | aliud] aliquid H KU *om.* NO | distincte] distinctum N   23 entis] eius FW | includatur] includitur N KU | autem *om.* N | habet *om.* U

[16]**Aristot.**, *Physic.* I c. 1 (AL VII¹ 8; A c. 1, 184*b* 10-12); *Physic.* I c. 2 (AL VII¹ 8; A c. 2, 184*b* 19-22).

conceptum nisi distinctum, quia non habet in quo possit confuse et indistincte cognosci; igitur, etc. Simile autem est de aliis universalibus: quanto enim aliquid est universalius, tanto potest plurium definitionem intrare; et[17] distinctius cognosci, quanto pauciora superiora habeat, in quibus cognoscatur confuse.

Item, secundum AVICENNAM,[18] metaphysica est prior secundum ordinem cognoscendi distincte, quae tamen est universalius; igitur, etc. Nec tamen contradicit sibi AVICENNA[19] dicens quod est postrema ordine doctrinae, quia ordine doctrinae procedimus a cognitione confusa ad distinctam. Modo ita est quod principia aliarum scientiarum prius ordine doctrinae sunt nobis nota ex confuso conceptu terminorum, sicut geometer ex confuso conceptu lineae et puncti procedit ad cognoscendum eius definitionem et passionem. Et ideo metaphysica est posterior ordine doctrinae, cuius tamen principia sunt distincte cognita. Sed scientia metaphysicae acquisita, revertendo ad alias scientias, magis distincte cognoscuntur earum principia, scientia metaphysicae prius distincte

---

1 conceptum] contradictorium O | possit] potest N posset HM | et] vel NO FW X Z 2 indistincte] distincte H F | cognosci] add. cum non habeat aliquod superius indistincte FW | igitur etc.] igitur L om. N X | autem est] inv. M FW X Z | aliis] istis NO 3 aliquid est] inv. X aliquod est L | universalius] universalis Z | tanto om. KU | plurium om. KU 4 distinctius] distincte X | cognosci] cognoscitur N KU cognoscit O | quanto] cum NO FW X Z om. U 5 superiora om. Z | habeat] habeant FW X | cognoscatur] cognoscitur NO FW X Z cognoscetur KU 6 Item] Praeterea NO K FW X Z | Avicennam] add. Metaphysicae K | est prior] inv. KU | secundum ordinem] ordine NO Z 7 distincte] definitione NO | tamen] causa NO | universalius] quia universalius est N universalior K universalium X | igitur etc.] etc. X om. K 8 Avicenna] ipsi KU | dicens] dicendo N | est om. F 9 doctrinae] naturae X | quia — doctrinae om. KU FW Z | procedimus] procedens KU add. enim quia (communi W) FW 10 cognitione confusa] inv. NO | ad] add. cognitionem KU | ita est] inv. Z | principia] principium omnium X 11 prius] priorum NO FW propriarum Z | sunt] est X Z | ex om. Z 12 conceptu] add. suo et U | geometer] geometria(!) F | confuso conceptu] inv. FW 13 cognoscendum] cognitionem HL X | eius definitionem] inv. NO | definitionem et passionem] definitionem a passione N definitionis et passionis L definitionem X 14 ideo] ita X | doctrinae] doctrina K add. (mg.) confuse concipiendi F² 15 cuius] cum X | tamen om. KU | sunt] sint X | cognita] cognoscenda Z om. X | scientia om. FW 16 metaphysicae] metaphysica KU add. alicuius H 17 cognoscuntur] cognoscitur N | earum] = NO sola HLM KU eorum FW X Z | scientia] = NO Z om. HLM KU F X | scientia metaphysicae] metaphysica W | prius om. L

[17] Subaudi: tanto potest.
[18] **Avicenna**, *Metaph.* I c. 3 (AviL 20): "Sicut enim haec scientia est principium essendi illas, sic scientia huius est principium certitudinis sciendi illas."
[19] Cf. **Avicenna**, *Metaph.* I c. 3 (AviL 20-1): "Ordo vero huius scientiae est ut discatur post scientias naturales et disciplinales."

cognita; et sic est[20] prius ordine distinctae cognitionis.[21] Sic in proposito: species prius cognoscitur indistincte — scilicet in cognoscendo quid dicitur per nomen vel in suo universali; sed cognito universali distincte, tunc per eius divisionem et contractionem — per additionem differentiae — fit reditus ad cognoscendum speciem distincte.

[Articulus 3: Illud quod prius est prioritate perfectionis a nobis cognoscitur]

Tertio, dico quod prius prioritate perfectionis cognoscitur a nobis.

Circa quod sciendum quod aliqua cognitio potest esse perfectior alia, vel secundum perfectionis complementum vel secundum proportionem ad obiectum, sicut visio aquilae primo modo est perfectior visione mea, sed visio mea respectu candelae est perfectior visione aquilae respectu solis. Ista divisio habetur II *De animalibus*[22] a PHILOSOPHO dicente quod magis desideramus scire modicum de substantiis separatis quam multum de inferioribus. Illud autem modicum attenditur secundum proportionem ad obiectum, non

---

1 est prius] inv. X est prior KU FW X Z   2 cognoscitur] cognoscuntur L | indistincte] distincte K *om.* L | scilicet in cognoscendo] *rep.* K *om.* X | in *om.* NO L FW Z   3 quid] *add.* est quod NO FW X Z | dicitur] dicit(!) U | vel] ut L | sed] *del.* Z²   4 distincte] distincto M | divisionem] definitionem L | contractionem] contradictionem L F contradictorium(!) U   5 fit] *del.* H   9 quod] quid HM *add.* magis universale K | perfectionis] perfectio Z | cognoscitur a nobis] *ant.* prioritate K a nobis cognoscitur NO M FW X Z   10 nobis] *add.* magis universalia NO   11 sciendum] sciendum est M F est sciendum K   12 secundum] *mg.* W | perfectionis] *mg.* Z² | perfectionis complementum] inv. H F | vel² *om.* X   13 obiectum] oppositum O | aquilae] *add. (mg.)* respectu solis F² | primo modo *post* perfectior FW X Z   14 visione *om.* KU | mea] mei L *add. (mg.)* respectu candelae F² | sed visio mea *om.* X   15 respectu] *add.* eiusdem vel respectu NO W X Z | Ista] Illa O FW Z Ideo X | divisio] distinctio (*lin.*) F² | habetur] *add.* in Z | II] "V" N W X "X" Z | a Philosopho] ab Aristotele FW   17 substantiis] *add.* id est O | multum *om.* U | de] *add.* substantiis KU | Illud] Idem(!) U   18 modicum] multum (*mg.*) F² | attenditur] attendit M | secundum — attingitur (par. 21) *rep. in ima col.* O | obiectum] oppositum(!) O

---

[20] Subaudi: metaphysica.
[21] Pro momento doctrinae totius paragraphi, cf. **Duns Scotus**, *Rep. Paris.* I-A prol. q. 2 n. 168 (ed. in praep.): "Ad auctoritatem Philosophi dico quod principia dupliciter possunt esse nota. Uno modo notitia confusa ut si termini confuse apprehendantur per sensum et experientiam — et hoc sufficit ad scientiam terminorum in scientia qualibet speciali ut quod linea sit longitudo, ignorando utrum quidditas eius sit substantia, quantitas, vel qualitas etc. Alio modo possunt cognosci notitia distincta, sciendo ad quod genus pertineat quidditas eorum, cum definitiones terminorum distincte cognoscuntur ex evidentia terminorum; et hoc contingit per scientiam metaphysicalem, dividendo et componendo, et sic omnes scientiae possunt dici sibi subalternatae VI Metaphysicae. Et ideo habita scientia metaphysicae perfectius cognoscuntur principia cuiuslibet scientiae quam nata sint cognosci in illa scientia per principia propria et per consequens perfectius habetur quaelibet alia scientia, habita metaphysica."
[22] *Auctoritates Aristotelis* (ed. J. Hamesse 165): "Melius est scire modicum de rebus nobilibus quam multum de rebus ignobilibus"; cf. **Aristot.**, *De part. anim.* I c. 5 (A c. 5, 644b 24-25, 31-33).

autem secundum naturam cognitionis absolute.

Ad propositum igitur dicendum quod illud quod a nobis cognoscitur prius prioritate perfectionis cognitionis in se et absolute consideratae est Deus, loquendo etiam de cognitione naturali et universali, tam causalitate quam praedicatione. Probatio primi: quia illa cognitio est perfectior in se per quam attingitur perfectius obiectum; sed haec est cognitio Dei, qui est obiectum perfectissimum; igitur, etc.

Item, PHILOSOPHUS X *Ethicorum*[23] ponit felicitatem humanam, quae ex puris naturalibus haberi potest, esse in cognitione substantiarum separatarum vel primae substantiae separatae, quae est Deus; sed ponit eam perfectissimam cognitionem; igitur eius cognitio, quae in via potest haberi perfectissima, est cognitio perfectior omni cognitione quorumcumque inferiorum, quia quodcumque individuum speciei nobilioris est nobilius quocumque individuo speciei inferioris.

Sed quae est cognitio perfectior secundum proportionem ad obiectum, id est respectu inferiorum, quae sunt intellectui nostro proportionata?

Dicendum quod cognitio illorum sensibilium quae fortius movent sensum est perfectior. Quia quae fortius movent sensum, fortius movent intellectum, licet altiori modo, quia universalius; quae autem fortius movent intellectum sunt magis proportionata

---

1 naturam] materiam K | cognitionis] *add.* (*lin. Z²*) in se FW X Z² *add.* ult. et X   2 igitur] est Z | dicendum] *add.* est M | quod² *om.* F | a nobis *post* cognoscitur KU   3 in se *post* absolute N | et *om.* NO F   4 etiam] et X *om.* Z   5 tam] aliqua X | causalitate] causatione KU | praedicatione] perfectione F | quia *om.* N   6 perfectior *post* se FW perfecta LM KU | attingitur] *add.* per se KU   7 obiectum perfectissimum] *inv.* Z   8 igitur etc.] igitur L U etc. X   9 Item] Praeterea NO KU FW X Z | X] "IV" HLM K Z "VIII" X | humanam] hominum FW X Z   10 haberi — esse] = H KU bene potest NO potest esse L haberi potest M FW X Z | substantiarum] scientiarum NO   11 vel] et X | primae] per se KU X | substantiae *om.* X | separatae *om.* L FW | est Deus] *inv.* O X Z   12 sed] *add.* non N | perfectissimam cognitionem] in perfectissimam in cognitionem NO in perfectissima cognitione KU FW X Z | igitur eius cognitio] perfecta eius X   13 quae] *add.* est H U X | perfectissima est] *inv.* NO FW Z | est *om.* X | cognitio] *add.* vel Z | omni] est NO enim M *om.* Z   14 quorumcumque *om.* X | quodcumque — nobilius] *in imo fol.* F²   15 nobilioris] superioris N | nobilioris — speciei *om.* X | quocumque individuo] indicio N   17 quae] qui Z | cognitio perfectior] *inv.* N H cognitio perfectioris Z | secundum] sed F   18 id est] in U *om.* N | respectu] scilicet N | inferiorum] inferioris N H U | sunt *post* nostro N | nostro *om.* L K W   19 proportionata] improportionata N   20 Dicendum] *add.* est M | illorum] istorum O X *om.* KU | quae fortius] *inv.* U   21 movent — fortius² *om.* Z | est — sensum] *rep.* W *om.* NO   22 fortius *om.* M KU | licet — intellectum *om.* O | universalius] universaliora K   23 autem *om.* K | fortius movent] *inv.* X magis movent Z

---

[23] **Aristot.**, *Eth. Nic.* X c. 7 (AL XXVI³ 358-359; K c. 7 1177a 12-13, 16-17); *Auctoritates Aristotelis* (ed. J. Hamesse 247): "Ultima felicitas hominis consistit in optima operatione."

intellectui; et ideo prius perfectione tali, scilicet secundum proportionem ad obiectum, intelligitur universale illius singularis sensibilis, quod fortius movet sensum.

[II. — Ad argumenta principalia]

25 Ad primum in oppositum,[24] dicendum quod PHILOSOPHUS I *Physicorum* intendit dare modum deveniendi in cognitionem distinctam; et hoc est per divisionem magis universalis et magis confusi, quod tamen est prius notum nobis cognitione distincta.

26 Ad aliud[25] dicendum quod ens et unum prius imprimuntur intellectui quoad eorum cognitionem distinctam quam alia; et ideo illa cognitione sunt nobis prius nota, quia non possunt notificari per priora; et hoc concedo.

27 Ad aliud[26] dicendum quod Thomas faciens illud argumentum deceptus fuit per hoc quod non distinxit inter cognoscere aliquid confuse et distincte et distinctum. Verum enim est quod cognoscere aliquid confuse, scilicet minus universale, est medium inter ignorantiam puram et cognitionem eius distinctam, et sic cognitio alicuius confusa prior est cognitione eius distincta. Sed propter hoc non sequitur quod cognitio confusi, id est magis universalis, sit prior cognitione distincti, id est minus universalis, nisi loquendo de cognitione distincta, ut dictum est[27] — immo est ibi fallacia consequentis a pluribus causis veritatis ad unam. Cognitio enim alicuius

---

1 prius *om.* K | tali *om.* F 2 intelligitur] intelligimus LM intellectus KU 3 sensibilis *om.* H K | sensum] *add.* perfectius cognoscitur K 5 dicendum] *add.* est M | Philosophus] *add.* in LM U | Philosophus — quod² (par. 26) *om.* N 6 intendit] intelligit FW | dare] docere M 7 et — distinctam (par. 26) *om.* X | divisionem] dictionem F conditionem Z 8 prius notum] magis notum et prius L | notum nobis] *inv.* KU | cognitione distincta] *inv.* Z 9 dicendum] *add.* est M 10 quoad] ergo ad L | quam] *add.* aliqua L 11 illa] ista X | nobis prius] *inv.* FW | prius *om.* X | possunt] *add.* nobis X 12 et] in L | concedo] *spat. vac.* Z 13 dicendum] *add.* est M F | Thomas] taliter(!) HLM KU | illud] hoc N M *om.* K 14 deceptus fuit] *inv.* K | per hoc *om.* Z | distinxit] distinguit Z 15 confuse et distincte et distinctum] = HM confuse (ant. aliquid N) et confusum et distincte et distinctum N L confuse (ant. aliquid) et cognoscere distincte confuse et distincte et distinctum O distincte et confuse et distinctum KU distincte et confuse F confuse et distincte W confusum et confuse et distincte et distinctum Z et X | Verum — quod *om.* X 16 aliquid] *rep.* H | confuse] commune W | scilicet] id est L K | est *om.* X | ignorantiam puram] *inv.* Z 17 alicuius] eius H 18 prior est] *inv.* NO FW prius est LM | eius] eiusdem M KU Z 20 id est] a U 21 ibi] in F *om.* N Z | fallacia] fallacitas U | consequentis *om.* N 22 enim] autem confusa KU

[24]Cf. supra n. 1.
[25]Cf. supra n. 2.
[26]Cf. supra n. 3.
[27]Cf. supra n. 18.

universalis minus est vel quando cognoscitur tantum de ipso "quid est" quod dicitur per nomen, vel quando cognoscitur in suo universaliori vel confuso; non igitur sequitur "cognitio confusa minus universalis est prior tempore quam distincta, igitur cognitio sui universalioris vel magis confusi est prior".

Ad ultimum[28] dicendum quod quando aliquod singulare est praesens sensui secundum debitam proportionem, tunc intellectus primo apprehendit speciem specialissimam eius; sed quando non est proportionatum sensui, ita quod non possit ipsum distincte cognoscere, tunc intellectus primo apprehendit speciem eius proximiorem quam potest, quia non movet sensum nisi sub ratione qua est singulare speciei communioris; ideo etc.

---

1 universalis minus] inv. KU minoris universalis N | est om. KU X | vel] et U om. N | quando] an X | cognoscitur post nomen FW | tantum post ipso NO add. quod H | quid] qui K   3 confuso] confuse N | igitur om. Z | sequitur] add. igitur NO LM Z | cognitio om. F | minus] minoris N minor O   4 prior] prius L | quam] quod O om. KU FW X add. eius NO Z   5 universalioris] superioris N | vel] et U   6 dicendum] add. est M F | quando om. X   8 primo om. M | specialissimam — speciem om. U | eius om. K | non om. N   9 proportionatum] improportionatum N | non] = N L K om. O HM FW X Z | possit] potest H | ipsum] ipsam L om. F X   10 intellectus om. K | apprehendit] comprehendit M | eius] ei H om. U Z | proximiorem] add. ei FW   11 potest] ponit NO M | sensum — ratione] nisi sensum rationem L | qua] quae Z | singulare] singularis Z   12 speciei om. Z | ideo etc.] etc. O U X om. N FW Z

[28] Cf. supra n. 4.

[QUAESTIO 17]

UTRUM IN INTELLECTU NOSTRO SINT SPECIES INTELLIGIBILES PRIORES NATURALITER ACTU INTELLIGENDI

Utrum[1] in intellectu nostro sint species intelligibiles priores naturaliter actu intelligendi.

[1] Videtur quod non:

1 Quia quandocumque aliqua species imprimitur ab obiecto in potentia repraesentat obiectum tantum sub illa ratione sub qua nata est imprimi ab obiecto, quia generatum est simile generanti secundum formam secundum quam generat; sed quaecumque species imprimitur ab obiecto in intellectu, sub ratione singularis imprimitur, quia obiectum extra vel phantasma a quo imprimitur est singulare — intellectus recipiens est singularis; igitur tantum repraesentat singulare, vel universale sub ratione singularis; hoc est falsum; igitur, etc.

2 Item, praesentia obiecti est causa praesentiae speciei, non autem e converso; cum autem obiectum intelligibile sit praesens in phantasmate, non requiritur species in intellectu propter praesentiam obiecti; sed non propter aliud ponitur species in intellectu; igitur frustra.

3 Item, si essent species in intellectu, plures possunt esse simul;

---

5 Utrum] *praem.* Quaeritur NO KU FW X Z *adnot. mg.* Quaestio 17 M | sint] sunt U *add.* plures U | intelligibiles] intelligentes Z   8 Quia] Quod Z | quandocumque] quantumcumque N antequam U   9 repraesentat] repraesentandum H *add.* illud L | tantum *om.* Q   10 generatum] generatio NO genitum KU FW X Z | simile] similis N sub X | generanti] generan*te* X   11 generat] generatur FW X | quaecumque] quocumque O   12 imprimitur] imprimuntur N imprimeretur O KU | in intellectu] intellecto K *om.* X | singularis] singularitatis KU | imprimitur] imprimetur K   13 obiectum] *add.* est O *add.* eius FW | imprimitur²] imprimeretur O | est singulare] ant. a KU *om.* O   14 singulare] *add.* et N | intellectus] *add.* etiam KU | intellectus — est] est intellectus recipiens intellectus O | est *om.* Q X | est — ratione] *mg.* Z² | singularis — repraesentat] *mg.* W *om.* F | igitur] ergo L Q X | repraesentat] repraesentaret N KU X   15 singularis] singulare Z | hoc] quod X   16 igitur etc.] etc. L ergo etc. FW Q Z *om.* X   17 Item] Praeterea N K FW Q X Z Prima(!) O | obiecti] oppositi O   18 autem obiectum] *inv.* M obiectum L igitur (ergo FW Q X) obiectum (oppositum O) NO FW Q X Z   19 requiritur] sequitur Q | species] *add.* esse Q | propter — intellectu *om.* X   20 obiecti] oppositi O | sed *om.* NO | non *om.* Q | ponitur species] *inv.* Z | species *om.* Q   21 igitur] ergo L FW Q X   22 Item] *mg.* Z² Praeterea NO KU FW Q X | essent] esset F | intellectu] *add.* igitur HM *add.* ergo L | plures *om.* NO | possunt] possent FW Q X Z

[1] Pro argumentis principalibus atque contextu totius quaestionis, cf. **Henricus de Gandavo**, *Quodl.* V q. 14 (f. 174rT—179vG).

consequens est falsum; igitur, etc. Probatio consequentiae: quia species talis habet esse permanens etiam absente actu intelligendi; tamen post unum actum intelligendi potest succedere alius respectu alterius obiecti, et sic esset alia species alterius cum prima simul. Probatio falsitatis consequentis: quia cum illa species non sit potentia rationalis vel libera sed naturalis, de necessitate est actu praesente obiecto; cum igitur semper repraesentet obiectum suum, semper homo intelligeret per eam actu, et sequeretur quod per plures species illas posset simul plura intelligere, quod falsum est; igitur, etc.

4   Item, potentia semper prius perficitur proprio actu; proprius autem actus potentiae apprehensivae est apprehendere, non autem species; igitur, etc.

5   Contra:

PHILOSOPHUS III *De anima*,[2] dicit quod "anima est locus specierum, non tota sed intellectus," et in eodem,[3] "lapis non est in anima, sed species" lapidis.

Item, in eodem:[4] "anima per intellectum est omnia intelligibilia,

---

1 est *om.* NO Q | igitur etc.] igitur L ergo et antecedens FW ergo Q ergo etc. Z *om.* X   2 talis habet] tales habent KU | etiam — actu] assumptum a casu N   3 tamen] cum N *om.* KU | tamen — intelligendi *om.* X Z | unum actum] *inv.* HLM | intelligendi *om.* F | alius] alia NO aliter U   4 et — alterius *om.* N | species] *add.* respectu HL | cum] lin. F   5 Probatio falsitatis] Probo falsitatem NO Sed probatur falsitas K Sed probatio falsitatis U FW Q X Z | quia] quod KU | cum — species] illa potentia cum N *spat. vac.* + illa species O cum ipsa (ista X) species Q X | sit] sint O   6 rationalis] realis N | vel] et U | est] *add.* in N | actu] activa Q   7 cum igitur] *inv.* N | igitur] ergo L FW Q X | repraesentet *post* suum Q praesentet NO F | obiectum suum] *inv.* HLM   8 semper homo] *inv.* KU | homo intelligeret] *inv.* H | intelligeret per eam] per illam (istam O F X) intelligeret NO FW Q X intelligeret per ipsum KU intelligeret per illam intellectum Z | actu] a casu N | quod] quia Z | per² *om.* Q   9 illas] *ant.* plures H istas O X illa U *om.* N L *add.* semper Z | posset] potest H | posset — intelligere] plura possit intelligere simul N | simul plura] *inv.* O plura KU Z vel plura X | falsum est] *inv.* Q   10 igitur etc.] igitur L ergo etc. FW Q Z *om.* X   11 Item] Praeterea NO KU FW Q X Z | potentia] *add.* prius U | semper prius perficitur] semper prius cognoscitur perficitur O prius semper perficitur H U semper perficitur prius K FW semper perficitur X Z | proprio actu] *inv.* F | proprius] prius Q *om.* F   12 autem] cum F *om.* X | autem²] nisi N   13 species] speciem NO | igitur etc.] igitur L ergo etc. FW Q etc. X Z   15 Philosophus *om.* NO | dicit] dicitur N *om.* O | est locus] *inv.* Q   16 intellectus] intellectiva X   17 sed — lapidis] etc. Z | lapidis] lapidum O   18 Item] Praeterea K Et Z | eodem] eadem W *add.* dicitur HLM

²**Aristot.**, *De an.* III c. 1 (Γ c. 4, 429a 27-28): "Et bene iam dicentes sunt animam esse locum specierum, nisi quod non tota, sed intellectiva ..."; *Auctoritates Aristotelis* (ed. J. Hamesse 186): "Anima intellectiva est specierum intelligibilium locus."
³**Aristot.**, *De an.* III c. 7 (Γ c. 8, 431b 29—432a 1): "Non enim lapis in anima est, sed species"; *Auctoritates Aristotelis* (ed. J. Hamesse 188): "Lapis non est in anima sed species eius."
⁴**Aristot.**, *De an.* III c. 7 (Γ c. 8, 431b 21-23): "Dicamus iterum quod omnia ea quae sunt quodam modo est anima: aut enim sensibilia quae sunt aut intelligibilia, est autem scientia quidem scibilia quodam modo, sensus autem sensibilia"; *Auctoritates Aristotelis* (ed. J. Hamesse 188): "Anima est quoddammodo omnia."

et per sensum sensibilia"; hoc autem non potest intelligi, quod sit omnia per essentiam; igitur per eorum species in anima exsistentes.

Item, per rationem sic: omne quod reducitur de potentia essentiali ad accidentalem, oportet quod hoc sit per aliquod sibi impressum formaliter; intellectus noster ante addiscere vel invenire cognitionem intellectualem est in potentia essentiali ad actum intelligendi, a qua postea reducitur ad potentiam accidentalem, qua scilicet potest intelligere cum voluerit[5]; igitur hoc est per aliquid sibi formaliter impressum, quod voco speciem; igitur, etc.

[I. — Opinio communis seu Commentatoris]

[3] Responsio: una opinio communis[6] est quod intellectus habet speciem sibi impressam necessario requisitam ad actum intelligendi. Quod potest sic probari ex praedictis: quia oportet quod universale, actu intellectum, actu sit praesens in ratione obiecti; sed non potest esse praesens nisi per speciem impressam; igitur, etc.

Maior patet: quia sicut obiectum est prius actu intelligendi ordine naturae, sic ratio obiecti. Probatio minoris: quia non potest aliter esse praesens nisi per speciem in phantasmate exsistentem, sed non per illam. Probo: quia una species non potest repraesentare obiectum aliquod sub oppositis rationibus; sed singulare et

---

1 sensum] *add.* omnia N X | sensibilia] intelligibilia Z *add.* licet HLM | hoc autem] *inv.* M | autem non] *inv.* F non NO *add.* ult. enim F *add.* esse non potest vel X | intelligi] intellectus NO | sit] est KU si X   2 omnia] opposita NO | per essentiam] essentiam U *om.* H | igitur] ergo FW Q X | eorum] earum FW Q X Z   3 Item] Et praeterea NO Praeterea KU FW Q X Z | omne] in omni KU   4 accidentalem] actualem U | accidentalem — ad[2] *om.* NO | aliquod] aliquid Q X | sibi impressum] *inv.* L | impressum formaliter] *inv.* F   5 intellectus] *add.* autem H | noster] autem FW | ante] non F | cognitionem intellectualem] cognitionem intelligibilem K intellectum X   7 potentiam accidentalem] *inv.* O actualem potentiam N potentiam actualem KU rationem accidentalem Z | qua[2]] quia X | scilicet] vero Q *om.* L   8 voluerit] voluerint O vult Q | igitur] ergo L FW Q X *om.* N | est] sit K *om.* U | aliquid] aliquod HL FW | formaliter] *ant.* sibi H *ant.* per U *om.* NO FW   9 quod] quo H | quod — impressam *om.* NO | igitur etc.] igitur L ergo etc. FW *om.* Q X   11 Responsio] Respondeo KU Z | communis] Commentatoris HLM | est] *ant.* opinio K | habet] habeat Q   12 speciem] *rep.* W | requisitam *post* intelligendi FW requisitum N   13 ex praedictis] ex dictis HL cum praedictis KU *add.* ult. primo H   14 intellectum] intellectui K | actu[2] *om.* NO FW Q X Z | praesens] *add.* intellectui FW Q X Z | in *om.* X Z   15 igitur etc.] igitur K ergo etc. FW etc. Q X   16 Maior] Minor NO LM | patet] probatur N | prius] praesens K   17 naturae *om.* X | ratio] ideo(?) O | Probatio — illam *om.* NO | minoris *om.* HLM | quia *om.* H   18 aliter] aliud Z | sed non] non autem HLM   19 per *om.* F | illam] istam Z *om.* FW | Probo] Probatio NO L W Q X Z Pro obiecto(!) F | quia *om.* Z | una] illa Z | non[2] *om.* FW   20 aliquod *om.* Z | singulare et universale] universale et singulare FW Z

---

[5] Cf. **Aristot.**, *Physica* VIII c. 4 (AL VII[1] 294; T c. 4, 255a 35—b 5).
[6] Cf. **Averroës**, *De an.* III com. 18 (AverL 438-439): "Neque etiam possumus dicere quod intentiones imaginatae sunt solae moventes intellectum materialem et extrahentes eum de potentia in actum; quoniam, si ita esset, tunc nulla differentia esset inter universale et individuum, et tunc intellectus esset de genere virtutis imaginativae"; cf. *De an.* II com. 60 (AverL 220-221)

universale habent oppositas rationes; species autem in phantasmate est repraesentativa obiecti ut singulare est, igitur non ut universale; igitur praeter illam est necessaria species in intellectu ad repraesentandum universale. Maior illius rationis confirmatur: quia idem non potest mensurari duabus mensuris totalibus, species autem mensuratur totaliter ab obiecto; igitur eadem species non est diversorum obiectorum, ut diversa sunt, repraesentativa.

[II — Reprobationes opinionis communis ex parte Henrici et redargutiones Scoti]

9 [PRIMA REPROBATIO HENRICI ET REDARGUTIONES SCOTI] Sed DICES[7] quod hoc verum est eodem lumine, sed luminibus diversis potest eadem species diversa repraesentare, ut patet de noctilucis, quae in die videntur colorata lumine solis sed de nocte lucentia lumine proprio; sic species in phantasmate lumine phantasiae vel virtutis sensitivae potest repraesentare singulare, lumine tamen intellectus agentis penetrante phantasma universale.

10 Sed hoc non valet:

---

2 repraesentativa] repraesentatum X | obiecti] add. sub ratione singularis Q | est² om. NO X | igitur] ergo L FW Q X | ut² om. Q   3 igitur] ergo L FW Q X | illam] illa U Q istam X | est necessaria] inv. HL est necessario FW | in intellectu post repraesentandum Q   4 illius rationis] istius opinionis K illius compositionis U istius rationis W X Z huiusmodi probationis Q | confirmatur] conceditur N consequitur(?) O | quia] sic KU   5 potest om. U | mensurari] add. diversis sive FW | duabus mensuris totalibus] totaliter duabus mensuris K   6 ab om. H | obiecto] opposito(!) O | igitur] ergo FW Q X | non est] ant. eadem HLM   11 dices] dicit X | verum est] inv. KU | eodem] eadem Z | luminibus diversis] inv. N H K Q   12 diversa] plura H | noctilucis] noctiluca NO nocte lucis X   13 quae] an X | in die] de die H om. N | videntur] videtur N H verum(?) O add. esse K | colorata] coloratae M | solis] solum X rep. Z | sed] sic X | de — lucentia] delucens N | nocte] add. (lin.) scilicet K² | lucentia om. L   14 lumine proprio] luce propria KU | sic] ut O | lumine phantasiae] inv. NO lumine phantasmate X Z   15 virtutis] virtute L | singulare] sine Z | tamen] tam Z om. X   16 penetrante] repraesentare potest N | phantasma] phantasmata Z add. apparet L add. repraesentat K add. spat. vac. U   17 Sed] Si Z | valet] videtur F

[7] Henricus de Gandavo, *Summa* a. 58 q. 2 ad 3 (II f. 129vE): "Videmus enim quod nocticulae de die non movent visum nisi sub forma coloris. Et sic lux quae est hypostasis coloris sub particularibus et materialibus condicionibus habet esse in noctilucis terminata in forma coloris. De nocte vero movent visum sub forma lucis purae quasi abstractae a materia et condicionibus particularibus corporis in quo est. Colores ergo in corpore non terminato, puta in ligno et lapide, sunt sub esse particulari et materiali quemadmodum phantasmata in phantasia, quae est de se et hic et ibi, non sunt nata movere nisi secundum esse materiale et particulare. Quemadmodum ergo si super colorem ligni aut lapidis lux aliqua temperata radians faceret colorem visum movere sub forma lucis quasi abstractae a materia et condicionibus particularibus eius ad videndum ipsam lucem specie sua, sic super phantasmata lux agentis radians quasi separat ipsa a materia et condicionibus particularibus et proponit ea intellectui possibili et per ea res universales et in eis eidem proponit propositum et sic secundum rationem universalis movet possibilem ad intelligendum universale."

Quia noctilucae repraesentant diversa obiecta de die et de nocte, quia lux et color sunt diversa, et tunc necessario hoc est per diversas species; vel si non sint diversa obiecta, oportet dicere quod huiusmodi habent aliquam qualitatem diversam a luce et colore, virtualiter tamen utrumque continentem; et ideo in die poterit gignere speciem repraesentativam unius, scilicet coloris, et in nocte repraesentativam lucis; sic igitur semper habebit diversas species in quantum repraesentantur in eo diversa. Sic in proposito de universali et singulari.

[4] Item, cuiuslibet potentiae realis activae est actio realis; intellectus agens est potentia activa realis; igitur operatio eius est realis et terminus realis. Sed intelligere non est operatio eius,[8] nec terminus suae operationis (saltem propinquus terminus) quia non intelligit, sed operatio eius est facere intelligibilia in potentia actu intelligibilia; fiunt autem aliqua intelligibilia actu per abstractionem speciei; abstrahere igitur speciem est actus eius et species intelligibilis abstracta est terminus eius. Non potest autem talis species in phantasia esse, quae corporalis est et extensa; non autem talis species; igitur oportet eam esse in intellectu possibili.

---

1 noctilucae repraesentant] noctiluca vel (*om*. KU) repraesentat (repraesentant K FW X Z) NO KU FW Q X Z | obiecta] opposita(!) O *add*. et K | de — obiecta *om*. X | de² *om*. N L KU FW Q Z 2 lux et color] color et lux O KU FW Q Z | diversa] *add*. de die et nocte Z | tunc] sic N | necessario *post* est HLM 3 species *om*. O | sint] sunt FW 4 habent] habeant U | aliquam qualitatem diversam] aliquam quantitatem diversam L diversas qualitates F qualitates diversas W | colore] *add*. et luce O 5 tamen] tantum F | continentem et ideo] continet quia H continet et ideo LM continentem et Q | in] de N | poterit gignere] potest sumere K poterit sumere U 6 speciem *om*. N | unius] huius HM huiusmodi L | scilicet] *lin*. K 7 igitur] autem L ergo FW Q X 8 repraesentantur] representatur M KU | Sic] Sicut O M Ergo F 9 et] *add*. particulari sive FW | singulari] singulare U *add*. etc. F *add*. ergo etc. W 10 Item] Praeterea N KU FW Q X Z Ipsa O | cuiuslibet] cuiuscumque FW | realis activae] *inv*. N KU | realis²] *add*. sed HLM *add*. et terminus realis KU FW *add*. et ens reale X 11 est *om*. O | activa] accipitur O actualis U | igitur] ergo L FW Q X | igitur — realis *om*. H | operatio eius] *inv*. FW Z | est realis] *inv*. L U | est — eius *om*. X 12 terminus] *add*. eius est (*om*. U) KU | realis²] *add*. sicut N *add*. (ant. realis FW Q Z) similiter O FW Z | Sed] Licet Q | operatio eius] *inv*. N 13 terminus *om*. X | suae *om*. FW | propinquus] propinquiores X | terminus² *om*. L KU X Z 14 potentia] potentiali U 15 intelligibilia — autem] intellecta (*om*. O) sunt autem NO fiunt autem FW Q *om*. Z | aliqua *om*. NO KU 16 igitur] autem NO U X ergo FW Q *om*. K | actus eius] eius operatio N actus Z 17 est] *rep*. H | terminus eius] *inv*. N | potest autem] *inv*. FW potest H | talis *om*. N 18 species *om*. N M | phantasia] phantasmate X | esse] ant. in KU Q X Z ant. talis F *post* extensa N *om*. W | quae] quia X | et] etiam X | non autem *om*. N 19 species] *add*. est huiusmodi K | igitur] ergo L FW Q X

---

[8] Cf. **Thomas**, *De an*. III c. 6 (XLV¹ 230a); **Henricus Gand.**, *Quodl*. V q. 14 in corp. (f. 175rD).

12 [SECUNDA REPROBATIO HENRICI ET REDARGUTIONES SCOTI] Sed DICES[9] quod universale, quod est obiectum intellectus, fulget in phantasmate per lumen intellectus agentis ad esse intelligibile actu.

13 Contra:

Esse splendens vel cognitum tantum est esse diminutum, non reale; igitur non potest esse terminus operationis realis intellectus agentis.

14 Item, obiectum universalius non potest repraesentari sub ratione sua universaliori per speciem obiecti particularis, quia obiectum universale in quantum huiusmodi est indifferens ad omnia particularia sub eo contenta; singulare autem est determinatum, et etiam universale, ut in singulari, non est universale ut universale, sed determinatum; sed phantasma, et quod est in eo, est tantum ut est singulare, quia hic et nunc; igitur species in eo exsistens non potest repraesentare obiectum universale; igitur oportet ad intelligendum universale ut universale speciem eius imprimi in intellectu possibili.

15 Item, ex nobilitate intellectus potest sic argui: si non requiritur ad intelligendum species in intellectu sed tantum in phantasmate, intellectus noster non habet operationem separabilem a corpore in

---

2 dices] dicit O | quod universale] rep. X | quod² post intellectus FW | obiectum] oppositum O 3 phantasmate] phantasia FW add. et K | agentis] add. et ducitur N add. et O FW Q X Z add. et hoc sufficit ad terminandum operationem intellectus agentis et U | ad esse] sit K | intelligibile] add. in K | actu] a casu N 4 Contra] add. hoc Q 5 Esse] add. cognitum M | splendens] fulgens N | vel] add. esse N | tantum est] inv. Z 6 igitur] ergo L FW Q X | non om. X | realis om. KU 8 Item] Praeterea NO KU FW Q X Z add. ult. in K | obiectum] oppositum O | universalius] universale N KU X universalis O Q | potest] est X | repraesentari] repraesentare U 9 universaliori om. X | obiectum] omne FW 10 omnia] obiecta NO 11 est om. NO | determinatum] terminatum KU | et etiam] et tamen N et caetera O et HL | et — determinatum om. N 12 ut] mg. W | singulari] add. est FW | universale³] ultimum X 13 sed] secundum M F | et] est Z FW | est post eo N om. O | tantum ut est] omnino N omnia O tantum K tantum et ut U tantum ut Z 14 igitur] ergo L FW Q X | exsistens] exsistunt U | potest repraesentare] repraesentat L repraesentare U 15 obiectum] oppositum O om. N | igitur] sed K ergo FW Q X om. U | oportet] rep. U 16 universale] lin. X universalia NO | eius] suam N | imprimi] imprimat N X 17 Item] Praeterea NO KU FW Q X Z adnot. mg. nota argumentum M 18 ad intelligendum post intellectu N F | tantum post phantasmate Z | phantasmate] add. sed K 19 intellectus] add. enim H | habet] add. per H

[9] Cf. **Henricus Gand.**, *Quodl.* V q. 14 in corp. (f. 176vO); "Et est respectus eius scilicet intellectus agentis ad intellectum possibilem, sicut est respectus lucis ad diaphanum; et ad phantasmata, sicut est respectus diaphani ad colores; praeter hoc quod lux est perfectio accidentalis diaphani et forma ei inhaerens; agens autem non est perfectio intellectus possibilis, nec ei inhaeret, sed solum vis et potentia activa consubstantialis ei, sicut et uterque scilicet intellectus agens et possibilis est consubstantialis animae intellectivae; et praeter hoc quod diaphanum actione lucis facientis colorem quantum est de se solum in potentia moventem esse in actu moventem diaphanum recipit speciem eius sibi impressam. Intellectus autem possibilis speciem impressam nullam recipit a phantasmate; sed actione agentis facientis phantasmata quantum est de se solum in potentia moventia intellectum esse actu moventia et exsistentia in eo ut in cognoscente solum — et hoc sub ratione universalis, quod idem re est ut est in cognoscente scilicet imaginativa sub ratione particularis et in intellectu sub ratione universalis ..."

quo est phantasia, quia habet organum; sed si non habet operationem separabilem, ipse non est separabilis a corpore, sicut ipse PHILOSOPHUS arguit I *De anima*;[10] igitur intellectus noster esset inseparabilis a corpore, et commixtus corpori, sicut potentia organica; hoc autem est contra PHILOSOPHUM, I, II et III *De anima*,[11] et XII *Metaphysicae*.[12] Hoc etiam est contra veritatem evangelii ponentis animam a corpore aliquando separari, et intelligere ea quae prius intellexit, ut patet de divite epulone[13] — hoc autem non esset, nisi remansissent in anima eius species in via acquisitae. Nec videtur verisimile quod anima exuta a corpore remaneat ita nuda, sicut in prima sui creatione, ita quod non possit intelligere nisi de novo species sibi imprimatur; sed rationale est ipsam per species acquisitas in via aliquid posse intelligere, ut dictum est. Haec autem positio confirmatur auctoritatibus praedictis pro illa parte.

---

1 phantasia] phantasma LM KU F X | quia — organum] quae habet organum KU om. L | sed om. U 2 operationem separabilem] operationem sensibilem separabilem K operationem sensibilem U | ipse] ipsa N | sicut — corpore om. FW 3 ipse om. KU Q X Z | Philosophus arguit] inv. M KU Q X arguit Aristoteles Z | I] II KU X | igitur] ergo Q X Z | noster om. NO 4 inseparabilis] non (*lin.*) separabilis Q | et] sed O H U FW Q X Z | commixtus] coniunctus H | sicut] ut L *add.* patet X | organica] regitiva X 5 autem est] inv. M U *add. seu rep.* est N *add.* inconveniens et H | Philosophum] *add.* et N | I] *add.* et N X | et III *post* De anima X 6 Hoc *om.* H | etiam est] inv. K est autem U | veritatem] mentem Z | evangelii] *spat. vac.* Z | ponentis] ponentem NO ponentes X 7 aliquando] *ant.* animam K *ant.* a FW *om.* U | et] vel KU | quae] etiam U 8 intellexit] intellexerit N intelligit Z | epulone] epul*ante* Q X | autem *om.* NO FW | esset] est X 9 remansissent] mansisset Z | in] *add.* eo vel Q | eius *om.* Z | acquisitae] acquisita HLM U | videtur] verum X 10 exuta] *add.* corpore U | a *om.* NO K FW 11 prima sui] sua prima NO prima sua H FW Q sua L | possit] potest H posset M KU 12 species sibi] *ant.* de KU *inv.* N FW | sibi] *rep.* Z sunt(!) O | imprimatur] imprimantur NO KU imprimuntur Q praesentantur X | rationale] rationabile K | ipsam] in ipsa F | ipsam — via] per ipsam speciem in via acquisita KU | species acquisitas] speciem acquisitam HL 13 Haec] Hic U | positio] opinio F ratio X 14 confirmatur auctoritatibus] inv. H auctoribus confirmatur L confirmatur auctoribus K FW Q X affirmatur auctoritatibus U | praedictis *om.* H | illa] ista O KU prima H

[10] **Aristot.**, *De an.* I c. 2 (A c. 1, 403*a* 7-8); *De an.* I c. 2 (A c. 1, 403*a* 10-12); *Auctoritates Aristotelis* (ed. J. Hamesse 174): "Unde nulla operatio animae est propria in qua communicetur corpori, unde ipsum intelligere non est proprium animae, sed totius coniuncti."
[11] **Aristot.**, *De an.* I c 4 (A c. 1, 402*a* 12-16); *De an.* I c. 1 (A c. 1, 402*a* 20-22); *De an.* II c. 1 (B c. 1, 412*a* 19-20); *De an.* III c. 7 (Γ c. 8, 431*b* 21-22).
[12] **Aristot.**, *Metaph.* XII c. 7 (AL XXV$^{3.2}$ 257; Λ c. 7, 1072*a* 30—*b* 3).
[13] **Luc.** 16: 19-31.

[III. — Ad argumenta principalia secundum opinionem communem]

16 Ad primum in oppositum,[14] MODERNI[15] dicunt quod differt ratio agendi et ratio agentis. Verum est autem quod species repraesentat obiectum in illa ratione agendi sub qua nata est imprimi; hoc autem est sub ratione naturae absolute consideratae, non autem sub ratione agentis, quod est particulare, et ideo species repraesentat universale. Vel aliter potest dici secundum ILLOS quod, licet phantasma a quo immediate imprimitur sit singulare, quod tamen non agit in possibilem virtute propria sed virtute intellectus agentis abstrahentis species universales a phantasmate, ideo potest illa species repraesentare universale.

17 Ad secundum[16] dicendum quod aequivocatio est de praesentia obiecti et speciei; obiectum enim est causa praesentiae realis speciei in intellectu in quo eam imprimit, in virtute tamen intellectus agentis; species autem impressa est causa praesentiae obiecti in esse intelligibili, et ut sic obiectum est praesens intellectui ratione speciei.

---

3 in oppositum *om.* FW | moderni dicunt] *inv.* H dicunt NO KU FW X Z | differt] differunt N L KU Q   4 autem] ad hoc N *om.* X | quod] aliqua X | repraesentat] repraesentant K   5 obiectum] oppositum O | agendi — ratione *om.* NO | hoc — consideratae *om.* KU   6 sub — non] *mg.* Z² | autem² *om.* Z   7 species] ibi Z *om.* N | repraesentat] repraesentant K   8 universale] obiectum(?) X | Vel] Quod U | postest dici] *inv.* Z | illos] istos NO KU W X Z   9 a quo] in alico N | immediate imprimitur] *inv.* Q intelligere imprimitur Z | sit] sic Q Z ut X | quod] = HM K F quia NO L U W Q X Z   10 in] *add.* intellectum HL KU | possibilem] possibile X Z *add.* in Q X | propria] prima NO | virtute² *om.* FW Q X Z   11 universales] universalis NO KU | a] in K | illa] ista X   13 secundum] primum FW | dicendum] *add.* est HM | est] *add.* ibi NO FW Q X Z   14 enim] non X | est *om.* H   15 quo] qua Z | in³ *om.* KU   16 autem] aut O *om.* X | obiecti *om.* Q   17 et] *lin.* Q etiam Z *add.* sic K | obiectum] oppositum O | est] sit X | intellectui] intellecti O FW X Z

---

[14]Cf. supra n. 1.
[15]Cf. **Aegidius Romanus**, *De cognitione angelorum* q. 5 (ed. Venice, 1503, f. 88*ra-b*): "Tertia autem via [ostendendi quomodo species intelligibilis possit movere intellectum angelicum] sumitur, prout illa species comparatur ad obiectum quod repraesentat. Nam illa species non agit [ita] quod ei attribuatur actio, sed agit quia est ratio agendi, sicut nec calor calefacit, sed est ratio calefaciendi. Nunc autem inter causas agendi videmus hanc distinctionem quod aliquid principaliter agit et aliquid agit in virtute alterius. Et hanc distinctionem quam videmus inter ipsas rationes actionum, nam aliquid est ratio agendi secundum se, aliquid vero est ratio agendi in virtute alterius. Dupliciter ergo in talibus potest esse defectus: primo, si non agat, sed sit solum ratio agendi; secundo, si non sit ratio agendi secundum se sed sit ratio agendi in virtute alterius. Utrumque defectum habet species intelligibilis. Primo non agit sed solum est ratio agendi … Secundo deficit huiusmodi species intelligibilis quia non solum non est agens, sed est ratio agendi; sed non est ratio agendi secundum se, sed magis est ratio agendi, ut est repraesentativa obiecti"; **Guil. de Ware**, *In II Sent.* d. 3 [sec. ennumerationem Daniels, q. 127] (cod. Vindobon. Nat. 1424 f. 104*vb*).
[16]Cf. supra n. 2.

[7]   Ad aliud[17] dicendum, concedendo consequentiam. Ad improbationem consequentis dicendum quod species, licet sit forma naturalis quoad actum intelligendi (quantum est de se) semper producendum, quia[18] tamen non est tota causa actus sed requiritur necessario intellectus, et principalius (ille autem non semper est in actu[19]), ideo non oportet quod semper intelligat. Similiter non oportet quod omnes simul causent actum intelligendi, sed illa tantum cuius phantasma fortius movet intelligentem ad actum primum intelligendi — ut patet cum homo excitatur a somno, tunc intelligit necessario illud quod prius occurrit — vel cuius phantasma fortius movet; sed post illum actum intelligit illud quod voluntas sibi imperat intelligendum, et hoc secundum speciem eius in intellectu conservatam.

Ad ultimum[20] dicendum quod potentia prius — prioritate perfectionis — perficitur actu proprio quam alieno, non autem semper prioritate generationis quando specialiter ad eius generationem plura alia requiruntur propter suam perfectionem. Sic est in proposito de actu intelligendi, qui prius ordine generationis requirit phantasma et cognitionem sensitivam, a qua originatur, et speciem intelligibilem, secundum quam intellectus formaliter intelligit.

---

1 dicendum] communiter X *om.* L *add.* est HM F | concedendo] concedo L KU F Q X | consequentiam] *add.* et per (*om.* NO KU FW Q) consequens NO KU FW Q X *add.* ult. et KU FW | Ad improbationem] In plures F *om.* X   3 quantum *om.* F | se *om.* O | semper] *add.* est KU   4 producendum] producens NO | quia] quando N | tota causa] *inv.* HLM X Z | causa] producens actus NO *om.* HLM   5 necessario] attentio KU intentio (*post* intellectus Z) FW X Z | et principalius] in principali X | ille] illa U FW Q ita X ista Z | autem *om.* X | semper est] *inv.* KU Q Z | in actu] *inv.* O   6 intelligat] intelligit X   7 quod omnes *om.* FW | causent] causant NO | sed] si X | sed — intelligendi *om.* F | illa] illud N   8 cuius] cum X | fortius movet] *inv.* M | intelligentem] intellectum H | intelligentem — movet *om.* KU | actum *om.* Z   9 homo excitatur] *inv.* F hoc excitatur Z | a somno] a se Z *om.* F | tunc] cum Z | intelligit] intelligitur F   10 prius] primo sibi FW | occurrit] occurrerit L | occurrit — post *om.* Z | cuius] cum X *add.* in FW | phantasma *om.* X   11 illum] ipsum U Q istum X | actum] *add.* tunc KU FW | intelligit illud] *inv.* H K intelligit idem N idem intelligit U intelligit Z | occurrit] occurrerit L | imperat] importat N M U *add.* ad K   12 hoc] *add.* est L | secundum] per FW | eius *om.* NO | in intellectum *post* conservatam KU   14 ultimum] aliud Z | dicendum] *add.* est HM F | potentia *om.* N | perfectionis — prioritate *om.* X   17 alia] autem X | requiruntur] requiritur O requiratur Q | propter suam perfectionem] semper (super O) anima perfectior NO | suam] sua L | perfectionem] imperfectionem X | Sic] Sicut Z | est *om.* N   18 requirit] requiritur NO Z   19 cognitionem sensitivam] cognitio sensitiva N | speciem — secundum] species intelligendi per N   20 intellectus formaliter] *inv.* FW Q X Z forma NO fortiter intellectus U

[17] Cf. supra n. 3.
[18] Legendum forsan potius: quae.
[19] Exempli gratia: quia attentio intellectus non semper adhibetur.
[20] Cf. supra n. 4.

[IV. — Opinio scholae antiquae Franciscanae et Olivianae redargutionesque Godefridi de Fontibus cum responsionibus ex parte scholae]

20 [OPINIO OLIVI ATQUE ALIQUORUM SCHOLAE ANTIQUAE FRANCISCANAE] Alia opinio[21] est quod nulla species a phantasmate vel obiecto extrinseco imprimitur in intellectu, nec etiam actus intelligendi.

Quod probatur sic: agens aequivocum est semper nobilius passo;[22] sed phantasma vel obiectum extrinsecum non est nobilius intellectu vel specie vel actu intelligendi; igitur, etc. Probatio maioris: si est aeque nobile, tunc non est aequivocum; similiter nec imperfectius, quia non esset causa unde effectus esset nobilior et perfectior; igitur est nobilius. Minor patet. Igitur, etc.

21 [REDARGUTIO PRIMA GODEFRIDI] Sed dices[23] quod vera est maior de agente aequivoco in virtute propria, non autem de instrumentali; modo phantasma agit in intellectu possibili virtute intellectus agentis penetrantis ipsum et abstrahentis quidditatem a condicionibus individualibus, quae sunt in phantasmate; sicut lumen attingens ipsum lac, quod est album et dulce, quodammodo

---

5 opinio est] inv. K | a] in N | vel obiecto] vel ab obiecto N vel opposito O om. X   6 in intellectu] intellectui U om. NO | intelligendi] intellectus agentis N intellectus agendi O   8 sic] quia Z | agens aequivocum] agens N agentis sic extrinsecum Z | est semper] inv. L KU FW Z est Q   9 vel] ut O | nobilius] add. in O   10 igitur etc.] ergo etc. L FW ergo Q om. X | Probatio — etc. om. L | maioris] minoris Z add. quia U   11 si] sic X | est om. NO | nobile] notabile O | non est] non N U om. O   12 imperfectius] superficitur FW imperfectior Q sufficit X super fan-ur(?) Z | quia] add. tunc HM K | non] rep. N nec X | esset causa] inv. F est causa NO esset causat(!) X | nobilior et perfectior] perfectior vel (et O) nobilior NO   13 igitur] ergo FW Q X add. ult. etiam X | nobilius] nobilis Z | Igitur etc.] Ergo etc. FW Q etc. N de se X   14 Sed dices] Si dicas (dices U) KU | vera est maior] maior est vera L   15 agente aequivoco] inv. N add. seu rep. agente O | in om. K | virtute] voluntate O | non] add. est N | de² om. K add. agente FW Q X Z add. ult. in virtute X   16 phantasma] phantasia NO W | in] de O om. X   17 et] ut N | abstrahentis] abstrahens Q | quidditatem] quidditatis X   18 individualibus] individuantibus W Q X Z | quae — individuantibus om. L   19 attingens] agentis Z | ipsum] illum Q | album] albus U | et om. X | quodammodo] modo N quod modo O et modo H quod non KU

[21]Cf. **Petrus I. Olivi**, *Summa* II q. 58 corp. (BFS V 463; 457); **Ioannes de Pecham**, *Tract. de an.* c. 4 (ed. Melani 16); **Rogerus Marston**, *Quaest. Disp. De anima* q. 8 (BFS VII 394-395); **Matthaeus ab Aquasparta**, *De cognitione* q. 3 (BFS I² 265).
[22]**Aristot.**, *De an.* III t. 19 (Γ c. 5, 430a 18-19); *Auctoritates Aristotelis* (ed. J. Hamesse 187): "Agens est nobilius passo et forma materia."
[23]**Godefridus de Fontibus**, *Quodl.* V q. 10 (PhB III 37): "Sicut enim si poneretur quod, cum albedo et dulcedo lactis simul sunt quod lac, per se ipsum absque praesentia luminis non posset se facere in medio secundum speciem coloris vel albi quin faceret se secundum speciem dulcis, sed lumine praesente facere posset se secundum speciem albi absque specie dulcis, et sic diceretur fieri abstractio albi a dulci non secundum rationem essendi sed secundum rationem immutandi ..."

abstrahit album a dulci, dum repraesentat visui lac sub ratione albi, non tamen sub ratione dulcis.

[RESPONSIONES EX PARTE SCHOLAE] Contra duo quae DICUNT,[24] primo quod intellectus agens subintrat phantasma sua actione et lumine; secundo, quod abstrahit quidditatem a condicionibus individuantibus, arguo sic:

Quaero utrum per actionem intellectus agentis in phantasma aliquid repraesentativum recipiatur in phantasmate aut non. Si sic, sequitur quod illud sit corporale sicut phantasma recipiens et extensum, et per consequens non poterit agere in intellectu possibili per rationem praedictam. Si nihil, igitur phantasma per illam actionem non erit virtuosius ad agendum in intellectu possibili, cuius contrarium DICEBANT.

Item, si DICUNT quod non solum phantasma agit in intellectum possibilem sed etiam intellectus agens, destruitur eorum principium quo DICUNT quod idem subiecto sunt intellectus agens et possibilis;[25] certum est autem quod agens et passum non sunt idem

---

1 dum] tantum HLM | repraesentat] repraesentans X | visui] in sui Z   3 dicunt] dicuntur N K Q dicantur U   4 phantasma] phantasmata N Q | sua] in X | actione] active(!) O | et] vel NO FW Q X Z   5 secundo] tertio(!) O | abstrahit quidditatem] inv. F abstrahit quantitatem(!) O | individuantibus] individualibus H K F om. X   6 sic] add. et K   7 per actionem] actione X | agentis om. X | in phantasma om. FW   8 aliquid] aut N ad O | repraesentativum recipiatur] inv. K receptum recipiatur NO positivum recipiatur L recipiatur positivum U principatum recipiatur Q praesentatum recipiatur X Z   9 illud] idem H U om. X | sit] est aequale X | corporale] corruptibile FW | sicut] sic U   10 poterit] posset L | agere om. FW | intellectu possibili] intellectum possibilem NO K   11 praedictam] positam U secundum dictam Z | nihil igitur] inv. KU non igitur N nihil ergo L FW Q X Z | per om. X | illam] aliam Q   12 erit] est X | virtuosius] virtuosus U FW Q | ad agendum] in agendo K | in om. Q | intellectu possibili] intellectum possibilem NO | dictum est N dicebatur FW dicunt Q   14 Item] Praeterea NO KU FW Q X Z | si om. H | quod om. X | agit post possibilem Q | intellectu possibili] intellectum possibili HLM   15 etiam om. KU | destruitur] destruit N U destruetur H destruunt K   16 quod om. H | idem — possibilis] intellectus agens et possibilis sunt idem subiecto FW | subiecto sunt] in substantia est N | et] lin. U add. intellectus N   17 certum] iterum N

[24]Cf. supra n. 21.
[25]**Godefridus de Fontibus**, *Quodl.* VI q. 7 (PhB III 172): "Quod autem dicitur quod intellectus agens est memoria cuius est agere et producere prolem in ipsa intelligentia et caetera, dicendum quod hoc dictum videtur originem sumpsisse a dictis meis alibi male tamen intellectis, quia non dixi asserendo quod intellectus agens sit omnino proprie et perfecte memoria nec quod aliquam actionem per se et proprie faciat in intellectu possibili, sed quod pro quanto pertinet ad naturam mentis in anima, secundum quam anima facta est ad Dei imaginem, debet ad imaginem pertinere; et cum sint tres partes imaginis, scilicet memoria, intelligentia et voluntas, et memoria secundum quod ad imaginem dicitur pertinere videtur habere rationem agentis et parentis, quod etiam ad intellectum agentem pertinet, videtur pro tanto quod sit idem quod intellectus agens; sed quomodo hoc sit intelligendum alterius est considerationis." Cf. *Quodl.* V q. 8 (PhB III 31); *Quodl.* VI q. 7 (PhB III 152, 154); *Quodl.* VIII q. 2 (PhB IV 26); cf. **Henricus de Gand.**, *Quodl.* XIII q. 8 (AmPh XVIII 53-56).

subiecto realiter; igitur, etc.

24 [REDARGUTIO SECUNDA GODEFRIDI] Si autem DICUNT[26] quod solum phantasma agit ut tactum ab intellectu agente, sequitur ut prius quod solum phantasma est nobilius intellectu possibili vel specie intelligibili per rationem praedictam. Habent autem alia verba:[27] DICUNT quod intellectus agens ut subintrat phantasma, quodammodo distinguitur subiecto ab intellectu possibili, sed potest talis responsio praedicto modo improbari.

[V. — Opinio Aegidii redargutionesque secundum mentem scholae Franciscanae antiquae]

25 [OPINIO AEGIDII] ALII[28] dicunt ad rationem principalem praedictam[29] quod intellectus agens agit in intellectum possibilem sicut causa partialis cum phantasmate, non autem sicut causa totalis, sed sicut causa principalis cum instrumentali.

26 [REDARGUTIONES AD MENTEM SCHOLAE FRANCISCANAE ANTIQUAE] Sed contra: causa aequivoca, habens in virtute sua totum

---

1 subiecto] substantiae N *om.* Z | realiter] reali NO KU FW *om.* X | igitur etc.] ergo etc. L FW Q Z *om.* X 2 autem *om.* NO | dicunt] dicant Q 3 ut] ad Q | tactum] actum Z *add.* est N 4 solum — quod *om.* K | nobilius] *add.* subiecto FW | possibili *om.* U 6 verba] vera L *add.* praedicta NO W *add.* praedicti F Q X Z | dicunt] dicendo L dicentes Q *om.* Z | ut *om.* X | subintrat] se intrat Z 7 distinguitur] *add.* a U | subiecto] subiecta Z | sed — praedictam *om.* L 8 responsio] modus N modo O sensus FW sensio(!) Q Z sensitio(?) X | improbari] reprobari NO FW Q Z 11 principalem *om.* Z | praedictam *om.* KU 12 agens *om.* NO LM Z | intellectum possibilem] intellectu possibili HLM *add.* illam (istam Q X *om.* Z) speciem FW Q X Z 13 partialis] *mg.* K principalis U Z *add.* ult. scilicet KU FW Q X Z | non] cum M | autem] sunt X *add.* sunt HLM | totalis] totale Z | sed] = HLM vel NO KU FW Q X Z 14 principalis] principali O 16 Sed *om.* HL | causa] cum X | habens] licet non N habent X | in virtute sua] in causa sua NO in se et sua virtute K in se totum virtute sua U

[26]**Godefridus de Fontibus**, *Quodl.* V q. 10 (PhB III 38): "... ita etiam separans ipsam [sc. quidditatem] sic secundum considerationem sive faciens quod id quod est in hoc lapide suae quidditatis substantialis absque condicionibus praedictis immutet aliquam potentiam, facit ipsum de potentia actu intelligibilem. Hoc autem fit quodam contactu spirituali et virtuali luminis intellectus agentis ... et hoc est in natura talis obiecti singularis scilicet quod sit praecise tactum sive quod virtute intellectus agentis suo lumine ipsum contingentis, secundum illud praecise scilicet secundum huiusmodi suam quidditatem, sic possit movere ipsum intellectum possibilem."
[27]Cf. **Godefridus de Fontibus**, *Quodl.* V q. 10 (PhB III 36-39); *Quodl.* VI q. 7 (PhB III 172); *Quodl.* VIII q. 2 (PhB IV 31-32).
[28]**Aegidius Romanus**, *Quodl.* V q. 21 in corp. (f. 67ra—va); **Bernardus de Trilia**, *Quaest. de cognitione animae coniunctae corpori* q. 1 (cod. Bibl. Vatic. Apost. 2188, f. 5rb): "Et ideo est tertius modus dicendi convenientior quod intellectus possibilis reducitur de potentia ad actum respectu omnium naturaliter cognoscibilium per duplex agens sibi proportionatum, scilicet, per intellectum agentem tamquam per agens principale ... et per potentias sensitivas organis corporalibus affixas tamquam per agens instrumentale."
[29]Cf. supra n. 20.

effectum, potest totum effectum producere in passo aeque disposito, vel sufficit quia plus non requiritur ad effectum quam quod dictum est; sed intellectus agens habet in virtute sua totali speciem intelligibilem (probatio: quia non habet aliquam actualitatem in phantasmate respectu talis speciei; ipse tamen continet in se totam virtutem phantasmatis respectu eiusdem, cum sit in eo virtuosius). Igitur sine phantasmate poterit illam speciem causare in intellectu possibili, qui est aeque dispositus ad recipiendum ab utroque.

Item, si causa imperfectior est totalis causa respectu perfectioris effectus, multo fortius causa perfectior erit totalis causa respectu effectus imperfectioris; sed intellectus agens est perfectior et nobilior intellectu possibili, ut dicitur III *De anima*;[30] tamen intellectus possibilis est causa totalis actus intelligendi, qui est perfectior effectus specie intelligibili; igitur multo fortius intellectus agens est totalis causa respectu speciei.

Item, inter duo agentia concurrentia ad unum effectum debet esse proportio; sed inter agens immateriale vel spirituale, quod est intellectus agens, et corporale, quod est phantasma, non est proportio; igitur, etc.

Item, licet activum sit aliquando imperfectius passivo, sicut obiectum sensibile sensu, tamen activum secundum quod agit est nobilius passivo secundum quod patitur —. exemplum de igne agente in corpus mixtum et igne infernali agente in spiritum

---

1 effectum] *add.* suum U | potest — effectum *om.* X | totum effectum *om.* N | aeque *om.* Z 2 sufficit] sufficienter NO KU FW Q Z | quia] quod X | plus non] *inv.* KU | requiritur] sequitur L Q | dictum est] *inv.* M U FW Q X Z dicitur K 3 totali] totalem H totaliter Q *add.* secundum NO 4 probatio] probo O LM | non] = HLM K *om.* NO U FW Q X Z | habet] licet Z | aliquam] aliam LM *om.* X Z | actualitatem] activitatem N Q auctoritatem Z | in] *add.* tali X 5 phantasmate] phantasma Q | talis] *rep.* W | tamen] non O M X enim HL | in se *om.* FW | totam *om.* F 6 eiusdem] eius Z | in eo] de se L eo KU FW Q X Z | virtuosius] virtuosus NO 7 Igitur] Ergo FW Q X | illam] eam U istam X 8 est *om.* Q | aeque dispositus] causa disponens Z 9 Item] Praeterea NO KU FW Q X Z | si causa] *lin.* O | est] esset Z | respectu *om.* KU FW Q X Z | perfectioris effectus] *inv.* L 10 erit] esset HM K | totalis] possibilis Z | causa² *om.* X 11 effectus *om.* KU FW Q X Z | nobilior] *add.* in H 12 dicitur] patet HLM *add.* ex M *add.* in X | III] II K | tamen] igitur cum N cum KU 13 est] *add.* totalis NO | qui — intelligibili *om.* FW 14 effectus] effectu X | intelligibili] intelligendi Q X Z | igitur] ergo L FW Q X 15 speciei] *add.* ergo etc. FW 16 Item] Praeterea N KU FW Q X Z Prima O | unum] eundem N | effectum] *add.* producendum NO 17 immateriale] materiale N Z | vel] et N Z sive X | quod — phantasma] quod est phantasma et intellectus agens Z 18 et — phantasma] vel phantasma quod est corporale N quod est corporale O | corporale] materiale KU 19 igitur etc.] ergo L W X Z ergo Q *om.* N 20 Item] Praeterea N KU FW Q X Z Prima O | activum] actus X | sit aliquando] *inv.* HL 21 obiectum] oppositum O 22 nobilius] perfectius M | passivo] passiva Z | secundum quod] in quantum Z 23 agente²] agenti Q | spiritum damnatum] animam Q damnatum Z

[30] **Aristot.**, *De an.* III c. 4 (Γ c. 5, 430*a* 18-19); *Auctoritates Aristotelis* (ed. J. Hamesse 187): "Agens est nobilius et honorabilius passo, et forma materia."

damnatum. Si igitur phantasma aliquo modo agit in intellectum possibilem, secundum illud quo agit, est perfectius illo quo intellectus possibilis patitur; omne autem illud quod est in phantasmate est corporale et omne illud quod est in intellectu possibili est spirituale. Igitur corporale erit nobilius spirituali, quod falsum est.

Item, quanto aliquod corporale est magis obediens spirituali, tanto magis spirituale, mediante illo corporali, potest effectum nobiliorem producere; sed corpora caelestia magis obediunt substantiis separatis quam phantasma intellectui agenti, tamen mediantibus illis substantiae separatae non possunt nisi aliquod corporale producere; igitur sic intellectus agens mediante phantasmate vel ipso coadiuvante non poterit speciem intelligibilem producere.

[VI. — Opinio quae negat speciem intelligibilem actui intellectus praeviam]

[RATIONES PRO OPINIONE] Item, ostendo quod non requiritur species, quod est ad principale,[31] quia species praecedit per te actum intelligendi et habitum; illa igitur species potest destrui, manente tamen habitu. Tunc quaero: aut intellectus est in potentia essentiali ad actum intelligendi, aut accidentali tantum. Non in potentia essentiali, quia habens habitum intellectualem potest eo uti, cum voluerit.[32] Est igitur in potentia accidentali sine specie; sed propter

---

1 igitur] ergo L FW Q X | aliquo] aliquando(?) F | agit] agat N M KU   2 illud] id M K F Z idem U | quo] quod NO KU FW Q | est] add. nobilius et L | illo quo] eo quod N   3 omne autem illud] = HLM FW illud autem omne N K Q illud autem esse(!) O idem esse(!) U autem illud omne X omne autem aliud Z | quod] quo Q | quod — illud om. HLM | est] habet N   4 illud] idem U | quod] quo Q   5 Igitur] Ergo L FW Q X | erit nobilius] inv. O nobilius N erit perfectius et nobilius M est nobilius KU Z | falsum est] inv. L Q   6 Item] Praeterea NO KU FW Q X Z | aliquod] aliquid L Z | corporale] corporalem U | est om. X | magis] ant. aliquod L   7 tanto] causato(!) O tantum U | spirituale] spirituali U X | illo om. F   8 producere om. Z   9 intellectui] in intellectu Q | agenti] agentis O   10 illis] illius X | substantiae separatae] substantiis separatis N | non possunt nisi] non possunt N H nisi possunt non O   11 igitur] ergo L FW Q X add. (mg. W) nec FW | sic] si NO nec KU | phantasmate om. FW | vel om. Z | ipso] illo Q   12 coadiuvante] adiuvante K coadunante U X | non om. KU FW X Z | poterit] possit N | producere om. X   15 Item] Praeterea NO KU FW Q X Z   16 species] add. ad actum intelligendi K | quod — principale] et hoc est contra principale Q | praecedit post te NO K X | actum om. FW   17 illa igitur] inv. U illa ergo FW Q X | potest destrui] destruitur KU | manente] manifeste O   18 tamen om. K | aut] an L add. tunc O U FW Q X Z | essentiali om. K   19 ad actum intelligendi post tantum K | aut — intelligendi om. NO | tantum om. Z | Non] Sed Q   20 quia] quod Z | habens] habent X | potest] poterit Z   21 Est igitur] inv. KU Ergo est F Est ergo W Q Ergo X Igitur Z

[31]Cf. supra, n. 1-4
[32]**Averroës**, De an. III com. 18 (AverL 438): "Haec enim est definitio habitus, scilicet ut habens habitum intelligat per ipsum illud quod est sibi proprium ex se et quando voluerit, absque eo quod indigeat in hoc aliquo extrinseco"; Auctoritates Aristotelis (ed. J. Hamesse 190): "Habitus est secundum quem habens ipsum potest agere quando vult."

aliud non ponit speciem necessariam ad actum intelligendi nisi ut reducat intellectum de potentia essentiali ad accidentalem; igitur frustra.

Item, phantasma non potest agere in voluntatem, igitur nec in intellectum. Antecedens patet per sanctos doctores. Probatio consequentiae: quia aut repugnat voluntati pati a phantasmate ratione suae immaterialitatis, aut ratione libertatis. Si primo modo, eadem ratione repugnat intellectui, quia aeque immaterialis est. Non autem ratione libertatis, quia illa non obstante primo recipit vel patitur ab obiecto.

Item, sicut se habent phantasmata ad intellectum, sic appetitus sensitivus et eius passio ad voluntatem; sed passio appetitus sensitivi non potest directe et per se agere in voluntatem, quia tunc homo necessario peccaret; igitur nec phantasma in intellectum.

Item, corporale ut corporale non agit in spirituale; phantasma ut phantasma est corporale, et intellectus est spiritualis; igitur, etc.

[AUCTORITATES PRO OPINIONE] Ad istam partem adducunt auctoritates:

Primo AUGUSTINUS, XII *Super Genesim*,[33] dicit quod "anima a corporali nihil facit in se"; et in eodem[34] dicit quod "anima rerum

---

1 ponit] potest F | necessariam *om.* KU | intelligendi *om.* Z | ut *om.* Z 2 accidentalem] actualem N accidentale Z | igitur] ergo FW Q X 3 frustra] fruitur Z *add.* ponitur Q 4 Item] Praeterea NO KU FW Q X Z | igitur] ergo FW Q X | in² *om.* O 5 per sanctos] per X *om.* Q *add.* et W Q Z | consequentiae] consequentis O 6 quia *om.* O 7 ratione] *add.* suae O FW X | libertatis] liberalitatis K | Si — libertatis *om.* NO | primo illo U 8 repugnat] repugnabit FW X | quia] qui X | autem *om.* M 9 ratione] *add.* suae F | libertatis] liberalitatis K | illa] illo U *add.* libertate L | primo recipit] *inv.* F primo percipit Z 10 obiecto] opposito O 11 Item] Praeterea NO KU FW Q X Z | sicut] si sic F | sic] ita KU Q | appetitus sensitivi] appetitus sensus H appetitivus sensus X appetitus sensitivi Z 12 eius] est X | passio — sed *om.* X | ad *om.* O | sed — in *om.* U | passio² *post* sensitivi Z | sensitivi] sensibilis H 13 potest] *add.* et Q | directe et per se] perfecte et directe N | homo necessario] *inv.* K 14 igitur] ergo FW X | nec] ut N | phantasma *om.* W 15 Item] Praeterea N KU FW Q X Z Prima O | agit] aget O | spirituale] spiritum O KU FW X *add.* in quantum spirituale sed Z 16 et *om.* Q Z | est² *om.* FW Q | igitur etc.] ergo etc. FW ergo Q *om.* X 17 istam] illam NO FW Q Z | adducunt] adducuntur LM FW inducunt KU adducit(?) Q 18 auctoritates] auctor(?) Q auctores X 19 Primo *om.* Q | Augustinus] beati Augustini F Augustini Q | XII *post* Genesim Q super septimo K septimo U *om.* X | Super] *rep.* O | dicit] dicentis HL Q dicens KU *om.* X | quod — dicit *om.* KU | anima] alia Q 20 dicit quod] dicitur quod M Z *om.* Q

---

[33] **Augustinus**, *De Genesi ad litteram* XII c. 16 [n. 32] (CSEL 28¹ 401, PL 34 466): "Quia vero spiritus omnis omni est corpore sine dubitatione praestantior, sequitur, ut non loci positione, sed naturae dignitate praestantior sit natura spiritualis isto corporeo caelo etiam illa, ubi rerum corporalium exprimuntur imagines."

[34] **Augustinus**, *De Genesi ad litteram* XII c. 18 [n. 40] (CSEL 28¹ 407, PL 34 469): "... quanta celeritate ac facilitate in se anima fabricetur imagines corporum ..."

imagines in se de se facit." ARISTOTELES etiam, III *De anima*,[35] dicit quod anima quidditates in phantasmatibus intelligit, non dicit autem in speciebus in ea exsistentibus. Hoc autem ideo dicit quia in phantasmate obiectum eius repraesentatur sufficienter. Quod patet, quia dicit ibidem,[36] quod sic se habent phantasmata ad intellectum sicut sensibilia ad sensum. Sensibilia autem sunt obiecta sensus, et ideo phantasmata sufficienter continent obiecta intellectus. Unde subdit[37] quod cum anima intelligit, necesse est phantasmata simul speculari. In primo autem phantasmate intuetur anima quidditatem speciei absolute et condiciones etiam individui. Quia sicut in singulari extra reservatur natura communis et sunt in eo condiciones individuales vel principia individualia, sicut in Socrate est humanitas et Socrateitas, sic in phantasmate ipsius singularis repraesentatur natura communis et singularis; et in repraesentativo singularis, quod est phantasma, continetur repraesentativum naturae communis.

---

1 imagines] imaginationes NO quiditates KU | se] *add.* et H KU | etiam] II X *add.* in F Z *add.* et Q X *om.* HL Z 2 anima] *lin.* N | non] nunc FW X | dicit autem] *inv.* FW 3 ea] se L | autem² *om.* FW | quia] quod Q | quia — dicit *om.* NO 4 obiectum eius] *inv.* Q 5 dicit ibidem] *inv.* KU dicit H ibi dicit Q | sic] sicut Z | habent] habet N | phantasmata] phantasma NO 6 sicut] ut HL FW X Z | obiecta] obiectum FW Z | sensus] sensuum Q | et ideo] igitur et N ideo HM Z 7 sufficienter continent] *inv.* KU Q X Z essent sufficienter N et tunc sufficienter O continent virtualiter FW | obiecta] obiectum FW 8 subdit] sub dicitur Q | est] *add.* et KU | phantasmata simul] *inv.* NO KU FW Q X Z 9 primo] ipso NO Z prima X | autem] enim H | phantasmate *om.* NO | quidditatem speciei] *inv.* Q 10 speciei] animae KU | etiam *om.* HL F X | individui] individuales FW | Quia] Qui O | sicut *om.* K 11 eo] ea L 12 individuales *om.* FW | vel] ut Z | individualia] individua NO individuantia KU FW Q X Z | in] *add.* corpore O | Socrate] Socratis O 13 et Socrateitas *om.* X | sic] sicut X | singularis *om.* M Z | repraesentatur — singularis² *om.* X 14 singularis] singulare Z | et²] *add.* ideo NO | in] *lin.* N *om.* O | repraesentativo] repraesentatur Q | singularis²] singulari W 15 continetur] continentur Z | repraesentativum] *add.* vero Z | naturae] ut X *add.* et K | communis] commune X

[35] **Aristot.**, *De an.* III c. 7 (Γ c. 8, 432a 5-7): "Et ab hoc neque non sentiens nihil, nihil utique addiscet neque intelliget, sed cum speculetur, necesse simul phantasma aliquod speculari ..."
[36] **Aristot.**, *De an.* III c. 7 (Γ c. 8, 432a 8-10): "... phantasmata autem sicut sensibilia sunt praeter quod sunt sine materia."
[37] Cf. **Aristot.**, *De an.* III c. 7 (Γ c. 8, 432a 8-9); melius in *Auctoritates Aristotelis* (ed. J. Hamesse 188): "Necesse est quemcumque intelligentem phantasmata speculari."

[VII. — Obiectiones contra opinionem negantium speciem intelligibilem actui intellectus praeviam]

Sed contra istam rationem potest sic argui:

Quia si universale est tantum in phantasmate repraesentatum, non in specie intelligibili, cum phantasma sit corporeum et organicum, universale non est in intellectu sed potius in sensu.

Item, anima, separata a corpore et phantasmate, et[38] per consequens non posset intelligere.

Item, intellectus ante intellectionem est indeterminatissimus. Oportet igitur quod determinetur ad intelligendum per aliquid sibi impressum, quod voco speciem.

[VIII. — Responsiones ad obiectiones ex parte negantium speciem intelligibilem actui intellectus praeviam]

Ad primum istorum[39] dicendum, secundum ISTOS,[40] quod universale accipitur aliquando pro intentione secunda, quae sequitur operationem primam intellectus qua intelligitur quidditas absolute, et hoc est quando intellectus, considerans illam quidditatem esse reperibilem et praedicabilem de multis, attribuit sibi rationem speciei vel generis; et isto modo est in intellectu tanquam aliquid factum per operationem intellectus. Unde de tali dicit THEMISTIUS,

---

3 istam] illam NO FW Q | rationem] responsionem H KU om. X | potest sic argui] potest argui sic NO sic potest argui L arguitur KU   4 Quia] Sed X | si] sic NO om. L | repraesentatum] repraesentativum U Q   5 non] sed X | intelligibili] intellectuali H | sit] est K | et] add. non FW 6 in om. W | sensu] sensus O   7 Item] Praeterea NO KU FW Q X Z | anima] aut X | separata] separatur repraesentata FW Z repraesentare(?) X | a om. X | phantasmate] phantasmata L | et per consequens] etiam per consequens NO per consequens W Q del. M om. KU   8 posset] possit N potest H add. ult. alia N add. anima O LM   9 Item] Praeterea N KU FW Q X Z Prima O | intellectus ante] inv. N intellectus autem H intellectus Z | intellectionem] intellectum U FW X intelligere Q om. N Z | indeterminatissimus] indeterminatus N Q indeterminatum F determinatissimus U 10 Oportet igitur] inv. NO Oportet ergo FW Q X | ad intelligendum om. Z | sibi om. L 14 istorum] illorum H F Z horum Q | dicendum om. H add. est M F add. quod X | istos] illos HLM F Q add. dicendum X   15 accipitur aliquando] inv. N | quae] et KU   16 qua] quia N | intelligitur] intelligit N X intellectus(!) O   17 quando om. FW | illam quidditatem] inv. FW istam quidditatem K ipsam quidditatem X   18 reperibilem] rem subicibilem FW resolubilem X re solutionem(?) Z add. in multis NO add. in pluribus KU | multis] pluribus KU Z   19 speciei vel generis] generis vel speciei FW | isto] illo O H K Q X | modo] tantum X | est om. X | aliquid factum] factum N exsistens K

---

[38]Subintellige: etiam.
[39]Cf. supra n. 36
[40]Cf. **Henricus de Gandav.**, *Summa* art. 53 q. 5 (II, f. 66r-v); **Simon de Faversham**, *Sophisma: Universale est intentio* (ed. Yokoyama 7-11).

I *De anima*,[41] quod intellectus est qui facit universalitatem in rebus, quia universale aut nihil est aut posterius est.[42] Aliquando autem universale accipitur pro re subiecta intentioni secundae, id est, pro quidditate rei absoluta, quae quantum est de se nec est universalis primo modo nec singularis, sed de se est indifferens, et tale est obiectum intellectus directum. Non autem est in intellectu subiective, sed obiective tantum.

40   Ad aliud[43] dicunt ALIQUI[44] quod anima separata intelligit per species sibi influxas a Deo. Vel potest dici quod ad praesentiam obiecti per suum actum elicit suam intellectionem, et post unam intellectionem relinquitur sibi habitus per virtutem illius actus. Qui habitus habet inclinare potentiam ad intelligendum alias eandem rem et ipsam repraesentare, sicut posset species impressa.

41   Ad aliud[45] dicendum quod potentia passiva determinatur per aliquid sibi impressum, sed potentia activa non, sed solum per praesentiam obiecti expressam, sicut sol habet glaciem dissolvere, non per aliquid sibi impressum, sed tantum praesentata sibi glacie.

---

1 est *om.* F | in rebus *om.* NO M *add.* et Aristoteles (*om.* X) primo De anima KU FW X Z *add.* et Q *add. ult.* quod intellectus est qui facit universalitatem in rebus et (*om.* U) KU *add. ult.* quod intellectus est qui facit universalitatem X Z   2 quia] quod KU FW Q | aut *om.* N | nihil est] *inv.* HLM nihil F Q Z | nihil ... posterius] posterius ... nihil Q | aut²] vel N quia U *add.* per HL | posterius est] posterius est singularis N praeteritus est O posterius singulari K | autem *om.* NO L FW   3 universale accipitur] *inv.* NO L universale sumitur U | intentioni] intuitio(!) O | id est] et H   4 absoluta] absolute L KU X | quae *om.* Z | se] *lin.* F *om.* W | nec — se] nec singularis nec universalis est (*mg.*) Z² 5 nec] *add.* est Q | singularis] singulare H | est indifferens] *inv.* M X | et tale] talis enim NO et talis FW | est² *om.* F   6 subiective *om.* U   7 sed —tantum] *mg.* Z² | obiective tantum] *inv.* O KU Q X Z²   8 aliqui quod] *inv.* X alii quod Z quod FW   9 sibi *om.* KU FW   10 per *om.* H | actum] obiectum FW *add.* activum W | suam] *rep.* N | intellectionem] intentionem NO L Z | post *om.* NO 11 intellectionem] intentionem NO L | relinquitur] resolvitur N | habitus] *add.* et N | actus] vel actus actionis F actionis W *add.* (*mg.*) alias actus W   12 habet] potest KU | inclinare *om.* X | potentiam] potentias K | ad — eandem] alias dandum rem U | alias *om.* FW   13 ipsam] ipsum NO | posset] potest H | impressa] expressa FW   14 dicendum] *add.* (*mg.* F) est M F | potentia *om.* O   15 potentia *om.* H | potentia — sed² *om.* X | sed² *om.* FW | solum] sola N | per *om.* U   16 obiecti] oppositi O | expressam] expressa Z | sol] solis Q | glaciem dissolvere] *inv.* U dissolvere K 17 non] nec Q *rep.* Z | aliquid] aliquod K | impressum] impressam(!) O | praesentata] repraesentata NO HM U | sibi² *om.* U | glacie] *add.* etc. K

[41]Potius **Averroës**, *De an.* I com. 8 (AverL I 12): "... sed intellectus est qui agit in eis universalitatem"; *Auctoritates Aristotelis* (ed. J. Hamesse 176): "Intellectus agens causat universalitatem in rebus."
[42]**Aristot.**, *De an.* I c. 1 (A c. 1, 402*b* 7-8); *Auctoritates Aristotelis* (ed. J. Hamesse 174): "Animal universale aut nihil est aut posterius est."
[43]Cf. supra n. 37
[44]**Thomas**, *Summa theol.* I q. 89 a. 1 ad 3 (V 371*b*): "Ad tertium dicendum quod anima separata non intelligit per species innatas, nec per species quas tunc abstrahit; nec solum per species conservatas ... sed per species ex influentia divini luminis participatas ..."; *Summa theol.* I q. 89 a. 3 in corp. (V 3767*a*).
[45]Cf. supra n. 38

[IX. — Ad argumenta principalia secundum opinionem negantium speciem intelligibilem actui intellectus praeviam]

Ad auctoritates PHILOSOPHI in contrarium adductas,[46] dicendum quod cum dicitur quod intellectus est locus specierum, per speciem intelligit PHILOSOPHUS actum intelligendi, qui est vera species et similitudo obiecti. Nec anima est locus specierum quasi subiectum, nec hoc ostendit PHILOSOPHUS. Sed pro tanto hoc dicitur quod, sicut locatum continetur in loco — non quidem subiective nec etiam quod informat locum, sed expressive —, sic in proposito de specie. Nec etiam dicit PHILOSOPHUS quod species lapidis sit in anima impressa, ipsam informans, sed expressa tantum obiective, ut dictum est. Similiter "anima est omnia intelligibilia" per actum intelligendi. Unde dicit in eodem libro[47] quod idem est scientia secundum actum rei scitae, sicut idem est sensibile in actu et sensus in actu; non autem concludit ILLA AUCTORITAS quod hoc sit per speciem impressam in intellectu.

[16] Ad rationem de reductione etc.[48] dicendum quod potentia passiva reducitur de potentia essentiali ad accidentalem per aliquid sibi impressum, non autem potentia activa, ut dictum est,[49] sed sufficit ad hoc praesentia obiecti; talis autem potentia est intellectus, ut

---

3 auctoritates] auctoritatem W | in — adductas *om.* FW | dicendum] *add.* est M F   4 quod *om.* O HL | quod² *om.* N | locus specierum] *inv.* O | specierum] ant. est K *add.* quod FW   5 qui] quae (*mg.* Z²) O U FW X Z²   6 Nec] Ut N | quasi] sicut X Z *om.* U | subiectum] *mg.* K obiectum H   7 nec] ad N ut O | ostendit] dicit NO FW Q X intendit K | Philosophus] *add.* ostendere K | Sed *om.* NO | quod] quia W Q   8 continetur] dicitur contineri N | subiective] informative NO obiective M | nec — locum] ut ita per locum informarent (informet O) NO ita quod informet M | nec — locum] ut ita per locum informet (instret(?) U informat X) locum (locus Z) KU FW X Z ita quod locum informet Q   9 sed] *add.* tantum KU FW X Z | sic] ita N   10 etiam] et U | in anima] animae NO   11 impressa] *lin.* K expressa U | expressa] expressam Q   12 est²] *lin.* X | omnia] obiecta O anima Q *om.* FW X Z | intelligibilia] intellectiva FW Q X   13 intelligendi] sciendi FW X Z speculandi Q *add.* sicut (sic U) sensibilia (sensitiva FW) per actum sentiendi KU FW X Z | Unde] Ut K Sicut U | in *om.* Q   14 secundum actum] *mg.* W | idem *post* actu X | est sensibile] scibile est M scibile KU sensibile Q est scibile X Z²   15 in] *rep.* Q | concludit] concedit HM | illa] ista M K ita Z   16 speciem impressam] species impressas X | in intellectu] intellectui L *om.* X | intellectu] intellectum F   17 etc.] et U *om.* N X | dicendum] *add.* est M F   18 ad] *add.* potentiam H | aliquid] aliquod L KU   19 sufficit] suscipit Z   20 praesentia] potentia Q | talis — intellectus *post* facta KU | autem *om.* KU | est intellectus] *inv.* Q erit intellectus U

[46]Cf. supra n. 5
[47]**Aristot.**, *De an.* III c. 7 (Γ c. 8, 431*b* 20—432*a* 3); *Auctoritates Aristotelis* (ed. J. Hamesse 188): "Scientiae secantur quemadmodum res de quibus sunt scientiae."
[48]Cf. supra n. 6.
[49]Cf. supra n. 41.

dictum est in alia quaestione de hoc facta;⁵⁰ igitur, etc.

[X. — Subquaestio: nulla specie impressa posita, quaeritur quomodo intellectus ab intelligibili patiatur]

44 Sed potest quaeri per quem modum patitur intellectus ab intelligibili, ex quo nihil ab illo sibi imprimitur.

45 Dicendum quod hoc ideo est, quia obiectum sibi repraesentatum et expressum per phantasma inclinat et excitat potentiam ad intelligendum, quem tamen actum elicit intellectus virtute sua propria. Exemplum⁵¹ de magistro excitante intellectum discipuli per exempla sensibilia, qui tamen nihil imprimit in eius intellectu. Exemplum etiam de primo movente quod movet ut amatum et desideratum per modum finis allicientis appetitum propter eius iustitiam et bonitatem, nihil tamen appetitui imprimendo.

[XI. — Epilogus Scoti]

46 Teneas quam partem volueris. Prima tamen videtur communior et verior, et "qui potest capere capiat".⁵²

---

1 est *om.* X | quaestione] conclusione(?) O | igitur etc.] ergo etc. W *om.* NO L Q X 4 intelligibili] intelligibilibus FW 5 ex quo] cum FW et Z | nihil *om.* L | ab illo sibi] sibi ex ipso N sibi ab illo (isto O alio Q) O KU FW Q X Z 6 Dicendum] Dicitur FW Q X Z *add.* est M K | ideo est] est H non est nisi L | quia *om.* X | sibi *om.* L | repraesentatum] praesentatum O KU Q Z plicatum FW explicatum X 7 et — propria] est virtute intellectus agentis N virtute intellectus O 8 quem] quod X Z | elicit] intendit(?) X elicitum Z | intellectus] *add.* non KU | virtute *post* propria Q | sua *om.* KU FW Q X Z 9 propria] *add.* sed aliunde (aliquando Q) excitatur sine specie sibi (*om.* FW) impressa KU FW Q X Z | Exemplum — intellectu *om.* X | intellectum discipuli] *inv.* Q *add.* ad intelligendum KU 10 qui *om.* HL F | nihil] non KU FW Q Z | imprimit] imprimunt H *add.* aliquid KU FW Q Z | in eius intellectu] eius intellectui NO in eius intellectum K FW Q Z eius intellectum U 11 etiam *om.* X | et] vel K 12 per modum] respectu FW | allicientis] ultimantis N elicientis KU | eius] illius FW 13 iustitiam et] sanctam(?) X *om.* FW Q *spat. vac.* Z | tamen] *add.* eius Q 15 Teneas] Tene Z | quam — volueris] quod placet Q | volueris] voluerit H velis FW | tamen *om.* N Q *add.* ult. positio Q | videtur *om.* KU | communior et verior] verior et communior NO FW Q X Z *add.* ult. etc. F 16 et — capiat] = HLM KU *om.* NO FW Q X Z | capiat] *add.* etc. H *add.* etc. quod Alygton M

⁵⁰Cf. supra q. 12 n. 30.
⁵¹Cf. **Iacobus de Viterbio**, *Quodl.* I q. 12 (ed. Ypma 177): "Dicitur etiam causari scientia a doctore, in quantum per signa sensibilia admovetur et excitatur aliquis ad considerandum aliquid, cuius habitualis notitia praeexsistit in ipso …"
⁵²**Matt.** 19, 12; cf. **Duns Scotus**, *Metaph.* VII q. 19 n. 57 (OPh IV 374).

[QUAESTIO 18]

UTRUM INTELLECTUS NOSTER POSSIT INTELLIGERE SINE PHANTASMATE

Utrum intellectus noster possit intelligere sine phantasmate.

[I. — Opinio Thomae]

[1] QUIDAM[1] dicunt quod non, propter istam rationem:
Quia obiectum intellectus viatoris, qui est corpori coniunctus, est quiditas materialis, sicut obiectum substantiae separatae est quiditas separata; sed de natura quiditatis materialis est quod sit in aliquo singulari, sicut natura lapidis quod sit in hoc lapide; igitur non potest perfecte eius natura intelligi vel cognosci, nisi cognoscatur in singulari. Cognitio autem singularis pertinet ad sensum exteriorem et phantasma; igitur ad hoc quod perfecte eius natura intelligatur, oportet quod intelligitur in phantasmate repraesentante eius singulare.

Aliae rationes sumuntur ex experimento,[2] quia experimur primo intellectum impediri in sua operatione, laeso organo phantasiae, ut in phreneticis. Ex hoc potest formari ratio sic: potentia

---

4 Utrum] *praem.* Quaeritur NO KU FW Q X Z Si U *adnot. mg.* Quaestio 18 M | noster *om.* X | possit] posset O potest H K | intelligere] recipere H   6 istam] illam NO H FW Q X   7 Quia *om.* Q | obiectum *om.* L | viatoris] viatorum U | est] enim X | corpori] communior X   8 quiditas] *add.* rei Q | materialis] naturalis U | separatae] incorporeae HM   9 quiditas] quantitas O | quiditatis] quantitas O | materialis *om.* F Z | sit] insit Q   10 natura] naturae N materia U | lapidis] lipidem(?) O | quod sit *om.* FW | igitur] ergo L FW Q X   11 eius natura] *inv.* Q | intelligi vel cognosci] intellectus vel cognitio O | cognoscatur] cognoscitur KU Z   12 in] a N | autem] in X   13 et] *add.* ad KU | phantasma] phantasiam KU FW X Z | igitur] ergo FW Q X | quod] ut Z | eius natura] *ant.* perfecte KU Q *inv.* L KU FW Q   14 intelligatur] intelligitur L KU *add. ult.* quod U | oportet — intelligitur *om.* Q | intelligitur] intelligatur L K FW X Z   16 ex experimento] experimento NO FW Q ab experimento KU Z *om.* L | quia] quod O | experimur] exprimuntur F | primo *om.* Z   17 impediri] experiri Q | in] a M | laeso] *add.* eius Q | organo] *mg.* Z² *add.* et Q   18 formari] *add.* talis X | sic] sicut FW X Z

[1]Cf. **Thomas**, *Summa theol.* I q. 84 a. 7 in corp. (V 325b): "De ratione autem huius naturae est, quod in aliquo individuo exsistat, quod non est absque materia corporali; sicut de ratione naturae lapidis est quod sit in hoc lapide ... Unde natura lapidis, vel cuiuscumque materialis rei, cognosci non potest complete et vere, nisi secundum quod cognoscitur ut in particulare exsistens. Particulare autem apprehendimus per sensum et imaginationem"; cf. etiam *Summa theol.* I q. 84 a. 8 in corp. (V 328a).

[2]Cf. **Thomas**, *Summa theol.* I q. 84 a. 7 in corp. (V 325a): "Videmus enim quod impedito actu virtutis imaginativae per laesionem organi, ut in phreneticis ... impeditur homo ab intelligendo in actu etiam ea quorum scientiam praeaccepit."

non-organica non impeditur in actu suo propter laesionem potentiae organicae, nisi ad actum suum indigeret actu illius potentiae organicae; sed intellectus est potentia non-organica, tamen impeditur in actu suo, laeso organo phantasiae; igitur ad actum intelligendi requiritur actus phantasiae.

3 Item, alio experimento:[3] quando aliquid intelligere volumus, formamus nobis exempla vel idola in phantasia, et tunc facilius intelligimus, sicut patet in docente discipulum, proponendo sibi exempla sensibilia.

4 Sed sciendum quod licet duae ultimae rationes valeant, prima tamen non videtur valere ALIQUIBUS,[4] quia supponit quod quiditas sensibilis tantum sit obiectum intellectus coniuncti, et quod de natura eius sit esse in singulari. Quae videntur esse falsa, ut postea[5] apparebit.

[II. — Opinio Avicennae]

5 AVICENNA[6] autem ponit quod, in prima intellectione rei

[2]

---

1 non] *mg.* X | propter] *add.* operationem Z 2 nisi — organicae *om.* Z | actu illius] operatione talis FW actum illius X | illius *om.* L 3 intellectus] missus X *add.* noster Q | tamen] cum U | in] ab KU *om.* Z 4 laeso] lexo Q | igitur] ergo N L Q X | ad *om.* O 6 Item] Praeterea NO KU FW Q X Z | alio] alius O *om.* N | aliquid] aliqua KU Z | intelligere] cognoscere N | volumus] voluimus Z 7 nobis] *add.* aliqua NO FW Q X | exempla vel] exempla sive N *om.* Z | phantasia] phantasiam X | et] sed L *add.* (*mg.*) per aliqua exteriora M | et — intelligimus] per aliqua exteriora Z 8 intelligimus] intelligemus O | patet] apparet Q | in] de KU | docente] docendo NO | proponendo] proponente Z | sibi *om.* N Z 9 exempla] *add.* singularia Q 10 sciendum] *add.* est M F | duae ultimae] *inv.* Z | rationes *om.* U | valeant] voleant Z *om.* X | prima tamen] *inv.* K propter ea tamen U 11 non — aliquibus] non videtur aliquibus valere NO L FW Z aliquibus non videtur valere Q videtur aliquibus non valere X | supponit] suspendunt O supponitur FW | quiditas] quantas O 12 tantum sit] *inv.* N K tantum sed O sit U | obiectum] oppositum O | intellectus] *rep.* O | quod *om.* Z 13 eius] *lin.* N | sit] est H | Quae] Quia Q *add.* omnia FW | esse[2]] eis O M Q Z ei X *om.* FW 14 apparebit] parebit X 16 autem] etiam HLM X | in] *add. spat. vac.* H *add.* ipsa Z | intellectione] intentione O KU *om.* H | rei cuiuslibet] *inv.* HL F

---

[3] Cf. **Thomas**, *Summa theol.* I q. 84 a. 7 in corp. (V 325*a-b*): "Secundo, quia hoc quilibet in seipso experiri potest, quod quando aliquis conatur aliquid intelligere, format aliqua phantasmata sibi per modum exemplorum, in quibus quasi inspiciat quod intelligere studet. Et inde est etiam quod quando alium volumus facere aliquid intelligere, proponimus ei exempla, ex quibus sibi phantasmata formare possit ad intelligendum."

[4] Cf. **Matthaeus ab Aquasparta** *Quaest. disp. de cognitione* q. 1 (ed. Gál BFS I² 209-215; q. 6 (ed. Gál BFS I² 327-332).

[5] Cf. infra n. 9.

[6] **Avicenna**, *De an.* pars V cap. 3 (AviL 105): "Hoc autem contingit in principio tantum et non postea, nisi parum. Cum autem proficit anima et roboratur, sola per se operatur actiones suas absolute. Virtutes autem sensibiles et imaginativae et caeterae virtutes corporales retrahunt eam a sua actione, verbi gratia, sicut homo qui aliquando indiget iumento et eius apparatu quo perveniat eo quo proponit; quo cum accesserit, sed ex illis causis acciderit non pervenire, causa quae fuit perveniendi eadem est prohibendi."

cuiuslibet, necessarium est phantasma, ut ab ipso quodammodo species imprimatur, ut dictum est supra;[7] sed quando est impressa, et homo vult postea idem intelligere, non est necessarium phantasma, sed magis est intellectui onus. Exemplum PONIT de iumento quod est homini necessarium in itinere, sed in termino est sibi in onus. Hoc etiam probatur sic: habitis omnibus necessariis ad operationem, statim sequitur operatio; sed actus intelligendi solum dependet, essentialiter loquendo, ab intellectu et obiecto — nisi addatur accidentaliter ab actu voluntatis imperantis, sed elicitive tantum dependet a praedictis; per speciem autem intelligibilem obiectum fit praesens intellectui; igitur non est necessarium recurrere ad phantasmata propter actum intelligendi.

[III. — Opinio aliorum]

Propter istam rationem dicunt ALIQUI[8] quod non est necessaria species impressa intellectui ad actum intelligendi. Quia, ad solam conversionem intellectus super phantasmata, intellectus elicit actum suum; et quia, transeunte actu, non manet species, ideo semper necesse est recurrere ad phantasmata in quolibet actu intelligendi.

---

1 ut] *lin.* Z² | ab ipso] ab eo N appositio Q | quodammodo species] *inv.* (*lin.* N) N HL quaedam modo species O 2 species imprimatur] *inv.* Q 3 homo] *add.* (*lin.*) quando Z² | vult] *mg.* Q | postea *om.* Z | idem intelligere] *inv.* K intelligere N F 4 est intellectui] *inv.* H est intellectum X intellectui Z *add.* in FW Q | onus] impedimentum cuius N HL cuius O *add.* et impedimentum KU | iumento] in mento(!) X 5 est *om.* U | homini necessarium] *inv.* Q | termino] terminos U | est sibi] qui O sibi Z | in³] *spat. vac.* Z 6 onus] unus O | Hoc] Igitur etc. N | habitis] corr. (*mg.*) W | omnibus] habitibus F 7 sequitur] requiritur K FW 8 essentialiter] essentia O | ab] de HL 9 ab actu] actu H ad actum K | elicitive] eliciative N elicite X 10 dependet] dependat O impendet Z | a praedictis] ab istis N ex praedictis M FW de praedictis KU 11 obiectum] oppositum O | fit] sit U X *rep.* Q | praesens] primum FW praesentatum X | intellectui] intellectu O intellectum W | igitur] ergo L FW Q X 12 recurrere] incurrere F | phantasmata] phantasma N K X 14 Propter] Praeter Q | Propter — intelligendi] *mg.* NO | istam] illam HL FW | aliqui] qui U | necessaria] necessarium FW 15 impressa intellectui] *inv.* Q 16 super phantasmata] sicut phantasma NO super phantasma K | intellectus² *om.* Q | elicit] *add.* ad W X | actum suum] *inv.* L 17 et *om.* Z | non] *mg.* Z² *om.* FW | manet] remanet KU FW 18 necesse est] *inv.* O Q X Z necessario est H est necessarium M necessarium est KU | recurrere] incurrere F *add.* in Z | phantasmata] phantasma K X

---

[7]Cf. supra q. 14, n. 13-15.
[8]Cf. **Henricus de Gandavo**, *Quodl.* V q. 14 (f. 176v O—177r O): "Intellectus autem possibilis speciem impressam nullam recipit a phantasmate, sed actione agentis facientis phantasmata quantum est de se solum in potentia moventia intellectum esse actu moventia et exsistentia in eo ut in cognoscente solum (et hoc sub ratione universalis quod idem re est ut est in cognoscente, scilicet imaginativa sub ratione particularis et in intellectu sub ratione universalis), ita quod in ipsum speculatur intellectus et imaginativa, nec est praesens intellectui nisi quia praesens est imaginativae ... Propter quod bene dixit Avicenna in suo libro *De anima* quod in intellectu possibili non manet intelligibile nisi cum actu intelligit, sed solum manet in potentia in phantasmatibus exsistentibus in vi sensitiva a quibus iterato abstrahitur actione agentis si intellectus noster aliquid debeat intelligere."

Et hoc dicunt PHILOSOPHUM intellexisse I et II *De anima*[9] cum dicit quod nihil intelligimus sine phantasmate.

7   Sed quia ALIIS[10] videtur quod species impressa intellectui requiritur ad intelligendum, et quod manet, cessante actu, ideo DICUNT quod fit recursus ad phantasmata, non ut iterum ibi species abstrahatur, quia iam habet, sed ut habita intendatur. Dicunt enim ALIQUI[11] quod species in intellectu habet debile esse, et transeunte actu, paulative remittitur, sicut calida aqua amoto igne tepescit. Quia igitur tunc species habet esse incompletum, ideo DICUNT quod necesse est intellectui recurrere ad phantasmata si debeat intelligere, ut species praehabita intendatur.

8   Sed licet illa via videatur rationalis, tamen consideranti

---

1 Et] Ut F | hoc dicunt] inv. NO Q sic dicunt K FW X Z sic debent U | intellexisse] *add.* in X | I et II] III U | cum] ubi N quando Q *om.* O   2 intelligimus] intelligemus O | phantasmate *om.* O   3 aliis] alius O | requiritur — habet² *om.* N   4 et *om.* O | manet] *add.* sentiente actu O | actu] *add.* etiam X   5 fit] sit X | recursus] cursus KU | phantasmata] phantasma K | ibi species] *inv.* L species KU FW X sibi species Q | abstrahatur] abstrahitur O   6 quia iam habet *om.* KU | habita] *lin.* Z | enim *om.* FW | aliqui] aliquid O alii X   7 in] *lin.* U | debile esse] *inv.* O Q X debile N   8 paulative] paulatim HL KU X | calida aqua amoto] aqua calida amoto (remoto KU) KU FW Q calido amoto X calida aqua amato(!) Z | igne] *add.* illa U   9 igitur] ergo L FW Q X | tunc *om.* F | species] *ant.* igitur Q | esse *om.* N | incompletum] incompletam O X *add.* et X   10 necesse] necessarium X | intellectui recurrere] intellectum recurrere (concurrere KU) KU FW Q X | phantasmata] phantasma K   11 species praehabita] praehabita FW   12 licet] *mg.* K si NO U FW Q X etsi Z | illa] ista X | videatur] videtur H Q X | rationalis] *add.* sufficienter NO FW X *add.* superfluit Q *add.* superficiatur Z | consideranti] considerata H considerari X

---

[9] Potius, cum codice U, nobis legendum est "III De anima"; cf. **Aristot.**, *De an.* III c. 6 (Γ c. 7, 431*a* 15-16); cf. **Thomas**, *De an.* III c. 6 (XLV¹ 229*a*): "… propter quod nequaquam sine phantasmate intelligit anima."

[10] **Aegidius Romanus**, *De cognitione angelorum* q. 4 (ed. 1503 f. 84*ra*); "Species ergo intelligibilis quamdiu est coniuncta phantasmati illustrato et irradiato per lumen intellectus agentis tamdiu est in esse perfectiori ut possit ex se causare actum intelligendi; sed statim cum desinit phantasma esse in phantasia non propter hoc desinit esse species in intellectu possibili, cum huiusmodi intellectus secundum Philosophum sit locus specierum et per consequens sit conservativus ipsarum. Sed licet non totaliter desinat esse species intelligibilis, desinente phantasmate, attamen non remanet in illa perfectione et in illo complemento in quo erat, phantasmate exsistente, id est quod non potest species illa ex se generare actum intelligendi nisi iterum fiat phantasma in phantasia et ipsa species per huiusmodi phantasma rursus fiat in esse perfecto."

[11] Cf. **Ioannes Parisiensis**, *In I Sent.* d. 3 q. 11 [q. 23] (ed. Muller 81): "Quid ergo dicemus? Si sunt species in memoria conservatae, quae est necessitas quod intellectus ad phantasmata convertatur? Ad quod dicendum quod intellectus potest dupliciter considerari, videlicet in generatione habitus scientialis, dum scilicet primo incipit intelligere; sic dico quod si non multum figatur acies cogitantis super rem cogitatam, sed figatur tenuiter, nihil remanet in acie cogitantis impressum. Si autem acies convertatur frequenter super phantasmata, vel in una conversione firmiter et diu teneatur ex forti impressione, bene, postquam non cogitat actu, remanet species impressa et efficitur habitus. Sed iste habitus potest dupliciter considerari: vel secundum communem modum habitus, qui secundum communem statum est in hominibus; vel secundum potissimum statum, in quo est perfectissimus habitus, qui est paucorum et non nisi in fine. Si primo modo, habebit ibi illa species vel habitus debilem impressionem, et ideo per se non est sufficienter immutativa acie intellectus; immo oportet quod intellectus ad phantasmata se convertat, si denuo vellet aliquid intelligere."

subtiliter includit inconvenientia:

Primum est quod intellectus possit iterare illum recursum in infinitum, sicut potest multiplicare actum intelligendi in infinitum, quantum est de se; et sequitur quod species illa posset intendi in infinitum. Ex hoc sequitur aliud inconveniens quod, cum per speciem magis intensam magis intelligamus et melius, si species semper potest intendi, semper poterit eadem res a nobis melius cognosci et intelligi; et sic nullam rem, quamcumque modicam et vilem, intellectus noster posset intelligere quantum intelligibilis esset; quod videtur inconveniens, cum sensus, qui est potentia inferior, possit sentire aliquod sensibile inquantum sensibile est.

[IV. — Opinio ab Augustino aliisque auctoritatibus fulcita]

[4] Ideo, omissis aliis necessitatibus, dicunt ALII[12] quod non est contra rationem actus intelligendi intellectus nostri absolute intelligere sine phantasmate, quia tunc recursus ad phantasmata esset necessarius animae separatae, ut dictum est;[13] nec contra rationem eius ut est corpori unitus absolute, quia etiam hoc esset necessarium si uniatur corpori glorioso post resurrectionem, quod falsum est; nec contra rationem eius ut viator est vel ut coniunctus corpori in via, quia hoc etiam esset necessarium homini in statu

---

1 inconvenientia] inconvenientiam U W   2 est om. L | possit] posset L potest KU | iterare] nascere X | illum] istum K X Z   3 sicut — infinitum om. H add. igitur H | potest om. U | multiplicare] intelligere KU X   4 quantum] quando X | est post se K | et sequitur] sequitur etiam N sequitur O X Z quare sequitur FW sequitur tunc Q | species om. Q | illa] ista X | posset] possit KU FW | intendi] multiplicari FW   5 infinitum] add. et Z | aliud inconveniens] inv. H maius inconveniens FW | cum] tamen FW | per speciem] inv. N speciem Q add. impressam FW   6 magis om. L | intensam] intensum NO | magis² om. H | intelligamus] intelligimus Q | melius] add. et KU | si] sed X | species — potest] semper species possit Q | semper potest] inv. NO FW   7 poterit] potest H | eadem — intelligi] a nobis res melius intelligi NO | res] ratio L | melius] ant. a FW | cognosci et om. KU FW Q X Z   8 rem] add. deus K | quamcumque] quantumcumque L KU FW Q X Z | et vilem om. KU   9 noster om. H | posset] possit N K potest H | quantum] quantumcumque Q   10 possit] posset N LM   11 inquantum] ut N primum O quantum FW Q X Z   13 Ideo] praem. Non FW Q | aliis] add. scilicet H | necessitatibus] necessariis H KU | dicunt] sicut N sunt O | quod] quando NO | est] lin. N   14 actus intelligendi] inv. KU intelligendi N | intellectus nostri] inv. NO   15 sine] absque KU | quia om. L | tunc] sic H | recursus] recursivus O | phantasmata] phantasma N K   16 animae separatae] ad animam separatam N non separatae L | dictum est] inv. H dictum Q add. supra K | nec] add. est H   17 est om. U | unitus] immixtus Q | etiam hoc] inv. X Z etiam si hoc N etiam hic O tunc hoc L | hoc esset] rep. NO   18 si uniatur] si unitus M sibi unito KU unire FW sibi unite Q sibi unire X Z | glorioso] glorificato N | post] propter O   19 eius] est Z | viator] viatoris N | est — via om. N | vel — etiam] spat. vac. O | ut²] non est X om. L Z   20 in via om. Q | hoc etiam] inv. FW tunc N etiam O | esset] fuisset NO Q | homini om. NO

[12] Cf. fontes citati infra, qui ex *Quaestionibus disputatis* Matthaei ab Aquasparta hauriuntur.
[13] Cf. supra q. 17 n. 37

innocentiae (quia tunc fuit viator) — hoc autem est falsum, cum anima eius quantum ad actum proprium in nullo fuisset corpori subiecta, sed super ipsum et sensus suos, tam quoad apprehensionem quam quoad appetitum, habuisset plenum dominium ita quod potuisset intellexisse sine phantasmate vel cum phantasmate sicut placuisset sibi; sed DICUNT quod necessitas recurrendi ad phantasma est nobis inflicta propter peccatum. Unde sequitur ad ignorantiam nobis inflictam, et hoc iuste, quia ex quo anima se deordinavit, dimittendo dominium divinum et se ab eius subiectione retrahendo, rationale fuit in poenam hanc incidere ut amitteret dominium proprium quod habebat super corpus suum et super sensum. Et haec est sententia beati AUGUSTINI in pluribus locis,[14] et HUGONIS *Super angelicam hierarchiam*,[15] et EUSTRATII

---

1 quia] qui KU FW cum (*mg.*) Z² *om.* O | viator] via O | hoc — falsum] quod falsum est N | autem *om.* O U | est falsum] *inv.* L | cum — quantum] quia tunc anima N quia anima Q 2 eius *post* actum Z | ad] *lin.* Z² | proprium] primum FW | in nullo fuisset] non (in O) fuit NO nulli fuisse X | corpori subiecta] *inv.* M 3 sed *om.* X | super] semper L | et] ut X 4 quam] quae (*lin.*) Z² | quoad] quo X | appetitum] appetitivum Q | habuisset] habuisse H | ita] *lin.* X 5 potuisset] posset X | intellexisse] *rep.* O | vel — phantasmate *om.* Q X | cum] non O 6 placuisset sibi] *inv.* W Q Z sibi placuit X | sed] *add.* (*mg.*) ecce M | dicunt] *add.* aliqui Q | necessitas *post* phantasma L 7 phantasma] phantasmata Q X | propter peccatum] per in poenitentiam peccati K per peccatum U per X | propter — inflictam] *mg.* H | ad *om.* H 8 ignorantiam] generationem (*lin.*) Z² | anima] *ant. ex* F animae Q 9 deordinavit] deordinant Q | dimittendo] amittendo K *om.* FW | dominium divinum] *inv.* Q dominium Domini O L dominium Dei FW divinum U | divinum — dominium] (*post* sensum) rationale fuit in hanc poenam incidere K | se] sic O | eius] eis NO | subiectione] subiectioni N 10 retrahendo] detrahendo N subtrahendo O FW Q Z *om.* X | fuit] facit Q *add.* ut N | poenam] speciem Q | incidere] incideret N | ut] et N H U Z quod FW Q X 11 amitteret] aiunt te L amittere H U Z amitterent Q *add. ult. spat. vac.* L | dominium] divinum U | habebat] habeat H | super] *mg.* W supra U | et — sensum] *mg.* W 12 sensum] *add.* suum L | haec] hoc U F Z | beati] sancti L *om.* Q 13 locis *om.* F | et Hugonis] *mg.* M *om.* KU | angelicam] evangelicam L angelicas X | hierarchiam] ferarchiam O vel arcam FW artes X *om.* Q | Eustratii] Eustatii M FW Q Z Eutratue U etiam X

[14]Cf. **Augustinus**, *De Trinitate* XV c. 27 (CCL 50A 533, PL 42 1097): "Quae igitur causa est cur acie fixa ipsam [lucem] videre non possis, nisi utique infirmitas? Et quid tibi eam fecit, nisi iniquitas"?; *De civ. Dei* XI c. 2 (CCL 48 322, PL 41 318). Eaedem auctoritates seriatim, Lincolniensi excepto, adhibentur a **Matthaeo ab Aquasparta**, *Quaest. de fide* q. 7 (ed. Gál BFS I² 173); cf. *Quaest. disp. de cognitione* q. 10 (ed. Gál BFS I² 388-406).

[15]Cf. **Hugo de S. Victore**, *Super de cael. hier.* VI (PL 175 975D—976A): "Homo enim sensum hominis habet, et sentit secundum sensum hominis, vel quod extra est secundum carnem, vel quod intus est secundum mentem, et non habet amplius homo. Oculus carnis quae ad carnem, oculus mentis quae ad mentem. Amplius quid? ... Est autem oculus triplex: oculus carnis, oculus rationis, oculus contemplationis. Oculus carnis apertus est, oculus rationis lippus, oculus contemplationis clausus et caecus. Oculo carnis videtur mundus, et ea quae sunt in mundo. Oculo rationis animus, et ea quae sunt in animo. Oculo contemplationis Deus, et ea quae sunt in Deo. Oculo carnis videt homo quae sunt extra se; oculo rationis quae sunt in se; oculo contemplationis quae sunt intra se et supra se."; *De sacramentis christ. fidei* I pars 10 c. 2 (PL 176 329C—330A).

Super libros Ethicorum,[16] et LINCOLNIENIENSIS *Super libros Posteriorum*[17] super illud verbum: "Deficiente nobis uno sensu, necesse est nobis deficere scientiam secundum illum sensum".

ARISTOTELES[18] autem, quia nihil scivit de illo peccato et invenit naturam taliter dispositam — procedens ex sensu tantum —, credidit hoc esse nobis naturale sicut intelligere; et ideo hoc posuit absolute, quia necesse est ad phantasmata recurrere volentem intelligere.

---

1 Super — Ethicorum *om.* N | libros] librum O Q X Z libro FW | libros²] librum O M K Q X Z primo FW *add.* ult. primum M K   2 super — illum] manifestum autem si aliquis sensus defecerit Q | illud verbum] hoc verbum KU illo verbo FW | Deficiente] Diffinite U *add.* in H | nobis *om.* N | uno sensu] *inv.* M sensu N L FW   3 scientiam] scientia O | secundum illum sensum] sensibilium N secundum istum sensum O X secundum sensum illum M per illum sensum FW   4 Aristoteles] Secundum Aristotelem H | autem] vero FW | quia] qui H | illo *post* peccato Z isto NO M X *om.* KU | et] vel L   5 taliter dispositam] *inv.* NO taliter disponi Q *add.* et X | ex] est F | sensu] sensibus KU | credidit — nobis] hoc credidit nobis esse L   6 hoc] huiusmodi Q | esse *post* naturale NO *post* nobis Z | nobis naturale] *inv.* KU | sicut] sic NO | intelligere] intellexit KU | et ideo] et sic N et O L tunc X | hoc² *om.* N FW *add.* esse Q | posuit] ponit Z   7 quia] quod N KU FW X | phantasmata] phantasma HM | intelligere] *add.* igitur etc. KU *add.* etc. X

[16] Cf. **Eustratius**, *In libros Ethicorum Aristotlelis* VI c. 3 (ed. Heylbut *Comm. in Aristot. graeca* vol. XX, 297). In translatione vero Roberti Grossetestae apud fontes in editione **Matthaei ab Aquasparta** *Quaest. disp. de fide* q. 7 (ed. Gál BFS I² 173 n. 4) adhibitos reperta: "Neque hoc novum prorsus est existimandum, neque ab primo hominis errore longe alienum. Perfectus enim a principio ab omnium opifice creatus est homo ... qui non cogitando solummodo, sed intelligendo etiam pro ratione naturalis sui status operaretur. Intelligendo autem operari nihil aliud est nisi absque ullo medio res ipsas simplici intellectus appulsione comprehendere. Quod si statum illum servasset, legemque a creatore acceptam non fuisset transgressus, sed animo ad superiora converso eorum frui consortio ardenter appetivisset, inferiora vero eatenus advertisset, quatenus prout ordini ac naturae eius conveniebat, curam eorum erat habiturus, stabilis ipsi ac perpetua perfectio hucusque permansisset. Sed quia ab inferioribus illectus sursum intendere vires neglexit vitamque sensualem concupivit, propterea a propria perfectione deiectus, generationi et corruptioni obnoxius factus est; atque ita crassitudine mortalis corporis offuscante ac turbante, intellectualis ei conclusus est atque opertus, ut sensuum cognitione postea indiguerit." Cf. VI c. 6 (ed. Heylbut, *Comm. in Aristot. graeca*, vol. XX, 318), in translatione Roberti Grossetestae apud praefationem editionis Leoninae, ed. Gauthier tom. XLVII 246*: "Animali enim substantia manente, impossibile operationem in hoc venire ut exaequetur ei operationi quae est naturae super illam, ut non causatur exsistens operatio substantiae ulterius generantis causa fiat, quod impossibile. Mensura enim unicuique profectus proportionalis substantiae nata est fieri." Cf. **Albertus Magnus**, *Super Ethica, commentum et quaestiones, libros VI-X* VI lect. 8 (ed. Kubel, Editio Coloniensis XIV pars 2, 453-4).

[17] Cf. **Robertus Grossatesta**, *Comm. in Post. An.* I c. 14 (ed. P. Rossi 213-214): "Et similiter si pars suprema animae humanae, quae vocatur intellectiva et quae non est actus alicuius corporis neque agens in operatione sui propria instrumento corporeo, non esset mole corporis corrupti obnubilata et aggravata, ipsa per irradiationem acceptam a lumine superiori haberet completam scientiam absque sensus adminiculo, sicut habebit cum anima erit exuta a corpore et sicut forte habent aliqui penitus absoluti ab amore et phantasmatibus rerum corporalium. Sed, quia puritas oculi animae per corpus corruptum obnubilata et aggravata est, omnes vires ipsius animae rationalis in homine nato occupatae sunt per molem corporis, ne possint agere, et ita quodammodo sopitae."

[18] Cf. **Aristot.**, *Anal. pos.* II c. 13 [t. 75] (AL IV³ 271, c. 13 97a 5-6): "Cum ergo incedimus hac via cadit scientia quod divisio non deficit in aliquo ..."

[QUAESTIO 19]

UTRUM QUIDITAS SENSIBILIS TANTUM SIT OBIECTUM INTELLECTUS

Utrum quiditas sensibilis tantum sit obiectum intellectus nostri.

[1]   Videtur quod sic: 1
Quia potentia passiva tantum se extendit ad illa recipienda ad quae potentia activa correspondens se extendit facienda; sed intellectus agens tantum illa quae in phantasmatibus praesentantur potest facere actu intelligibilia; igitur intellectus possibilis est in potentia tantum ad illa intelligenda.[1]

Item, si quiditas sensibilis non esset eius adaequatum obiectum, tunc posset intelligere substantias separatas et Deum; consequens est falsum; igitur, etc. Falsitas consequentis patet per PHILOSOPHUM IX et XII *Metaphysicae*,[2] et per rationem specialiter de Deo: quia si possemus Deum per essentiam intelligere, tunc esset idem obiectum et sub eadem ratione et eadem potentia absolute in intellectione nostra et beatorum; actus igitur isti essent eiusdem rationis, et per consequens viatores essent beati.   2

---

4 Utrum] *praem.* Quaeritur NO KU FW Q X *adnot. mg.* Quaestio 19 M | Utrum quiditas] *inv.* F | tantum sit] *inv.* N | obiectum] oppositum O | intellectus *om.* Z | nostri *om.* O FW Q X Z 5 Videtur *post* sic HLM *om.* X 6 illa] alia U | ad quae] a X 7 activa] *add.* sibi KU 8 in *om.* U | phantasmatibus] phantasmate F | praesentantur] praesentatur O 9 intelligibilia] intellecta F Z 10 tantum *post* illa O KU Q X | intelligenda] intelligibilia HLM 11 Item] Praeterea NO KU FW Q X Z *add.* quia O | eius *om.* HL KU | ,adaequatum obiectum] *inv.* K Q 12 substantias] *add.* sed U | et Deum] ut dictum(!) K ut Deum U *om.* Z | consequens est] *inv.* K consequens N H Q est Z 13 etc.] et antecedens F *om.* Q | patet] ant. falsitas O *om.* H | per *om.* O FW | Philosophum *om.* F 14 IX et XII] IX et VII NO XI et XII U II F II et IX W IX et II Q IX et IV Z | specialiter] *add.* patet Q 15 possemus] possumus N possimus H | Deum] *add.* scilicet H | intelligere] *add.* et F | tunc] igitur O cum M FW Q X Z | esset idem] *inv.* X | obiectum] oppositum O 16 sub] scilicet secundum NO | eadem ratione] eandem rem N eadem re O *add.* ult. absolute N | et²] *add.* sub X *om.* Z | eadem potentia absolute] eodem gradu ab L eadem possibilitate et KU | in] et NO *om.* U X 17 et] *add.* aliorum et X | beatorum *om.* NO | igitur *om.* FW Q X Z | isti] ille NO | essent] esset N | et² *om.* U 18 beati] boni X

[1] **Aristot.**, *De an.* III c. 7 (Γ c. 8, 432a 3-10); **Aristot.**, *De an.* III c. 6 (Γ c. 7, 431a 16-17); **Aristot.**, *De an.* III c. 6 (Γ c. 7, 431b 2).
[2] Pro primo textu citato, cf. potius **Aristot.**, *Metaph.* II c. 1 (AL XXV³ 43; α c. 1, 993b 9-11): "Sicut enim nicticoracum oculi ad lucem diei se habent, sic et animae nostrae intellectus ea quae sunt omnium naturae manifestissima"; cf. infra n. 31; cf. *Metaph.* XII c. 6 (AL XXV³ 254; Λ c. 6, 1071b 12-20). Cf. **Duns Scotus**, *Metaph.* II q. 2-3 n. 5-6 (OPh III 201); *Lectura* I d. 3 p. 1 q. 1 n. 1-2 (XVI 223); *Ordinatio* I d. 3 p. 1 q. 1-2 n. 2 (III 2).

3 Contra:

Habitus metaphysicae informans intellectum nostrum excedit quiditates sensibiles quoad obiectum, quia ens inquantum ens est eius obiectum; igitur intellectus noster habet obiectum excedens quiditatem sensibilem.

4 Item, PHILOSOPHUS XII *Metaphysicae*³ multa concludit de substantiis separatis — quod non faceret si eas non intelligeret —, et II *Ethicorum*⁴ ponit ARISTOTELES felicitatem consistere in earum cognitione; felicitas autem potest a nobis adipisci; igitur, etc.

[I. — Ad quaestionem]
[A. — Opinio Thomae]

5 Ad hoc dicunt QUIDAM, scilicet THOMAS,⁵ quod quiditas rei sensibilis est obiectum adaequatum intellectus nostri, quod sic probant.

---

2 metaphysicae] immediate NO   3 quiditates sensibiles] quiditatem sensibilis L | quoad] quoque ad K | obiectum] obiecta HLM *add.* et FW | quia] *add.* omne H | inquantum] *add.* est X   4 eius obiectum] *inv.* Q eius oppositum O | igitur] ergo Q W X *add.* et M KU X | noster *om.* KU FW | obiectum²] oppositum O   5 quiditatem sensibilem] quiditates sensibiles X   6 XII] II NO Q | substantiis] subiectis K   7 quod] quae HM KU | faceret] fieret NO | si — intelligeret] si non eas intelligeret M nisi intelligeret eas KU | eas] ea Z *om.* H | II] I NO "X" Q   8 Ethicorum] Ethicis Q W | Aristoteles *om.* X | felicitatem *post* cognitione Z | cognitione] cognitionem NO   9 felicitas] illa L | potest *post* nobis K X ant. autem L | a *om.* FW Q X | adipisci] advenire FW Q X Z | igitur etc. *om.* NO L X   12 quidam scilicet Thomas] aliqui (*om.* M) theologi HLM quidam Q quidam secundum D. Thomam Z *add.* et caeteri KU   13 obiectum adaequatum] *inv.* X | adaequatum] adest tum(!) O   14 probant] probat U FW Q Z

³**Aristot.**, *Metaph.* XII c. 7-8 (AL XXV³ 256-261; Λ c. 7-8, 1072a 20—1073b 1).
⁴Potius cf. **Aristot.**, *Eth. Nic.* X c. 7 (AL XXVI³ 358-359, K c. 7 1177a 12-13, 16-17); *Auctoritates Aristotelis* (ed. J. Hamesse 247): "Ultima felicitas hominis consistit in optima operatione."
⁵**Thomas**, *Summa theol.* I q. 85 art. 1 in corp. (V 330b—331a): "Respondeo dicendum quod ... obiectum cognoscibile proportionatur virtuti cognoscitivae. Est autem triplex gradus cognoscitivae virtutis. Quaedam enim cognoscitiva virtus est actus organi corporalis, scilicet sensus. Et ideo obiectum cuiuslibet sensitivae potentiae est forma prout in materia corporali exsistit. Et quia huiusmodi materia est individuationis principium, ideo omnis potentia sensitivae partis est cognoscitiva particularium tantum. Quaedam autem virtus cognoscitiva est quae neque est actus organi corporalis, neque est aliquo modo corporali materiae coniuncta, sicut intellectus angelicus. Et ideo huius virtutis cognoscitivae obiectum est forma sine materia subsistens. Etsi enim materialia cognoscant, non tamen nisi in immaterialibus ea intuentur, scilicet vel in seipsis vel in Deo. Intellectus autem humanus medio modo se habet; non enim est actus alicuius organi, sed tamen est quaedam virtus animae, quae est forma corporis ... Et ideo proprium eius est cognoscere formam in materia quidem corporali individualiter exsistentem, non tamen prout est in tali materia. Cognoscere vero id quod est in materia individuali, non prout est in tali materia, est abstrahere formam a materia individuali quam repraesentant phantasmata. Et ideo necesse est dicere quod intellectus noster intelligit materialia abstrahendo a phantasmatibus; et per materialia sic considerata in immaterialium aliqualem cognitionem devenimus, sicut e contra angeli per immaterialia materialia cognoscunt." Cf. **Rogerus Marston**, *Quaest. disp. de anima* q. 2 (BFS VII 231-232) ubi idem textus Sancti Thomae allegatur ad quaestionem utrum obiectum intellectus humani sit quiditas materialis disceptandam.

Obiectum proportionatur potentiae cognitivae. Modo ita est quod quaedam potentia cognitiva est organica, et ideo eius obiectum est materiale, et quia materia est principium individuationis secundum EOS, ideo earum obiectum est signatum; alia autem potentia est omnino immaterialis et secundum esse et secundum operationem, sicut intellectus angeli, et ideo primum eius obiectum est quiditas omnino immaterialis; alia est potentia cognitiva, quae est quidem secundum esse in materia, sed secundum operationem non, sicut intellectus humanus qui secundum esse corpus informat, non tamen utitur organo in sua operatione, et ideo obiectum eius proprium est quiditas exsistens in materia secundum esse, quam tamen non intelligit ut in materia, sed ut abstractam secundum rationem ab ea.

[B. — Obiectiones contra opinionem Thomae et responsiones pro ea]

Sed contra conclusionem[6] qua dicitur quod sola quiditas materialis est obiectum intellectus nostri, arguitur sic:

Nulla potentia eadem manens habet actum circa aliquid quod non sit eius obiectum vel sub obiecto eius contentum; sed intellectus beatus et viatoris est eadem potentia; tamen intellectus beatus intelligit divinam essentiam; igitur Deus saltem continetur sub obiecto intellectus viatoris, non autem sub quiditate materiali; igitur, etc.

---

1 proportionatur] debet esse proportionatum KU | cognitivae] organicae X   2 quod] quam X | ideo om. H   3 et om. X | principium] mg. Z² 4 ideo] ita K in U | earum] eorum L FW | obiectum] oppositum O | signatum] singulare N | autem om. H X   5 potentia est inv. H K X | omnino immaterialis] inv. KU immutabilis omnino N | et] vel U | et² om. O   6 primum eius obiectum] verum eius obiectum H eius primum obiectum L   7 omnino immaterialis] inv. KU | alia] praem. sed KU | cognitiva] cognoscitiva W om. L   8 quidem secundum esse] = HM Q secundum esse NO L FW quodammodo secundum esse KU quaedam sensus est X secundum esse quidem Z | sed] et L | secundum²] per K   9 sicut] sic X | qui] quae O add. est X | informat] actum N   10 tamen om. N | ideo om. K | obiectum] add. est O | obiectum — esse] quiditas exsistens in materia secundum esse est proprium eius obiectum Z | eius proprium] inv. NO eius proprie L   11 exsistens post materia KU | in materia om. L | secundum — materia om. N | esse om. KU   12 tamen om. FW Z | intelligit] intellexit O | sed] igitur L | abstractam] = L KU FW abstracta NO X Z abstractum HM abstractiva Q   16 conclusionem] positionem NO consequentiam FW X Z rationem Q | qua] quia Z | dicitur] dicit O   17 intellectus nostri] inv. Z   18 aliquid] aliquod N   19 sit] est HL | obiectum] oppositum O | eius om. FW   20 beatus] beati N M | et — beatus²] mg. Z² | viatoris] viator O FW | est] possunt esse (mg.) F² in W | tamen] cum N L KU | intellectus² om. NO   21 intelligit] intellexit NO iam Z | divinam om. Z | Deus saltem] inv. M   22 intellectus] vite cum O om. FW | igitur etc. om. X

[6]Cf. supra n. 5.

7 Sed dices⁷ quod⁸ intelligit divinam essentiam per lumen gloriae quod non est in via; igitur, etc. [3]

8 Sed quod non valet, probo:

Quia obiectum primum alicuius habitus exsistentis in aliqua potentia non excedit potentiam illam — quia si excederet potentiam, habitus eius cognoscitivus excederet etiam potentiam illam et eam informare non posset; sed quiditas Dei et substantiarum separatarum est obiectum luminis gloriae informantis intellectum; per te, igitur, Deus non excedit potentiam intellectivam nostram.

9 Item, omnis habitus exsistens in intellectu praesupponit eius obiectum; igitur lumen illud, cum sit in intellectu nostro respectu Dei, praesupponit quod Deus sit eius obiectum.

10 Item, anima naturaliter desiderat, cognito effectu, cognoscere causam; sed omnia alia ab ipso sunt effectus Dei; igitur ad ipsum cognoscendum habemus naturale desiderium; sed naturale desiderium non est ad impossibile; igitur Deus etiam naturaliter potest aliqualiter a nobis cognosci.

11 Sed diceret DOCTOR ille⁹ quod potest cognosci ab intellectu separato, non tamen a coniuncto corpori.

12 Sed hoc non valet secundum positionem suam, nam via sua procedit de intellectu nostro secundum naturam suam vel naturalem modum eius essendi, sicut procedit de naturali modo essendi et

---

1 quod *om.* X *add.* intellectus H *add.* intellectus beatus KU FW Q X Z | intelligit] intellexit NO | divinam essentiam] *inv.* FW | per lumen] in lumine KU FW Q X Z   2 igitur etc.] igitur L ergo etc. W ideo etc. Q *om.* NO X   3 quod] hoc NO | valet] valeat Q | probo] probatur KU   4 Quia *om.* L KU | primum *om.* X | aliqua] alia N   5 potentia] materia Z | non *om.* NO | illam] istam X | excederet] excedat H excedit LM Z   6 cognoscitivus] cognitivus L F | excederet] excederetur N excedere O | etiam] in NO *om.* KU | illam *om.* FW Q X Z | eam] eum HLM *om.* X   8 est obiectum] est oppositum O *om.* N | luminis] lumine U   9 igitur] ergo W Q X   10 habitus] actus N | exsistens *om.* Z | intellectu] actu NO *add.* nostro FW | praesupponit — intellectu *om.* X | eius] idem F illud W   11 obiectum] oppositum O | illud *om.* H | cum sit *post* nostro KU | sit *om.* F | in] *lin.* F²   12 Dei] rei N | praesupponit] supponit Z | obiectum] oppositum O   13 Item] Praeterea NO KU FW Q X Z | anima *om.* N   14 sed *om.* Q | ipso] ipsa N illo FW   15 cognoscendum] *mg.* F² cognitum W X | habemus] habuit FW X Z | naturale — sed *om.* X | sed — desiderium] *mg.* Z²   16 etiam *om.* N L | naturaliter — cognosci] = H KU naturaliter aliqualiter potest (posset N) a nobis cognosci NO Q X Z potest naturaliter aliqualiter cognosci a nobis L naturaliter aliqualiter a nobis potest cognosci M naturaliter aliqualiter potest cognosci FW   18 ille] iste L K | potest] posset N L KU |· cognosci] intelligere U   19 separato *om.* Z | a *om.* NO L F Q | coniuncto corpori] *inv.* Q coniuncto corpore X   20 hoc] haec N *om.* X | valet] *add.* quia Q | secundum — nostro *om.* X | positionem] potentiam(?) O FW Z | suam] finitam FW | via sua] *inv.* Q   21 de] ab N | nostro] non K | naturam] speciem X | suam *om.* N H   22 modum eius] *inv.* HLM U Q

---

⁷Cf. **Thomas**, *Summa theol.* I q. 12 a. 5 in corp. (IV 123*a*-*b*).
⁸Subaudi: intellectus beatus.
⁹Cf. **Thomas**, *Summa theol.* I q. 89 art. 1-2 in corp. (V 370*a*—375*b*).

cognoscendi angeli et potentiae sensitivae. Modo ita est quod non est natus ita semper esse separatus, sed naturaliter appetit corpori uniri; igitur, secundum IPSUM, naturale obiectum eius, in quocumque statu sit, erit quiditas materiae coniuncta secundum esse, licet sit separabilis secundum rationem — quod est improbatum.

[4] Item, intellectus noster etiam in via potest cognoscere ens sub ratione entis, quae est universalior quam ratio quiditatis sensibilis; igitur quiditas sensibilis non est obiectum adaequatum intellectus nostri. Antecedens patet, quia aliqua scientia humana est de ente secundum quod ens. Probatio consequentiae: quia nulla potentia potest cognoscere aliquid universalius obiecto sibi adaequato; tunc enim obiectum non esset sibi adaequatum. Exemplum de visu, qui non potest cognoscere aliquid universalius colore vel luce.

Sed adhuc diceret THOMAS[10] quod Deum non cognoscimus nisi discurrendo a notitia sensibilium ad ipsum et per sensibilia tantum.

Sed tunc quaero ab eo utrum in fine huius discursus intelligimus Deum secundum conceptum proprium vel in conceptu alicuius creati tantum. Si primo modo, habetur propositum; si secundo modo tantum, non quietatur appetitus naturae nec per consequens cessat, sed ulterius procedit usque ad cognitionem Dei vel procedit in infinitum — quod non est dicendum. Nec valet ratio sua[11] de

---

1 et] vel N | sensitivae] sensationis O   2 ita *om.* KU FW Q X | ita — separatus] esse separatus (*lin.*) Z² | separatus] paratus N | naturaliter appetit] *inv.* L naturaliter ei competit Q   3 obiectum] oppositum O | eius] illius NO *add.* scilicet H   4 statu sit] *inv.* N | materiae] materialis L   5 separabilis] spiritualis N | secundum rationem] ratione U FW Q X Z *om.* K | quod] *add.* non X   6 Item] Praeterea NO KU Q X Z | etiam *om.* N H | ens] *add.* in quantum ens et L   7 quae] quod N Z | est] *add.* ratio L | universalior] universalius N   8 sensibilis *om.* Q X   9 Antecedens] Consequens(!) FW | quia] quod X | aliqua] alia N | scientia] sua O | humana] humano (*post* ente) H | est] ant. aliqua HLM X   10 quod] *add.* est N HL   11 potest cognoscere] *inv.* NO | aliquid] aliquod NO | obiecto — adaequatum] quam obiectum sibi adequatum FW | sibi] suo N   12 obiectum *om.* Z   13 aliquid *om.* NO Q X Z | universalius] a K *om.* U | vel] universalius O et L   14 adhuc] ad hoc Q | diceret] *add.* Sanctus K | Thomas] = KU FW X Z taliter NO HM talis L opinans Q | quod] quia O   15 a *om.* W | notitia] natura L | tantum] tamen O   16 tunc *om.* NO | huius] illius FW huiusmodi Q | huius discursus] *inv.* KU huius discursivus O | intelligimus] cognoscimus L intellectus intelligit K intellectus U intelligamus FW   17 Deum] eum N enim O | secundum] per L | conceptum proprium] *inv.* HL | in conceptu] in convenienti(!) N secundum conceptum Z | alicuius] alicis O *om.* N   19 modo *om.* H | tantum *om.* Z | appetitus] appetibile O | naturae] *add.* et O | nec] et L   20 cessat] cessabit HM nec cessabit L | sed] quod U | procedit — vel *om.* X | usque] vel KU | cognitionem] conceptum KU FW | procedit²] procedet L   21 sua *om.* NO

[10] **Thomas**, *Summa theol.* I q. 85 art. 1 in corp. (V 331*a*): "Et ideo necesse est dicere quod intellectus noster intelligit materialia abstrahendo a phantasmatibus; et per materialia sic considerata in immaterialium aliqualem cognitionem devenimus …"; cf. q. 84 art. 7 ad 3 (V 326*a-b*).
[11] Cf. supra n. 5.

proportione illa; immo sequitur magis oppositum, scilicet si est proportio inter potentiam et obiectum, quod non sint similia in natura, quia materia et forma sunt sibi invicem proportionata et tamen sunt maxime ab invicem disparata. Proportio autem potentiae ad obiectum, etiam secundum ISTOS, est sicut motivi ad mobile. Illa autem sunt dissimilia, immo quoad hoc opposita.

16 Sed DICES quod potentia activa assimilatur obiecto, licet non passiva activae.

17 Hoc non valet, quia differt assimilari in modo essendi et quantum ad actum intelligendi. Non enim oportet quod intellectus sit similis in natura vel quantum ad modum essendi obiecto, sed sufficit quantum ad actum intelligendi, ut scilicet similitudinem, scilicet speciem obiecti recipiat vel actum ipsum. Exemplum de visu, qui licet sit potentia materialis, non tamen recipit species cum materia; ideo multo minus recipit speciem vel immutatur ab obiecto etiamsecundum modum essendi eius. Sicut igitur non est alius visus qui videt coelum et inferiora, quae tamen differunt secundum corruptibile et incorruptibile, sic idem intellectus potest multo fortius intelligere sensibile et non-sensibile.

[II. — Solutio quaestionis]

18 Dicendum igitur ad quaestionem quod via generationis vel acquirendo scientiam prius apprehendimus quiditates sensibilium,

[5]

---

1 illa] ista X | immo sequitur] inv. O semper immo N enim sequitur U | sequitur magis] inv. H K Z sequeretur magis FW | oppositum] obiectum O U | scilicet *om.* U | est] sit (*post mg.*) proportio F²) HLM F² 2 proportio] proportionem X | obiectum] causam NO | quod] quae N | sint] sunt N KU sit Z 3 quia] quod X | sunt *post* invicem FW Q X 4 tamen *om.* Z | ab] ad NO | potentiae ad obiectum] inter potentiam et obiectum L 5 *om.* O | etiam] et X *om.* NO | istos] illos HLM F | motivi ad] motio ad N inter motum (motivum M) et HLM motus ad X 6 Illa] Ista L KU W Alia X Ita Z | sunt dissimilia] inv. Z | immo *om.* NO | hoc] haec N | opposita] potentia N opponitur Z 7 Sed] Si U | dices] dicit NO diceres K Q dicens U diceret FW Z | quod *om.* Z | assimilatur] similatur N | obiecto] oppositum O *om.* KU 8 passiva] potentia N | activae] actio U activo FW X Z *om.* K 9 Hoc] Haec U | valet] videtur Q | differt] dicitur O deberet F | assimilari *om.* KU | et] etiam FW 10 Non] Et X | intellectus *om.* KU 11 ad modum] in (*om.* O) omni modo NO | obiecto] obiective N 12 quantum *om.* Z | intelligendi] *add. seu rep.* non tantum (enim FW *om.* K) oportet quod intellectus noster (*om.* FW) KU FW *add.* ult. sit similis FW | ut *om.* KU | ut scilicet] *lin.* N | scilicet] *mg.* Z² *om.* L KU X | similitudinem scilicet speciem] speciem vel similitudinem N similem scilicet speciem HL 13 obiecti] *add.* realis HLM | ipsum] illum HLM *add.* (*mg.*) secundum modum essendi F² 14 qui] quod H | species] speciem Q *om.* KU 15 ideo] *lin.* H immo N | minus] minori N | obiecto] opposito O | obiecto] = etiam LM et NO *om.* H KU FW Q X Z | eius *om.* KU FW Z | igitur *om.* KU 17 quae *om.* FW | tamen] tantum O L | differunt] dicunt O | secundum] sicut L K X sed U 18 et incorruptibile] *mg.* Z² | sic] *sic* O X | sic — non-sensibile *om.* KU | idem intellectus] inv. O M KU W Q X Z intellectus F | potest *post* fortius L KU Z 19 fortius] *add.* recipere et Q | et non-sensibile] *mg.* F²W² Z² et insensibile NO 21 Dicendum] *add.* est O M KU FW | quod] *add.* in HLM X 22 prius] *add.* acquirimus seu X | quiditates] *add.* sensibiles X

quia pro statu naturae lapsae nihil intelligimus nisi cum ministerio sensibilium; tamen illa non sunt proprium et adaequatum obiectum intellectus nostri, sed etiam possumus intelligere substantias separatas. Et tale obiectum est prius via perfectionis et simpliciter, quia per talem cognitionem attingitur obiectum perfectissimum quod est Deus et substantiae separatae aliae, etiam pro statu viae; et licet talis cognitio sit aenigmatica, tamen perfectior est omni alia cognitione nostra respectu inferioris creaturae.

Sed contra:

Aut cognoscimus Deum distincte aut confuse, scilicet in communi conceptu entis. Si primo modo, tunc essemus beati in via, quia talis cognitio debetur beatis. Si secundo modo, tunc cognitio eius est imperfectior cognitione cuiuscumque creaturae distincte cognitae.

Dicendum quod aliquid potest cognosci quadrupliciter:

Uno modo per comparationem ad aliud, ut cognoscitur hominem esse perfectissimum animalium; talem autem cognitionem necessario praecedit alia absoluta.

Secundo modo potest aliquid cognosci per accidens suum, ut homo per risibile; et haec non potest esse prima, quia necessarium est, si cognoscam dispositionem, quod cognoscam subiectum sibi substratum, saltem confuse.

Tertio modo potest aliquid cognosci per conceptum

communem sibi et aliis, ut cognosco hominem per animal. Et sic cognoscere Deum est imperfecte cognoscere, scilicet per conceptum communem sibi et aliis; hoc enim imperfectius est quam cognoscere lapidem distincte, quia per illum conceptum communem non magis cognoscitur Deus quam aliud, et ideo non sortitur nobilitatem ex Deo talis cognitio.

23 Quarto modo cognoscitur aliquid conceptu quiditativo, sed ille est duplex: unus est primo primus, qui scilicet non est in alios conceptus resolubilis, quo scilicet res cognoscitur intuitive in se ut est talis natura, et talem conceptum non possumus habere de Deo in via, immo nec de anima nostra nec de aliqua spirituali substantia. Cuius ratio est, quia de Deo nullam habemus cognitionem naturaliter nisi per creaturas; nulla autem creatura, nec etiam omnes simul, possunt sufficenter divinam essentiam repraesentare quiditative, id est, ut natura haec vel essentia.

24 Alius autem conceptus quiditativus rei nec est omnino simplex nec primus, sed resolubilis in alios, ut est definitio rei composita ex diversis conceptibus. Talem autem conceptum possumus habere naturaliter de anima nostra, scilicet considerando quod entium quaedam sunt entia in potentia, quaedam in actu; et illud ens actu habet duas partes integrales, quarum una est actus, et sic apprehendimus quod est actus. Ulterius procedimus, dividendo, quod

---

23 communem — aliis] sui superioris N   1 et] in O | cognosco] cognoscendo KU | hominem] homo O | Et *om.* K   2 est] esse est N esse O *add.* ipsum O FW Q X Z   3 imperfectius est] *inv.* U est imperfectior K   4 lapidem] *add.* et FW | illum] istum LM X ipsum Z   5 Deus *om.* H | aliud] alia L   6 talis cognitio] *ant.* non L   7 modo] = L KU F *om.* NO HM W Q X Z | sed] si O | ille] iste U F   8 est duplex] *inv.* Q | est²] autem KU | primo *om.* FW | primus] *mg.* Z² | qui scilicet] = O FW Q X qui N K Z quia H quia scilicet M scilicet quia L qui et quia id est U | alios] alius O | conceptus] consequens N *om.* L Q   9 resolubilis] resolvere U | quo scilicet] quas N quo X | in se] naturarum(!) F   10 natura] vera F *om.* Q | habere *post* via X   11 nec] *mg.* M | Cuius — est *om.* X   12 quia] qui O | cognitionem] cognoscibilitatem L | naturaliter *om.* NO | nisi] *lin.* K²   13 creaturas — essentiam] effectum non est eius causa nec etiam ens potest simul esse naturam divinam sufficienter N | autem] enim L | creatura] creatur H | etiam] = NO M KU X *om.* HL FW Q Z | omnes] deus O | possunt] *add.* simul O M *om.* L   14 sufficenter] sufficere HM sufficierent L *om.* U | divinam essentiam] *inv.* U | essentiam] *add.* cognoscere vel F | repraesentare] *add.* sufficienter et HLM | quiditative] *add. seu adnot.* vel quietative L   15 natura haec vel] vera (vere Q) haec KU FW Q X Z | essentia] *add.* haec etc. N *add.* est O² KU FW Q X Z   16 autem *om.* L *add.* est HLM K | conceptus] compositus O | quiditativus] *mg.* Z² | nec] non NO ut Q | omnino] materiae N modo O | simplex] simpliciter FW supra(?) Q   17 nec] ut FW X Z *om.* Q | primus] prius U | sed] *add.* compositus et FW X Z | in alios *om.* FW | est *om.* N | composita] concepta U compositae X Z | ex] *add.* a O   18 Talem autem] Et talem K | habere naturaliter] *inv.* L FW habere de Deo in via N habere U Q   19 de] et (*lin.*) N | scilicet considerando] *inv.* N sic resolvendum K considerando Q Z *add. seu rep.* scilicet O   20 quaedam] quae N | entia] in natura et NO *om.* K FW X | in potentia] imposita N | potentia ... actu] a. ... p. K | in² *om.* O Z | et illud] et idem(?) N H et illus(!) O *om.* K | ens] *add.* in H   21 apprehendimus] habemus K *add.* prima X   22 quod] quid N KU FW Q X Z | actus — est² *om.* X | Ulterius] Ultimus et F | procedimus] procedamus K | quod²] quia HM

actuum quidam primus, quidam secundus, et sic apprehendimus postea quod est actus primus. Postea dividimus illa quae actuantur, et sic, illa componendo ad invicem, tandem deveniemus ad hoc quod illud est corpus organicum physicum quod ab anima actuatur.
5 Et sic, illa componendo ad invicem, habemus conceptum quiditativum animae nostrae. Hic autem conceptus est animae proprius ita quod nulli alii substantiae spirituali convenit, sed per hoc non cognosco animam meam vel in se intuitive et in speciali ut haec anima est, sicut nec illud quod numquam vidi.

10 Exemplum ponitur ad hoc: ponamus quod nunquam viderim triangulum — viderim autem tetragonum et pentagonum etc. —, tunc possum abstrahere ab omnibus huiusmodi quod est figura; deinde possum scire quod non est processus in infinitum in descendendo, sicut nec in numeris, ex quo possum scire quod oportet dare aliquam primam. Ulterius dividendo figuram in circularem et rectilinearem, et componendo rectilinearem cum figura prima, intelligo quiditatem trianguli, quae convenit triangulo soli ita quod non alii; non tamen per hunc conceptum compositum possum intelligere triangulum, ut triangulus est, sub propria forma per se et
20 intuitive.

Similiter a pluribus entibus possumus abstrahere hoc quod est

---

1 quidam] *add.* est HL | primus quidam *om.* U | et sic] nec H sic Q et sicut Z   2 postea *om.* N | quod] quid U Q qui Z | quod — postea *om.* O FW | actus primus] *inv.* M Z prius actus U | dividimus] dicimus F | illa] ea N H FW ista X | actuantur] dividuantur U aduantur(!) Q   3 illa — sic *om.* FW | deveniemus] devenimus M U Q deveniremus X Z | hoc] idem H   4 illud] ideo U *om.* H | est] sit K | quod²] et H   5 illa componendo] *inv.* N ista componendo ista K componendo H X | habemus *om.* H   6 animae nostrae] de anima nostra FW | Hic] Hoc N | conceptus est] *inv.* NO | animae proprius] animae nostrae proprius HL F | ita] sic K *om.* X   7 nulli] nullius X | substantiae spirituali] *inv.* L U FW Q X Z | convenit *om.* X   8 cognosco] cognoscimus K cognoscendo U | animam *om.* N | meam] naturaliter Z *om.* NO FW | vel *post* se N ut M *om.* HL Z *add.* illam K *add.* tuam U *add.* etiam X | intuitive] motive N movitive(!) O | et] vel N FW sed H | in speciali] spiritualiter FW spirituali X | ut] et X   9 est *om.* Z | nec] hoc FW homo Q X Z | illud] id N *om.* X | vidi] vidit H KU Z   10 ad] in HLM de FW | ponamus] ponitur N | quod] ut N *om.* X | nunquam *om.* N X   11 triangulum] *add.* tamen ergo quod K | autem tetragonum] *inv.* H enim tetragonum NO tetragonum K autem tetrangulum F tamen tetragonum Z *add.* et caetera N *add. (mg.)* ponit in conclusionem Z² | et pentagonum *om.* Z | etc.] et HLM *add.* id est Z² | tunc] sic L   12 possum] possumus L KU possimus Z | abstrahere *om.* H | ab omnibus huiusmodi] = HLM ab omnibus NO huiusmodi figuras KU ab omnibus figuris FW Q X Z | quod] hoc quod O FW Q X Z quod hoc K quod haec U | est *om.* U   13 est *om.* X | in² *om.* NO L X *add.* figuris FW Q Z   14 nec *om.* K Q | aliquam] aliam O K   15 primam] partem NO primum KU potentiam F | in — figura *om.* X | circularem et *om.* KU | et rectilinearem] et rectilineam N Q Z et rectam H *om.* Z   16 et — rectilinearem *om.* NO Z | componendo] ponendo HL | rectilinearem²] rectilineam Q | cum] in NO | prima] primam X *om.* KU   17 intelligo] intelligendo M KU Z | quiditatem] naturam L | trianguli] *add.* sive quiditatem L *add.* id est KU FW Z *add.* et Q | quae] qui H *add.* non X | convenit] continet O | soli] solum FW   18 alii] aliis NO | possum] possumus H   19 propria forma] *inv.* H ipsa forma Z | per se *om.* N L X | et *om.* NO X   21 a] in H | possumus] possum L KU X *add.* intelligere O | abstrahere *post* absolute NO Q | quod est] commune K

ens absolute; et a pluribus bonis, ipsum bonum. Et quia entia et bona sunt ordinata, tandem possumus devenire ad hoc quod intelligam summum bonum, quia non est in eis processus in infinitum. Sic ergo possum illa ad invicem componere per intellectum et dicere aliquod ens esse summum bonum, qui conceptus sic compositus soli Deo convenit. Et ideo de Deo possumus naturaliter habere conceptum quiditativum, compositum tamen; sed per talem conceptum non cognoscimus eum in se, ut est talis naturae determinatae, tamen sic eum cognoscere perfectius est simpliciter quam cognoscere quodcumque aliud a Deo, ut dictum est supra.[12] Sic igitur patet quod obiectum adaequatum intellectui nostro non est quiditas materialis, quia Deum et substantias spirituales aliqualiter cognoscere possumus, ut dictum est.

[III. — Ad rationes principales]

27 Ad rationes in oppositum:

Ad primam dicendum[13] quod maior est vera quantum ad primam receptionem potentiae passivae et primam operationem activae; potentia tamen passiva informata prima receptione potest in plura quam activa potuit in prima operatione. Supposito igitur quod intellectus agens sit aliquid animae, non est omnino adaequatus possibili, sed tantum quantum possibilis est, scilicet

---

1 et] *lin.* M | bonis] *add.* et X | Et quia entia *om.* U | entia] *mg.* Z² 2 sunt ordinata] ordinantur N | tandem] eadem X *om.* N | possumus] possum NO U FW Q Z | devenire — intelligam] intelligere K | intelligam] possum intelligere X 3 bonum *om.* O Q Z | quia — bonum *om.* N | quia] quod Z | in eis *om.* KU | infinitum] eis O *add.* mensuram(?) O 4 Sic] Aut(?) O | ergo] igitur H U Z autem X | possum] possumus HL | illa] ista O L KU Z *om.* Q | ad invicem *post* componere FW | dicere] dico O 5 aliquod ens esse] = HM W esse aliquod ens O Q aliquod ens est L esse ens K esse U aliquod esse ens esse F aliquod esse ens X Z | summum] summe L X | bonum] *add.* per intellectum L | qui] quia HLM quae O X | conceptus] *mg.* F² | compositus] *add.* conceptus X | soli] solius O 6 Deo²] eo HM | naturaliter habere] *inv.* K X naturaliter U 7 tamen sed] tamen N Z tamen si O cum H sed K | per] *add.* illum F | conceptum²] compositionem O 8 cognoscimus] possumus cognoscere U | in se *om.* Q | est talis] *inv.* N | naturae] nec NO | determinatae] determin*ante* L 9 tamen] cum H et non Z *om.* NO | cognoscere] *add.* componendo U FW Q X Z | perfectius est] *inv.* N HL 10 quodcumque] quodque O | dictum est] *inv.* H | supra *om.* HLM | Sic — est² *om.* Z 11 nostro] modo NO 12 spirituales] separatas et (*om.* Q) spirituales HLM Q | aliqualiter cognoscere possumus] = NO KU possumus aliquo modo intelligere (cognoscere H) HLM aliqualiter intelligere possumus FW Q X aliqualiter cognoscimus Z 13 ut dictum est *om.* FW 15 in oppositum] in obiectum O in contrarium X *om.* H 16 Ad primam *post* dicendum L Ad primum NO *om.* H | dicendum] *add.* est HLM F | maior] minor O | quantum] quod Z 17 operationem] *add.* per U 18 tamen] autem K | potest] ponit U 19 quam] qua W | activa potuit in prima] = KU Q X Z activa ponit in prima NO activa potentia in secunda HLM potentia activa in prima FW | igitur] ergo Q W X 20 sit] est M | aliquid] *mg.* Z² | animae] *add.* nostrae L K 21 possibili] potentiali F | sed *om.* N | possibilis] potentialis F | est *om.* U | scilicet] sed N

[12]Cf. supra n. 18.
[13]Cf. supra n. 1.

quantum ad primam operationem eius, quae est abstrahere a sensibilibus phantasmatibus speciem, quam intellectus possibilis recipit; sed postquam est factus in actu per speciem, tunc potest abstrahere conceptus et intentiones et ad invicem copulare modo praedicto,[14] usquequo habeat conceptum proprium Dei vel spiritualium substantiarum. — Vel dicendum ad minorem quod, licet Deus non habeat phantasma, tamen ad hoc quod Deum intelligamus, oportet quod phantasia formet sibi aliquod idolum, et ab hoc intellectus agens abstrahit aliquo modo et alii componit, modo praedicto.[15]

Ad aliud[16] dicendum quod eadem difficultas videtur esse de actu diligendi sicut de actu cognoscendi. Si enim est actus eiusdem speciei in via et in patria, viator habens caritatem esset beatus, licet non aequaliter sicut comprehensor. Ideo videtur quod nec actus cognoscendi nec diligendi sunt eiusdem speciei in viatore et comprehensore; quia, dato quod sit idem obiectum, eadem potentia et idem habitus — quia caritas numquam excidit —, quia tamen alia est approximatio obiecti ad potentiam hic et ibi, et lumen aliud et repraesentativum, ideo possunt differre specie. Exemplum de igne calefaciente tantum lignum a longe, igniente tamen ipsum de prope, qui actus differunt specie et genere.

---

1 quantum] quam O | operationem eius] inv. HLM operationem NO | a — conceptus] conceptum (mg.) Z² 2 sensibilibus phantasmatibus] inv. N sensibus phantasmatibus F sensibilibus a phantasmatibus X | intellectus] speciem NO M FW Q X Z add. (mg.) intellectus F 3 est factus] inv. HLM factus N | in actu post speciem Q 4 conceptus et] alias N alius et O | et² om. NO Z | copulari] copulari O 5 usquequo] usque N M W quousque L | usquequo — praedicto om. X | proprium] add. ipsius L | vel] et H ut O 6 Vel] Et N | dicendum] add. est M KU F | Deus om. H 7 habeat] habet K | tamen] cum U | Deum om. N | intelligamus] intelligimus Q Z 8 phantasia] = FW Q Z phantasma NO HLM KU | formet sibi] inv. L faciat sibi N formaret sibi KU | ab hoc] ad hoc L om. F 9 abstrahit] abstrahat N add. de obiecto U add. ab eo FW add. ab Z | modo om. Z | alii] aliis NO Z 10 praedicto] add. scilicet componendo L 11 dicendum] add. est M F | videtur esse] videtur O Q X Z est L dicitur FW om. N 12 diligendi] = (mg. F²) M F² Q X Z intelligendi NO HL KU W | Si] Verus N Vi(!) O | enim] illi KU | est om. HM | est actus] actus esset L actus essent KU 13 in] et X | caritatem] talitatem NO | licet] mg. Z² 14 aequaliter] essentialiter L KU | sicut] sic Q | nec] ant. videtur Q | actus om. X 15 cognoscendi ... diligendi] diligendi ... cognoscendi X | diligendi] intelligendi U deliberandi Z | sunt] sint FW Q Z | et] add. in U 16 quia om. Q | sit] si U | obiectum] subiectum FW add. (lin. F²) et F² Z 17 idem habitus] inv. O W Q X Z habitus N | caritas] habitus correspondens N | excidit] extendit NO excedit U | quia² om. FW | alia est] inv. NO 18 approximatio] add. subiecti(?) Q | obiecti ad potentiam om. KU | ad] per H | et² om. Q | aliud] ad N | et³ om. NO 19 repraesentativum] repraesentatum N F Z add. et X | specie om. K 20 calefaciente tantum lignum] = O LM Q Z tantum lignum calefaciente H tantum calefaciente lignum N calefaciente lignum(mg. F² om. W) KU FW X | a] de N | ipsum] illum Q | de] sic N a Q 21 qui] quia NO F | specie et genere] genere et specie L specie igitur etc. NO add. et caetera K

[14]Cf. supra n. 24
[15]Cf. supra n. 24.
[16]Cf. supra n. 2.

[IV. — Obiectiones earumque redargutiones]

29 Sed contra dicta[17] potest sic argui:

Secundum PHILOSOPHUM[18] sic se habent phantasmata ad intellectum, ut sensibilia ad sensum; sed non sentimus nec possumus sentire nisi quod est sensibile; igitur nec intelligere nisi quod est phantasiabile et ideo quia speculamur intelligibilia in phantasmatibus, ut dicitur III *De anima*.[19]

30 Dicendum quod pro tanto est simile: quia nos non possumus sentire nisi ad praesentiam sensibilis, sic nec intelligere communiter nisi phantasma sit in actu suo; tamen phantasma non est obiectum intellectus sicut sensibile sensus.

31 Item, contra principale:[20] 'sicut oculi noctuae se habent ad lucem diei, sic animae nostrae intellectus ad manifestissima naturae';[21] sed oculus noctuae non potest videre solem; igitur nec intellectus noster intelligere substantias separatas.

32 Dicendum est quod verum est intuitive pro statu viae, tamen potest hoc abstractive et compositive, ut dictum est;[22] sicut noctua potest videre lucem diei, obscuratam tamen.

---

2 potest *om.* N | sic argui] *inv.* O arguitur sic N   3 sic ... ut] sicut ... sic X | habent] habet L | phantasmata] phantasma L | ad *om.* O   4 ut] sicut L KU Z | non] nec X | sentimus nec *om.* NO   5 est sensibile] *inv.* Q | igitur] ergo W Q X | nec] non FW *add.* intelligimus nec possumus FW | est²] *add.* in O   6 ideo quia] iterum quia NO iterum quod FW Q X quod KU iterum Z | intelligibilia *om.* K   7 dicitur] *add.* in N M | III] I O | anima] *add.* et caetera L   8 Dicendum] Igitur idem N *add.* est M F | quia] quod N *add.* sicut U FW Q X Z | nos *om.* H K X   9 sentire] sensus(?) X | ad] in L *om.* N | praesentiam] praesentia L | sic] sicut KU | communiter *om.* L   10 sit] fuerit M | suo *om.* NO   11 sicut] *mg.* Z²   12 Item *om.* NO | principale] *add.* sic HL KU | se habent] *ant.* oculi KU *post* solis Q   13 lucem] lumina H lumen L KU | diei] sol(!) L solis Q | sic] sicut O | nostrae *om.* N F | intellectus] *ant.* animae L *om.* X | manifestissima] maxima NO *add.* et X   14 videre solem] *inv.* NO | igitur] ergo W Q X   15 intelligere *post* separatas NO videre U *om.* HM Q X Z   16 est *om.* O L W Q X Z | intuitive *om.* X | statu] *add.* illo F Q *add.* isto W | viae *om.* Q   17 potest] praeter(!) F | abstractive] *add.* pro statu viae N | compositive] composita est U *add.* scilicet H | noctua *om.* NO   18 lucem] lumen NO U solem L | diei] Dei N licet L solis Q | obscuratam] obscuratum NO FW obscure L ab scuratum(!) U obscuram Z | tamen] tantum X Z *om.* N L Q *add.* ergo et caetera H *add.* igitur et caetera K *add.* etc. U

---

[17] Cf. supra n. 27.
[18] **Aristot.**, *De an.* III c. 1 (Γ c. 4, 429a 16-18); *Auctoritates Aristotelis* (ed. J. Hamesse 185): "Sicut se habet sensus ad sensibilia, sic se habet intellectus ad intelligibilia."
[19] **Aristot.**, *De an.* III c. 7 (Γ c. 8, 432a 3-9): 'Quoniam autem neque res nulla est praeter magnitudinem, sicut videntur sensibilia separata, in speciebus sensibilibus intelligibilia sunt, et quae abstractione dicuntur et quaecumque sensibilium habitus et passiones. Et ab hoc neque non sentiens nihil, nihil utique addiscet neque intelliget, sed cum speculetur, necesse simul phantasma aliquod speculari; phantasmata autem sicut sensibilia sint praeter quod sunt sine materia'; *Auctoritates Aristotelis* (ed. J. Hamesse 188): 'Necesse est quemcumque intelligentem phantasmata speculari.'
[20] Cf. supra n. 18.
[21] Cf. supra n. 2.
[22] Cf. supra n. 25-26.

[QUAESTIO 20]

UTRUM VERUM VEL ENS SUB RATIONE VERI SIT OBIECTUM PRIMUM INTELLECTUS

Utrum verum vel ens sub ratione veri tantum sit obiectum primum intellectus.

[1] Videtur quod sic:

Quia potentiae distinctae habent distincta obiecta; intellectus et voluntas sunt potentiae distinctae, ens autem inquantum ens est indistinctum; igitur non potest esse ut sic utriusque obiectum, sed per hoc quod distinguitur in ratione veri et boni.

Item, obiectum appropriari debet potentiae; sed ens inquantum ens est commune ad ens sensibile et intelligibile; igitur si ens debet poni obiectum intellectus, oportet quod contrahatur ad intelligibile; non autem contrahitur ad hoc nisi per rationem veri; igitur, etc.[1]

Contra:

Obiectum formale est prius ipso actu, II *De anima*;[2] sed verum non est prius actu intelligendi; igitur non est primum obiectum intellectus. Minor patet, quia intellectus facit rationem veri.

Item, quod non attingitur a potentia actu directo, non est primum eius obiectum; sed ipsum verum attingitur ab intellectu actu

---

4 Utrum] *praem.* Quaeritur N KU FW Q X Z *praem.* Quaero O *adnot. mg.* Quaestio 20 HM | ratione veri tantum] ratione veri N Q tantum sub O | obiectum primum] inv. Q oppositum primum O 5 intellectus] *add.* non sub ratione boni N *add.* ratione O *add.* nostri KU 6 Videtur *om.* N 7 distincta obiecta] inv. K | et] *lin.* N *om.* O 8 voluntas] bonitas Q | potentiae distinctae] inv. H U *add.* sed K *add.* etc. X | autem *om.* X | ens²] *add.* non Z 9 indistinctum] distinctum Q X Z | indistinctum — ens *post* nisi K | igitur] ergo L FW Q X | esse *post* sic N HL | ut sic] ut sit U *om.* K | utriusque obiectum] inv. NO | sed] ergo Q 10 quod distinguitur] inv. O | ratione] rationi O rationem KU Q Z 11 Item] Praeterea NO KU FW Q X Z | obiectum] subiectum O | appropriari debet] inv. KU Q Z appropinquari debet O approximari debet FW | sed] *add.* li X 12 ens *om.* N K | ens — ens³ *om.* X | commune causae U | commune — nisi] rep. K | ens² *om.* N F | intelligibile] intelligibili O | igitur] ergo L FW Q | ens debet] inv. U 13 intellectus *om.* N | ad intelligibile] per (ad O) intelligibilia NO ad ens intelligibile U FW Q X Z 14 contrahitur] contrahatur Z | per rationem] in ratione N L ratione U | veri] verbi U | igitur etc.] ergo etc. L FW Q *om.* X 16 ipso] illo Q | ipso — prius *om.* X | II] I FW Z *spat. vac.* O 17 prius] *add.* in N | intelligendi *om.* HM | igitur] ergo FW Q X Z | primum obiectum] inv. HL obiectum KU 18 facit] terminat KU | rationem veri] inv. Q | veri] unam N verbi U *add.* igitur Q 19 Item] Praeterea NO KU FW Q X Z | potentia] *add.* nec N | primum *post* eius HL praesens X 20 eius obiectum] obiectum intellectus Q | ipsum] primum KU FW X Z | intellectu] *add.* ipso O M | actu *om.* FW

[1]Cf. **Henricus Gand.**, *Summa* a. 34 q. 3 in corp. (AMPh s.2 XXVII 191).
[2]**Aristot.**, *De an.* II c. 26 (Γ c. 2, 426*b* 8-11).

reflexo tantum, quia ratio veri est ratio intellecti vel intelligibilis; ratio autem intelligibilis non intelligitur nisi per reflexionem; igitur, etc.

[I. — Opinio Henrici et redargutiones eius]

5   Ad hoc dicunt QUIDAM[3] quod intellectus et voluntas tantum distinguuntur per respectus ad obiecta sua quae sunt verum et bonum. Quod declarant sic: anima enim secundum se est indeterminata, sed determinatur ad potentias organicas aliter quam ad non-organicas, quia ad organicas determinatur per determinationem organorum. Unde potentia sensitiva, quae est organica, non est potentia propria animae sed coniuncti ex anima et corpore. Ad non-organicas vero determinatur non per organa nec per qualitates absolutas, igitur per respectum ad distincta obiecta; illa autem formalia obiecta distincta sunt verum et bonum; igitur, etc.

---

1 reflexo] inflexo W | tantum *om.* U | ratio²] in U *om.* H *add.* ipsius Q | intellecti vel] intellecti et H ipsius K intellectu ipsius U *add.* ipsius FW X Z   2 igitur etc.] ergo etc. L FW X igitur Q   5 hoc] illam quaestionem Q | dicunt] dicit Q | quod] quod (*om.* X Z) scilicet Henricus quod FW X Z | tantum] = HLM *om.* NO KU FW Q X Z   6 distinguuntur] distinguitur Q *om.* O | respectus] respectum FW *add.* ab K | quae] *add.* non U | verum] obiectum O | et *om.* O   7 Quod] Et NO | declarant] declarat Q declaratur H F | sic] se O *om.* F | anima enim] enim FW anima Q Z etiam tantum X | est] *ant.* enim FW   8 ad] per L | aliter] *ant.* determinatur NO FW Q (aliqua Q) X Z | quam] quod Q   9 ad *om.* N FW X Z | quia — organicas] *mg.* Z² | per *om.* X | determinatinem organorum] *inv.* Q   10 sensitiva] organica F passiva X   11 propria] propriae F | coniuncti] composita N coniunctum O coniuncta H FW X Z coniunctim K   12 non-organicas] nos organicas O | vero *om.* N X | determinatur non] *inv.* N X *add.* ult. nec X | non *om.* O U | per *om.* U | organa] organica H   13 igitur] ergo L FW Q X | respectum] *add.* distinctum K *add.* ad distinctum U | ad distincta] *mg.* F² distinguitur L ad diversa KU | obiecta] opposita O | illa autem] *inv.* L illa a O ista autem Z   14 formalia obiecta distincta] distincta obiecta NO formalia L distincta formalia obiecta KU | sunt] *add.* unum FW | verum ... bonum] bonum ... verum Q | igitur etc.] ergo etc. L FW igitur Q *om.* X

[3]Cf. **Henricus Gand.**, *Quodl.* III q. 14 (f. 68rZ; f. 69rA); (f. 70rC): "Quare cum illud quod potest sentire potentia sensitiva tamquam potentia propinqua solum eget unica transmutatione ut ex ipso per potentiam eliciatur actio, non est nisi compositum ex ipsa substantia animae et organo corporali sua dispositione determinante animam ut est in organo determinato ad rationem potentiae determinatae et ad determinatum actum ..., potentia igitur sentiendi per se in organo composito ex substantia animae et corpore determinante animam sua dispositione ad rationem determinatae potentiae et ad determinatum actum ..."; (f. 71rE): "Secundum ergo hunc modum quia intellectus est quasi media ratio omnium specierum intelligibilium per hoc quod omnino immunis est a materia et nulli aliquid habet commune, ut habetur III *De anima*: 'omnium specierum est susceptivus', in sua nuda substantia et per ipsas determinabilis ad diversas operationes. Et sic potest per specierum determinationem diversarum in ratione intelligibilis sicut sunt species veri sub ratione veri vel sub ratione boni aut huiusmodi assumere in se rationem diversarum potentiarum quarum nullam sibi determinat. Et sic omnes accidunt essentiae eius non quia sunt re aliud ab ea sed quia est respectus ei additus extra intentionem essentiae suae, sicut primae materiae accidunt potentiae ad formas."

[2]   Contra:

Unum quod supponit, scilicet quod potentiae distinguuntur per obiecta, est alibi reprobatum,⁴ et potest sic argui: primum non distinguitur per posterius; sed potentia est prior actu et obiecto; igitur, etc.

Contra principale⁵ sic:

Ista diversitas obiectorum aut est per respectus aut per absoluta. Non per absoluta, quia idem absolutum potest immediate attingi a duabus potentiis, sicut idem absolutum potest immediate intelligi et amari. Nec per respectus, quia nulla potentia potest attingere obiectum suum sine ratione formali obiecti; sed intellectus potest attingere quodcumque absolutum sine respectu aliquo, voluntas amare bonum absolute sine quocumque respectu; igitur respectus non est ratio formalis obiecti intellectus vel voluntatis.

Item, obiectum sub ratione formali movet potentiam; sed impossibile est primum movere sub ratione respectiva, quia respectus non est principium operandi vel movendi, sicut nec terminus;⁶ igitur, etc.

Item, obiectum quod est principium operationis debet esse ens per se sicut unum per se; sed compositum ex obiecto et respectu non est unum per se sed per accidens tantum; igitur non potest esse principium simplicis operationis intellectus.

---

2 Unum] Primum KU Verum X Z | quod] add. sic F | supponit] supponitur L 3 est om. Q Z | reprobatum] improbatum U Q reprobatur Z | potest sic] inv. H | primum] prius Q 4 est prior] inv. HL est prius Q 5 igitur etc.] ergo etc. L FW igitur Q etc. X 6 principale] add. arguitur M | sic om. X 7 Ista diversitas] Diversitas illa NO Illa diversitas FW | aut om. NO | respectus] respectum X | per² om. L X 8 Non] lin. O | Non — absoluta om. U X | quia quod O | idem] illud N HM | immediate attingi] inv. N immediate intelligi L 9 duabus] diversis HL | intelligi] intendi U 10 nulla om. L FW | obiectum — attingere om. NO L 11 obiecti om. X 12 quodcumque] quod tenet(!) N | absolutum] obiectum H | respectu aliquo] inv. Z respectu alicuius H add. ergo et L add. (lin. F) et KU F | voluntas] voluntatis Z add. (mg. F²) potest N F² 13 absolute] absoluto Z om. N FW | igitur] ergo L FW Q X 14 est om. Q | obiecti intellectus] inv. Z intellectus K | vel] et N KU X Z 15 Item] Praeterea NO KU FW Q X Z | sub] mg. W² om. X | formali] add. obiecti K 16 est om. O | primum] principium N ipsum KU add. (mg. F²) obiectum L F² Q | movere] moveri L 17 operandi vel movendi] movendi sed operandi N movendi vel operandi Q | vel — sicut om. L | nec] non Q | terminus om. X | igitur etc.] ergo etc. L FW igitur Q etc. X 19 Item] Praeterea N KU FW Q X Z Primum O | obiectum om. L FW | debet] sed U | ens ... unum] unum ... est ens N unum ... ens O 20 sicut — se om. Z | obiecto] absoluto KU FW Q X Z 21 igitur] ergo FW Q X

⁴Cf. **Duns Scotus**, *Metaph.* I q. 6 n. 18-20 (OPh III 139-140); n. 42 (OPh III 145); cf. **Aristot.**, *De an.* II c. 6 (B c. 4, 415a 17-22); cf. *Auctoritates Aristotelis* (ed. J. Hamesse 179): "Potentiae cognoscuntur per actus, actus vero per obiecta."
⁵Cf. supra n. 1.
⁶**Aristot.**, *Physica* V c. 3 (AL VII¹ 196; E c. 3, 225b 11-16).

10   Sed DICES ad omnia ista⁷ quod verum non habet virtutem movendi intellectum sed determinativum entis quod est primum movens intellectum in habitudine ad intellectum, ita quod ens sub ratione habitudinis, quae est ratio veri determinans ipsum ens, movet intellectum.

11   Contra:

Ista habitudo aut est principalis ratio obiecti aut consequens; non principalis, quia tunc respectus esset principium movendi, quod est superius improbatum;⁸ si consequens — sicut propria passio — et ratio entis esset principalis, secundum eamdem rationem ens moveret intellectum et voluntatem, quia illa ratio est indistincta et per consequens, secundum ILLOS, esset eadem potentia intellectus et voluntas.

12   Item, obiectum visus est visibile per se secundo modo; visibile autem importat illam habitudinem obiecti ad visum; igitur illa habitudo non est de ratione obiecti essentiali sed consequens, cum non insit ei primo modo dicendi per se, sed tantum secundo modo.

---

1 dices] diceres KU | ad] quod H | ista] illa O H FW Q X   2 intellectum *om.* L | sed] *add.* est HL | sed — intellectum²] *mg.* Z² | determinativum] de termino tantum(!) NO *add.* (*mg.* Z²) est X Z² | quod] *add.* (*mg.* Z²) non X Z² | est primum] *inv.* H est primo L   3 ad intellectum] ad totum NO ad intelligibile Q *om.* X | ita] ista Z | ens] species F | sub] in Q   4 est *post* veri K | veri] verum Q *add.* est U   7 Ista habitudo] Illa habitudo NO H FW Q Istam habitudinem X | aut] autem L | est] esset NO FW X Z *om.* Q | principalis ratio] *inv.* Q principalis N principalis ideo O principali ratio X | obiecti *om.* Z   8 tunc *om.* O FW Q X Z | respectus esset] *inv.* (*post* movendi) N principalis ratio esset respectus et L   9 superius] iam Q | improbatum] probatum X | si] sicut O M X sic F | sicut *om.* Q Z   10 et] tunc N | entis] entitatis Z | principalis] principium X *add.* vel X | principalis — voluntatem] *mg.* Z² | secundum eamdem rationem] sed eadem ratione N per eamdem rationem KU   11 illa] ista M K Z | indistincta] distincta FW   12 illos] istos N M Z eos H illas F istas W   13 et *om.* U | voluntas] voluntatis NQ   14 Item] Probo N Ponitur O Praeterea KU FW Q X Z | visibili Q | per — importat] autem X | modo *om.* H. *add.* aut N *add.* autem O | visibile²] *add.* autem Q Z   15 illam] istam HM Z | igitur] ergo L FW Q | igitur — obiecti] quia ergo illa habitudo non est de ratione obiecti ad visum ergo illa habitudo essentiali X | illa] ista LM   16 obiecti essentiali] *inv.* M X essentiali X   17 non] *add. scilicet* H | insit] sit X | ei] sibi Q *om.* NO *add.* in L | sed] hoc Z | secundo modo] ratione materiae NO secundo FW

⁷Cf. **Henricus Gand.**, *Summa* a. 34 q. 3 in corp. (AMPh s. 2, XXVII 191): "… oportet igitur quod super rationem entis, ut determinetur ad rationem intelligibilis, sit ratio apprehensibilis, qua ens respectum habet ad intellectum ut motivum intellectus, ita quod ratio entis apprehensibilis ab intellectu non esset, nisi huiusmodi rationis in se esset susceptibilis. Haec enim ratio est in ente per hoc quod est natum sibi assimilare intellectum. Assimilatio enim intellectus ad cognitum est causa et ratio cognitionis prima. Prima ergo ratio, qua ens secundum rationem suam absolutam absque omni conditione assumit supra se intellectus considerationem, est ratio conformandi sibi intellectum. Conformatio autem huiusmodi adaequatio quaedam est et rectitudo, qua intellectus per id quod concipit de re ipsa, rei adaequatur et correspondet. Haec autem ratio est illa a qua imponitur hoc nomen 'verum' sive 'veritas', et addit eam super ens …"

⁸Cf. supra n. 7-8.

Simile est de obiecto intellectus et aliis obiectis in comparatione ad potentias.

Item, sequeretur quod, ad determinationem de obiecto alicuius potentiae, sufficeret dicere quod illud esset obiectum quod haberet habitudinem ad potentiam; sed si in hoc consisteret ratio formalis obiecti, nec esset ultra quaerendum cuius naturae esset in speciali; quod falsum est, ut patet per inquisitionem PHILOSOPHI.

[II. — Opinio propria]

[4] Dicendum ergo ad quaestionem quod verum non est primum obiectum intellectus sub ratione veri. Probo: quia quod secundum propriam rationem intelligi potest, ut distinguitur ab alio, non intelligitur sub ratione eius a quo distinguitur; sed bonum, ut distinguitur a vero sub ratione propria boni, potest intelligi; igitur non intelligitur sub ratione veri; sed omne quod intelligitur, intelligitur sub ratione formali obiecti intellectus. Ergo ratio veri non est formalis ratio obiecti intellectus. Maior patet. Minor probatur: quia intellectus potest cognoscere differentiam formalem inter verum et bonum; formalis enim ratio boni non est ratio veri, ut dicunt ALII;[9] igitur bonum potest intelligi ut differens a vero.

Item, quidquid est volitum sub aliqua ratione, sub eadem ratione potest esse intellectum, quia impossibile est aliquid esse volitum

---

1 et] *add.* de Q | obiectis] oppositis O potentiis X | in comparatione] = HL KU per comparationem NO M FW Q X Z *add. ult.* ad comparationem U   3 Item] Praeterea NO KU FW Q X Z | sequeretur] sequitur HLM | quod] *lin.* N *om.* O | ad *om.* U X | de *om.* Q X Z | obiecto] obiecti Z   4 illud] idem H | obiectum] ens NO   5 potentiam] potentias KU | sed] = LM X semper H *om.* NO KU FW Q Z | si in] suam F in X | consisteret] consistit O consistat HM | ratio formalis] *inv.* FW Q X Z   6 nec] non HL | nec — quaerendum *om.* FW | ultra quaerendum] *inv.* Q ulterius quaerendum NO KU *ultra* accidentium X | cuius] cuiusmodi (*mg.* W²) FW² Q X *add.* in U | naturae esset] *inv.* KU esset N | in — Philosophi] *mg.* Z²   7 ut] unde NO | inquisitionem] *add.* hi K | inquisitionem — secundum *om.* NO   9 Dicendum *post* quaestionem W dicendum est (*post* quaestionem F) M F | ergo] igitur H Z *om.* FW | non est] *inv.* X | primum obiectum] *inv.* HL   10 Probo] Probatio L KU Z | quod *om.* H FW   11 propriam rationem] *inv.* N | potest *om.* N | distinguitur *post* alio H   12 intelligitur] intelligibili FW | eius] illius NO *om.* Z | sed *om.* H | ut] non XZ   13 sub ratione propria] secundum rationem N | ratione propria] *inv.* K | propria — ratione] ergo non intelligitur sub ratione veri *mg.* Z² | propria boni] *inv.* FW Q Z | potest intelligi] *inv.* M intelligi U | igitur] ergo L FW Q X *add.* hoc H   14 intelligitur *om.* O   15 formali] formalis X | obiecti *om.* FW Q | Ergo] Igitur K | Ergo —intellectus] = L KU FW X Z *om.* NO HM Q | ratio veri] verum L | est] *lin.* F²   16 obiecti intellectus] obiectalis L intellectus obiecti X obiecti Z | patet] est nota L *add.* et HL | probatur] patet L *om.* N   17 potest] habet M | formalem] *rep.* U | verum ... bonum] bonum ... verum Q   18 enim] autem X *om.* N | est] *add.* formalis HL Q   19 igitur] ergo L FW Q X | bonum potest intelligi] = HLM bonum intelligi potest NO potest bonum intelligi KU FW Q X Z | differens] distinguitur NO differentiis X   20 Item] Praeterea NO KU FW Q X Z | volitum] *add.* est L | ratione] oratione U | ratione *om.* O U FW Q X Z   21 aliquid esse] *inv.* Q

[9] Richardus de Mediav., *Sent.* II d. 24 p. 1 q. 5 (97*va*—*b*).

sub aliqua ratione quae prius non sit cognita ab intellectu; sed voluntas potest velle bonum sub ratione boni et non sub ratione veri; igitur intellectus potest ipsum intelligere bonum, non intelligendo rationem veri. Maior patet per AUGUSTINUM, X *De Trinitate*.[10]

16 Item, passio est extra rationem sui subiecti; verum autem est passio entis; igitur differt a ratione entis, sed compositio differentium constituit ens per accidens, quod non potest esse obiectum, ut dictum est;[11] igitur, etc.

17 Item, obiectum alicuius habitus non excedit nec praecedit naturaliter obiectum potentiae, in qua est habitus, immo magis ipsum praesupponit; sed obiectum scientiae metaphysicalis est ens in quantum ens, quod praecedit naturaliter rationem veri, sicut subiectum passionem vel sicut absolutum contractum; igitur verum non est primum obiectum intellectus nostri in quo est metaphysica.

18 Item, obiectum primum alicuius potentiae debet praedicari primo modo dicendi per se — sicut genus de specie — de omnibus quae per se cadunt sub actu illius potentiae, sicut color de albo et nigro; sed verum de nullo intellecto a nobis praedicatur per se primo modo sed tantum secundo modo, quia dicit habitudinem ad intellectum quae consequitur illud quod est intellectum nec est de intellectu eius essentiali, sicut visibile praedicatur de colore per se secundo modo tantum; igitur, etc.

---

1 quae cognita] quod cognitum HLM | sit] sint K | ab] sub H 2 voluntas] volens N 3 igitur] ergo FW Q X | igitur — veri *om.* U Z | ipsum intelligere] *inv.* NO K | bonum] *add.* sub ratione boni et K | intelligendo] sub K 4 per] *add.* beatum L | per — Trinitate *om.* N | X] IV L X Z 5 Item] Praeterea NO KU FW Q X Z | extra] *add* scilicet H | rationem] essentiam H | sui subiecti] sui obiecti O H Q obiecti L obiecti sui U | verum] utrum F | autem] *lin.* Q *om.* H U 6 igitur] ergo L FW Q X | a] q(!) O 7 constituit ens] consistit ens O constituens(!) F | obiectum] *add.* intellectus N 8 est] esse Z | igitur etc.] ergo etc. L FW igitur Q *om.* X 9 Item] Praeterea O KU FW Q | Item — metaphysica *om.* Z | habitus] virtutis W | excedit] exstitit(!) X 10 obiectum potentiae] poni O | potentiae in qua] potentiam quae X | ipsum praesupponit] *inv.* KU 11 obiectum] subiectum N L K | metaphysicalis] metaphysicae Q 12 ens *om.* U | naturaliter rationem] naturale ratione X 13 subiectum] obiectum O FW X *add.* suam KU | igitur] ergo L FW Q X 14 est *om.* Q | primum *post* nostri KU | primum obiectum] *inv.* O H FW X | quo] qua U | metaphysica] *add.* igitur Q 15 Item] Praeterea O KU FW Q X Z | debet praedicari] praedicare debet F *add.* per se O FW Q Z *add.* in L 16 modo *om.* O | dicendi] dicendum O | sicut — nigro *om.* K | specie] se X *add.* et H U | de²] in FW | omnibus] *add.* aliis N L *add.* illis U 17 sub actu] sub statu H *om.* O | sicut] *add.* obiecto X 18 de *om.* Q | praedicatur] *mg.* Z² primo O | per — modo] in primo modo dicendi per se KU 19 primo] obiecto O 20 quae] qui X | consequitur illud] *spat. vac.* U | intellectum²] in intellectu O 21 visibile] sensibile Z | per se *om.* FW Q X Z 22 igitur etc.] ergo etc. L FW ergo Q *om.* X

[10]**Augustinus**, *De Trinitate* X c. 2 (CCL L 315-6).
[11]Cf. n. 9.

[III. — Ad argumenta principalia]

Ad primum in oppositum,[12] dicendum quod magis concludit propositum quam oppositum, quia impossibile est aliquid esse volitum sub aliqua ratione, quae prius non fuit cognita ab intellectu; igitur non oportet quod habeant distincta obiecta.

[6] Dicendum igitur quod potentiarum animae quaedam sunt disparatae, quaedam subordinatae; et istarum quaedam sunt in eodem genere ut apprehensivae, quaedam in diversis ut apprehensivae cum appetitivis. Si autem sint potentiae disparatae, habent obiecta omnino disparata, sicut quinque sensus particulares. Si autem sint subordinatae et in eodem genere, habent obiecta subordinata, quia obiectum primum et adaequatum potentiae superioris sub se continet obiectum inferioris, quod tamen est obiectum per se, licet non primum nec adaequatum potentiae superioris, quia potentia superior potest habere actum suum circa obiectum adaequatum potentiae inferioris et ipsum perfectius cognoscit quam potentia inferior. Sicut sensus communis album perfectius cognoscit quam visus quia cognoscit ipsum ut distinctum a dulci, sic intellectus cognoscit quidquid sensus cognoscit, et perfectius quam sensus. Si autem potentiae subordinatae sint alterius generis, sicut intellectus et voluntas, tunc dicendum quod si sint adaequatae — id est, si in tot potest una, in quot potest alia —, tunc habent idem obiectum formale. Si autem non sint adaequatae (quia voluntas non habet

---

2 in oppositum] obiectum K | dicendum] *add.* est N M F   3 propositum ... oppositum] oppositum ... propositum FW | aliquid] aliquod O | esse] commune(?) O   4 aliqua ratione] inv. N | quae] quod L | fuit] sit O KU FW Q X Z | cognita] cognitum L   5 igitur non] = N HM non igitur O KU Z ergo non L non ergo FW Q non X | habeant] habent M K habeat W   6 Dicendum] *add.* est N M F | igitur] ergo L FW Q X | animae *om.* K | disparatae quaedam] disparatae et quaedam KU *om.* Z   7 istarum] illarum O H F Q *add.* potentiarum L | eodem genere] inv. Q   8 quaedam — cum *om.* L   9 appetitivis] appetitis O | sint] sunt NO FW Q X Z | obiecta omnino] inv. K obiecta O obiecta omnia (*lin.* F²) F²W Z   10 disparata] *mg.* F² disposita W | sicut] *add.* sunt F | particulares] particularis O | autem *om.* X | sint] sunt O FW Q X sit Z   11 et *om.* H FW | obiecta] subiecta W   12 primum et *om.* KU | potentiae *om.* O | sub se *post* continet Z sub U   13 obiectum] *add.* adaequatum potentiae N M *add.* adaequatum FW Q X Z | inferioris — nec *om.* O | quod] quia F   14 quia — inferioris *om.* Z   15 circa] aliqua O   16 potentiae] *add. seu rep.* superioris quia potentia superior circa obiectum adequatum potentiae O   17 perfectius cognoscit] inv. O | quam] *lin.* F² quod O *om.* W   18 quia] quod O | dulci] dulce H   19 cognoscit] intelligit K cognitis Z | cognoscit²] cognitis Z *om.* FW   20 autem] iam Z | sint] essent K esset U sunt FW Q X Z   21 dicendum] *add.* est N M F | quod *om.* K | si *om.* Q | sint] sunt O FW Q X Z | id est] et KU | si²] quod (*lin.* F²) O F²W Q X Z *om.* KU | in tot] intelligit(!) O   22 potest] possit FW Q X Z | in quot potest] quot potest N sicut KU in quod posset X | obiectum *om.* Q   23 sint] sunt O K FW Q X Z

[12]Cf. supra n. 1.

actum suum nisi circa finem et ea quae sunt ad finem, non autem circa necessaria et impossibilia quae sunt tantum speculativa, ut conclusiones geometricae), tunc dicendum quod obiectum voluntatis continetur sub obiecto intellectus.

21 Sed contra:

Potentiae distinguuntur per actus, et actus per obiecta, ut videtur III *De anima*[13].

22 Dicendum quod hoc non dicit PHILOSOPHUS, sed quod prius oportet considerare actus quam potentias et obiecta quam actus, quia sunt priora quoad cognitionem nostram obiecta quam actus et actus quam potentiae; tamen actus non est principium essendi potentiae vel prius perfectione, immo posterior, quia sunt effectus potentiarum. Bene igitur sequitur, si obiecta sint diversa, quod potentiae sint diversae, sed non e converso. Nec sequitur si obiecta sint idem et non differunt, quod potentiae non differunt. Sed est fallacia consequentis ad destructionem antecedentis; plura enim requiruntur ad identitatem aliquorum quam ad distinctionem eorum. Exemplum: motus distinguuntur penes terminos, ita quod si termini ubi sint distincti, et motus; sed non sequitur quod si terminus est idem, quod motus sit idem. Diversi enim motus specie possunt esse ad eundem terminum, sicut circularis et rectus ad

---

1 suum nisi circa] primum aliqua O nisi circa X | et] *add.* (*lin.* F²) circa L F² | ad] *lin.* F² *om.* W 2 impossibilia] *add.* (*mg.*) aliter se habere F² | sunt tantum] *inv.* H KU X | speculativa] speculabilia FW Q X Z 3 dicendum] *add.* est N M F 5 Sed *om.* H | contra *om.* X 6 Potentiae] Potentia O | distinguuntur] distinguitur NO | videtur] dicitur FW habetur Q X *add.* ex Q Z 7 III] "II" O M X Z "I" FW Q 8 Dicendum] Dicitur (*lin.*) F² Dicit W *add.* est N M | Philosophus] *add.* quia primum non distinguitur per posterius potentia est prior actu et obiecto K | prius *post* considerare FW *post* oportet X 9 oportet] *add.* nos L | obiecta — actus] *del.* F² *et add. mg.* et prius obiecta quam actus et prius actus quam obiecta F² | obiecta — nostram *om.* O U 10 priora] propria H propinquiora L | quoad] *add.* nos K | nostram *om.* L | obiecta — actus *om.* Q X Z | obiecta — et *om.* FW 11 actus] *add.* et X | tamen] tunc O | principium] prius X 12 potentiae] potentia FW | posterior] posterioris L W Q posteriores F X Z | quia] et Z 13 Bene] Unde H KU | igitur] ergo L K FW Q X | si] quod O | sint] sunt O K FW Q X Z 14 sint] sunt O K FW Q X | sed] et L Q X | Nec] Non H *om.* X 15 sint] sunt O FW Q X Z | idem] eadem KU | et] vel FW Q X Z | differunt²] differant O FW Q X Z | est] *lin.* F² 16 ad destructionem] a destructione O FW Q X Z | antecedentis] *add.* (*mg.*) ad destructionem consequentis F² 17 identitatem] entitatem W | aliquorum] contentorum O obiectorum Z | ad² *om.* X 18 eorum *om.* FW | distinguuntur] distinguitur NO L W X Z | penes] per KU | si] *lin.* M *om.* O 19 ubi *om.* L KU FW Q X Z | sint] sunt O FW Q X | quod *om.* FW Q X Z 20 est] sit L KU Z | quod] et KU | sit] sunt O est U | Diversi enim] Quia diversi termini F"W *sed del.* "termini" F² Diversi termini X 21 possunt] possent Q | terminum] *lin.* F² motum W numerum X | sicut] *add. mg.* motus F² | circularis] circularem O | et rectus] *lin* F² et rectitudo W X *add.* et KU X *om.* Z | ad² *om.* U

[13]Potius **Aristot.**, *De an.* II c. 6 (B c. 4; 415*a* 16-21); *Auctoritates Aristotelis* (ed. J. Hamesse 179): "Potentiae cognoscuntur per actus, actus vero per obiecta."

eundem punctum. Ita est in proposito.

Ad aliud[14] dicendum est quod obiectum adaequatum potentiae superiori est commune obiecto adaequato potentiae inferiori. Si igitur intellectus est potentia superior, et obiectum eius est communissimum.

Sed dicis:
Oportet obiectum determinari ad potentiam per respectum.

Dicendum quod indeterminatio obiecti intellectus per respectum ad alia obiecta, id est communitas eius, est determinatio sua ad intellectum, si sit potentia superior; non autem per aliquid contrahens ipsum ad specialius obiectum, cum sit obiectum potentiae communissimae, ut suppono. Et si dicatur quod obiectum movet cum habitudine ad intellectum, dicendum quod verum est, non quia respectus ad intellectum sit principium movendi vel concausatio, sed tantum forma absoluta.[15] Sed pro tanto: quia actum intelligendi bene sequitur respectus actualis obiecti ad potentiam, et non e converso. Ante autem actum intelligendi erat ille respectus in potentia tantum in obiecto ad potentiam. Non igitur ens sub ratione veri vel ipsum verum ut verum est primum obiectum intellectus, ut visum est.

---

1 punctum] puncta U | Ita] Sicut L | est *om.* Q   2 est *om.* O H KU W Q X Z   3 superiori] superioris KU | commune] communis FW communius Z | obiecto adaequato] inv. H | potentiae inferiori] inv. L potentiae inferioris H KU   4 igitur] ergo (ant. si L) L FW X | est²] et N *om.* LU Q   6 Sed] Si U | dicis] dices O L K FW Q Z   7 Oportet] Quod KU | obiectum determinari] inv. Q obiectum determinatur KU | respectum] *add.* ad potentiam L   8 Dicendum] *add.* est N M | quod *om.* U F | indeterminatio] determinatio N | obiecti intellectus] = KU FW Z obiecti et intellectus NO HLM intellectus obiecti Q intellectus X *add.* ult. est K | per respectum *om.* X   9 alia obiecta] inv. Q illa obiecta L aliqua obiecta X | id est] et K | communitas] *mg.* Z² | eius] sua KU | est² *om.* Q | sua] eius (ant. determinatio) L   10 aliquid] aliquod H K | contrahens] *add.* per Q   11 cum — obiectum *om.* H FW Z   12 ut suppono] ut suppositum O *om.* K FW | dicatur] dicitur N | movet] manet H   13 dicendum] *add.* est N M | est *om.* K   14 sit] sicut U | movendi] *add.* ipsum O KU FW Q X Z   15 concausatio] = N HM a causa O concausa L W Q communicatio KU cum causa F X communicandi Z *add.* debet X | sed *om.* Z | quia] quod N KU   16 actum] actus Q | respectus] *add.* actus L | obiecti *om.* X   17 non *om.* U FW Q X | Ante] Cum O Non U F | autem] *add.* omnem KU *om.* H | erat] esset Q   18 ille] iste LM Q | in²] *lin.* M | Non] Cum U Nisi Q   19 igitur] ergo O L FW X autem H | ens] est Z | sub] est O | verum *om.* X | ut verum] *rep.* U | verum²] *add.* est FW | primum obiectum] inv. KU falsum obiectum O obiectum FW Q X Z   20 ut — est] ut dictum Z *om.* L *add.* igitur etc. K *add.* Deo gratias amen Q

[14]Cf. supra n. 2.
[15]Subintellige: est principium movendi intellectum.

[QUAESTIO 21]

UTRUM ENS SIT OBIECTUM PRIMUM INTELLECTUS NOSTRI

Utrum ens sit primum obiectum intellectus nostri.

[1] Videtur quod non:

Quia omnis potentia habens aliquod commune pro primo obiecto potest per se naturaliter tendere in quodcumque per se contentum sub illo, sicut in per se obiectum licet non primum; si ergo ens est obiectum primum intellectus nostri, tunc, cum quaelibet substantia tam creata quam increata sub propria et distincta ratione contineatur per se sub ente, intellectus noster potest per se tendere in cognitionem determinatam cuiuscumque substantiae tam separatae quam corporalis, cuius oppositum experimur; igitur, etc. Probatio maioris exemplo: quia hoc videmus de visu respectu coloris et suorum inferiorum; secundo, ratione: si enim non posset in omnia contenta sub primo obiecto vel si posset in plura tantum, tunc illud commune non esset obiectum adaequatum potentiae nec per consequens primum eius obiectum.

Item, primum obiectum intellectus debet habere unum per se conceptum, quia movet secundum unam formam; sed ens non habet unum conceptum per se; igitur, etc. Probatio maioris: quia potentia potest obiectum suum primum unico actu attingere, quod

---

4 Utrum] *praem.* Quaeritur O KU FW Q X *adnot. mg.* Quaestio 21 M | primum] proprium Q | nostri *om.* KU X   5 Videtur *om.* X   6 omnis] communis O *om.* L | aliquod] aliud Q aliquid Z | primo obiecto] *inv.* K obiecto FW X   7 per se *om.* KU | naturaliter] *ant. per* L | tendere] intendere O tandem X   8 contentum] *ant. per* KU FW conceptum Z | illo] eo FW | per se] *mg.* O   9 ergo] igitur O KU Q Z | est] *lin.* Q *om.* X | obiectum primum] *inv.* L Q | tunc *om.* FW Q X | cum *post* increata N LM *om.* KU | quaelibet] quaecumque FW X quacumque Q Z   10 sub] super X   11 contineatur] continentur U | noster *om.* L | potest] posset L *om.* Q   12 tendere] tenderet Q intendere FW tandem X | determinatam] terminatam U   13 corporalis] inseparatae H | experimur] exprimimur K | igitur etc.] ergo etc. L FW ergo Q *om.* X   14 Probatio maioris] Maior probatur O X Probo maiorem H Probatio minoris U Probatur maior Q *add.* in KU X *add. et* FW | exemplo] exemplum (*mg.* M²) HM² | hoc videmus] *inv.* X hic videmus O hoc apparet Q   15 secundo] et FW Q X Z | secundo — obiecto *om.* O | posset] possit KU | in omnia] in substantia FW *om.* X *spat. vac.* Z   16 contenta — obiecto] sibi contenta FW Z sub eo (*om.* Q) sibi contenta Q X | primo] proprio H KU | tantum *om.* O KU FW Q X Z   17 illud] idem H | commune *om.* O | esset] esse U | obiectum adaequatum] *inv.* O adaequatum Q | potentiae] *add.* nostrae FW X Z   18 eius *om.* L   19 Item] Praeterea O KU FW Q X Z | primum obiectum] *inv.* X primum Z | debet] oportet Q   20 conceptum] *ant. per* F | quia] quod H qui X | movet] moveret L | secundum] sibi (*post* formam Z) FW Z   21 habet] movet KU *add.* secundum K | unum *om.* O | igitur] ergo FW Q *om.* X | Probatio maioris] Maior probatur X   22 potest] ponit Q habet X | actu] *rep.* N *mg.* Z

non posset intellectus nisi obiectum eius haberet de se unum conceptum tantum. Probatio minoris: quia ens non dicitur univoce de omnibus entibus, et ideo non uno actu potest intellectus noster attingere omnia entia nec ens commune; igitur, etc.

3 Item, sicut aliqua se habent ad esse, sic ad intelligi vel cognosci, ex II *Metaphysicae*.[1] Quod igitur est primum ens, est primum intelligibile; sed Deus est primum ens, quia est per suam essentiam — alia per participationem — et est aliis causa essendi; igitur est primum intelligibile intellectus nostri, non igitur ens commune.

4 Contra, AVICENNA:[2]

Ens et unum sunt quae primo imprimuntur in intellectu; igitur sunt primum obiectum.

5 Item, per rationem sic: illud est primum obiectum intellectus nostri sub cuius ratione alia intelliguntur; sed ens in communi est huiusmodi, quia praedicatur essentialiter de omnibus per se intellectis, non autem Deus; igitur, etc.

[I. — Ad quaestionem]

6 Ad istam quaestionem dicendum quod "primum" accipitur generatione vel perfectione vel adaequatione. De duobus primis modis non est intentio, sed de tertio tantum, utrum ens sit primum obiectum intellectus nostri, id est adaequatum eius obiectum. Circa

---

1 obiectum eius] *inv.* HL   2 tantum *om.* Q | Probatio minoris] Minor probatur X | dicitur] videtur X   3 non *post* actu KU | uno *om.* X | potest] posset U | noster *om.* KU   4 entia] etiam Z | igitur etc.] ergo etc. L F Q ideo etc. W *om.* X   5 Item] Praeterea O KU FW Q X Z | habent] haberet Z | sic] ita LM FW Q X Z *add.* se habent O H | intelligi vel cognosci] cognosci vel (et FW) intelligi O FW Q Z intelligi K cognosci X   6 ex *om.* O FW Q X Z | igitur] ergo L FW Q X *om.* O | ens — primum] *mg.* Z²   7 primum ens] *inv.* M FW X Z primum Q *add. seu rep.* igitur est primum intelligibile minor per H | est²] *add.* ens FW | alia] aut Q   8 est] cum X | causa] *ant.* est Q | essendi] causandi O | igitur] ergo L FW Q X   9 non igitur] non ergo L W X ergo non F | non — nostri] *mg.* W | commune] = HL KU in communi NO M FW Q X Z   10 Contra] *add.* secundum L K | Avicenna] *add.* dicit H   11 in intellectu] intellectui O in intellectum F intellectu X | igitur] ergo N L FW X   13 Item] Praeterea O KU FW Q X Z | Item — obiectum *om.* L | rationem] rationes FW | illud] idem H U   14 sub *om.* Z | cuius] quorum L *lin.* X | alia] illa U *add.* omnia Q | in communi] commune FW   15 huiusmodi] huius O | omnibus] entibus O | intellectis] intellectivis U intellectus X   16 igitur] ergo L FW Q *om.* X   18 istam] primam O illam H FW X Z | dicendum] *add.* est N M F | accipitur] *add.* vel O U FW X Z *add.* tripliciter vel K   19 duobus primis] *inv.* O FW Q X Z   20 intentio] *add.* quaestionis O FW Q X Z | tantum utrum] *inv.* U utrum O tantum sicut utrum L | primum *om.* KU FW Q X Z   21 id est *om.* KU | adaequatum] adaequati X | eius] *add.* subiectum sive F *add.* subiectum si non W | eius obiectum *om.* KU

---

[1] **Aristot.**, *Metaph.* II c. 1 (AL XXV³·² 44; α c. 1, 993b 30-32): "Quare unumquodque sicut se habet ut sit, ita et ad veritatem."
[2] **Avicenna**, *Metaph.* I c. 5 (AviL 31-32): "Dicemus igitur quod res et ens et necesse talia sunt quod statim imprimuntur in anima prima impressione, quae non acquiritur ex aliis notioribus se …"

quod sciendum quod duplex est adaequatio obiecti: una secundum virtutem, alia secundum praedicationem. Illud autem dicitur obiectum adaequatum potentiae adaequatione secundum virtutem, quod per se ipsum solum potest movere intellectum ad notitiam sui et aliorum; sicut essentia divina est primum obiectum adaequatum intellectus divini, quia est sufficienter movens intellectum divinum ad notitiam sui primo et aliorum ex consequenti, et substantia movet intellectum nostrum ad notitiam sui primo et propriae passionis vel accidentis ex consequenti. Obiectum autem adaequatum secundum praedicationem est quod per se et essentialiter praedicatur de omnibus quae possunt a potentia cognosci, sicut lux vel color vel aliquid commune utrique praedicatur essentialiter de omnibus visibilibus.

Utraque autem primitate adaequationis ens est primum obiectum intellectus nostri, ut declarabo primo indirecte, removendo alia ab illa prioritate, de quibus magis posset videri; secundo directe probando propositum.

[II. — Probationes indirectae adaequationis entis ad intellectum utroque modo]

Primum sic ostendo: ens est illud primum obiectum vel verum vel Deus vel substantia; sed neutrum trium ultimorum[3]; igitur primum, scilicet ens.

---

1 sciendum] *add.* est N LM F | adaequatio obiecti] *inv.* Q adaequatio subiecti U   2 Illud] Idem H | obiectum *om.* FW   3 potentiae] *ant.* obiectum HL KU | adaequatione *om.* L   4 solum *om.* H K   5 aliorum] aliarum U | primum obiectum] *inv.* H KU Z obiectum FW | primum — adaequatum] obiectum adaequatum et primum L | adaequatum] *add.* potentiae divinae Q   6 divini] Dei H | est sufficienter] *inv.* Q | divinum *om.* Q   7 sui primo] *inv.* Q | et *om.* KU | et — consequenti *om.* Z   8 sui primo] *inv.* H | propriae — accidentis] aliorum N | passionis *om.* X   9 accidentis] actionis O M X Z | autem *om.* O   10 secundum praedicationem] *mg.* F² *om.* W | per se et *om.* FW | essentialiter praedicatur] *inv.* FW | praedicatur] praedicare X   11 quae] *mg.* O | vel] et KU   12 aliquid] aliquod L KU | utrique] utrumque Q *om.* FW | essentialiter *om.* KU FW   13 visibilibus] *add.* et FW   14 Utraque] Nunc X | autem] enim O KU *om.* FW | primitate] primum X | adaequationis] adaequationes Z | ens *om.* X | primum obiectum] *inv.* L   15 declarabo] declarabitur Q | primo] *add.* vero L | indirecte *om.* O   16 ab] a X | illa *post* prioritate X illo O ista M Q | magis posset] *inv.* O L X magis potest H magis possit KU   17 secundo] *add.* magis Q | probando] producendo O praedicando F Q   20 Primum] *praem.* Et Q | sic ostendo] *inv.* Q | illud primum] *inv.* K primum N idem primum H primum idem U | vel *om.* K | verum] unum N   21 vel] *add.* domus U | ultimorum] = K FW Z vel duorum NO LM Q vel ultimorum U *dub.* H *om.* X | igitur] ergo L FW Q X   22 primum] *add.* obiectum O | scilicet] si U

[3]Hic codices meliores perperam 'vel duorum' tradunt, litteris exemplaris modo anglicano confectis male intellectis.

9   Quod non verum, ostensum est in quaestione immediate praecedente.[4]

10   Quod non Deus, probatio: non enim potest esse primum obiectum adaequatione secundum praedicationem, quia non praedicatur essentialiter de omnibus intelligibilibus. Nec secundum virtutem, quia non movet intellectum primo ad sui notitiam et aliorum ex consequenti. Probatio: quia aut hoc esset secundum suum conceptum simplicem et quidditativum, aut secundum conceptum abstractum a creaturis. Non primo modo, quia ille conceptus est essentiae divinae ut intuitivus est, et talis conceptus beatificat — quod non convenit viatoribus. Nec secundo modo, quia includit oppositum in adiecto; prius enim occurrit intellectui conceptus eorum a quibus fit abstractio quam eius quod abstrahitur.

11   Item, obiectum naturale habet habitudinem et proportionem ad potentiam; Deus autem nullam habet habitudinem nec proportionem ad intellectum nostrum, saltem pro statu viae, quia omnis nostra cognitio naturalis intellectiva oritur a cognitione sensitiva;[5] igitur, etc.

12   Sed quod substantia non possit esse obiectum primum, probo: non enim est primum secundum praedicationem, quia non praedicatur essentialiter de omnibus intelligibilibus, quia non de

---

1 non] *add. est* X | verum] unum X | immediate praecedente] *inv.* KU *add. et* L 3 Quod] *lin.* Z | non Deus] *inv.* Z | probatio] probo LM U Q probatur K | primum obiectum] *inv.* L Z 4 adaequatione] adaequationis L adaequatum X 5 omnibus *om.* KU | intelligibilibus] intentionibus L 6 non *om.* X | intellectum] *add.* nostrum K FW | primo *post* notitiam O nostrum X nostri Z | sui *om.* X | et *om.* X | ex consequenti *om.* FW Q X Z 7 Probatio] Probo KU Primo Q | esset] *add.* falsum F | suum] sui L 8 conceptum²] *add.* communem FW 9 a *om.* F | creaturis] aliis O | Non] *add. enim* Z | ille] iste Q *om.* X | conceptus] commune O 10 essentiae] convenientiae H | intuitivus est] *inv.* O Q intuitus est K est intuitiva (intuitam W) FW est simpliciter X intuitivus Z *add. ult. (mg.)* vel ut Z² | talis] ille H 11 quod] et U | convenit] contingit NO Q Z 12 oppositum] *mg.* F² | occurrit] occurret U | intellectui] intellectus O intellectu X | conceptus eorum] eorum conceptui O 13 a] in Z | fit] sit X | eius] est O | abstrahitur] astrahit Q 14 Item] Praeterea O KU FW Q X Z | naturale habet] naturaliter habet L habet (*om.* U) naturalem KU | habet *post* proportionem FW Q X Z | ad — proportionem *om.* L 15 Deus *om.* U | autem] aut U | habet *post* proportionem O | habitudinem ... proportionem] proportionem ... habitudinem KU | nec] aut U et X 17 nostra cognitio] *inv.* L | cognitio naturalis] *inv.* K cognitio Q | naturalis intellectiva] *inv.* F naturalis K X | oritur] ortum habet KU | cognitione sensitiva] sensu KU 18 igitur etc.] ergo etc. L FW Q *om.* X 19 Sed] Et KU | possit] potest HL K posset M | obiectum primum] *inv.* NO M FW Q X Z | probo] probatio NO M FW Q X Z 20 enim *om.* N Q | est *om.* K | secundum praedicationem] per praedicationem HLM *om.* N 21 essentialiter *post* intelligibilibus O | omnibus] *add.* scilicet O | intelligibilibus *om.* L | non] nec L

[4] Cf. supra q. 20 n. 14-18.
[5] Cf. **Aristot.**, *Anal. post.* I c. 18 (AL IV¹ 40; c. 18, 81b 6-9): "Inducere autem non habentes sensum impossibile est. Singularium enim sensus est; non enim contingit accipere ipsorum scientiam. Neque enim ex universalibus sine inductione, neque per inductionem sine sensu"; *Anal. post.* I c. 2 (AL IV² 113; c. 2, 71b 33—72a 5); *De sensu et sensato* c. 6 (c. 6, 445b 16-17): "Nec enim intelligit intellectus quae exterius nisi cum sensu."

accidentibus. Nec secundum virtutem, quia non movet intellectum sufficienter ad sui notitiam et aliorum. Quod probatur sic:⁶ quia hoc esset tantum secundum conceptum simplicem et quiditativum et intuitive; hoc autem sic esse primum est impossibile, quia quidquid intellectus noster potest sic intuitive cognoscere per eius praesentiam, eius absentiam cognoscere potest per naturam; sed intellectus noster non potest cognoscere per naturam absentiam substantiae panis in sacramento Altaris, sed tantum per fidem — aequaliter enim cognoscitur substantia panis quando non est ibi, sicut quando est ibi; igitur, etc. Maior patet per exemplum et auctoritatem PHILOSOPHI⁷ dicentis quod visus est perceptivus lucis et tenebrae, quae est absentia lucis. Minor est declarata. Igitur, etc.

[4] Cum igitur nec Deus nec verum nec substantia sit primum obiectum intellectus, sequitur quod ens sit illud primum obiectum.

[III. — Probationes directae adaequationis entis ad intellectum utroque modo
A. — De primitate entis secundum adequationem ad intellectum nostrum]

Secundo, hoc idem potest ostendi directe sic: illud quod est primum adaequatione secundum virtutem respectu potentiae est primum obiectum eius; sed ens in comparatione ad verum et bonum est primum adaequatione secundum virtutem respectu

---

1 Nec] Non F | intellectum sufficienter] *inv.* L K intellectum nostrum sufficienter FW Q X Z 2 ad] secundum F | probatur sic] *inv.* Q probatur L 3 esset tantum] *inv.* HL | conceptum] *add.* (*ant.* conceptum FW) eius O KU FW Q X Z | et *om.* F | et² *om.* F Z 4 hoc] hanc L | autem sic] *inv.* O autem sicut U | primum] *add.* obiectum L 5 potest] possit X | sic *om.* K X | per] *add.* naturam O | praesentiam] *add.* per K 6 absentiam] essentiam X | cognoscere potest] *inv.* KU FW Q 7 noster] *rep.* K | non potest] non habet H *om.* FW | cognoscere *post* naturam L KU W Q *om.* X | naturam] *add.* basc(!) U | substantiae *om.* N HM Z 8 panis *om.* L | in — panis *om.* O | aequaliter] essentialiter F 9 cognoscitur] cognoscit L | substantia] substantiam L | quando] quia X | non *post* quando K 10 ibi *om.* O FW Q X Z | igitur] ergo L FW Q *om.* X | Maior patet] *inv.* O | et] *add.* per X *om.* FW Z | auctoritatem] auctoritate KU FW Z 11 dicentis] dicens U quia dicit Q *om.* X | et — lucis *om.* K | est²] sunt U 12 Igitur etc.] Ergo etc. FW Q *om.* L X 13 Cum igitur] Igitur O Cum ergo L X Ergo cum FW | sit] sint FW X 14 intellectus] lucis U *add.* nostri Q | illud primum] *inv.* K eius primum HL primum idem U | obiectum² *om.* FW Z *add.* intellectus X 19 hoc idem potest] potest hic idem O hoc potest L potest FW | sic] *ant.* ostendi Z *om.* L | illud] idem H U 20 primum] principium U | est *om.* X 22 secundum virtutem] secundum H tali Q *om.* FW X Z | respectu *om.* L KU *add.* seu rep. potentiae est primum obiectum O

⁶Cf. **Richardus de Mediav.**, *Sent.* II d. 24 p. 3 q. 3 in corp. (II f. 100*va*—101*ra*).
⁷Cf. **Aristot.**, *De an.* II c. 15 (B c. 15, 418*b* 26—419*a* 6); cf. **Thomas**, *De an.* II c. 15 (XLV¹ 132*a-b*).

intellectus nostri; igitur, etc. Maior patet ex praemissis. Minor probatur: ens est subiectum respectu veri et boni, quae sunt passiones entis, secundum AVICENNAM[8] et PHILOSOPHUM IV *Metaphysicae*.[9] Sed respectu illorum non est primum adaequatione secundum praedicationem. Probatio: quia primum tali adaequatione praedicatur de posterioribus essentialiter; sed ens non praedicatur essentialiter et in quid de vero et bono, et aliis; igitur, etc. Maior patet per praedicta. Minor patet: quia talia, verum et bonum, sunt entis; ens autem vel quodcumque aliud subiectum non praedicatur de propria passione in quid, quia subiectum cadit in definitione passionis sicut aliquid additum, non autem sicut aliquid de eius essentia; igitur, etc.

Item, in praedicationibus per se non est conversio, ut dicitur I *Posteriorum*,[10] ut cum dicitur "animal est homo", licet haec sit per se "homo est animal"; sed passio praedicatur per se de subiecto; igitur subiectum non praedicatur per se de passione; igitur nec ens de vero et bono, licet unum, verum et bonum praedicentur de ente per se. Dicitur enim IV *Metaphysicae*[11] quod substantia

---

1 igitur] ergo L FW Q *om.* X | ex praemissis] per praemissa L | Minor probatur] = L U X *praem.* Et H K Minorem probo quia N M Probatio minoris (consequentis Q) quia O FW Q Z 2 subiectum] obiectum L | veri et boni] boni et veri Q | passiones] *add.* respectu K 3 Avicennam et Philosophum] Philosophum et Avicennam O | et] *add.* secundum L K 4 illorum] eorum O FW Q X Z istorum KU | est *om.* Q 5 secundum] *add.* virtutem U | Probatio] Probo HL Probatur KU | quia *om.* L | primum tali] praedicamentali F 6 posterioribus] passionibus F speciebus Q | essentialiter] *ant. de* FW *add.* et in quid L | sed — essentialiter *om.* N H | ens *om.* O 7 et² *om.* HM X | vero et bono] bono et vero Q | et³] *add.* de H U X *add.* sic de K | aliis] substantia FW *add.* etc. N M X | igitur etc.] ergo etc. L FW Q *om.* X 8 praedicta] *add.* et KU | patet² *om.* O | quia] per Q | talia] tam U *om.* K | et] quam U | sunt entis] sunt passiones entis L sunt passiones KU 9 ens *om.* Z | aliud subiectum] *inv.* X | praedicatur] ponitur Z 10 passione] *add.* et Q | in quid] *ant. de* KU | quia] *add.* proprium X | subiectum] *lin.* X | cadit] est (*post* passionis) K *om.* U 11 aliquid] aliquod H *om.* Q X | additum — aliquid *om.* O | sicut²] tamquam L sic X | aliquid *om.* KU Z | aliquid — essentia] substantiale eius Q Deus X | eius essentia] *inv.* FW 12 igitur etc.] ergo etc. FW Q *om.* X 13 Item] Praeterea O KU FW Q X Z | non] *rep.* Z | est] *add.* per se O 14 cum] tamen X | dicitur] conceditur Z | est *om.* X | licet *om.* O | haec] hoc FW *om.* L | sit *post se* FW 15 sed] si ergo L | praedicatur per se] = O HL U Q per se praedicatur N M FW X Z praedicatur K *add.* ult. conversim O 16 igitur] ergo L FW Q X | per se] *ant.* non Z | de] *add.* propria L | igitur²] ergo L FW Q X 17 unum *om.* H | unum verum et bonum] illa K | praedicentur] praedicatur H 18 per se] *ant.* praedicentur FW Q X Z *om.* O KU

---

[8]**Avicenna**, *Metaph.* VII c. 1 (AviL 349): "Scias autem quod unum et ens iam parificantur in praedicatione sui de rebus, ita quod, de quocumque dixeris quod est ens uno respectu, illud potest esse unum alio respectu. Nam quidquid est, unum est, et ideo fortasse putatur quia id quod intelligitur de utroque sit unum et idem, sed non est ita; sunt autem unum subiecto, scilicet quia, in quocumque est hoc, est et illud."
[9]**Aristot.**, *Metaph.* IV c. 2 (AL XXV$^{3.2}$ 70; Γ c. 2 1004b 5-6); *Auctoritates Aristotelis* (ed. J. Hamesse 122): "Prima philosophia, id est metaphysica, considerat ens et passiones et principia entis secundum quod ens."
[10]Cf. **Aristot.**, *Anal. post.* I c. 4 (AL IV^1 13; A c. 4, 73b 16-18).
[11]Cf. **Aristot.**, *Metaph.* IV c. 1 (AL XXV$^{3.2}$ 68; Γ c. 1, 1003b 16-18).

uniuscuiusque est ens et una per se, et non per accidens.

Item, quando aliquid praedicatur de alio per se primo modo, nugatio est addendo unum alii, ut animal homo, et homo animal; sed non est nugatio dicendo ens unum, nec e converso; igitur, etc.

[5] Item, ens sufficienter dividitur in ens creatum et ens increatum, quod ens creatum iterum subdividitur in decem praedicamenta, ita quod quidquid est ens per se et essentialiter oportet quod sit ens creatum vel ens increatum; sed unum non potest esse ens creatum tantum, cum dicatur de ente increato; igitur de ipso non praedicatur ens per se primo modo, id est essentialiter et in quid.

Item, si ens praedicatur essentialiter de uno, tunc aut unum dicit praecise ipsum ens aut cum hoc aliquid additum. Non praecise, quia tunc unum non esset magis passio entis quam e converso, et essent aliter nomina synonyma, quod negat PHILOSOPHUS in IV *Metaphysicae*,[12] et esset nugatio dicendo ens unum, et e converso. Si aliquid addit supra ens, tunc quaero utrum illud additum sit essentialiter ens vel non; si sic, tunc unum dicit ens bis, semel ratione entis inclusi in uno, alias ratione additi, si sit additio; si autem illud additum non includat essentialiter ens, sequitur propositum, scilicet quod unum, in quantum unum, id est ut differt ab ente, non

---

1 uniuscuiusque est] *inv.* K uniuscumque est F | non] *add.* per Q | per²] secundum NO M FW Q   2 Item] Praeterea O KU FW Q X Z | quando] quod non X | aliquid] unum KU FW Q X Z *add.* (*post* praedicatur U) per se KU | de alio *om.* L *add.* et X | modo *om.* H   3 nugatio est] *inv.* K | est — nugatio] *mg.* Z² | addendo unum] addere unum KU FW Q unum addere X Z² | alii] alteri Q | animal — animal] homo animal et homo O homo animal animal homo L | et] *lin.* F | homo²] hoc N   4 dicendo] dicere K FW Q X *om.* O U | unum] *add.* igitur H U *add.* ult. etc. U | e] *lin.* Q | igitur etc.] igitur L ergo etc. FW Q *om.* X   5 Item] Praeterea O KU FW Q X Z | ens *om.* O | creatum] increatum O | creatum ... increatum] increatum ... creatum KU X | et] *add.* in HM FW | ens *om.* Q Z | ens — est *om.* O | increatum] creatum W   6 quod] et X | quod — iterum] quorum alterum Z | ens creatum *om.* KU FW Q X | iterum] ita (*ant.* quod) F verum X | subdividitur] dividitur HL Q | decem] quattuor L | ita quod] quia L   7 sit] *add.* vel O KU FW X   8 creatum] causatum M | ens *om.* L KU FW Q X Z | increatum] incausatum M | sed — dubius et certus sed (n. 26) *om.* X | ens² *om.* HL K   9 ente *om.* FW | increato] *add.* nec ens increatum tantum cum dicatur de ente (*om.* FW) creato FW Q Z | igitur] ergo (*post* ipso FW) L FW Q   10 ens *om.* F | per se *om.* Q | modo *om.* O H | id est] et H KU scilicet FW | et *om.* O   11 Item] Praeterea O K FW Q Z | si *om.* H | praedicatur] ponitur O | essentialiter *om.* O Q | tunc *om.* HL KU   12 hoc] *mg.* O W | aliquid] aliquod FW | quia tunc] tunc enim L quia FW Q Z   13 unum *om.* KU | non — magis] *rep.* O | esset magis] *inv.* L | entis *om.* KU   14 aliter *om.* O FW Q Z | in *om.* O L FW Q | IV] 'X' FW   15 nugatio] magis FW Q Z | dicendo] dicere FW Q Z | et²] vel O FW Q Z | Si] *add.* autem NO M FW Q Z | aliquid addit] *inv.* N M K W Q Z addidit aliquid O   16 supra] super O F Z | ens *om.* N | tunc — ens] essentialiter O | utrum] an KU | illud] idem H U | additum] superadditum KU | sit] esset KU | essentialiter ens] *inv.* N M FW Q Z   17 si] scilicet Z *om.* H | sic] sit N L | semel] solum FW   18 inclusi] inclusum F | in] *add.* alia U | alias — additio] sibi sic addito FW | si] etsi O | additio] additum H | illud] idem H sic Z   19 non *om.* Z | includat] includit O L FW Q Z sit H | ens] *ant.* essentialiter L est (*ant.* essentialiter) O *om.* N FW Z   20 quod *om.* L U | id est] scilicet Z *om.* FW | non] hoc FW

[12]Cf. **Aristot.**, *Metaph.* IV c. 1 (AL XXV^{3.2} 68; Γ c. 1, 1003b 23-25).

includit ens essentialiter

19 Sed dices quod hoc est propter diversitatem rationum. [6]

20 Dicendum quod bene verum est quod dicunt eandem rem absolutam, tamen rationes eorum sunt ita disparatae quod una non includit essentialiter aliam, et hoc sufficit ad impediendum praedicationem essentialem; sicut "animal" et "rationale", licet dicant eandem rem, unum tamen non praedicatur de alio per se. Et hoc concordat proposito nostro, scilicet quod unum prout distinguitur ab ente dicit aliquod accidens per passionem entis — accipiendo large accidens cum AVICENNA[13] pro omni eo quod est extra rationem essentialem alicuius. Patet quod non valet ratio COMMENTATORIS facta IV *Metaphysicae*[14] contra AVICENNAM, quia bene concludit si unum diceret accidens reale distinctum contra substantiam quod dividitur in novem praedicamenta accidentium, sed non concludit quod unum dicat tale accidens quod est extra rationem formalem entis. Sic igitur patet quod ens respectu unius, veri et boni, quae sunt eius passiones, est primum obiectum intellectus primitate adaequationis secundum virtutem sicut subiectum respectu suae propriae passionis.

[B. — De primitate entis secundum praedicationem]

21 Sed quod sit etiam obiectum respectu suorum inferiorum, scilicet Dei et creaturae, primitate praedicationis, ostendo: quia ad [7]

---

1 essentialiter] esse O   2 Sed dices] Sed dicit O Si dicas K Sed dicis U Sed dicet F | hoc est] *inv.* F | rationum] *add.* scilicet (*om.* Z) quod impeditur praedicatio essentialis (*add.* entis FW Q Z) vel (et U) e converso KU FW Q Z   3 Dicendum] *add.* est N M *add.* tamen H | bene *om.* H | bene — quod] unum verum et ens KU | rem] rationem Q   4 absolutam] absolute H | sunt] sint H | ita disparatae] *inv.* HL KU | non] *mg.* F²   5 includit] includat KU | essentialiter] ant. non HL U ant. includit K formaliter O   6 essentialem] = N M K F essentialiter O HL U Q Z essentiale W *add.* aliam F | sicut *om.* U   7 rem] naturam Z | unum *post* praedicatur K *om.* U | unum tamen] *inv.* Z | de alio *post* se L de illo K | hoc *om.* FW   8 concordat] concedatur Q *add.* cum F | scilicet] sed N M Q licet KU | quod — distinguitur] divino potest distingui O | prout] ut HL   9 dicit] contingit FW | accidens] ens Q | per] vel KU   10 cum] sed O   11 alicuius] *add.* unde O KU FW Q Z   12 facta *om.* L | IV] 'X' FW | IV Metaphysicae *post* Avicennam Q   13 reale *om.* Z | distinctum *post* substantiam Q *om.* K   14 praedicamenta] genera Q Z *add.* sive in novem genera FW   15 concludit] contingit N W | quod] quoniam K F quando Q si Z | unum] *add.* non O | dicat] dicit O K | tale *om.* Z | extra *om.* K   16 Sic] Sicut U | igitur] ergo L FW   17 sunt *om.* Q   18 intellectus] *add.* non Q | primitate] primitive U *om.* O   19 subiectum] solum O obiectum H Z | suae *om.* O KU FW Q Z | propriae passionis] *inv.* Q   21 sit etiam] *inv.* KU sint etiam O *add.* primum F Q Z | obiectum] subiectum L   22 Dei] Deo K | creaturae] creatione (*lin.*) O M

---

[13] **Avicenna**, *Metaph*. V c. 1 (AviL 232-236).
[14] Cf. **Averroës**, *Metaph*. IV com. 3 (ed. Iuntina VIII f. 67r B).

hoc requiritur, ut dictum est,¹⁵ quod tale obiectum praedicetur essentialiter et per se de omnibus intelligibilibus, et per consequens univoce aliqua univocatione; sed ens est huiusmodi; igitur, etc. Minorem ostendo per intentionem PHILOSOPHI II *Metaphysicae*¹⁶ dicentis quod "unumquodque est maxime tale inter alia quod est causa quod alia sunt talia univoce, ut ignis est calidissimus, quia est causa univoca caloris in aliis"; non autem hoc est verum de causa analogica vel aequivoca, quia sic sol esset calidissimus, et subdit quod "prima principia oportet esse verissima, quia sunt causae veritatis in aliis", quod non sequitur nisi veritas diceretur in utrisque univoce; sed subdit:¹⁷ "sicut se habent ad esse, sic ad veritatem". Igitur quod est causa entitatis aliis est maxime ens, si tamen¹⁸ ens dicatur de eis univoce et non aliter. Cum igitur Deus sit causa entitatis creaturae et dicatur maxime ens, oportet quod ens dicatur de Deo et creatura univoce; et hoc est quod dicit AVICENNA in *Metaphysica* sua,¹⁹ quod conceptus entis est communis omnibus

---

1 est *om.* N | quod] ut Z | praedicetur] praedicatur KU   2 essentialiter] aequaliter K   3 univoce] unitate F | univocatione] universalissime F univoce Z | ens *om.* O | igitur] ergo L FW Q   4 Minorem] Maiorem K | ostendo] primo O | intentionem Philosophi] Philosophum L *add.* in N M | II] III Z   5 dicentis quod] ait (*post* unumquodque) Q | maxime tale] *inv.* Q maximum tale U | alia] aliqua HL U talia FW | quod²] quia O *add.* illud O   6 quod] et N quare KU Q | talia univoce] *inv.* Z | ut ignis] uti aliquis Z   7 causa univoca] *inv.* F causa analogica vel aequivoca Z | non — est] hoc autem non est KU *rep.* W | autem hoc] *inv.* F | est] ant. autem O Q   8 analogica] analoga HL FW | sic *om.* FW Q Z | subdit] suddit(!) H   9 prima principia] *inv.* L | causae] causa O FW Q Z   10 in *om.* FW | sequitur] sequeretur N M FW Q Z *add.* ut dictum est O FW Q Z | in²] de K | utrisque] utriusque Z   11 sed] et L KU | habent] *add.* aliqua L | sic] ita N M FW *add.* se habent K | ad²] *add.* virtutem Z   12 Igitur] Ergo L FW Q | aliis] in aliis Q | aliis — entitatis *om.* N HLM | tamen] tantum Q | ens dicatur] *inv.* K   13 et *om.* KU Z | igitur] ergo FW Q | causa] ei Q   14 creaturae] creaturis M | et *om.* L | dicatur] dicitur N HLM | ens *om.* F   15 et] *add.* de FW | creatura] creaturis KU FW Z | Avicenna] *add.* de U   16 sua *om.* KU | quod] et in U | conceptus] *add.* mentis qui sunt quasi species eius W | entis *om.* Q

¹⁵Cf. supra n. 6. 9.
¹⁶Cf. **Aristot.**, *Metaph.* II c. 1 (XXV³·² 44; α c. 1 993b 24-32): "Unumquodque vero maxime ipsum aliorum secundum quod et aliis inest univocatio, puta ignis calidissimus; et enim est causa aliis hic caloris. Quare et verissimum quod posterioribus est causa ut sint vera. Quapropter semper exsistentium principia semper esse verissima est necesse; non enim quandoque vera nec illis causa aliquid est ut sint, sed illa aliis. Quare unumquodque sicut se habet ut sit, ita et ad veritatem"; cf. *Auctoritates Aristotelis* (ed. J. Hamesse 118): "Quidquid est causa aliorum ut tale, illud est maxime tale ..."; cf. **Thomas**, *Metaph.* II lect. 2 n. 292 (ed. Cathala-Spiazzi 85): "Unumquodque inter alia maxime dicitur ex quo causatur in aliis aliquid univoce praedicatum de eis ..."
¹⁷Cf. **Aristot.**, *Metaph.* II c. 1 (XXV² t. 4; α c. 1 993b 30-32): "... quare unumquodque sicut habet esse, ita et veritatem.": cf. *Auctoritates Aristotelis* (ed. J. Hamesse 118): "Unumquodque sicut se habet ad entitatem, sic se habet ad veritatem."
¹⁸Subaudi: dummodo.
¹⁹Cf. **Avicenna**, *Metaph.* I c. 2 (AviL 12-13): "Igitur ostensum est tibi ex his omnibus quod ens, inquantum ens, est commune omnibus his et quod ipsum debet poni subiectum huius magisterii ... Ideo primum subiectum huius scientiae est ens, inquantum est ens; et ea quae inquirit sunt consequentia ens, inquantum est ens, sine condicione. Quorum quaedam sunt ei quasi species, ut substantia, quantitas et qualitas, quoniam esse non eget dividi in alia priusquam in ista, sicut substantia eget dividi in alia antequam perveniat ad dividendum in hominem et non-hominem."

praedicamentis, quae sunt quasi eius species. Idem patet per COMMENTATOREM IV *Metaphysicae* commento 2,[20] ubi dicit quod simile est de illo genere quod est ens et aliis generibus univocis, quia ens praedicatur de illis univoce et essentialiter sicut genera alia; certum est autem quod aequivocum non praedicatur essentialiter de aequivocatis, igitur, etc.

22 Item, per rationem sic: non dices ens aequivoce vel analogice praedicari de aliis nisi quia conceptus entis convenit Deo per essentiam, aliis autem per participationem. Sed quod non convenit Deo per essentiam, probo: intellectus enim, habens conceptum proprium alicuius obiecti, potest illud per illum conceptum distinguere[21] ab omni alio, quia ille conceptus, qui est uni proprius, est alteri impossibilis; sed si conceptus entis non est communis Deo et creaturae, ille est proprius Dei, saltem si conveniat Deo tantum per essentiam et principaliter, ut supponis; igitur intellectus noster per conceptum entis potest distinguere Deum a creatura — quod falsum est (per conceptum enim entis cognoscimus Deum confuse tantum prout habet esse cum aliis); igitur, etc.

23 Item, nullus conceptus creaturae facit conceptum proprium Dei; sed facit conceptum entis; igitur conceptus entis non est conceptus proprius Dei. Maior probatur: quia nihil potest facere conceptum

[8]

---

1 praedicamentis] praedicabilibus H | quae] qui W | eius species] *inv.* W | patet *om.* U Q 2 IV] 'IX' O 'X' KU | 2] 20 Z | ubi *om.* O H KU FW Q 3 illo] isto O KU W Q Z | et] *add.* de FW 4 illis] eis N aliis FW | et *om.* Z 5 est autem] *inv.* L 6 aequivocatis] aequivocis H U FW Z univocis Q | igitur etc.] ergo etc. L FW Q Z *om.* N M 7 Item] Praeterea O KU FW Q Z | dices] diceres O KU FW diceretur Q diceret Z | ens *om.* L 8 praedicari] praedicare U | nisi] non F *om.* Z | quia] quod N M | entis] ens U 9 autem] vero F nota W *om.* L | participationem] *spat. vac.* O | convenit] conveniat N M FW Q cum O 10 per essentiam *om.* L | probo] = HLM probatio NO Q Z probatur KU FW 11 potest illud per illum conceptum distinguere] = FW Q Z per illum conceptum distinguitur N HLM KU potest illud per illum conceptum distincte O | illum] illud O istum KU Q | conceptum] compositum O 12 alio] alia re O | quia] qui U | est alteri impossibilis] alteri est incompossibilis O et alteri impossibilis U est incompossibilis alii FW Z est impossibilis alii Q 13 non] nec O | communis] aliquid O *add.* univoce Q Z | creaturae] creaturis K 14 ille] iste Q | est] esset KU | Dei] Deo L Q *add.* conceptus KU | conveniat] convenit O H FW Q Z | tantum] *lin.* W *om.* F Z | essentiam] essentialem Z 15 supponis] suppositum KU *add.* est K | igitur] ergo L FW Q | intellectus noster] *inv.* KU | per conceptum] in conceptu FW 16 entis] ens U *om.* O | creatura] creaturis H KU | falsum est] *inv.* Q falsum W 17 confuse tantum] *inv.* FW 18 habet esse] *inv.* H habet FW Z habet conceptum communem Q | igitur etc.] ergo etc. L FW Q *om.* O 19 Item] Praeterea KU FW Q Z | conceptus] *add.* communis Z 20 igitur] ergo L FW Q | conceptus proprius Dei] = HL FW proprius Dei NO M Z conceptus Dei proprius K proprius conceptus Dei U Q 21 Maior probatur] *inv.* N Minor probatur L | quia] quod F | nihil] non O | conceptum proprium] *inv.* KU

---

[20]Cf. **Averroës**, *Metaph.* IV com. 2 (ed. Iuntina VIII f. 65r D-E).
[21]Hic plures codices, et antiqui et meliores, pro verbis 'potest illud per illum conceptum distinguere' ea verba 'per illum conceptum distinguitur' exhibent. Attamen revera, ut opinamur, Scotus in lectionibus suis probabiliter dixit: 'per illum conceptum distinguit illud'; error autem tranmissionis ex litteris male intellectis forsan ortus est.

proprium de aliquo quod non contineat essentialiter vel virtualiter; essentialiter sicut homo animal, virtualiter ut subiectum propriam passionem; sed creatura nulla per se nec omnes simul continent Deum nec virtualiter nec essentialiter; igitur, etc. Ex creaturis autem possumus formare de Deo quod sit ens; igitur conceptus entis non est Deo proprius.

Item, ille conceptus, cui alii conceptus attribuuntur, est perfectior aliis. Exemplum: conceptus sanitatis in animali est perfectior conceptu sanitatis in cibo vel in urina vel in diaeta, qui omnes primo conceptui attribuuntur; similiter, conceptus substantiae perfectior est conceptu accidentis. Sed si per conceptum entis haberemus conceptum proprium de Deo, illi attribuerentur omnes conceptus creaturarum. Igitur ille esset perfectior; sed nullum conceptum perfectiorem conceptu creaturae possumus habere pro statu viae — nec de Deo nec de alio — nisi creatum ex conceptu tantum creaturae, qui conceptus est causa aequivoca; omnis autem causa aequivoca est perfectior causato vel non imperfectior; igitur nullus conceptus perfectior est conceptu creaturae; conceptus igitur entis quem habemus de Deo non est perfectior conceptu creaturae, et per consequens nec Deo proprius.

---

1 quod non] nisi HL *add.* intelligat O | contineat] continet F *add.* vel O KU *add.* illud H FW *add.* illud vel Q | essentialiter ... virtualiter] virtualiter ... essentialiter L   2 essentialiter] *add.* ut H | sicut] ut K | virtualiter] *add.* sicut O | ut] sicut N U *om.* Q | propriam passionem] *inv.* U propriam habet passionem O   3 creatura nulla] *inv.* HL Q creatur(!) nulla Z | omnes simul] *inv.* N omnis simul U | continent Deum] *rep.* W   4 Deum *om.* L | virtualiter ... essentialiter] essentialiter ... virtualiter FW | igitur] ergo L FW Q | etc.] *add.* probatio quod non essentialiter quia negas univocum quod non virtualiter quia perfectius non continetur in minus perfecto Q | creaturis] causis O | autem] in O etiam (ant. Ex) L   5 igitur] ergo L FW Q | non *om.* L   6 est] *add.* de H FW   7 Item] Praeterea O KU FW Q Z | ille] iste KU Q | alii *om.* Q | conceptus²] conceptu Q *om.* O KU FW Z | attribuuntur] ant. alii H | perfectior aliis] *inv.* O KU FW Q Z   9 conceptu sanitatis] *inv.* U | in² *om.* L Q | in³ *om.* L U Q   10 conceptui] *add.* primo H   11 perfectior est] *inv.* O KU FW Z perfectior Q | Sed] *add.* se O | per *om.* Z | conceptum] conceptum F   12 haberemus] habere H | conceptum proprium] *inv.* FW conceptum entis proprium O | Deo] *add.* et L | illi] alii F alli(!) W ibi Q | attribuerentur] attribuuntur U | omnes conceptus] conceptus omnium FW   13 Igitur] Ergo L FW Q Quibus KU   14 perfectiorem — creaturae] in via F | conceptu] respectu L | creaturae] crearetur Z | habere *post* viae KU   15 viae *om.* Z *add.* seu *rep.* quia nullum conceptum in via (eis Z) possumus habere pro statu viae W Q Z | creatum *om.* Z | conceptu] u O | tantum] ant. ex Z *post* creaturae L *om.* FW Q   16 autem] enim L   17 vel] et H | non] *lin.* Q | imperfectior] *lin.* Q | igitur] ergo L FW Q | nullus — creaturae] nullum conceptum perfectiorem conceptu creaturae possumus habere O FW Q   18 perfectior est] *inv.* HL KU | creaturae] creaturarum H | conceptus²] quibus O | igitur] ergo (ant. conceptus FW) FW Q   19 de *om.* O   20 nec] non N M FW *add.* est FW | Deo proprius] de propriis O

[IV. — De univocatione entis]

25 Quod etiam conceptus entis sit communis univoce substantiae et accidenti, probo: quia si non, nullum conceptum de substantia haberemus. Aut enim haberemus de substantia conceptum proprium et quidditativum et intuitivum, aut abstrahibilem; non primum, ut probatum est;[22] igitur conceptum abstrahibilem a substantia et accidente et communem utrique; sed nullus est conceptus communis utrique nisi conceptus entis; igitur, etc. Quod autem substantiam in via non possumus conceptu simplici et primo cognoscere, patet ex hoc quod omnis nostra cognitio oritur a sensu; substantia autem per se non est sensibilis; et ideo intuitive vel conceptu simplici non possumus eam cognoscere, sed per illum modum: quia ab accidentibus nobis sensibilibus abstrahimus conceptum entis, dicendo quod sunt entis, et ulterius inquirendo invenimus quod est tale ens quod est alteri inhaerens; illud autem alterum oportet esse subsistens, et tali subsistenti imponimus nomen substantiae. Et ideo sic confuse cognoscimus substantiam, componendo ipsi enti subsistentiam, dicendo quod est ens per se subsistens; non autem de ipsa habemus in via conceptum intuitivum, quo cognoscimus ipsam esse hoc ens nisi modo praedicto, ut experientia docet.

26 Item, omnis intellectus certus de uno et dubius de duobus

---

2 Quod] *lin.* Z Praeterea O | communis univoce] unicus H univocus L KU | univoce *post* accidenti Q 3 accidenti probo] = LM Q accidenti probatio N H FW Z arguit primo O accidenti probatur KU | quia — haberemus *om.* FW | substantia] *add.* proprium Q 4 haberemus] *add.* primo Q *add.* probatio KU Z *add.* ult. quod K | enim] igitur O | haberemus² *post* substantia L | conceptum *om.* O KU FW Q Z 5 quidditativum ... intuitivum] intuitivum ... quidditativum H | et² *om.* O FW Q Z | abstrahibilem] abstahibile Z | non — abstrahibilem *om.* O 6 est] *add.* supra FW Q Z | igitur] ergo L FW Q | conceptum *om.* FW 7 communem] commune KU | conceptus communis] *inv.* FW Z conceptus commune O communis Q 8 conceptus *om.* FW Q Z | igitur] ergo L FW Q 9 substantiam *post* via Q differentia O | conceptu] intellectu Z | et] a N 10 nostra *om.* Q | oritur *om.* Z | sensu] sensibile M 11 autem *om.* H *add.* ut patet FW Z | per se *post* est K de se FW ex se Q | non] *rep.* N | et *om.* KU | vel] et K in U 12 conceptu] intellectu Z | simplici] *mg.* W | possumus] possimus O | eam cognoscere] *inv.* Z ea cognoscere O | per] super U | illum] istum HM W hunc Q 13 nobis] neque U non F | sensibilibus] sensibilis Z 14 dicendo] de Deo(!) O Q Z dicendum FW 15 invenimus *om.* Q | quod] quia Z | est] sunt O KU FW Z | est²] sunt U | alteri] alicui Z | illud] idem H U 16 esse] omne U 17 substantiam *om.* O 18 componendo] cognoscendo FW | ipsi] ipsius F | enti] entis L FW | subsistentiam] subsistentia KU | dicendo] de Deo(!) F Q Z | ens *om.* K 19 non] *rep.* Z | ipsa] ipso KU | habemus] ant. de H | intuitivum] in talibus O 20 cognoscimus] cognoscamus Z | ipsam] eam O FW Q Z ipsum KU | ens *om.* FW | nisi] non F 21 experientia] apparentia H | docet *om.* Z 22 Item] Praeterea O KU FW Q Z | intellectus] *add.* (*lin.* W) creatus FW | duobus] diversis FW

[22]Cf. supra n. 12.

oportet quod habeat alium conceptum de certo et alium de duobus, quia aliter per eundem conceptum idem intellectus esset dubius et certus; sed aliquis potest esse certus de aliquo quod sit ens, dubius autem utrum sit substantia vel accidens — sicut de potentiis animae patet, et de primo principio, ut dubitaverunt antiqui philosophi, ut patet I *Physicorum*,[23] et de luce; igitur alius est conceptus entis, alius substantiae et accidentis; sed ille est communis utrique et non importat illos conceptus plures; igitur est communis univoce.

[10] Item, omnis ille conceptus qui sufficit ad contradictionem est univocus, quia contradictio est affirmatio et negatio circa idem univocum — hic enim non est contradictio: canis currit, canis non currit;[24] sed conceptus entis sufficit ad contradictionem secundum PHILOSOPHUM VIII *Metaphysicae*[25] — immo prima contradictio est formata de ente, sicut de quolibet esse vel non esse; igitur, etc.

Item, primum principium debet esse firmissimum secundum PHILOSOPHUM IV *Metaphysicae*;[26] sed primum principium formatur de ente, sicut dictum est, igitur firmissime; sed si ens diceret plures conceptus, non esset certum de quo conceptu esset verum, immo semper esset distinguendum; igitur, etc.

---

1 oportet quod habeat] habet L oportet habere H | alium conceptum] *inv.* O aliquem conceptum K | certo] uno L | et alium] alium O U Z alium autem Q | duobus] dubio FW Z dubitationis Q *add.* dubiis KU 2 conceptum] *rep.* H *add.* cognosceret dubium et certum et sic FW | idem *om.* O Q Z | intellectus] intellectum O | esset] *ant.* idem K | dubius et certus] certus et dubius O L 3 certus²] certum X | de aliquo] de alio O de uno K *om.* X | ens] *add.* et H 4 autem utrum] *inv.* O tamen an L an H KU autem quod Q et utrum X | sit substantia] *inv.* F | de] *lin.* X | potentiis] potentia O 5 et *om.* U | de primo] de O FW X de hoc H *om.* Z | ut *om.* F Q | dubitaverunt] dubitaverant Q | antiqui] aliqui H HM | philosophi *om.* X 6 patet *om.* U | et] *add.* patet HL | igitur] ergo L FW Q X | entis — conceptus] *rep.* X 7 et] alius N H U | ille] iste L | est *om.* FW | utrique] utroque U utrisque F | et²] ut X | non *om.* U Z 8 illos] alios H istos K X | igitur] ergo L FW Q X | est *om.* X | univoce] unitatem X 9 Item] Praeterea O KU FW Q X Z | omnis *om.* O KU FW Q X Z | ille] iste K Q X *om.* H 10 est affirmatio *om.* X | est — currit *om.* O | negatio] nugatio X 11 univocum *om.* Q | hic] ut X | enim *post* est F *om.* KU X | currit] *add.* et KU F | canis non] nullus canis L 13 VIII] IV FW X | prima] propterea U primae X 14 quolibet] *add.* dicitur K | igitur etc.] ergo etc. L FW etc. Q *om.* X 15 Item] Praeterea O KU FW Q X Z | debet] oportet X 16 IV] 'X' Z | primum principium] *inv.* Q | formatur] formaliter Q 17 ente] essente U | sicut] *add.* quod FW | igitur] ergo L FW Q X | firmissime] firmissimum FW Q X Z *add.* est Q Z 18 certum] certus U | esset²] essent X 19 distinguendum] verum dicendum H dubitandum L | igitur etc.] ergo etc. L FW Q *om.* X

[23] Cf. **Aristot.**, *Physic.* I c. 2 (AL VII¹ 8; A c. 2 184b 15-22).
[24] Subaudi: canis, qui sidus in caelo est, non currit.
[25] Cf. potius **Aristot.**, *Metaph.* IV c. 3 (AL XXV^{3.2} 73; Γ c. 3 1005b 19-25).
[26] Cf. **Aristot.**, *Metaph.* IV c. 3 (AL XXV^{3.2} 73; Γ c. 3 1005b 12-15).

[V. — Obiectiones contra univocationem entis earumque redargutiones]
[A. — Obiectiones]

29 Contra praedicta potest sic argui:

Quia si esset univocum, aut sicut genus, differentia vel species; non potest esse species, quia non habet superius et quia substantia et accidens non sunt individua sed genera generalissima; nec differentia, quia esset una substantiae vel accidenti et haberet genus supra se; nec genus, ut probatur III *Metaphysicae*,[27] quia genus habet differentias quae sunt extra rationem generis — nihil autem est quod subterfugiat rationem entis. Hoc idem dicit PORPHYRIUS:[28] dicit quod ens non est genus, sed dicitur aequivoce de substantia et accidente.

30 Item, omne commune indeterminatum descendit in inferiora per aliquid additum sibi contrahens ipsum, sicut genus per differentias, species per principia individuantia; sed enti non potest fieri talis additio contrahens. Probatio: quia illud additum esset ens vel non-ens. Si sic, igitur substantia, quae includit illud additum, esset ens bis, et sic esset nugatio dicere "substantiam tantum".[29] Si vero non sit ens, tunc non descendit ens in substantiam per aliquid sed per non-ens, et etiam illud non-ens esset de ratione substantiae per

---

4 praedicta] dicta W | potest sic argui] potest argui NO M FW X potest argui sic L sic argui potest Q 5 si] aut FW add. ens KU | aut] add. esset L | genus] add. vel O FW Q X Z | differentia ... species] species ... differentia L FW add. ult. et L 6 potest esse] sicut FW | et] etiam N om. O | quia²] lin. F 8 quia] add. tunc K | una] add. vel U Q add. propria vel FW X Z | vel] et N K | accidenti] accidentem X 9 se om. L | nec] add. ut FW | genus] igitur Z | probatur post Metaphysicae H | habet] habent X 10 autem est] inv. K aliud est X 11 subterfugiat] subterfugiet N subterfugit L | rationem] add. generis K | idem] autem L | dicit²] dicens KU om. O Q X Z add. enim FW 12 quod] quia Q | est] lin. X 14 Item] Praeterea O KU FW Q X Z | omne om. H Q | in] ad X 15 aliquid] aliquod H add. quod O | additum sibi] inv. O L FW Q Z sed additum X add. ult. per O X add. ult. scilicet Q | sicut] si est X om. Q | genus] add. per species X | differentias species] inv. F differentias et species K 16 individuantia] individua F X 17 talis] tali H | quia] aut X om. Z add. aut KU FW | illud] idem H U | additum] ens] spat. vac. O | vel] aut FW | vel — ens² om. X 18 non-ens] non KU FW Z | sic] ens L | igitur] ergo L FW Q | substantia quae] idem quod H substantia quae incluserat quae Q | includit illud] includit idem H includeret illud (idem U) KU FW illud incluserat Z add. ult. ens FW Q | additum om. FW Z 19 ens bis] inv. H KU | sic] lin. X | esset nugatio] inv. L esse nugatio H nugatio Q | dicere] de O diceret Q | substantiam] substantia O | vero] nullo O autem Z om. KU X 20 non sit] inv. O L FW non Q esset non Z | non²] mg. W | descendit] descenderet FW descendet Z | in substantiam om. N M | per] in O | sed — non-ens om. FW Q X Z 21 etiam illud] inv. O FW Q X etiam idem H illud K idem U etiam Z | non-ens] non Q | substantiae] add. quod O

---

[27] Cf. **Aristot.**, *Metaph.* III c. 3 (AL XXV³·² 56; c. 3 998b 23-26).
[28] Cf. **Porphyrius**, *Liber praedicabilium* cap. 'De specie' (AL I⁶ 12; c. 6 8-9); cf. *Auctoritates Aristotelis* (ed. J. Hamesse 299): "Si aliquis omnia praedicamenta entia vocet aequivoce et non univoce ea nuncupabit, id est analogice."
[29] Cf. **Aristot.**, *Metaph.* VII c. 3 (AL XXV³·² 139; E c. 3 1030b 29-36).

quod descenderet in eam, et sic quaererem sicut prius et esset processus in infinitum.

Item, si ens praedicatur in quid de substantia et accidente, oportet quod sit per rationem alicuius praedicabilis, scilicet generis vel differentiae, et ceterorum. Non differentiae, quia non praedicatur in quale. Igitur hoc esset per rationem generis, sed hoc est falsum, quia descenderet in substantiam et accidens tanquam in species per differentias quae essent extra rationem entis, quod falsum est — immo ens statim est illa in quae descendit sine expectatione differentiae, sicut etiam dicitur de uno, VIII *Metaphysicae*.[30] Non est igitur genus et per consequens non praedicatur de eis univoce.

Item, expresse IV *Metaphysicae*[31] dicitur quod ens dicitur de multis non univoce, sed ad unum, sicut sanum, id est analogice.

[B. — Redargutiones]

[12]   Ad primum istorum[32] dicendum quod in III *Metaphysicae* ARISTOTELES nihil dicit assertive, sed arguit ad utramque partem contradictionis; unde COMMENTATOR dicit ibidem[33] quod prima ratio PHILOSOPHI ibi posita peccat secundum accidens sive continet fallaciam accidentis. Argumentum enim PHILOSOPHI[34] ad contrarium est tale: si ens non dicat unum conceptum decem

---

1 descenderet] descendit H | et sic] tunc O KU FW Q X et tunc Z | quaererem] quaere FW 3 Item] Praeterea O K FW Q X Z 4 quod] *add.* hoc FW X Z | per] secundum F X | scilicet] ut K | generis] *add.* speciei L 5 differentiae *om.* O | et ceterorum *om.* O KU FW Q X Z | non *om.* O K Q | praedicatur *post* quale O 6 Igitur *post* esset U Ergo L FW Q Z Genus X | per] secundum FW Q X Z | est] *mg.* M esset NO W Q 7 quia] quod O Q *add.* tunc N M | descenderet] descendit H | et accidens *om.* FW Z | in² *om.* N L X 8 essent] *add.* per O | entis] generis FW 9 est²] *ab* Z | illa] in substantia Q | quae] qua Q Z 10 dicitur] dicuntur Z *om.* X | de uno *om.* U | VIII] IV FW 11 Non — univoce *om.* O | est *post* genus Q *om.* M K | igitur] *rep.* M ergo (ant. non L *lin.* X) L FW X | et] nec X | non — univoce] = N HM non praedicatur univoce L nec univoce praedicatum (praedicatur F) de eis KU FW Z non praedicatur univoce de eis Q praedicatur unvoce de eis X 13 Item] Praeterea O KU FW Q X Z | dicitur] ant. IV N | dicitur — ens] *mg.* Z² *om.* O FW *add.* quod X 14 non *om.* U | ad unum *om.* HL KU | sanum] sana X Z 16 istorum dicendum] *inv.* Z istorum dicendum est N M illorum dicendum H FW Z horum dicendum Q | in *om.* Z | III] I N HM KU | Aristoteles] ant. III Z *post* dicit O Q 17 nihil] non U Z *om.* X | dicit] dicitur X | ad utramque] ut ad magnam X 18 ibidem] ibi HL KU | prima ratio] *inv.* X 19 ibi posita] imposita Q | peccat — sive *om.* FW Q X Z | sive] seu L 20 ad] in HL KU 21 dicat] dicit N M | unum conceptum] *inv.* X conceptum K *add.* univocum KU FW Q X Z

---

[30]Cf. **Aristot.**, *Metaph.* VIII c. 1 (AL XXV[3.2] 168; H c. 1 1042a 21-22).
[31]Cf. **Aristot.**, *Metaph.* IV c. 2 (AL XXV[3.2] 67; Γ c. 2 1003a 32—1003b 1).
[32]Cf. supra n. 29.
[33]Cf. **Averroës**, *Metaph.* III com. 3 (ed. Iuntina VIII f. 40v M—41r B).
[34]Cf. **Aristot.**, *Metaph.* III c. 3 (AL XXV[3.2] 56; c. 3 998b 17-23).

generibus sed cuilibet proprium, sequitur quod ens non tantum sit genus sed etiam decem genera. Dicendum ergo quod illud non dicit Philosophus determinative, scilicet quod ens non sit genus, sed arguendo. Ad dictum autem Porphyrii dicendum quod, licet fuerit logicus, multa tamen dixit non logice, specialiter illud quod pertinet ad praedicamenta; ens enim, prout praedicatur de decem praedicamentis metaphysice vel naturaliter, non dicit unum conceptum — nec genus est naturale eorum nec metaphysicum; est tamen univocum, logice loquendo.

34 Ad aliam confirmationem de differentia quae est extra rationem generis,[35] dicendum quod licet genus et differentia non sunt idem formaliter, quia ratio formalis differentiae non includit rationem formalem generis, tamen sunt idem realiter vel identice. Quandocumque enim aliqua sunt idem formaliter, si iungantur sine medio, est ibi nugatio, ut "color albedo"; non tamen si sint idem identice solum et non formaliter, ut "color albus" — licet album sit idem in re quod albedo, quia tamen album significat suam rem denominative vel in concreto — non est nugatio. Sic autem iungitur differentia generi in definitione quod differentia denominative sive in concreto significatur, ut "animal rationale", et sic est idem generi identice tantum et non formaliter. Sic in proposito est de ente respectu unius, quia dicendo "ens unitas" est nugatio. Sic ergo illud

---

1 cuilibet *om.* Z | sequitur] sequetur Q 2 sed etiam] etiam O sed FW immo KU Q X Z | decem] quattuor X *om.* Z | Dicendum] *add.* est N M F | ergo] igitur NO K Q Z *om.* U | quod] non Q | illud] idem U *om.* Z | non *om.* O 3 Philosophus *om.* Q | determinative] determinate N M KU Q X determinare O | quod ens] *rep.* Z | sit] est O | genus] *add.* tantum Q 4 arguendo] arguitive X ordo Z *add. spat. vac.* X | dicendum] *add.* (ant. dicendum L) est N ML | licet *om.* X *add.* multa L 5 logicus] locutus N HL locus O | multa tamen] *inv.* L | dixit] dicit O L FW Q Z dicitur X | logice] logica KU | specialiter] *add.* sed H | illud] idem U id W 6 praedicatur] praedicare K praedicari U 7 vel *om.* N M | non] *add.* tamen K | unum] *lin.* X 8 genus est] *inv.* K Q genus U *add. ult.* nec KU | naturale] *add.* est KU | nec[2]] vel Q *om.* FW X Z | metaphysicum] analogicum K | est tamen] *inv.* X | univocum] unicum O *add.* locutum HL 9 logice] loquendo(!) M 11 dicendum] *add.* est N M F | sunt] sint O FW Q Z 12 non] *lin.* Z[2] 13 realiter] formaliter L | vel identice] vel redemptior U *om.* Z | Quandocumque] Quandoque O Quando Q | Quandocumque — identice *om.* X 14 enim *om.* H | aliqua sunt] *inv.* Q | sunt] *rep.* N | formaliter] *add.* quae Q | si] sine K | iungantur] coniungantur H iungatur Z 15 ibi nugatio] *inv.* K aliquando nugatio O nugatio H | non — identice] *mg.* Z[2] | sint] sunt FW Q Z[2] 16 non] tamen U | ut] et U | sit] sint X | sit — albedo] et albedo sint idem re O | in *om.* FW Q X Z 17 quod] et Q | tamen] tunc KU | album *om.* FW Q X Z | suam rem] *inv.* KU 18 vel] et L *om.* O | in concreto] in contrario X in contrario concreto *mg.* Z[2] | non *om.* X | Sic] Sicut K Si Z | iungitur] coniungitur O H 19 differentia generi *om.* X | quod] = O HL F Q X quia N M KU W Z | sive] vel O FW Q X Z 20 in concreto] increato U | significatur] significat L sumatur similatur Z | ut] vel Q | generi] genere Q Z genus X 21 identice] identitate F | et] vel U | Sic — formaliter *om.* KU | est] *ant.* in HL Q 22 quia] quod N Q Z | dicendo] ordo Q | nugatio] *lin.* Z[2] | Sic *om.* N | ergo] igitur NO H Z

[35]Cf. supra n. 29.

additum enti effugit rationem entis, quod significatur modo differentiae quae est idem generi, identice tantum et non formaliter.

[13] Ad aliud[36] de descensu indeterminati in inferiora, dicendum quod duplex est indeterminatum. Unum quod descendit in inferiora per aliquid additum, et tale dicit totum quod inferius, tamen per modum partis determinabilis ut genus, vel per modum partis determinantis ut differentia — et tale non est ipsum ens. Aliud est commune indeterminatum, quod dicit totum illud quod inferiora per modum totius nec expectat terminari per aliud — ut species respectu individuorum, duo enim individua se totis in specie conveniunt et numero differunt —, et tale commune non descendit in inferiora per aliquid additum. Sic autem ens est commune ad Deum et decem praedicamenta, ad substantiam et accidens; nihil enim est in substantia et accidente quod non sit ens, et ideo statim seipso sine addito est substantia vel accidens; non igitur reducitur ad praedicabile generis vel differentiae, sed speciei specialissimae.

Vel potest dici,[37] sustinendo, quod sit genus, vel quasi genus secundum Avicennam et Averroëm, quod descendit in inferiora per addita, quae sunt entia identice vel realiter, non tamen formaliter. Nec sequitur sic quod secundum se sint non-entia, sicut non sequitur "homo non secundum se est albus, igitur secundum se est non-albus", quia nec ex ratione humanitatis habet quod sit albus,

---

1 quod] quae L si Z | significatur] sumitur Z 2 differentiae] differre H | quae] quod F | generi] genere Q X 3 aliud *om.* L | de] *rep.* N | descensu] sensu H specie Q | indeterminati] indeterminata Q | in] ad L K Q X | dicendum] *add.* est F 4 est] *ant.* quod N M | indeterminatum] determinatum (*lin.*) Z² | in] ad Q 5 et tale] *mg.* Z² | totum *om.* Z | inferius] *add.* idem quod dicit inferius U | tamen] *add.* (*mg.*) vel F² 6 partis *om.* FW X | determinabilis] indeterminabilis X *add.* vel X | partis² *om.* L | determinantis] determinabilis Q determinatis Z 7 ut] *add.* est O | differentia] *add.* (*mg.*) vel per modum F² | et — modum *om.* F | Aliud] *add.* autem O Q Z | Aliud — totum *om.* X 8 illud] idem U id X *om.* Q | quod²] *add.* dicit K | inferiora] inferius K U *add.* dicit U 9 totius] *add.* determinati FW | nec — aliud *om.* FW | expectat] expectatur Q | terminari] determinari Q 10 individuorum] inferiorum K | se totis] *inv.* O *om.* Z | in *om.* O X 11 commune] continue O | descendit] distinguunt Z | in] *lin.* X *om.* Z 12 aliquid] *add.* commune O | Sic] Sicut X Si Z | ens est] *inv.* O Q 13 et] *add.* ad H FW | decem] quattuor X *om.* L | praedicamenta ad] = NO HM praedicamenta et ad K Q praedicamenta et L U FW X Z | enim est] *inv.* Z est X 14 sit] est X | et² *om.* X | ideo] *add.* se U | seipso] ipsis FW 15 sine *om.* Q Z | igitur] ergo K FW X 16 sed *om.* X 17 dici *om.* X | sustinendo] sciendum O | sit] est L KU 18 descendit] decendit(!) H 19 addita] additamenta Q | vel] et M | non tamen] *inv.* O 20 Nec] *add.* tamen L | sic quod secundum se] si non sunt secundum se entia igitur secundum se O sic quod se K si non secundum se sint entia ergo secundum se FW si non secundum se quod (*om.* Z) Q Z si non per se X | sint] sunt O L FW U X | non²] nec O L FW illud X 21 non *post* (*lin.* F) se N KU F Q | est] *ant.* secundum L | albus] album K FW | igitur] ergo L FW Q X | secundum²] *add.* quod Z 22 non-albus] non-album FW | quia — non-albus *om.* Z | nec] non O | humanitatis] communitatis O | habet *om.* Q X | albus²] album FW

[36]Cf. supra n. 30.
[37]Cf. supra n. 30.

nec non-albus. Istae igitur differentiae per rationem differentiae non sunt entia, nec tamen sequitur quod secundum rationem differentiae sunt non-entia.

37 Ad aliud de IV *Metaphysicae*[38] dicendum quod secundum PHILOSOPHUM in IV *Metaphysicae* non est contra rationem unitatis generis quod omnia illius generis dicantur per attributionem ad unum, ut patet de genere coloris in quo tamen species coloris omnes attributionem habent ad albedinem, quae est primum et mensura omnium colorum; et simile est in quolibet genere, ut dicitur ibidem.[39] Sic in proposito: omnia entia habent attributionem ad ens primum, quod est Deus, vel entia creata ad substantiam; tamen, hoc non obstante, potest ab omnibus istis entibus abstrahi unus communis conceptus significatus nomine entis, qui est univocus logice loquendo, licet non naturaliter vel metaphysice loquendo.

[VI. — Ad argumenta principalia]

38 Ad primum principale[40] dicendum quod primum obiectum potentiae debet accipi secundum adaequationem ad potentiam secundum se, non pro statu aliquo determinato tantum; ens autem

---

1 non-albus] non-album FW non X | Istae] Illae F Q | igitur] ergo L FW X | non²] ant. per O KU FW Q X Z 2 entia — sunt *om.* Z | nec] non KU | nec — entia *om.* X | secundum] per O KU FW Q | differentiae] *add. seu rep.* non per rationem differentiae O 3 sunt] sint O M FW Q 4 dicendum] *ant. de* Q *add.* est N M F | quod *om.* K | Philosophum] *rep.* N 5 in *om.* L FW Q Z | IV] 'X' O | unitatis] unitatem K 6 ad unum] ut unum U *om.* Z 7 genere] generatione Q | coloris] colorum F X | tamen] = O FW Q X tantum N HLM *om.* KU Z | coloris²] colorum F *om.* L | omnes] = N LM *ant.* species O FW Q X Z *ant.* coloris KU omnis (ant. species) H | attributionem habent] *inv.* L Z 8 omnium colorum] omnium aliorum O aliorum colorum L omnium aliorum colorum KU 9 et simile] similisque L sed similiter Q | est *om.* O X Z | in] de KU | Sic in proposito *om.* FW 10 entia] *add.* creata L | ens primum] *inv.* L 11 entia] essentia Q | ad substantiam *om.* Q | hoc *om.* K 12 ab *om.* O | istis] ipsis N | communis conceptus significatus] conceptus communis significatus L conceptus significatus communis KU 13 entis] dictis K | qui] quae O | univocus] univoce O M unicus Z | logice loquendo] *inv.* N loquendo M | licet non] vel X | licet — loquendo *om.* Q 14 loquendo *om.* L FW 16 dicendum] *mg.* Z² *add.* est N M F | primum obiectum] *inv.* N M 18 non] *lin.* Z² *om.* Q | aliquo determinato] *inv.* FW Q X Z | tantum] tamen O | autem *om.* H

[38]Cf. supra n. 32.
[39]Cf. **Aristot.**, *Metaph.* II c. 1 (XXV$^{3.2}$ 44; α c. 1 993b 24-32): "Unumquodque vero maxime ipsum aliorum secundum quod et aliis inest univocatio, puta ignis calidissimus; et enim est causa aliis hic caloris. Quare et verissimum quod posterioribus est causa ut sint vera. Quapropter semper exsistentium principia semper esse verissima est necesse; non enim quandoque vera nec illis causa aliquid est ut sint, sed illa aliis. Quare unumquodque sicut se habet ut sit, ita et ad veritatem"; cf. *Auctoritates Aristotelis* (ed. J. Hamesse 118): "Quidquid est causa aliorum ut tale, illud est maxime tale …"; cf. **Thomas**, *Summa theol.* I q. 2 a. 3 in corp. (IV 32a): "Quod autem dicitur maxime tale in aliquo genere, est causa omnium quae sunt illius generis …".
[40]Cf. supra n. 1.

secundum se et secundum quodlibet suppositum eius est naturaliter immutativum intellectus nostri secundum se, id est in quantum intellectus humanus. Unde Deus est etiam secundum se ab ipso intelligibilis, quantum est ex parte potentiae intellectivae, et sine medio aliquo vel lumine vel specie, quia Deus ipse est lumen et praesentialiter potest adesse intellectui humano, sicut in beatis. Si autem non potest intelligi a nobis pro statu viae, hoc est ratione phantasmatis nobis coniuncti in nostro modo intelligendi pro statu viae, sed hoc est nobis inflictum in poenam peccati, non autem secundum naturam quiditativam, ut dictum est.[41]

[15] Ad aliud[42] dicendum: concedendo maiorem et probationes eius, sed negando minorem. Ad auctoritatem qua dicitur quod dicitur aequivoce: verum est metaphysice loquendo vel naturaliter, non tamen verum est logice loquendo; immo dicit unum communem conceptum omnibus entibus.

Ad aliud[43] dicendum quod cognoscibilitas secundum se sequitur entitatem, non autem respectu cuiuscumque intellectus vel pro quocumque statu, sed tantum respectu illius intellectus qui potest cognoscere ens secundum suam totam communitatem, et hoc est Deus. Unde bene sequitur quod essentia divina est primum obiectum intellectus sui, cum sit primum ens; non autem oportet quod sit primum obiectum intellectus nostri.

---

1 quodlibet] quoddam L *add.* suum F | suppositum eius] *inv.* O | est *om.* Q | naturaliter immutativum] *inv.* Q immutativum O naturaliter mutatum X 2 immutativum] *mg.* Z² | id est] et KU 3 est etiam] *inv.* O KU W Z est N etiam Q X *add.* obiectum L | secundum se] per se (*post* ipso) O KU Q X Z *om.* FW | ipso] *add.* est per se X 4 intelligibilis] *add.* in L | et] etiam KU 5 aliquo *om.* K | ipse est] ille est N est H est illud L ille M ipse X | et] a O *om.* N 6 praesentialiter] principaliter L K | sicut] *add.* patet Q | in *om.* K | Si] Sic Z 7 intelligi *post* nobis O KU FW Q Z | viae] *add.* sed N | hoc — viae] *rep.* O *om.* Z 9 poenam] poenitentiam N HM Q | autem *om.* F 10 secundum — quiditativam] unitati quod dicam X | quiditativam] quaesitiva(!) F quaesitam W *om.* L KU 11 dicendum *om.* Q *add.* est N M *add.* quod X | concedendo] concedo W Q | eius *om.* O X 12 sed] et O U X | negando] nego L | auctoritatem] auctoritates O | qua] quando Q | dicitur aequivoce] = N HM non dicitur univoce dicendum quod O KU FW Q X Z non dicitur univoce L 13 loquendo *post* naturaliter L 14 tamen] autem O | verum est] *inv.* L verum F subiectum est Z *om.* O | logice] *ant.* verum Q | loquendo *om.* O KU FW Q Z | communem conceptum] *inv.* O H verum conceptum KU conceptum L conceptum univocum FW communem Z 16 dicendum] *add.* est M F | quod *om.* Q | secundum se *om.* FW | sequitur] *add.* ad KU 17 autem *om.* H | cuiuscumque] cuicumque O | intellectus] intellectu O | pro] *rep.* U 18 illius] istius Z 19 suam totam] *inv.* U W Q suam O | communitatem] entitatem FW 20 bene *om.* O KU | quod] *add.* ipsa Z | primum] ipsum Z 21 sui — intellectus *om.* X | autem *om.* FW 22 primum *om.* Q | obiectum] subiectum O | nostri] *add.* igitur etc. L KU *add.* Deo gratias Q *add.* ult. leva oculos L

[41] Cf. supra q. 18 n. 9-10.
[42] Cf. supra n. 2.
[43] Cf. supra n. 3.

[QUAESTIO 22]

UTRUM SINGULARE SIT AB INTELLECTU NOSTRO PER SE INTELLIGIBILE

Utrum[1] singulare sit ab intellectu nostro per se intelligibile.

[1] Videtur quod non:

Quia "quod quid est" est obiectum intellectus nostri; singulare autem in quantum singulare non habet quiditatem; igitur, etc. Probatio minoris. Quia si haberet quiditatem, esset definibile, et de ipso posset haberi scientia; hoc autem falsum est, quia scientia esset corruptibilis sicut et scibile. Similiter essent scientiae infinitae, sicut singularia possunt multiplicari in infinitum.

Item, sensus est singularium, intellectus universalium, ex II *De anima*,[2] et sic de multis aliis auctoritatibus.[3]

Item, diversorum obiectorum formaliter sunt diversae potentiae cognitivae; sed universale et singulare sunt obiecta formaliter distincta; igitur, etc.

Item, si singulare posset intelligi a nobis, tunc habens perfectam cognitionem de specie specialissima nondum intelligeret singulare,

---

4 Utrum] *praem.* Quaeritur O KU FW Q Z *adnot. mg.* Quaestio 22 M | ab — nostro *post* se Q *post* intelligibile X | se *om.* U | intelligibile *om.* Q 5 Videtur *post* non U Dicitur (*post* non) O *om.* X 6 Quia *om.* X | quod] *lin.* Z² | est²] *mg.* U² *om.* O K Q Z *add.* (*post* obiectum FW X Z *mg.* U²) proprium FW U² X Z | nostri *om.* X 7 autem — singulare *om.* X | singulare] huiusmodi N | igitur etc.] ergo etc. L etc. Z *om.* X 8 Probatio minoris] Probatur X | esset] esse U | definibile] difficile Z 9 ipso] eo L *add.* (*post* scientia FW Z) per consequens FW Q Z | posset haberi] posse esse O possit haberi U | scientia] demonstratio L | hoc] quod X | autem *om.* K X | falsum est] *inv.* O falsum esset FW | quia] *add.* tunc HL *add.* sic X | esset] *add.* tantum K 10 sicut *om.* X | et *om.* Z | scibile] sensibile U | scibile — essent] dicunt X | scientiae infinitae] *inv.* X | sicut — infinitum] cum sint infinita singularia X 11 possunt — infinitum *om.* L 12 Item] Praeterea O KU FW Q X Z | sensus] *mg.* (*post* est) O² | ex] in X *om.* O L KU | II De anima *om.* Q 13 et — etc. *om.* X | sic — auctoritatibus] sic de multis auctoritatibus H U sic de multis auctoritatibus aliis L multis aliis auctoritatibus K sic multae auctoritates aliae Q 14 Item] Praeterea O K FW Q X Z | obiectorum] oppositorum O | sunt diversae] *inv.* L 15 formaliter] omnino L 16 igitur] ergo L U W Q 17 Item] Praeterea O KU FW Q X Z | posset] possit U | a nobis *om.* O KU | tunc *om.* FW | habens perfectam] *inv.* F 18 nondum] non X

[1] Cf. pro tota hac quaestione *Correctorium corruptorii "Quare"* In primam partem Summa theol. [q. 14 a. 2] (ed. Glorieux 12-17).

[2] **Aristot.**, *De an.* II c. 12 (B c. 5, 417b 22-23): "Causa autem est quoniam singularium qui 'secundum actum' sensus, scientia autem universalium"; *Auctoritates Aristotelis* (ed. J. Hamesse 179): "Anima intelligit quando vult, sed non sentit quando vult, quia obiectum intellectus est in anima, ut universale, obiectum sensus est extra animam, ut particulare."

[3] Cf. **Averroës**, *De an.* II com. 60 (AverL I 220-1); **Aristot.**, *Anal. post.* I c. 31 (A c. 31, 87b 37-39); *Auctoritates Aristotelis* (ed. J. Hamesse 319): "Sensus est singularium, scientia vero universalium."

sed esset adhuc in potentia ad intellectionem eius, quod falsum est. Quia agens artificiale non dirigitur in agendo nisi cognoscat agibile perfecte; sed artifex habens cognitionem domus in universali potest perfecte et directe facere domum;[4] igitur ad cognitionem intellectualem speciei specialissimae sequitur sufficiens cognitio intellectus singularis, immo in ea includitur.[5]

5   Item, aut per eandem speciem intelligerentur[6] cum universali, aut per aliam. Non per eandem, quia eadem species non potest repraesentare diversa sub oppositis rationibus, quales sunt ratio distincti et indistincti, quae conveniunt universali et singulari. Si etiam esset eadem et esset universalis primo, illa non posset repraesentare distincte singularia, quia esset indistincta et confusa. Si autem esset ipsius singularis primo et ex consequenti universalis, quot essent species singularium tot essent universalia, et multiplicarentur species in infinitum, si debeant cognosci omnia singularia.

6   Si autem dicas quod non est eadem species utriusque: sicut per unum singulare generatur species universalis, sic per omnia alia et sic unius universalis essent infinitae species, vel eadem intendetur, cum possunt esse singularia infinita.

7   Contra:
Quidquid perfectionis est in potentia inferiori, scilicet sensitiva,

---

1 esset adhuc] *inv.* KU X | falsum est] *inv.* O H K   2 agens *om.* K | artificiale] accidentale O actuale F | artificiale — facere] per actionem universalem potest se dirigere faciendo X | agendo] agenda L   3 habens] habet O *add.* tantum KU FW   4 perfecte et directe] directe (*post* facere) O directe et perfecte KU | domum] *add.* (*ante* domum FW Q X) hanc KU FW Q X Z | igitur] ergo L | igitur — includitur] absque eo quod prius novisset eam et ita singulare non est difficile X   5 speciei] *add.* substantialis KU   6 includitur] inconcluditur O   7 Item] Praeterea O K FW Q Z | aut] *lin.* N | intelligerentur] intelligentur H intelliguntur L intelligeretur KU   9 repraesentare] repraesentari KU | sub] ab L | oppositis] obiectis O | rationibus] modis L | quales] qualia K | ratio *post* distincti K *lin.* U duo N Z rationes HL   10 distincti] distincta K FW Z | et *om.* K | indistincti] *mg.* U² indistincta FW Z *om.* K | quae] quia O | conveniunt] *add.* in K | universali et singulari] singulari et universali KU Q | Si] Sic F   11 esset² *om.* KU | illa *post* posset KU | posset] possit KU   12 distincte singularia] *inv.* FW distincta singularia U Q | indistincta et confusa] confusa et distincta F distincta et confusa W Q Z   14 multiplicarentur] multiplicatur H   15 species *om.* F | debeant cognosci] dicunt cognosci O cognoscerentur L debent cognosci FW Z | cognosci] *lin.* U²   16 dicas] dicat KU | utriusque] *add.* sed H | sicut] sic Z   18 unius] unus O *om.* K | universalis] vel O | species *om.* O Q | intendetur] intenderetur L *add.* in infinitum KU   19 cum] tamen H | possunt] possint O K possent U   21 Quidquid] quod L | perfectionis est] *inv.* H KU perfectius est Q | sensitiva] sensibila(!) O insensitiva W

[4] Cf. **Aristot.**, *Physica* II c. 22 (AL VII¹ 53; B c. 22 194a 23-25); **Thomas**, *Summa theol.* I q. 85 a. 4 arg. 3 (V 339a).
[5] Quia hic et deinceps codex X textum, qui minime conferri potest textui ab aliis codicibus tradito, exhibet, ideo deinde lectiones eius non referrimus.
[6] Subaudi: singularia.

est in intellectiva quae superior est; sed perfectionis est cognoscere singularia distincte, quae conveniunt sensui; igitur, etc.

Item, intellectus compositus praesupponit simplicem; sed intellectus componit universale singulari et cognoscit compositionem, ut cum dicit "Socrates est homo"; igitur cognoscit utrumque.

Item, proprium motivum intellectus est phantasma, quod est singulare; sed quod movet intellectum est eius obiectum; igitur, etc.

[I. — Ad quaestionem
A. — Solutio secundum opinionem Thomae]

Ad quaestionem dicit THOMAS[7] quod intellectus noster pro statu viae non potest cognoscere singulare directe, sed secundum IPSUM materia est principium singularis; sed intellectus noster nihil intelligit nisi per abstractionem a materia et condicionibus materiae; abstractum autem a materia individuali est universale; igitur tantum universale est ab intellectu nostro primo intelligibile.

DICUNT[8] tamen quod per reflexionem potest cognoscere singulare, quia licet species intelligibiles sint in intellectu nostro, tamen per eas non possumus intelligere nisi intuendo obiectum universale in

---

1 in *om.* O *add.* superiori scilicet L | quae — est *om.* L | perfectionis] perfectius Q   2 singularia] *add.* et O | quae] quod O | conveniunt] convenit O | igitur] ergo L | etc.] et intellectum Q   3 Item] Praeterea O KU FW Q Z   4 et] quod N   5 dicit] dicat H dicitur U | igitur] ergo L | utrumque] *add.* extremum L *add.* igitur KU *add.* ult. etc. U   6 Item] Praeterea FW Q Z *om.* O | Item — etc. *om.* KU   7 sed] *mg.* O | eius *om.* O | igitur] ergo L   10 Ad] *add.* illam FW *add.* hanc Q *add.* istam Z | dicit] dicunt quidam scilicet (*om.* Z) FW Z dicit quidam Q *add.* ult. *mg.* aliqui Z | Thomas] Themistius(!) (*mg.* F²) F²W Doctor Q | intellectus — sed *om.* O   11 cognoscere] intelligere KU | singulare directe] *inv.* FW singularia directe Q | sed] quia KU FW Z | ipsum] eum Q   12 singularis] singularitatis N individuationis L | nihil] non HL Q   13 nisi] *lin.* U | per abstractionem] abstractionem H ut abstractum Z | et] *add.* a N M FW | materiae] *lin.* U² animateria(!) O *om.* K   14 a] *lin.* F² U² | igitur] ergo L | tantum *post* est N M   15 primo intelligibile] *inv.* FW   16 Dicunt] Dicit Z | tamen] *add.* aliqui L | cognoscere] intelligere HL   17 per eas *post* possumus L   18 possumus] potest O FW Q Z | nisi] non F | intuendo] intelligendo O | universale] singulare Z | in] sub L

---

[7] Cf. **Thomas**, *Summa theol.* I q. 86 a. 1 in corp. (V 347a): "Respondeo dicendum singulare in rebus materialibus intellectus noster directe et primo cognoscere non potest. Cuius ratio est, quia principium singularitatis in rebus materialibus est materia individualis; intellectus autem noster, sicut supra dictum est, intelligit abstrahendo speciem intelligibilem ab huiusmodi materia. Quod autem a materia individuali abstrahitur, est universale. Unde intellectus noster directe non est cognoscitivus universalium."

[8] Cf. **Thomas**, *Summa theol.* I q. 86 a. 1 in corp. (V 347a-b): "Indirecte autem, et quasi per quandam reflexionem potest cognoscere singulare, quia, sicut supra dictum est, etiam postquam species intelligibiles abstraxit, non potest secundum eas actu intelligere nisi convertendo se ad phantasmata, in quibus species intelligibiles intelligit, ut dicitur in III *De anima*. Sic igitur ipsum universale per speciem intelligibilem directe intelligit; indirecte autem singularia, quorum sunt phantasmata."

phantasmate, quod est repraesentativum singularis primo.

[B. — Obiectiones contra opinionem Thomae]

12   Sed contra hoc procedendum est primo destruendo suum principium, quod materia non est principium individuationis — immo excommunicatus est Parisius articulus: quod non possunt esse plura individua eiusdem speciei propter defectum materiae.[9]

13   Item, IPSIMET[10] concedunt quod singularitas secundum se non repugnat intellectui, cum anima se possit intelligere; sed materia individualis non addit supra materiam speciei nisi singularitatem; materia autem specifica est intelligibilis, quia est de quiditate speciei materialis, quae primo est intelligibilis secundum IPSUM; igitur materiae singulari non repugnat intelligibilitas.

14   Item, contra modum abstrahendi quem PONUNT, sic: abstractio universalis a singulari fit ab intellectu possibili, non ab agente cuius est abstrahere species a phantasmatibus tantum; sed impossibile est abstrahere universale a singulari nisi cognoscendo singulare, aliter enim abstraheret ignorans a quo abstraheret; igitur, etc.

15   Item, secundum IPSOS[11] intellectus noster non potest

---

1 repraesentativum] repraesentatum O | singularis primo] *inv.* FW singulare primo Z   3 hoc *om.* H | procedendum est] *inv.* O | est] *lin.* U | primo *om.* H | destruendo] contra L   4 quod — principium *om.* FW | non *om.* L | est] sit O | immo] unde FW   5 excommunicatus est] *inv.* Q excommunicatus O Z | Parisius articulus] *inv.* O Z Parisius articulus ille (*om.* H) scilicet HL Parisiis articulus M Parisius articulus iste K Parisius Q | quod] qui K *add.* (*lin.*) scilicet U | possunt esse] possent esse N M essent L posuit esse KU possint esse FW Z   6 individua *om.* O | speciei] materiae KU   7 Item] Praeterea O KU FW Q Z | secundum] per H   8 repugnat] impugnat Q | cum *om.* Z | se possit intelligere] possit intelligere se O se posset intelligere L possit se intelligere KU possit intelligere ea Q   9 non] *rep. post* addit FW | supra] super O | materiam] naturam O Q | singularitatem] singulare FW Z   10 materia] natura Q | intelligibilis] intelligere O | quia — intelligibilis *om.* Z   11 quae] sed Q | primo est] *inv.* K | igitur] ergo L Q Z   12 singulari] singularis(!) Z | repugnat] repugnabit Z | intelligibilitas] intellectus Q   13 Item] Praeterea O KU FW Q Z | abstrahendi] abstrahendo O | ponunt] *add. arguitur* N M Q | abstractio] abstractus O   14 singulari] singulare L | ab intellectu possibili] per intellectum possibilem L | ab agente] per agentem L agente FW Q Z   15 species] speciem U FW Z | phantasmatibus] phantasmate O sensibus K   16 universale] universali K | nisi] non O U FW Z | cognoscendo] agendo cognoscendo O | aliter] supra(!) Q   17 ignorans] ignorantiam FW | igitur] ergo L Q   18 Item] Praeterea O FW Q Z

[9] Cf. D. Piché, *La condamnation parisienne de 1277* n. 81 (43) 104 "Quod quia intelligentiae non habent materiam, Deus non posset plures eiusdem speciei facere"; R. Hissette, *Enquête sur le 219 articles condamnés à Paris le 7 mars 1277* n. 43, 82.
[10] Cf. **Thomas**, *Summa theol.* I q. 86 a. 1 ad 3 (V 347b): "Ad tertium dicendum quod singulare non repugnat intelligibilitati in quantum est singulare, sed in quantum est materiale, quia nihil intelligitur nisi immaterialiter. Et ideo si sit aliquod singulare immateriale, sicut est intellectus, hoc non repugnat intelligibilitati."
[11] Cf. *supra* n. 10.

cognoscere nisi convertendo se ad phantasmata; sed convertendo se ad phantasmata, intelligit singulare; igitur non potest intelligere universale nisi intelligendo simul singulare; igitur non tantum per reflexionem.

Item, si intelligitur singulare, scilicet per reflexionem tantum, aut hoc esset per speciem intelligibilem aut phantasiabilem; non primo modo, quia illa est in intellectu repraesentativa quiditatis absolute; nec secundo modo, quia illud tantum movet phantasiam, non intellectum, cum illa non sit in intellectu, et per consequens non potest esse principium intelligendi singulare.

[II. — Solutio propria]
[A. — Singulare est a nobis intelligibile secundum se]

[4]   Dicendum igitur quod singulare est a nobis intelligibile secundum se, quia intelligibilitas sequitur entitatem. Quod igitur secundum se non diminuit de ratione entis, nec intelligibilitatis; sed singulare secundum se non diminuit de ratione entis, immo est ens actu perfectum — unde in *Praedicamentis* et in VII *Metaphysicae*[12] dicitur quod singulare subiectum est maxime substantia; igitur, etc.

Item, illud quod secundum se non est intelligibile, a nullo intellectu potest intelligi; sed singulare, ut singulare, ab aliquo

---

18 cognoscere] intelligere O FW Q Z   1 se *om.* O | phantasmata] *lin.* U² phantasma NO M K | sed] *add.* sic H | sed — intelligit *om.* O | se² *om.* L   2 phantasmata intelligit] phantasma intelligit K *om.* L | igitur] ergo L FW Q Z   3 universale] *mg.* Z | intelligendo simul] *inv.* O KU | igitur non] ergo non L Q igitur K non ergo FW Z | non] *lin.* U²   5 Item] Praeterea O FW Q Z | si *om.* FW Z | intelligitur] intelligere KU | singulare *om.* O | scilicet *om.* NO L Q | tantum] *ante* per N   6 aut *om.* KU | esset] est N FW Q Z | phantasiabilem] phantasmabilem L   7 in *om.* Q Z | quiditatis] quiditas O *add.* | tantum Z   8 nec] non FW quia Q *add.* movet Z | tantum movet] *inv.* O KU Q   9 non] in Q | illa *post* sit H ista Q | sit] *add.* tantum Q | et] sed O   10 singulare] singulari Q *add.* et sic positio illa falsa K   13 Dicendum] *praem.* Responsio Q *add.* est N M F Q | igitur] ergo L FW Q Z | est] *lin.* Q | secundum] per Q   14 Quod] *coni. cum* Q Z Quia (*lin.* U²) NO HLM KU² FW | igitur] ergo L FW Z   15 non] *ante* secundum F | de ratione] = O U F Q Z a ratione N M K W rationem HL | entis] entitatis O L KU | intelligibilitatis] intelligentis O Q   16 diminuit] *add.* aliquid Q | entis] entitatis O KU Q   17 perfectum] perfectio H | et] *rep.* O | in² *om.* L U W Q Z | VII] IX O   18 singulare] *add.* et Q | est *post* substantia L | maxime] maxima U F | igitur] ergo L FW Q Z   19 Item] Praeterea O KU FW Q Z | illud] idem H *om.* N | quod *post* se O | nullo] aliquo K   20 intellectu potest intelligi] intelligitur FW intellectu est intelligibile vel potest intelligi Q intelligi potest Z | sed — angelico] nec ab intellectu divino nec angelico sed singulare intelligitur ab illis Z | singulare²] *add.* potest K | aliquo *om.* H

[12] Cf. **Aristot.**, *Praedic.* c. 5 (AL I² 50; c. 5, 2b 15-18): "Amplius principales substantiae, eo quod aliis omnibus subiectae sint et alia omnia de his praedicentur aut in eis sunt, ideo maxime dicuntur substantiae"; *Metaph.* VII t. 22 (AL XXV² 133; Z c. 7 1032a 16-20): "Generationes naturales quidem hae sunt quarum generatio ex natura est, 'ex quo' fit, quam dicimus materiam, 'a quo' natura quid entium, 'quid' vero homo aut planta aut aliud quid talium, quae maxime dicimus substantias esse."

intellectu potest intelligi, ut ab intellectu divino et angelico;[13] igitur, etc.

19 Item, singulare nihil addit ultra universale nisi gradum singularitatis; sed non excluditur ab intelligente ratione universalitatis in eo contentae, nec etiam ratione gradus singularitatis, quia multa singularia, ut angeli et animae separatae et alia inferiora, intelliguntur ab intellectu divino vel angelico; igitur, etc.

[B. — Singulare est a nobis intelligibile pro statu isto]

20 Secundo, dico quod singulare est a nobis intelligibile pro statu isto. Probo: sicut enim conclusionem intelligimus sive cognoscimus in syllogismo, ita principia inductive, II *Posteriorum*;[14] sed inductio est processus a singularibus ad universale, sic autem discurrere pertinet tantum ad intellectum; igitur cognoscit singularia.

21 Item, incognita non possumus diligere, secundum AUGUSTINUM;[15] sed per prius diligimus singulare quam universale, quia praeceptum de dilectione est magis respectu singularis quam universalis; unde in I *Canonica* IOANNIS:[16] 'Qui non diligit fratrem suum, quem videt, Deum quem non videt quomodo potest

---

1 potest] *ante* ab HL U | ut] scilicet FW | ab *om.* FW | igitur] ergo L FW Z 2 etc. *om.* L 3 Item] Praeterea O FW Q Z *add.* ult. si Q | nihil addit] non additur (addit W) aliquid FW | ultra] super K supra N L Q ad U | singularitatis] singularis U 4 intelligente] intellectu L intelligibilitate W *add.* animae KU | ratione *om.* U 5 contentae] contiente(!) N contenta W | etiam] cum Q *om.* F | ratione *om.* Z | gradus singularitatis] *inv.* K gradus singularis O Q singularitatis U 6 angeli] spirituali O | animae] substantiae L *add.* substantiae Q 7 igitur] ergo FW Z 9 Secundo] *praem.* Item K | est *om.* O | a] *lin.* O 10 isto *om.* Q *add.* sicut U | Probo] Probatio Z | conclusionem] quoque O conclusiones KU FW Q Z | intelligimus sive] intelleximus sive O intelligimus vel L *om.* FW Q Z 11 in *om.* O U Q Z | principia] *add.* in K | inductive] inductione O KU FW Q Z | II] I (*lin.*) Z | Posteriorum] Physicorum N HLM | sed] dicitur quod Z | inductio] induto O 12 processus] progressus Q | singularibus] singulari H | universale] universalia KU | autem] *rep.* M | discurrere] discurrem Z 13 pertinet tantum] *inv.* L pertinet K Q | igitur] ergo L FW Z | cognoscit] cognoscimus FW 14 Item] Praeterea O K FW Q Z | incognita] cognita H | diligere] cognoscere Q 15 Augustinum] Augustinus O | per *om.* H FW Z | singulare] particulare Q | singulare ... universale] universale ... singulare O 16 est magis] *inv.* Q 17 in *om.* U FW Q Z | I *post* Ioannis F Q | Canonica *om.* O FW Q Z *add.* Sancti U | Ioannis] Ioanne Q 18 videt] *add.* non diligit O | Deum — etc.] Quomodo etc. Z | potest diligere] *inv.* L

---

[13] Cf. **Aegidius Romanus**, *Quodl.* I q. 9 (f. 6ra-va); *Quodl.* V q. 28 (f. 70ra—f. 71ra). In locis citatis autem multa reperiuntur eadem ad sensum, minime tamen verbotenus. Multa attamen verbotenus eadem inveniuntur apud **Gonsalvum Hispanum**, *Quodl.* q. 10 (BFS IX 419).
[14] **Aristot.** *Anal. post.* II c. 19 (AL IV² 182; **B** c. 19, 100*b* 3-5); *Auctoritates Aristotelis* (ed. J. Hamesse 321): "Principia non cognoscimus per demonstrationem, sed per inductionem via sensus et memoriae."
[15] **Augustinus**, *De Trinitate* X c. 3 (CCL 50 315, PL 42 975): "'Amat incognita'; illud enim fieri potest ut amet quisque scire incognita, ut autem amet incognita non potest."
[16] I Ioh. 4:20.

diligere?'; igitur, etc.

[5] Si dicas quod ad dilectionem singularis sufficit cognitio universalis: non valet, quia sic sequeretur quod cognitio universalis sufficeret ad diligendum tale singulare quod numquam fuit cognitum a sensu, quod videtur absurdum.

Item, cognoscens differentiam extremorum, cognoscit extrema; sed intellectus cognoscit differentiam universalis a singulari; igitur, etc.

Item, nulli non-intellecto a nobis possumus nomen imponere; voces enim sunt notae earum passionum quae sunt in anima;[17] sed intellectus noster, vel nos mediante intellectu, imponimus nomina singularibus; igitur, etc.

Item, experimur nos cognoscere singularia vel cognoscimus; hoc autem non est per potentiam sensitivam, quia non est reflexiva super suum actum; igitur per intellectum cognoscimus nos cognoscere singulare; sed intellectus non potest cognoscere se cognoscere singulare nisi ipsum singulare cognoscat, quia actus quo cognoscitur singulare est repraesentativum singularitatis tamquam eius similitudo vera magis quam species singularis; igitur, etc.

[C. — Nulla potentia cognitiva nostra potest singulare cognoscere sub propria ratione singularitatis]

[6] Tertio, dico quod nulla potentia nostra, nec intellectiva nec

---

1 igitur etc.] ergo etc. L FW *om.* Q   2 Si dicas] Sed dices Z | dilectionem singularis] singulare FW cognitionem singularis Q   3 quia] *add.* si L | sequeretur] sequitur L | universalis²] *lin.* H | sufficeret] sufficit L Q   4 diligendum] intelligendum FW   5 videtur] est H dicitur FW Z | absurdum] *add.* esse FW   6 Item] Praeterea O KU FW Q Z | extremorum] inter (*lin.*) extrema U   7 universalis a singulari] inter universale et singulare KU | igitur etc.] ergo L ergo etc. Q   9 Item] Praeterea O FW Q Z | nulli non-intellecto] non-intellecto nulli N nulla non-intellecto O universali non-intellecto H nulli intellecto W | a nobis *om.* H   10 passionum *post* anima Q   11 noster] sive O | nos] *lin.* U² | nomina] *add.* scilicet H   12 singularibus] significatis K | igitur] ergo L Q   13 Item] Praeterea O KU FW Q Z | cognoscimus] *add.* vel non Z | hoc] illud FW   14 autem *om.* Q | non] *lin.* M | est] cognoscimus Q   15 super] supra K | suum actum] *inv.* L K FW Z actum Q | igitur] ergo L FW Q Z | cognoscimus] possumus cognoscere U   16 singulare] singulari O singularia FW Q *om.* L | potest] *add.* (*post* cognoscere U) nos KU | se cognoscere] cognoscere U *om.* K   17 singulare] singulari (*ante* cognoscere) O singularia L *om.* Z | ipsum singulare] ipsa singularia L | cognoscat] cognoscatur FW Z | quo] primo(!) FW | cognoscitur] cognoscimus Q   18 singulare *om.* O | repraesentativum] repraesentativus O K FW Z | singularitatis] singularis L KU Q | eius] *add.* sunt O   19 igitur etc.] ergo etc. L FW Z ergo Q *om.* K   22 dico] dicitur Z | nostra *om.* Z | intellectiva ... sensitiva] sensitiva ... intellectiva Z

[17] **Aristot.**, *De interpr.* I c. 1 (AL II¹ 5; c. 1, 16a 3-4): "Sunt ergo ea quae sunt in voce earum quae sunt in anima passionum notae, et ea quae scribuntur eorum quae sunt in voce."

sensitiva, potest cognoscere singulare sub propria ratione singularitatis. Quia potentia cognoscens aliquod obiectum sub propria ratione potest ipsum cognoscere et ab aliis distinguere, circumscripto quocumque alio non habente illam rationem; sed manente propria ratione singularitatis, amotis aliis, non possumus distinguere inter duo singularia, nec per sensum nec per intellectum; igitur, etc. Probatio minoris: quia potentia cognoscens obiectum suum secundum aliquam unitatem, potest illud distinguere ab omni alio quod non habet illam unitatem; sed unum singulare non habet unitatem essentialem alterius, et tamen nec sensu nec intellectu possumus distinguere inter duo singularia, circumscripta distinctione accidentali quae est per locum, figuram, tempus, magnitudinem, colorem, et sic de aliis.[18]

27   Exemplum: si ponantur visui duo alba vel intellectui duo singularia quaecumque quae in rei veritate essent distincta essentialiter, si tamen haberent omnino consimilia accidentia ut locum — utpote duo corpora in eodem loco vel duo radii in medio illorum — et haberent figuram omnino consimilem et magnitudinem et colorem et sic de aliis, nec intellectus nec sensus inter illa distingueret, sed iudicaret esse unum; igitur neutrum[19] eorum cognoscit quodlibet illorum singularium secundum propriam rationem singularitatis.

---

1 singulare *om.* O Z | propria *om.* K   2 singularitatis] singularis O KU FW Q singularia Z | cognoscens] agens O | aliquod obiectum] *inv.* O FW Q Z   3 propria ratione] *inv.* L | ipsum] illud Q | distinguere] *add.* sibi Z   4 circumscripto] *add.* omni FW | alio *om.* H   5 propria] quam O | singularitatis] singularis Q | possumus] possemus FW Z   7 igitur] ergo L FW Q Z | minoris] maioris K | quia] *add.* omnis Q | potentia] *add.* communis O *add.* omnis F Z   8 obiectum suum] subiectum N | illud] ipsum (*post* distinguere) L idem U   9 ab — distinguere *om.* O | alio] tali L | illam *om.* Q | unum singulare] *inv.* FW   10 non habet *om.* H | tamen] *mg.* L | nec] non Z   11 possumus] possimus Q | singularia] *add.* distincta Q | circumscripta *om.* N HLM   12 distinctione] distinctio O | locum figuram] *inv.* Z locum et figuram H | magnitudinem *om.* Z *add.* et N HM   14 ponantur] ponatur U proponantur O proponuntur Z | vel] et KU   15 quaecumque] *add.* fuerint K | quae *om.* HL Q | essent] sunt N M | distincta essentialiter] *inv.* Q realiter distincta O   16 tamen *om.* H | haberent — et *om.* O | omnino *post* accidentia FW omnia HL Q | consimilia] *add.* ut Q | ut] vel Q | locum] loco U | utpote] ut principio(!) F   17 vel] et L | radii *om.* F | illorum] eodem (*ante* medio FW) KU FW Z eorum Q | et] sed K   18 omnino *om.* K | consimilem] similem N   19 nec *om.* O | illa] ista L ea KU   20 iudicaret] iudicarent Q | esse unum] *rep.* O | igitur] ergo L W Q Z unde F | neutrum] nullum H neuter K W Z | eorum] illorum L | cognoscit] cognitio(!) O | quodlibet illorum singularium] quodlibet singularium illorum L quidlibet illorum singularium (sensibilium K) M K singulare quodlibet F quodlibet singulare W quodlibet eorum singularium (singulare Q) Q Z   21 secundum] sed U

[18]Cf. **Porphyrius**, *Liber praedicabilium* cap. 'De specie' (AL I⁶, 13-14; ed. Busse 7.21-23): "Individua ergo dicuntur huiusmodi quoniam ex proprietatibus consistit unumquodque eorum quorum collectio numquam in alio eadem erit"; cf. *Auctoritates Aristotelis* (ed. J. Hamesse 300): "Et sunt septem proprietates, ut dicit Boethius, scilicet forma, figura, locus, stirps, nomen, patria, tempus. Haec septem propria continet omnis homo."

[19]Lege: neuter; cf. lectiones variantes K W Z.

Cuius causa est principium agendi-assimilandi, quia agens intendit assimilare patiens sibi, et hoc specialiter est verum in cognitione quae fit per assimilationem; sed principium assimilandi non est singulare ut singulare est, immo magis[20] distinguendi (quia in singularitate differunt[21]), sed magis natura communis[22] in qua singularia conveniunt; igitur singulare ut singulare non est principium agendi nec in sensu nec in intellectu.

[7]   Contra hoc posset sic argui:

Numerus est sensibile per se, cum sit sensibile commune; sed numerus non est nisi pluralitas unitatum; igitur quaelibet unitas est sensibilis per se; igitur, etc.

Item, species gignitur ab obiecto in quantum singulare est, quia actiones sunt singularium; sed species repraesentat illud a quo gignitur, et sub eadem ratione; igitur, etc.

Item, secundum praedicta sequitur quod sensus non magis determinate cognosceret singulare quam intellectus, quod est contra PHILOSOPHUM in pluribus locis[23].

Ad primum[24] dicendum est quod sensibile commune non facit propriam speciem in sensu per quam faciat ad substantiam immutationis, sicut sensibilia propria, sed tantum facit ad modum et differentiam immutationis, et ideo non sentitur numerus nec eius

---

.1 Cuius causa] Causa huius NO M Causa huius autem FW Q Z | agendi-assimilandi] agendi scilicet assimilando H agendi est principium assimilandi K agendi et assimilandi FW   2 assimilare] assimilari O H U | patiens sibi] *inv.* Q | specialiter est] *inv.* NO M FW Z specialiter Q | verum *om.* F   3 assimilationem] *add.* quia obiectum agens in veritatem assimilat sibi potentiam etc. K   4 singulare] singularis U | magis] *add.* est (*om.* L) principium L K | singularitate] *add.* vel in haecceitate quae facit unum singulare differre ab alio K   5 communis] generis est K | singularia *om.* L   6 conveniunt] conveniuntur U | igitur] ergo L FW Q Z   7 nec *om.* O Q | sensu — intellectu] sensum nec in intellectum K | in² *om.* Z   8 posset sic argui] arguitur sic L posset sic arguitur(!) U potest sic argui Q   9 sensibile] sensibilis L FW | sensibile — sit *om.* Z | per se *om.* U | sit sensibile] *inv.* Q dicitur sensibile O sit singulare(!) Z   10 igitur] ergo L FW Q Z | est²] esset N   11 igitur etc.] ergo etc. L *om.* FW Q Z   12 Item] Praeterea O KU FW Q Z | est *om.* K FW Q Z | quia — singularium *om.* FW   13 sed] quia O | repraesentat illud] *inv.* L repraesentant illud O Q repraesentat idem U | gignitur] gignuntur K   14 igitur] ergo L FW Q Z   15 Item] Praeterea O K FW Q Z | sequitur] sequeretur FW Z   16 cognosceret] cognoscit KU FW Q   17 pluribus] multis L | locis] *lin.* F *add.* ergo etc. F Q *add. spat. vac.* W   18 est *om.* HL W Q Z   19 sensu] sensum O | faciat] facit O | substantiam] rationem Z   20 sicut] *add.* faciunt L | sicut — imutationis *om.* Z | modum et *om.* FW | et] vel Q

[20]Subaudi: singulare est principium.
[21]Subaudi: singularia.
[22]Subaudi: est principium assimilandi.
[23]**Aristot.**, *Anal. post.* I c. 31 (A c. 31, 87*b* 37-39); *Auctoritates Aristotelis* (ed. J. Hamesse 319): "Sensus est singularium, scientia vero universalium"; **Aristot.**, *Metaph.* I c. 1 (A c. 1, 981*a* 15-16); *Auctoritates Aristotelis* (ed. J. Hamesse 115).
[24]Cf. supra n. 28.

unitates nisi mediantibus qualitatibus sensibilibus; sic igitur non sentimus unitates ratione suae singularitatis ut duo substantiá in quantum duo, sed ut distincta subiecto, vel loco vel tempore vel aliis accidentibus.

32 Ad secundum[25] dicendum quod singularitas bene est ratio vel condicio agentis, sed non est ratio agendi, immo formalis natura quae est similis in diversis; et haec est ratio quam debet repraesentare species genita, non autem condicio agentis.

33 Ad aliud[26] dicendum quod sensus tantum cognoscit singulare intuitive et non abstractive, sed intellectus utroque modo; et ideo dicitur per appropriationem quod sensus est singularium, quia non est universalium cognoscitivus sicut intellectus qui est utriusque cognoscitivus; et ideo sensus magis determinate cognoscit singulare, quia cognoscit eius essentiam praesentem et actualem, non autem eius quiditatem absolutam.

[D. — Quomodo singulare intelligitur]

34 Quarto dicendum, quantum ad modum intelligendi singulare, quod, si non ponimus speciem in intellectu sed tantum in phantasia, sicut natura in agendo non intendit universale — quia generato corpore, quod est universalius quam animatum vel homo, non procederet[27] ad generationem animalis vel hominis —, nec primo intendit singulare signatum vel expressum — quia tunc

---

1 unitates] unitate O | nisi — unitates om. O H | sic om. Z | igitur] ergo L FW Q Z | non] nec (ante igitur Z) FW Z 2 suae om. H 3 subiecto] subiecta O FW substantia H | vel] et L om. KU FW Z | vel³] = H FW Z et L Q om. NO M KU 4 accidentibus] add. igitur etc. K 5 secundum] aliud O FW Q Z | dicendum] add. est N M F | bene est] inv. N M | ratio — agentis] condicio cognoscentis et ratio Q 6 formalis] formaliter(!) W | natura] non O 7 et — ratio] quia et haec est species Q | repraesentare species genita] species generata repraesentare N M 8 autem om. B 9 aliud om. Q | dicendum om. F add. est N M | sensus] sensu Z | tantum cognoscit] inv. FW tantum continuit(?) O tantum cognoscimus Z 10 et om. Q | intellectus post modo Q | ideo] ita L 11 per] propter O | quod] quia L | sensus est] rep. N 12 est om. O | qui est om. Z | est utriusque] inv. K 13 determinate cognoscit] inv. U determinate continuit(?) O definitive cognoscit Z 14 cognoscit post actualem Z | eius essentiam] exsistentiam eius KU | actualem] accidentalem HL accidentem O 15 eius quiditatem] inv. Q | absolutam] add. quod primo in corpus est singulare O 17 dicendum] dico O FW Q Z add. est N M add. quod Q | intelligendi] intelligi debet Q | singulare] add. dicendum FW Z 18 quod] quia L om. Q | si non] non H om. O | ponimus] ponamus O M FW Q Z | speciem] mg. U² om. K | sed tantum] sive O | tantum] rep. O 20 est universalius] inv. Q ulterius(!) FW Z 21 procederet] procedit Z | generationem] congenerationem FW 22 signatum om. L | tunc om. O FW Q Z

[25] Cf. supra n. 29.
[26] Cf. supra n. 30.
[27] Subaudi: natura.

generato unico singulari, cessaret actio naturae (quae ambo[28] sunt falsa ut patet ad sensum), sed primo intendit producere naturam in aliquo supposito (et hoc est individuum vagum):[29] sic in repraesentando species in phantasia primo repraesentat singulare vagum in quod primo fertur cognitio intellectus (et hoc patet, quia aliquando intelligimus aliquod singulare, ignorando in qua specie est); secundo repraesentat naturam absolute (quando, scilicet, intellectus fertur in naturam non considerando eius singularitatem); tertio, reflectendo considerationem naturae ad circumstantias signatas ad ipsam (per illas determinando) individuum signatum possumus intelligere, utpote quia est hic et nunc et cum tali figura et magnitudine et colore et ceteris.

Descriptio autem talis quam possumus habere in via de singulari, vel conceptus quicumque, non repugnat contradictorie[30], sed conceptus proprius sub propria singularitate alteri repugnat; modum autem praedictum intelligendi singulare ponit AVICENNA I *Physicorum*.[31] Dictus autem modus intelligendi singulare non est simplex, ut dictum est,[32] sed est compositus ex conceptibus multarum circumstantiarum universali conceptui additarum. Et hoc patet experimento: sicut enim res intelligimus, sic eas significamus et aliis exprimimus; sed conceptum singularis signati nullo alio modo exprimimus quam praedicto nec alios aliter scimus docere. Unde dicimus "Socrates est unus homo albus, crispus, longus, blaesus" et

---

1 unico] unice O | singulari] sensibil(!) Q | actio] et actus F | sunt falsa] *inv.* NO M FW Q Z   3 sic] sicut O | repraesentando] praesentando H   4 singulare vagum] individuum signatum O *add.* sed Q | in²] secundum FW Z | in — intellectus *om.* O   5 quod] *add.* in FW Z | et hoc] quod O | aliquando intelligimus] *inv.* L aliquando O   6 aliquod singulare *om.* Q | ignorando] ignoro O | est] sit NO M FW Q Z   7 repraesentat *om.* O | quando scilicet] *inv.* H quando KU quando etiam Z | intellectus] *add.* noster U   8 considerando] cognoscendo Z | singularitatem] *mg.* U² singulare Q | reflectendo] repraesentando O *add.* eius O   9 considerationem] considerationes K | naturae *om.* K | circumstantias] circumstans O | ad²] et FW Q Z | ipsam] *add.* et O   10 illas] ipsas O Q illa U   11 utpote] ut patet Q | est *om.* Z | tali] talia O | figura et magnitudine] figura H figura magnitudine FW magnitudine figura Z   12 et ceteris *om.* O L   13 autem] enim Q | in via *post* singulari FW   14 quicumque] quocumque O | non *om.* O | repugnat] repugnant H | contradictorie] *spat. vac.* L *add.* alteri O FW Q Z   15 alteri repugnat] *inv.* Q alteri non repugnat F   16 modum — praedictum] modum alteri praedicto Q praedictam autem modum Z | singulare] universale HM K   17 Dictus] Dicit O   18 est *om.* L | est² *om.* Q   19 universali] vel(!) FW   20 sicut] sic O | intelligimus] cognoscimus L | eas *om.* H | significamus] signamus K consignificamus Q | aliis *om.* FW Z   21 sed — exprimimus *om.* F | signati] significati Z   22 praedicto] *add.* modo K | nec] et L | dicimus] *add.* quod K   23 unus *om.* O K | crispus longus blaesus] blaesus longus L longus crispus blaesus K crispus et longus Q | et] et cetera O FW Z

---

[28]Scilicet, duo consequentia, quae inter lineolas rectas planas longiores ponuntur, sunt falsa.
[29]Cf. **Avicenna**, *Liber primus naturalium* I tr. 1 c. 1 (AviL 8-9).
[30]Subintellige: alteri; cf. lectiones variantes.
[31]Cf. **Avicenna**, *Liber primus naturalium* I tr. 1 c. 1 (AviL 12-14).
[32]Cf. supra n. 34.

huiusmodi, ut quilibet experitur in seipso et ceteris.[33]

36 Si vero ponamus speciem in intellectu, dicendum quod huiusmodi species duplicem singularitatem habet: unam a subiecto, quia est in subiecto singulari, et hanc semper habet; et aliam ab obiecto a quo imprimitur saltem primo, licet per operationem intellectus agentis abstrahatur a condicionibus individuantibus. Et sic primo repraesentat naturam in supposito vago, quia illud se primo offert intellectui; secundo, naturam absolute; tertio, ipsam intellectus determinat, addendo sibi circumstantias singulares praedictas. Et sic intelligit singulare signatum, non sub propria ratione singularitatis, ut dictum est.[34]

37 Quod autem tali ordine fiat cognitio intellectus patet per praedicta, quia scilicet ars et cognitio intellectualis imitatur naturam.[35] Dictum autem est quod natura primo intendit individuum vagum; secundo, naturam in ipso; tertio, individuum signatum, quod est terminus generationis; igitur talis erit modus intelligendi, sive species ponatur in intellectu sive non.[36]

[III. — Ad argumenta principalia]

38 Ad rationes principales in oppositum:
Dicendum ad primam[37] quod verum est "quod quid" est prius

---

1 experitur *post* seipso FW | et ceteris *om.* O L KU Q   2 vero] ergo Z | ponamus] ponimus Q | dicendum] *add.* est N M | quod] *add.* si FW | huiusmodi] secundum omnes Q   3 species] *add.* habet K | quia] quod U quae O | quia — subiecto] *mg.* U² *om.* K   4 in *om.* U² | subiecto] intellectus U² intellectu FW Q Z *add.* in intellectu O *add.* in quo U² | semper habet] *inv.* F | et²] *rep.* Z | et aliam] aliam W quia Q | a] et N in Q   5 quo] quomodo N | operationem] operationes Z   6 abstrahatur] abstrahitur N | condicionibus] *add.* materialibus vel KU | sic] si N   7 supposito] individuo O KU FW Q Z | vago *om.* K | illud se] *inv.* Q | se primo] *inv.* HL K FW   8 secundo] et O | ipsam intellectus] *inv.* N L   10 intelligit] intelligo N | non *om.* O | propria ratione] *inv.* NO M FW Q Z | singularitatis] singularis Z   11 est *om.* O   12 intellectus] intellectiva Q Z | patet *om.* O | per] *mg.* U² *lin.* Q *om.* K   13 scilicet] omnis KU *om.* O | intellectualis] intelligibilis O FW Q   14 autem est] *inv.* L FW Q Z est KU | quod natura] quamvis O | primo intendit] *inv.* NO M intendit KU   15 secundo] et O | quod] quia O Q | est] erit K   16 igitur] ergo L FW Z | erit] est O FW | modus] motus O   17 species ponatur] *inv.* Q ponatur K   19 rationes principales] re principali O | in oppositum] in obiectum O   20 Dicendum] *add.* est N M K F | ad primam] ad primum HL K *om.* U | quid] quidquid N Q quod quid L Z | est²] *lin.* O *add.* est FW | prius *post* nostri Q primum K FW

[33] Cf. **Duns Scotus**, *Lectura* I d. 7 q. un. n. 54-56 (XVI 492-493).
[34] Cf. supra n. 35.
[35] Cf. **Aristot.**, *Physica* II c. 22 (AL VII¹ 52-53; B c. 22 194a 21-22): "Si autem ars imitatur naturam, eiusdem autem scientiae est cognoscere speciem et materiam..."; *Auctoritates Aristotelis* (ed. J. Hamesse 145): "Ars imitatur naturam in quantum potest."
[36] Cf. **Duns Scotus**, *Lectura* I d. 7 q. un. n. 54-56 (XVI 492-493).
[37] Cf. supra n. 1.

obiectum intellectus quam singulare signatum vel singulare sub propria ratione singularitatis — immo sic non est obiectum intellectus per se, et ideo singulare non definitur nec cadit per se sub scientia —, tamen aliquo modo cognoscimus ipsum reflectendo, ut dictum est.[38]

Ad omnes auctoritates PHILOSOPHI[39] dicendum quod sensus singularium est cum praecisione, quia non est universalium; intellectus non, quia est cognoscitivus utriusque; et sic ad alias.

[10] Ad aliud[40] dicendum quod maior est vera de obiectis omnino disparatis, ut color et sonus, non autem de obiectis subordinatis — immo quod est primum obiectum potentiae inferioris est per se obiectum, licet non primum, potentiae superioris, ut patet de obiecto sensus particularis et sensus communis; sic est in proposito.

Ad aliud[41] dicendum quod artifex primo intendit naturam domus in supposito vago, et ex consequenti hanc domum et per accidens, et ideo, cognito universali, per accidens cognoscitur singulare. Vel aliter dicendum quod artifex, cognito universali per intellectum, intelligit singulare signatum, circumstantiando universali modo praedicto.

Ad aliud[42] dicendum quod per eandem speciem, aliter tamen consideratam, intelligimus universale et singulare, quia illa species repraesentat naturam primo in aliquo supposito vago; secundo, naturam absolute; tertio autem cum designationibus particularibus circumstantibus naturam et singulare signatum. Et sic patet solutio quaestionis. Vel potest dici quod, si intellectus non indiget nisi

---

1 intellectus] add. nostri N M add. (mg. K) prius K FW | signatum om. KU | vel singulare om. KU F 2 propria ratione] inv. K | immo] quamvis L add. ut O FW Q Z | est] add. proprium KU Q 3 singulare om. O FW Q Z | non] nec O FW Q Z | nec cadit] nisi cadat L | per se] ante cadit Q post scientia KU | sub scientia] ad suam O 4 tamen] cum KO | aliquo] alio O | modo om. U | ut] lin. Z 6 omnes auctoritates] inv. O | dicendum] add. est N M K F 7 singularium est] inv. KU FW Q Z | singularium — quia² om. O | intellectus] add. autem O KU FW Z 8 non om. H | est cognoscitivus] inv. F est cognitivus HL | utriusque] uterque O | et — alias om. Z | alias] alios O H FW add. omnes KU 9 dicendum] add. est N M F | maior] minor N 10 disparatis] add. et Q | et om. W 11 primum om. L 12 obiectum] oppositum O | licet] vel H | primum] primo HL 13 est om. FW 14 dicendum] add. est N M F | quod om. W | primo] prius FW | naturam] materiam(!) Z 15 per] secundum Z 16 cognito] add. per accidens W | cognoscitur] intelligitur KU Q Z intelligit FW 17 universali om. L 19 universali] = N HLM universale O KU FW Q Z 20 dicendum] add. est N M F 22 repraesentat] mg. F om. W Z add. illam L | primo] ante repraesentat K ante naturam U W Q Z om. F | vago] vagi O om. W Q Z 23 particularibus] partibus U 24 et] vel N om. KU 25 quod om. N LM | indiget] indigeret KU | nisi specie] inv. N LM

[38] Cf. supra n. 25. 34. 36.
[39] Cf. supra n. 2.
[40] Cf. supra n. 3.
[41] Cf. supra n. 4.
[42] Cf. supra n. 5.

specie in phantasmate, per speciem singularis intelligitur universale. Nec sequitur quod quot sunt singularia tot sunt universalia, quia species omnium singularium non repraesentant nisi unum universale.

43 Ad rationem THOMAE[43] dicendum quod materia non est principium individuationis, ut supponit; sed quando PHILOSOPHUS[44] loquitur de illa materia, vocat materiam designationes singulares vel materiales. Unde dicit in VII[45] quod in dictis secundum accidens non est idem "quod quid est" cum eo cuius est; et vocat postea[46] dicta per accidens materialia.

44 Item, dato quod materia esset principium individuationis, tamen non sequitur quod individuum sit ignotum sicut materia. Si enim materia dicitur ignota quia non est aeque primo nota ut forma et cognoscitur, prius cognita forma, sic etiam singulare signatum intelligitur, ut dictum est,[47] prius cognita natura, circumstantiando eam, ut dictum est supra.[48]

---

1 specie] *add.* quae est KU FW Q Z | intelligitur] intelligit Z 2 sequitur *om.* U | quod *om.* Z | singularia] *add.* quod O Q | sunt²] sint FW Q 3 species omnium] omnes species FW species Z | non *om.* L | unum *om.* O Q | universale] singulare L 5 Thomae] oppositam Q | dicendum] *add.* est N M F 6 Philosophus loquitur] *inv.* KU 7 illa] ista L KU Z | materiam] materias Z | vel] et U 8 materiales] *mg.* Z | dicit *post* VII H ait Q | VII] *add.* Metaphysicae K Q | secundum] per O FW Q Z 9 non — materialia *om.* Z | idem] id O | eo] *mg.* Q | et *om.* K | postea] praeterea N LM praeterita H 10 dicta] diversas(?) O | per] secundum L 11 Item] Praeterea FW Q Z Prima(?) O | dato quod] dico quod licet N M | esset] sit H U est K | tamen non] *inv.* O 13 materia *om.* L | dicitur] dicatur L sit Q | est *om.* Q | aeque] aquae O | primo nota] prima L | forma] facta O | et] etiam K 14 forma *om.* L | sic] sicut N H si Q | etiam] et KU autem Q 15 circumstantiando] circumstando HL | eam] ipsam Z 16 supra *om.* L *add.* Explicit doctor subtilis se anima O *add.* etc. H F *add.* Amen Q

[43]Cf. supra n. 10.
[44]Cf. **Aristot.**, *Metaph.* VII c. 8 (AL XXV³ 147; Z c. 8 1034*a* 4-8).
[45]Cf. **Aristot.**, *Metaph.* VII c. 6 (AL XXV³ 141; Z c. 6 1031*b* 18-21).
[46]Cf. **Aristot.**, *Metaph.* VII c. 11 (AL XXV³ 155-6; Z c. 11 1031*b* 22-27).
[47]Cf. supra n. 34. 36. 37.
[48]Cf. supra n. 34. 36. 37.

[QUAESTIO 23]

UTRUM IN ELICITIONE ACTUS INTELLIGENDI INTELLECTUS SIT MOVENS MOTUM AB OBIECTO VEL INTELLECTUS ET OBIECTUM RELUCENS IN SPECIE CONCURRANT AD ACTUM INTELLIGENDI

Utrum[1] in elicitione actus intelligendi intellectus sit movens motum ab obiecto, vel quod intellectus et obiectum relucens in specie concurrant ad actum intelligendi ut duo agentia partialia perfecte in suo ordine et sua causalitate, quorum causalitas unius non dependet a causalitate alterius, licet unum sit principalius movens alio.

[1] Et quod intellectus non sit movens-motum videtur:

Quia effectus magis assimilatur causae propinquae quam remotae; sed actus intelligendi magis assimilatur obiecto quam intellectui, quia per actum attingit obiectum; igitur obiectum est causa propinquior respectu elicitionis actus intelligendi quam intellectus. Sed causa propinqua est magis movens-motum quam causa remota. Igitur intellectus non est movens-motum, sed potius obiectum. Maior patet in naturalibus actionibus, quod quando duae causae concurrunt ad aliquem effectum subordinatae, quod effectus magis assimilatur causae propinquae quam remotae; nam ignis generatur ab igne et a sole, magis autem assimilatur igni quam soli. Similiter in artificialibus: impressio in cera magis assimilatur sigillo quam manui, quae est causa remota. Sed manifestum est quod obiectum et intellectus concurrunt ad actum intelligendi, et de intellectu manifestum est, et de obiecto dicit AUGUSTINUS IX *De*

---

6 Utrum] *praem.* Quaeritur KU *adnot. mg.* Quaestio 23 M | intelligendi] *add.* actus L   7 quod *om.* L | relucens] *add.* in phantasmate W   8 concurrant] occurrant H K | actum] actus FW   9 perfecte] perfecta FW X | et] in X | sua *om.* U | causalitas *om.* X   10 dependet] depende N | a] ex FW | unum] unus L KU   12 intellectus *om.* U | non] *lin.* K² *om.* U   13 causae — assimilatur *om.* L   14 assimilatur] similatur N   15 obiectum *om.* U | igitur] sed KU   17 propinqua] propinquior N | est magis] *inv.* N M FW X   19 actionibus] accidentibus H *add.* est L | quod ... quod] quia ... K quod ... U quod ... quodam FW   20 aliquem] unum K | subordinatae] sub ordine N M FW X   22 generatur] generatus N M FW X | a *om.* L K FW | autem *om.* N M FW X   23 artificialibus] artibus H K X   26 et *om.* U

[1] Deficiunt codices O Q Z.

Trinitate[2] "a cognoscente et cognito paritur notitia," et similiter dicit quod "omnis generat sui notitiam". Minor etiam conceditur ab omnibus.

2 Item, si obiectum splendens in specie moveret intellectum ad actum intelligendi, quaero quid causaretur in intellectu per illam actionem et motionem. Si nihil causaretur, intellectus non est movens-motum. Et non causat potentiam intellectivam, quia praesupponitur; nec etiam speciem intelligibilem, quia ponitur quod illa species quae imprimitur in intellectu sit ultimate repraesentans obiectum, igitur illa non movebit intellectum causando in illo novam speciem; nec actum intelligendi, quia tunc intellectus nihil faceret ad actum intelligendi, sed tantum reciperet, cuius oppositum praesupponit quaestio. Igitur intellectus non est movens motum ab obiecto.

[I. — Responsio]

3 Dicitur quod intellectus est movens motum ab obiecto ad hoc quod eliciat actum intelligendi, quia quando aliquid est in potentia essentiali ad aliquem actum, non reducitur de potentia ad actum nisi per aliquid sibi impressum; sed intellectus, antequam recipiat speciem, est in potentia essentiali ad actum intelligendi; igitur ad hoc quod concurrat ad actum intelligendi requiritur quod sit motus ab alio per aliquid sibi impressum. Maior patet[3] per PHILOSOPHUM II *De anima*,[4] quia in hoc distinguitur potentia accidentalis a potentia essentiali. Minor etiam patet per PHILOSOPHUM III *De anima*,[5]

---

2 quod omnis] ens KU quod omne L | sui] sibi N 4 in specie *om.* K 5 causaretur] causetur KU | illam *om.* KU 6 causaretur] causetur U *add.* tunc KU 7 movens-motum] movens et motum U | causat] causam U | quia] *add.* illa N M FW X 8 etiam] et U | intelligibilem *om.* KU | ponitur] ponatur HL 9 imprimitur *post* intellectu H est K *om.* U | sit *om.* KU 10 movebit] moveret KU | intellectum *om.* KU | illo] illa H 11 novam] non album K 12 oppositum] obiectum K 13 movens motum] motus KU 16 Dicitur] Dico M FW X Dicendum est K 17 aliquid] aliquis H 18 reducitur] producitur H | de potentia *om.* H KU 22 Maior] Minor L M U | patet per — etiam *om.* N HLM KU 23 II De anima *om.* X | a potentia] ab X 24 III De anima *om.* X

[2]**Augustinus**, *De Trinitate* IX c. 12 (CCL 50 309, PL 42 970): "Unde liquido tenendum est quod omnis res quamcumque cognoscimus congenerat in nobis notitiam sui; ab utroque enim notitia paritur, a cognoscente et cognito"; Cf. **Scotus**, *Lectura* II d. 3 pars 2 q. 1 (XVIII 314).
[3]Quaenam verba ab "Maior" usque ad "III *De anima*" legenda sint, coniecimus cum codicibus FW, errore homeoteleutico in codicibus principalibus commisso.
[4]**Aristot.**, *De an.* II c. 11 (B c. 11, 417b 12-16.)
[5]**Aristot.**, *De an.* III c. 3 (Γ c. 4, 429b 30—430a 2); *Auctoritates Aristotelis* (ed. J. Hamesse 186): "Intellectus possibilis est primo tanquam tabula rasa in qua nihil est depictum."

quia anima est sicut tabula nuda etc., et in potentia essentiali.

[II. — Ad argumenta principalia]

Ad argumentum[6] dicendum quod minor est falsa, immo actus intelligendi magis assimilatur intellectui quam obiecto; et ideo intellectus denominatur ab actu intelligendi et non obiectum.

Ad secundum[7] dicendum quod species non movet intellectum sed est sibi ratio movendi; perficit enim intellectum in actu primo, et sic perfectus elicit actum secundum. Unde illa impressio non est motio, sicut nec impressio formae in materia nec est motio per quam forma illa movet materiam; sed movetur ab obiecto in phantasmate, quod movet intellectum possibilem, gignendo ibi suam similitudinem.

Contra: minor illa[8] ostenditur dupliciter:

Primo, quia sic ex actibus generatur habitus et habitus inclinat in similitudinem actus ex quo generatur; sed habitus magis assimilatur obiecto secundum actus in quos inclinat quam intellectui, quia habitus declinat in obiectum et principia eius, non autem in intellectum; igitur actus magis assimilatur obiecto quam intellectui.

Item, ad idem, motus denominatur a termino a quo, et magis quam a termino ad quem; igitur actus intelligendi quo attingitur ipsum obiectum magis assimilatur termino a quo quam termino ad quem — et praecipue in proposito[9] ab obiecto, cum ipsum sit terminus a quo et non ad quem.

---

1 sicut] tamquam FW | nuda] rasa FW X | etc.] in qua etc. N U in qua nihil depingitur (est H) H K | et] ut F ita W *om.* U | essentiali] *add.* ad actum intelligendi H   3 argumentum] secundum L | minor] maior K | est falsa] *inv.* M   5 denominatur] = FW X non N HL omnino est KU | denominatur] denominatur — obiectum] *ocellus spat. vac.* non ab *spat. vac.* M | actu — obiectum *om.* M | non] *add.* ab X   6 dicendum] dicitur X *add.* est N M FW X   7 sibi] si H | in *om.* H   8 perfectus] perfectius HL K | non — impressio *om.* L | est *om.* U   9 materia] materiam KU | nec²] non N M FW X | motio²] motus L | per — illa] illa forma per quam H forma per quam illa L forma illa per quam U   10 movet] moveret L   11 movet *post* possibilem H | ibi] sibi K   12 similitudinem] *add.* et cetera L   13 minor illa] *inv.* H U ista minor K   14 sic *om.* HL KU   15 in] ad HL KU | actus] *ante* similitudinem K | ex] a HL KU   16 in *om.* HL KU   19 ad idem motus *om.* KU *add.* magis K | denominatur] determinatur L | et *om.* L KU   21 assimilatur] *add.* a N M U FW X | a — termino] = KU *om.* N HLM FW X | quam] *add.* a U   22 et praecipue] et praecise L praecise etiam KU | ipsum *om.* H   23 non] = KU *om.* N HLM FW X

[6]Cf. supra n. 1.
[7]Cf. supra n. 2.
[8]Cf. supra n. 1, scilicet "actus intelligendi magis assimilatur obiecto quam intellectui."
[9]Subaudi: denominatur.

[III. — Argumenta altera intellectum non esse "movens motum" probantia]

8   Item, potentia activa non requirit aliquid sibi impressum ad hoc quod eliciat actum. Et hoc patet inductive: in omni potentia activa est[10] eius potentia simul, tam perfecta (quae non requirit nisi praesentiam diversorum obiectorum ad hoc quod determinetur ad agendum) quam potentia imperfecta (ut in calore). Igitur, cum intellectus eliciat actum intelligendi effective, sequitur quod non requiritur aliquid sibi impressum ad hoc quod intelligat.

9   Item, sicut aliquid se habet ad agere, sic ad esse; sicut igitur dat agere, ita dabit esse. Si igitur species in intellectu sit ratio agendi ipsi intellectui, igitur est magis intellectum et magis habebit de esse intelligibili; et per consequens esset species magis intelligibilis quam intellectus, cum sit magis intellectus.

10   Item, si sit ipsi intellectui ratio intelligendi, sicut calor ligno calefaciendi, et principium, tunc species separata intelligeret, sicut si calor esset separatus, calefaceret.

11   Item, quod potest plus, et minus; sed in visione beatifica potest intellectus sine specie intelligere, nec requiritur aliquid informans, secundum COMMENTATOREM,[11] sed essentia divina est in loco speciei, quae non informat; igitur similiter intellectus in cognitionem sibi naturalem potest sine specie.

12   Ad confirmationem autem opinionis praedictae[12] adducebatur

---

5 est — simul] post perfecta N HM FW X om. L KU | tam perfecta] mg. U | quae om. KU | requirit] add. aliquid sibi U 6 diversorum obiectorum] inv. K | hoc om. H 7 potentia] lin. H om. L KU | calore] colore L | cum] si L 8 non] = HL om. N M KU FW X 9 aliquid sibi] inv. U sibi aliquod K | sibi impressum] inv. N 10 sicut] si H | se habet] inv. K | sicut igitur] inv. KU | dat] debet U 11 ita dabit] sic dat KU ita dat L | igitur] ergo N | ratio] passio N | agendi] intelligendi L 12 magis habebit] inv. KU | habebit] habet X 13 intelligibili] intellectu L 14 intellectus² om. L 15 ipsi] ipsa L | ratio] in ratione K rationem U | intelligendi] agendi L 16 si om. KU 17 calor] color U | esset om. KU 18 et] potest KU | minus] add. potest L | sed] add. si L KU | visione beatifica] visionem beatificam X 19 aliquid om. L 20 secundum] sed U | Commentatorem] conclusionem U 22 sibi] add. essentialem sive L 23 autem om. KU X | opinionis] oppositis H

[10] Verba 'est eius potentia simul', quae nobis originem sumpsisse in codice primordio in margine videntur, omnes codices qui ea exhibent perperam transposuerunt post 'perfecta'. Cf. Praefatio nostra., 114*-118*.
[11] Cf. **Averroës**, De an. III c. 36 (AverL 500-501); Metaph. XII c. 51 (ed. Iuntina VIII 335rD—337rC).
[12] Cf. supra n. 8-11.

auctoritas COMMENTATORIS super III *De anima*, commento 2;[13] dicit quod necesse est inveniri in parte animae una pars quae dicitur intellectus, secundum quod facit illum intellectum qui est in potentia intelligere esse in actu; causa enim quae facit intellectum, qui est in potentia, intelligere omnia in actu nihil aliud est nisi quia sit in actu. Hoc enim, quia est in actu, est causa ut intelligat in actu omnia.

In hac auctoritate nominatur primo quod intellectus possibilis sit in actu per actionem intellectus agentis imprimentis speciem; et quando sic est in actu, tunc potest actu intelligere et speciem elicere — moveri igitur ab obiecto — et species obiecti est ratio sibi intelligendi per quam est in actu; igitur etc.

13

---

1 De anima *om.* KU | 2] *add.* ubi L *add.* qui K 2 inveniri] invenire H U | in] *add.* una K *add.* vita U | animae *om.* N H | una] secunda N M FW X *add.* est KU 3 intellectus] natus L | illum intellectum] *inv.* H istum intellectum L 4 intellectum] intelligit N 5 sit] fuit H fit L 6 in actu omnia] actu L 8 hac] *add.* autem L | nominatur primo] *inv.* KU notatur primo L 9 sit] fit HM FW X 10 et] vel U 12 quam] quem L | igitur etc. *om.* KU | etc] *add.* Expliciunt quaestiones Doctoris Subtilis super 2m et 3m De anima N *add. ult.* etiam Magister Bentley N² *add.* Expliciunt quaestiones D. super II et III libros De anima amen etc. H *add.* Expliciunt quaestiones Doctoris Subtilis super II et III De anima Oxoniensis scriptae per fratrem Petrum Pauli de Nycopia(?) L *add. ult.* Lord Iesus mercy L² *add.* Quod Esyche M *add. ult.* Expliciunt quaestiones super 2m et 3m libros De anima secundum Scotum alias doctorem subtilem M² *add.* Expliciunt quaestiones Doctoris Subtilis super II et III libros De anima (Oxoniensis) scriptae a domino Iohanne Saundri etc. K *add.* Expliciunt quaestiones secundum doctorem subtilem super duos libros De anima U *add.* Expliciunt quaestiones venerabilis D. subtilis magistri Ioannis Scoti de ordine minorum super 2 et 3 De anima etc. scriptae per me Maffenanthonem de Perabiago Mediolanens F *add. ult.* Expliciunt quaestiones venerabilis doctoris subtilis magistri Ioannis Scoti de ordine minorum super primo et secundo et tertio De anima etc. Et sunt ad usum fratris Guidonis de Alba ordinis minorum MCCCC4 F² *add.* Expliciunt quaestiones venerabilis doctoris magistri Johannis Scoti de ordine fratrum minorum super secundum et tertium De anima amen W

[13]Potius **Averroës**, *De an.* III c. 5 (AverL 406): "Et ideo opinandum est, quod iam apparuit ex sermone Aristotelis, quod in anima sunt duae partes intellectus, quarum una est recipiens ... alia autem est agens, et illud quod facit intentiones quae sunt in virtute imaginativa esse moventes intellectum materialem in actu postquam erant moventes in potentia."

INDICES

INDEX I: INDEX CODICUM

INDEX II: INDEX NOMINUM ANTIQUORUM
ET MEDIAEVALIUM (IN INTRODUCTIONE)

INDEX III: INDEX AUCTORUM

INDEX IV: INDEX DOCTINALIS

I: INDEX CODICUM

ASSISI, Biblioteca del Sacro Convento de S. Francesco, Ms. 136: 100*
ASSISI, Biblioteca del Sacro Convento de S. Francesco, Ms. 137: 100*
AVIGNON, Bibliothèque Municipale, Ms. 328 [= A]: 28*-29*, 35*, 55*, 114*, 117*, 119*, 127*
BASEL, Universitätsbibliothek (Öffentliche Bibliothek der Universität Basel), B.V.31 [= B]: 21*, 29*-30*, 55*, 114*, 117*, 119*, 127*
BOLOGNA, Biblioteca Comunale dell'Archiginnasio, Ms. A.162: 23* n. 29
CAMBRIDGE, Gonville and Caius College Library, Ms. 335 [= C]: 2*, 24*, 31*-33*, 39*, 44*, 48*, 53*, 55*, 70*, 114*, 117*, 119*, 121*, 127*
CAMBRIDGE, Gonville and Caius College Library, Ms. 369: 4*
CAMBRIDGE, Peterhouse Library, Ms. 239 [= D]: 14*, 33*-34*, 48*, 55*, 70*, 114*, 117*, 119*, 127*
CAMBRIDGE, University Library, Ms. 1234 (III.26): 29* n. 35
MILANO, Biblioteca Ambrosiana, C.62 sup. [= E]: 29*, 34*-35*, 55*, 70*, 114*, 117*, 119*, 127*
MODENA, Biblioteca Estense, Cod. α. M.5.29 (Lat. 302) [= F]: 1*-2*, 24*, 32*, 53*, 55*-56*, 59*-62*, 69*-75*, 77*-83*, 86*-95*, 99*, 101*-12*, 115*-17*, 119*, 127*-28*, 145*
MÜNCHEN, Bayerische Staatsbibliothek, Clm 8717 [= Z^2]: 2*, 24*, 26*, 29*, 32*, 51*-53*, 55*, 57*, 70*, 115*, 117*, 121*, 127*
OXFORD, All Souls College Library, Ms. 87 [= G]: 3*, 5*, 35*-37*, 55*, 70*, 114*, 117*, 119*, 127*
OXFORD, All Souls College Library, Ms. 88: 4*
OXFORD, Balliol College Library, Ms. 93: 4*
OXFORD, Balliol College Library, Ms. 117 [= H]: 2*-4*, 9*, 11*, 16*, 18*, 36*, 55*, 57*-59*, 61*, 69*, 73*, 77*-83*, 86*-95*, 98*, 101*-12*, 115*-17*, 119*, 127*-28*, 144*-45*
OXFORD, Bodleian Library, Ms. Canon Misc. 402 [= J]: 37*-40*, 55*, 70*, 114*, 117*, 119*, 127*
OXFORD, Bodleian Library, Ms. Digby 44 [= K]: 4*-7*, 15*-16*, 21*, 36*, 55*-56*, 59*-62*, 66*-69*, 72*-73*, 77*-83*, 86*-95*, 98*-99*, 101*-12*, 115*-17*, 119*, 127*-28*, 144*-45*
OXFORD, Corpus Christi College Library, Ms. 227 [= L]: 3*, 8*-9*, 11*, 15*, 22*, 55*, 57*-61*, 65*, 69*, 73*, 77*-83*, 86*-95*, 98*, 101*-12*, 115*-17*, 119*, 127*-28*, 144*-45*
OXFORD, Corpus Christi College Library, Ms. 228: 8* n. 8
OXFORD, Magdalen College Library, Ms. lat. 16 [= M]: 9*-16*, 44*, 55*, 57*-61*, 66*, 69*, 73*, 77*-83*, 86*-95*, 97*-99*, 101*-13*, 115*-16*, 119*, 121*, 127*-28*, 144*-45*
OXFORD, Magdalen College Library, Ms. lat. 80 [= N]: 2*-3*, 6*-7*, 9*-10*, 13*-18*, 34*, 48*, 55*-56*, 59*-66*, 69*, 73*, 75*, 77*-83*, 86*-97*, 99*, 101*-17*, 119*, 127*-28*, 144*-45*
OXFORD, Merton College Library, Ms. 59: 130*

OXFORD, Oriel College Library, Ms. 35 [= O]: 2*-3*, 9*, 13*, 16*-19*, 55*-56*, 59*-66*, 71*, 73*, 75*, 77*-83*, 86*-96*, 99*, 101*-17*, 119*, 127*-28*, 144*-45*

PADOVA, Biblioteca Antoniana, Ms. 173 Scaff. IX [= P]: 40*-43*, 49*, 55*, 70*, 114*, 117*, 119*, 121*, 127*

PRAHA, Knihovna Metropolitní Kapituli, Cod L.51: 134*-35*

PRAHA, Knihovna Metropolitní Kapituli, Cod M.89: 134*-35*

ROMA, Biblioteca Angelica, Ms. 953 (R.5.4) [= Q]: 19*-21*, 30*, 55*-56*, 59*-63*, 69*-75*, 77*-83*, 86*-95*, 99*, 101*-112*, 114*, 117*, 119*, 127*, 145*

ROMA, Biblioteca Angelica, Ms. 1034 (R.7.15) [= R]: 44*, 55*, 70*, 115*, 117*, 119*, 121*, 127*

SCHLÄGEL, Prämonstratenser-Stiftsbibliothek, Cod. 140: 29* n. 35

TORINO, Biblioteca Nazionale Universitaria, Ms. 1046 (G.IV.16) [= S et Z^3]: 44*, 53*, 55*, 70*, 115*, 117*, 119*, 127*

TORINO, Biblioteca Nazionale Universitaria, Ms. 1260 (H.111.43) [= T]: 45*-46*, 55*, 70*, 117*, 119*, 127*

TORTOSA, Biblioteca de la Catedral y del Cabildo de la Santísima Iglesia Catedral (Archivo Capitular de Tortosa), Cód. 201 [= Z^1]: 51*, 55*, 115*, 117*-127*

UPPSALA, Universitetsbibliotek, Hs. C.627: 54* n. 71

VATICANO (CITTÀ DEL), Biblioteca Apostolica Vaticana, Cod. Ottobonianus latinus 1442: 122*

VATICANO (CITTÀ DEL), Biblioteca Apostolica Vaticana, Cod. Urbinas latinus 1406 [= U]: 21*-22*, 55*, 56* n. 72, 59*-62*, 66*-75*, 77*-83*, 86*-92*, 93*-95*, 98*-99*, 101*-12*, 115*-17*, 119*, 127*, 144*-45*

VATICANO (CITTÀ DEL), Biblioteca Apostolica Vaticana, Cod. Vaticanus latinus 869 [= V]: 2*, 24*, 40*-41*, 46*-49*, 55*, 70*, 84*, 115*, 117*, 119*, 127*

VATICANO (CITTÀ DEL), Biblioteca Apostolica Vaticana, Cod. Vaticanus latinus 889: 23* n. 29

VATICANO (CITTÀ DEL), Biblioteca Apostolica Vaticana, Cod. Vaticanus latinus 890 [=W]: 2*, 22*-24*, 32*, 50*, 53*, 55*-56*, 59*-62*, 69*-75*, 77*-84*, 86*-95*, 99*, 101*-12*, 115*-17*, 119*, 121*, 127*, 133*, 145*

VATICANO (CITTÀ DEL), Biblioteca Apostolica Vaticana, Cod. Vaticanus latinus 3092 [= X]: 24*-25*, 39*, 55*-57*, 59*-61*, 66*, 69*-74*, 77*-84*, 86*-95*, 99*, 101*-10*, 112*, 115*-17*, 119*, 127*, 145*

VATICANO (CITTÀ DEL), Biblioteca Apostolica Vaticana, Cod. Vaticanus latinus 12995: 100*

VENEZIA, Biblioteca Nazionale Marciana, Cod. lat. III.230 [= Y]: 23*, 50*-51*, 55*, 96*, 115*, 117*, 119*, 133*

WIEN, Österreichische Nationalbibliothek, Cod. lat. 1447 [= Z]: 25*-27*, 55*-56*, 59*-62*, 66*, 69*-75*, 77*-83*, 86*-95*, 99*, 101*-12*, 114*, 117*, 119*, 145*

WORCESTER, Cathedral and Chapter Library, Ms. F.86: 4*

II: INDEX NOMINUM ANTIQUORUM ET MEDIAEVALIUM
(IN INTRODUCTIONE)

ADAMUS DE WODEHAM: 123*, 133*-35*, 142* n. 136
AEGIDIUS ROMANUS: 10*, 136*, 139*, 142*
ALBERTUS MAGNUS: 38*-39*
ALBERTUS METENSIS: 53*
ALDOBRANDINUS DE TUSCANELLA: 42*
ALEXANDER BONINI DE ALEXANDRIA: 14*-15*, 26*, 34*, 43*, 48*, 52*
ALEXANDER HALENSIS: 15*, 34*
ANONYMI ET AUCTORES FRANCISCANI, *Quaestiones miscelleneae*: 48*
ANONYMUS:
    Ars grammatica per interrogationes de responsiones: 22*
    Bona quaestio metaphysicalis de ente: 12*
    Casus papales, episcopales et abbaciales: 22*
    De propositionibus, etc.: 21*
    Duae quaestiones ordinariae de conceptibus transcendentibus et quaestiones miscellaneae de formalitatibus: 47*
    Expositio super libellum De sex principiis: 30*
    Fragmenta grammaticales: 21*
    Quaestio de Categoriis: 20*
    Quaestio de essentia et essaentia prima: 27*
    Quaestio optima metaphysicalis: 12*
    Quaestio utrum actio et passio constituunt diversa praedicamenta vel unum: 21*
    Quaestio utrum privatio sit existens extra animam: 37*
    Quaestio utrum theologia sit scientia proprie dicta: 27*
    Quaestiones: 47*
    Quaestiones de cognitione Dei: 1*-2*, 23*, 31*-32*, 47*, 52*-53*
    Quaestiones in libros I et II De anima: 47*
    Quastiones logicales: 19*-20*
    Quaestiones medicinales: 6*
    Quaestiones super libros De generatione et corruptione: 30*
    Quaestiones super libros De somno et vigilia: 5*
    Quaestiones super librum de memoria et reminiscentia: 6*
    Sermones et notae sermonum: 30*
ANONYMUS ET AUCTORES VARII, *Quaestiones logicales, de animalibus, physicales et metaphysicales*: 42*
ANTONIUS ANDREAE: 3*, 8*-9*, 11*, 16*, 31*, 34*, 44*-45*, 100* n. 94, 115* n. 99, 121*-23*, 123* n. 111, 128*, 134*-35*
ARISTOTELES: 4*-5*, 7*, 15*, 17*, 18* n. 21, 18* n. 22, 21*, 32*, 34*, 35* n. 43, 35* n. 44, 37*, 40*, 45*, 53* n. 70, 54*-55*, 58*, 72*, 78*, 80*, 85*, 114*-15*, 122* n. 109, 125*, 127*-128*, 133*-34*, 136*, 139*, 144*
ASTON, JOHN (scriptor): 50*-51*
AUFREDUS GONTERI: 47*-48*, 52*
AVERROES: 39*, 72* n. 74, 136*

AVICENNA: 59*, 134*

BENTLEY, JOHN (possessor): 13*-15*, 99*
BONAVENTURA A BAGNOREA: 41* n. 51

CROMWELL, THOMAS: 83*

DIONYSIUS DE BURGO SANCTI SEPULCHRI: 32*

FRANCISCUS DE MARCHIA: 24*
FRANCISCUS DE MAYRONIS: 24*-25*, 28*

GARSDALE, RICHARD (possessor): 16*, 19*, 99*
GASCOIGNE, THOMAS: 10*
GEDEON PARISIENSIS: 24*
GERARDUS DE BURGO SANCTI DONNINI: 140*
GERARDUS ODONIS: 24*-25*, 43*
GODEFRIDUS DE FONTIBUS: 100*, 134*, 136*, 139*, 142*
GOMETIUS HISPANUS: 54*
GONSALVUS HISPANUS: 97* n. 81, 123*-26*, 136*, 139*-40*, 143*
GUALTERUS BURLAEUS: 6*-7*, 10*-11*, 14*-15*, 24*-25*, 37*
GUILLELMUS DE ALNWICK: 24*, 42*, 47*, 51*, 135*
GUILLELMUS DE CONCHIS: 34*
GUILLELMUS DE LAMARA: 127*
GUILLELMUS MILVERLEY: 17*-18*
GUILLELMUS DE MISSALI: 23*, 41*, 50*-51*, 115*, 117*, 133*, 135*
GUILLELMUS DE OCKHAM: 16* n. 14, 24*, 100*, 123* n. 112, 134*, 139* n. 118
GUILLELMUS DE WARA: 136*

HENRICUS DE GANDAVO: 10*, 96* n. 77, 99*-100*, 134*, 136*, 139*, 142*
HERVAEUS NATALIS: 51* n. 67, 52*-53*
HUGO DE HARTLEPOOL: 141*
HUGO DE NOVO CASTRO: 47*-48*

IACOBUS DE AESCULI: 26*
IACOBUS DE CARSETO: 48* n. 60
IACOBUS DE PRAETO (scriptor): 45*
IACOBUS DE TURBIO: 122*
IACOBUS DE VITERBIO: 100*, 122*, 136*
IOANNES CANONICUS: 3*, 11*, 35* n. 43, 36*, 123*, 135*
IOANNES DEDECUS: 3*-4*
IOANNES DEE (possessor): 8*
IOANNES DUNS SCOTUS: *passim*
IOANNES DUNS SCOTUS (pseudo-): 3*, 9*, 48*
IOANNES DE EVERISDEN: 22*
IOANNES DE LYTHONA SCOTUS: 18*

IOANNES DE MERCURIA (MONACHUS): 42*
IOANNES PARISIENSIS: 136*
IOANNES PECHAM: 127*, 136*
IOANNES DE PISA: 6*
IOANNES DE RADINGIA: 47*
IOANNES DE RUPELLA: 39*
IOANNES SCOTUS IUNIOR: 18*
IOANNES SHARPE: 17*-18*
IOANNES VITALIS A FURNO (VITAL DU FOUR): 122*-23*, 136*, 139*
IOANNES WYCLIF: 16*
IODICUS WEILER DE HAILPRUNNA (possessor): 26*

LAW, ROBERT (scriptor et possessor): 9*-10*, 12*-13*
LAYTON, RICHARD: 83*, 99* n. 91

MAFFENANTHONES DE PERABIAGO MEDIOLANENSE (scriptor): 1*
MATTHAEUS DE AQUASPARTA: 136*
MAURITIUS DE PORTU: 121*
MORE, JOHN (Stationarius): 10*

NICOLAUS BONETUS: 1*
NICOLAUS COMPARINI DE ASSISI: 22*
NICOLAUS DE GORHAM: 18*
NICOLAUS DE LYRA: 41*, 45* n. 55, 48*-49*
NICOLAUS DE ORBELLIS: 122*

PAULUS NICCOLETTI VENETUS: 44*
PETRUS AUREOLUS: 42*-43*, 53*, 99*
PETRUS IOANNES OLIVI: 136*, 142*
PETRUS LOMBARDUS: 32* n. 38, 41*, 136*
PETRUS PAULI DE NYCOPIA (scriptor): 8*, 22*, 128*
PETRUS THOMAE: 10*-14*, 20*, 48*
PHILIPPUS DE BRIDLINGTON: 141*
PHILIPPUS DE MELDUNO: 14*-15*
PLATO: 30*
PORPHYRIUS: 21*, 51*

RICHARDUS ARMACHANUS: 12*
RICHARDUS DE CONINGTON: 52*
RICHARDUS DE MEDIAVILLA: 48*-49*, 136*
RICHARDUS DE NORHAUTONIA: 43*
ROBERTUS ALINGTON: 17*-18*
ROBERTUS COWTON: 10*, 12*
ROBERTUS GROSSETESTE: 98*, 134*
ROBERTUS KILWARDBY: 10*
ROGERUS MARSTON: 136*

SALIMBENE PARMENSIS: 140*
SAUNDER, JOHN (scriptor et possessor): 4*-7*, 21*, 35*-36*, 99*, 128*
SCOTULUS: 3*, 11*, 16*, 121*, 128*

THOMAS DE AQUINO: 71*, 127* n. 115, 136*, 139*
THOMAS BARNEBY: 48* n. 60
THOMAS STAKKYS: 22*
THOMAS SUTTON: 136*
THURSKE, CHRISTOPHER (possessor): 9*

VAVASOR, WILLIAM (scriptor): 8*-9*
VITAL DU FOUR, *vide* IOANNES VITALIS A FURNO

WYCHE, THOMAS (scriptor et possessor): 9*-12*, 16* n. 16, 99*, 102*, 110*, 113*

III: INDEX AUCTORUM

ADAM DE WODEHAM

Lectura secunda in librum primum Sententiarum (ed. Rega Wood et Gedeon Gál, S. Bonaventurae 1990. 3 vol.) prol. q. 3 n. 9: 9:16

AEGIDIUS ROMANUS

Expositio in libros De anima Aristotelis (Venice, 1496) II com. 108: 1:2; 1:5; 1:13; 1:16; 2:6 | II com. 109: 2:1 | II com. 111: 2:10 | II com. 113: 3:5; 3:6; 3:14| II com. 115: 3:1, 3:18; II com. 116: 3:1; 3:18 | II com. 118: 3:16 | II com. 119: 12:1 | II com. 121: 3:13, 4:1 (bis), 4:5, 4:6, 4:10 (ter), 4:11 (bis), 5:1, 5:2, 5:6 | II com. 128: 6:1, 9:11 | II com. 135: 10:16 | II com. 136: 9:4 | III com. 17: 13:11, III com. 18: 13:8

De cognitione angelorum (ed. Venice, 1503) q. 1: 12:13 | q. 4: 4:8; 18:7 | q.. 5: 17:16

Quodlibeta (Venetiis 1502) I q. 9: 22:18 | III q. 13: 12:19; 12:20; 14:21 | V q. 21: 17:25 | V q. 28: 22:18

ALBERTUS MAGNUS

(*Opera omnia*, ed. Institutum Alberti Magni Coloniense 1951-)

De Anima (ed. C. Stroick, Monasterii Westfalorum 1968. *Opera omnia*, editio Coloniensis VII[1]) II tr. 3 c. 27: 6:4 | c. 30: 1:3 | c. 31: 2:1 | c. 32: 3:2 | c. 32, 33: 3:1 | c. 33: 3:5; 3:6 | c. 34: 4:1; 4:8 | c. 35: 4:2 | tr. 4 c. 1: 5:1; 6:13 | c. 3: 6:1 | c. 6: 6:13 | c. 7-11: 9:1 | c. 8 : 9:3 | c. 11: 8:1; 9:10 (bis); 10:5; 10:8; 10:10

De animalibus (BGPTH 15 864-6). 2:7

De animalibus (BGPTH 15 865) 2:4

De generatione et corruptione (ed. P. Hossfeld, Monasterii Westfalorum 1980. *Opera omnia*, editio Coloniensis V2) I tr. 6 c. 9: 3:7

Physica (ed. P. Hossfeld, Monasterii Westfalorum 1987-1993. *Opera omnia*, editio Coloniensis VI[1-2]) V tr. 2 c. 3: 2:3 || VII tr. 1 c. 4: 6:12

Super Ethica, commentum et quaestiones, libros VI-X VI lect. 8 (ed. Kubel, Editio Coloniensis XIV pars 2, 453-4) 18:9

ALCHER

Liber de spiritu et anima (PL 40, 794): 2:8

ALFREDUS ANGLICUS

De motu cordis (BGPTH 23[1] 14-15): 2:7 | c. 16 (BGPTH 23[1] 88); 10:9

ANONYMUS : (JACOBUS DE DUACO?)

Quaestiones De anima (ed. Bazàn) II q. 30: 1:2; 1:9; 1:17 | q. 39: 9:1 | q. 40 : 10:1; 10:5; 10:9 (bis); 10:10; 10:13 | | III q. 1: 12:27

ANONYMUS: MAGISTER ARTIUM

Lectura in librum De anima (ed. Gauthier) II, 20: 1:5; 1:6 | II, 24: 9:1; 9:4

ANONYMUS

Quaestiones De anima (ed. Bazàn) III q. 1: 12:26

ANONYMUS

Quaestiones De anima (ed. Van Steenberghen) III q. 3: 12:1

ANONYMUS

Quaestiones in tres libros de anima (ed. J. Vennebusch) II q. 52: 1:5 | q. 55: 9:1 | q. 56 [1] : 10:1 (ter)

ANONYMUS

Sententia super II et III De anima (ed. Bazàn) II lect. 19: 1:2 | lect. 21: 1:6; 1:2 | lect. 24: 1:1

ARISTOTELES

(*Aristoteles latinus*. Corpus philosophorum medii aevi, Academiarum consociatarum auspiciis et consilio editum, 1939-; *Aristotelis opera cum Averrois commentariis*, latine, ed. Iuntina, Venetiis 1550-1552, 11 voll.; *Opera*, graece, ed. I. Bekker, Berolini 1831, 2 voll.)

Analytica posteriora (AL IV$^{1-4}$) I c. 2: 21: 11 | c. 4: 16:8; 21:15 | c. 18: 21:11 | c. 31: 22: 2; 22:30 | | II c. 13 [t. 75]: 18:10 | c. 19: 22:20

Analytica priora (AL III^1) I c. 15: P,13:15 | c. 46: 2PI,4:1. 4; 2PII,2-5:4 (bis). 7. 16. 18 | | II c. 15: P,5-8:39; 2PI,4:8

De anima (inter opera Sancti Thomae, ed. Leonina 45^1, Romae 1984) I c. 1 (☐ c. 1, 402a 12-16); 17:15 (bis); 17:39 | c. 2: 17:15 (bis) | c. 5: 12:2 | c. 10: 12:28 | | II c. 1: 17:15 | c. 2: 5:7; 12:21 | c. 3: 1:4 (bis); 1:16; 1:19 | c. 4: 12:21 | c. 5: 1:16; 2:2; 2:4 (bis) | c. 6: 2:2; 20:6; 20:21 | c. 11: 12:27 (bis); 23:3 | c. 12: 14:16; 22:2 | c. 13: 8:11; 10:17 | c. 15: 4:5 (bis); 4:10; 13:9; 21:12 | c. 21: 1:15; 6:4 | c. 22: 1:1; 1:2 (bis); 1:5; 1:6 (ter); 1:17; 2:1; 2:5; 3:1; 6:3; 10:1; 10:3 | c. 23: 2:9; 3:4; 3:5; 3:18; 4:1; 10: 1; 10:18; 12:1; 12:16; 14:2 | c. 24: 5:1; 5:4; 7:20; 8:12; 12:42 | c. 25: 1:1; 2:7; 5:4; 6:1; 6:5; 6:6; 6:13; 10:18; 10:27 | c. 26: 2:7; 7:1; 7:2; 7:20; 9:3; 9:4; 12:14; 20:3 | c. 27: 8:1 (bis); 8:3; 8:10; 9:1; 9:7; 9:17; 10:1; 10:4; 10:6 (ter) | c. 28: 11:2; 11:4; 11:6 | c. 30: 2:2 | | III c. 1: 9:10; 10:8; 12:1; 12:28 (bis); 15:1; 17:5; 19:29 | c. 2: 15:7 | c. 3: 23:3 | c. 4: 12:23; 13:1 (bis); 13:2; 13:3; 13:4; 13:5; 13:6; 13:7; 13:9;

13:11; 13:12; 13:13; 15:33; 17:20; 17:27 | c. 6: 12:43; 18:6; 19:1 (bis) | c. 7: 17:5 (bis); 17:15; 17:35 (ter); 17:42; 19:1; 19:29 | c. 8: 9:11 | c. 10: 1:4 | c. 12: 1:4

De caelo et mundo (ed. Iuntina V 1550) I c. 11: 15:33

De generatione et corruptione (AL IX¹) I c. 2: 3:9 (bis) || II c.1: 1:13 | c. 2: 1:5 (bis) | c. 4: 1:13 | c. 9: 15:31

De hist. animal. (ed. Iuntina VI¹) I c. 4: 2:7

De interpr. I c. 1 (AL II¹ 5): 22:24

De iuventute et senectute III c.2: 10:9; 10:13

De part. animal. (ed. Iuntina VI¹) I c. 5: 16:20 || II c. 1: 2:7 | c. 8 : 1:2; 1:4; 2:1; 2:4; 2:7 | c. 10: 2:7; 10:13

De sensu et sensato (ed. Iuntina VI 1550) c. 2: 10:9 | c. 4: 2:6; 4:4 | c. 6: 21:11 | c. 7: 8:10 | c. 8: 8:1 (bis); 8:2; 8:3

De somno et vig. (ed. Iuntina VI 1550) c.3: 10:11

Aristot., *Eth. Nich.* (AL XXVI³) I c. 3: 12:29 || II c. 1: 12:11 || III c. 5: 11:8 || VI c. 2: 13:13; 14:20| c. 3: 14:1 || VII c. 3: 11:4 || X c. 6: 4:11 | c. 7: 16:22; 19:4

Metaph. (AL XXV²⁻³) I c. 1: 22:30 | c. 2: 16:7 | c. 8:15:30 || II c.1: 1:18; 19:2; 21:3; 21:21 (bis); 21:37 || III c. 3: 21:29; 21:33 || IV c. 1: 21:15; 21:18 | c. 2: 21:14; 21:32 | c. 3: 21:27; 21:28 | c. 7: 1:13 || V c. 15: 7:11 (bis); 12:3; 12:26 | c. 28: 1:13 || VII c. 3: 21:30 | c. 6: 22:43 | c. 7: 15:31 | c. 8: 22:43 | c. 11: 11:13; 22:43 | c. 22: 22:17 || VIII c. 1: 21:31 | c. 6: 11:13; 15:20 || IX c. 2: 12:26 | c. 8 7:4; 15:36; 16:8 || X c. 4: 1:13 (bis); 13:8 | c.7: 1:13 | c.10: 15:20 || XII c. 6: 19:2 | c. 7: 17:15 | c. 7-8: 19:4 | c. 8: 15:10

Meteor. (ed. Iuntina V 1550) IV c. 4: 3:15

Physic. (AL VII¹) I c. 1: 16:1 (bis); 16:4; 16:6; 16:17 | c. 2: 16:17; 21:26 | c. 4: 16:5 | c. 6: 1:13 (bis)|| II. c. 22: 22:4; 22:37 || III c. 3: 7:1; 7:2; 7:8 | c. 5: 8:11 || IV c. 6: 8:11 | c. 8: 8:11 || V c. 1: 15:4 | c. 2: 7:3; 7:25 | c. 3: 20:8 | c. 5: 3:3 (bis) || VII c. 1: 15:4 | c. 3: 6:12 | c. 4: 1:13 (bis) || VIII c. 4: 15:4; 17:6 | c. 9: 11:3

Politica (AL XXIX¹) I c. 2: 9:11

Praedic. (AL I²) c. 5: 22:17 | c.7: 7:12 | c. 8 1:8; 6:12; 14:1 | c. 12: 16:6

AUCTORITATES ARISTOTELIS

Les Auctoritates Aristotelis (ed. J. Hamesse, Philosophes Médiévaux XVII, Lovaniensis-Parisiis 1974) p. 115: 22:30 | p. 117: 15:29 | p. 118: 1:18; 21:21 (bis); 21:37| p. 121: 15:20 |p. 122: 21:14 | p. 129: 15:31 | p. 133: 12:26 | p. 134: 7:4 | p. 136: 13: 8 | p. 140: 16:1; 16:4 | p. 145: 22:37 | p. 152: 7:13 | p. 153: 3:3 | p. 155: 1:13; 6:12 | p. 162: 12:21; 15:33 | p. 165: 16:20| p. 174: 17:15; 17:39 | p. 176: 17: 39 | p. 178: 1:4; 2:2 | p. 179: 1:1; 6:1; 10:17; 20:6; 20:21; 22:2| p. 180: 4:5; 8:11 | p. 182: 1:2; 5:4; 12:27 | p. 185: 3:5; 9:1; 12:1; 19:29 | p. 186: 23:3; 17:5 | p. 187: 12:23; 13:4; 17:20; 17:27

| p. 188: 9:11; 17:5 (bis): 17:35; 17:42; 1929 | p. 189: 1:4 | p. 190: 12:30; 13:8; 14:6; 17:31 | p. 196: 4:4 | p. 198: 4:4; 8:2 | p. 202: 10:11 | p. 218: 1:2; 2:1 | p. 231: 11:14 | p. 232: 4:2 | p. 233: 12:29 | p. 234: 12:11 | p. 240: 12:30 | p. 247: 16:22; 19:4 | p. 252: 9:11 | p. 299: 21:29 | p. 300: 22:26 | p. 303: 7:12 | p. 307: 8:11 | p. 319: 22:2; 22:30 | p. 321: 22:20

AUGUSTINUS

Confess. (CCL 27; PL 32) XII c. 7: 15:26

De civ. Dei (CCL 48, PL 41) XI c. 2. 18:9

De Genesi ad litteram (CSEL 28^1, PL 34) XII c. 16 [n. 32]: 17:35 | c. 18 [n. 40]: 17:35

De libero arbitrio (CCL 29, PL 32) III c. 25: 11:9

De Trinitate (CCL 50; PL 42) III c. 4. 11:3 || IX c. 3: 14:21 | c. 12: 23:1 || X c.2: 20:15 | c. 3: 22:21 || XI c. 2: 12:15 || XII c. 4: 13:13 || XV c. 27: 18:9

De vera relig. (CCL 32; PL 34) c. 3 n. 3. 15:38 | c. 24-25 n. 45-46: 15:39

AVERROËS

(*Aristotelis opera cum Averrois commentariis*, latine, ed. Iuntina, Venetiis 1550-1552, 11 vol.)

De anima (ed. F. S. Crawford, AverL IV^1, Cantabrigiae [Cambridge, Massachussets] 1956; ed. Iuntina VI 1550) I com. 8: 17:39 | com. 53: 15:12 || II com. 9: 5:7 | com. 36: 15:12 | com. 60: 17:7; 22:2 | com. 107: 1:2; 1:5; 10:1 | com. 108: 1:2; 1:8; 2:7; 2:11; 6:14 | com. 109: 1:8; 2:1; 2:5 | com. 109: 1:8; 2:1; 2:5 | com. 111: 2:8; 4:9 | com. 113: 3:1; 3:13 | com. 115: 3:4; 3:5; 3:6; 3:18 | com. 116: 2:5 | com. 121-124: 5:1 | com. 133: 5:4 | com. 136: 9:3 | com. 139: 7:2 | com. 144-147: 9:1 | com. 146: 9:18; 10:1; 10:16 | com. 148: 10:1; 10:19 | com. 149: 9:10; 10:8 || III com. 4: 11:2; 12:5; 12:21; 12:22; 15:1 | com. 5: 23:12 | com. 6: 9:5; 10:9 | com. 18: 12:30; 13:8; 14:6; 17:7; 17:31 | com. 36: 23:11 | com. 66: 3:1 | com. 128: 1:1

De caelo et mundo (ed. Iuntina V 37vb) I com. 117: 15:33

De part. animal. (ed. Iuntina VI^1 ff. 129D) II c. 1: 1:2; 1:4

De sensu (ed. Shields 8) 1:2

Liber sex principiorum (AL I^7 39) c. 2 n. 20: 7:13

Metaph. (ed. Iuntina VIII) I com. 17: 15:29 || III com. 3: 21:33 || IV com.2 : 21:21 | com. 3: 21:20 || VI com. 3: 16:12 || VIII com. 4: 15:22 | com.7: 12:9 || IX com. 2: 12:1 || XII com. 51: 23:11

Physica (ed. Iuntina IV) I com. 3: 16:5 | com. 50: 1:13 || III com. 3: 7:13 | com. 4: 7:17 | com. 18: 7:20 | com 19: 7:2; 7:13 | com. 76: 8:11

AVICENNA

(*Avicenna latinus*. Lovaniensis–Leidae 1968-; *Opera*, latine, Venetiis 1508, 2 vol.)

De an. (AviL) I c. 5: 1:1; 2:7 (bis); 9:12; 10:9; 10:10 || II c. 2: 5:1 | c. 3: 1:4; 2:1; 2:5; 2:9 | c. 4: 4:4|| III c. 7: 9:12; 10:10 || IV c. 1: 2:2; 9:9; 9:11 (bis); 9:12; 10:7 (bis); 10:8; 10:10; 10:16; 10:27 | V c. 2: 9:10; 9:16 | c. 3: 18:5 | c. 6: 14:4; 14:11; 14:13 (bis) | c. 8: 2:13; 10:15

Liber primus naturalium (AviL) I tr. 1 c. 1: 16:4; 22:34 (bis) | c. 3: 15:30; 15:35

Metaphysica (*Liber de philosophia prima sive scientia divina*, ed. S. Van Riet et G. Verbeke, *AviL*, Lovaniensis–Leidae 1977-1983, 3 vol.) I c. 2: 21:21 | c. 3: 16:12; 16:19 (bis) | c. 5: 16:2; 21:4 || V c. 1: 21:20 || VII c. 1: 21:14 || VIII c. 7: 9:10

Sufficientia (ed. Venetiis I 1508) II c. 1: 7:16

BERNARDUS DE TRILIA

Quaest. de cognitione animae coniunctae corpori q. 1 (cod. Bibl. Vatic. Apost. 2188, f. 5rb: 17:25

BIBLIA SACRA

Esth. 5, 1: 10:8
Ioh. 1:9: 13:12; 14:14 || 4:20. 22:21
Gen. 2, 7: IX,12:3
Luc. 16: 19-31. 17:15
Matt. 19, 12: 17:46
Ps. 4:6. 13:12 || 11, 8: 11:9
Prov. 20, 8: 10:8
3 Reg. 22, 10: 10:8
Sap. 11, 21: VIII,2-3:195

BOETHIUS

Commentarium in Categorias Aristotelis (PL 64) c. 1: 15:23
De Trinitate (ed. R. Peiper in Bibliotheca Teubneriana, Lipsiae 1871; *PL* 64): c. 2: 15:8 | c. 4: 7:12

CALCIDIUS

Commentarius in Platonis Timaeum (*Timaeus a Calcidio translatus commentario- que instructus*, ed. J. H. Waszink in *Plato latinus* IV, Corpus Platoni- cum medii aevi, Auspiciis Academiae Britannicae adiuvantibus, Instituto Warburgiano Londinensi unitisque academiis, Londinii-Leidae 1975): 10:9

CONDEMNATIONES PARISIENSES: (ed. D. Piché, *La condamnation parisienne de 1277*): 4:12 | 22:12

CONSTANTINUS AFRICANUS, *De nervis* 34-35: 2:7

COSTA BEN LUCA, *De differentia animae et spiritus* c. 3 (ed. Barach et Wrobel 126): 2:7 | 10:9

DOMINICUS GUNDISSALINUS

De immortalitate animae (BGPTH 2^3 20-1): 2:7
De unitate et uno (ed. P. Correns in BGPTM I^1): 15:24

DUNS SCOTUS *vide* IOANNES DUNS SCOTUS

EUCLIDES

Elementa I def. 14 (ed. H. Busard 31): 5:4

EUSTRATIUS

In libros Ethicorum Aristotlelis VI c. 3: 18:9 | c. 6: 18:9

GALIENUS

Opera I (ed. Lyon 1528, 224): 10:9

GODEFRIDUS DE FONTIBUS

Quodlibeta (PhB II-V, XIV, Lovaniensis 1904-1937) V q. 8: 17:23 | V q. 10: 17:21; 17: 24 (bis) | VI q. 7: 17:21; 17:23; 17;24 | VII q. 5: 15:10 | VIII q. 2: 17:23; 17:24 | VIII q. 1: 12:29 | IX q. 19: 12:29

GONSALVUS HISPANUS

(*Quaestiones disputatae et de Quodlibet*, ed. L. Amorós in *BFS* IX, ad Claras Aquas 1935)
Quaestiones disputatae: q. 10: 5:10 | q. 11: 15:25
Quodlibet q. 10: 22:18 | q. 11: 15:25

GUILELMUS DE ALVERNIA PARISIENSIS

De immortalitate animae, (BGPTH 2^3 57): 2:7

GUILLELMUS DE LA MARE

Correctorium, in primam partem *Summae theologiae fratris Thomae*, art. 10: 15:24; 15:25
Correctorium, in *Qq. de anima fratris Thomae*, art. 6: 15:21 | art. 7: 15:25
Scriptum in secundum librum Sententiarum (ed. H. Kraml, Veröffentlichungen der Kommission für die Herausgabe unde-

gedruckter Texte aus der mittelalterlichen Geisteswelt XVIII, Monachii 1995) I d. 7 p.1 q. 3: 15:25 || II d. 12 q. 2: 15:37

GUILLELMUS DE WARE

Commentarium in Sententias I (cod. Vindebon. nat. 1424) d. 3 q. 127 [secundum numerationem Daniels]: 17:16

HALI IBN ABBAS, *Liber regalis disp. (=Pantegni)*: 10:9

HENRICUS GANDAVENSIS

(*Opera omnia*, editio Lovaniensis, AMPh s.2, Lovaniensis-Leidae 1979-)
Quodlibeta (AMPh s. 2, V-XIV) X q. 9: 9:10 | q. 9: IX,14:51. 76. 88 || XII q. 9: 4:11 || XIII q. 8: 17:23
Quodlibeta (ed. Parisiis 1518, reimpr. Lovaniensis 1961) III q. 14: 20: 5 || V q. 6: 7:18 | q. 14: 17:1; 17:11; 17:12; 18:6 || XI q. 5: 12:21; 12:27 | XI q. 8: 4:12 (bis)
Summa quaestionum ordinarium art. XXXI-XXXIV (AMPh s. 2, XXVII 1991) a. 32 q. 5: 7: 18|| a. 34 q. 3: 20:2; 20:10
Summa quaestionum ordinarium (ed. Parisiis 1520, 2 voll.) a. 53 q. 5: 17:39|| a. 58 q. 2: 17:9

HISSETTE, ROLAND

Enquête sur le 219 articles condamnés à Paris le 7 mars 1277 n. 43, 82. 22:12

HUGO DE S. VICTORE

De sacramentis christ. fidei I pars 10 c. 2 (PL 176 329C—330A). 18:9
Super de cael. hier. VI (PL 175 975D—976A): 18:9

IACOBUS DE VITERBIO

Quodl. I q. 12 (ed. Ypma 177): 17:45

IOANNES BLUND

Tractatus de anima c. 16. 2:1; 2:5; 2:9; 2:10 | c. 17: 1:14; 2:7; 9:12; 10:10 (bis)

IOANNES DUNS SCOTUS

(*Opera omnia*, ed. L. Vivès, Parisiis 1891-1895, 26 voll.; *Opera omnia*, editio Vaticana 1950-; *Opera philosophica*, editio Instituti Franciscani Universitatis S. Bonaventurae atque Universitatis Catholicae Washingtoniensis, 1997-2006)
Lectura I d. 3 p. 1 q. 1 n. 1-2: 19:2 | I d. 7 q. un. n. 54-56: 22:35; 22:37 || II d. 3 pars 2 q. 1: 22: 35: 14:21; 23:1

Ordinatio (ed. Vaticana I-, 1950-; ed. Vivès VIII-XXI, 1893-1894) I d. 3 p. 1 q. 1-2: 19:2 || II d. 3 pars 2 q. 1: 6:9 || III d. 1 q. 1 a. 1: 7:18 (bis) | III d. 15 q. un: 4:12 || *Ordinatio* IV d. 12 q. 3: 5:6

Quaestiones super libros Metaphysicorum Aristotelis (ed. R. Andrews, G. Etzkorn, G. Gál, R. Green, F. Kelley, T. Noone, R. Wood, *Opera philosophica* III-IV, S. Bonaventurae 1997-1998) *Metaph.* I q. 6: 20:6 || II q. 2-3: 19:2 || V q. 11: 7:11: 7:18 || VII q. 14: 12:38 | q. 19: 17:46

Quaestiones super Praedicamenta Aristotelis q. 30-36: 6:12; 6:13

Reportatio (ed. Vivès XXII-XXIV, 1894) prol. q. 2 (ed. in praep.): 16:19

IOANNES DE RUPELLA

Summa de anima q. 94 (ed. Bougerol 238) 2:10 | c. 97: 9:1; 9:12; 10:10

Tractatus II c. 3-4 1:1 | II c. 6: 9:1 | II c. 21

IOANNES PARISIENSIS

In I Sent. d. 3 q. 11 [q. 23] :18:7

IOANNES PECKHAM

Quaestiones de anima. q. 6 n. 52-53 (ed. Etzkorn, BFS XXVIII 402): 13:4 | q. 7: 13:4

Quodl. I q. 3: 12:27 | III q. 9: 12:27 | IV q. 4: 13:2

Tractatus de anima c. 3-4: 12:27 | c. 4: 17:20 c. 10: 1:3; 10:5; 10:10

Liber sex principiorum (Gilberto Porretae ascriptus) c. 1 n. 13 (AL I^7 38): 7:18

MATTHAEUS DE AQUASPARTA

(*Quaestiones disputatae de fide et de cognitione*, ed. PP. Collegii S. Bonaventurae in *BFS* I, ed. 2, ad Claras Aquas 1957)

Quaestiones disputatae de cognitione q. 1: 18:4 | q. 3: 17:20 | q. 6: 18:4 | q. 7: 18:9 | q. 10: 18:9

Quaestiones disputatae de fide q. 7: 18:9

(*Quaestiones disputatae de productione rerum et de providentia*, ed. G. Gál in BFS XVII, ad Claras Aquas 1956)

Quaestiones de providentia q. 5: 11:1

NEMESIUS, *De natura hominis* c. V, XI-XII: 10:9

PETRUS DE TRABIBUS, *Quodl.* I q. 14: 11:1

PETRUS HISPANUS

Scientia libri De anima tr. 7 c. 1: 9:1; 9:10; 10:1; 10:8: 10:10 | c. 2: 10:5 | c. 10: 1:2; 2:10

PETRUS IOANNIS OLIVI

Summa quaestionum in libros Sententiarum (II: ed. B. Jansen in *BFS* IV-VI, ad Claras Aquas 1922-1926, 3 voll.) q. 58: 12:23; 12:24; 12:28; 13:4; 17:20 | q. 60: 6:11 | q. 61: 3:13; 4:11; 4:12

PETRUS LOMBARDUS

Sent. IV, d. 44 c. 7 (SB V.2 520-521): 4:12

PHILIPPUS CANCELLARIUS

Quaestiones de anima q. 29 (ed. Keeler 91): 2:7

PSEUDO-ARISTOTELES

Liber de causis prop. 1: 11:14 | prop. 23: 4:2

PSEUDO-PETRUS HISPANUS

Expositio libri De anima c. 6 (ed. Alonso 173): 10:5 | c. 11: 1:5; 3:11; 5:3

PTOLEMAEUS

Almagestum dictio 5; 11:12

PORPHYRIUS

Liber praedicabilium cap. 'De specie' 21:29; 22:26

PROCLUS

Elementatio theologica prop. 15: 9:10

RADULPHUS BRITO

In Aristot. librum III De an. q. 2: 12:29

RICHARD KNAPWELL

Le Correctorium Corruptorii "Quare" I a. 2: 22:1.

RICHARDUS DE MEDIAVILLA

Quaestiones disputatae q. 5 (Vat. Lat. 868, f. 13v): 15:2 5 | q. 9: 5:10
Super quattuor libros Sententiarum Petri Lombardi quaestiones subtilissimae (Brixiae 1591, 4 voll.) II d. 24 p. 1 q. 5: 20:14 | d. 24 p. 3 q. 3: 21:12

RICHARDUS RUFUS DE CORNUBIA

Abbreviatio, II, d. 24, q. 6 (Civitas Vaticana, Bibliotheca Apostolica Vaticana cod. 12993, f. 237ra): 13:13

ROBERTUS GROSSATESTA

Comm. in Post. An. I c. 14 (ed. P. Rossi 213-214): 18:9

Rogerus Marston
: *Quaest. disp. de anima* q. 2: 19:5 | q. 3: 13:2; 13:6; 13:12 | q. 8: 17:20

Simon de Faversham
: *Sophisma: Universale est intentio* (ed. Yokoyama 7-11). 17:39

Simplicius
: *In Praedicamenta*, praed. 'De facere et pati': 7:20

Themistius
: *De an.* I: 2:1: 3:18 | III: 9:1 | IV: 1:6; 2:5; 5:8; 6:3 | V: 9:1; 9:10; 10:5; 10:8

Thomas Aquinas
: (*Opera*, ed. Parmae 1852-1869, 24 vol.; *Opera*, ed. Leonina, Romae 1882-)
Commentum in quattuor libros Sententiarum (ed. Parmen. VI-VII 1856-1858): I d. 3 q. 5: 12:6 | d. 14 q. 1 a. 4: 3:7 | d. 17 q. 1 a. 5: 9:10 || II d. 13 q. 1 a. 3: 4:7 | d. 15 q. 1 a. 3: 11:1; 11:3; 11:10 | d. 19 q. 1 a. 1: 9:10 | d. 19 q. 1 a. 2: 1:13 || III d. 15 qc. 3: 11:16 | d. 22 q. 1 a. 2: 9:9 || IV d. 12 q. 1 a. 1 q.3 : 15:10 | d. 44 q. 1 a. 3: 4:12 | d. 48 q. 2 a. 4: 4:11
In Metaphysicam Aristotelis Commentaria (ed. Marietti; Cathala 1935): I lect. 1: 4:11 || II lect. 2: 21:21 || IV lect. 16: 1:13 || X lect. 5: 1:13 (bis) | lect. 9: 1:13
In Octo Libros Physicorum Aristotelis Expositio (ed. Marietti 1965): I lect. 11: 1:13 || II
lect. 11: 1:13 || VII lect. 4: 1:13 || VIII lect. 4: 3:12 | lect. 19: 11:3
Quaestiones disputatae De anima (XXIII 1982) q. 3: 15:11 || q. 6: 15:11 || q. 13: 1:13
Sentencia libri De anima (XLV^1 1984): I c. 10: 4:11 || II c. 2: 5:7 | c. 5: 1:16 | c. 11: 12:27 | c. 14: 4:11 (bis); 6:11 | c. 15: 21:12 | c. 17: 4:7 | c. 19: 1:19 | c. 21: 1:13; 1:17 | c. 22: 1:7; 1:9; 1:13; 1:17; 1:18 | c. 23: 2:6; 3:1 (bis); 3:5; 3:6; 3:7; 3:8; 3:9; 3:14; 3:15 | c. 24: 5:1 (bis); 5:2; 5:6 (bis); 5:7; 5:8; 5:13; 5:14; 5:16 | c. 25: 5:4; 6:1 | c. 26: 9:1; 9:3 | c. 27: 8:3; 9:9; 9:10; 9:18; 10:1; 10:5 (bis); 10:6 (ter); 8:1; 10:8 | c. 28: 11:1 (bis); 11:7; 11:10 || III c. 1: 6:7; 12:1; 12:2 | c. 2: 7:1; 11:13 | c. 4: 13:8; 13:8; 13:12 | c. 6: 17:11; 18:6
Sentencia libri De sensu et sensato (XLV^2 1985): tr. I c. 4: 10:9 | c. 18: 8:1; 8:10
Sententia libri Ethicorum (XLVII^2 1969): IV lect. 17: 10:9, 10:12 || VI lect. 6: 10:9
Summa theologiae (IV-XII 1888-1906): I q. 2 a. 3 in corp.; 21:37 | q. 7 a. 3:

15:10 | q. 12 a. 5: 19:7 | q. 14 a. 2: 12:10 | q. 14 a. 11: 22:1| q. 56 a. 1: 12:6; 12:7 | q. 58 a. 2: 8:11; 8:15 | q. 75 a. 5: 15:3 | q. 76 a. 2: 15:10 | q. 77 a. 1: 5:7 | q. 78 a. 1: 1:16 | q. 78 a. 3: 1:15; 1:18; 6:1 (bis); 6:2; 6:3; 6:4; 6:9 (quatter) 6:11 (ter); 6:12; 6:13; 6:14 (bis); 10:3 | q. 78 a. 4: 2:7 (bis); 9:1; 9:11 (bis); 9:17; 10:5; 10:6; 10:9; 10:14 | q. 79 a. 2: 12:6; 12:26; 12:27 | q. 79 a. 3: 13:1 | q. 79 a. 6: 14:1; 14:4; 14:9; 14:10 | q. 83 a. 3: 4:11 | q. 84 a. 6: 13:4 | q. 84 a. 7: 18:1; 18:2; 18:3; 19:14 | q. 84 a. 8: 18:1 | q. 85 a. 1: 19:5; 19:14 | q. 85 a. 3: 16:3 | q. 85 a. 4: 8:12; 22:4 | q. 86 a. 1: 22:10; 22:11; 22:13 | q. 86 a. 2: 8:11 | q. 89 a. 1-2: 17:40; 19:11 | q. 89 a. 3: 17:40 | q. 115 a. 4: 11:1; 11:10; 11:12 | I-II q. 9 a. 5: 11:1; 11:3 (bis); 11:10; 11:12 | I-II q. 83 a. 4: 4:11

THOMAS SUTTON

Quaest. ordinariae (ed. Schneider BAW III 39) q. 2: 9:10 | q. 15: 4:10; 12:13; 12:15

VITAL DU FOUR (IOANNES VITALIS A FURNO)

Quaest. disput. de cognitione (ed. Delorme) q. 2: 4:8

IV: Index Doctrinalis

Accidens: Modo ita est quod accidens absolutum potest per miraculum a subiecto absolvi quantum ad inesse actu, et ideo, si potentia sit absoluta qualitas, potest agere sine eius subiecto, quod est anima: q. 5 n. 10

Accidens: v. Miraculum

Actio: Dico ... actio, secundum quod est praedicamentum, est in agente; secundo, quod aliquo modo actio et passio sunt in patiente: q. 7 n. 10; omnis respectus realis est in eo quod realiter refertur ad aliud per illum, licet hoc non oportet de respectu rationis, sicut patet de scibili quod non refertur ad scientiam, sed scientia ad scibile; actio autem est quidam respectus realis agentis ad patiens; igitur est in agente sicut relatio: q. 7 n. 12; impossibile est aliquod creatum fieri de non-agente agens nisi mutetur ad aliquam formam in eo exsistentem — forma enim secundum quam est mutatio est in eo quod mutatur; sed illa mutatio non est ad formam absolutam, quia de non-agente non fit aliquid agens per aliquid exsistens in eo absolutum; sed certum est quod non fit agens formaliter nisi per actionem; igitur actio est forma respectiva exsistens in agente: q.7 n. 13; Dicendum igitur est secundum praedicta quod actio est respectus agentis ad passum in agente exsistens, et passio respectus patientis ad agens in patiente exsistens; motus autem est forma fluens media inter utrumque vel est fluxus formae secundum quod ponit istos duos modos intelligendi motum Commentator III Physicorum; dicit quod 'iste secundus modus est famosior, sed primus est verior.' Secundum primum modum, motus est in genere sui termini vel formae secundum quam est motus; secundum autem alium modum est in genere 'ad aliquid', in primo modo relationis, quae sumitur secundum quod fundatur super multitudinem vel unum, quia respectu termini 'a quo' importat talis fluxus multitudinem, respectu termini 'ad quem' unitatem: q. 7 n. 17; est sciendum quod est actio quaedam de genere actionis et illa est proprie dicta actio, de qua dictum est immediate, et est quaedam actio acta seu producta, quae non est de genere actionis, sicut intelligere et velle sunt quaedam formae absolutae non de genere actionis; sed sunt actiones actae vel productae per actiones intellectus et voluntatis, quae sunt de genere actionis: q. 7 n. 20; Certum est enim quod effectus actionis est actio, non quae est praedicamentum, sed factio facta: q. 7 n. 20; Est igitur duplex actio secundum iam dicta; sed actio acta est illa quae est in patiente, quae est effectus actionis proprie dictae, et ideo non est actio praedicamentum nisi quae est in agente; nihil enim est causa sui ipsius. Et differunt in hoc quod actio, quae est praedicamentum, est secundum quam vel per quam ab aliquo est aliud; actio autem acta est secundum quam aliquid est ab alio; esse enim a quo est aliud et quod est ab alio sunt rationes oppositae, nec eidem possunt convenire, sicut idem per se non potest esse producens et productum: pater et filius respectu eiusdem — pater enim est a quo est filius, et filius qui est a patre: q. 7 n. 22; dicendum quod actio illa quae est in agente non est motus, et ideo non sequitur quod omne agens in quantum huiusmodi moveatur, sed potius quod sit motivum: q. 7 n. 24; utraque enim actio tam manens in agente, sicut intelligere et velle, quam transiens est actio producta. Sed differentia est quantum ad hoc: quod talium actionum quaedam est perfectio agentis — licet non secundum quod agens est sed secundum quod perfectibile est — ita quod idem secundum diversas rationes sit agens et recipiens; quaedam est perfectio extrinseci operati, sicut transiens: q. 7 n. 27; dicendum quod actio quae est praedicamentum, quae est respectus adveniens extrinsecus manens in agente, non est successiva quia mensuratur tempore vel quia sit tempus, sed tantum quia coexsistit tempori: q. 7 n. 28; actio debet magis attribui formali principio agendi quam materiali: q. 12 n. 9

Actio: v. Passio, Relatio, Respectus

Actus: sunt igitur duo actus perfectissimi [sensus], quorum unus ab alio non dependet: q. 1 n. 10; respectu obiectorum formaliter diversorum non est idem actus: q. 1 n. 11; dicendum quod verum est quod idem est actus motivi effective, qui actus est passivi vel mobilis formaliter; sed ille actus non est actio quae est praedicamentum quae est in agente formaliter, sed est actio producta effective ab agente: q. 7 n. 23; Dicendum ergo quod quando unus actus est ita intensus, indivisus quod adaequat sibi potentiam, tunc evacuat totaliter alium actum eiusdem potentiae; si autem sit minus intensus et citra terminum potentiae, licet aliqualiter impediat alium et e converso, tamen non totaliter depellit, sed secum compatitur. Unus actus sentiendi unum obiectum obtenebrat alium, non tamen semper obfuscat; ideo possunt simul esse etc.: q. 8 n. 21; Modo ita est quod actus a voluntate elicitus non est liber per essentiam sed tantum potentia volitiva, et ideo non oportet quod si sit liber participatione quod actus volendi vel causatus a corpore caelesti sit liber, dato quod sit eiusdem rationis — immo esset non-liber quia haberet causam necessariam: q. 11 n. 14; sed per solam potentiam intenditur actus cognoscendi, quia, organo, specie, medio, et obiecto stantibus in eadem dispositione in uno actu cognoscendi sicut in alio, sola potentia intensius se ferente ad cognitionem obiecti, et ab aliis attentionibus se retrahente, sequitur intensior actus cognoscendi; igitur, etc.: q. 12 n. 11; Sic est in proposito de actu intelligendi, qui prius ordine generationis requirit phantasma et cognitionem sensitivam, a qua originatur, et speciem intelligibilem, secundum quam intellectus formaliter intelligit: q. 17 n. 19; Utrum in elicitione actus intelligendi intellectus sit movens motum ab obiecto, vel quod intellectus et obiectum relucens in specie concurrant ad actum intelligendi ut duo agentia partialia perfecte in suo ordine et sua causalitate, quorum causalitas unius non dependet a causalitate alterius, licet unum sit principalius movens alio: q. 23 n. 1

Actus: v. Species, Voluntas

Adaequatio: sciendum quod duplex est adaequatio obiecti: una secundum virtutem, alia secundum praedicationem. Illud autem dicitur obiectum adaequatum potentiae adaequatione secundum virtutem, quod per se ipsum solum potest movere intellectum ad notitiam sui et aliorum; sicut essentia divina est primum obiectum adaequatum intellectus divini, quia est sufficienter movens intellectum divinum ad notitiam sui primo et aliorum ex consequenti, et substantia movet intellectum nostrum ad notitiam sui primo et propriae passionis vel accidentis ex consequenti. Obiectum autem adaequatum secundum praedicationem est quod per se et essentialiter praedicatur de omnibus quae possunt a potentia cognosci, sicut lux vel color vel aliquid commune utrique praedicatur essentialiter de omnibus visibilibus: q. 21 n. 6

Agens: Si autem intelligatur sic quod agens non agit nisi secundum quod est in actu, non secundum quod est in potentia, et per consequens patiens non recipit aliquid ab agente nisi secundum quod est in actu, ita quod receptum est procedens ab actualitate agentis, non potentialitate, verum est, sed non concludit propositum sub illo intellectu: q. 5 n. 13; sicut se habet agens increatum ad actionem suam, ita agens creatum ad actionem suam: q. 7 n. 15; sciendum est quod agens potest comparari vel ad terminum productum vel ad passum. Si comparetur ad terminum productum — sive sit in fieri sive in facto esse — ut calefaciens ad calefactionem sive ad calorem (quod est idem quantum ad hoc), tunc sic includit relationem vel refertur ad ipsum productum relatione, quae est de genere 'ad aliquid', quae advenit, positis extremis, de necessitate; positis enim agente et patiente et producto, necessario est relatio agentis ad effectum. Si comparetur ad patiens, ille respectus quem includit non est de genere 'ad aliquid'; non enim, posito igne agente absolute et lignis, de necessitate sequitur calefactio vel talis relatio, sed requiritur appropinquatio extremorum; non est igitur de genere 'ad aliquid,' sed de genere actionis; talis ergo respectus extrinsecus adveniens, qui est agentis ad patiens, in agente exsistens est actio quae est praedicamentum, et simile est de passione: q. 7 n. 19

Album: Exemplum: si ponantur visui duo alba vel intellectui duo singularia quaecumque quae in rei veritate essent distincta essentialiter, si tamen haberent omnino consimilia accidentia ut locum — utpote duo corpora in eodem loco vel duo radii in medio illorum — et haberent figuram omnino consimilem et magnitudinem et colorem et sic de aliis, nec intellectus nec sensus inter illa distingueret, sed iudicaret esse unum; igitur neutrum eorum cognoscit quodlibet illorum singularium secundum propriam rationem singularitatis: q. 22 n. 27

Album: v. Ens, Visus

Index Doctrinalis

Analogia entis: non dices ens aequivoce vel analogice praedicari de aliis nisi quia conceptus entis convenit Deo per essentiam, aliis autem per participationem. Sed quod non convenit Deo per essentiam, probo: q. 21 n. 22

Anima: anima potest mediante corporeo organo aliquid recipere ab obiecto corporeo, licet anima non posset immediate: q. 5 n. 8

Animal: Si igitur in animali sunt plures sensus tactus, animal erit plura animalia, quod est falsum: q. 1 n. 4

Aqua: aqua pura potest calefieri cuius contrarium dicit [Averroes], licet ignis non possit infrigidari, quia ignis inter elementa est maxime activus: q. 3 n. 15

Aristoteles (Philosophus): tamen potest curalius dici, excusando Philosophum, quod non contradixit sibi, quia statim post in De animalibus subdit quod caro non est primum organum tactus sicut nec pupilla est primum organum visus — immo est intus; est tamen aliqualiter instrumentum; ita etiam caro est instrumentum, scilicet sicut medium: q. 2 n. 11; Et ideo secundum hoc, est propositio Philosophi vera quod sensibilia tangentia sensum non faciunt sensum: quia ratione immutationis naturalis, secundum quam tangunt organum, non faciunt sensum: q. 4 n. 14; dicendum quod probatio Philosophi non est a priori, quia probat propositum ex numero organorum; organa autem sunt propter sensum, non e converso: q. 6 n. 6; Secundum Philosophi habentur duae viae ad investigandum necessitatem sensus communis per duas operationes praedictas: q. 9 n. 8; Oppositum huius vult Philosophus in De somno et vigilia, dicens quod primum sensitivum in corde est: q. 10 n. 11

Articuli Parisius condemnati: contra hoc procedendum est primo destruendo suum principium, quod materia non est principium individuationis — immo excommunicatus est Parisius articulus: quod non possunt esse plura individua eiusdem speciei propter defectum materiae: q. 22 n. 12

Articuli Parisius condemnati: v. Individuatio, Parisius

Astrologi: Astrologi praedicunt multa vera de agibilibus ab homine quae dependent a voluntate et intellectu (opinio Thomae) q. 11 n. 1. si astrologi, ut in pluribus, verum dicunt, hoc ideo accidit quia homines, ut in pluribus, sequuntur suas phantasias et passiones in quae possunt directe agere corpora caelestia; tamen hoc non est necessarium — immo homines virtuosi sequentes iudicium rationis reprimunt huiusmodi passiones.: q. 11 n. 13

Averroes (Commentator): Potest tamen sua [sc. Averrois] ratio sic colorari: quia praeter utramque univocationem est una metaphysicalis, secundum quam aliqua uniuntur in genere propinquo, et est media inter utramque praedictam — est enim maior primā et minor secundā. Et de ista univocatione habet maior sua veritatem, ut patet ratione superius posita pro ista parte ante responsionem: q. 1 n. 13; ut Commentator dicit, Aristoteles tunc nescivit naturam nervorum, postea autem inquisivit per rationem et investigavit naturam et probat, II De anima, carnem non esse organum: q. 2 n. 11; Responsio Commentatoris est quod animal vivens in aere non patitur ab aere, nec animal vivens in aqua patitur ab aqua. Cuius ratio est: quia passio naturalis est a contrario; locus autem non est contrarius, sed conformis locato: q. 3 n. 5; [secundum Averroem] si esset vacuum, ibi posset esse motus animalis progressivus ubi pes tangeret terram et eius frigiditatem, non autem aerem vel aquam; ideo potest elementum simplex immutare sensum tactus: q. 3 n. 12

Averroes (Commentator): v. Colorari

Avicenna: Praedictae viae sumuntur a Philosopho, sed consequenter ab Avicenna. Prima sic: 'natura non deficit in necessariis';[1] sed ad vitam animalis perfectam necessario requiritur conservatio specierum sensibilium, etiam in eorum absentia, quia aliter non possent moveri progressive ad sensibile distans et absens. Et mediantibus speciebus sic reservatis, fit apprehensio sensibilis absentis per aliquam potentiam sensitivam; non autem est particularis, quia talis sentit praesente sensibili tantum; igitur vel illa est communis sensus, vel saltem praesupponit ipsum, sicut imaginativa, rememorativa : q. 9 n. 11; Alia autem via Avicennae accipitur ex eo quod ad sensum videmus, scilicet quod si attendamus ad guttas pluviae sibi mutuo succedentes, apparebit nobis una linea de omnibus illis guttis quasi continua. Similiter, si moveatur circulariter aliqua virga in cuius summitate est aliquis color, apparebit nobis circulus quidam in summitate eius propter motum circularem summitatis vel coni illius virgae. Ex hoc potest sic argui: impossibile est sensum particularem percipere suum sensibile ubi non est; sed summitas virgae motae non est semper in eodem loco in quo apparet circulus, quia circulus apparet quasi immobilis, illa autem semper movetur. Simile est de guttis. Igitur ille circuls vel illa linea non percipitur a sensu particulari: igitur a communi. Simile est de homine exsistente in navi mota, qui iudicat ad sensum ripam moveri: q. 9 n. 12

Avicenna: v. Sensus communis

Caelestia: corpora caelestia non possunt movere intellectum nostrum nec voluntatem directe: q. 11 n. 10

Caro: quaecumque pars c. sentit unam contrietatem, sentit et aliam: q. 1 n. 2; caro est instrumentum tactus, sicut pupilla visus: q. 2 n. 1 (dictum Aristotelis); caro non est organum sensus tactus, sed aliquid infra carnem, scilicet nervus, vel aliquid loco nervi coextensum corpori: q. 2 n. 6 (doctrina Scoti);; caro non continuatur organo sensus communis, quod est in cerebro vel in corde — immo nervi vel venae, derivatae a corde secundum Philosophum vel a cerebro secundum medicos, continuant organa sensuum particularium organo sensus communis, et ipsi nervi vel venae eius continuantur.: q. 2 n. 7; quaedam est caro nervosa, quaedam pura; nervosa autem non tantum est medium, sed etiam organum: q. 2 n. 9; Caro autem pura est tantum medium in tangendo: q. 2 n. 9

Caro: v. Instrumentum

Cartilagines: in cerebro sunt cartilagines loco nervorum: q. 2 n. 13

Cartilagines: v. Cerebrum

Cerebrum: in cerebro sunt cartilagines loco nervorum: q. 2 n.13

Cerebrum: v. Cartilagines

Certus: omnis intellectus certus de uno et dubius de duobus, oportet quod habeat alium conceptum de certo et alium de duobus, quia aliter per eundem conceptum idem intellectus esset dubius et certus; sed aliquis potest esse certus de aliquo, quod sit ens, dubius autem utrum sit substantia vel accidens — sicut de potentiis animae patet, et de primo principio, ut dubitaverunt antiqui philosophi, ut patet I Physicorum, et de luce; igitur alius est conceptus entis, alius substantiae et accidentis; sed ille est communis utrique et non importat illos conceptus plures; igitur est communis univoce: q. 21 n. 26

Cognitio: Quod autem tali ordine fiat cognitio intellectus patet per praedicta, quia scilicet ars et cognitio intellectualis imitatur naturam.[34] Dictum autem est quod natura primo intendit individuum vagum; secundo, naturam in ipso; tertio, individuum signatum, quod est terminus generationis; igitur talis erit modus intelligendi, sive species ponatur in intellectu sive non: q. 22 n. 37

Cognitum: v. Primum cognitum, Obiectum adaequatum

Cognoscere: Ulterius sciendum quod non est idem cognoscere confusum et confuse, nec distinctum et distincte. Nam confusum potest distincte cognosci, sicut 'animal' quod est confusum respectu hominis. Similiter distinctum potest confuse cognosci, sicut 'homo', cognoscendo animal vel quod sit animal. Illud autem est confusum quod est indistinctum, distinguibile tamen sicut genus. Cognoscere autem confuse est cognoscere quid est quod dicitur per nomen, vel cognoscere in suo universali tantum; sed cognoscere quid distincte est cognoscere illud per principia propria posita in sua definitione: q. 16 n. 9

Cognoscere: v. Confusum, Distinctum

Color: Dicendum quod sicut appropinquans agens ad patiens dicitur agere vel disponens materiam ultimate dicitur informare, quia statim sequitur actio vel informatio, sic lumen dicitur facere colores actu, id est actu visibiles, in quantum disponit medium, quo facto, statim color potest movere visum; sic movens visum est actu color, non quidem actu primo tantum sed etiam actu secundo: q. 13 n. 10

Colorari: Potest tamen sua [Averrois] ratio sic colorari: quia praeter utramque univocationem est una metaphysicalis, secundum quam aliqua uniuntur in genere propinquo, et est media inter utramque praedictam — est enim maior primā et minor secundā. Et de ista univocatione habet maior sua veritatem, ut patet ratione superius posita pro ista parte ante responsionem: q. 1 n. 13

Colarari: v. Averroes

Commentator: v. Averroes

Commune: possibile est intelligere minus commune, ignorando magis commune; igitur non oportet semper universalius prius cognosci ab intellectu. Probatio antecedentis: quia geometer cognoscit lineam et multa de linea probat, et tamen nescit utrum sit substantia vel accidens; igitur, etc.: q. 16 n. 16; commune indeterminatum: omne commune indeterminatum descendit in inferiora per aliquid additum sibi contrahens ipsum, sicut genus per differentias, species per principia individuantia; sed enti non potest fieri talis additio contrahens. Probatio: quia illud additum esset ens vel non ens. Si sic, igitur substantia, quae includit illud additum, esset ens bis, et sic esset nugatio dicere 'substantiam tantum'. Si vero non sit ens, tunc non descendit ens in substantiam per aliquid sed per non-ens, et etiam illud non-ens esset de ratione substantiae per quod descenderet in eam, et sic quaererem sicut prius et esset processus in infinitum: q. 21 n. 30

Conceptus: conceptus communis: Tertio modo potest aliquid cognosci per conceptum communem sibi et aliis, ut cognosco hominem per animal: q. 19 n. 22; conceptus quiditativus duplex: Quarto modo cognoscitur aliquid conceptu quiditativo, sed ille est duplex: unus est primo primus, qui scilicet non est in alios conceptus resolubilis, quo scilicet res cognoscitur intuitive in se ut est talis natura, et talem conceptum non possumus habere de Deo in via, immo nec de anima nostra nec de aliqua spirituali substantia. Cuius ratio est, quia de Deo nullam habemus cognitionem naturaliter nisi per creaturas; nulla autem creatura, nec etiam omnes simul, possunt sufficenter divinam essentiam repraesentare quiditative, id est, ut natura haec vel essentia est: q. 19 n. 23; Alius autem conceptus quiditativus rei nec est omnino simplex nec primus, sed resolubilis in alios, ut est definitio rei composita ex diversis conceptibus: q. 19 n. 24; conceptus univocus: omnis ille conceptus qui sufficit ad contradictionem est univocus, quia contradictio est affirmatio et negatio circa idem univocum — hic enim non est contradictio: canis currit, canis non currit; sed conceptus entis sufficit ad contradictionem secundum Philosophum VIII Metaphysicae — immo prima contradictio est formata de ente, sicut de quolibet esse vel non esse; igitur, etc.: q. 21 n. 27; Sic in proposito: omnia entia habent attributionem ad ens primum, quod est Deus, vel entia creata ad substantiam; tamen, hoc non obstante, potest ab omnibus istis entibus abstrahi unus communis conceptus significatus nomine entis, qui est univocus logice loquendo, licet non naturaliter vel metaphysice loquendo: q. 21 n. 3

Confusum: Ulterius sciendum quod non est idem cognoscere confusum et confuse, nec distinctum et distincte. Nam confusum potest distincte cognosci, sicut 'animal' quod est confusum respectu hominis. Similiter distinctum potest confuse cognosci, sicut 'homo', cognoscendo animal vel quod sit animal. Illud autem est confusum quod est indistinctum, distinguibile tamen sicut genus. Cognoscere autem confuse est cognoscere quid est quod dicitur per nomen, vel cognoscere in suo universali tantum; sed cognoscere quid distincte est cognoscere illud per principia propria posita in sua definitione: q. 16 n. 9

Confusum: v. Cognoscere, Distinctum

Conservatio: Ad consequendum igitur convenientia ad conservationem animalis, et fugiendum nociva, est organum tactus ita extensum, et etiam est intrinsecum propter eandem causam, ne de facili corrumpatur ab excellenti tangibili: q. 2 n. 10

Conservatio: v. Tactus

Contraria: Dicendum quod aliquando una sensatione sentitur utrumque [scilicet, contrariorum], sicut quando cognoscit unum in aliqua habitudine ad alterum, scilicet ut differentia vel contraria vel similia, si sint similia; aliquando autem pluribus, scilicet quando sentit utrumque absolute et secundum se: q. 8 n. 13

Contrareitas: dicendum quod non sufficit contrarietas qualitatis activae et passivae, quae non communicant in uno genere naturali, sed tantum logico. Secundum autem genus naturale differunt, ut contrarietas tangibilium qualitatum: q. 1 n. 20

Conversio intellectus: Sed ad modum positionis suae (sc. Avicennae) sciendum quod ponit duplicem conversionem intellectus: unam ad sensibilia, a quibus recipit species intelligibiles, quae sunt singulares respectu intellectus quem informant, universales respectu singularium quae universaliter repraesentant; aliam conversionem ponit respectu intelligentiae separatae, a qua etiam recipit species. Sed illae non manent nisi ad praesentiam influentiae illius intelligentiae vel intellectus agentis, quod idem est secundum ipsum 'quia ipse Deus est lux illa quae illuminat omnem hominem' etc. Sicut igitur lux aerem illuminat, et ad eius praesentiam tantum manet lumen in aere, sic, secundum ipsum, ipsa lux quae est Deus vel intelligentia separata illuminat de necessitate naturae animas nostras se ad eam convertentes, suae lucis speciem imprimendo, praesente actu animae et obiecto: q. 14 n. 14

Corporale: pure corporale non potest agere directe in pure spirituale, eo quod agens est nobilius patiente: q. 11 n. 10

Corporale: v. Spirituale

Corpus: corpora nostra non habent locum naturalem nisi ratione elementi dominantis in eis: q. 3 n. 7; quod est in potentia tale, patitur ab eo quod est in actu tale; corpora nostra sunt in potentia ad excellentias qualitatum tangibilium, cum sint ad medium reducta et comparata: q. 3 n. 8; si duo corpora se tangentia sint sicca in ultimis, tangunt se sine medio et sunt contigua et eorum ultima sunt simul; si autem humida sunt, eorum ultima non tangunt se immediate, sed mediante corpore humido: q. 3 n. 17; omne corpus corruptibile movet de necessitate in virtute corporis incorruptibilis: q. 11 n. 7

Cultellus: cultellus scindens nervum causat maximum dolorem, maiorem quam si scinderet carnem: q. 4 n. 1; ALIQUI dicunt quod si cultellus scinderet immediate nervum, in quo est sensus tactus, homo non sentiret: q. 4 n. 5 (Opinio Aegidii); Quod probant dicentes oportere sensum habere proportionem non tantum ad obiectum sed ad medium: q. 4 n.6 (Opinio Aegidii)

Delectatio: Probo: quia eorum contraria, scilicet odium et tristitia, non sunt idem, nec sunt ambo a voluntate causata, sed alterum tantum, scilicet odium. Quod patet per hoc quod voluntas complacet sibi in actu proprio ab ipsa causato — voluntas enim non complacet sibi in tristitia, immo est voluntati contraria, et quilibet invite tristatur; sed bene complacet sibi odium; igitur tristitia causatur tantum ab obiecto et non a voluntate, et per consequens nec delectatio. Sed obiectum conveniens cum perceptione, dum tamen sit praesens, causat delectationem, et obiectum contrario modo tristitiam: q. 11 n. 16; delectatio non immediate causatur ab apprehensione convenientis, sed mediante actu dilectionis coniungente potentiam volitivam obiecto sibi convenienti. Quae quidem coniunctio est prior origine naturae ipsa delectatione, licet simul sint tempore; eodem enim instanti quo voluntas coniungitur obiecto suo praesenti per actum dilectionis vel fruitionis, stillat quaedam dulcedo ab obiecto in potentia volitiva, et haec est delectatio: q. 11 n. 17

Delectatio: v. Odium, Tristitia

Desiderium: Item, anima naturaliter desiderat, cognito effectu, cognoscere causam; sed omnia alia ab ipso sunt effectus Dei; igitur ad ipsum cognoscendum habemus naturale desiderium; sed naturale desiderium non est ad impossibile; igitur Deus etiam naturaliter potest aliqualiter a nobis cognosci: q. 19 n. 10

Deus: Quod non Deus [sit obiectum primum intellectus nostri], probatio: non enim potest esse primum obiectum adaequatione secundum praedicationem, quia non praedicatur essentialiter de omnibus intelligibilibus. Nec secundum virtutem, quia non movet intellectum primo ad sui notitiam et aliorum ex consequenti. Probatio: quia aut hoc esset secundum suum conceptum simplicem et quidditativum, aut secundum conceptum abstractum a creaturis. Non primo modo, quia ille conceptus est essentiae divinae ut intuitivus est, et talis conceptus beatificat — quod non convenit viatoribus. Nec secundo modo, quia includit oppositum in adiecto; prius enim occurrit intellectui conceptus eorum a quibus fit abstractio quam eius quod abstrahitur: q. 21 n. 10; obiectum naturale habet habitudinem et proportionem ad potentiam; Deus autem nullam habet habitudinem nec proportionem ad intellectum nostrum, saltem pro statu viae, quia omnis nostra cognitio naturalis intellectiva oritur a cognitione sensitiva; igitur, etc.: q. 21 n. 11

Dilectio: …dilectio et delectatio sunt actus diversi: q. 11 n. 15; dilectio est in voluntate et a voluntate; delectatio est in voluntate, et non a voluntate, sed potius ab obiecto: q. 11 n. 16

Distinctum: Ulterius sciendum quod non est idem cognoscere confusum et confuse, nec distinctum et distincte. Nam confusum potest distincte cognosci, sicut 'animal' quod est confusum respectu hominis. Similiter distinctum potest confuse cognosci, sicut 'homo', cognoscendo animal vel quod sit animal. Illud autem est confusum quod est indistinctum, distinguibile tamen sicut genus. Cognoscere autem confuse est cognoscere quid est quod dicitur per nomen, vel cognoscere in suo universali tantum; sed cognoscere quid distincte est cognoscere illud per principia propria posita in sua definitione: q. 16 n. 9

Distinctum: v. Confusum

Diversitas: aliquid potest diversificare potentiam inferiorem, quod non potest superiorem diversificare. Diversitas igitur generis propinqui sensibilium diversificat potentias sensitivas proprias, vel saltem ostendit earum diversitatem non esse diversitatem sensus communis: q. 1 n. 14

Divina potentia: remota frigiditate ab aqua (per impossibile vel potentiam divinam) adhuc tactus sentit humiditatem: q. 1 n. 10

Elementum: quando unum elementum locatur in altero, alteratur ab eo. elementa enim alterant se secundum extremitates, secundum quas se invicem locant: q. 3 n. 7; elementa possunt considerari secundum suas qualitates activas et passivas, et sic non sunt similia sed contraria se invicem alterantia; vel secundum quod unum continet et locat aliud, et sic sunt partes universi: q. 3 n. 14

Ens: utrum ens sit obiectum primum intellectus nostri: q. 21 n. 1; Utraque autem primitate [scilicet, secundum virtutem et secundum praedicatioem] adaequationis ens est primum obiectum intellectus nostri, ut declarabo primo indirecte, removendo alia ab illa prioritate, de quibus magis posset videri; secundo directe probando propositum: q. 21 n. 7; ens sufficienter dividitur in ens creatum et ens increatum, quod ens creatum iterum subdividitur in decem praedicamenta, ita quod quidquid est ens per se et essentialiter, oportet quod sit ens creatum vel ens increatum; sed unum non potest esse ens creatum tantum, cum dicatur de ente increato; igitur de ipso non praedicatur ens per se primo modo, id est essentialiter et in quid: q. 21 n. 17; si ens praedicatur essentialiter de uno, tunc aut unum dicit praecise ipsum ens aut cum hoc aliquid additum. Non praecise, quia tunc unum non esset magis passio entis quam e converso, et essent aliter nomina synonyma, quod negat Philosophus in IV Metaphysicae, et esset nugatio dicendo ens unum, et e converso. Si aliquid addit supra ens, tunc quaero utrum illud additum sit essentialiter ens vel non; si sic, tunc unum dicit ens bis, semel ratione entis inclusi in uno, alias ratione additi, si sit additio; si autem illud additum non includat essentialiter ens, sequitur propositum, scilicet quod unum, in quantum unum, id est ut differt ab ente, non includit ens essentialiter: q. 21 n. 18; Sed quod sit etiam obiectum respectu suorum inferiorum scilicet Dei et creaturae, primitate praedicationis, ostendo: quia ad hoc requiritur, ut dictum est,[15] quod tale obiectum praedicetur essentialiter et per se de omnibus intelligibilibus, et per consequens univoce aliqua univocatione; sed ens est huiusmodi; igitur, etc: q. 21 n. 21; ens enim, prout praedicatur de decem praedicamentis, metaphysice vel naturaliter non dicit unum conceptum — nec genus est naturale eorum nec metaphysicum; est tamen univocum, logice loquendo: q. 21 n. 33; Vel potest dici, sustinendo, quod sit genus, vel quasi genus secundum Avicennam et Averroëm, quod descendit in inferiora per addita, quae sunt entia identice vel realiter, non tamen formaliter. Nec sequitur sic quod secundum se sint non-entia, sicut non sequitur 'homo non secundum se est albus, igitur secundum se est non-albus', quia nec ex ratione humanitatis habet quod sit albus, nec non-albus. Istae igitur differentiae non per rationem differentiae sunt entia, nec tamen sequitur quod secundum rationem differentiae sint non-entia: q. 21 n. 36; Sic in proposito: omnia entia habent attributionem ad ens primum, quod est Deus, vel entia creata ad substantiam; tamen, hoc non obstante, potest ab omnibus istis entibus abstrahi unus communis conceptus significatus nomine entis, qui est univocus logice loquendo, licet non naturaliter vel metaphysice loquendo: q. 21 n. 37

Ens: v. Album, Obiectum, Univocatio, Unum

Exemplum: Et hoc videtur ad sensum ex hoc quod homo exsistens in navi mota iudicat res exteriores moveri, quae tamen sunt immobiles; hoc autem non est per sensus exteriores, ut probatum est supra, nec per motum cordis, sed per motum capitis; igitur sensus communis, qui hoc iudicat, est in capite. Hoc etiam patet ex hoc quod homines dolent caput ex studio vehementi in quo vires sensitivae inferiores multum laborant, non autem ita sentiunt dolorem cordis: q. 10 n. 15; Exemplum: si ponantur visui duo alba vel intellectui duo singularia quaecumque quae in rei veritate essent distincta essentialiter, si tamen haberent omnino consimilia accidentia ut locum — utpote duo corpora in eodem loco vel duo radii in medio illorum — et haberent figuram omnino consimilem et magnitudinem et colorem et sic de aliis, nec intellectus nec sensus inter illa distingueret, sed iudicaret esse unum; igitur neutrum eorum cognoscit quodlibet illorum singularium secundum propriam rationem singularitatis: q. 22 n. 27

Experientia: experimur nos cognoscere singularia vel cognoscimus; hoc autem non est per potentiam sensitivam, quia non est reflexiva super suum actum; igitur per intellectum cognoscimus nos cognoscere singulare; sed intellectus non potest cognoscere se cognoscere singulare nisi ipsum singulare cognoscat, quia actus quo cognoscitur singulare est repraesentativum singularitatis tamquam eius similitudo vera magis quam species singularis; igitur, etc.: q. 22 n. 25

Figura: Quia figura cerae non est forma absoluta sicut species, ut bene probatum est, sed est similitudo ita quod sicut, mediante figura, cera assimilatur anulo et cera figurata est similitudo formae anuli non materiae (quia recipit tantum formam, non materiam), ita, mediante specie, sensus assimilatur obiecto et species tantum repraesentat formam obiectivam, sicut species coloris tantum colorem, non parietem vel superficiem, quia per se non faciunt ad substantiam immutationis, licet magnitudo et figura faciant ad differentiam eius; aliter enim immutat magna quantitas quam parva, quia fortius, et plura alba vel colorata quam unum; ideo, etc: q. 5 n. 16

Generatio: generatio potest fieri sine mixtione in simplicibus; sed generatio requirit alterationem; igitur potest fieri alteratio in aqua et ab aqua sine admixtione alterius corporis: q. 3 n. 9

Gradus: dicendum quod sicut sunt quattuor gradus viventium,[41] tamen sunt quinque genera potentiarum — quia appetitivum non constituit distinctum gradum a sensitivo, quia ubi est appetitivum, et sensitivum: q. 1 n. 16

Gustus: Exemplum de sapore, qui fundatur in tangibilibus qualitatibus ex quibus causatur tanquam qualitas secunda. Ideo gustus, cuius obiectum est sapor, fundatur in tactu — immo est quidam tactus causaliter loquendo, sicut 'gustabile est quoddam tangibile'.: q. 1 n. 15; dicendum quod quantum ad modum immutandi, qui est realis in utroque, gustus est tactus, quia gustabile tangit realiter, vel medium gustus gustatur tangendo; tamen, quantum ad obiecta formalia, sunt diversi sensus; sapor enim est obiectum gustus, qui sapor est qualitas secunda causata a primis, sed obiecta tactus sunt qualitates primae: q. 6 n. 15

Gustus: v. Tactus

Guttae: Alia autem via Avicennae accipitur ex eo quod ad sensum videmus, scilicet quod si attendamus ad guttas pluviae sibi mutuo succedentes, apparebit nobis una linea de omnibus illis guttis quasi continua: q. 9 n. 12

Hiems: in hieme sentimus frigiditatem aeris immediate sine corpore alio ab aere quod sit medium vel obiectum: q. 3 n. 2

Humor: In lingua autem secundum aliam et aliam qualitatem est organum gustus et tactus, et sic humor et potus per aliam qualitatem et aliam est gustabilis et tangibilis: q. 1 n. 17; aliquis humor potabilis positus supra medium gustus, scilicet super carnem linguae, sentitur; igitur multo magis positus super organum: q. 4 n. 2; species potabilis recepta in medio causat gustum, multo fortius potabile immediate positum super organum causat gustum; q. 4 n. 2.

Humor: v. Lingua

Idem: Quandocumque enim aliqua sunt idem formaliter, si iungantur sine medio, est ibi nugatio, ut 'color albedo'; non tamen si sint idem identice solum et non formaliter, ut 'color albus' — licet album sit idem in re quod albedo, quia tamen album significat suam rem denominative vel in concreto — non est nugatio. Sic autem iungitur differentia generi in definitione quod differentia denominative sive in concreto significatur, ut 'animal rationale', et sic est idem generi identice tantum et non formaliter. Sic in proposito est de ente respectu unius, quia dicendo 'ens unitas' est nugatio. Sic ergo illud additum enti effugit rationem entis, quod significatur modo differentiae quae est idem generi, identice tantum et non formaliter: q. 21 n. 34

Identitas: identitas obiecti non sufficit ad identitatem actus, quia intelligere et velle sunt respectu unius obiecti formalis, scilicet entis in actu in quantum huiusmodi; sed diversitas obiecti bene sufficit ad diversitatem actus: q. 11 n. 15

Imaginatio: dicendum quod imaginatio sentit actum proprium; imaginamur enim nos imaginari vel imaginatum fuisse, et memoramur nos memoratum fuisse, et somniamus nos somniare, sicut experimur manifeste: q. 9 n. 16

Immutatio: duplex est immutatio ipsius sensibilis. Una est naturalis, quando scilicet immutatur sensus a sensibili secundum idem vel tale esse, vel secundum eundem modum essendi quo est in re extra ut cum sensus tactus calefit vel alius sensus aliqualiter alteretur vel movetur secundum locum. Alia est immutatio animalis secundum quam immutatur intentionaliter vel spiritualiter a sensibili, licet habeat modum essendi extra realem sive materialem: q. 4 n. 11; in damnatis post resurrectionem generalem erit sensus tactus et omnes sensus in actu suo, et tunc tactus non immutabitur naturaliter (quia illa immutatio est corruptiva); igitur tantum intentionaliter. Tamen illa erit maxime afflictiva: igitur verissime ibi poterit esse una sine alia. Tamen in statu isto non est intentionalis immutatio sine reali et naturali immutatione, quia causatur ab ea: q. 4 n. 13; Si autem sit immutatio animalis in organo tactus vel aliorum, bene facit sensum, non autem naturalis; quia immutatio naturalis in organo non facit sensum — immo magis impedit —, quia si sine naturali posset esse intentionalis, magis sentiretur sensibile, sicut patet in damnatis. Tamen immutatio naturalis in carne, quae est medium, bene facit sensum, causando immutationem similem in organo, non de se tantum: q. 4 n. 13; Est autem duplex immutatio in genere: quaedam naturalis, quaedam animalis. Naturalis est secundum quam vel per quam forma recipitur in patiente secundum esse reale, et secundum dispositionem materiae, consimilem illi quae est in agente. Animalis autem secundum quam recipitur secundum esse intentionale species obiecti agentis in potentiam animalem.: q. 6 n. 7; Si autem immutentur aliqui sensus naturaliter, cum hoc tamen immutantur intentionaliter — immo magis intentionaliter quam naturaliter; immutatio enim naturalis impedit animalem sensationem, ut visum est. Si enim esset immutatio intentionalis sine naturali, sicut est in visu, magis sentiretur et verius quam cum ea: q. 6 n. 8; Ex diversitate ergo immutationis organi ab obiecto et conformationis sumitur sic sufficientia sensuum: q. 6 n. 9

Immutatio: v. Sensus, Tactus

Indeterminatum: de descensu indeterminati in inferiora, dicendum quod duplex est indeterminatum. Unum quod descendit in inferiora per aliquid additum, et tale dicit totum quod inferius, tamen per modum partis determinabilis ut genus, vel per modum partis determinantis ut differentia — et tale non est ipsum ens. Aliud est commune indeterminatum, quod dicit totum illud quod inferiora per modum totius nec expectat terminari per aliud — ut species respectu individuorum, duo enim individua se totis in specie conveniunt et numero differunt —, et tale commune non descendit in inferiora per aliquid additum. Sic autem ens est commune ad Deum et decem praedicamenta, ad substantiam et accidens; nihil enim est in substantia et accidente quod non sit ens, et ideo statim seipso sine addito est substantia vel accidens; non igitur reducitur ad praedicabile generis vel differentiae, sed speciei specialissimae: q. 21 n. 35

Individuatio: contra hoc procedendum est primo destruendo suum principium, quod materia non est principium individuationis — immo excommunicatus est Parisius articulus: quod non possunt esse plura individua eiusdem speciei propter defectum materiae: q. 22 n. 12

Individuatio: v. Articuli Parisius

Instrumentum: caro est instrumentum tactus, sicut pupilla visus: q. 2 n. 1 (dictum Aristotelis)

Instrumentum: v. Caro

Intellectus: intellectus noster unica intellectione non potest plura obiecta intelligere si sint disparata, sed hoc tamen potest sub una ratione obiectiva; sicut etiam visus potest album et nigrum cognoscere simul secundum quod conveniunt in quadam differentia vel contrarietate, quae est una ratio obiectiva cognoscendi simul utrumque: q. 8 n. 14; intellectus est summe dispositus ad recipiendum intellectum, quia non habet contrarium: q. 12 n. 31; videtur aliquibus secundum Philosophum [intellectum agentem] esse aliquid animae nostrae (opinio Thomae): q. 13 n. 1; Sed contrarium videtur aliis esse de intentione Philosophi (opinio Ioannis Peckham discipulique sui Rogeri Marston de intellectu agente): q. 13 n. 2-7; alii dicunt quod [intellectus agens] est habitus principiorum. Quod sic potest intelligi quod sit 'habitus': 'habitus est quo quis utitur cum voluerit'; ita intellectus agens est quo homo utitur respectu possibilis cum voluerit se et intellectum possibilem ad illum convertere (opinio Themistii quae apud opera Aegidii Romani recitabatur): q. 13 n. 8; Modo ita est secundum PHILOSOPHUM, quod intellectus agens movet intellectum possibilem ad actum primum, non tamen ad actum secundum, ideo realiter differunt secundum eum, et ideo si intellectus possibilis est aliquid animae nostrae, oportet ponere intellectum agentem esse quandam substantiam separatam secundum ipsum.: q. 13 n. 12; alii tamen dicunt, et probabiliter, quod intellectus agens et possibilis idem sunt in re, differunt tamen ratione vel officiis, quia intellectus, ut eliciens actum intelligendi, dicitur agens, ut recipiens autem intellectionem, dicitur possibilis (opinio Ioannis de Rupella et Richardi Rufi de Cornubia): q. 13 n. 13; Ad aliud dicendum quod intellectus noster est in potentia naturali, et desiderium naturale habet ad omnia intelligibilia intelligenda et ad beatitudinem consequendam; secundum Augustinum tamen ex natura propria nec potentia cuiuscumque creaturae potest ad hoc attingere: q. 15 n. 38; omne agens secundum ultimum suae potentiae producit perfectissimum effectum quem potest producere, quia da oppositum, quod non producat effectum perfectissimum quem potest, sequitur quod agit citra ultimum potentiae suae; sed omne agens naturale est agens secundum ultimum potentiae suae, quia non agit deliberative, determinando sibi quantitatem effectus, sed determinatur ab alio; igitur agit perfectissimum effectum quem potest. Intellectus autem quantum ad primum actum intelligendi et etiam omnia quae concurrunt ad causandum intellectionem effective — sive phantasia sive species intelligibilis — sunt agentia naturalia; igitur intellectus in primo actu intelligendi praecedente omnem actum volendi intelligit perfectissimum intelligibile in quod potest, quia terminat actionem perfectissimam quam habere potest; tale autem intelligibile est species specialissima; igitur, etc.: q. 16 n. 11; sed potest quaeri per quem modum patitur intellectus ab intelligibili, ex quo nihil ab illo sibi imprimitur: q. 17 n. 44; intellectus noster non potest sine phantasmate intelligere (opinio Thomae): q. 18 n. 1-3; quamvis intellectus phantasmate in prima intellectione rei indigeat, tamen homo postea sine phantasmate intelligere potest (opinio Avicennae): q. 18 n. 5; Ideo, omissis aliis necessitatibus, dicunt alii quod non est contra rationem actus intelligendi intellectus nostri absolute intelligere sine phantasmate (opinio Augustino atque aliis auctoritatibus gravioribus attributa): q. 18 n. 9; Quia Aristoteles nihil de peccato originali scivit, ideo hoc posuit absolute, quia necesse est ad phantasmata recurrere volentem intelligere: q. 18 n. 10; quod intellectus non sit movens-motum videtur: q. 23 n. 1; Dicitur quod intellectus est movens motum ab obiecto ad hoc quod eliciat actum intelligendi, quia quando aliquid est in potentia essentiali ad aliquem actum, non reducitur de potentia ad actum nisi per aliquid sibi impressum; sed intellectus, antequam recipiat speciem, est in potentia essentiali ad actum intelligendi; igitur ad hoc quod concurrat ad actum intelligendi requiritur quod sit motus ab alio per aliquid sibi impressum: q. 23 n. 3

Intelligere: intelligere et sentire sunt actiones immanentes in agente. Certum est autem quod manent in sentiente et intelligente, non autem in obiecto extrinseco; igitur obiectum non est activum talium, sed potius homo sentiens et intelligens, mediantibus suis potentiis animae: q. 20 n. 21; si sentire sit pati, sentiri est agere; sed agere est nobilius quam pati; si obiectum igitur intelligi est nobilius quam intelligere, per illud inanimata, quae non intelligunt sed intelliguntur, sunt perfectiora quam homo qui intelligit: q. 12 n. 25

Lingua: In lingua autem secundum aliam et aliam qualitatem est organum gustus et tactus, et sic humor et potus per aliam qualitatem et aliam est gustabilis et tangibilis: q. 1 n. 17

Lingua: v. Humor

Materia: Ad aliud dicendum quod condiciones materiae possunt accipi prout opponuntur universalitati et sunt condiciones singularitatis: et sic verum est quod sensus recipit speciem cum condicionibus materiae. Alio modo pro dispositione reali qua materia recipit formam naturalem et realem, quae dispositiones sunt qualitates activae et passivae; illo modo non est verum quod sensus, in quantum huiusmodi et per se, recipiat speciem: q. 5 n. 14; Respondeo quod probabiliter potest dici quod in anima est materia, et secundum fundamenta Philosophi et eorum qui ponunt contrarium (opinio quae apud mentem Guillelmi de la Mare et aliorum recitatur): q. 15 n. 10; sicut operatio arguit formam, ita proprietas materiae materiam; sed proprietas materiae quantum ad suum esse et fieri suum reperiuntur verius in spiritualibus quam corporalibus Proprietas enim materiae, quantum ad esse, est quod est ingenerabilis et incorruptibilis; sed quantum ad fieri, quod tantum producitur per creationem. Haec autem maxime reperiuntur in spiritualibus. Similiter substare accidentibus; sicut enim corpus subest qualitatibus corporalibus, ita anima spiritualibus, sicut habitibus animae. (arg. pro op. recitata): q. 15 n. 19; Dicendum est ad quaestionem quod si in anima vel angelo est materia, quod est eiusdem rationis cum materia corporalium (opinio Duns Scoti): q. 15 n. 25

Medietas: dicendum quod non quaecumque medietas vel propinquitas facit ad hoc quod propinquum sentiatur, sed tantum proportionalis, quia nec nimis propinqua nec nimis remota.: q. 9 n. 13

Medium: Medium debet esse denudatum a sensibilibus illius sensus, cuius est medium: q. 3 n. 1; si sentirentur talia media, hoc non est ut pura sunt, sed propter admixtionem alicuius vaporis vel alterius corporis cum ipsis: q. 3 n. 6 (opinio Averrois)

Miraculum: Modo ita est quod accidens absolutum potest per miraculum a subiecto absolvi quantum ad inesse actu, et ideo, si potentia sit absoluta qualitas, potest agere sine eius subiecto, quod est anima: q. 5 n. 10

Miraculum: v. Accidens

Moderni: moderni dicunt quod differt ratio agendi et ratio agentis. Verum est autem quod species repraesentat obiectum in illa ratione agendi sub qua nata est imprimi; hoc autem est sub ratione naturae absolute consideratae, non autem sub ratione agentis, quod est particulare, et ideo species repraesentat universale. Vel aliter potest dici secundum ILLOS quod, licet phantasma a quo immediate imprimitur sit singulare, quod tamen non agit in possibilem virtute propria sed virtute intellectus agentis abstrahentis species universales a phantasmate; ideo potest illa species repraesentare universale: q. 17 n. 16

Motus: duo motus reales corporales se impediunt, non autem intentionales sicut in proposito: q. 8 n. 19

Movens: Dicendum igitur quod movens ad actum primum, quod est generans realiter differt a moto, quia nihil generat seipsum; sed ad actum secundum aliquid potest movere seipsum, sicut grave movet seipsum ad ubi, licet non ad formam substantialem gravis; sic etiam intellectus et voluntas movent se ad actus suos: q. 13 n. 12

Necessitas: illud quod movet, motum ab alio tantummodo, movet de necessitate, si moveatur de necessitate: q. 11 n. 9

Nervus: nervus est unum organum tactus: q. 1 n. 2; organum tactus est nervus extensus toti corpori, et non caro, sed est medium in tangendo: q. 2 n. 5 (dictum Averrois); caro non continuatur organo sensus communis, quod est in cerebro vel in corde — immo nervi vel venae, derivatae a corde secundum Philosophum vel a cerebro secundum medicos, continuant organa sensuum particularium organo sensus communis, et ipsi nervi vel venae eius continuantur; igitur, etc.: q. 2 n. 7; Per istos autem nervos vel ramusculos derivatur virtus tactiva a corde vel a cerebro per totum corpus: q. 2 n. 9; non autem requiritur quod ibi sit nervus formaliter in qualibet parte carnis, sed sufficit quod sit prope vel iuxta realiter vel formaliter, et sic in qualibet parte virtualiter, quia virtute nervi prope exsistentis quaelibet pars potest sentire tangibile: q. 2 n. 13; in cerebro sunt cartilagines loco nervorum: q. 2 n. 13

Nervus: v. Ramusculi nervorum

Obiectum: obiectum debet corresponder potentiae, vel esse determinativum potentiae, et est eiusdem generis determinati: q. 1 n. 13; Potentiae distinguuntur per actus, et actus per obiecta, ut videtur III De anima. Dicendum quod hoc non dicit Philosophus, sed quod prius oportet considerare actus quam potentias et obiecta quam actus, quia sunt priora quoad cognitionem nostram obiecta quam actus et actus quam potentias; tamen actus non est principium essendi potentiae vel prius perfectione, immo posterior, quia sunt effectus potentiarum. Bene igitur sequitur, si obiecta sint diversa, quod potentiae sint diversae, sed non e converso. Nec sequitur si obiecta sint idem et non differunt, quod potentiae non differunt. Sed est fallacia consequentis ad destructionem antecedentis; plura enim requiruntur ad identitatem aliquorum quam ad distinctionem eorum: q. 20 n. 21-22; Cum igitur nec Deus nec verum nec substantia sit primum obiectum intellectus, sequitur quod ens sit illud primum obiectum: q. 21 n. 13; illud quod est primum adaequatione secundum virtutem respectu potentiae est primum obiectum eius; sed ens in comparatione ad verum et bonum est primum adaequatione secundum virtutem respectu ntellectus nostri; igitur, etc.: q. 21 n. 14; Sed quod sit etiam obiectum respectu suorum inferiorum scilicet Dei et creaturae, primitate praedicationis, ostendo: quia ad hoc requiritur, ut dictum est, quod tale obiectum praedicetur essentialiter et per se de omnibus intelligibilibus, et per consequens univoce aliqua univocatione; sed ens est huiusmodi; igitur, etc: q. 21 n. 21

Obiectum: v. Ens

Odium: Probo: quia eorum contraria, scilicet odium et tristitia, non sunt idem, nec sunt ambo a voluntate causata, sed alterum tantum, scilicet odium. Quod patet per hoc quod voluntas complacet sibi in actu proprio ab ipsa causato — voluntas enim non complacet sibi in tristitia, immo est voluntati contraria, et quilibet invite tristatur; sed bene complacet sibi odium; igitur tristitia causatur tantum ab obiecto et non a voluntate, et per consequens nec delectatio. Sed obiectum conveniens cum perceptione, dum tamen sit praesens, causat delectationem, et obiectum contrario modo tristitiam: q. 11 n. 16

Odium: v. Delectatio, Tristitia

Operationes: operationes vitales sunt effectivae a principio vitali et intrinseco, si sint naturales; actus sentiendi et intelligendi sunt operationes vitales, et etiam substantiales sentienti et intelligenti; igitur a principio intrinseco effectivo: q. 12 n. 24

Opinio communis seu Commentatoris: Responsio: una opinio communis est quod intellectus habet speciem sibi impressam necessario requisitam ad actum intelligendi: q.17 n. 7

Ordo potentiarum sensitivarum: Ex praedictis patet ordo potentiarum, quia visus, cum immutetur tantum intentionaliter, est sensus nobilior et certior; post hunc autem auditus, qui minus materialiter immutatur, quia mediante motu locali tantum qui est primus motuum; post hunc olfactus, qui immutatur materialiter ex parte obiecti, quod est remotius a potentia quam organum; post hunc gustus, qui immutatur materialiter ex parte organi, sed non immediate cum suo obiecto, sed mediante humore intrinseco; ultimus autem quantum ad cognitionis nobilitatem est tactus, qui ab obiecto suo immediate immutatur; est tamen prius ordine generationis vel imperfectionis vel communitatis, qui est fundamentum aliorum[22] et communis omnibus habentibus sensum, etiam imperfectis: q. 6 n. 11

Organum: organum tactus est unum, quia est corpus mixtum quod habet unitatem ab una perfectione dominante in eo: q. 1 n. 2; dicendum quod organum non est unum formaliter sed tantum materialiter. Unde in eodem nervo est alia qualitas secundum quam est discretio humidi et sicci, et alia secundum quam est discretio frigidi et calidi; q. 1 n. 17; dicendum quod organum est aliqualiter coloratum per speciem et per visionem, quae multum assimilatur colorato a quo est primogenita, et per consequens potest dici sensibile; potest igitur dici quod non tantum est sensibile per se qualitas prima aut secunda, sed etiam aliquid causatum a qualitate prima vel secunda, ut sensatio vel visio.: q. 9 n. 14; Dicendum est igitur quod organum eius [scilicet sensus communis] est unum unitate naturae, non quidem simplicis, sed mixtae et quasi mediae inter naturas aliorum organorum. Sic enim se habet organum sensus communis ad alia ut centrum ad lineas procedentes ab eo ad circumferentiam, vel ad ipsum terminatas quasi sit radix communis organorum sensuum particularium, et potentia sensus communis in eo exsistens est sicut rex sedens in solio, iudicans de actibus particularium sensuum ad ipsum terminatorum repraesentantium sibi propria obiecta: q. 10 n. 8; Sed ubi est situatum illud organum? De hoc est controversia inter medicos et philosophos. Dicunt enim medici quod in capite, quorum ratio est quia sensus communis accipit suam immutationem ex sensibus particularibus, et ideo debet esse situatum eius organum prope organa sensuum particularium; sed organa omnium sensuum particularium sunt in capite: q. 10 n. 9; Imaginandum est igitur quod a corde ad cerebrum procedunt quaedam venae vel nervi, in quibus originaliter continentur organa omnium sensuum, sed in cerebro faciunt conum; a cerebro autem procedunt quinque nervi ad organa exteriora, facientes basim; et sic organum sensus communis habet ortum a corde, sed in cerebro habet suum complementum: q. 10 n. 15; Ita organum sensus communis, cum sit radix aliorum, est continens virtualiter omnia organa secundum suam complexionem; est tamen formaliter determinatae complexionis et distinctae a praedictis: q. 10 n. 19; organum phantasiae est corpus corruptibile et phantasia est potentia organica: q. 11 n. 7; phantasia proprie non movet intellectum, nec aliquid in ipso imprimit, sed tantum repraesentat sibi obiectum.: q. 11 n. 13

Organum: v. Sensus communis, Phantasia

Parisius: contra hoc procedendum est primo destruendo suum principium, quod materia non est principium individuationis — immo excommunicatus est Parisius articulus: quod non possunt esse plura individua eiusdem speciei propter defectum materiae: q. 22 n. 12

Parisius: v. Articuli Parisius

Passio: Dico ... actio, secundum quod est praedicamentum, est in agente; secundo, quod aliquo modo actio et passio sunt in patiente: q. 7 n. 10; dicendum quod est una passio realis, quae est abiectio formae a contrario, et a passione tali non patiuntur potentiae huiusmodi, ut patet II De anima alia est passio quae est perfectio patientis, ut patet ibidem. Et illa subdividitur, quia quaedam est perfectio prima, sicut actus primus habilitans et inclinans potentiam ad actum; alia est perfectio quae est operatio: q. 12 n. 27

Passio: v. Actio

Pati: quandocumque aliqua duo sunt eiusdem speciei, a quocumque potest pati unum, et aliud: q. 1 n. 3

Patiens: aliquando patiens recipit formam secundum eundem modum essendi quo est in agente, et hoc est quando est eodem modo dispositum ad formam quo est forma in agente, vel quo modo materia agentis est disposita ad eam; et illud accidit in actione naturali, in qua agens et patiens communicant in materia. Aliquando patiens non est eodem modo dispositum, et tunc recipit sine materia, non quia forma in ipso recepta sit sine materia, vel prius fuerit sine materia, sed quia recipit formam non cum materiali dispositione praecedente, vel non recipiendo dispositionem materiae praecedentis (per oppositum ad alium modum quo patiens recipit realem formam vel materialem, quia cum dispositione materiae praecedente): q. 5 n. 6; dicendum quod si intelligatur maior quod patiens formam recipiat secundum eandem dispositionem qua est in agente, non est verum, nisi de patiente passione naturali et univoca, non autem de intentionali, sicut est in proposito de sensu: q. 5 n. 13

Perfectio: quod est perfectionis in potentia inferiori, debet esse in potentia superiori; sed perfectionis est in imaginativa potentia habere obiectum praesens in sua specie, absente obiecto reali extrinseco — hoc patet quia in hoc excedit potentias sensitivas particulares et exteriores; igitur potentia intellectiva potest habere obiectum praesens in specie, remota eius actuali consideratione: q. 14 n. 18

Phantasia: organum phantasiae est corpus corruptibile et phantasia est potentia organica: q. 11 n. 7; si ipsa sola [sc. phantasia] movet intellectum et non intellectus seipsum et intellectus sic motus movet voluntatem, sequitur quod directe corpus caeleste, in cuius virtute movet, possit utrumque movere, licet mediante phantasmate — et tunc sequitur ulterius quod mala phantasia de necessitate causabit malam voluntatem: q. 11 n. 7; phantasia proprie non movet intellectum, nec aliquid in ipso imprimit, sed tantum repraesentat sibi obiectum.: q. 11 n. 13

Phantasia: v. Organum

Phantasma: Quo praesente, intellectus ex virtute sua activa elicit actum suum, sicut praesente sensibili sensus elicit actum sentiendi, et in hoc est convenientia, non quia phantasmata sunt obiectum intellectus, sicut sensibilia sensus... tamen requiritur phantasma ad intelligendum obiectum, quia sicut quidditas absoluta vel universale, quod est directum obiectum intellectus, non habet esse extra nisi in singulari, ut homo in Socrate, ita non potest repraesentari intellectui secundum speciem intelligibilem pro statu viae nisi in repraesentatione similitudinis ipsius singularis, quod fuit in phantasmate.: q. 11 n. 13

Phantasmata: ..si sola phantasmata moverent intellectum et voluntatem et per consequens, ita quod intellectus et voluntas essent potentiae pure passivae, nec moverent seipsas ad actus suos, sequeretur quod corpora caelestia possunt illas potentias directe movere: q. 11 n. 7

Philosophus: v. Aristoteles

Pisces: sunt aliqua animalia quae non habent nervos, ut pisces, tamen habent sensum tactus: q. 2 n. 4; in piscibus est aliquid proportionale nervis, et hoc sufficit: q. 2 n. 14

Potentia: omnis potentia una habet obiectum unum sibi adaequatum: q. 1 n. 7; omnis potentia una est respectu unius generis univoce praedicati de omnibus quae ab illa potentia cognoscuntur: q. 1 n. 8; una potentia particularis sensitiva est respectu unius generis determinati: q. 1 n. 13; si potentia immutatur a sensibili mediante alio, prius immutatur a medio quam a sensibili: q. 3 n. 4; Licet igitur non prius tempore et causalitate immutatur potentia tactiva a medio extrinseco quam obiecto, prius tamen secundum situm immutatur, et hoc sufficit ad tale medium: q. 3 n. 18; Quia igitur potentia sensitiva propinqua non est anima tantum, immo includit organum, ideo potest ab obiecto speciem recipere, stante identitate reali ipsius potentiae cum animae essentia. Immo, si esset diversa essentia ab anima, sicut qualitas quaedam absoluta, sequeretur quod ipsa cum organo, sine essentia animae, posset sentire, quia posita causa totali, ponitur et eius effectus: q. 5 n. 8; Sed forte tu dicis quod potentia sensitiva non possit exire in actum nisi virtute animae, quae est principalis, dato quod sit eius qualitas absoluta. Contra: quod per se potest habere esse qualitercumque, sive per naturam sive per miraculum, per se naturaliter -- sine alio -- potest agere sine alio, sicut patet de accidente in sacramento Altaris, quod non habet esse in subiecto, et tamen naturaliter agit: q. 5 n. 9-10; Sed contra: potentia sensitiva non est separabilis a corpore; anima secundum suam essentiam est separabilis a corpore. Dicendum quod potentia propinqua ad sentiendum quae est totalis causa eliciendi actum, supposito obiecto, non est separabilis, quia talis includit organum corporeum, quod est aliud ab essentia animae, et sic ipsa potentia differt ab anima. Sed potentia sensitiva, praecise quae est remota, talis est separabilis, sicut et essentia, quia idem sunt: q. 5 n. 11-12; Sed causa quare magis dicitur sensitiva inseparabilis, quam intellectiva, est quia sensitiva dicitur per respectum ad actum sentiendi, quia potentia sensitiva est qua homo potest sentire, et intellectiva per quam potest intelligere; modo ita est quod ad actum sentiendi concurrunt per se duae causae partiales ex parte hominis, scilicet potentia sensitiva et organum, et ideo utraque requiritur et neutra sufficit, et ideo sensitiva potentia ut sic est inseparabilis ab organo; sed potentia intellectiva est totalis causa intelligendi, nec requirit aliam causam per se ex parte hominis, ideo dicitur separabilis, non enim per se utitur organo tanquam instrumento: q. 5 n. 12; omnis potentia cognitiva elicit operationem suam per quamdam conformitatem ad obiectum. Quod non potest facere potentia organica nisi per receptionem speciei, in organo, sui obiecti. Quae species est conformis obiecto, et etiam determinativa potentiae ad cognoscendum hoc vel illud obiectum, secundum quod a diversis obiectis imprimitur diversa species in organo per diversas immutationes organi ab obiecto: q. 6 n. 7; Sed dices quod licet eiusdem potentiae sit discernere album a dulci, alterius est discernere album a sono. Contra: si alia potentia discerneret album a dulci quam illa quae discernit album a sono, tunc sequitur quod eadem ratione duae potentiae insubordinatae discernerent sive cognoscerent album, quia nulla potentia discernit aliqua, quae non cognoscit utrumque illorum: q. 10 n. 6; ... sed per solam potentiam intenditur actus cognoscendi, quia, organo, specie, medio, et obiecto stantibus in eadem dispositione in uno actu cognoscendi sicut in alio, sola potentia intensius se ferente ad cognitionem obiecti, et ab aliis attentionibus se retrahente, sequitur intensior actus cognoscendi; igitur, etc.: q. 12 n.11; Dicendum igitur quod potentiae animae respectu suarum operationum sunt activae; aliter nimis vilescerent, ut patebit: q. 12 n. 21; differentia nobilior alicuius generis constituit speciem nobiliorem, sicut rationale respectu hominis, irrationale respectu bruti; sed potentia activa est nobilior differentia quam passiva, ut patet V et IX Metaphysicae; sed vegetativa est potentia activa; si igitur potentia intellectiva et sensitiva sunt tantum passivae, vegetativa erit nobilior, quod falsum est: q. 12 n. 26; ... est duplex modus ponendi dictas potentias esse passivas. Unus enim est quod potentia recipit immediate secundum actum evocatum, et determinatur a specie sibi praesentata sui obiecti in organo potentiae sensitivae ad sentiendum vel in phantasmate ad intelligendum, illa tamen specie in potentia nullatenus exsistente. Istum autem secundum actum elicit ipsa potentia ex virtute sua activa, sicut specie sibi praesentata ipsam potentiam evocante et determinante ad cognoscendum illud obiectum cuius est species, non tamen aliqualiter ipsam potentiam informante: q. 12 n. 27; Quia igitur potentia sensitiva vel intellectiva dicitur formaliter sentiens vel intelligens vel homo per eas (et ut sic denominantur ab eis) — loquitur PHILOSOPHUS — et ideo magis attribuit pati talibus potentiis vel recipere quam agere, quia notum est magis tales actus esse in potentiis subiective quam a potentiis effective, sicut de motu gravis, qui magis patet esse in gravi, quam ab ipso effective causatus: q. 12 n. 28; dicendum quod pro tanto dicuntur pati, quia huiusmodi potentiae non dicuntur formaliter sentire et intelligere in quantum eliciunt, sed in quantum illos actus recipiunt, vel secundum ALIQUOS propter hoc quod in potentiis sunt duae passiones: una respectu obiecti a quo recipiunt speciem, et haec est prima, et secunda est respectu sui ipsius, ut elicit actum cognoscendi, et haec est receptio cognitionis; una autem tantum a quo sit iudicium de obiecto: q. 12 n. 38; Non igitur omni potentiae passivae naturali correspondet potentia activa naturalis, quae posset effective ipsam reducere ad actum; sed sufficit potentiae passivae naturali quod ex natura sua habeat quod possit recipere illam perfectionem ad quam habet potentiam naturalem — et hoc sive ab agente naturali sive supernaturali: q. 15 n. 38; Nulla potentia eadem manens habet actum circa aliquid quod non sit eius obiectum vel sub obiecto eius contentum; sed intellectus beatus et viatoris est eadem potentia; tamen intellectus beatus intelligit divinam essentiam; igitur Deus saltem continetur sub obiecto intellectus viatoris, non autem sub quiditate materiali; igitur, etc.: q. 19 n. 6; quia nulla potentia potest attingere obiectum suum sine ratione formali obiecti; sed intellectus potest attingere quodcumque absolutum sine respectu aliquo, voluntas amare bonum absolute sine quocumque respectu; igitur respectus non est ratio formalis obiecti intellectus vel voluntatis: q. 20 n. 7

Potentia: v. Sensus

Primitas: Dicendum quod aliquid dicitur prius alio tripliciter, scilicet generatione, perfectione et adaequatione. De duobus primis habetur IX Metaphysicae; de tertio I Posteriorum ubi dicitur quod universale est quod convenit alicui primo. Et vocat universale et primum adaequatione ipsam propriam passionem quae praedicatur convertibiliter de subiecto. De duobus primis modis dicendum est ad praesens.: q. 16 n. 8

Primum cognitum: Dicendum igitur ad quaestionem primo quod minus universale est prius notum nobis prioritate generationis et cognitione confusa quam magis universale: q. 16 n. 10; dico quod prius cognoscitur magis universale a nobis cognitione distincta. Probatio: prius distincte illud cognoscitur quod intrat definitionem alterius, per quod aliud distincte cognoscitur; sed ens quod est universalissimum intrat definitionem omnium, cum conceptus entis includatur in conceptu cuiuslibet — ipsum autem non habet conceptum nisi distinctum, quia non habet in quo possit confuse et indistincte cognosci; igitur, etc. Simile autem est de aliis universalibus: quanto enim aliquid est universalius, tanto potest plurium definitionem intrare; et distinctius cognosci, quanto pauciora superiora habeat, in quibus cognoscatur confuse: q. 16 n. 18; Ad propositum igitur dicendum quod illud quod a nobis cognoscitur prius prioritate perfectionis cognitionis in se et absolute consideratae est Deus, loquendo etiam de cognitione naturali et universali, tam causalitate quam praedicatione. Probatio primi: quia illa cognitio est perfectior in se per quam attingitur perfectius obiectum; sed haec est cognitio Dei, qui est obiectum perfectissimum; igitur, etc: q. 16 n. 21; Sed quae est cognitio perfectior secundum proportionem ad obiectum, id est respectu inferiorum, quae sunt intellectui nostro proportionata? Dicendum quod cognitio illorum sensibilium quae fortius movent sensum est perfectior. Quia quae fortius movent sensum, fortius movent intellectum, licet altiori modo, quia universalius; quae autem fortius movent intellectum sunt magis proportionata intellectui; et ideo prius perfectione tali, scilicet secundum proportionem ad obiectum, intelligitur universale illius singularis sensibilis, quod fortius movet sensum: q. 16 n. 23-24

Primum principium: Item, primum principium debet esse firmissimum secundum PHILOSOPHUM IV Metaphysicae; sed primum principium formatur de ente, sicut dictum est, igitur firmissime; sed si ens diceret plures conceptus, non esset certum de quo conceptu esset verum, immo semper esset distinguendum; igitur, etc.: q. 21 n. 28

Principia: Modo ita est quod principia aliarum scientiarum prius ordine doctrinae sunt nobis nota ex confuso conceptu terminorum, sicut geometer ex confuso conceptu lineae et puncti procedit ad cognoscendum eius definitionem et passionem. Et ideo metaphysica est posterior ordine doctrinae, cuius tamen principia sunt distincte cognita. Sed scientia metaphysicae acquisita, revertendo ad alias scientias, magis distincte cognoscuntur earum principia, scientia metaphysicae prius distincte cognita; et sic est prius ordine distinctae cognitionis. Sic in proposito: species prius cognoscitur indistincte — scilicet in cognoscendo quid dicitur per nomen vel in suo universali; sed cognito universali distincte, tunc per eius divisionem et contractionem — per additionem differentiae — fit reditus ad cognoscendum speciem distincte: q. 16, n. 19

Proportio: Et tu dicis quod aeque perfecte sentit unus suum obiectum sicut alius. Dicendum quod hoc est verum secundum aequalitatem proportionis, non tamen secundum aequalitatem adaequationis et perfectionis, quia perfectior est immutatio a calido et frigido quam ab humido et sicco: q. 1 n. 18

Qualitas: Sicut igitur se habent ad invicem obiecta sensus tactus, quae sunt qualitates activae et passivae, ita et potentiae tactivae. Modo ita est quod qualitates activae fundantur in passivis et se invicem concomitantur, sicut forma in materia fundatur, et se concomitantur quia qualitates activae consequuntur compositum ratione formae, et passivae ratione materiae; ergo et potentiae tactivae se invicem consequuntur, ut ubicumque et in quocumque est una potentia, foret et alia: q. 1 n. 15

Quandocumque: quandocumque aliqua duo sunt eiusdem speciei, a quocumque potest pati unum, et aliud: q. 1 n. 3

Quiditas: utrum quiditas rei sensibilis sit obiectum intellectus nostri: Ad hoc dicunt quidam, scilicet, Thomas, quod quiditas rei sensibilis est obiectum adaequatum intellectus nostri: q. 19 n. 5; intellectus noster etiam in via potest cognoscere ens sub·ratione entis, quae est universalior quam ratio quiditatis sensibilis; igitur quiditas sensibilis non est obiectum adaequatum intellectus nostri. Antecedens patet, quia aliqua scientia humana est de ente secundum quod ens. Probatio consequentiae: quia nulla potentia potest cognoscere aliquid universalius obiecto sibi adaequato; tunc enim obiectum non esset sibi adaequatum. Exemplum de visu, qui non potest cognoscere aliquid universalius colore vel luce: q. 19 n. 13; Dicendum igitur ad quaestionem quod via generationis vel acquirendo scientiam prius apprehendimus quiditates sensibilium, quia pro statu naturae lapsae nihil intelligimus nisi cum ministerio sensibilium; tamen illa non sunt proprium et adaequatum obiectum intellectus nostri, sed etiam possumus intelligere substantias separatas. Et tale obiectum est prius via perfectionis et simpliciter, quia per talem cognitionem attingitur obiectum perfectissimum quod est Deus et substantiae separatae aliae, etiam pro statu viae; et licet talis cognitio sit aenigmatica, tamen perfectior est omni alia cognitione nostra respectu inferioris creaturae: q. 19 n. 18

Ramusculi nervorum: nervi coextenduntur toti carni animalis, non quia sunt in qualibet parte carnis quantumcumque modica nervi — aut quod non sit caro pura in animali — sed quia prope vel iuxta quamlibet partem carnis sicut aliqui ramusculi nervorum coextenduntur per corpus ad modum retis, et hoc patet in folio arborum ad sensum. Per istos autem nervos vel ramusculos derivatur virtus tactiva a corde vel a cerebro per totum corpus: q. 2 n. 9

Ramusculi nervorum: v. Nervus, Relatio

Relatio: relatio non separatur a subiecto et fundamento suo vel a ratione fundandi. Aliqua autem relativa, ut de ecundo modo, fundantur super actionem et passionem, scilicet relatio calefacientis ad calefactum, patris ad filium; vel saltem rationes fundandi illas relationes sunt actio et passio: vel secundum suum esse, sicut in patre et filio, vel secundum fieri, ut in calefaciente et calefacto, vel secundum factivum ad faciendum, ut calefactivum ad calefactibile, ut patet V Metaphysicae.[10] Igitur talis relatio non potest separari ab actione et passione in subiecto; sed talis relatio est in agente quae est agentis ad patiens, vel in patiente quae est patientis ad agens — paternitas enim est in patre, filiatio in filio; igitur et actio est in agente: q. 7 n. 11; omnis respectus realis est in eo quod realiter refertur ad aliud per illum, licet hoc non oportet de respectu rationis, sicut patet de scibili quod non refertur ad scientiam, sed scientia ad scibile; actio autem est quidam respectus realis agentis ad patiens; igitur est in agente sicut relatio: q. 7 n. 12

Relatio: v. Actio

Respectus: omnis respectus realis est in eo quod realiter refertur ad aliud per illum, licet hoc non oportet de respectu rationis, sicut patet de scibili quod non refertur ad scientiam, sed scientia ad scibile; actio autem est quidam respectus realis agentis ad patiens; igitur est in agente sicut relatio: q. 7 n. 12; Respectus quoad praesens est in duplici differentia. Est enim quidam respectus intrinsecus adveniens, qui de necessitate advenit, positis extremis, et talis est tantum de genere relationis, sicut, positis duobus albis, de necessitate sequitur similitudo. Similiter, posita activa et passiva generatione in facto esse, de necessitate ponitur paternitas et filiatio. Alius est respectus importatus extrinsecus adveniens, qui non ponitur de necessitate, positis extremis. Talis est respectus importatus in sex aliis praedicamentis relativis; posita enim re quandali vel temporali et tempore, non de necessitate ponitur quando', sed requiritur adiacentia temporis vel aliquid aliud temporale: q. 7 n. 18

Respectus: v. Actio

Sapor: Exemplum de sapore, qui fundatur in tangibilibus qualitatibus ex quibus causatur tanquam qualitas secunda. Ideo gustus, cuius obiectum est sapor, fundatur in tactu — immo est quidam tactus: q. 1 n. 15

Sensibile commune: Circa quod sciendum quod sensibilia communia sunt quasi media inter sensibilia propria, quae immutant sensus proprios per se et proprie, et sensibilia per accidens, quae nec per se nec primo immutant sensus, quia sensibilia communia immutant per se sensus proprios quia faciunt ad differentiam immutationis; aliter enim immutat magnitudo magna et parva, et unum quam multa, et circulare et triangulare, et quiescens et motum; sed non faciunt ad substantiam immutationis sensus proprii nisi mediante sensibili proprio, et ideo secundum illa non debet sumi aliqua potentia sensitiva propria: q. 6 n. 13

Sensibile proprium: dicendum quod obiectum sensus est tantum accidens de tertia specie qualitatis ... illae autem qualitates differunt formaliter quantum ad immutationem sensuum, et ideo secundum hoc accipiuntur diversi sensus, non autem secundum genera accidentium...: q. 6 n. 12

Sensus: ubi est sensus tactus, ibi est organum tactus: q. 2 n. 3; aliquid potest esse prius alio vel causalitate vel tempore vel situ. Ita dico quod 'potentia prius immutatur per medium extrinsecum quam per obiectum' potest esse verum, et hoc secundum situm et secundum causalitatem in aliis sensibus a tactu, sicut in visu. Immutatur enim primo medium a visibili secundum situm, quod est ei propinquius; etiam secundum causalitatem, quia immutatio medii est causa immutationis organi; licet non prius tempore, quia visio fit in instanti. In auditu etiam est prior immutatio medii et causalitate et situ et tempore — etiam in aliqua sui parte, scilicet in remota ab organo, quia sonus se multiplicat mediante motu locali. Sic etiam in olfactu et gustu, in quo — gustu — medii extrinseci immutatio est causa immutationis organi, licet simul tempore immutetur saliva — quae est medium extrinsecum — et organum. Sed in tactu medium extrinsecum prius quidem secundum situm immutatur, quia est propinquius, non tamen prius tempore, sicut simul tempore percutitur clypeus et clypeatus, non autem prius causalitate (non enim clypeus percussus percutit clypeatum): q. 3 n. 18; sensus non est eodem modo dispositus ad recipiendum speciem vel formam obiecti sensibilis sicut materia prima, et ideo recipit speciem eius sine materia, id est sine dispositione materiae: q. 5 n. 6; Quia igitur potentia sensitiva propinqua non est anima tantum, immo includit organum, ideo potest ab obiecto speciem recipere, stante identitate reali ipsius potentiae cum animae essentia. Immo, si esset diversa essentia ab anima, sicut qualitas quaedam absoluta, sequeretur quod ipsa cum organo, sine essentia animae, posset sentire, quia posita causa totali, ponitur et eius effectus: q. 5 n. 8; Sed forte tu dicis quod potentia sensitiva non possit exire in actum nisi virtute animae, quae est principalis, dato quod sit eius qualitas absoluta. Contra: quod per se potest habere esse qualitercumque, sive per naturam sive per miraculum, per se naturaliter -- sine alio -- potest agere sine alio, sicut patet de accidente in sacramento Altaris, quod non habet esse in subiecto, et tamen naturaliter agit: q. 5 n. 9-10; Sed contra: potentia sensitiva non est separabilis a corpore; anima secundum suam essentiam est separabilis a corpore. Dicendum quod potentia propinqua ad sentiendum quae est totalis causa eliciendi actum, supposito obiecto, non est separabilis, quia talis includit organum corporeum, quod est aliud ab essentia animae, et sic ipsa potentia differt ab anima. Sed potentia sensitiva, praecise quae est remota, talis est separabilis, sicut et essentia, quia idem sunt: q. 5 n. 11-12; Sensus autem non tantum immutatur naturaliter ab obiecto, quia tunc inanimata, quae sic naturaliter immutantur, possent sentire: q. 6 n. 7; Si autem immutentur aliqui sensus naturaliter, cum hoc tamen immutantur intentionaliter — immo magis intentionaliter quam naturaliter; immutatio enim naturalis impedit animalem sensationem, ut visum est. Si enim esset immutatio intentionalis sine naturali, sicut est in visu, magis sentiretur et verius quam cum ea: q. 6 n. 8; Ex diversitate ergo immutationis organi ab obiecto et conformationis sumitur sic sufficientia sensuum: quia aliquando sensus immutantur intentionaliter tantum, aliquando cum hoc naturaliter. Si primo modo, sic est visus; si secundo modo, aut est transmutatio naturalis ex parte obiecti, aut ex parte organi. Si ex parte obiecti, aut fit talis immutatio mediante motu locali, et sic est auditus, qui immutatur a sono se multiplicante in aere usque ad auditum mediante motu locali; aut fit mediante motu alterationis, et sic est odoratus, qui sentit odorem procedentem ab odorabili secundum quod est alteratum per calefactionem — unde in hieme male odoratur corpus odorabile, specialiter si sit congelatum ... Si autem immutatio sit naturalis ex parte organi, sic habemus gustum et tactum. Sed differunt, quia organum tactus immutatur a calore et qualitate sensibili quae est eius obiectum immediate, vel saltem potest ab ea immediate immutari; gustus autem non potest immediate immutari a sapore, qui est eius obiectum, sed mediante humore coniuncto linguae: q. 6 n. 9; Ex praedictis patet ordo potentiarum, quia visus, cum immutetur tantum intentionaliter, est sensus nobilior et certior; post hunc autem auditus, qui minus materialiter immutatur, quia mediante motu locali tantum qui est primus motuum; post hunc olfactus, qui immutatur materialiter ex parte obiecti, quod est remotius a potentia quam organum; post hunc gustus, qui immutatur materialiter ex parte organi, sed non immediate cum suo obiecto, sed mediante humore intrinseco; ultimus autem quantum ad cognitionis nobilitatem est tactus, qui ab obiecto suo immediate immutatur; est tamen prius ordine generationis vel imperfectionis vel communitatis, qui est fundamentum aliorum et communis omnibus habentibus sensum, etiam imperfectis: q. 6 n. 11; ... omnes sensus habent unum genus innominatum, quod potest dici sensus in communi: q. 6 n. 14; dicendum quod sensus non movetur propter hoc contrariis motibus, quia motus contrariorum in sensu non sunt contrarii, sicut nec in medio (immo minus quam in medio, et tamen in eodem puncto medii potest esse species albi et nigri), et hoc ideo est quia species sensibilium non recipiuntur materialiter in sensu sicut in re extra, ubi tantum sunt contraria: q. 8 n. 18

Sensus: v. Immutatio, Potentia

Sensus communis: Igitur sensus communis tantum est cognoscitivus operationis sensus particularis. Hoc autem habet fieri per hunc modum: primo enim sensus proprius a sensibili proprio immutatur; immutatio cuiuslibet sensus proprii ad sensum communem terminatur; sicut plures lineae ductae a circumferentia ad idem centrum terminantur; sensus autem communis sic immutatus a diversis sensationibus vel immutationibus particularibus iudicat et cognoscit actum cuiuslibet sensus particularis, et ulterius cognoscit differentiam sensibilium propriorum: q. 9 n. 10; Et mediantibus speciebus sic reservatis, fit apprehensio sensibilis absentis per aliquam potentiam sensitivam; non autem est particularis, quia talis sentit praesente sensibili tantum; igitur vel illa est communis sensus, vel saltem praesupponit ipsum, sicut imaginativa rememorativa: q. 9 n. 11; dicendum quod sensus communis sentit et visionem et colorem: q. 9 n. 15; Dicendum quod sicut ab actu imaginationis defluit quaedam species in organo alicuius sensus, sive exterioris sive interioris, in qua specie est similitudo actus illius, a qua specie potest potentia imaginativa sic immutari; sic est de sensu communi, quod ab eius actu defluit quaedam species in organo sensus particularis interius, a qua specie, retinente similitudinem actus eius, potest sensus communis immutari.: q. 9 n. 16; dicendum quod sensus communis non est potentia collativa proprie, sicut memorativa vel cogitativa. Memorativa cognoscit suum obiectum ut distans a praesenti nunc, cogitando tempus medium. Est enim praeteriti ut praeteritum est. Sed sensus communis sic confert unum sensibile alteri quod simul sentit ipsa sensibilia, et sentit ipsa differre sine intermedio aliquo, et talis collatio, id est compositio et divisio taliter, non repugnat ei, sicut non repugnat sensui proprio affirmare vel negare proprium obiectum de aliquo: q. 9 n. 17; licet sensus communis cognoscat illa quae differunt, et cognoscat album a dulci differre, non tamen cognoscit habitudinem differentiae secundum se, sed tantum in fundamento.: q. 9 n. 18; sensus communis non est unus unitate praedicationis sed unitate singularitatis et causalitatis; est enim radix et causa omnium sensuum particularium: q. 10 n. 5; sensus communis habet operationem distinctam ab operationibus sensuum particularium, scilicet distinguere inter sensibilia diversorum sensuum: q. 10 n. 5; Est etiam unus unitate actus qui est discernere inter album et dulce, quod est actus eius: q. 10 n. 6; Est etiam sensus communis potentia una unitate organi:

q. 10 n. 7; Dicendum est igitur quod organum eius [scilicet sensus communis] est unum unitate naturae, non quidem simplicis, sed mixtae et quasi mediae inter naturas aliorum organorum. Sic enim se habet organum sensus communis ad alia ut centrum ad lineas procedentes ab eo ad circumferentiam, vel ad ipsum terminatas quasi sit radix communis organorum sensuum particularium, et potentia sensus communis in eo exsistens est sicut rex sedens in solio, iudicans de actibus particularium sensuum ad ipsum terminatorum repraesentantium sibi propria obiecta: q. 10 n. 8; Imaginandum est igitur quod a corde ad cerebrum procedunt quaedam venae vel nervi, in quibus originaliter continentur organa omnium sensuum, sed in cerebro faciunt conum; a cerebro autem procedunt quinque nervi ad organa exteriora, facientes basim; et sic organum sensus communis habet ortum a corde, sed in cerebro habet suum complementum: q. 10 n. 15; Dicendum est igitur quod aliquod sensibile commune communitate praedicationis — non autem sensibile commune ut ait PHILOSOPHUS II De anima, sicut magnitudo et figura — potest dici obiectum proprium sensus communis: q. 10 n. 18; Ad aliud, dicendum quod plus requiritur ad diversitatem sensus superioris quam inferioris, quia superius est quasi ligamentum sensibus propriis; unde, licet proprius non sit cognitivus proprie nisi unius contrarietatis, sensus tamen communis potest esse respectu plurium contrarietatum: q. 18 n. 25; Tres sunt actus sensus communis: q. 18 n. 26-28

Sensus communis: v. Avicenna, Organum

Sensus particularis: oportet organum sensuum particularium continuari organo sensus communis, quia sensus communis habet iudicare de speciebus receptis in organis sensuum particularium q. 2 n. 7; hoc [sc. sensum particularem simul posse contraria sentire] est possibile, quia possibile est duo sensibilia contraria simul offerri sensui. Aut igitur utrumque sensus sentit, et sic habeo propositum; si alterum, igitur eadem ratione et alterum, quia suppono quod sint aeque propinqua et aequalis virtutis ad movendum: q. 8 n. 4

Sentire: intelligere et sentire sunt actiones immanentes in agente. Certum est autem quod manent in sentiente et intelligente, non autem in obiecto extrinseco; igitur obiectum non est activum talium, sed potius homo sentiens et intelligens, mediantibus suis potentiis animae: q. 20 n. 21; si sentire sit pati, sentiri est agere; sed agere est nobilius quam pati; si obiectum igitur intelligi est nobilius quam intelligere, per illud inanimata, quae non intelligunt sed intelliguntur, sunt perfectiora quam homo qui intelligit: q. 12 n. 25

Singulare: Utrum singulare sit ab intellectu nostro per se intelligibile: q. 22 n. 1; Ad quaestionem dicit Thomas quod intellectus noster pro statu viae non potest cognoscere singulare directe: q. 22 n. 10; dicunt [sc. Thomas] tamen quod per reflexionem potest cognoscere singulare, quia licet species intelligibiles sint in intellectu nostro, tamen per eas non possumus intelligere nisi intuendo obiectum universale in phantasmate, quod est repraesentativum singularis primo: q. 22 n. 11; Dicendum igitur quod singulare est a nobis intelligibile secundum se, quia intelligibilitas sequitur entitatem. Quod igitur secundum se non diminuit de rationem entis, nec intelligibilitatis; sed singulare secundum se non diminuit de ratione entis, immo est ens actu perfectum — unde in Praedicamentis et in VII Metaphysicae dicitur quod singulare subiectum est maxime substantia; igitur, etc: q. 22 n. 17; Secundo, dico quod singulare est a nobis intelligibile pro statu isto. Probo: sicut enim conclusionem intelligimus sive cognoscimus in syllogismo, ita principia inductive, II Posteriorum; sed inductio est processus a singularibus ad universale, sic autem discurrere pertinet tantum ad intellectum; igitur cognoscit singularia: q. 22 n. 20; incognita non possumus diligere, secundum AUGUSTINUM; sed per prius diligimus singulare quam universale, quia praeceptum de dilectione est magis respectu singularis quam universalis: q. 22 n. 21; Tertio dico quod nulla potentia nostra, nec intellectiva nec sensitiva, potest cognoscere singulare sub propria ratione singularitatis. Quia potentia cognoscens aliquod obiectum sub propria ratione potest ipsum cognoscere et ab aliis distinguere, circumscripto quocumque alio non habente illam rationem; sed manente propria ratione singularitatis, amotis aliis, non possumus distinguere inter duo singularia, nec per sensum nec per intellectum; igitur, etc. Probatio minoris: quia potentia cognoscens obiectum suum secundum aliquam unitatem, potest illud distinguere ab omni alio quod non habet illam unitatem; sed unum singulare non habet unitatem essentialem alterius, et tamen nec sensu nec intellectu possumus distinguere inter duo singularia, circumscripta distinctione accidentali quae est per locum, figuram, tempus, magnitudinem, colorem, et sic de aliis: q. 22 n. 26; Quarto dicendum, quantum ad modum intelligendi singulare, quod, si non ponimus speciem in intellectu sed tantum in phantasia, sicut natura in agendo non intendit universale ... sic in repraesentando species in phantasia primo repraesentat singulare vagum in quod primo fertur cognitio intellectus (et hoc patet, quia aliquando intelligimus aliquod singulare, ignorando in qua specie est); secundo repraesentat naturam absolute (quando, scilicet, intellectus fertur in naturam non considerando eius singularitatem); tertio, reflectendo considerationem naturae ad circumstantias signatas ad ipsam (per illas determinando) individuum signatum possumus intelligere, utpote quia est hic et nunc et cum tali figura et magnitudine et colore et ceteris: q. 22 n. 34; [Quarto] Si vero ponamus speciem in intellectu, dicendum quod huiusmodi species duplicem singularitatem habet: unam a subiecto, quia est in subiecto singulari, et hanc semper habet; et aliam ab obiecto a quo imprimitur saltem primo, licet per operationem intellectus agentis abstrahatur a condicionibus individuantibus. Et sic primo repraesentat naturam in supposito vago, quia illud se primo offert intellectui; secundo, naturam absolute; tertio, ipsam intellectus determinat, addendo sibi circumstantias singulares praedictas. Et sic intelligit singulare signatum, non sub propria ratione singularitatis, ut dictum est: q. 22 n. 36

Sonus: sonus habet esse reale in omni parte medii; sed auris potest audire in omni parte medii exsistente, igitur in parte sibi coniuncta; igitur, etc.: q. 4 n. 3

Species: species in organo est principium actus, vel formale vel inclinativum: q. 1 n. 12; species in organo habet esse ab obiecto; igitur mediante corpore medio in quo habet esse minus materiale quam in obiecto — magis tamen quam in organo —, causatur species ita intentionalis in organo, quia ab extremo in extremum devenitur per medium: q. 4 n. 8 (Opinio Aegidii); Deus potest actum imaginandi et intelligendi sine specie obiectorum causata ab obiectis in potentiis causare: q. 12 n. 20; Dicendum quod, secundum aliquos opinio Avicenna VI Naturalium est quod species non sit in intellectu nostro nisi quando actu considerat per hunc modum, quia quando intellectus noster convertit se ad intelligentiam separatam, tunc tantum intelligit, quia tunc speciem ab ea recipit (opinio Avicennae apud mentem Thomae): q. 14 n. 4; Dicendum igitur quod opinio Avicennae fuit aliquas species esse in intellectu, etiam cessante actu. Dicit enim quod in intellectu sunt species ipsum decorantes, et subdit quod, cum recipit intellectus aliquam speciem ab imaginibus, non recipit aliam eiusdem speciei (opinio Avicennae apud mentem Scoti): q. 14 n. 13; Respondeo quod species [intelligibilis[potest manere, cessante actu. Quod probatur sic: quod est causa alterius et prius naturaliter eo, non tamen necessaria, potest esse sine effectu; sed species intelligibilis est causa prior actu intelligendi nec est causa necessaria — quia quod est formale principium intelligendi quo elicitur actus intelligendi, sive sit intelligere sive species, est liberum per participationem a sua causalitate, ut scilicet producat effectum; igitur non est causa necessaria producendi effectum. Intelligimus enim cum volumus, ut dicitur II De anima. Potest enim liberum per essentiam, scilicet voluntas, impedire liberum per participationem a sua causalitate ne scilicet producat effectum suum. Igitur species potest esse sine actu: q. 14 n. 16; utrum in intellectu nostro sint species intelligibiles priores naturaliter actu intelligendi: q. 17 n. 1; una species non potest repraesentare obiectum aliquod sub oppositis rationibus; sed singulare et universale habent oppositas rationes; species autem in phantasmate est repraesentativa obiecti ut singulare est, igitur non ut universale; igitur praeter illam est necessaria species in intellectu ad repraesentandum universale: q. 17 n. 8; Sed dices quod hoc verum est eodem lumine, sed luminibus diversis potest eadem species diversa repraesentare, ut patet de noctilucis, quae in die videntur colorata lumine solis sed de nocte lucentia lumine proprio; sic species in phantasmate lumine phantasiae vel virtutis sensitivae potest repraesentare singulare, lumine tamen intellectus agentis penetrante phantasma universale: q. 17 n. 9; Sed dices quod universale, quod est obiectum intellectus, fulget in phantasmate per lumen intellectus agentis ad esse intelligibile actu: q. 17 n. 12; dicendum quod species, licet sit forma naturalis quoad actum intelligendi (quantum est de se) semper producendum, quia tamen non est tota causa actus sed requiritur necessario intellectus, et principalius (ille autem non semper est in actu), ideo non oportet quod semper intelligat Similiter non oportet quod omnes simul causent actum intelligendi, sed illa tantum cuius phantasma fortius movet intelligentem ad actum primum intelligendi — ut patet cum homo excitatur a somno, tunc intelligit necessario illud quod prius occurrit — vel cuius phantasma fortius movet; sed post illum actum intelligit illud quod voluntas sibi imperat intelligendum, et hoc secundum speciem eius in intellectu conservatam: q. 17 n. 18; Sic est in proposito de actu intelligendi, qui prius ordine generationis requirit phantasma et cognitionem sensitivam, a qua originatur, et speciem intelligibilem, secundum quam intellectus formaliter intelligit: q. 17 n. 19; Sed dices quod vera est maior de agente aequivoco in virtute propria, non autem de instrumentali; modo phantasma agit in intellectu possibili virtute intellectus agentis penetrantis ipsum et abstrahentis quidditatem a condicionibus individualibus, quae sunt in phantasmate; sicut lumen attingens ipsum lac, quod est album et dulce, quodammodo abstrahit album a dulci, dum repraesentat visui lac sub ratione albi, non tamen sub ratione dulcis (opinio Godefredi): q. 17 n. 21; alii dicunt ad rationem principalem praedictam quod intellectus agens agit in intellectum possibilem sicut causa partialis cum phantasmate, non autem sicut causa totalis, sed sicut causa principalis cum instrumentali (opinio Aegidii): q. 17 n. 25; Teneas quam partem volueris. Prima tamen videtur communior et verior, et 'qui potest capere capiat': q. 17 n. 46; Propter istam rationem dicunt aliqui quod non est necessaria species impressa intellectui ad actum intelligendi. Quia, ad solam conversionem intellectus super phantasmata, intellectus elicit actum suum; et quia, transeunte actu, non manet species, ideo semper necesse est recurrere ad phantasmata in quolibet actu intelligendi (opinio Henrici): q. 18 n. 6; Sed quia aliis videtur quod species impressa intellectui requiritur ad intelligendum, et quod manet, cessante actu, ideo dicunt quod fit recursus ad phantasmata, non ut iterum ibi species abstrahatur, quia iam habet, sed ut habita intendatur. Dicunt enim aliqui quod species in intellectu habet debile esse, et transeunte actu, paulative remittitur, sicut calida aqua amoto igne tepescit. Quia igitur tunc species habet esse incompletum, ideo dicunt quod necesse est intellectui recurrere ad phantasmata si debeat intelligere, ut species praehabita intendatur (Opinio Aegidii aliorumque): q. 18 n. 7

Species: v. Actus

Spirituale: pure corporale non potest agere directe in pure spirituale, eo quod agens est nobilius patiente: q. 11 n. 10

Spirituale: v. Corporale

Substantia: Sed quod substantia non possit esse primum obiectum, probatio: non enim est primum per praedicationem, quia non praedicatur essentialiter de omnibus intelligibilibus, quia non de accidentibus. Nec secundum virtutem, quia non movet intellectum sufficienter ad sui notitiam et aliorum: q. 21 n. 12; Quod autem substantiam in via non possumus conceptu simplici et primo cognoscere, patet ex hoc quod omnis nostra cognitio oritur a sensu; substantia autem per se non est sensibilis; et ideo intuitive vel conceptu simplici non possumus eam cognoscere, sed per illum modum: quia ab accidentibus nobis sensibilibus abstrahimus conceptum entis, dicendo quod sunt entis, et ulterius inquirendo invenimus quod est tale ens quod est alteri inhaerens; illud autem alterum oportet esse subsistens, et tali subsistenti imponimus nomen substantiae, et ideo sic confuse cognoscimus substantiam, componendo ipsi enti subsistentiam, dicendo quod est ens per se subsistens: q. 21 n. 25

Sufficientia sensuum: Ex diversitate ergo immutationis organi ab obiecto et conformationis sumitur sic sufficientia sensuum: quia aliquando sensus immutantur intentionaliter tantum, aliquando cum hoc naturaliter. Si primo modo, sic est visus; si secundo modo, aut est transmutatio naturalis ex parte obiecti, aut ex parte organi. Si ex parte obiecti, aut fit talis immutatio mediante motu locali, et sic est auditus, qui immutatur a sono se multiplicante in aere usque ad auditum mediante motu locali; aut fit mediante motu alterationis, et sic est odoratus, qui sentit odorem procedentem ab odorabili secundum quod est alteratum per calefactionem — unde in hieme male odoratur corpus odorabile, specialiter si sit congelatum ... Si autem immutatio sit naturalis ex parte organi, sic habemus gustum et tactum. Sed differunt, quia organum tactus immutatur a calore et qualitate sensibili quae est eius obiectum immediate, vel saltem potest ab ea immediate immutari; gustus autem non potest immediate immutari a sapore, qui est eius obiectum, sed mediante humore coniuncto linguae: q. 6 n. 9

Sufficientia potentiarum cognitivarum: Dicendum igitur quod potentiarum animae quaedam sunt disparatae, quaedam subordinatae; et istarum quaedam sunt in eodem genere ut apprehensivae, quaedam in diversis ut apprehensivae cum appetitivis. Si autem sint potentiae disparatae, habent obiecta omnino disparata, sicut quinque sensus particulares. Si autem sint subordinatae et in eodem genere, habent obiecta subordinata, quia obiectum primum et adaequatum potentiae superioris sub se continet obiectum inferioris, quod tamen est obiectum per se, licet non primum nec adaequatum potentiae superioris, quia potentia superior potest habere actum suum circa obiectum adaequatum potentiae inferioris et ipsum perfectius cognoscit quam potentia inferior. Sicut sensus communis album perfectius cognoscit quam visus quia cognoscit ipsum ut distinctum a dulci, sic intellectus cognoscit quidquid sensus cognoscit, et perfectius quam sensus. Si autem potentiae subordinatae sint alterius generis, sicut intellectus et voluntas, tunc dicendum quod si sint adaequatae — id est, si in tot potest una, in quot potest alia —, tunc habent idem obiectum formale. Si autem non sint adaequatae (quia voluntas non habet actum suum nisi circa finem et ea quae sunt ad finem, non autem circa necessaria et impossibilia quae sunt tantum speculativa, ut conclusiones geometricae), tunc dicendum quod obiectum voluntatis continetur sub obiecto intellectus: q. 20 n. 20

Tactus: sensus tactus facit animal esse animal, quia est primus sensus: q. 1 n. 4; sensus tactus sunt formaliter duo, non tamen ita diversi vel divisi sicut alii ab invicem: q. 1 n. 9; impossibile est unum sensum tactus habere simul et semel duos perfectissimos actus: q. 1 n. 10; tactus simul sentit aquam humidam et frigidam esse: q. 1 n. 10; dicendum quod ideo tactus facit esse animal quia est communior[51] sensuum et est fundamentum aliorum, sicut anima vegetativa facit corpus esse animatum, non quia sit perfectior anima nec quia tactus sit perfectior sensus: q. 1 n. 19; ubi est sensus tactus, ibi est organum tactus: q. 2 n.3; ; Necessitas autem ponendi sensum vel organum tactus esse extensum toti corpori est quia qualitates tangibiles possunt agere in quamcumque partem corporis, cum quaelibet pars sit mixta ex quattuor elementis, in qua reducuntur ad medium, et per consequens est in potentia ad receptionem et passionem naturalem ab excellentiis qualitatum: q. 2 n. 10; Ad consequendum igitur convenientia ad conservationem animalis, et fugiendum nociva, est organum tactus ita extensum, et etiam est intrinsecum propter eandem causam, ne de facili corrumpatur ab excellenti tangibili: q. 2 n. 10; tactus potest comparari ad qualitatem aliquam accidentalem inhaerentem vel adhaerentem, id est, non exsistentem in suo proprio subiecto sed in alio sibi coniuncto. Primo modo potest fieri tactus sine corpore medio extrinseco, sicut patet de dolore apostematis, qui sentitur vehementer non nisi per tactum, ut patet inductive... Loquendo autem de qualitate adhaerente, quodammodo sentitur immediate sine corpore medio, alio a corpore cui adhaeret sed immediate tangente, sicut patet de qualitate exsistente in corpore non-terminato sed fluido ut est aer vel aqua, quorum qualitates immediate tanguntur sine corpore medio alio a propriis subiectis: q. 3 n. 13; Licet igitur non prius tempore et causalitate immutatur potentia tactiva a medio extrinseco quam obiecto, prius tamen secundum situm immutatur, et hoc sufficit ad tale medium: q. 3 n.18; Tactus autem utraque immutatione immutatur realiter et naturaliter. Probo: quia organum tactus est corpus mixtum, sicut medium quod est caro, igitur est passivum naturale et receptivum actionis naturalis; qualitates autem tangibiles sunt naturaliter activae; igitur, etc. Similiter, immutatur intentionaliter: quia, si tantum immutaretur naturaliter ratione qua mixtum naturale, non plus sentiret qualitates tangibiles quam lignum vel lapis, quae naturaliter immutantur; quia igitur tactus sentit huiusmodi qualitates; ideo, etc.: q. 4 n. 11; in damnatis post resurrectionem generalem erit sensus tactus et omnes sensus in actu suo, et tunc tactus non immutabitur naturaliter (quia illa immutatio est corruptiva); igitur tantum intentionaliter. Tamen illa erit maxime afflictiva: igitur verissime ibi poterit esse una sine alia. Tamen in statu isto non est intentionalis immutatio sine reali et naturali immutatione, quia causatur ab ea: q. 4 n. 12; in damnatis post resurrectionem generalem erit sensus tactus et omnes sensus in actu suo, et tunc tactus non immutabitur naturaliter (quia illa immutatio est corruptiva); igitur tantum intentionaliter. Tamen illa erit maxime afflictiva: igitur verissime ibi poterit esse una sine alia. Tamen in statu isto non est intentionalis immutatio sine reali et naturali immutatione, quia causatur ab ea: q. 4 n. 13; dicendum quod tactus in quantum sensus non recipit calorem materialiter vel realiter, sed immutatur intentionaliter tantum in quantum sensus (licet illa immutatio non possit separari a naturali immutatione pro statu viae), et ideo recipit speciem sine materia ut sic: q. 5 n. 15 ;... dicendum quod tactus est plures sensus secundum speciem, non autem secundum genus; ideo sunt tantum quinque genera sensuum, sicut sunt quinque genera potentiarum, licet non sint nisi quattuor gradus viventium: q. 6 n. 14; dicendum quod quantum ad modum immutandi, qui est realis in utroque, gustus est tactus, quia gustabile tangit realiter, vel medium gustus gustatur tangendo; tamen, quantum ad obiecta formalia, sunt diversi sensus; sapor enim est obiectum gustus, qui sapor est qualitas secunda causata a primis, sed obiecta tactus sunt qualitates primae: q. 6 n. 15

Tactus: v. Conservatio, Gustus, Immutatio

Tristitia: Probo: quia eorum contraria, scilicet odium et tristitia, non sunt idem, nec sunt ambo a voluntate causata, sed alterum tantum, scilicet odium. Quod patet per hoc quod voluntas complacet sibi in actu proprio ab ipsa causato — voluntas enim non complacet sibi in tristitia, immo est voluntati contraria, et quilibet invite tristatur; sed bene complacet sibi odium; igitur tristitia causatur tantum ab obiecto et non a voluntate, et per consequens nec delectatio. Sed obiectum conveniens cum perceptione, dum tamen sit praesens, causat delectationem, et obiectum contrario modo tristitiam: q. 11 n. 16

Tristitia: v. Delectatio, Odium

Universale: Item, si semper intelligamus magis universale prius quam singulare aliquod quod subito movet sensum, erit magnum tempus antequam possumus cognoscere eius speciem specialissimam, quia oportet prius cognoscere omnia eius superiora essentialia, quae cum sint multa non possunt in instanti cognosci; hoc autem manifeste patet esse falsum: q. 16 n. 13; dico quod prius cognoscitur magis universale a nobis cognitione distincta. Probatio: prius distincte illud cognoscitur quod intrat definitionem alterius, per quod aliud distincte cognoscitur; sed ens quod est universalissimum intrat definitionem omnium, cum conceptus entis includatur in conceptu cuiuslibet — ipsum autem non habet conceptum nisi distinctum, quia non habet in quo possit confuse et indistincte cognosci; igitur, etc. Simile autem est de aliis universalibus: quanto enim aliquid est universalius, tanto potest plurium definitionem intrare; et distinctius cognosci, quanto pauciora superiora habeat, in quibus cognoscatur confuse: q. 16 n. 18

Univocatio: Est enim duplex univocatio: una est logica, secundum quam plura conveniunt in uno conceptu communi tantum; alia est naturalis, secundum quam aliqua conveniunt in aliqua natura reali ad extra, ut in specie atoma, de qua loquitur PHILOSOPHUS VII Physicorum[33] — illud est univocum secundum quod aliqua sunt comparabilia: q. 1 n. 13; Sed quod sit etiam obiectum respectu suorum inferiorum scilicet Dei et creaturae, primitate praedicationis, ostendo: quia ad hoc requiritur, ut dictum est, quod tale obiectum praedicetur essentialiter et per se de omnibus intelligibilibus, et per consequens univoce aliqua univocatione; sed ens est huiusmodi;

igitur, etc: q. 21 n. 21; Quod etiam conceptus entis sit communis univoce substantiae et accidenti, probo: q. 21 n. 25

Univocatio: v. Ens

Unum: si ens praedicatur essentialiter de uno, tunc aut unum dicit praecise ipsum ens aut cum hoc aliquid additum. Non praecise, quia tunc unum non esset magis passio entis quam e converso, et essent aliter nomina synonyma, quod negat Philosophus in IV Metaphysicae, et esset nugatio dicendo ens unum, et e converso. Si aliquid addit supra ens, tunc quaero utrum illud additum sit essentialiter ens vel non; si sic, tunc unum dicit ens bis, semel ratione entis inclusi in uno, alias ratione additi, si sit additio; si autem illud additum non includat essentialiter ens, sequitur propositum, scilicet quod unum, in quantum unum, id est ut differt ab ente, non includit ens essentialiter: q. 21 n. 18; unum prout distinguitur ab ente dicit aliquod accidens per passionem entis — accipiendo large accidens cum Avicenna pro omni eo quod est extra rationem essentialem alicuius; patet quod non valet ratio Commentatoris facta IV Metaphysicae contra Avicennam, quia bene concludit, si unum diceret accidens reale distinctum contra substantiam, quod dividitur in novem praedicamenta accidentium, sed non concludit quod unum dicat tale accidens quod est extra rationem formalem entis. Sic igitur patet quod ens respectu unius, veri et boni, quae sunt eius passiones, est primum obiectum intellectus primitate adaequationis secundum virtutem sicut subiectum respectu suae propriae passionis: q. 21 n. 20

Unum: v. Ens

Vena: caro non continuatur organo sensus communis, quod est in cerebro vel in corde — immo nervi vel venae, derivatae a corde secundum Philosophum vel a cerebro secundum medicos, continuant organa sensuum particularium organo sensus communis, et ipsi nervi vel venae eius continuantur.: q. 2 n. 7

Verum: utrum verum sit obiectum intellectus nostri: q. 20 n.1; Ad hoc dicunt quidam quod intellectus et voluntas tantum distinguuntur per respectus ad obiecta sua quae sunt verum et bonum. Quod declarant sic: anima enim secundum se est indeterminata, sed determinatur ad potentias organicas aliter quam ad non-organicas, quia ad organicas determinatur per determinationem organorum. Unde potentia sensitiva, quae est organica, non est potentia propria animae sed coniuncti ex anima et corpore. Ad non-organicas vero determinatur non per organa nec per qualitates absolutas, igitur per respectum ad distincta obiecta; illa autem formalia obiecta distincta sunt verum et bonum; igitur, etc (opinio Henrici): q. 20 n. 5; Dicendum ergo ad quaestionem quod verum non est primum obiectum intellectus sub ratione veri. Probo: quia quod secundum propriam rationem intelligi potest, ut distinguitur ab alio, non intelligitur sub ratione eius a quo distinguitur; sed bonum, ut distinguitur a vero sub ratione propria boni, potest intelligi; igitur non intelligitur sub ratione veri; sed omne quod intelligitur, intelligitur sub ratione formali obiecti intellectus. Ergo ratio veri non est formalis ratio obiecti intellectus: q. 20 n. 14

Virtus: quaedam sunt virtutes naturales, quaedam animales. Naturales bene fundantur in carne, quae est corpus mixtum in quo sunt qualitates activae et passivae, saltem virtute; virtutes autem animales fundantur in venis et nervis: q. 2 n. 8; virtus tactiva est virtus animalis: q. 2 n. 8

Visus: in uno sensu, scilicet visu, est causa specialis, quare sensibile positum supra sensum non sentitur, quia 'color non videtur sine lumine', et adhuc requiritur quod videatur per medium illuminatum; si autem color poneretur supra organum visus, obumbraret ipsum, et ideo sequitur quod non potest videri: q. 4 n. 10; aliquis sensus immutatur spiritualiter tantum, ut visus: q. 4 n. 11; Unde visus non dicitur coloratus proprie, sicut paries dicitur coloratus, quia recipit colorem realiter; q. 6 n. 7; potentia, discernens inter duo et cognoscens eorum differentiam, necessario cognoscit utrumque; sed visus cognoscit differentiam albi et nigri; igitur, etc: q. 8 n. 6; Dicendum quod sicut appropinquans agens ad patiens dicitur agere vel disponens materiam ultimate dicitur informare, quia statim sequitur actio vel informatio, sic lumen dicitur facere colores actu, id est actu visibiles, in quantum disponit medium, quo facto, statim color potest movere visum; sic movens visum est actu color, non quidem actu primo tantum sed etiam actu secundo: q. 13 n. 10; Exemplum: si ponantur visui duo alba vel intellectui duo singularia quaecumque quae in rei veritate essent distincta essentialiter, si tamen haberent omnino consimilia accidentia ut locum — utpote duo corpora in eodem loco vel duo radii in medio illorum — et haberent figuram omnino consimilem et magnitudinem et colorem et sic de aliis, nec intellectus nec sensus inter illa distingueret, sed iudicaret esse unum; igitur neutrum eorum cognoscit quodlibet illorum singularium secundum propriam rationem singularitatis: q. 22 n. 27

Visus: v. Album

Volitio: …dicendum quod volitio qua dicitur volens est quaedam qualitas habitualis spiritualis, libera tantum per participationem, vel quia in subiecto libero essentialiter quod est voluntas, vel quia a principio elicitivo libere, scilicet voluntate, sicut alii actus imperati a voluntate dicuntur liberi per participationem. Dicendum igitur quod si ly in quantum teneatur reduplicative, ita quod dicat illud, cui additur, esse causam inhaerentiae praedicati ad subiectum, falsa est maior, quia volitio non est causa quare voluntas est libera, sed e converso. Si autem ly in quantum teneatur specificative, hoc est dupliciter: aut enim specificat voluntatem ad hoc quod sit eliciens volitionem, et sic maior est vera, quia voluntas sub illa ratione determinata qua eliciens volitionem est libera; si autem ut recipiens formaliter volitionem, ut accipitur in minori, tunc maior est falsa, quia necessario, non libere, recipit volitionem elicitam libere a se ipsa: q. 12 n. 37

Voluntas (sive potentia volitiva): Modo ita est quod actus a voluntate elicitus non est liber per essentiam sed tantum potentia volitiva, et ideo non oportet quod si sit liber participatione quod actus volendi vel causatus a corpore caelesti sit liber, dato quod sit eiusdem rationis — immo esset non-liber quia haberet causam necessariam: q. 11 n. 14;… si voluntas moveretur a corpore caelesti, sicut posset moveri a Spiritu Sancto, quod actus eius esset eiusdem rationis cum actu a voluntate tantum elicito, quia quod potest causa prima mediante secunda, illud idem et eiusdem rationis potest sine secunda. Et ideo si voluntas potest elicere actum volendi, cum sit causa secunda, actum eiusdem rationis potest elicere Spiritus Sanctus qui est causa prima; et si corpus caeleste haberet causalitatem supra illam, eliceret actum eiusdem rationis cum ipsa.: q. 11 n. 14

Voluntas: v. Actus

INDEX GENERALIS

FOREWORD..	v

QUAESTIONES SUPER SECUNDUM ET TERTIUM DE ANIMA

INTRODUCTION..	1*
1. DESCRIPTIONS OF THE MANUSCRIPTS.................................	1*
2. MANUSCRIPT TRADITION..	55*
3. AUTHENTICITY..	121*
4. NATURE, FUNCTION AND CHRONOLOGY OF THE *QUAESTIONES SUPER SECUNDUM ET TERTIUM DE ANIMA*......	139*
5. EDITORIAL PRINCIPLES...	144*
SIGLORUM INTERPRETATIO...	145*
SIGNORUM INTERPRETATIO...	147*
ABBREVIATIONUM INTERPRETATIO..	148*

QUAESTIONES SUPER SECUNDUM ET TERTIUM DE ANIMA

QUAESTIO 1: Utrum sensus tactus sit unus vel plures...............	1
QUAESTIO 2: Utrum caro sit organum tactus...........................	13
QUAESTIO 3: Utrum ad tactum requiratur medium extrinsecum in quo fiet..	19
QUAESTIO 4: Utrum sensibile positum supra sensum vel organum sensus sentiatur..	27

QUAESTIO 5: Utrum sensus sit receptivus specierum sine materia.. 35

QUAESTIO 6: Utrum sint tantum quinque sensus...................... 43

QUAESTIO 7: Utrum ratione huius quod dicitur in littera quod 'idem est actus sensibilis et sensitivi', actio et passio sint idem actus sive motus.. 51

QUAESTIO 8: Utrum sensus particularis possit simul sentire contraria.. 63

QUAESTIO 9: Utrum sit ponere sensum communem................. 69

QUAESTIO 10: Utrum sensus communis sit unus vel plures......... 79

QUAESTIO 11: Utrum corpora caelestia possint agere in intellectum vel voluntatem nostram................................... 89

QUAESTIO 12: Utrum potentiae animae, scilicet intellectiva et sensitiva, sint tantum passivae.................................. 97

QUAESTIO 13: Utrum de intentione Philosophi fuerit ponere intellectum agentem aliquid animae nostrae vel potius substantiam separatam...................................... 113

QUAESTIO 14: Utrum species maneant in intellectu, cessante actu intelligendi... 119

QUAESTIO 15: Utrum intellectus noster sit immaterialis........... 129

QUAESTIO 16: Utrum magis universale prius intelligatur a nobis quam minus universale..................................... 145

QUAESTIO 17: Utrum in intellectu nostro sint species intelligibiles priores naturaliter actu intelligendi......... 157

QUAESTIO 18: Utrum intellectus noster possit intelligere sine phantasmate... 177

QUAESTIO 19: Utrum quiditas sensibilis tantum sit obiectum intellectus.. 185

QUAESTIO 20: Utrum verum vel ens sub ratione veri sit obiectum primum intellectus.. 197

QUAESTIO 21: Utrum ens sit obiectum primum intellectus nostri.. 207

QUAESTIO 22: Utrum singulare sit ab intellectu nostro per se intelligibile.. 227

QUAESTIO 23: Utrum in elicitione actus intelligendi intellectus sit movens motum ab obiecto vel intellectus et obiectum relucens in specie concurrant ad actum intelligendi.. 241

I: INDEX CODICUM.. 249

II: INDEX NOMINUM ANTIQUORUM ET MEDIAEVALIUM (IN INTRODUCTIONE).. 251

III: INDEX AUCTORUM... 255

IV: INDEX DOCTRINALIS... 267

V: INDEX GENERALIS.. 293